THIRD EDITION

NEW AFFINITIES

ANCA ROSU

PEARSON

Custom
Publishing

Cover Image: *Ray,* by Jason Fieldman.

Printed in the United States of America

10 9 8 7 6 5 4 3 2

ISBN 0-536-81866-5

2004240021

BK/GM

Please visit our web site at *www.pearsoncustom.com*

PEARSON CUSTOM PUBLISHING
75 Arlington Street, Suite 300, Boston, MA 02116
A Pearson Education Company

This book is dedicated to past, present, and future students of DeVry University, North Brunswick.

Acknowledgments

This book would not have been possible without the contributions of the English Composition Committee members. Thanks are due to Jeanne Baptiste, Barry Batorski, Barbara Burke, Barbara Goldberg, Kelly Hogan, Randall Spinks, Andrew Scoblionko, Rose Vydelingum, and Paul Winters for their suggestions, text contributions, and discussions. Special thanks to Mark Geller for his choice of poems and to Kathy Wagner for inspiring the assignments. A debt of gratitude goes to Martin Gloege and especially to Wendolyn Tetlow, who initiated and substantially contributed to this project. Christine Grexa and Antoinette Payne from Pearson Custom Publishing deserve the warmest thanks for their readiness to help and their encouragement.

Instead of Introduction: Write On!

What do they teach in a writing class? What do we learn in a writing class? In a writing class we just write, right? But that means we know how to write, why do we have to take a class anyway? We are not here to become writers, are we? One can ask such questions and invoke their obvious answers, only if one has never seriously thought of writing and its reason to be. Pause to think about it, and writing unfolds as a complicated business. There are as many varieties of writing as there are purposes and audiences for it. However, all these kinds of writing share two important characteristics: they result from deeply personal, natural thought processes, and they take on widely public, conventional forms.

Although we think of it as remote from everything technical, writing is actually a technology. It was invented for the purpose of simplifying record keeping in commercial transactions. Thus, one of the first achievements of writing was to make it possible for some people to leave a record for the future. It also made it possible for others to look back on the records of the past.

This victory against time may be the reason why, in his essay "The Faces of Ants," the poet and artist Breyten Breytenbach brings up writing as he explores the relation between past and future: "The past is the ink with which we write the present—and in the process and the flow of writing the words, the concepts and ideas, the images, the flights become…just ink. Whereas what we'd probably like to write would be an open hand wherein time, which is the future of the present movement, could find its fit and its fist" (34). While struggling with metaphors for our sense of history, Breytenbach also creates a metaphor of writing. The passage from the past to the present, or the continuity of past, present, and future is seen as writing. Writing is a way of representing ourselves in time, and if we think of it functionally, keeping records, (or aiding memory) is perhaps the first thing that comes to mind. When we write, we are, in a sense, historians.

Although the record keeping function seems the most obvious, when we say "writing," we most often have in mind works of literature. Writers fall into the same category with poets. In this case, writing is an artistic activity, one that produces, like painting or carving, images of the world for our understanding and delight. Art requires talent and dedication, and this is perhaps why those of us who do not write professionally tend to think of writing as some mystical gift. "I cannot write. I am no good at it." I have heard these sentences from my students more often than I care to remember. They share the belief that writing is an art, made possible by some divine gift. But as Ved Mehta points out in his essay "Lightning and the Lightning Bug," "for every natural writer there are ten or more writers that have to labor over their craft" (191). Mehta talks about craft, not art, suggesting that we can all learn to write.

What his essay describes is a learning experience, which embraces both writing and other kinds of knowledge. In trying to perfect his writing style, Mehta reads and learns to appreciate the best-known authors of English literature, for instance. Most interestingly, he talks about how the writing and learning processes are hard to distinguish from each other: "I found I had first to decide what, exactly, I wanted to say, even if in the course of writing I should find myself saying something totally different. (All ideas grow and develop as one writes, I learned, since one's memory expands through the process of association)" (190). Mehta's experience reveals to us yet another dimension of writing, where beyond record keeping and artistry, a learning process emerges. Associations that expand memory develop as one writes. It is perhaps this aspect of writing that should interest us most when we are students: writing as learning and discovery of new ideas.

Mehta's experience, however, is marked by labor and constraint. In spite of the passion he develops for writing, one cannot ignore his struggle. What is most striking in this struggle is perhaps the feeling of inferiority. He continuously evaluates himself as he writes: "I remember that I was struck by the elegance and luster of many of the essays written by my English contemporaries. Compared to theirs, my best efforts came across as dull and lame" (190). Mehta's feeling may have to do with the fact that he was not born English, although he learned the language early enough in his life to call it his own. But beyond his origin, the inferiority complex is fostered, if not even created, by his teacher: "My tutor's questioning of one infelicitous word effectively unraveled my confidence in my writing even as it began to sensitize me to the nuances of words. For some time thereafter, whenever I wrote a sentence, I would read it as my tutor might, and conclude that almost everything was wrong with it" (190). Even when the tutor is absent, his presence is felt by the student writer. In his imagination, the tutor's intervention is magnified and becomes an obstacle in the way of his desire to write. The student's inner self seems to be invaded by the voice of the tutor.

Mehta's teacher appears more as a censor than as a mentor. The way Mehta internalized the opinion of his tutor looks quite similar to the way writers internalize the point of view of the censors described by J.M. Coetzee it in his essay "Emerging from Censorship." Coetzee shows how censorship is fueled by paranoia, an irrational fear of whatever may question the power of the authorities. Censors are watchdogs set against opinions contrary or irreverent to political authority. But the restrictions they impose on writers become part of the writer's consciousness: "By forcing the writer to see what he has written through the censor's eyes, the censor forces him to internalize a contaminating reading" (65). The contamination consists, according to Coetzee, in the writer becoming as paranoid as the censor. And indeed Mehta's state of mind as he writes could well be called paranoia.

This paranoia involves a hostile relationship with the reader, a relationship perverted, according to Coetzee, precisely because, even though we always write for someone else, we conceive of that someone as a beloved. Writing is, according to Coetzee, "a transaction with some such figure of the beloved, that tries to please her (but that also tries continually though surreptitiously to revise and recreate her as the-one-who-will-be-pleased)" (66). Coetzee's image of writing here is personalized, a transaction that takes place between two people, although obviously the writer is writing alone. The second figure, the reader, is created and recreated as someone who will not censor but will appreciate the writing.

Perhaps the censorship exercised by Mehta's teacher is partly due to Mehta's own inner effort to create his reader. Because he is a student in a foreign university of great prestige, he imagines his reader as intimidating and censorious. Instead of recreating the reader into "the-one-who-will-be-pleased," Mehta recreates himself into the inferior, submissive student, who must study the masters in order to form his own style. Although he becomes a good writer, Mehta seems to be adversely affected by the process. Mehta is not the only one to make this mistake. Many students write only to please their teacher, and the effort leaves them depleted of the ability to deal with other writing situations. Too often, the relationship between the mentor and the pupil becomes too personal, and both lose sight of what is at stake in writing. In a sense, the teacher must be pleased, but only in so far as he or she represents the reading public. But even in an ideal situation the writing self may still be hurt in the process.

The most difficult task of the writer is thus to balance the two aspects of writing: the personal and the public. On the one hand, writing is personal, intimate, private. It is, as Coetzee's metaphor suggests, an act of love. To an extent, it is useful to think about writing that way. Love not only endows the beloved with the best qualities, but it also brings up the best in us. When we fall in love, we are excited and elated, we want to show and give what we have best. Unlike the student, as portrayed by Mehta, the lover is confident, daring, and creative. Many of my students feel that way: "I can write when I am interested in the topic"; "I can write well about what I like." In such statements, writing seems to be no more than a fine romance, where the writer finds self-fulfillment. But notice that the satisfaction does not quite take the other, the beloved reader, into account. It is the topic, or the theme that my students are infatuated with, not the audience for whom they write. The readers, because they are not present, are banished from the student writers' minds.

It is, however, dangerous to forget the audience. Writing becomes then a closed self-reflection. Here is how Breytenbach, with his unchecked metaphors, intuits the impulse to make writing an affair with oneself: "You must polish the word—not to have it shiny or smooth but to make it as clear as a mirror or a pebble in which you can see your face, and may see that your face is death" (34). Why is death the ultimate reflection? Though the writer polishing the words seems to be a solitary creature, he or she looks in the mirror he has created and sees something or someone else— death. What we may learn from Breytenbach's turn of words is that whenever we write, no matter how joyfully alone we feel doing it, we establish a relation with another. The other is imagined here as death, probably because as long as the reader has not been created by the writer, there is nothing there but death. An uncalled reader, or worse, one that does not feel welcome to the text, can be as harsh and censorious as Mehta's Oxford tutor. But is any reader, an actual, not an imagined reader, any better than Mehta's teacher, any better than a reflection of death? Where are we to find the benevolent beloved who will indeed help us accomplish the writing romance?

To Coetzee, the reader is someone the writer creates and re-creates in his mind while he writes. In real life situations, however, a writer encounters people, who are not always willing to let themselves be recreated by his or her will. Romance itself does not take place in a vacuum, and its relation to social norms is not always easy. Romance shares with writing the impossibility of separating its public from its private aspect. Though we think of it as intimate and personal, it is, in so far as it includes another, a social form. If the intimate and personal aspect flourishes in romance, it is because it is socially sanctioned. But when fantasy takes over, romance becomes antisocial.

It is hard, if one thinks of writing as the form of self-reflection, as a romance with oneself, to suffer anyone else to read it. One can see this reluctance in the jealousy with which teenagers guard their personal journals. One should perhaps keep separate the writing done for oneself, the writing with maximum personal involvement, and the other writing, the writing for others, for the public. Some people do just that. I have read as many impersonal, cold, and indifferent papers, as I have read confessions, so personal as to make me feel embarrassed. Where does this split come from? What are we sometimes too afraid and sometimes too willing to expose?

Past rhetoricians thought of writing as exclusively public, and the desire to assert oneself (and sometimes expose oneself) in writing may have to do with the delicate balance between the private and the public spheres in our times. As Jonathan Franzen points out in "Imperial Bedroom," today everyone feels that privacy is threatened. But in Franzen's opinion, "What is threatened isn't the private sphere. It's the public sphere" (118). Franzen attracts our attention to the counterpart of privacy, the seldom-mentioned public domain in which we live. Without the public sphere, the private sphere does not make sense, and ultimately it does not exist. The reason why the threat is differently understood by the public and by Franzen may have to do with the fact that it comes from a cancellation of differences. What is threatened, I would say, is the difference between what is private and what is public.

Much of the erasure of differences is due to new technologies like the computer, the personal phone, the TV, VCR, etc., which enable us to do our job from home, or enjoy entertainment that once was available only in public, in the comfort of our bedroom. Ellen Ullman sees the progress of such technologies, especially of the Internet, as a threat to shared experience:

> The Net ideal represents a retreat not only from political life but also from culture—from that tumultuous conversation in which we try to talk to one another about our shared experience. As members of a culture, we see the same movie, read the same book, hear the same string quartet. Although it is difficult for us to agree on what we might have seen, read or heard, it is out of that difficult conversation that real culture arises. Whether or not we come to an agreement or understanding, even if some decide that understanding and meaning are impossible, we are still sitting around the same campfire. (349)

Ullman sees in the new technology of the Internet the same threat that our ancestors must have seen when writing came about. Before writing was invented, people talked to each other, they shared news, traditions, emotions, and experiences. One can say that inventing writing was the first step toward becoming the solitary creatures we are today. But we do not feel so solitary when we pick up a book. The very nature of language has made it possible to preserve the relation with another even in writing. Our ability to speak is inextricably related to our social nature. No one speaks, or writes, exclusively for oneself.

As Ullman notes, though, the social relation, the cultural conversation is not easy. Sharing is hard. Making others understand us is harder. It is as hard as understanding others. Breytenbach's metaphors let us see this difficulty in its tragic dimension: "The recognition and the acceptance of the Other's humanity (or humanness) is a maiming of the self. You have to wound the self, cut it in strips, in order to know that you are similar and of the same substance as shadows" (34). It seems paradoxical and sacrificial, but Breytenbach's insight applies to our everyday transactions with each other. Whenever we listen to others, we have to keep our selves silent. Does this mean that the self is sacrificed on the altar of knowledge and of community? Does this mean that in order to know and speak to others, we have to annihilate the self? Notice that Breytenbach says only maim, cut into strips. From those strips we can weave another self, one that has the knowledge of oneself and of the other.

Breytenbach is not the only one to describe the contact between self and other as hurtful. Certainly Mehta's self as a student seems maimed in spite of the fact that the maiming leads to his achievement as a writer. Robert Scholes also describes the relation with the other in a negative metaphor. In "On Reading a Videotext," he speaks of reading as surrender. Although he refers to videotexts, which are, in his opinion, more powerful seducers than written texts, his image of reading as surrender to another's voice, another's view, another's thought is quite appropriate for any kind of text. For sheer understanding of what someone else says, we have to listen passively. Scholes warns us, however, that from surrender we must recover, and that "Recovery, in fact, may depend upon critical analysis" (274). Scholes speaks at once about the personal side of processing texts and the relationship implied in this process. When we read, as when we write, something happens to us, but it happens in relation to another. Whether it is a maiming or a surrender of the self, we need to recover as ourselves again. However, when we do, what do we do with our new critical knowledge if not share it, yet again, with another?

With Scholes, the reading and writing appear as parts of a never-ending cycle, in which knowledge is circulating both *within* and *between* persons. It is easy to see the importance of being part of such a cycle: the very act of being human, no matter how much technology is involved, is a shared and sharing experience. The self does not make sense without its opening to another, without its maiming, surrender, and recovery, any more than the private can make sense without the public. No matter how self-sufficient and independent we are, we do not make sense without others. We make sense from others and for others.

Scholes's lesson about reading videotexts is also explaining to us the process by virtue of which we become willing to surrender. We are in possession of a culture, of a shared experience, even as, if we are to trust Ullman, we are in danger of losing it. We draw our opinions and beliefs from that culture. Ultimately thus, our selves have always been made up of others. Coetzee sees it that way: "The self, as we understand the self today, is not the unity it was assumed to be by classical rationalism. On the contrary, it is multiple and multiply divided against itself. It is, to speak in figures, a zoo in which a multitude of beasts have residence, over which the anxious, overworked zookeeper of rationality exercises a rather limited control" (66). Perhaps what we ordinarily call self is the zookeeper that tries to exercise control. When we write and address others, it is important to achieve not only control but unity as well. There should be some consensus among the animals of the zoo in order for the keeper to be able to report to someone outside.

Let us imagine ourselves ready to write, to address an audience that for the moment will remain imaginary, an audience that shares our culture and can therefore understand us. What do we have to tell this audience? Where do we start? To be part of the great conversation, of the culture Ullman talked about, we have to pick up where others left off. Before we write for others, we have to read others. Many times, we tend to see the reading as an imposition, as something we would rather not do. But that is unfair. If we write, and implicitly, we want someone else to read our writing, then we have to reciprocate, and read what others have written. Sometimes, what we read goes directly to our heart. The writer seems to be of one mind with ourselves, and we are ready to surrender. Scholes thinks the cause of this readiness to surrender is cultural reinforcement. And he explains: "By cultural reinforcement, I mean the process through which video texts confirm viewers in their ideological positions and reassure them as to their membership in a collective cultural body" (272). Scholes refers to videotexts, of course, but the same is true about written texts. We are all satisfied and reassured when someone agrees with us. As Ullman argues, we need such reassurance in order to share experience.

The question is, however, what would happen if our opinions were constantly reinforced, and we would continue to reinforce them for others? We would probably be happy, but nothing new would ever emerge. The critical analysis, I have to agree with Scholes, is indeed the necessary means not only to recover from the surrender to the text but also to be able to create something new. Analysis means separating things into their component elements to see what they are made of, or what their nature is. It comes from a Greek word that means to undo, to loosen throughout. And although we usually think of "critical" as judging, we must not forget that it comes from crisis, which means a crucial point, or a turning point. We thus have to undo first what the others have done in order to turn it around and recreate it in our own way.

This description of our job as writers seems focused only on its public side, on the relationship with other authors we read and with our prospective readers. It would appear that nothing is in it for the self, that when recreating, we cannot create. But that is a one-sided view. In critically processing others' ideas, we enrich ourselves, bring more animals to our inner zoo, if we are to stick with Coetzee's metaphor. Once we know these animals well, we are free to steer and control our zoo the way we want to. And it is not only in the interest of our beloved reader that we have to harness the force of our inner zoo, but also in our own interest. Inner order makes us more secure even as it makes us more capable and ready to meet the others.

You may have noticed that in the course of this essay I have referred to many sources. I have deliberately chosen sources from this book, because I want you, my audience, to be able to consult them easily. Much of the essay's shape has been determined by you and by the sources. In spite of my reliance on these sources though, I can claim this essay for my own, and it is indeed the result of my experience in writing. By opening myself to the texts and to you, I have been able to shape an argument that gives a richer meaning to my experience as a writer. I can understand now why criticism has always hurt, and why it has been so hard to satisfy my audiences. I have also learned that reading others critically, carefully, considerately can make me richer intellectually. I know now how to respect my readers, to share my experience in reading with care and clarity. The notes I write for myself are animals from my inner zoo. What I write for the public though is measured and under control.

Control is difficult to achieve these days, when we are bombarded with information. If you have ever worked on a research project, you know that the problem with information is not that it is too scarce but that it is too abundant. Some people become complacent, because information is so readily available, especially on the Internet. But information does not help, unless it is organized into some meaningful whole. To appropriate information and call it knowledge, we have to give it meaning. In order to have meaning, we have to manage information, to include, but also to exclude, and above all, to make connections between the pieces of information we have and to bring them together.

To achieve this meaningful whole is to write. To write is thus to abandon oneself to reading and readers and to recover oneself from reading for one's readers. It is to undo and remake the readings and oneself; therefore, it is the most intensely private and the most riskily public experience and the most exhilarating. Whether we are writing a poem, a novel, an essay, a report, or a memo, the process is the same. We gather information from without, make it meaningful within, and write it out again for our readers.

My colleagues and I have gathered here a number of texts for your reading. Some will please you, some will challenge you, but we hope you will read them all with curiosity and an open mind. We hope you will surrender to them temporarily and then recover your stance through critical analysis. We also hope you are ready to cut the self into strips and reweave it into a new and richer you. And we hope that writing will be the process by which you enrich yourselves and enrich the world. Write on!

Anca Rosu

Teachers' Orientation

New Affinities is a collection of texts dedicated to DeVry students. In recognition of our students' diversity, the book includes texts on a wide range of topics. The texts are also of various lengths, genres, and difficulty levels. In order to enable a course to follow a thematic content, the texts have been selected according to their potential to be related to other texts. To allow for freedom in choosing and arranging the themes of particular classes, the texts have been arranged in alphabetical order, and a brief synopsis for each title has been provided in the table of contents. However, the texts are richer in implications than a synopsis can show, and have many off-shoots that can relate them to other texts in the book. As you read through the book to make your selections for a semester, you will discover you can group the texts in many interesting ways. The book contains contemporary short stories, personal essays, academic essays, journalistic pieces, as well as poems. Thematic links are possible across genres. Our students relate well to short stories; therefore, you may want to start with a piece of fiction and progress toward the more difficult pieces such as poems, and personal or academic essays.

It is important for our students to integrate reading and writing. Reading can easily be seen as passive, but one of the objectives of the class is precisely to teach students to read actively and respond to the texts critically. Active reading becomes a necessity when the students write about what they have read, whether responding to the text in a journal, or in an electronic threaded discussion, or in papers that use the texts as sources. The way to read actively may vary from an emotional response that needs explanation, to an analytical probing, to an evaluation, or a more extended interpretive activity. Interpretation is the process that enables students to connect the reading to their experience and to develop original ideas of their own, starting from and in relation to a text. Through interpretation, the students can learn how to develop their own voices and how to place themselves within the context of a larger reading/writing community.

The possibilities of relating the texts within this collection create a synergetic effect, and reading any text within a context enriches the intellectual experience of the class. To some extent, the collection is a *hyper*text, in the sense that we can relate the texts to one another by following key words or concepts, and thus we can generate new pathways of reading, in the way we do when we follow hot links in the Internet. Hypertext is often being blamed for encouraging superficiality in reading, but we should remember that how we read depends on our attitude and purposes. Any kind of reading can be seen as passive, and can remain on the surface, unless we make it active and purposefully look for depth. Hypertext can encourage active reading through the unexpected juxtapositions, which demand interpretations and explanations, which in turn can prompt extensive writing. This is why the assignments at the end of the book are called *links*, to suggest connections between texts that need to be interpreted and explained. Such interpretation/explanation encourages original thinking.

The groups of assignments are called *concatenations,* because the way of thinking encouraged by hypertext, and by analogy by this book, does not follow a linear sequence. The links of a concatenation relate to each other loosely, forming a chain, which often veers off from the initial direction and follows a new pathway through the reading context. The analogy with hypertext serves the task of creating assignments, but the similarities stop there. This class is about writing in textual, not hypertextual form. Nevertheless, the curriculum guide recommends the construction of a website as an assignment for the class. One exercise could be to create hot links between several texts from the book and make a website focused on a theme. Establishing the links, the students can ponder on the relations they are creating or suggesting.

In addition to the website assignment, the curriculum guide also recommends an oral presentation using Power Point. Such a presentation can be used as an intermediary stage in completing one paper. It offers an opportunity for the student writer to organize the material in order to fit it on slides and to address a live audience as well. Another recommendation of the curriculum guide is the use of research in one paper. The final link in each concatenation includes some research, which does not have to be extensive, but it has to give students an opportunity to get acquainted to the library.

You may use the concatenations in various ways. A concatenation can serve as a backbone for an entire semester. Each assignment can lead to a paper varying in length from 3 to 5 pages. The individual links can alternately be used as separate assignments. The texts on which each assignment is based may be read by the whole class, or individually, by each student, depending on your teaching style. Alternately, you can use the concatenations as bases for class discussions. Obviously, you are free to create other types of assignments starting from the texts as well.

The book's attributes can be useful to most teaching approaches. The texts vary in difficulty; therefore we can adjust to the students' needs by choosing the kind of texts that our students will be able to handle. The genres represented in the book allow us to emphasize one branch of the humanities and social sciences or another according to our inclinations and backgrounds. The thematic content allows us to deal with contemporary or historical issues. The stories, essays, poems, and the more academic pieces can also serve as models for the students' writing.

Approaches to Writing

Writing is being taught in many different ways, and each method can be effective, if the teacher believes in what he or she teaches. Approaches to teaching rely on approaches to writing. Below are several approaches to writing that are practiced by our faculty here at DeVry.

The Rhetorical Approaches

When writing, many of us are influenced by rhetoric, which is the art of speaking. Rhetoric has its virtues, especially because it encourages awareness of an audience and recommends ways in which a speaker could keep an audience's attention focused on his or her main point. On the negative side, rhetoric can lead to less attention to reading and steer writers toward common places. The origin of rhetoric in cultures where books were rare and knowledge was all memorized explains why it does not insist on interpretation of text. The oral/aural orientation does not prevent us, however, from adapting rhetoric to our cultural environment. Instead of resorting exclusively to what we remember, we can easily read and research in order to find support for our arguments. What rhetoricians call invention can be stimulated by the reading and interpretation of texts.

The structuring of speech or writing is also an important aspect of rhetoric, which sometimes degenerates into an exaggerated emphasis on the form at the expense of the content. The prescribed forms of rhetoric give the impression that writing an essay is like filling a vessel. This dominance of the form may seem constraining to some writers, who prefer to develop their own forms. Nevertheless, the challenge of fitting self-expression in a prescribed form can be exhilarating. A rhetorical approach balanced by attention to self-expression and to the process of invention based on research can work quite nicely.

There is another approach related to rhetoric, which is known as "rhetorical modes." This approach considers writing in its detailed operations, asking writers to practice a mode (a description, a comparison, a narrative, an analysis, etc.) in a full essay. It also has positive and negative aspects and needs careful implementation. Writers may learn to excel in a particular mode, but remain unable to integrate several modes in a more complex essay, and the purpose of their writing seems to be constrained by the form. Ignoring the fact that a piece of writing may result from a combination of several modes, they may be puzzled by writing tasks that do not lend themselves a particular mode. If one practices modes, one has to take care to integrate the skills and consider the way in which the separate operations contribute to the whole. One also needs to emphasize one's personal stakes as a writer, and pursue the thought beyond the mode. Writers need to learn to subordinate the rhetorical tools to their creativity and self-expression.

The Personal Approach

Personal essays are meant to develop self-reflection, self-awareness, and they are especially valued for helping us find our personal voices. When the emphasis on the personal goes too far, however, the balance tips in favor of self-indulgence, rather than self-reflection. This imbalance originates perhaps in confusing the personal with the private and confessional discourse. As Harriet Malinowitz put it, the personal essay, "doesn't have to be—*certainly should not be*—self-indulgent or derivative of an Oprah-show confession, as some reflexively presume. Nor is it even necessarily about oneself. Its essence is subjectivity, not autobiography"(317). Many great writers use the personal essay as a means to reveal social problems and debate cultural issues. Scott Russell Sanders and Patricia Williams are two good examples in this book. A thoughtful use of readings can help a writer develop a more challenging self-reflective process. Inspired by the issues debated in the texts, a writer can start exploring his/her personal experiences in new ways. From personal experience, writers can progress to larger topics, in which they can invest attention and study, and become able to integrate academic knowledge in their personal preoccupations. The idea is to relate new concepts derived from reading to personal experience, without actually writing only for oneself. To be effective, personal essays should be reader-centered rather than writer-centered.

The Scholarly/Academic Approach

For those of us who emulate scholarly writing, the danger is to generate impersonal and unengaged essays. This happens when, uninitiated in the academic reasoning process, we substitute academic parlance for actual thinking. Too often, we start out to demonstrate a thesis for which we have no foundation. For if the form of such essays is generally top-down, starting with a thesis and supporting it, it does not mean that the process of writing them follows the same path. On the contrary, the thesis is the final result of a lot of questioning, searching, and experimentation. Nor does such an essay need to claim the kind of total objectivity that translates into impersonal writing. As Peter Elbow defines it, the academic discourse is, "giving reasons and evidence, yes, but doing so as a person speaking with acknowledged interests to others—whose interest and position one acknowledges and tries to understand" (142). Academic thinking is exploratory in its main aspect and cultivates respect for other people's work. It focuses on problems and looks for solutions. If properly prepared, an academic essay has the virtue of fostering not only interpretation, but also original thinking. Engaged in interpretation of multiple texts and from various points of view, writers can earn a position among other writers, and they can also learn to assert their own voices among the voices of others. The best academic essays are engaged and personal, and they make complicated concepts clear and easy to understand for the layman. Good examples of academic essays in this book are Michael Dorris's "Indians on the Shelf" and J. M. Coetzee's "Emerging from Censorship," which are, in obvious ways, related to the authors' backgrounds.

Approaches to Teaching Writing

The descriptions above apply to kinds or genres of essays that imply different approaches to writing, rather than to the teaching of writing. All these approaches to writing can lead to comparable results. The best samples of each are equally good and effective. What makes the approaches different is the road taken by the writer to reach the final goal. How to help a student do his or her best depends on the approach to writing, and pedagogy may vary with the kind of writing one wants to teach. There are a few things that all approaches have in common though. They all encourage the writers to be active readers and to appropriate the author position. They all respect the individuality of the writer even as they emphasize the importance of the audience.

One thing I would not recommend teachers is to mix approaches to writing in the same class. It is very difficult and disorienting for our students to learn to write in different genres within the short period of time of a semester, especially if they are not aware of the change from one type of essay to another. None of the approaches can teach the students to write in a single trial, so I recommend writing four or five papers, which give the students similar tasks and help them perfect their techniques. Since our purpose is to enable students to tackle writing in other classes, we have to bring them to a point where they will be able to do that, in whatever genre we have chosen to teach them. Whether they learn to use the concepts from the readings to interpret their own experience, or to defend a thesis in a rhetorically effective manner, or to produce coherent interpretations, they will be able to approach any writing task with the skills they have acquired. We have to teach them that, irrespective of approach, all the essays they write must be personal, engaged, thoughtful, coherent, well formed, and capable to reach their audience.

A similar classification by genre of essays is to be found on the Website called **Paradigm** (*http//:www.powa.org*) authored by Chuck Guilford. His list includes informal essays, thesis/support essays, exploratory essays, and argumentative essays. One point he makes about this division into genres is that they share characteristics, but one characteristic or another comes to dominate and defines the genre. The same holds true for the types of writing I described above. No matter how we approach writing, we aim at teaching the students to read attentively and interpret what they read—which means relating what they read to personal experience—to construct coherent wholes in their papers, and to consider the audience for whom they write.

It is important to tell the students what the qualities of good writing are, and how we aim to reach them through our particular approach to writing. Too many times, students seem to think that every teacher appreciates a different kind of writing, and that they have to learn everything over again. That is damaging to them and to us. On the contrary, if we are aware of the other approaches, and we can see what their strengths and weaknesses are, we can help our students become better writers. We may want to identify the way the students have been taught to write and encourage them to use the skills they have acquired in new ways. Such encouragement may also teach them to transfer the writing skills from one type of course to another.

The Writing Process

The type of essay we emulate is not the only aspect of our teaching, although it can influence the way we work with the students. Writing pedagogy has changed lately from attention to the finished product to the so called process-oriented approach. It would seem that the rhetorical approach to writing lends itself better to a product-oriented pedagogy. The personal or academic approaches to writing seem better served by a process-oriented pedagogy. The product-oriented pedagogy emphasizes the form that writing must achieve, whereas the process-oriented approach focuses on the process of composition.

Process-oriented pedagogy is interpreted in very different ways by teachers, probably because the process of writing itself is highly individual and depends on previous education. Generally, the approach encourages writing numerous drafts and performing substantial revisions. It also includes free writing, in-class writing, and personal writing. However, we cannot be sure about what happens in the process of writing. Indeed, many times, thoughts do not come to mind, unless we have the possibility to write them down, but this may have to do with a habit of not thinking about important matters, unless we have a pen in hand, or are seated in front of a computer. The more traditional method of drawing an outline first can also have good and bad effects. Each writer makes choices in this regard, and our students are best off discovering their own process.

Instead of trying to figure out the process in the abstract, we can look closely at what our students are doing. Reading a student paper is not a simple task. Of course, we notice the mistakes, the awkward phrasings, the misunderstandings of concepts, but that is not what we are there to do. When she visited us, Ann Raimes said something interesting about reading student papers: look for what they do well, instead of looking for the errors. Indeed, if we approach the task from that direction, we are more open to see what the students are trying to do. In general, they are willing to comply with the teacher's requests and are doing their best to please us. But things can go wrong in the execution of any assignment. If we pay close attention to what the student is trying to accomplish, we will be able to intervene in the proper way. It's not enough for the students to find out that their sentences are awkward; they should know why they appear that way.

It bears repeating that none of the genres described above is more effective than the others as a teaching tool. The informal, personal essay may seem so, but unless strictly autobiographical, this type of essay will also create problems for the beginning students. When we read our students' essays, our task is to see where they have problems and why. Sometimes, such problems derive from a misunderstanding of our own instructions, but simpler instructions will not necessarily lead to better papers. Instructions, as well as the texts students read, are to be interpreted. They actually should allow for several interpretations, and we should be open to them all. It is best when the assignment itself presents a problem to solve, but the solutions can be many. We have to figure out what the student writer is up to and help him or her achieve whatever purpose he or she had in mind. The comments on the paper should open a dialogue with the student rather than judge his or her performance.

But beyond the assignment itself, the student may have problems understanding the concepts he or she is working with. This problem is not easily solved by telling them what the concepts mean, because making sense of them is precisely what the students should do for themselves. We can tell them to go back to the texts and probe a little deeper, or we can ask them to produce examples from their own experience to see how the concepts work.

At other times, students start writing, before they have completely solved the problem the assignment raises. They have started thinking about something, but the thought is not completely clear to them. In such cases, we are best off asking for clarifications and talking to the students individually, until they manage to figure things out. (Lab time is ideal for such discussions). Their dilemmas often show themselves in what we misleadingly identify as grammar errors. Those are errors all right, but no amount of grammar rules enforcement would put an end to them. To solve his or her conceptual dilemmas, the student can benefit from thinking out loud in conversation with a teacher or a tutor. Determination to communicate to an audience can play a crucial role. Another whole series of errors arise from not taking the audience into account, or rather not knowing for whom to write. The conventions of academic writing are familiar to us, and we often take them for granted. However, our students think of the teacher as their only audience. Some protest against peer group review, because they are interested solely in the response of the teacher. Often they think of such response as corrective, and they write to achieve some kind of abstract rectitude. Peer group reviews, when guided by specific questions, can be quite effective in making the students aware of an audience. However, there is familiarity and common knowledge in the class, and the students tend to think of their audience as someone close to them. They need an audience from outside the classroom. The students' audience should be their peers, but peers from another school, peers who are not familiar with everything that went on in class. Sometimes, writers need to think of a more knowledgeable and more experienced audience as well.

The advantage of thinking of an audience outside the class is that students will be less tempted to resort to shortcuts in expression, or to half-formed thoughts, of the kind only people sitting in the same class can understand. They will learn to fully express an opinion and support it with evidence. They will learn to convert emotional response into reasoned statement. They will learn how to make reference to a reading without actually summarizing the whole of it. They will learn how to support their interpretations of readings and parts of readings. Simply put, awareness of the audience and determination to communicate can transform thoughtless or formless writing into well-formed, thoughtful essays. Even when not prescribed, form emerges in writing, when the writer masters what he or she has to say. Besides, awareness of the audience can also take care of such little, but important, details like mentioning the authors and titles referred to, giving the piece a title, or voicing one's writing, so as to make it distinct from the sources.

Given the types of errors described above, it is important to point them out to the students in ways that mobilize their energies rather than make them give up in despair. We all know by now that we have to start with a positive comment, and that is indeed a useful rule. However, the positive reinforcement is not enough. The comments must address the macro level of the paper first. A thoughtless first draft, received from a careless student needs a comment that addresses the macro level: the preparation of the paper, the purpose, and the personal involvement. The editing errors at this stage may be many, but addressing them will not help. On a thoughtful final draft, however, we may need to point out the editing errors and stylistic awkwardness.

One word of caution about good papers: we often reward the student with a good grade and a 'Well done' remark at the end of the paper. Sometimes the students are not sure about what we liked in the paper, and may not be able to repeat performance. It's as valuable for a student to know why a paper is good as it is to know why a paper is bad.

The pedagogies sketched above are derived from the conversations we carry on in the Composition and Communications Committee meetings, on our listserv called *engtalk,* and informally, whenever at least two of us meet. A quick perusal of the latest articles in such journals as *College English* and the CCCC publication shows that the disputes among the supporters of one kind of writing or another, one kind of teaching or another, rage on a national level. Our innovative idea is to see the good side of every approach, understand them all, and practice the one we are best at. This is why, our conversations must continue and you are invited to join them.

Further Reading in Composition

Bean, John C. *Engaging Ideas: The Professor's Guide to Integrating Writing, Critical Thinking, and Active Learning in the Classroom*. San Francisco: Jossey-Bass, 1996.

Berlin, James A. *Rhetoric and Reality. Writing Instruction in American Colleges, 1900-1985*. Carbondale: Southern Illinois U P, 1987.

Bizzell, Patricia. *Academic Discourse and Critical Consciousness*. Pittsburgh: University of Pittsburgh P, 1993.

Bloom, Lynn Z., Donald A. Daiker, and Edward M. White, Eds. *Composition in the Twenty-First Century: Crisis and Change*. Carbondale: Southern Illinois UP, 1996.

Bolter, Jay David. *Writing Space: The Computer, Hypertext, and the History of Writing*. Fairlawn, N.J.: Erlbaum, 1991.

Dillon, George. *Contending Rhetorics: Writing in Academic Disciplines*. Bloomington: Indiana University Press, 1991.

Dombek, Kristin, and Scott Herndon. *Critical Passages: Teaching the Transition to College Composition*. New York: Teachers College P, 2003.

Elbow, Peter. "Ranking, Evaluating, and Liking: Sorting out Three Forms of Judgment." *College English* 55.2 (1993): 187-207.

_____. "Reflections on Academic Discourse: How It Relates to Freshmen and Colleagues." *College English* 53.2 (1991): 135-56.

_____. *Writing with Power. Techniques for Mastering the Writing Process*. New York: Oxford U P, 1998.

_____. *Writing without Teachers*. New York: Oxford U P, 1998.

Flower, Linda. *Problem Solving Strategies for Writing in College and the Community*. 4th ed. New York: Heinle, 1997.

Harkin, Patricia, and John Schlib, Eds. *Contending with Words. Composition and Rhetoric in the Postmodern Age.* New York: MLA, 1991.

Malinowitz, Harriet. "Business, Pleasure, and the Personal Essay." *College English* 65.3 (2003): 305-22.

Perl, Sondra. *Landmark Essays on the Writing Process.* Hermagoras P, 1995.

Rose, Mike. *Lives on the Boundary.* New York: Penguin, 1990.

Shaughnessy, Mina. *Errors and Expectations.* New York: Oxford U P, 1979.

Spellmeyer, Kurt. *Common Ground: Dialogue, Understanding, and the Teaching of Composition.* Boston: Prentice Hall, 1993.

Contents

who were once pushed to the margins of society have become the most important persons due to the rise of computers. The essay raises issues about growing up, forming an identity, and negotiating between work and personal life.

Kipnis makes an argument about the social construction of the notion of love and the problems it raises for contemporary couples.

Kohn considers issues in education, and questions the definition of an educated person.

Lewontin argues that scientific discoveries, such as the discovery of the DNA, and the human genome project are often used to revive reactionary ideologies. In the process, he mentions Hobbes, and some other political theories. He criticizes the media for popularizing science the wrong way.

The story deals with the unusual discovery of a young man. It covers issues about family structure, relationships between parents and children, responsibility, tolerance, etc.

This is a poem about mothers and daughters, ethnic identity, and the transmission of values form one generation to the next.

Mehta talks about his experience with writing in college as well as his career as a writer.

A wonderful portrayal of "femininity" and what such a notion does to women comes from Toni Morrison. It may also raise issues about violence, love, and consumerism.

Mosley's story reveals the complexity of interracial relationships in today's society and sheds some extra light on sexual politics as well.

This is a Vietnam story, gruesome in its details. It includes issues about war violence, ethics, and mortality as well as questions about the telling of stories and the representation of historical events.

This article combines scientific method and reportage to contextualize issues about genetic history, the human diversity genome project, and controversial theories of race.

Requiem for the Twin Towers

Jean Baudrillard

Jean Baudrillard is a well known French sociologist and theorist of contemporary culture. Born in Reims in 1929, he moved to Paris, where he taught at the Nanterre University, Paris X. Among his works translated into English are Simulacra and Simulation, Seduction, America, Cool Memories, The Transparency of Evil, Impossible Exchange, The Perfect Crime, Screened Out, *and the more recent, The Spirit of Terrorism, from which the following essay has been excerpted. His current interests lie in the influence of technology on society, globalization, mass communication, and mass consumption.*

A version of this paper was Baudrillard's contribution to a debate on the events of September 11 2001, the 'Rencontres philosophiques outre-Atlantique,' organized jointly by New York University and France Culture in Washington Square, Manhattan. The formal contributions were broadcast on France Culture on the afternoon of February 23 2002. The debate, which was largely conducted in French, was chaired by Tom Bishop; other participants were Jacques Rancière, Charles, Larmore and Mark Lilla. The footnotes, which refer to slight variations between the written text and the version delivered in New York, are my own [Trans.].

The September 11 attacks also concern architecture, since what was destroyed was one of the most prestigious of buildings, together with a whole (Western) value-system and a world order.[1]

It may, then, be useful to begin with a historical and architectural analysis of the Twin Towers, in order to grasp the symbolic significance of their destruction.

Reprinted from *The Spirit of Terrorism,* translated by Chris Turner, (2002), by permission of Verso Ltd.

First of all, why the *Twin* Towers? Why *two* towers at the World Trade Center?

All Manhattan's tall buildings had been content to confront each other in a competitive verticality, and the product of this was an architectural panorama reflecting the capitalist system itself—a pyramidal jungle, whose famous image stretched out before you as you arrived from the sea. That image changed after 1973, with the building of the World Trade Center. The effigy of the system was no longer the obelisk and the pyramid, but the punch card and the statistical graph. This architectural graphism is the embodiment of a system that is no longer competitive, but digital and countable, and from which competition has disappeared in favour of networks and monopoly.

Perfect parallelepipeds, standing over 1,300 feet tall, on a square base. Perfectly balanced, blind communicating vessels (they say terrorism is 'blind', but the towers were blind too—monoliths no longer opening on to the outside world, but subject to artificial conditioning[2]). The fact that there were two of them signifies the end of any original reference. If there had been only one, monopoly would not have been perfectly embodied. Only the doubling of the sign truly puts an end to what it designates.

There is a particular fascination in this reduplication. However tall they may have been, the two towers signified, none the less, a halt to verticality. They were not of the same breed as the other buildings. They culminated in the exact reflection of each other. The glass and steel façades of the Rockefeller Center buildings still mirrored each other in an endless specularity. But the Twin Towers no longer had any façades, any faces. With the rhetoric of verticality disappears also the rhetoric of the mirror. There remains only a kind of black box, a series closed on the figure two, as though architecture, like the system, was now merely a product of cloning, and of a changeless genetic code.

New York is the only city in the world that has, throughout its history, tracked the present form of the system and all its many developments with such prodigious fidelity. We must, then, assume that the collapse of the towers—itself a unique event in the history of modern cities—prefigures a kind of dramatic ending and, all in all, disappearance both of this form of architecture and of the world system it embodies. Shaped in the pure computer image of banking and finance, (ac)countable and digital, they were in a sense its brain, and in striking there the terrorists have struck at the brain, at the nerve-centre of the system.

The violence of globalization also involves architecture, and hence the violent protest against it also involves the destruction of that architecture. In terms of collective drama, we can say that the horror for the 4,000 victims of dying in those towers was inseparable from the horror of living in them—the horror of living and working in sarcophagi of concrete and steel.

These architectural monsters, like the Beaubourg Centre, have always exerted an ambiguous fascination, as have the extreme forms of modern technology in general—a contradictory feeling of attraction and repulsion, and hence, somewhere, a secret desire to see them disappear. In the case of the Twin Towers, something particular is added: precisely their symmetry and their twin-ness. There is, admittedly, in this cloning and perfect symmetry and aesthetic quality, a kind of perfect crime against

2

form, a tautology of form which can give rise, in a violent reaction, to the temptation to break that symmetry, to restore an asymmetry, and hence a singularity.

Their destruction itself respected the symmetry of the towers: a double attack, separated by a few minutes' interval, with a sense of suspense between the two impacts. After the first, one could still believe it was an accident. Only the second impact confirmed the terrorist attack. And in the Queens air crash a month later, the TV stations waited, staying with the story (in France) for four hours, waiting to broadcast a possible second crash 'live'. Since that did not occur, we shall never know now whether it was an accident or a terrorist act.

The collapse of the towers is the major symbolic event. Imagine they had not collapsed, or only one had collapsed: the effect would not have been the same at all. The fragility of global power would not have been so strikingly proven. The towers, which were the emblem of that power, still embody it in their dramatic end, which resembles a suicide. Seeing them collapse themselves, as if by implosion, one had the impression that they were committing suicide in response to the suicide of the suicide planes.

Were the Twin Towers destroyed, or did they collapse? Let us be clear about this: the two towers are both a physical, architectural object and a symbolic object[3] (symbolic of financial power and global economic liberalism). The architectural object was destroyed, but it was the symbolic object which was targeted and which it was intended to demolish. One might think the physical destruction brought about the symbolic collapse. But in fact no one, not even the terrorists, had reckoned on the total destruction of the towers. It was, in fact, their symbolic collapse that brought about their physical collapse, not the other way around.

As if the power bearing these towers suddenly lost all energy, all resilience; as though that arrogant power suddenly gave way under the pressure of too intense an effort: the effort always to be the unique world model.

So the towers, tired of being a symbol which was too heavy a burden to bear, collapsed, this time physically, in their totality. Their nerves of steel cracked. They collapsed vertically, drained of their strength, with the whole world looking on in astonishment.

The symbolic collapse came about, then, by a kind of unpredictable complicity—as though the entire system, by its internal fragility, joined in the game of its own liquidation, and hence joined in the game of terrorism. Very logically, and inexorably, the increase in the power of power heightens the will to destroy it. But there is more: somewhere, it was party to its own destruction. The countless disaster movies bear witness to this fantasy, which they attempt to exorcize with images and special effects. But the fascination they exert is a sign that acting-out is never very far away—the rejection of any system, including internal rejection, growing all the stronger as it approaches perfection or omnipotence. It has been said that 'Even God cannot declare war on Himself.' Well, He can. The West, in the position of God (divine omnipotence and absolute moral legitimacy), has become suicidal, and declared war on itself.

Even in their failure, the terrorists succeeded beyond their wildest hopes: in bungling their attack on the White House (while succeeding far beyond their objectives on the towers), they demonstrated unintentionally that that was not the essential target, that political power no longer means much, and real power lies elsewhere. As for what should be built in place of the towers, the problem is insoluble. Quite simply because one can imagine nothing equivalent that would be worth destroying—that would be worthy of being destroyed. The Twin Towers were worth destroying. One cannot say the same of many architectural works. Most things are not even worth destroying or sacrificing. Only works of prestige deserve that fate, for it is an honour. This proposition is not as paradoxical as it sounds, and it raises a basic issue for architecture: one should build only those things which, by their excellence, are worthy of being destroyed. Take a look around with this radical proposition in mind, and you will see what a pass we have come to. Not much would withstand this extreme hypothesis.

This brings us back to what should be the basic question for architecture, which architects never formulate: is it normal to build and construct? In fact it is not, and we should preserve the absolutely problematical character of the undertaking. Undoubtedly, the task of architecture—of good architecture—is to efface itself, to disappear as such. The towers, for their part, have disappeared. But they have left us the symbol of their disappearance, their disappearance as symbol. They, which were the symbol of omnipotence, have become, by their absence, the symbol of the possible disappearance of that omnipotence—which is perhaps an even more potent symbol. Whatever becomes of that global omnipotence, it will have been destroyed here for a moment.

Moreover, although the two towers have disappeared, they have not been annihilated. Even in their pulverized state, they have left behind an intense awareness of their presence. No one who knew them can cease imagining them and the imprint they made on the skyline from all points of the city. Their end in material space has borne them off into a definitive imaginary space. By the grace of terrorism, the World Trade Center has become the world's most beautiful building—the eighth wonder of the world![4]

ENDNOTES

[1] In the New York debate, Baudrillard prefaced his talk with the following comments: 'There is an absolute difficulty in speaking of an absolute event. That is to say, in providing an analysis of it that is not an explanation—as I don't think there is any possible explanation of this event, either by intellectuals or by others—but its *analogon*, so to speak; an analysis which might possibly be as unacceptable as the event, but strikes the . . . let us say, symbolic imagination in more or less the same way.'

[2] In New York, Baudrillard here glossed: 'Air conditioning, but mental conditioning too'.

[3] In New York, Baudrillard added: 'symbolic in the weak sense, but symbolic, for all that'.

[4] After delivering a slightly modified version of this last paragraph in New York, Baudrillard closed with the comment: 'So I set out to produce a Requiem, but it was also, in a way, a Te Deum.'

Blood Music

Greg Bear

Greg Bear is a well-known science fiction writer, winner of many prizes and awards. He was born in San Diego, California and started writing at a very early age. His first novel, Hegira, *was published in 1979. Among his best known novels are:* Eon *(1985),* The Forge of God *(1986),* Queen of Angels *(1990),* Anvil of the Stars *(1992),* Dinosaur Summer *(1998),* Darwin's Radio *(1999), and* Darwin's Children *(2003). "Blood Music" was first published as a short story and later expanded into a novel. The novel was published in 1985. Greg Bear's work is remarkable for the well researched and imaginative use of biology, genetics, and evolution in stories that are both insightful and cautionary.*

There is a principle in nature I don't think anyone has pointed out before. Each hour, a myriad of trillions of little live things—bacteria, microbes, "animalcules"—are born and die, not counting for much except in the bulk of their existence and the accumulation of their tiny effects. They do not perceive deeply. They don't suffer much. A hundred billion, dying, would not begin to have the same importance as a single human death.

Within the ranks of magnitude of all creatures, small as microbes or great as humans, there is an equality of "elan," just as the branches of a tall tree, gathered together, equal the bulk of the limbs below, and all the limbs equal the bulk of the trunk.

That, at least, is the principle. I believe Vergil Ulam was the first to violate it.

It had been two years since I'd last seen Vergil. My memory of him hardly matched the tan, smiling, well-dressed gentleman standing before me. We had made a lunch appointment over the phone the day before, and now faced each other in the wide double doors of the employee's cafeteria at the Mount Freedom Medical Center.

Reprinted from *The Ultimate Cyberpunk*, edited by Pat Cadigan, (2002), Simon & Schuster.

"Vergil?" I asked. "My God, Vergil!"

"Good to see you, Edward." He shook my hand firmly. He had lost ten or twelve kilos and what remained seemed tighter, better proportioned. At the university, Vergil had been the pudgy, shock-haired, snaggle-toothed whiz kid who hot-wired doorknobs, gave us punch that turned our piss blue, and never got a date except with Eileen Termagent, who shared many of his physical characteristics.

"You look fantastic," I said, "Spend a summer in Cabo San Lucas?"

We stood in line at the counter and chose our food. "The tan," he said, picking out a carton of chocolate milk, "is from spending three months under a sun lamp. My teeth were straightened just after I last saw you. I'll explain the rest, but we need a place to talk where no one will listen close."

I steered him to the smoker's corner, where three diehard puffers were scattered among six tables.

"Listen, I mean it," I said as we unloaded our trays. "You've changed. You're looking good."

"I've changed more than you know." His tone was motion-picture ominous, and he delivered the line with a theatrical lift of his brows. "How's Gail?"

Gail was doing well, I told him, teaching nursery school. We'd married the year before. His gaze shifted down to his food—pineapple slice and cottage cheese, piece of banana cream pie—and he said, his voice almost cracking, "Notice something else?"

I squinted in concentration. "Uh."

"Look closer."

"I'm not sure. Well, yes, you're not wearing glasses. Contacts?"

"No. I don't need them anymore."

"And you're a snappy dresser. Who's dressing you now? I hope she's as sexy as she is tasteful."

"Candice isn't—wasn't—responsible for the improvements in my clothes," he said. "I just got a better job, more money to throw around. My taste in clothes is better than my taste in food, as it happens." He grinned the old Vergil self-deprecating grin, but ended it with a peculiar leer. "At any rate, she's left me, I've been fired from my job, I'm living on savings."

"Hold it," I said. "That's a bit crowded. Why not do a linear breakdown? You got a job. Where?"

"Genetron Corp.," he said. "Sixteen months ago."

"I haven't heard of them."

"You will. They're putting out common stock in the next month. It'll shoot off the board. They've broken through with MABs. Medical—"

"I know what MABs are," I interrupted. "At least in theory. Medically Applicable Biochips."

"They have some that work."

"What?" It was my turn to lift my brows.

"Microscopic logic circuits. You inject them into the human body, they set up shop where they're told and trouble-shoot. With Dr. Michael Bernard's approval."

That was quite impressive. Bernard's reputation was spotless. Not only was he associated with the genetic engineering biggies, but he had made news at least once a year in his practice as a neurosurgeon before retiring. Covers on *Time, Mega, Rolling Stone.*

"That's supposed to be secret—stock, breakthrough, Bernard, everything." He looked around and lowered his voice. "But you do whatever the hell you want. I'm through with the bastards."

I whistled. "Make me rich, huh?"

"If that's what you want. Or you can spend some time with me before rushing off to your broker."

"Of course." He hadn't touched the cottage cheese or pie. He had, however, eaten the pineapple slice and drunk the chocolate milk. "So tell me more."

"Well, in med school I was training for lab work. Biochemical research. I've always had a bent for computers, too. So I put myself through my last two years—"

"By selling software packages to Westinghouse," I said.

"It's good my friends remember. That's how I got involved with Genetron, just when they were starting out. They had big money backers, all the lab facilities I thought anyone would ever need. They hired me, and I advanced rapidly.

"Four months and I was doing my own work. I made some breakthroughs," he tossed his hand nonchalantly, "then I went off on tangents they thought were premature. I persisted and they took away my lab, handed it over to a certifiable flatworm. I managed to save part of the experiment before they fired me. But I haven't exactly been cautious . . . or judicious. So now it's going on outside the lab."

I'd always regarded Vergil as ambitious, a trifle cracked, and not terribly sensitive. His relations with authority figures had never been smooth. Science, for him, was like the woman you couldn't possibly have, who suddenly opens her arms to you, long before you're ready for mature love—leaving you afraid you'll forever blow the chance, lose the prize, screw up royally. Apparently, he had. "Outside the lab? I don't get you."

"Edward, I want you to examine me. Give me a thorough physical. Maybe a cancer diagnostic. Then I'll explain more."

"You want a five-thousand-dollar exam?"

"Whatever you can do. Ultrasound, NMR, thermogram, everything."

"I don't know if I can get access to all that equipment. NMR full-scan has only been here a month or two. Hell, you couldn't pick a more expensive way—"

"Then ultrasound. That's all you'll need."

"Vergil, I'm an obstetrician, not a glamour-boy lab-tech. OB-GYN, butt of all jokes. If you're turning into a woman, maybe I can help you."

He leaned forward, almost putting his elbow into the pie, but swinging wide at the last instant by scant millimeters. The old Vergil would have hit it square. "Examine me closely and you'll . . ." He narrowed his eyes and shook his head. "Just examine me."

"So I make an appointment for ultrasound. Who's going to pay?"

"I'm on Blue Shield." He smiled and held up a medical credit card. "I messed with the personnel files at Genetron. Anything up to a hundred thousand dollars medical, they'll never check, never suspect."

He wanted secrecy, so I made arrangements. I filled out his forms myself. As long as everything was billed properly, most of the examination could take place without official notice. I didn't charge for my services. After all, Vergil had turned my piss blue. We were friends.

He came in late at night. I wasn't normally on duty then, but I stayed late, waiting for him on the third floor of what the nurses called the Frankenstein wing. I sat on an orange plastic chair. He arrived, looking olive-colored under the fluorescent lights.

He stripped, and I arranged him on the table. I noticed, first off, that his ankles looked swollen. But they weren't puffy. I felt them several times. They seemed healthy, but looked odd. "Hm," I said.

I ran the paddles over him, picking up areas difficult for the big unit to hit, and programmed the data into the imaging system. Then I swung the table around and inserted it into the enameled orifice of the ultrasound diagnostic unit, the hum-hole, so called by the nurses.

I integrated the data from the hum-hole with that from the paddle sweeps and rolled Vergil out, then set up a video frame. The image took a second to integrate, then flowed into a pattern showing Vergil's skeleton.

Three seconds of that—my jaw gaping—and it switched to his thoracic organs, then his musculature, and finally, vascular system and skin.

"How long since the accident?" I asked, trying to take the quiver out of my voice.

"I haven't been in an accident," he said. "It was deliberate."

"Jesus, they beat you, to keep secrets?"

"You don't understand me, Edward. Look at the images again. I'm not damaged."

"Look, there's thickening here," I indicated the ankles, "and your ribs—that crazy zigzag pattern of interlocks. Broken sometime, obviously. And—"

"Look at my spine," he said. I rotated the image in the video frame.

Buckminster Fuller, I thought. It was fantastic. A cage of triangular projections, all interlocking in ways I couldn't begin to follow, much less understand. I reached around and tried to feel his spine with my fingers. He lifted his arms and looked off at the ceiling.

"I can't find it," I said. "It's all smooth back there." I let go of him and looked at his chest, then prodded his ribs. They were sheathed in something rough and flexible. The harder I pressed, the tougher it became. Then I noticed another change.

"Hey," I said. "You don't have any nipples." There were tiny pigment patches, but no nipple formations at all.

"See?" Vergil asked, shrugging on the white robe. "I'm being rebuilt from the inside out."

In my reconstruction of those hours, I fancy myself saying, "So tell me about it." Perhaps mercifully, I don't remember what I actually said.

He explained with his characteristic circumlocutions. Listening was like trying to get to the meat of a newspaper article through a forest of sidebars and graphic embellishments.

I simplify and condense.

Genetron had assigned him to manufacturing prototype biochips, tiny circuits made out of protein molecules. Some were hooked up to silicon chips little more than a micrometer in size, then sent through rat arteries to chemically keyed locations, to make connections with the rat tissue and attempt to monitor and even control lab-induced pathologies.

"*That* was something," he said. "We recovered the most complex microchip by sacrificing the rat, then debriefed it—hooked the silicon portion up to an imaging system. The computer gave us bar graphs, then a diagram of the chemical characteristics of about eleven centimeters of blood vessel . . . then put it all together to make a picture. We zoomed down eleven centimeters of rat artery. You never saw so many scientists jumping up and down, hugging each other, drinking buckets of bug juice." Bug juice was lab ethanol mixed with Dr Pepper.

Eventually, the silicon elements were eliminated completely in favor of nucleoproteins. He seemed reluctant to explain in detail, but I gathered they found ways to make huge molecules—as large as DNA, and even more complex—into electrochemical computers, using ribosome-like structures as "encoders" and "readers," and RNA as "tape." Vergil was able to mimic reproductive separation and reassembly in his nucleoproteins, incorporating program changes at key points by switching nucleotide pairs. "Genetron wanted me to switch over to supergene engineering, since that was the coming thing everywhere else. Make all kinds of critters, some out of our imagination. But I had different ideas." He twiddled his finger around his ear and made theremin sounds. "Mad scientist time, right?" He laughed, then sobered. "I injected my best nucleoproteins into bacteria to make duplication and compounding easier. Then I started to leave them inside, so the circuits could interact with the cells. They were heuristically programmed; they taught themselves more than I programmed them. The cells fed chemically coded information to the computers, the computers processed it and made decisions, the cells became smart. I mean, smart as planaria, for starters. Imagine an *E. coli* as smart as a planarian worm!"

I nodded. "I'm imagining."

"Then I really went off on my own. We had the equipment, the techniques; and I knew the molecular language. I could make really dense, really complicated biochips by compounding the nucleoproteins, making them into little brains. I did some research into how far I could go, theoretically. Sticking with bacteria, I could make them a biochip with the computing capacity of a sparrow's brain. Imagine how jazzed I was! Then I saw a way to increase the complexity a thousandfold, by using something we regarded as a nuisance—quantum chitchat between the fixed elements of the circuits. Down that small, even the slightest change could bomb a biochip. But I developed a program that actually predicted and took advantage of electron tunneling. Emphasized the heuristic aspects of the computer, used the chitchat as a method of increasing complexity."

"You're losing me," I said.

"I took advantage of randomness. The circuits could repair themselves, compare memories, and correct faulty elements. The whole schmeer. I gave them basic instructions: Go forth and multiply. Improve. By God, you should have seen some of the cultures a week later! It was amazing. They were evolving all on their own, like little cities. I destroyed them all. I think one of the petri dishes would have grown legs and walked out of the incubator if I'd kept feeding it."

"You're kidding." I looked at him. "You're not kidding."

"Man, they *knew* what it was like to improve! They knew where they had to go, but they were just so limited, being in bacteria bodies, with so few resources."

"How smart were they?"

"I couldn't be sure. They were associating in clusters of a hundred to two hundred cells, each cluster behaving like an autonomous unit. Each cluster might have been as smart as a rhesus monkey. They exchanged information through their pili, passed on bits of memory, and compared notes. Their organization was obviously different from a group of monkeys. Their world was so much simpler, for one thing. With their abilities, they were masters of the petri dishes. I put phages in with them; the phages didn't have a chance. They used every option available to change and grow."

"How is that possible?"

"What?" He seemed surprised I wasn't accepting everything at face value.

"Cramming so much into so little. A rhesus monkey is not your simple little calculator, Vergil."

"I haven't made myself clear," he said, obviously irritated. "I was using nucleo-protein computers. They're like DNA, but all the information can interact. Do you know how many nucleotide pairs there are in the DNA of a single bacteria?"

It had been a long time since my last biochemistry lesson. I shook my head.

"About two million. Add in the modified ribosome structures—fifteen thousand of them, each with a molecular weight of about three million—and consider the combinations and permutations. The RNA is arranged like a continuous loop paper tape, surrounded by ribosomes ticking off instructions and manufacturing protein chains . . ." His eyes were bright and slightly moist. "Besides, I'm not saying every cell was a distinct entity. They cooperated."

"How many bacteria in the dishes you destroyed?"

"Billions. I don't know." He smirked. "You got it, Edward. Whole planetsful of *E. coli.*"

"But they didn't fire you then?"

"No. They didn't know what was going on, for one thing. I kept compounding the molecules, increasing their size and complexity. When bacteria were too limited, I took blood from myself, separated out white cells, and injected them with the new biochips. I watched them, put them through mazes and little chemical problems. They were whizzes. Time is a lot faster at that level—so little distance for the messages to cross, and the environment is much simpler. Then I forgot to store a file under my secret code in the lab computers. Some managers found it and guessed what I was up to. Everybody panicked. They thought we'd have every social watchdog in the country on our backs because of what I'd done. They started to destroy my work and wipe my programs. Ordered me to sterilize my white cells. Christ." He pulled the white robe off and started to get dressed. "I only had a day or two. I separated out the most complex cells –"

"How complex?"

"They were clustering in hundred-cell groups, like the bacteria. Each group as smart as a ten-year-old kid, maybe." He studied my face for a moment. "Still doubting? Want me to run through how many nucleotide pairs there are in a mammalian cell? I tailored my computers to take advantage of the white cells' capacity. Ten billion nucleotide pairs, Edward. Ten E-f—ing ten. And they don't have a huge body to worry about, taking up most of their thinking time."

"Okay," I said. "I'm convinced. What did you do?"

"I mixed the cells back into a cylinder of whole blood and injected myself with it." He buttoned the top of his shirt and smiled thinly at me. "I'd programmed them with every drive I could, talked as high a level as I could using just enzymes and such. After that, they were on their own."

"You programmed them to go forth and multiply, improve?" I repeated.

"I think they developed some characteristics picked up by the biochips in their *E. coli* phases. The white cells could talk to one another with extruded memories. They almost certainly found ways to ingest other types of cells and alter them without killing them."

"You're crazy."

"You can see the screen! Edward, I haven't been sick since. I used to get colds all the time. I've never felt better."

"They're inside you, finding things, changing them."

"And by now, each cluster is as smart as you or I."

"You're absolutely nuts."

He shrugged. "They fired me. They thought I was going to get revenge for what they did to my work. They ordered me out of the labs, and I haven't had a real chance to see what's been going on inside me until now. Three months."

"So …" My mind was racing. "You lost weight because they improved your fat metabolism. Your bones are stronger, your spine has been completely rebuilt—"

"No more backaches even if I sleep on my old mattress."

"Your heart looks different."

"I didn't know about the heart," he said, examining the frame image from a few inches. "About the fat—I was thinking about that. They could increase my brown cells, fix up the metabolism. I haven't been as hungry lately. I haven't changed my eating habits that much—I still want the same old junk—but somehow I get around to eating only what I need. I don't think they know what my brain is yet. Sure, they've got all the glandular stuff—but they don't have the *big* picture, if you see what I mean. They don't know *I'm* in there. But boy, they sure did figure out what my reproductive organs are."

I glanced at the image and shifted my eyes away.

"Oh, they look pretty normal," he said, hefting his scrotum obscenely. He snickered. "But how else do you think I'd land a real looker like Candice? She was just after a one-night stand with a techie. I looked okay then, no tan but trim, with good clothes. She'd never screwed a techie before. Joke time, right? But my little geniuses kept us up half the night. I think they made improvements each time. I felt like I had a god-damned fever."

His smile vanished. "But then one night my skin started to crawl. It really scared me. I thought things were getting out of hand. I wondered what they'd do when they crossed the blood-brain barrier and found out about *me*—about the brain's real function. So I began a campaign to keep them under control. I figured, the reason they wanted to get into the skin was the simplicity of running circuits across a surface. Much easier than trying to maintain chains of communication in and around muscles, organs, vessels. The skin was much more direct. So I bought a quartz lamp." He caught my puzzled expression. "In the lab, we'd break down the protein in biochip cells by exposing them to ultraviolet light. I alternated sun lamp with quartz treatments. Keeps them out of my skin, so far as I can tell, and gives me a nice tan."

"Give you skin cancer, too," I commented.

"They'll probably take care of that. Like police."

"Okay, I've examined you, you've told me a story I still find hard to believe . . . what do you want me to do?"

"I'm not as nonchalant as I act, Edward. I'm worried. I'd like to find some way to control them before they find out about my brain. I mean, think of it, they're in the trillions by now, each one smart. They're cooperating to some extent. I'm probably the smartest thing on the planet, and they haven't even begun to get their act together yet. I don't really want them to take over." He laughed very unpleasantly. "Steal my soul, you know? So think of some treatment to block them. Maybe we can starve the little buggers. Just think on it." He buttoned his shirt. "Give me a call." He handed me a slip of paper with his address and phone number. Then he went to the keyboard and erased the image on the frame, dumping the memory of the examination. "Just you," he said. "Nobody else for now. And please . . . hurry."

It was three o'clock in the morning when Vergil walked out of the examination room. He'd allowed me to take blood samples, then shaken my hand—his palm damp, nervous—and cautioned me against ingesting anything from the specimens.

Before I went home, I put the blood through a series of tests. The results were ready the next day.

I picked them up during my lunch break in the afternoon, then destroyed all the samples. I did it like a robot. It took me five days and nearly sleepless nights to accept what I'd seen. His blood was normal enough, though the machines diagnosed the patient as having an infection. High levels of leukocytes—white blood cells— and histamines. On the fifth day, I believed.

Gail was home before I, but it was my turn to fix dinner. She slipped one of the school's disks into the home system and showed me video art her nursery kids had been creating. I watched quietly, ate with her in silence.

I had two dreams, part of my final acceptance. The first that evening—which had me up thrashing in my sheets—I witnessed the destruction of the planet Krypton, Superman's home world. Billions of superhuman geniuses went screaming off in walls of fire. I related the destruction to my sterilizing the samples of Vergil's blood.

The second dream was worse: I dreamed that New York City was raping a woman. By the end of the dream, she was giving birth to little embryo cities, all wrapped up in translucent sacs, soaked with blood from the difficult labor.

I called him on the morning of the sixth day. He answered on the fourth ring. "I have some results," I said. "Nothing conclusive. But I want to talk with you. In person."

"Sure," he said. "I'm staying inside for the time being." His voice was strained; he sounded tired.

Vergil's apartment was in a fancy high-rise near the lake shore. I took the elevator up, listening to little advertising jingles and watching dancing holograms display products, empty apartments for rent, the building's hostess discussing social activities for the week.

Vergil opened the door and motioned me in. He wore a checked robe with long sleeves and carpet slippers. He clutched an unlit pipe in one hand, his fingers twisting it back and forth as he walked away from me and sat down, saying nothing.

"You have an infection," I said.

"Oh?"

"That's all the blood analyses tell me. I don't have access to the electron microscopes."

"I don't think it's really an infection," he said. "After all, they're my own cells. Probably something else . . . sign of their presence, of the change. We can't expect to understand everything that's happening."

I removed my coat. "Listen," I said, "you have me worried now." The expression on his face stopped me: a kind of frantic beatitude. He squinted at the ceiling and pursed his lips.

"Are you stoned?" I asked.

He shook his head, then nodded once, very slowly. "Listening," he said.

"To what?"

"I don't know. Not sounds . . . exactly. Like music. The heart, all the blood vessels, friction of blood along the arteries, veins. Activity. Music in the blood." He looked at me plaintively. "Why aren't you at work?"

"My day off. Gail's working."

"Can you stay?"

I shrugged. "I suppose." I sounded suspicious. I was glancing around the apartment, looking for ashtrays, packs of papers.

"I'm not stoned, Edward," he said. "I may be wrong, but I think something big is happening. I think they're finding out who I am."

I sat down across from Vergil, staring at him intently. He didn't seem to notice. Some inner process was involving him. When I asked for a cup of coffee, he motioned to the kitchen. I boiled a pot of water and took a jar of instant from the cabinet. With cup in hand, I returned to my seat. He was twisting his head back and forth, eyes open. "You always knew what you wanted to be, didn't you?" he asked me.

13

"More or less."

"A gynecologist. Smart moves. Never false moves. I was different. I had goals, but no direction. Like a map without roads, just places to be. I didn't give a shit for anything, anyone but myself. Even science. Just a means. I'm surprised I got so far. I even hated my folks."

He gripped his chair arms.

"Something wrong?" I asked.

"They're talking to me," he said. He shut his eyes.

For an hour he seemed to be asleep. I checked his pulse, which was strong and steady, felt his forehead—slightly cool—and made myself more coffee. I was looking through a magazine, at a loss what to do, when he opened his eyes again, "Hard to figure exactly what time is like for them," he said. "It's taken them maybe three, four days to figure out language, key human concepts. Now they're on to it. On to me. Right now."

"How's that?"

He claimed there were thousands of researchers hooked up to his neurons. He couldn't give details. "They're damned efficient, you know," he said. "They haven't screwed me up yet."

"We should get you into the hospital now."

"What in hell could they do? Did you figure out any way to control them? I mean, they're my own cells."

"I've been thinking. We could starve them. Find out what metabolic differences—"

"I'm not sure I want to be rid of them," Vergil said. "They're not doing any harm."

"How do you know?"

He shook his head and held up one finger. "Wait. They're trying to figure out what space is. That's tough for them. They break distances down into concentrations of chemicals. For them, space is like intensity of taste."

"Vergil—"

"Listen! Think, Edward!" His tone was excited but even. "Oh-serve! Something big is happening inside me. They talk to one another across the fluid, through membranes. They tailor something—viruses?—to carry data stored in nucleic acid chains. I think they're saying 'RNA.' That makes sense. That's one way I programmed them. But plasmid-like structures, too. Maybe that's what your machines think is a sign of infection—all their chattering in my blood, packets of data. Tastes of other individuals. Peers. Superiors. Subordinates."

"Vergil, I'm listening, but I still think you should be in a hospital."

"This is my show, Edward," he said. "I'm their universe. They're amazed by the new scale." He was quiet again for a time. I squatted by his chair and pulled up the sleeve to his robe. His arm was crisscrossed with white lines. I was about to go to the phone and call for an ambulance when he stood and stretched. "Do you realize," he said, "how many body cells we kill each time we move?"

"I'm going to call for an ambulance," I said.

"No, you aren't." His tone stopped me. "I told you, I'm not sick; this is my show. Do you know what they'd do to me in a hospital? They'd be like cavemen trying to fix a computer the same way they fix a stone ax. It would be a farce."

"Then what the hell am I doing here?" I asked, getting angry. "I can't do anything. I'm one of those cavemen."

"You're a friend," Vergil said, fixing his eyes on me. I had the impression I was being watched by more than just Vergil. "I want you here to keep me company." He laughed. "But I'm not exactly alone."

He walked around the apartment for two hours, fingering things, looking out windows, making himself lunch slowly and methodically. "You know, they can actually feel their own thoughts," he said about noon. "I mean, the cytoplasm seems to have a will of its own, a kind of subconscious life counter to the rationality they've only recently acquired. They hear the chemical 'noise' or whatever of the molecules fitting and unfitting inside."

At two o'clock, I called Gail to tell her I would be late. I was almost sick with tension but I tried to keep my voice level. "Remember Vergil Ulam? I'm talking with him right now."

"Everything okay?" she asked.

Was it? Decidedly not. "Fine," I said.

"Culture!" Vergil said, peering around the kitchen wall at me. I said good-bye and hung up the phone. "They're always swimming in that bath of information. Contributing to it. It's a kind of gestalt-thing, whatever. The hierarchy is absolute. They send tailored phages after cells that don't interact properly. Viruses specified to individuals or groups. No escape. One gets pierced by the virus, the cell blebs outward, it explodes and dissolves. But it's not just a dictatorship, I think they effectively have more freedom than in a democracy. I mean, they vary so differently from individual to individual. Does that make sense? They vary in different ways than we do."

"Hold it," I said, gripping his shoulders. "Vergil, you're pushing me close to the edge. I can't take this much longer. I don't understand, I'm not sure I believe—"

"Not even now?"

"Okay, let's say you're giving me the, the right interpretation. Giving it to me straight. The whole thing's true. Have you bothered to figure out all the consequences yet? What all this means, where it might lead?"

He walked into the kitchen and drew a glass of water from the tap, then returned and stood next to me. His expression had changed from childish absorption to sober concern. "I've never been very good at that."

"Aren't you afraid?"

"I was. Now I'm not sure." He fingered the tie of his robe. "Look, I don't want you to think I went around you, over your head or something. But I met with Michael Bernard yesterday. He put me through his private clinic, took specimens. Told me to quit the lamp treatments. He called this morning, just before you did. He says it all checks out. And he asked me not to tell anybody." He paused and his expression became dreamy again. "Cities of cells," he continued. "Edward, they push pili-like tubes through the tissues, spread information—"

"Stop it!" I shouted. "Checks out? What checks out?"

"As Bernard puts it, I have 'severely enlarged macro-phages' throughout my system. And he concurs on the anatomical changes. So it's not just our common delusion."

"What does he plan to do?"

"I don't know. I think he'll probably convince Genetron to reopen the lab."

"Is that what you want?"

"It's not just having the lab again. I want to show you. Since I stopped the lamp treatments. I'm still changing." He undid his robe and let it slide to the floor. All over his body, his skin was criss-crossed with white lines. Along his back, the lines were starting to form ridges.

"My God," I said.

"I'm not going to be much good anywhere else but the lab soon. I won't be able to go out in public. Hospitals wouldn't know what to do, as I said."

"You're . . . you can talk to them, tell them to slow down," I said, aware how ridiculous that sounded.

"Yes, indeed I can, but they don't necessarily listen."

"I thought you were their god or something."

"The ones hooked up to my neurons aren't the big wheels. They're researchers, or at least serve the same function. They know I'm here, what I am, but that doesn't mean they've convinced the upper levels of the hierarchy."

"They're disputing?"

"Something like that. It's not all that bad, anyway. If the lab is reopened, I have a home, a place to work." He glanced out the window, as if looking for someone. "I don't have anything left but them. They aren't afraid, Edward. I've never felt so close to anything before." The beatific smile again. "I'm responsible for them. Mother to them all."

"You have no way of knowing what they're going to do."

He shook his head.

"No, I mean it. You say they're like a civilization—"

"Like a thousand civilizations."

"Yes, and civilizations have been known to screw up. Warfare, the environment—"

I was grasping at straws, trying to restrain a growing panic. I wasn't competent to handle the enormity of what was happening. Neither was Vergil. He was the last person I would have called insightful and wise about large issues.

"But I'm the only one at risk."

"You don't know that. Jesus, Vergil, look what they're *doing* to you!"

"To me, all to me!" he said. "Nobody else."

I shook my head and held up my hands in a gesture of defeat. "Okay, so Bernard gets them to reopen the lab, you move in, become a guinea pig. What then?"

"They treat me right. I'm more than just good old Vergil Ulam now. I'm a goddamned galaxy, a super-mother."

"Super-host, you mean." He conceded the point with a shrug.

I couldn't take any more. I made my exit with a few flimsy excuses, then sat in the lobby of the apartment building, trying to calm down. Somebody had to talk some sense into him. Who would he listen to? He had gone to Bernard . . .

And it sounded as if Bernard was not only convinced, but very interested. People of Bernard's stature didn't coax the Vergil Ulams of the world along, not unless they felt it was to their advantage.

I had a hunch, and I decided to play it. I went to a pay phone, slipped in my credit card, and called Genetron.

"I'd like you to page Dr. Michael Bernard," I told the receptionist.

"Who's calling, please?"

"This is his answering service. We have an emergency call and his beeper doesn't seem to be working."

A few anxious minutes later, Bernard came on the line. "Who the hell is this?" he asked quietly. "I don't have an answering service."

"My name is Edward Milligan. I'm a friend of Vergil Ulam's. I think we have some problems to discuss."

We made an appointment to talk the next morning.

I went home and tried to think of excuses to keep me off the next day's hospital shift. I couldn't concentrate on medicine, couldn't give my patients anywhere near the attention they deserved.

Guilty, anxious, angry, afraid.

That was how Gail found me. I slipped on a mask of calm and we fixed dinner together. After eating, we watched the city lights come on in late twilight through the bayside window, holding on to each other. Odd winter starlings pecked at the yellow lawn in the last few minutes of light, then flew away with a rising wind which made the windows rattle.

"Something's wrong," Gail said softly. "Are you going to tell me, or just act like everything's normal?"

"It's just me," I said. "Nervous. Work at the hospital."

"Oh, lord," she said, sitting up. "You're going to divorce me for that Baker woman." Mrs. Baker weighed three hundred and sixty pounds and hadn't known she was pregnant until her fifth month.

"No," I said, listless.

"Rapturous relief," Gail said, touching my forehead lightly. "You know this kind of introspection drives me crazy."

"Well, it's nothing I can talk about yet, so …" I patted her hand.

"That's disgustingly patronizing," she said, getting up. "I'm going to make some tea. Want some?" Now she was miffed, and I was tense with not telling.

Why not just reveal all? I asked myself. An old friend of mine was turning himself into a galaxy.

I cleared away the table instead. That night, unable to sleep, I looked down on Gail in bed from my sitting position, pillow against the wall, and tried to determine what I knew was real, and what wasn't.

I'm a doctor, I told myself. A technical, scientific profession. I'm supposed to be immune to things like future shock.

Vergil Ulam was turning into a galaxy.

17

How would it feel to be topped off with a trillion Chinese? I grinned in the dark, and almost cried at the same time. What Vergil had inside him was unimaginably stranger than Chinese. Stranger than anything I—or Vergil—could easily understand. Perhaps ever understand.

But I knew what was real. The bedroom, the city lights faint through gauze curtains. Gail sleeping. Very important. Gail, in bed, sleeping.

The dream came again. This time the city came in through the window and attacked Gail. It was a great, spiky lighted-up prowler and it growled in a language I couldn't understand, made up of auto horns, crowded noises, construction bedlam. I tried to fight it off, but it got to her—and turned into a drift of stars, sprinkling all over the bed, all over everything. I jerked awake and stayed up until dawn, dressed with Gail, kissed her, savored the reality of her human, unviolated lips.

And went to meet with Bernard. He had been loaned a suite in a big downtown hospital; I rode the elevator to the sixth floor, and saw what fame and fortune could mean.

The suite was tastefully furnished, fine serigraphs on wood-paneled walls, chrome and glass furniture, cream-colored carpet, Chinese brass, and wormwood-grain cabinets and tables.

He offered me a cup of coffee, and I accepted. He took a seat in the breakfast nook, and I sat across from him, cradling my cup in moist palms. He was dapper, wearing a gray suit; had graying hair and a sharp profile. He was in his mid-sixties and he looked quite a bit like Leonard Bernstein.

"About our mutual acquaintance," he said. "Mr. Ulam. Brilliant. And, I won't hesitate to say, courageous."

"He's my friend. I'm worried about him."

Bernard held up one finger. "Courageous—and a bloody damned fool. What's happening to him should never have been allowed. He may have done it under duress, but that's no excuse. Still, what's done is done. He's talked to you, I take it."

I nodded. "He wants to return to Genetron."

"Of course. That's where all his equipment is. Where his home probably will be while we sort this out."

"Sort it out—how? What use is it?" I wasn't thinking too clearly. I had a slight headache.

"I can think of a large number of uses for small, super-dense computer elements with a biological base. Can't you? Genetron has already made breakthroughs, but this is something else again."

"What do you envision?"

Bernard smiled. "I'm not really at liberty to say. It'll be revolutionary. We'll have to get him in lab conditions. Animal experiments have to be conducted. We'll have to start from scratch, of course. Vergil's . . . um . . . colonies can't be transferred. They're based on his white blood cells. So we have to develop colonies that won't trigger immune reactions to other animals."

"Like an infection?" I asked.

"I suppose there are comparisons. But Vergil is not infected."

"My tests indicate he is."

"That's probably the bits of data floating around in his blood, don't you think?"

"I don't know."

"Listen, I'd like you to come down to the lab after Vergil is settled in. Your expertise might be useful to us."

Us. He was working with Genetron hand in glove. Could he be objective? "How will you benefit from all this?"

"Edward, I have always been at the forefront of my profession. I see no reason why I shouldn't be helping here. With my knowledge of brain and nerve functions, and the research I've been conducting in neurophysiology—"

"You could help Genetron hold off an investigation by the government," I said.

"That's being very blunt. Too blunt, and unfair."

"Perhaps. Anyway, yes. I'd like to visit the lab when Vergil's settled in. If I'm still welcome, bluntness and all." He looked at me sharply. I wouldn't be playing on *his* team; for a moment, his thoughts were almost nakedly apparent.

"Of course," Bernard said, rising with me. He reached out to shake my hand. His palm was damp. He was as nervous as I was, even if he didn't look it.

I returned to my apartment and stayed there until noon, reading, trying to sort things out. Reach a decision. What was real, what I needed to protect.

There is only so much change anyone can stand. Innovation, yes, but slow application. Don't force. Everyone has the right to stay the same until they decide otherwise.

The greatest thing in science since . . .

And Bernard would force it. Genetron would force it. I couldn't handle the thought. "Neo-Luddite," I said to myself. A filthy accusation.

When I pressed Vergil's number on the building security panel, Vergil answered almost immediately. "Yeah," he said. He sounded exhilarated now. "Come on up. I'll be in the bathroom. Door's unlocked."

I entered his apartment and walked through the hallway to the bathroom. Vergil was in the tub, up to his neck in pinkish water. He smiled vaguely at me and splashed his hands. "Looks like I slit my wrists, doesn't it?" he said softly. "Don't worry. Everything's fine now. Genetron's going to take me back. Bernard just called." He pointed to the bathroom phone and intercom.

I sat down on the toilet and noticed the sun lamp fixture standing unplugged next to the linen cabinets. The bulbs sat in a row on the edge of the sink counter. "You're sure that's what you want," I said, my shoulders slumping.

"Yeah, I think so," he said. "They can take better care of me. I'm getting cleaned up, go over there this evening. Bernard's picking me up in his limo. Style. From here on in, everything's style."

The pinkish color in the water didn't look like soap. "Is that bubble bath?" I asked. Some of it came to me in a rush then and I felt a little weaker: what had occurred to me was just one more obvious and necessary insanity.

"No," Vergil said. I knew that already.

"No," he repeated, "it's coming from my skin. They're not telling me everything, but I think they're sending out scouts. Astronauts." He looked at me with an expression that didn't quite equal concern; more like curiosity as to how I'd take it.

The confirmation made my stomach muscles tighten as if waiting for a punch. I had never even considered the possibility until now, perhaps because I had been concentrating on other aspects. "Is this the first time?" I asked.

"Yeah," he said. He laughed. "I've half a mind to let the little buggers down the drain. Let them find out what the world's really about."

"They'd go everywhere," I said.

"Sure enough."

"How . . . how are you feeling?"

"I'm feeling pretty good now. Must be billions of them." More splashing with his hands. "What do you think? Should I let the buggers out?"

Quickly, hardly thinking, I knelt down beside the tub. My fingers went for the cord on the sun lamp and I plugged it in. He had hot-wired doorknobs, turned my piss blue, played a thousand dumb practical jokes and never grown up, never grown mature enough to understand that he was just brilliant enough to really affect the world; he would never learn caution.

He reached for the drain knob. "You know, Edward, I—"

He never finished. I picked up the fixture and dropped it into the tub, jumping back at the flash of steam and sparks. Vergil screamed and thrashed and jerked and then everything was still, except for the low, steady sizzle and the smoke wafting from his hair.

I lifted the toilet and vomited. Then I clenched my nose and went into the living room. My legs went out from under me and I sat abruptly on the couch.

After an hour, I searched through Vergil's kitchen and found bleach, ammonia, and a bottle of Jack Daniel's. I returned to the bathroom, keeping the center of my gaze away from Vergil. I poured first the booze, then the bleach, then the ammonia into the water. Chlorine started bubbling up and I left, closing the door behind me.

The phone was ringing when I got home. I didn't answer. It could have been the hospital. It could have been Bernard. Or the police. I could envision having to explain everything to the police. Genetron would stonewall; Bernard would be unavailable.

I was exhausted, all my muscles knotted with tension and whatever name one can give to the feelings one has after—

Committing genocide?

That certainly didn't seem real. I could not believe I had just murdered a hundred trillion intelligent beings. Snuffed a galaxy. It was laughable. But I didn't laugh.

It was not at all hard to believe I had just killed one human being, a friend. The smoke, the melted lamp rods, the drooping electrical outlet and smoking cord.

Vergil.

I had dunked the lamp into the tub with Vergil.

I felt sick. Dreams, cities raping Gail (and what about his girlfriend, Candice?). Letting the water filled with them out. Galaxies sprinkling over us all. What horror. Then again, what potential beauty—a new kind of life, symbiosis and transformation.

Had I been thorough enough to kill them all? I had a moment of panic. Tomorrow, I thought, I will sterilize his apartment. Somehow. I didn't even think of Bernard.

When Gail came in the door, I was asleep on the couch. I came to, groggy, and she looked down at me.

"You feeling okay?" she asked, perching on the edge of the couch. I nodded.

"What are you planning for dinner?" My mouth wasn't working properly. The words were mushy. She felt my forehead.

"Edward, you have a fever," she said. "A very high fever."

I stumbled into the bathroom and looked in the mirror. Gail was close behind me. "What is it?" she asked.

There were lines under my collar, around my neck. White lines, like freeways. They had already been in me a long time, days.

"Damp palms," I said. So obvious.

I think we nearly died. I struggled at first, but within minutes I was too weak to move. Gail was just as sick within an hour.

I lay on the carpet in the living room, drenched in sweat. Gail lay on the couch, her face the color of talcum, eyes closed, like a corpse in an embalming parlor. For a time I thought she was dead. Sick as I was, I raged—hated, felt tremendous guilt at my weakness, my slowness to understand all the possibilities. Then I no longer cared. I was too weak to blink, so I closed my eyes and waited.

There was a rhythm in my arms, my legs. With each pulse of blood, a kind of sound welled up within me. A sound like an orchestra thousands strong, but not playing in unison; playing whole seasons of symphonies at once. Music in the blood. The sound or whatever became harsher, but more coordinated, wavetrains finally cancelling into silence, then separating into harmonic beats.

The beats seemed to melt into me, into the sound of my own heart.

First, they subdued our immune responses. The war—and it was a war, on a scale never before known on Earth, with trillions of combatants—lasted perhaps two days.

By the time I regained enough strength to get to the kitchen faucet, I could feel them working on my brain, trying to crack the code and find the god within the proto-plasm. I drank until I was sick, then drank more moderately and took a glass to Gail. She sipped at it. Her lips were cracked, her eyes bloodshot and ringed with yellowish crumbs. There was some color in her skin. Minutes later, we were eating feebly in the kitchen.

"What in hell was *that*?" was the first thing she asked. I didn't have the strength to explain, so I shook my head. I peeled an orange and shared it with her. "We should call a doctor," she said. But I knew we wouldn't. I was already receiving messages; it was becoming apparent that any sensation of freedom we had was illusory.

The messages were simple at first. Memories of commands, rather than the commands themselves, manifested themselves in my thoughts. We were not to leave the apartment—a concept which seemed quite abstract to those in control, even if undesirable—and we were not to have contact with others. We would be allowed to eat certain foods, and drink tap water, for the time being.

With the subsidence of the fevers, the transformations were quick and drastic. Almost simultaneously, Gail and I were immobilized. She was sitting at the table, I was kneeling on the floor. I was able barely to see her in the corner of my eye.

Her arm was developing pronounced ridges.

They had learned inside Vergil; their tactics within the two of us were very different. I itched all over for about two hours—two hours in hell—before they made the break-through and found me. The effort of ages on their time scale paid off and they communicated smoothly and directly with this great, clumsy intelligence which had once controlled their universe.

They were not cruel. When the concept of discomfort and its undesirability was made clear, they worked to alleviate it. They worked too effectively. For another hour, I was in a sea of bliss, out of all contact with them.

With dawn the next day, we were allowed freedom to move again; specifically, to go to the bathroom. There were certain waste products they could not deal with. I voided those—my urine was purple—and Gail followed suit. We looked at each other vacantly in the bathroom. Then she managed a slight smile. "Are they talking to you?" she asked. I nodded. "Then I'm not crazy."

For the next twelve hours, control seemed to loosen on some levels. During that time, I managed to pencil the majority of this manuscript. I suspect there was another kind of war going on in me. Gail was capable of our previous limited motion, but no more.

When full control resumed, we were instructed to hold each other. We did not hesitate.

"Eddie . . ." she whispered. My name was the last sound I ever heard from outside.

Standing, we grew together. In hours, our legs expanded and spread out. Then extensions grew to the windows to take in sunlight, and to the kitchen to take water from the sink. Filaments soon reached to all corners of the room, stripping paint and plaster from the walls, fabric and stuffing from the furniture.

By the next dawn, the transformation was complete.

I no longer have any clear view of what we look like. I suspect we resemble cells—large, flat and filamented cells, draped purposefully across most of the apartment. The great shall mimic the small.

I have been asked to carry on recording, but soon that will not be possible. Our intelligence fluctuates daily as we are absorbed into the minds within. Each day, our individuality declines. We are, indeed, great clumsy dinosaurs. Our memories have been taken over by billions of them, and our personalities have been spread through the transformed blood.

Soon there will be no need for centralization.

I am informed that already the plumbing has been invaded. People throughout the building are undergoing transformation.

Within the old time frame of weeks, we will reach the lakes, rivers, and seas in force.

I can barely begin to guess the results. Every square inch of the planet will teem with thought. Years from now, perhaps much sooner, they will subdue their own individuality—what there is of it.

New creatures will come, then. The immensity of their capacity for thought will be inconceivable.

All my hatred and fear is gone now.

I leave them—us—with only one question.

How many times has this happened, elsewhere? Travelers never came through space to visit the Earth. They had no need.

They had found universes in grains of sand.

Filling Station

Elizabeth Bishop

Elizabeth Bishop was born in Worcester, Massachusetts, but she grew up in Canada, traveled all over the world, and lived in Brazil for sixteen years. She was educated at Vassar, where she met and befriended Marianne More, who was already an established poet. Starting with her first book, her work was honored with numerous prizes for poetry. Her volumes include: North & South *(1946),* Questions of Travel *(1965),* The Complete Poems *(1969, and* Geography III *(1976). Posthumous works include:* The Complete Poems, 1927–1979 *(1983) and* The Collected Prose *(1984).*

Oh, but it is dirty!
—this little filling station,
oil-soaked, oil-permeated
to a disturbing, over-all
black translucency.
Be careful with that match!

Father wears a dirty,
oil-soaked monkey suit
that cuts him under the arms,
and several quick and saucy
and greasy sons assist him
(it's a family filling station),
all quite thoroughly dirty.

Do they live in the station?
It has a cement porch
behind the pumps, and on it
a set of crushed and grease—
impregnated wickerwork;
on the wicker sofa
a dirty dog, quite comfy.

Some comic books provide
the only note of color—
of certain color. They lie
upon a big dim doily
draping a taboret
(part of the set), beside
a big hirsute begonia.

Why the extraneous plant?
Why the taboret?
Why, oh why, the doily?
(Embroidered in daisy stitch
with marguerites, I think,
and heavy with gray crochet.)

Somebody embroidered the doily.
Somebody waters the plant,
or oils it, maybe. Somebody
arranges the rows of cans
so that they softly say:
ESSO—SO—SO—SO

to high-strung automobiles.
Somebody loves us all.

If the River Was Whiskey

T. Coraghessan Boyle

*Born in the Hudson Valley of New York State, T. Coraghessan Boyle
is the author of numerous short stories and novels. His novels include* East Is East *and* The Road to Wellville *(1993), and his novel*
World's End *won the 1988 PEN/Faulkner Award for Fiction. Boyle's
short fiction has been published in* The New Yorker, Harper's, The
Atlantic, *and* Playboy, *and collected in* Without A Hero *and* If the
River Was Whiskey. *He lives near Santa Barbara, California.*

The water was a heartbeat, a pulse, it stole the heat from his body and pumped it to
his brain. Beneath the surface, magnified through the shimmering lens of his face
mask, were silver shoals of fish, forests of weed, a silence broken only by the distant
throbbing hum of an outboard. Above, there was the sun, the white flash of a faraway sailboat, the weatherbeaten dock with its weatherbeaten rowboat, his mother
in her deck chair, and the vast depthless green of the world beyond.

He surfaced like a dolphin, spewing water from the vent of his snorkel, and
sliced back to the dock. The lake came with him, two bony arms and the wedge of
a foot, the great heaving splash of himself flat out on the dock like something thrown
up in a storm. And then, without pausing even to snatch up a towel, he had the spinning rod in hand and the silver lure was sizzling out over the water, breaking the surface just above the shadowy arena he'd fixed in his mind. His mother looked up at
the splash. "Tiller," she called, "come get a towel."

His shoulders quaked. He huddled and stamped his feet, but he never took his
eyes off the tip of the rod. Twitching it suggestively, he reeled with the jerky, hesitant
motion that would drive lunker fish to a frenzy. Or so he'd read, anyway.

"Tilden, do you hear me?"

"I saw a Northern," he said. "A big one. Two feet maybe." The lure was in. A flick
of his wrist sent it back. Still reeling, he ducked his head to wipe his nose on his wet

---

shoulder. He could feel the sun on his back now and he envisioned the skirted lure in the water, sinuous, sensual, irresistible, and he waited for the line to quicken with the strike.

The porch smelled of pine—old pine, dried up and dead—and it depressed him. In fact, everything depressed him—especially this vacation. Vacation. It was a joke. Vacation from what?

He poured himself a drink—vodka and soda, tall, from the plastic half-gallon jug. It wasn't noon yet, the breakfast dishes were in the sink, and Tiller and Caroline were down at the lake. He couldn't see them through the screen of trees, but he heard the murmur of their voices against the soughing of the branches and the sadness of the birds. He sat heavily in the creaking wicker chair and looked out on nothing. He didn't feel too hot. In fact, he felt as if he'd been cored and dried, as if somebody had taken a pipe cleaner and run it through his veins. His head ached too, but the vodka would take care of that. When he finished it, he'd have another; and then maybe a grilled swiss on rye. Then he'd start to feel good again.

His father was talking to the man and his mother was talking to the woman. They'd met at the bar about twenty drinks ago and his father was into his could-have-been, should-have-been, way-back-when mode, and the man, bald on top and with a ratty beard and long greasy hair like his father's, was trying to steer the conversation back to building supplies. The woman had whole galaxies of freckles on her chest, and she leaned forward in her sundress and told his mother scandalous stories about people she'd never heard of. Tiller had drunk all the Coke and eaten all the beer nuts he could hold. He watched the Pabst Blue Ribbon sign flash on and off above the bar and he watched the woman's freckles move in and out of the gap between her breasts. Outside it was dark and a cool clean scent came in off the lake.

"Uh huh, yeah," his father was saying, "the To the Bone Band. I played rhythm and switched off vocals with Dillie Richards. . . ."

The man had never heard of Dillie Richards.

"Black dude, used to play with Taj Mahal?"

The man had never heard of Taj Mahal.

"Anyway," his father said, "we used to do all this really outrageous stuff by people like Muddy, Howlin' Wolf, Luther Allison—"

"She didn't," his mother said.

The woman threw down her drink and nodded and the front of her dress went crazy. Tiller watched her and felt the skin go tight across his shoulders and the back of his neck, where he'd been burned the first day. He wasn't wearing any underwear, just shorts. He looked away. "Three abortions, two kids," the woman said. "And she never knew who the father of the second one was."

"Drywall isn't worth a damn," the man said. "But what're you going to do?"

"Paneling?" his father offered.

The man cut the air with the flat of his hand. He looked angry. "Don't talk to me about paneling," he said.

Mornings, when his parents were asleep and the lake was still, he would take the rowboat to the reedy cove on the far side of the lake where the big pike lurked. He didn't actually know if they lurked there, but if they lurked anywhere, this would be the place. It looked fishy, mysterious, sunken logs looming up dark from the shadows beneath the boat, mist rising like steam, as if the bottom were boiling with ravenous, cold-eyed, killer pike that could slice through monofilament with a snap of their jaws and bolt ducklings in a gulp. Besides, Joe Matochik, the old man who lived in the cabin next door and could charm frogs by stroking their bellies, had told him that this was where he'd find them.

It was cold at dawn and he'd wear a thick homeknit sweater over his T-shirt and shorts, sometimes pulling the stretched-out hem of it down like a skirt to warm his thighs. He'd take an apple with him or a slice of brown bread and peanut butter. And of course the orange lifejacket his mother insisted on.

When he left the dock he was always wearing the lifejacket—for form's sake and for the extra warmth it gave him against the raw morning air. But when he got there, when he stood in the swaying basin of the boat to cast his Hula Popper or Abu Reflex, it got in the way and he took it off. Later, when the sun ran through him and he didn't need the sweater, he balled it up on the seat beside him, and sometimes, if it was good and hot, he shrugged out of his T-shirt and shorts too. No one could see him in the cove, and it made his breath come quick to be naked like that under the morning sun.

"I heard you," he shouted, and he could feel the veins stand out in his neck, the rage come up in him like something killed and dead and brought back to life. "What kind of thing is that to tell a kid, huh? About his own father?"

She wasn't answering. She'd backed up in a corner of the kitchen and she wasn't answering. And what could she say, the bitch? He'd heard her. Dozing on the trundle bed under the stairs, wanting a drink but too weak to get up and make one, he'd heard voices from the kitchen, her voice and Tiller's. "Get used to it," she said, "he's a drunk, your father's a drunk," and then he was up off the bed as if something had exploded inside of him and he had her by the shoulders—always the shoulders and, never the face, that much she'd taught him—and Tiller was gone, out the door and gone. Now, her voice low in her throat, a sick and guilty little smile on her lips, she whispered, "It's true."

"Who are you to talk?—you're shit-faced yourself." She shrank away from him, that sick smile on her lips, her shoulders hunched. He wanted to smash things, kick in the damn stove, make her hurt.

"At least I have a job," she said.

"I'll get another one, don't you worry."

"And what about Tiller? We've been here two weeks and you haven't done one damn thing with him, nothing, zero. You haven't even been down to the lake. Two hundred feet and you haven't even been down there once." She came up out of the corner now, feinting like a boxer, vicious, her sharp little fists balled up to drum on him. She spoke in a snarl. "What kind of father are you?"

He brushed past her, slammed open the cabinet, and grabbed the first bottle he found. It was whiskey, cheap whiskey, Four Roses, the shit she drank. He poured out half a water glass full and drank it down to spite her. "I hate the beach, boats, water, trees. I hate you."

She had her purse and she was halfway out the screen door. She hung there a second, looking as if she'd bitten into something rotten. "The feeling's mutual," she said, and the door banged shut behind her.

There were too many complications, too many things to get between him and the moment, and he tried not to think about them. He tried not to think about his father—or his mother either—in the same way that he tried not to think about the pictures of the bald-headed stick people in Africa or meat in its plastic wrapper and how it got there. But when he did think about his father he thought about the river-was-whiskey day.

It was a Tuesday or Wednesday, middle of the week, and when he came home from school the curtains were drawn and his father's car was in the driveway. At the door, he could hear him, the *chunk-chunk* of the chords and the rasping nasal whine that seemed as if it belonged to someone else. His father was sitting in the dark, hair in his face, bent low over the guitar. There was an open bottle of liquor on the coffee table and a clutter of beer bottles. The room stank of smoke.

It was strange, because his father hardly ever played his guitar anymore—he mainly just talked about it. In the past tense. And it was strange too—and bad—because his father wasn't at work. Tiller dropped his bookbag on the telephone stand. "Hi, Dad," he said.

His father didn't answer. Just bent over the guitar and played the same song, over and over, as if it were the only song he knew. Tiller sat on the sofa and listened. There was a verse—one verse—and his father repeated it three or four times before he broke off and slurred the words into a sort of chant or hum, and then he went back to the words again. After the fourth repetition, Tiller heard it:

> *If the river was whiskey,*
> *And I was a divin' duck,*
> *I'd swim to the bottom,*
> *Drink myself back up.*

For half an hour his father played that song, played it till anything else would have sounded strange. He reached for the bottle when he finally stopped, and that was when he noticed Tiller. He looked surprised. Looked as if he'd just woke up. "Hey, ladykiller Tiller," he said, and took a drink from the mouth of the bottle.

Tiller blushed. There'd been a Sadie Hawkins dance at school and Janet Rumery had picked him for her partner. Ever since, his father had called him ladykiller, and though he wasn't exactly sure what it meant, it made him blush anyway, just from the tone of it. Secretly, it pleased him. "I really liked the song, Dad," he said.

"Yeah?" His father lifted his eyebrows and made a face. "Well, come home to Mama, doggie-o. Here," he said, and he held out an open beer. "You ever have one of

29

these, ladykiller Tiller?" He was grinning. The sleeve of his shirt was torn and his elbow was raw and there was a hard little clot of blood over his shirt pocket. "With your sixth-grade buddies out behind the handball court, maybe? No?"

Tiller shook his head.

"You want one? Go ahead, take a hit."

Tiller took the bottle and sipped tentatively. The taste wasn't much. He looked up at his father. "What does it mean?" he said. "The song, I mean—the one you were singing. About the whiskey and all."

His father gave him a long slow grin and took a drink from the big bottle of clear liquor. "I don't know," he said finally, grinning wider to show his tobacco-stained teeth. "I guess he just liked whiskey, that's all." He picked up a cigarette, made as if to light it, and then put it down again. "Hey," he said, "you want to sing it with me?"

All right, she'd hounded him and she'd threatened him and she was going to leave him, he could see that clear as day. But he was going to show her. And the kid too. He wasn't drinking. Not today. Not a drop.

He stood on the dock with his hands in his pockets while Tiller scrambled around with the fishing poles and oars and the rest of it. Birds were screeching in the trees and there was a smell of diesel fuel on the air. The sun cut into his head like a knife. He was sick already.

"I'm giving you a big pole, Dad, and you can row if you want."

He eased himself into the boat and it fell away beneath him like the mouth of a bottomless pit.

"I made us egg salad, Dad, your favorite. And I brought some birch beer."

He was rowing. The lake was churning underneath him, the wind was up and reeking of things washed up on the shore, and the damn oars kept slipping out of the oarlocks, and he was rowing. At the last minute he'd wanted to go back for a quick drink, but he didn't, and now he was rowing.

"We're going to catch a pike," Tiller said, hunched like a spider in the stern.

There was spray off the water. He was rowing. He felt sick. Sick and depressed.

"We're going to catch a pike, I can feel it. I know we are," Tiller said, "I know it. I just know it."

It was too much for him all at once—the sun, the breeze that was so sweet he could taste it, the novelty of his father rowing, pale arms and a dead cigarette clenched between his teeth, the boat rocking, and the birds whispering—and he closed his eyes a minute, just to keep from going dizzy with the joy of it. They were in deep water already. Tiller was trolling with a plastic worm and spinner, just in case, but he didn't have much faith in catching anything out here. He was taking his father to the cove with the submerged logs and beds of weed—that's where they'd connect, that's where they'd catch pike.

"Jesus," his father said when Tiller spelled him at the oars. Hands shaking, he crouched in the stern and tried to light a cigarette. His face was gray and the hair beat crazily around his face. He went through half a book of matches and then threw the cigarette in the water. "Where are you taking us, anyway," he said, "—the Indian Ocean?"

"The pike place," Tiller told him. "You'll like it, you'll see."

The sun was dropping behind the hills when they got there, and the water went from blue to gray. There was no wind in the cove. Tiller let the boat glide out across the still surface while his father finally got a cigarette lit, and then he dropped anchor. He was excited. Swallows dove at the surface, bullfrogs burped from the reeds. It was the perfect time to fish, the hour when the big lunker pike would cruise among the sunken logs, hunting.

"All right," his father said, "I'm going to catch the biggest damn fish in the lake," and he jerked back his arm and let fly with the heaviest sinker in the tackle box dangling from the end of the rod. The line hissed through the guys and there was a thunderous splash that probably terrified every pike within half a mile. Tiller looked over his shoulder as he reeled in his silver spoon. His father winked at him, but he looked grim.

It was getting dark, his father was out of cigarettes, and Tiller had cast the spoon so many times his arm was sore, when suddenly the big rod began to buck. "Dad! Dad!" Tiller shouted, and his father lurched up as if he'd been stabbed. He'd been dozing, the rod propped against the gunwale, and Tiller had been studying the long suffering-lines in his father's face, the grooves in his forehead, and the puffy discolored flesh beneath his eyes. With his beard and long hair and with the crumpled suffering look on his face, he was the picture of the crucified Christ Tiller had contemplated a hundred times at church. But now the rod was bucking and his father had hold of it and he was playing a fish, a big fish, the tip of the rod dipping all the way down to the surface.

"It's a pike, Dad, it's a pike!"

His father strained at the pole. His only response was a grunt, but Tiller saw something in his eyes he hardly recognized anymore, a connection, a charge, as if the fish were sending a current up the line, through the pole, and into his hands and body and brain. For a full three minutes he played the fish, his slack biceps gone rigid, the cigarette clamped in his mouth, while Tiller hovered over him with the landing net. There was a surge, a splash, and the thing was in the net, and Tiller had it over the side and into the boat. "It's a pike," his father said, "goddamnit, look at the thing, look at the size of it."

It wasn't a pike. Tiller had watched Joe Matochik catch one off the dock one night. Joe's pike had been dangerous, full of teeth, a long, lean, tapering strip of muscle and pounding life. This was no pike. It was a carp. A fat, pouty, stinking, ugly mud carp. Trash fish. They shot them with arrows and threw them up on the shore to rot. Tiller looked at his father and felt like crying.

"It's a pike," his father said, and already the thing in his eyes was gone, already it was over, "it's a pike. Isn't it?"

It was late—past two, anyway—and he was drunk. Or no, he was beyond drunk. He'd been drinking since morning, one tall vodka and soda after another, and he didn't feel a thing. He sat on the porch in the dark and he couldn't see the lake, couldn't hear it, couldn't even smell it. Caroline and Tiller were asleep. The house was dead silent.

Caroline was leaving him, which meant that Tiller was leaving him. He knew it. He could see it in her eyes and he heard it in her voice. She was soft once, his soft-eyed lover, and now she was hard, unyielding, now she was his worst enemy. They'd had the couple from the roadhouse in for drinks and burgers earlier that night and he'd leaned over the table to tell the guy something—Ed, his name was—joking really, nothing serious, just making conversation. "Vodka and soda," he said, "that's my drink. I used to drink vodka and grapefruit juice, but it tore the lining out of my stomach." And then Caroline, who wasn't even listening, stepped in and said, "Yeah, and that"—pointing to the glass—"tore the lining out of your brain." He looked up at her. She wasn't smiling.

All right. That was how it was. What did he care? He hadn't wanted to come up here anyway—it was her father's idea. Take the cabin for a month, the old man had said, pushing, pushing in that way he had, and get yourself turned around. Well, he wasn't turning around, and they could all go to hell.

After a while the chill got to him and he pushed himself up from the chair and went to bed. Caroline said something in her sleep and pulled away from him as he lifted the covers and slid in. He was awake for a minute or two, feeling depressed, so depressed he wished somebody would come in and shoot him, and then he was asleep.

In his dream, he was out in the boat with Tiller. The wind was blowing, his hands were shaking, he couldn't light a cigarette. Tiller was watching him. He pulled at the oars and nothing happened. Then all of a sudden they were going down, the boat sucked out from under them, the water icy and black, beating in on them as if it were alive. Tiller called out to him. He saw his son's face, saw him going down, and there was nothing he could do.

Write and Wrong

Breyten Breytenbach

Breyten Breytenbach is a South African writer, painter, and performing artist. He made his literary debut with a volume of prose, Katastrofes, *and poetry,* Die ysterkoei moet sweet, *in 1964. Due to his marriage to a Vietnamese woman, Breytenbach was persecuted by the Apartheid regime and was not allowed to visit his own country. He returned to South Africa with a false passport in 1975, but was arrested after a few weeks. He was charged with and convicted of terrorism, an experience upon which he based his memoir,* The True Confessions of an Albino Terrorist.

A large number of articles, essays, academic dissertations, doctoral theses and books have been written and published—in Afrikaans, English, French, Dutch, German, Russian, Chinese and Arabic, among others—on Breytenbach's literary and visual work. Several documentaries have been made about his life and work, including the 1998 film, Vision from the Edge: Breyten Breytenbach Painting the Lines.

Breytenbach has published numerous literary works, the most recent being the 1999 prose work, Woordwerk. *He has also won a number of international prizes and awards for literature and art, including the Alan Paton Award for Literature (South Africa), the Libyan Jurists Association Award (Libya) and the Prix d'Ivry pour la Peinture (France).*

I don't know whether I've written this before. One plunders the notebook again and again.

I find: "The past is the ink with which we write the present—and in the process and the flow of writing the words, the concepts and ideas, the images, the flights become . . . just *ink*. Whereas what we'd probably like to write would be an open hand wherein time, which is the future of the present movement, could find its fit and its fist."

A little further I find: "You must polish the word—not to have it shiny or smooth but to make it as clear as a mirror or a pebble in which you can read your face, and may see that your face is death." And then: "The recognition and the acceptance of the Other's humanity (or humanness) is a maiming of self. You have to wound the self, cut it in strips, in order to *know* that you are similar and of the same substance of shadows."

These reflections surface during a visit to Weimar, where I'm to be a member of the jury deciding which philosophical essay best answers the question of how to free the future from the past and the past from the future. It is a curious town, the small provincial capital of Thüringen; egg-yellow facades are washed to keep up a sun-splashed face of classicism and quaint comfort and the late bourgeois charms of GDR democracy—but in the back streets houses are rotting from neglect and decay. The town is flooded with Goethe; he is on every menu; the dogs don't piss against trees and lampposts, they bark snippets of the great man's wisdom. And to a lesser extent there are Schiller and Herder and Liszt, who played his piano in a big room with an ornate ceiling, and Nietzsche, who stroked his madness in his mother's house as if it were a mustache. Their spirits flutter above the rooftops and the steeples the way banners are the remembrance of republics and of battles.

It is dark when we visit the replica of Goethe's *Gartenhaus*. A blonde lady architect guides us through the low-beamed rooms of the exact copy of the small house where the master used to work. Look, she says and points, we photographed the floor tiles of the original dwelling so that we could faithfully reproduce the spots and the scratches; and look, this is the identical copy of his writing desk where we made precisely the same ink stains blot by blot. When she turns her back to escort us to the next room, Andrei Bitov, the Russian author, slips a kopeck into one of the desk's small drawers, "to fuck up the symmetry and destroy the German soul."

But why this? Because we wanted to see if it could be done, the girl guide says. It cost nearly two million deutsche marks to assemble. Now you see it, now you don't. The original, nearby in the dark garden of the night, is for pious ogling; the clone you can run your hands over. But is that not the definition of totalitarianism, "the repetition of the same"? And now, what about aging? Will they touch up the copy to show, in time, the same wear and tear as the original? Or will the original be brought into line with its monstrous shadow?

On Sunday, after adjudicating an essay called "A Dictionary of Winds" the best entry, we go up the hill to visit Buchenwald. It is so close by, a raven could bridge the distance like an open hand writing without thinking a single line of invisible ink! And yet, how distant it is.

There are trees up there, many trees, and clouds racing through a high-domed light-soaked sky, and birds being fluttered by the wind, and probably insects in the soil too. There's a breathtaking view over the gentle surroundings of flowing valleys and peaceful towns where Goethe must have taken his walks. And suddenly it is cold, so desperately cold—as if we'd moved into another world. We shouldn't have come.

A young man takes us through the camp. He is thickset and has dark half-moons under his eyes; he speaks English with a Scottish accent, probably that of a soccer fan, but the German breaks through painfully. He blurts out figures and facts relentlessly. This was a training ground for the SS, he tells us. As early as 1934. They came here young, sometimes only sixteen years old. They were to be the new elite to revolutionize society. The New Man could be unshackled only in a hierarchy of self-abnegation and arbitrary violence and torture. He saw this job as a guide advertised in the newspaper, the young man says, and so he applied. Sometimes he wonders. He has met survivors. He asked them: "What were your first thoughts when you woke up in the mornings here?"

We are shown the barracks. We see the exact replica of the small zoo where officials brought their families on Sunday outings—hardly three meters away from the barbed-wire enclosure keeping in the inmates. We pass through the narrow wrought-iron gate to the inner camp, with its mocking iron letters: *Jedem das Seine* ("To each his own"). Then we see the bare expanse, the broad view from up here overlooking the world with its harvests.

And then we're taken to the execution block, the tiles of the autopsy room, the furrows to sluice away the blood, the instruments shiny and elegant like slivered mirrors or like pebbles. Then the ovens and the urns and in the basement the hooks and the piano wire. . . . We should not have come.

But this I cannot look at. This then is the Other. This is Me. This is what we do. This is what we're like. Vietnam. Rwanda. Kosovo.

We cling to one another. The wind is in our eyes and our throats. A beautiful sunset purples the sky. Grandfather sky and father sky and son sky, and man. Grandmother wind and mother tree and daughter bird and grandchild insect through all the ages, and man once only. Once is enough.

Back in the hotel Andrei Bitov gives me a full glass of vodka, "to take the shiver out of the soul." He clumsily cuts up an apple with a bottle opener. "One must always have an apple with the vodka," he says. "Now go and take a hot bath."

Immediately I fall into a bottomless sleep. I have a first dream.

A bright, sylvan scene. A clearing in the forest. We hear, at the periphery of our eyesight, a thrashing in the undergrowth. As if someone (or something) is observing us from the invisibleness, but clumsily now camouflaging its presence. We then know it is an immortal. How can he be lured forth? Only one thing will work. We peg down a book in the sun-filled glade. This will be the irresistible bait. We know he/she is desperate to know what's written. Does the wind turn over the leaves of the book? Can the wind read? And what is the title?

How rotten with memory this earth is! And how the one thing slides over the other! When does memory become obliterated? Can we write everything? Are we not obliged to approach obliquely, camouflaging our presence, turning away our faces? Can we see Goethe whole?

It should have been burned to the ground and left to the wind. The town, too, should have been given over to the dark ink of time. No memorial, no ceremonies, just the salted earth forever. Because we have no right to remember.

Thereafter the night turns, and it is empty. And when we take leave the next day to return to our respective cities of time and of rhythm, Andrei Bitov and I, as writers from nowhere at the end of this century, exchange the empty bound books that we had been given by the organizers. He writes in the copy that he gives me: *I would like to present you something. But we, in our monastery, have nothing. . . .* Underneath he notes: *For writing nothings.* And in my copy to him I jot: *1. Thou shalt not kill. 2. Thou shalt laugh with thy whole mouth and thy whole belly. 3. Thou shalt study the expressions on the faces of ants.*

The Videotapes

Brooks Brown and Rob Merritt

Brooks Brown was a student at Columbine when the incident, for which the school is now famous, happened. Brown had been friends with Dylan Klebold and Eric Harris, the two students who shocked the world by shooting to death twelve other students and a teacher, and finally committing suicide. As a friend of the shooters, Brown was able to disclose some of the warning signs, which had been previously ignored, and to give a unique account of the events. He wrote the book No Easy Answers, *from which this fragment is taken, together with the journalist Rob Merritt. The story does not claim to have found a complete explanation of the events at Columbine, but rather demonstrates how difficult it is to explain such events. Brooks Brown has also consulted with director Michael Moore for the latter's Academy Award winning documentary,* Bowling for Columbine.

On the first day of school in the fall of 1999, Columbine held a "Take Back the School" ceremony. It was the first time classes had resumed at the building since April 20. Repair crews had spent the summer removing all evidence of Eric and Dylan's rampage. Ceiling tiles were replaced, water damage from the fire sprinklers was repaired, and bullet holes and broken glass were removed. A wall of lockers was installed in front of the entrance to the library, which had been permanently sealed.

Brook's brother Aaron, a junior, had to return to Columbine. He remembers the bizarre atmosphere of the first day. Media trucks filled nearby Clement Park. Principal Frank DeAngelis's welcoming speech was carried live by CNN. Parents

Reprinted from *No Easy Answers: The Truth Behind Death at Columbine,* (2002), Lantern Books.

stood side by side in front of the entrance to shield students from the media as they entered the school.

Once inside, though—where cameras were banned—things were more subdued.

"Things were better at Columbine, as far as how people treated one another," Aaron recalls. "At least, that's how it was for the first month or so. But by two or three months after we got back, things were back to the way they had been before. The name-calling started up all over again. Some people had changed a lot, but others hadn't changed at all."

I was worried about my brother when he went back into that school. Principal DeAngelis repeatedly denied to the media that he saw any bullying going on. He kept making "We Are Columbine" speeches and talking about how the school was coming together. The administration wasn't facing the fact that kids were still as cruel to one another as ever.

Meanwhile, different organizations were using Eric and Dylan to promote their causes. Gun-control advocates arguing for more restrictive gun laws rose up against legal gun owners, starting with a protest outside the National Rifle Association's convention in Denver shortly after Columbine.

But tougher gun laws wouldn't have stopped Eric and Dylan. They went around one law by using Robyn Anderson to buy weapons at a gun show, and broke another entirely by buying their TEC-9 from a friend. All that gun-control advocates were doing was punishing law-abiding gun owners for Eric and Dylan's misdeeds.

Some tried to say Eric and Dylan were out to kill minorities, because they called Isaiah Shoels a "nigger" and then killed him. It's true Eric posted criticisms of other races on his Web site from time to time, and I have no doubt that they did call Isaiah what they did. However, they also killed twelve other people who were white. It seems clear that racist feelings weren't the motivating force behind the shootings.

Rather, I think Eric and Dylan were determined to humiliate all their victims, no matter who they were. Library witnesses said they made fun of another kid because of his glasses. They said they wanted to kill "anyone with a white hat," because athletes wore white hats. They found some way to mock or degrade each person before they fired the fatal shot. It was one big game to them.

Along the same lines, it doesn't seem that Eric and Dylan specifically targeted people because of their religion. Witnesses remember them asking several people whether they "believed in God" before shooting them. Those stories were repeated throughout the media.

As a result, religious organizations quickly picked up on Columbine. They tried to make people believe the shooting represented a "crisis of faith," that Eric and Dylan had gone into Columbine for the sole purpose of killing as many Christians as possible.

One of the best-known examples they held up is Cassie Bernall, who was killed in the library. More than one witness there claimed that Eric and Dylan asked Cassie if she believed in God, and that when she said yes, she was shot. Her parents wrote a book entitled *She Said Yes: The Unlikely Martyrdom of Cassie Bernall*, which became a bestseller.

However, according to the *Rocky Mountain News*, a student named Emily Wyant—who was crouched down next to Cassie underneath a table—told police that the exchange never happened.

Another library witness, Craig Scott (Rachel's brother), was one of the kids who told police he had heard Cassie say yes. According to a December 14 *Rocky Mountain News* article, "Inside the Columbine Investigation," police took Craig into the library and asked him what direction the question had come from.

"When he revisited the library, he realized the voice had come from another direction—from the table where student Valeen Schnurr had been shot," Dan Luzadder and Kevin Vaughn wrote. "Investigators came to believe it was probably Valeen, who survived, who told the gunmen of her faith in God."

Author P. Solomon Banda of the Associated Press wrote a Dec. 27, 1999 article entitled "Who Said 'Yes' To Columbine Gunmen? Faithful Say It's Immaterial." In the article, Schnurr said she was "blown out from underneath a table by a shotgun blast" from Eric or Dylan.

"One of the gunmen asked her if she believed in God and she said 'yes,' crawling away as he reloaded," Banda wrote.

TIME Magazine shared a different scenario in its Dec. 20, 1999 cover story, "The Columbine Tapes." Author Tim Roche wrote, "When Harris found Cassie Bernall, he leaned down. 'Peekaboo,' he said, and killed her. His shotgun kicked, stunning him and breaking his nose."

Yet even when these doubts surfaced, there were some who said the question was irrelevant. Banda wrote:

> *"It doesn't matter who said it or if no one said it," [church volunteer Sara] Evans said. "But if people believe in God, that's what's important." Doug Clark, director of field ministries of San Diego-based National Network of Youth Ministries, said he encourages other students to follow the teens' example of boldness. "Mincing words over what was said in the library is a minor part," Clark said. "The greater part is how they lived their lives, and it's not going to change anything."*
>
> *Religious experts said attempts to clarify the confusion surrounding the stories of Christian faith actually could help embed the story in religious circles.*
>
> *"This rethinking can be chalked up to media scrutiny, which I think the faithful would dismiss as a cynical attempt to debunk the story," said Randall Balmer, professor of American Religious Studies at Barnard College. "In some ways, it may make the faithful dig in a little bit deeper and resist those attempts."* ("Who Said 'Yes' To Columbine Gunmen?" P. Solomon Banda, Associated Press, 12/27/99)

Balmer's assessment was accurate. On the Web site cassie-bernall.org, Christian author Wendy Murray Zoba posted an article entitled "Did She or Didn't She?" with a clear slant against any reporter who questioned the story. She criticized *Salon.com* writer Dave Cullen for airing doubts, writing, "In fact, it is Cullen's piece—and the Jefferson County Sheriff's Department information office—that should be called into account."

Zoba's article showed a clear double standard. On the one hand, she tried to debunk witnesses like Emily Wyant by quoting trauma recovery expert Dee Dee McDermott:

> *[McDermott] says, "Some people have a great capacity for processing the trauma and are able to stay, what we call, 'fully present.' They have a high level of recall. Other students are so traumatized, they do not have the capacity to process all the information. Those students would be the ones who would have what we would call memory blocks. A diagnosis for this is Post Traumatic Stress Disorder. There was smoke [in the library] which was disorienting, and they were in study [carrels] with hard wood sides. . . . People who are interviewing these kids need to understand the dynamics of what trauma does and how they're processing it."* ("Did She or Didn't She?" Wendy Murray Zoba, cassiebernall.org.)

In other words, library witnesses like Emily were suffering from "stress disorder" that affected their memory.

On the other hand, witnesses like Craig Scott and Josh Lapp, whom she cited as remembering the exchange, suffered from no such disorientation—except that Scott was "disoriented" when he heard the question come from Valeen Schnurr's direction rather than from Cassie Bernall's. Zoba quoted Craig Scott as saying, "The whole world can say Cassie never said 'yes' to the gunmen, and I'd still stand by my knowledge that she did."

People were turning my high school's tragedy into a tool for their political causes. Zoba was not an objective third party. She was the associate editor for *Christianity Today* and the author of their Oct. 4, 1999 cover story, "Do You Believe In God? How Columbine Changed America." She has written an entire book about faith in regard to Columbine, entitled *Day of Reckoning*.

I'm not claiming that Eric and Dylan didn't have a certain hatred for religion. They did. In fact, we had many discussions about how difficult it could be for a non-Christian at Columbine. Many Littleton residents equate Christianity with being a good person, and they look down on those who are not members of the church. It was hard for Eric and Dylan to watch self-proclaimed "Christians" who pushed other kids around, shoved them into lockers and call them faggots, then got up later and talked about how "important" their faith was. I know for a fact that things like that made Eric and Dylan angry.

Yet, even if it is true that Cassie and Rachel said "yes," it doesn't mean Eric and Dylan's sole intention was to kill Christians. Eleven other people were shot without even being asked the question. Also, there were no stories of kids who said no and were allowed to live.

Zoba concluded her article with the following quote from investigator Gary Muse: "If Cassie's exchange with the gunmen is not germane to the investigation—and I don't believe it is—why are people so interested in debunking the account?"

My answer is simple: It isn't anti-Christian to have questions about Cassie's exchange. It's insulting to suggest that I shouldn't be allowed to seek clarity, in the wake of all the controversy surrounding the story. Cassie was my classmate. I have a right to try to learn the reasons for her death.

By December we would get our first glimpse of those reasons—from Eric and Dylan themselves.

That fall, we learned that *TIME Magazine* was working on an in-depth story about the Columbine investigation. Reporter Tim Roche, who wanted to know more about Eric's Web pages, contacted my family.

Roche conducted several interviews with us at our home. When he came over for the last one, he had a stunned look on his face. "You're not going to believe what the cops just showed me," he said.

Roche had just viewed Eric and Dylan's basement videotapes.

The tapes, which were found by the police in Eric's home on the day of the massacre, had been a well-guarded secret in the months since then. We knew they existed, and the police had read excerpts from them during a sentencing hearing for one of the gun suppliers, but when members of the media and the families of the victims asked to view them, they were denied. Now, however, Roche had seen them.

Apparently his access was very generous. On December 20, 1999, *TIME* printed its exclusive story, "The Columbine Tapes: The Killers Tell Why They Did It." The story featured extensive quotes from the videos, as well as Roche's assessment of them:

> *The tapes were meant to be their final word, to all those who had picked on them over the years, and to everyone who would come up with a theory about their inner demons. It is clear listening to them that Harris and Klebold were not just having trouble with what their counselors called 'anger management.' They fed the anger, fueled it, so the fury could take hold, because they knew they would need it to do what they set out to do. "More rage. More rage," Harris says. "Keep building it on," he says, motioning with his hands for emphasis.*
>
> *Harris recalls how he moved around so much with his military family and always had to start over, "at the bottom of the ladder." People continually made fun of him—"my face, my hair, my shirts." As for Klebold, "If you could see all the anger I've stored over the past four f—ing years . . ." he says. . . . As far back as the Foothills Day Care center, he hated the "stuck-up" kids he felt hated him. "Being shy didn't help," he admits. "I'm going to kill you all. You've been giving us s— for years." ("The Columbine Tapes," TIME, 12/20/99)*

Sheriff Stone came under heavy criticism for having ignored repeated pleas from the families to see the videotapes but allowed a reporter from *TIME* to see them. Stone countered by claiming that Roche had agreed never to quote from them, and had broken the agreement.

TIME denied that any such agreement had ever been entered into. Roche told my mother that the accusations were not only false, but were ruining his credibility as a journalist, because now people believed that he was willing to burn a source for the sake of a story. I knew he would not have lied about how things happened. He was a great guy, and an honest reporter. The police were rolling over him to protect themselves—just like they'd done with me.

Stone made another attempt at damage control. This time, he said he hadn't yet viewed the tapes himself, so he didn't know what they contained when he gave Roche permission to see them. This was hardly a good way to avoid criticism; as *Denver Post* columnist Chuck Green pointed out, "Although he is in charge of the Columbine investigation, Sheriff Stone hadn't taken the time to sit in a chair and watch the remarkable videotapes of Harris and Klebold planning the crime."

After it became known that Stone had allowed a reporter to view the tapes, other members of the media demanded the right to see them as well. In a last-ditch effort to defuse the situation, Stone proposed two screenings of the videos—one for the media and the other for the families. My parents got wind of this, and they headed over to the sheriff's office to see the tapes for themselves.

Randy and Judy Brown followed the arrows that led them through the Dakota Building, near the Jefferson County Sheriff's Office, until they reached the room where the videos were to be screened. As the tapes were about to begin, the police asked to see press credentials.

"We don't have any," Judy said.

The officer demanded their names. When the Browns told him, he replied that they couldn't be there.

"Yes, we can," Randy replied. "We're citizens and we're going to see those tapes."

"No, you're not," the officer replied.

Randy didn't back down. "Are you going to arrest me if I go in that room?" he asked. Behind the officer, members of the press were watching the exchange with interest.

"No," the officer replied after a moment.

With that, Randy marched past. "Rather than have a knock-down drag-out fight with them, we allowed them in," Deputy Wayne Holyerson told Holly Kurtz and Lynn Bartels of the Denver Rocky Mountain News. *"They wanted to watch the tapes, and we figured this was as good a time as any."*

One of the officers spoke with Judy in the hallway while Randy went into the screening room. The officer warned her that the tapes were "extremely disturbing," but he recognized her right to see them.

The officer called detective Kate Battan over to meet Judy. "She was so friendly, and said hello," Judy recalls. "Then the officer said, 'This is Judy Brown.' Kate just threw her hands in the air and walked away. The officer said, 'Well, I don't know what that was about.' She clearly didn't want to talk to me."

Judy rejoined her husband inside the screening room just as the first tape was beginning. What she saw, she says, horrified her.

Eric and Dylan's basement tapes have never been released for viewing by the general public—at least, as of the writing of this book. However, I've been able to learn a lot about them from what my parents remember seeing, as well as by reading the police summary of their contents (contained in a report released by the sheriff's office in November, 2000). This is what I have been able to put together.

On the first tape, Eric and Dylan are seated in the basement of Eric's house, with Eric holding a shotgun he calls "Arlene," named after a character in *Doom*. Eric is wearing a Rammstein T-shirt with "Wilder Wein"—German for "Wild Wine"—written on it. He and Dylan are drinking a bottle of Jack Daniels as they speak.

At first they talk about weapons. "Thanks to Mark John Doe and Philip John Doe," they say, referring to Mark Manes and Philip Duran, who provided them with their TEC-9. "We used them; they had no clue. If it hadn't been them, it would have been someone else over twenty-one."

Eric tells how close he came to being caught when the Green Mountain Guns store called his house. His father answered, and the clerk said, "Your clips are in." His father replied that he hadn't ordered any clips and left the matter there. Eric laughs as he recounts the story. He also mentions the time when his parents found a pipe bomb but never searched for others. He recalls the time he walked past his mother when his shotgun was "in my terrorist bag sticking out." She thought it was his pellet gun, he says.

The two are still angry about their arrest for the van break-in over a year before. "Fuck you, Walsh," Dylan says, a reference to the officer who caught them.

Eric and Dylan get up to take a tour of Eric's bedroom, "to see all the illegal shit." Eric shows off his stash of weapons; "Thanks to the gun show, and to Robyn," he says. "Robyn is very cool."

Eric then shows off how he's managed to keep his weapons hidden. My mom specifically remembers Eric pulling out a desk drawer filled with clocks of different sizes and shapes, along with batteries and solar igniters, which Eric planned to use for the propane bombs. Eric has pipe bombs hidden behind his CD collection; inside a "Demon Knight" CD is his receipt from Green Mountain Guns for nine ammunition magazines. However, he also has "fifty feet of cannon fuse" hanging on the wall in plain sight.

Eric holds up some of his gear in front of the camera. "What you will find on my body in April," he says.

The two appear in a second video dated March 18, once again seated in the basement. Writers Karen Abbott and Dan Luzadder of the Denver *Rocky Mountain News* viewed the tapes during the media screening and offered the following observation in their December 13, 1999 story, "War Is War":

> *They explain over and over why they want to kill as many people as they can. Kids taunted them in elementary school, in middle school, in high school. Adults wouldn't let them strike back, to fight their tormenters, the way such disputes once were settled in schoolyards. So they gritted their teeth. And their rage grew. "It's humanity," Klebold says, flipping an obscene gesture toward the camera." Look at what you made," he tells the world. "You're fucking shit, you humans, and you deserve to die.". . .*
> *They speak at length about all the people who wronged them. "You've given us shit for years," Klebold says. "You're fucking going to pay for all the shit. We don't give a shit because we're going to die doing it." (*"War Is War," *Rocky Mountain News, 12/13/99)*

Dylan asks Eric if he thinks the cops will listen to the entire video. Eric replies that he believes the cops will chop the video up into little pieces, "and the police will just show the public what they want it to look like." They suggest delivering the videos to TV stations right before the attack. After all, they want people to know that they feel they have their reasons.

"We are but aren't psycho," they say.

On another tape, at Dylan's house, Eric videotapes Dylan trying on his weapons. Dylan is wearing a black T-shirt with "Wrath" written on it—the same shirt he would wear on the day of the attack.

Dylan promises his parents that there was nothing they could have done to stop him. According to the *Rocky Mountain News* article "War Is War," "You can't understand what we feel," he says. "You can't understand, no matter how much you think you can."

The *Rocky Mountain News* quoted Eric as offering praise for his parents. "My parents are the best fucking parents I have ever known," he says. "My dad is great. I wish I was a fucking sociopath so I don't have any remorse, but I do. This is going to tear them apart. They will never forget it."

According to police reports, Eric expresses regret on another tape as well. He recorded one segment while driving alone in his car. "It's a weird feeling, knowing you're going to be dead in two and a half weeks," he says to the camera. He talks about the co-workers he will miss, and says he wishes he could have revisited Michigan and "old friends." The officer who viewed this tape wrote that "at this point he becomes silent and appears to start crying, wiping a tear from the side of his face. . . . [H]e reaches toward the camera and shuts it off."

Their final tape is less than two minutes long. Eric, behind the camera, tells Dylan to "say it now."

"Hey, Mom. Gotta go," Dylan says to the camera. "It's about half an hour before our little judgment day. I just wanted to apologize to you guys for any crap this might instigate as far as (inaudible) or something. Just know that I'm going to a better place than here. I didn't like life too much and I know I'll be happier wherever the fuck I go. So I'm gone."

My parents have only seen the tape once. The police refuse to release it to the public, citing fears of copycats. However, it is clear simply from the tapes' excerpts that much could be learned from them about Eric and Dylan's true motives.

What angers me about the videotapes is that none of Eric and Dylan's friends have ever been allowed to see them. Think about it. You have three hours of video, recorded by two teenagers full of rage about our school. They reference song lyrics. They reference things at Columbine. Who is going to understand those references? Other kids.

But at this time—three years after the shootings—the only people who have seen the videotapes are detectives, reporters, and the families of the victims. These adults won't catch the references that Eric and Dylan's friends and classmates will.

I believe the tapes can help us understand what happened and should be released to the public. However, if the judge isn't willing to do that, the police should at least put together a group of high school students, as well as some of Eric and Dylan's friends, and have them watch the tapes. It amazes me that investigators have not done this, because who knows what clues are flying right over their heads?

The police don't think people need to know anything more about Eric and Dylan's motives. But I want a chance to learn from those tapes for myself.

It remains to be seen whether any of us will have that chance.

Shortly after the *TIME* article about the videotapes was released, a small item appeared in the media. Undersheriff John Dunaway formally announced that I had nothing to do with the attack on Columbine.

"There is no evidence suggesting Brooks Brown was in any way involved in these murders," Dunaway said on December 21.

Nonetheless, the damage had already been done, and my family would never forget. And before long, we would be given the chance to fight back.

The Day the Martels Got the Cable

Pat Cadigan

Pat Cadigan was born in Schenectady, New York in 1954, but grew up in Fitchburg, Massachusetts. She attended the University of Massachusetts on a scholarship, majoring in theater, and eventually transferred to the University of Kansas, where she received her degree. Cadigan was an editor and writer for Hallmark Cards in Kansas City for ten years before embarking on her career as a Science Fiction writer in 1987. Cadigan is the only writer to have won the prestigious Arthur C. Clarke Award twice, in 1992 for Synners *and in 1995 for* Fools. *Her most recent novel is* Tea from an Empty Cup. *She now lives in England with her second husband, Chris Fowler.*

Cadigan's work is part of a special kind of Science Fiction called cyberpunk, which deals with the impact of technology on the future of mankind. The following story is from her first volume entitled Patterns.

Lydia had stayed home from work to take delivery on the washer and dryer. So this time David would have Lydia call him in sick and would wait for the cable TV people to come. Sitting at the kitchen table enjoying the luxury of a second cup of coffee, he skimmed the front page of the newspaper as Lydia hurriedly made herself up in the tiny downstairs bathroom.

"You sure you don't want me to drive you in?" he called over his shoulder.

Lydia poked her head out of the bathroom, holding a mascara brush between two fingers. "Not unless you want the car for some reason. Do you?"

Reprinted from *Patterns,* (1989), by permission of the author.

"Nah. I was just thinking though, I always do the driving and you're not really used to the rush-hour traffic. Awake, anyway."

She stuck her tongue out at him. *"That* to you. I was driving in rush hour long before I hooked up with you and I'll be driving in it long after you run off and leave me for a younger woman." She disappeared back into the bathroom.

"That will be the day." He got up and went to the doorway of the bathroom. "When I go, I'm taking the car with me."

"Men," Lydia said, staring down at the hand mirror as she worked her eyelashes. "You're all alike."

"We attend a special school for it when we're young." David looked at her admiringly. She had on what she called her dress-for-success get-up, tailored navy-blue jacket and skirt with a soft white blouse. What the well-dressed board chairperson was wearing this year. David had asked her once if it wasn't a bit overwhelming for an office manager. All in fun, of course. Truth to tell, her career was outstripping his own.

He reached out and stopped her as she was about to apply her lipstick. "Sure you don't want me to call you in sick, too? We could wait for the cable people together and then afterwards not watch the movie channel."

"That would look good, wouldn't it?" She gave him a quick but thorough kiss before she put on her lipstick. "I mean, the both of us working at the same company and we both happen to come down with stomach flu—ho, ho—on the same day. They'd buy that, for sure."

David shrugged. "So? We've got two bathrooms. Two toilets, no waiting. They can send the corporate secret police out to check if they want."

"David."

"I know, I know." He sighed. "It was worth a try."

"Don't think I don't appreciate it." She grinned redly, looking him up and down. "And don't think I'm not tempted. Say, poppa, did anyone ever tell you you do things for a bathrobe and pajamas that no other man can do?"

"Plenty of women, all the time." He stepped in and posed behind her in the mirror over the sink. They made a perfect portrait of the odd married couple, one with her blonde, chin-length hair carefully combed and the other with his tangled hair standing on end and morning stubble shading his cheeks. "Hey, if this were 1956, you'd be the one in the bathrobe, you know."

Lydia looked pained. "Promise me that after we get the cable, you won't tune in Channel 87 in Dry Rot, Egypt, for old *Leave It To Beaver* reruns."

"How about *Ozzie and Harriet?*"

"I *never* liked them." She gave him a push. "Let me out. I gotta go set the world on fire."

David backed up and blocked the doorway. "Last chance, woman. Eight hours of work or sixteen hours of ecstasy—the choice is yours." He made a thrusting motion with his hips.

"Sixteen hours of ecstasy or twenty-six weeks of paid unemployment. Outta my way, hot pajamas." She honked him as she slipped past and he chased her into the living room.

"Anything I should know about this cable thing?" he asked as she rummaged through her shoulder bag for her car keys.

"Like what?"

"I dunno. You're the one who filled out all the forms and made the arrangements. Am I supposed to do anything with the TV before they get here?"

"Not that I know of." Lydia hooked the keyring around her little finger and pushed several papers back into her purse. "Just stand back and don't get in anybody's way."

David put his hands on his hips. "Well, if they come during *Donahue,* they're just going to have to *wait!"* He tossed his head.

"I never liked him either. He's insincere." Lydia offered her cheek a kiss. Instead, he bit her on the neck and gave her an impertinent squeeze.

"Don't you love permanent press?" he whispered in her ear. "You do all sorts of things and your clothes never wrinkle."

She poked his ticklish spot and squirmed away. "Try not to eat too many chocolate-covered cherries while you're watching the soaps this afternoon, dear. And be dressed for when the cable people come, will you?"

"Yes, dear," he said nasally. "Honestly, work, work, work—that's all I ever *do* around this place."

Lydia's smile was only half amused. "And take the chicken out to thaw for supper tonight."

"I will."

"I mean it. Don't forget."

"All right, already. I'll take the chicken out to thaw. I was taking chicken out to thaw long before I hooked up with you and I'll be taking it out to thaw long after you run off and leave me to find yourself."

"Just make sure that you do it *today."*

"I will. I *promise.* Now go to work before I rip all your clothes off." He did another bump and grind and she escaped out the door, laughing.

He watched from the living room window as she maneuvered the car out of the cramped parking lot in front of the townhouse. Then he went upstairs to take a quick shower, keeping one ear cocked for the sound of the doorbell in case the cable people came early. Why was it cable installers and delivery people could never give you a definite time when they would arrive at your home? They'd just tell you the date and you had to be there. Of course, they didn't come on a Saturday. They worked a straight Monday-to-Friday week, God *forbid* they should arrange their time to accommodate customers with like schedules.

Decadently, he decided not to shave after dressing and went back downstairs to pour himself a fresh cup of coffee and finish the newspaper. At ten o'clock he was fresh out of lazy things to do and just beginning to feel hungry. Well, what the hell— this was a free day. If he wanted to eat lunch early, he could.

The house seemed so quiet, he thought, as he flopped down on the couch with a magazine and a sandwich. As he ate, he turned pages without really looking at them. Playing hooky from work wasn't much fun when there was no one else to share it with.

He laughed at himself. *You sound like an old married man, fella.* An old married man. That wasn't such a bad description, considering whom he was married to. How did that old song go? *Lydia, ho, Lydia . . .* something, something. The Marx Brothers had done it in one of their movies, hadn't they?

Lydia. He'd had some kind of industrial-strength good luck going for him when he'd met her. Everything had just fallen into place—their relationship had progressed to marriage without missing a beat, and their marriage hadn't had anything missing in three and a half years. Companionship, love, sex, and everything in between—it was all there, just the way he might have imagined it. He *had* imagined it a few times, but in an abstract sort of way. There had been no one he would have filled in the woman's part with until Lydia had come into his life.

Not that he was living some kind of fairy tale, though. They had their problems, they argued, and Lydia had the ability to play the bitch just as well as he could be the bastard. But there was nothing seriously wrong, nothing that threatened them. Hell, he didn't even feel funny about her making more money than he did. They were beyond that kind of macho silliness.

David got up and looked out the window at the parking lot. No sign of the cable truck yet. He supposed they would come in a truck with all kinds of equipment, ready to plug him into the wonderful world of pay-TV. He'd had a few misgivings, about it when Lydia first suggested they subscribe to the cable. The image of himself and Lydia sitting in front of the TV, slaves of the tube and its programming hadn't been terribly appetizing. As a rule, they weren't much for TV watching. But there was the movie channel, and the idea of being able to watch uncut films at home appealed to him. It would probably make them lazy about getting out to the theaters, but that wouldn't be so bad. During the week they were both tired, and on the weekends they had to fight the crowds—the terminal acne couples, the families with the restless kids and/or squalling babies, and let's not forget the inveterate chatterboxes who seemed to think they were in their living rooms and didn't refrain from adding their stupid comments at the tops of their lungs. Yeah, cable TV would be worth it if it would spare them that.

At 11 o'clock, when he was already giving thought to having another sandwich, the doorbell rang. "Hallelujah," he muttered and went to answer it.

The small woman smiling up at him on the doorstep had a wildly growing-out permanent and a broad, plain face. There was a length of black cable coiled around one shoulder and she held a bag of tools in her hand. "You Mr. Martel?"

He blinked. "Can I help you?"

"Cable-Rama. I'm here to put in your cable."

David looked past her, saw the truck sitting in their usual parking place. "Oh. Sure. C'mon in."

The woman gave him a big grin, the skin around her eyes crinkling a thousand deep lines. "Every time." She walked in, looked around, and went immediately to the television. David hesitated.

"Just you?" he asked. "I mean, did they send you out all by yourself?"

"Every time," she said again and dropped her tool bag on the carpet.

"Every time what?" David asked, closing the door.

49

The woman never stopped grinning, even as she rolled the television on its cart out from the wall and knelt behind it. "Every time they open the door and see the cable guy's a woman, their mouth falls open. Or they blink a lot." She showed her teeth cheerily. "Like you. They can't believe I can do it all alone."

David felt his face grow slightly warm. "That's not it at all. I just—well, these days you know, sending a woman by herself to people's houses is a risky kind of thing. I mean, times being what they are." The woman detached the rabbit ears and UHF antenna and set them aside. "Yeah? You mean, like if somebody tries something funny or like that?" She picked up a tool David couldn't imagine a use for, a thing that seemed to be a cross between a wrench and a pair of pliers. "Anybody tries something, I adjust their fine tuning. See?" She wiggled her eyebrows. "They said you guys seemed to be okay."

"Oh, we are, but I thought they'd have to send three, four g—people out to do this."

"Oh, yeah. Back in the early days." She kept working on the back of the television set as she spoke, occasionally reaching for a different tool or gadget from her bag. "Now it's easy. Someday the technology's gonna get so good, you'll be able to install this stuff yourself. Just click it onto the back of your set or something." She grimaced at the tip of a Phillips-head screwdriver and wiped it on her workshirt. "You guys into video games?"

David shook his head.

"Ah. That's good. Video games are shit. Burn your goddam tube out quicker. So do those videotape recorders. But you got a good cable-ready set here, you know that?"

"No."

"Yeah, you do. So you don't have to go unhooking this and hooking it back up again if you get a VCR. Better if you just leave it, unless the set has to go in for servicing."

"I wouldn't know how to remove it anyway."

"S'easy. But best not to fool with it. Play around back here, don't know what you're doing, next thing you know—*zzzzt!* Fried poppa." She raised one eyebrow. "Kids. You got any?"

"Nope."

"Good. I mean, well, you want 'em, you have 'em, I don't care. But if you have any in visiting or anything sometime, don't let them fool with this."

"*Zzzzt,*" said David, smiling.

"You got it." She picked up one end of the cable which she had let slide off her shoulder onto the floor and began connecting it to the back of the television. The other end she screwed into a silvery outlet in the wall. Then she got to her feet. "Gonna play outside for a few minutes now. Don't touch anything. Don't turn the set on, okay? I'll try to get this finished up by the time *Donahue* comes on."

"We don't like him," David said. "We think he's insincere."

"Suit yourself. Half the women in this town get cable just so they can see him better. It's all the same to me." Still grinning, she stepped over the tools and let herself out.

All delivery and service people, David decided, had to go to some kind of training camp for vocational-quirkiness lessons. Then again, maybe if he made a living connecting people to *Donahue,* he'd be a character himself. He couldn't wait to tell Lydia about this one. Lydia had thought the two guys who had delivered the washer and dryer had been lunatics.

When the woman hadn't returned for several minutes, he went to the window to check on her. She was standing at the open back of the truck with some kind of meter in her hand. It was attached to a cable that ran out of the truck over the sidewalk and around the side of the house. She seemed to be muttering to herself as she twisted a button or dial on the meter. David raised the window.

"Are you sure you don't need me to turn on the set?" he called.

She looked up at him, startled. "Don't touch it! You *didn't* touch it, did you? Well, don't! Can't take any power right now; you'll blow up all my equipment!"

"Okay." He left the window up and wandered into the kitchen. Was it considered improper to fix yourself something to eat while a service person who was probably dying for lunch herself was still on the premises? Almost certainly. His stomach growled. He snagged a piece of cheese out of the refrigerator and then crammed the whole thing into his mouth as he heard her come back into the house.

"Almost done," she sang. "Few more adjustments, you're ready for the glory of Living Room Cinema. Trademarked."

He went back to the living room, trying to chew inconspicuously. The woman glanced up at him as she connected wires from a small brown box to the back of the set.

"Ah. Lunch. I'm dyin' for lunch. That's what I'm goin' for next, you bet." She pushed her frizz back from her forehead. "Okay. C'mere. I'm gonna show you."

David swallowed the cheese and wiped his hand across his mouth.

"This here on top of the cable selector. S'got two buttons, A and B. One group of stations is on A, the other's on B. A is simple, mostly the local stations. B is complex—satellite stations and movie channel, sports and news networks, that stuff."

"How do I know what channels to turn to?"

"I'll give you a card before I leave, it's got all that stuff on it. And here's a free program guide. Right now, we wanna see how good it comes in, okay? Great. Go for it and turn her on."

David laughed a little and turned on the television. A game show sprang into life on the screen, looking a bit purple.

"Okay. You're on A right now, see? The A button is pushed in. Flip around the dial and let's see everything else."

More game shows, some soap operas and a flurry of commercials lashed on the screen before David returned to the original game show.

"Great picture, huh?" said the woman, tapping his arm lightly with screwdriver. *"Purple* picture."

"You can fix that yourself later. Right now we're just interested in your reception. No snow, no rolling. Great. Isn't that great?"

"It's great," David said. Strange how service people always seemed to crave praise for whatever company they represented. "Do *you* have the cable?"

The woman's eyes widened as though he had asked her about her sex life. "Do I look like someone who would need the cable? Try the B channels. No, keep your hand on the dial, in case you've got to fine tune."

David opened his mouth to tell her there was no fine tuning connected with the channel selector and decided to humor her. Then perhaps she'd take her quirky little self out of his living room faster. He was beginning to tire of her and her jackrabbity conversational style.

He reached up with his left hand and touched the box on top of the TV set. It was warm and tingly on his fingertips, and he almost snatched his hand back. The woman shifted her weight impatiently, and he thumbed down the B button.

Something hot and sizzling jumped into his left hand and shot up his arm. To his horror, he couldn't let go of the box. The hot, sizzling feeling hit his chest and streaked down his other arm before it began to burn through his torso. His last thought, as he turned his head toward the woman, was that she was reacting awfully nonchalantly to the electrocution of one of her customers.

The woman stood staring at David with, her arms folded. The fading expression on his face was typical—shock, panic, maybe a little betrayal. Probably thought he was being electrocuted. She'd heard the final connection was something like that, getting fried. *Zzzzt!* She grinned.

When the last bit of emotion had drained from David's face and his eyes had gone opaque, she produced something that might have been a lecturer's metal pointer form her back pocket and stepped around behind the television again. She did something else to the connections she had made, and the TV screen went dark: David's arms dropped abruptly. The woman punched the A button. "Straighten up," she ordered.

David did so, his head still facing where she had been standing previously. She moved back in front of the TV and twisted the channel selector. David took three steps backwards and bumped into the coffee table.

"Easy there, poppa." She patted her pockets and found the small white card she needed. "Okay. Here we go. Channel 4, right. Channel 5." David held his arms out to his sides as if waiting either to catch someone up in a hug or be crucified. She changed the channel again and he bent forward at the waist.

"Lotta talent there." The woman flipped through the channels, watching closely as David bent forward at the waist, bobbed up again, combed his hair with his fingers, pinched his nose and opened his mouth. "Siddown on the couch. Stand up. Stand on your left foot." David obeyed, his movements smooth and almost graceful. "Okay. Now the B channels. Do your stuff, poppa."

David walked around the room, turned on a lamp and shut it off again, mimed opening a drawer and searching through some files and danced a few shuffling steps.

"Great reception," the woman said. "One more and you're set." She consulted the card and turned to Channel 9. David did a bump and grind, slow and then fast. "Relax.

This is only a test." She laughed and switched back to the A button. He stood motionless again, awaiting instructions. "You're doin' great. Siddown."

David collapsed to the floor cross-legged. "Oops. Shoulda told you to sit on the couch. Hell. Just stay there. Gonna take care of momma next. After lunch." She went into the kitchen and found the cheese in the refrigerator. She nibbled at it while she got the peanut butter and a loaf of bread out of the cupboard. As an afterthought, she opened a can of black olives.

Lydia Martel was having a carton of strawberry yogurt for lunch at her desk when the phone rang. She dabbed at her lips with a napkin before picking up the receiver.

"Lydia Martel." She paused, sitting back. "Oh, good. Any problems? How's the reception, any static?" She paused again, listening. "Good. Good. Now, how much did you say the installation fee would be? Uh-huh. And the regular monthly charge is what?" She scribbled the figures on a memo pad. "Yes, it *is* reasonable. That includes everything, right?" Lydia laughed a little indulgently. "I *can't* get away before 4:30.— Yes, there is something. Put him on vacuum before you leave. He knows where it is, even if he's never touched it. *All* the rooms. After that he can clean up the kitchen, I'm sure he left a mess from lunch. Have him take the chicken out to thaw, I'm positive he forgot.

"And, oh, yes—have him shave, will you? Thanks."

San

Lan Samantha Chang

Lan Samantha Chang attended the Iowa Writers' Workshop where she began working on "San." At one point, the story was thirty pages long, at another seven pages. After much revision and a two-year period during which she waited for her perspective on the material to mature, Chang finished the story. Her other fiction has appeared in Prairie Schooner, The Atlantic Monthly, *and* The Best American Short Stories 1994. *She has received support for her fiction writing from the Michener-Copernicus Foundation, the Henfield Foundation, and the estate of Truman Capote. She teaches fiction writing at Stanford University.*

My father left my mother and me one rainy summer morning, carrying a new umbrella of mine. From our third-floor window I watched him close the front door and pause to glance at the sky. Then he opened my umbrella. I liked the big red flower pattern—it was *fuqi,* prosperous—but in the hands of a man, even a handsome man like my father, the umbrella looked gaudy and ridiculous. Still, he did not hunch underneath but carried it high up, almost jauntily.

As I watched him walk away, I remembered a Chinese superstition. The Mandarin word for umbrella, *san,* also means "to fall apart." If you acquire an umbrella without paying for it, your life will fall apart. My father had scoffed at such beliefs. The umbrella had been a present from him. Now I stood and watched it go, bright and ill-fated like so many of his promises.

Later that morning the roof of our apartment sprang a leak. Two tiles buckled off the kitchen floor, revealing a surprising layer of mud, as if my mother's mopping over the years had merely pushed the dirt beneath the tiles and all along we'd been living over a floor of soot.

Reprinted from *Hunger*, (1998), by permission of W.W. Norton & Company.

My mother knelt with a sponge in one hand. She wouldn't look at me. Her heavy chignon had come undone and a thick lock of hair wavered down her back.

"Can I help?" I asked, standing over her. She did not answer but stroked the tiles with her sponge.

I put the big rice cooker underneath the leak. Then I went to my room. All morning, I studied problems for my summer-school math class. I heard my mother, in the kitchen, start to sob. I felt only fear—a dense stone in my chest—but I put even this aside so I could study. My father had taught me to focus on the equations in front of me, and so I spent the hours after he left thinking about trigonometry, a subject he had loved.

My mathematical talent had sprung from an early backwardness. As a child I could not count past three: my father, my mother, and me.

"Caroline is making progress in her English lessons, but she remains baffled by the natural numbers," read an early report card. "She cannot grasp the *countability* of blocks and other solid objects. For this reason I am recommending that she repeat the first grade."

This comment left my father speechless. He believed I was a brilliant child. And mathematics had been his favorite subject back in China, before the political trouble had forced him to quit school.

"Counting," he said in English, when he was able to talk again. His dark eyebrows swooped over the bridge of his aquiline nose. Despite his drastic ups and downs, bad news always caught him by surprise. But he recovered with typical buoyancy. "Don't worry, Lily," he told my mother. "It's those western teachers. *I'll* teach her how to count."

And so my father, himself an unreliable man, taught me to keep track of things. We counted apples, bean sprouts, grains of rice. I learned to count in pairs, with ivory chopsticks. We stood on the corner of Atlantic Avenue, counting cars to learn big numbers. We spent a lovely afternoon in Prospect Park, counting blades of grass aloud until we both had scratchy throats.

"Keep going," he urged me on as the shadows lengthened. "I want you to be able to count all the money I'm going to make, here in America."

By the time I was seven I had learned the multiplication tables to twenty-times-twenty. In the following year I learned to recite the table of squares and the table of cubes, both so quickly that the words blended together into a single stream, almost meaningless: "Oneeighttwentysevensixtyfouronetwentyfivetwosixteenthree-fortythree . . ."

As I chanted, my father would iron the white shirt and black trousers he wore to his waiter's job, a "temporary" job. Or he stood in the kitchen, Mondays off, with three blue balls and one red ball, juggling expertly beneath the low tin ceiling. Each time the red ball reached his hand I was ordered to stress a syllable. Thus "One, *eight*, twenty-*sev*en, sixty-*four*."

"Pro*nounce*," said my father, proud of his clear *r*'s. To succeed in America, he was sure, required good pronunciation as well as math. He often teased my mother for pronouncing my name *Calorin,* "like a diet formula," he said. They had named me Caroline after Caroline Kennedy, who was born shortly before their arrival in the States. After all, my father's name was Jack. And if the name was good enough for a president's daughter, then certainly it was good enough for me.

After I learned to count I began, belatedly, to notice things. Signs of hard luck and good fortune moved through our apartment like sudden storms. A pale stripe on my father's tanned wrist revealed where his watch had been. A new pair of aquamarine slippers shimmered on my mother's feet. A beautiful collection of fourteen cacti, each distinct, bloomed on our fire escape for several summer months and then vanished.

I made careful explorations of our apartment. At the back of the foyer closet, inside the faded red suitcase my mother had brought from China, I discovered a cache of little silk purses wrapped in a cotton shirt. When I heard her footsteps I instinctively closed the suitcase and pretended I was looking for a pair of mittens. Then I went to my room and shut the door, slightly dizzy with anticipation and guilt.

A few days later when my mother was out, I opened one purse. Inside was a swirling gold pin with pearl and coral flowers. I made many secret visits to the closet, a series of small sins. Each time I opened one more treasure. There were bright green, milky white, and blood red jade bracelets. Some of the bracelets were so small I could not fit them over my hand. There was a ring with a pearl as big as a marble. A strand of pearls, each the size of a large pea. A strand of jade beads, each of them green as grass, carved in the shape of small buddhas. A rusty key.

"Do you still have keys to our old house in China?" I asked my father.

"That's the past, Caroline," he said. "*Wanle.* It is gone."

Surrounded by questions, I became intrigued by the answers to things. My report cards showed that I became a good student, a very good student, particularly in math. At twelve, I was the only person from my class to test into a public school for the "gifted" in Manhattan. My father attended the school event where this news was announced. I remember his pleased expression as we approached the small, crowded auditorium. He had piled all of our overcoats and his fedora over one arm, but with the other he opened the door for my mother and me. As I filed past he raised his eyebrows and nodded—proud, but not at all surprised by my achievement.

He believed in the effortless, in splurging and quick riches. While I studied, bent and dogged, and my mother hoarded things, my father strayed from waitering and turned to something bigger. He had a taste for risk, he said to us. A nose for good investments. Some friends were helping him. He began to stay out late and come home with surprises. On good nights, he brought us presents: a sewing kit, a pink silk scarf. Once he climbed out of a taxicab with a hundred silver dollars in my old marble bag.

On bad nights, my father whistled his way home. I sometimes woke to his high music floating from the street. I sat up and spied at him through the venetian blinds. He no longer wore his waiter's clothes; his overcoat was dark. I could just make out the glitter of his shiny shoes. He stepped lightly, always, on bad nights, although he'd whistled clear across the bridge to save on subway fare. He favored Stephen Foster tunes and Broadway musicals. He flung his head back on a long, pure note. When he reached our door he stood still for a moment and squared his shoulders. My mother, too, knew what the whistling meant.

"Stayed up for me?"

"I wasn't tired."

I crept to my door to peek at them. My mother staring at her feet. My father's hopeful face, his exaggerated brightness. My mother said, "Go to sleep, Caroline."

But I had trouble sleeping. I could feel him slipping away from us, drifting far in search of some intoxicating music. Each time he wandered off, it seemed to take more effort to recall us. He began to speak with his head cocked, as if listening for something. He often stood at the living room window, staring at the street.

"Does Baba have a new job?" I asked my mother.

"No." She looked away.

I felt sorry I'd asked. Questions caused my mother pain. But I was afraid to ask my father. In his guarded face he held a flaming knowledge: a certain concentration, a hunger for opportunities that lay beyond my understanding.

All that year I hunted clues, made lists of evidence.

> *Missing on February 3:*
>   *carved end table*
>   *painting of fruit (from front hallway)*
>   *jade buddha*
>   *camera (mine)*

I followed him. One evening after I missed my camera, I heard the front door slam. I grabbed my coat and bolted down the stairs. I dodged across the street half a block back, peering around pedestrians and traffic signs, my eyes fixed on his overcoat and fedora. At the subway station I waited by the token booth and dashed into the car behind him, keeping track of his shiny shoes through the swaying windows. I almost missed him when he left the train. Outside it was already dusk. The tall, cold shapes of City Hall and the courthouses loomed over us and I followed at a distance. I felt light as a puff of silk, breathing hard, excited, almost dancing.

Past the pawnshops, the offtrack betting office with its shuffling line of men in old overcoats, toward the dirty, crowded streets of Chinatown, its neon signs winking on for the night. Groups of teenagers, chattering in Cantonese, looked strangely at me and kept walking.

"Incense, candles, incense, *xiaojie?*" A street vendor held a grimy handful toward me.

"No, thanks," I panted. I almost lost him, but then ahead I recognized his elegant stride. He turned into a small, shabby building, nodding to an old man who stood at the door. I hung around outside, stamping my shoes on the icy sidewalk.

After a minute the old man walked over to me. "Your father does not know you followed him," he told me in Chinese. "You must go home. Go home, and I will not tell him you were here."

For a minute I couldn't move. He was exactly my height. His short hair was white but his forehead strangely unlined, and he wore well-fitting western clothes. It was his expensive tweed overcoat that made me turn around. That and the decaying, fetid odor of his teeth, and the fact that he knew my father well enough to recognize my features, knew he would not have wanted me to follow him. I reboarded the train at the Canal Street station. Back in the apartment, I stayed up until well past midnight, but I didn't hear him come home.

I should not have followed him. I should have known that eventually he would show his secret to me, his one pupil. A few months later, on the night before my fourteenth birthday, he motioned me to stay seated after supper. The hanging lamp cast a circle of light over the worn kitchen table.

"I'm going to teach you some math," he said.

I glanced at his face, but his eyes glowed black and expressionless in their sockets, hollow in the lamplight.

Over his shoulder I saw my mother check to see that we were occupied. Then she walked into the foyer and opened the closet door, where the jewelry was. I felt a tingle of fear, even though I had concealed my visits perfectly.

"Concentrate," said my father. "Here is a penny. Each penny has two sides: heads and tails. You understand me, Caroline?"

I nodded. The dull coin looked like a hole in his palm.

"Hao," he said: good. His brown hand danced and the penny flipped onto our kitchen table. Heads. "Now, if I throw this coin many many times, how often would I get heads?"

"One-half of the time."

He nodded.

"Hao," he said. "That is the *huo ran lu.* The *huo ran lu* for heads is one-half. If you know that, you can figure out the *huo ran lu* that I will get two heads if I throw twice in a row." He waited a minute. "Think of it as a limiting of possibilities. The first throw cuts the possibilities in half."

I looked into the dark tunnel of my father's eyes, and following the discipline of his endless drilling, I began to understand where we had been going. Counting, multiplication, the table of squares. "Half of the half," I said. "A quarter."

He set the coins aside and reached into his shirt pocket. Suddenly, with a gesture of his hand, two dice lay in the middle of the yellow circle of light. Two small chunks of ivory, with tiny black pits in them.

"Count the sides," he said.

The little cube felt cold and heavy. "Six."

My father's hand closed over the second die. "What is the *huo ran lu* that I will get a side with only two dots?"

My mind wavered in surprise at his intensity. But I knew the answer. "One-sixth," I said.

He nodded. "You are a smart daughter," he said.

I discovered that I had been holding onto the table leg with my left hand, and I let go. I heard the creak of the hall closet door but my father did not look away from the die in his hand.

"What is the *huo ran lu* that I can roll the side with two dots twice in a row?" he said.

"One thirty-sixth."

"Three times in a row?"

"One two-hundred-and-sixteenth."

"That is very good!" he said. "Now, the *huo ran lu* that I will be able to roll a two is one-sixth. Would it be a reasonable bet that I will not roll a two?"

I nodded.

"We could say, if I roll a two you may have both pennies."

I saw it then, deep in his eyes—a spark of excitement, a piece of joy particularly his. It was there for an instant and disappeared. He frowned and nodded toward the table as if to say: pay attention. Then his hand flourished and the die trickled into the light. I bent eagerly over the table, but my father sat perfectly still, his face impassive again. Two dots.

When I looked up at him in astonishment I noticed my mother standing in the doorway, her two huge eyes burning in her white face.

"Jack."

My father started, but he didn't turn around to look at her. "Yes, Lily," he said.

The die grew wet in my hand.

"What are you doing?"

"Giving the child a lesson."

"And what is she going to learn from this?" My mother's voice trembled but it did not rise, "Where will she go with this?"

"Lily," my father said.

"What will become of us?" my mother almost whispered. She looked around the kitchen. Almost all of the furniture had disappeared. The old kitchen table and the three chairs, plus our rice cooker, were virtually the only things left in the room.

I grabbed the second die and left the table. In my room as I listened to my parents next door in the kitchen I rolled one die two hundred and sixteen times, keeping track by making marks on the back of a school notebook. But I failed to reach a two more than twice in a row.

"The suitcase, Jack. Where is it?"

After a moment my father muttered, "I'll get it back. Don't you believe me?"

"I don't know." She began to cry so loudly that even though I pressed my hands against my ears I could still hear her. My father said nothing. I hunched down over my knees, trying to shut them out.

"You promised me, you promised me you'd never touch them!"

"I was going to bring them back!"

"We have nothing for Caroline's birthday . . ."

Something crashed against the other side of my bedroom wall. I scuttled to the opposite wall and huddled in the corner of my bed.

For a long period after I heard nothing but my mother's sobbing. Then I heard them leave the kitchen. The house was utterly silent. I realized I had wrapped my arms around my knees to keep from trembling. I felt strange and light-headed: oh, but I understood now. My father was a gambler, a *dutu,* an apprentice of chance. Of course.

With the understanding came a desperate need to see both of them. I stood up and walked through the living room to my parents' bedroom. The door was ajar. I peered in.

The moonlight, blue and white, shifted and flickered on the bed, on my mother's long black hair twisting over her arm. Her white fingers moved vaguely. I felt terrified for her. He moved against her body in such a consuming way, as if he might pass through her, as if she were incorporeal, I watched for several minutes before my mother made a sound that frightened me so much I had to leave.

The next morning my eyes felt sandy and strange. We strolled down Atlantic Avenue, holding hands, with me in the middle because it was my birthday. My mother's stride was tentative, but my father walked with the calculated lightness and unconcern of one who has nothing in his pockets. Several gulls flew up before us, and he watched with delight as they wheeled into the cloudy sky. The charm of Brooklyn, this wide shabby street bustling with immigrants like ourselves, was enough to make him feel lucky.

He squeezed my hand, a signal that I should squeeze my mother's for him. We'd played this game many times over the years, but today I hesitated. My mother's hand did not feel like something to hold onto. Despite the warm weather her fingers in mine were cold. I squeezed, however, and she turned. He looked at her over the top of my head, and my mother, seeing his expression, lapsed into a smile that caused the Greek delivery boys from the corner pizza parlor to turn and watch as we passed. She and my father didn't notice.

We walked past a display of furniture on the sidewalk—incomplete sets of dining chairs, hat stands, old sewing table—and I stared for a minute, for I thought I saw something standing behind a battered desk: a rosewood dresser my parents had brought from Taiwan; it used to be in my own bedroom. I once kept my dolls in the bottom left drawer, the one with the little scar where I had nicked it with a roller skate. . . . Perhaps it only had a similar shape. But it could very well be our dresser. I knew better than to point it out. I turned away.

"Oh, Jack, the flowers!" my mother exclaimed in Chinese. She let go of my hand and rushed to DeLorenzio's floral display, sank down to smell the potted gardenias with a grace that brought my father and me to a sudden stop.

My father's black eyebrows came down over his eyes. "*Ni qu gen ni mama tan yi tan,* go talk to your mother," he said, giving me a little push. I frowned.

"Go on."

She was speaking with Mr. DeLorenzio, and I stood instinctively on their far side, trying to act cute despite my age in order to distract them from what my father was doing. He stood before the red geraniums. He picked up a plant, considered it, and set it down with a critical shake of his head.

"And how are you today, sweetheart?" Mr. DeLorenzio bent toward me, offering me a close-up of his gray handlebar mustache. Behind him, my father disappeared from view.

"She's shy," said my mother proudly. After a few minutes I tugged her sleeve, and she said good-bye to the florist. We turned, continued walking down the street.

"Where is your father?"

"I think he's somewhere up there."

I pulled her toward the corner. My father stepped out from behind a pet store, smiling broadly, holding the pot of bright geraniums.

"It's going to rain," he proclaimed, as if he'd planned it himself.

It started to rain. The drops felt light and warm on my face. We ran to the nearest awning, where my mother put on her rain bonnet. Then my father disappeared, leaving us standing on the sidewalk. I didn't notice him leave. All of a sudden he was just gone.

"Where's Baba?" I asked my mother.

"I don't know," she said, calmly tucking her hair into the plastic bonnet. The geraniums stood at her feet. I looked around us. The sidewalks had become slick and dark; people hurried along. The wind blew cool in my face. Then the revolving doors behind us whirled and my father walked out.

"There you are," my mother said.

"Here, Caroline," said my father. He reached into his jacket and pulled out the umbrella. It lay balanced on his palm, its brilliant colors neatly furled, an offering.

I wanted to refuse the umbrella. For a moment I believed that if I did, I could separate myself from both of my parents, and our pains, and everything that bound me to them.

I looked up at my father's face. He was watching me intently. I took the umbrella.

"Thanks," I said. He smiled. The next day, he was gone.

My mother had her hair cut short and dressed in mourning colors; this attitude bestowed on her a haunting, muted beauty. She was hired for the lunch shift at a chic Manhattan Chinese restaurant. Our lives grew stable and very quiet. In the evenings I studied while my mother sat in the kitchen, waiting, cutting carrots and mushroom caps into elaborate shapes for our small stir-frys, or combining birdseed for the feeder on the fire escape in the exact proportions that my father had claimed would bring the most cardinals and the fewest sparrows. I did the homework for advanced placement courses. I planned to enter Columbia with the academic standing of a sophomore. We spoke gently to each other about harmless, tactful things. "Peanut sauce," we said. "Shopping." "Homework." "Apricots."

I studied trigonometry. I grew skillful in that subject without ever liking it. I learned calculus, linear algebra, and liked them less and less, but I kept studying, seeking the comfort that arithmetic had once provided. Things fall apart, it seems, with terrible slowness. I could not see that true mathematics, rather than keeping track of things, moves toward the unexplainable. A swooping line descends from nowhere, turns, escapes to some infinity. Centuries of scholars work to solve a single puzzle. In mathematics, as in love, the riddles matter most.

In the months when I was failing out of Columbia, I spent a lot of my time on the subway. I rode to Coney Island, to the watery edge of Brooklyn, and stayed on the express train as it changed directions and went back deep under the river, into Manhattan. Around City Hall or 14th Street a few Chinese people always got on the train, and I sometimes saw a particular kind of man, no longer young but his face curiously unlined, wearing an expensive but shabby overcoat and shiny shoes. I would watch until he got off at his stop. Then I would sit back and wait as the train pulsed through the dark tunnels under the long island of Manhattan, and sometimes the light would blink out for a minute and I would see blue sparks shooting off the tracks. I was waiting for the moment around 125th Street where the express train rushed into daylight. This sudden openness, this coming out of darkness into a new world, helped me understand how he must have felt. I imagined him bending over a pair of dice that glowed like tiny skulls under the yellow kitchen light. I saw him walking out the door with my flowery umbrella, pausing to look up at the sky and the innumerable, luminous possibilities that lay ahead.

Emerging from Censorship

J. M. Coetzee

J. M. Coetzee was born in Cape Town, South Africa in 1940. He studied first at Cape Town, and later earned a Ph.D. degree in literature from the University of Texas at Austin. He returned to South Africa and joined the faculty of the University of Cape Town in 1972.

His first novel, actually two novellas, Dusklands *(1974), examines the parallels between Americans in Vietnam and the early Dutch settlers in South Africa.* Waiting for the Barbarians *(1980), the story of a government magistrate, who questions the government for which he works, won South Africa's highest literary honor, the Central News Agency (CNA) Literary Award, in 1980. He won the premier British award, the Booker Prize, for the first time in 1983, for the* Life and Times of Michael K. *In the same year he was appointed Professor of General Literature at the University of Cape Town, a post he still holds.*

On October 25th 1999, Coetzee became the first author to win the prestigious Booker award twice in its 31-year history, for his current novel, Disgrace. *In addition to novels, he has written several volumes of critical essays. The following essay is part of a chapter in* Giving Offence: Essays on Censorship.

From the early 1960s until about 1980, the Republic of South Africa operated one of the most comprehensive censorship systems in the world. Called in official parlance not censorship but "publications control" (*censorship* was a word it preferred to censor from public discourse about itself),[1] it sought to control the dissemination of signs in whatever form. Not only books, magazines, films, and plays, but T-shirts, key-rings,

Reprinted from *Giving Offence: Essays on Censorship*, (1996), by permission of University of Chicago Press.

dolls, toys, and shop-signs—anything, in fact, bearing a message that might be "undesirable"—had to pass the scrutiny of the censorship bureaucracy before it could be made public. In the Soviet Union, there were some 70,000 bureaucrats supervising the activities of some 7,000 writers. The ratio of censors to writers in South Africa was, if anything, higher than ten to one.

Paranoids behave as though the air is filled with coded messages deriding them or plotting their destruction. For decades the South African state lived in a state of paranoia. Paranoia is the pathology of insecure regimes and of dictatorships in particular. One of the features distinguishing modern from earlier dictatorships has been how widely and rapidly paranoia can spread from above to infect the whole of the populace. This diffusion of paranoia is not inadvertent: it is used as a technique of control. Stalin's Soviet Union is the prime example: every citizen was encouraged to suspect every other citizen of being a spy or saboteur; the bonds of human sympathy and trust between people were broken down; and society fragmented into tens of millions of individuals living on individual islets of mutual suspicion.

The Soviet Union was not unique. The Cuban novelist Reinaldo Arenas wrote of an atmosphere of "unceasing official menace" in his country that made a citizen "not only a repressed person, but also a self-repressed one, not only a censored person, but a self-censored one, not only one watched over, but one who watches over himself."[2] "Unceasing official menace" punctuated with spectacles of exemplary punishment inculcates caution, watchfulness. When certain kinds of writing and speech, even certain thoughts, become surreptitious activities, then the paranoia of the state is on its way to being reproduced in the psyche of the subject, and the state can look forward to a future in which the bureaucracies of supervision can be allowed to wither away, their function having been, in effect, privatized.

For it is a revealing feature of censorship that it is not proud of itself, never parades itself. The archaic model for the censor's ban is the ban on blasphemy, and both bans suffer an embarrassing structural paradox, namely, that if a crime is to be satisfactorily attested in court, the testimony will have to repeat the crime. Thus it used to be that in the public sessions of the rabbinical courts witnesses to blasphemy were supplied with codified euphemisms to utter in place of the banned name of the Holy; if the actual blasphemy had to be repeated to make conviction conclusive, the court moved into closed session, and testimony was followed by rituals of purgation on the part of the judges. Embarrassment went even further: the very notion that the name of the Holy as a blasphemous word could curse the Holy was so scandalous that for "curse" the word "bless" had to be substituted.[3] Just as a chain of euphemisms came into being to protect the name of the Holy, so in an age when the state was worshipped the office that protected its name had to be euphemized. That office waits for the day when, its functions having been universally internalized, its name need no longer be spoken.

The tyrant and his watchdog are not the only ones touched by paranoia. There is a pathological edge to the watchfulness of the writer in the paranoid state. For evidence one need only go to the testimony of writers themselves. Time and again they record the feeling of being touched and contaminated by the sickness of the state. In a move typical of "authentic" paranoids, they claim that their minds have been invaded; it is against this invasion that they express their outrage.

The Greek writer George Mangakis, for instance, records the experience of writing in prison under the eyes of his guards. Every few days the guards searched his cell, taking away his writings and returning those which the prison authorities—his censors—considered "permissible." Mangakis recalls suddenly "loathing" his papers as he accepted them from the hands of his guards. "The system is a diabolical device for annihilating your own soul. They want to make you see your thoughts through their eyes and control them yourself, from their point of view."[4] By forcing the writer to see what he has written through the censor's eyes, the censor forces him to internalize a contaminating reading. Mangakis's sudden, revulsive moment is the moment of contamination.

Another passionate account of the operations of introverted censorship is given by Danilo Kis:

> The battle against self-censorship is anonymous, lonely and unwitnessed, and it makes its subject feel humiliated and ashamed of collaborating. [It] means reading your own text with the eyes of another person, a situation where you become your own judge, stricter and more suspicious than anyone else. . . .
>
> The self-appointed censor is the *alter ego* of the writer, an alter ego who leans over his shoulder and sticks his nose into the text. . . . It is impossible to win against this censor, for he is like God—he knows and sees all, he came out of your own mind, your own fears, your own nightmares. . . .
>
> This *alter ego* . . . succeeds in undermining and tainting even the most moral individuals whom outside censorship has not managed to break. By not admitting that it exists, self-censorship aligns itself with lies and spiritual corruption.[5]

The final proof that something has, so to speak, gone wrong with writers like Arenas or Mangakis or Kis is the excessiveness of the language in which they express their experience. Paranoia is not just a figurative way of talking about what has afflicted them. The paranoia is there, on the inside, in their language, in their thinking; the rage one hears in Mangakis' words, the bafflement in Kis's, are rage and bafflement at the most intimate of invasions, an invasion of the very style of the self, by a pathology for which there may be no cure.

Nor am I, as I write here, exempt. In the excessive insistency of its phrasing, its vehemence, its demand for sensitivity to minutiae of style, its overreading and overwriting, I detect in my own language the very pathology I discuss. Having lived through the heyday of South African censorship, seen its consequences not only on the careers of fellow-writers but on the totality of public discourse, and felt within myself some of its more secret and shameful effects, I have every reason to suspect that

65

whatever infected Arenas or Mangakis or Kis, whether real or delusional, has infected me too. That is to say, this very writing may be a specimen of the kind of paranoid discourse it seeks to describe.

For the paranoia I address is not the imprint of censorship on those writers alone who are singled out for official persecution. All writing that in the normal course of events falls under the censor's eye may become tainted in the manner I have described, whether or not the censor passes it. All writers under censorship are at least potentially touched by paranoia, not just those who have their work suppressed.

Why should censorship have such contagious power? I can offer only a speculative answer, an answer based in part on introspection, in part on a scrutiny (perhaps a paranoid scrutiny) of the accounts that other writers (perhaps themselves infected with paranoia) have given of operating under regimes of censorship.

The self, as we understand the self today, is not the unity it was assumed to be by classical rationalism. On the contrary, it is multiple and multiply divided against itself. It is, to speak in figures, a zoo in which a multitude of beasts have residence, over which the anxious, overworked zookeeper of rationality exercises a rather limited control. At night the zookeeper sleeps and the beasts roam about, doing their dreamwork.

In this figural zoo, some of the beasts have names, like figure-of-the-father and figure-of-the-mother; others are memories or fragments of memories in transmuted form, with strong elements of feeling attached to them; a whole subcolony are semi-tamed but still treacherous earlier versions of the self, each with an inner zoo of its own over which it has less than complete control.

Artists, in Freud's account, are people who can make a tour of the inner menagerie with a degree of confidence and emerge, when they so wish, more or less unscathed. From Freud's account of creative work I take one element: that creativity of a certain kind involves inhabiting and managing and exploiting quite primitive parts of the self. While this is not a particularly dangerous activity it is a delicate one. It may take years of preparation before the artist finally gets the codes and the keys and the balances right, and can move in and out more or less freely. It is also a very private activity, so private that it almost constitutes the definition of privacy: how I am with myself.

Managing the inner selves, making them work for one (making them productive) is a complex matter of pleasing and satisfying and challenging and extorting and wooing and feeding, and sometimes even of putting to death. For writing not only comes out of the zoo but (to be hypermetaphorical) goes back in again. That is to say, insofar as writing is transactional, the figures *for whom* and *to whom* it is done are also figures in the zoo: for instance, the figure-of-the-beloved.

Imagine, then, a project in writing that is, at heart, a transaction with some such figure of the beloved, that tries to please her (but that also tries continually though surreptitiously to revise and recreate her as the-one-who-will-be-pleased); and imagine what will happen if into this transaction is introduced in a massive and undeniable way another figure-of-the-reader, the dark-suited, baldheaded censor, with his pursed lips and his red pen and his irritability and his censoriousness—the censor, in fact, as parodic version of the figure-of-the-father. Then the entire balance of the carefully constructed inner drama will be destroyed, and destroyed in a way that is hard to repair, since the more one tries to ignore (repress) the censor, the larger he swells.

Working under censorship is like being intimate with someone who does not love you, with whom you want no intimacy, but who presses himself in upon you. The censor is an intrusive reader, a reader who forces his way into the intimacy of the writing transaction, forces out the figure of the loved or courted reader, reads your words in a disapproving and *censorious* fashion.

ENDNOTES

[1] Though by no means as extreme, the South African system showed odd parallels with the Soviet system. Andrei Sinyavsky recollects finding no entry for *tzenzura*, "censorship," in a 1977 dictionary of foreign-derived words in Russian: "The word 'censorship' was itself censored." Quoted in Marianna Tax Choldin and Maurice Friedberg, eds., *The Red Pencil* (Boston: Unwin Hyman, 1989), p. 94.

[2] Quoted in Carlos Ripoll, *The Heresy of Words in Cuba* (New York: Freedom House, 1985), p. 36.

[3] Leonard W. Levy, *Treason against God* (New York: Schocken, 1981), pp. 25–26.

[4] George Mangakis, "Letter to Europeans" (1972) in George Theiner, ed., *They Shoot Writers, Don't They?* (London: Faber, 1984), p. 33.

[5] Kis, Danilo. "Censorship/Self-Censorship." *Index on Censorship* 5/1 (January 1986): 45.

The Mathematics of Kindness: Math Proves the Golden Rule

K. C. Cole

K. C. Cole is a science writer for Los Angeles Times, *who lives in Santa Monica, California. In 1995, she won the American Institute of Physics Award for Best Science Writing. She wrote* Sympathetic Vibrations *(1984), a book that explores creativity, art and beauty in relation to physics. In* The Universe and the Teacup: The Mathematics of Truth and Beauty *(1998), from which the following essay was excerpted, she continues to explore the same themes in relation to mathematics.*

Surprisingly, there is a single property which distinguishes
the relatively high-scoring entries from the relatively low-scoring
entries. This is the property of being NICE. . . .
　　　　　　　—Robert Axelrod, in The Evolution of Cooperation

Life did not take over the globe by combat, but by networking.
　　　　　　　—Lynn Margulis and Dorion Sagan in Microcosmos

"Do unto others as you would have others do unto you." "An eye for an eye." "Get it while the getting's good." "He ain't heavy, he's my brother."

Selfishness and altruism have always been uneasy partners in human affairs. Churches and scout troops exhort us to lend a helping hand to those in need; at the same time, advertisers and politicians encourage us to be as greedy as humanly possible. Indeed, the idea that greed is all to the good has become encoded in a kind of

---

Reprinted from *The Universe and the Teacup: The Mathematics of Truth and Beauty*, (1998), by permission of Harcourt Inc.

religion of U.S.-style capitalism: The more you're out for yourself, the better off the whole society will be.

This win-at-all costs strategy gains strength because it appears to be founded on Mother Nature's own laws. Charles Darwin's idea of survival of the fittest suggests that only the meanest, most competitive, most selfish individuals will make it to the top of the evolutionary heap. Compromise, cooperation, and kindness are for losers and wimps. In a capitalistic society, failure to be selfish is akin to economic treason.

For a long time, people have accepted this philosophy as undeniably true. But for the past two decades, mathematicians have been studying survival strategies to find out which are truly best. To almost everyone's surprise, they have found that nice guys can and frequently do finish first. In tournaments designed to pick out winners in a variety of conflict situations, the top dog turns out to be not the most ferocious but the most cooperative. Ironically, the strategies that have emerged from the mathematical research sound a lot like old-fashioned homilies: think ahead, cooperate, don't covet your neighbor's success, and be prepared to forgive those who trespass against you.

Much work in game theory has focused on one of the most unsettling paradoxes of all, the so-called prisoner's dilemma. It's usually explained as a familiar cop show scenario. Two partners in crime are kept in isolated cells. Each is told that if he blows the whistle on the other, he might be able to go free. If he remains mute, each prisoner knows, the authorities might not have enough evidence to convict him—unless, of course, the other prisoner rats on him first. Which strategy works best—keep silent or strike a deal?

Variations on this theme, I think, make the inherent paradox even clearer. Assume, for example, that you've outgrown your old car but desperately want a family sailboat for Sunday afternoon excursions. Another person—whom you contact through the newspaper—desperately needs a car like yours and has exactly the sailboat you crave—a boat she no longer uses. You both agree that a swap would be a fair trade.

Now assume for some reason that the trade needs to be kept secret. You both agree to put the car/boat in predesignated places. The problem is: What happens if you leave behind your car, and the boat isn't where it's supposed to be? You've been cheated!

The boat owner faces exactly the same dilemma.

Logically, you might add up the pros and cons this way: If you leave the car, but the other person doesn't leave the boat, you get robbed. If you don't deliver the car, and she doesn't deliver the boat, then you come out even. If you don't leave the car and she does deliver the boat, you get something for nothing.

Logic points you to an inescapable conclusion: No matter what the other person does, you're better off not leaving your car. The other person's logic leads her to the same destination. Outcome? Neither of you gets what you wanted.

A prisoner's dilemma pops up anytime going after your own immediate interests results in disaster if everyone does it. Should you throw your trash out the window, or wait until you find a garbage can? Listen to public radio for free, or pay your way? Abide by disarmament agreements, or cheat and hide your arsenals?

Clearly, if one party cooperates while the other cheats, the cooperator is a sucker. But if both cheat, no one gets anything.

Looking in on the situation from the outside, it may be clear that cooperation is a better tactic for both sides. But from an individual player's point of view, there's always temptation to try to get the better of the other guy; you always have a chance of winning more by *not* cooperating.

Why, then, do people cooperate at all? This is the question that intrigued political scientist Robert Axelrod of the University of Michigan in the 1980s. If dog eat dog is the law of the jungle, why is cooperation so common among humans and other species as well? During trench warfare in World War I, Axelrod points out, soldiers on opposite sides of the front lines formed tacit agreements to live and let live—in direct defiance of orders from commanders. An officer in the British army, writing in his diary in August 1915, recounts how after a Prussian shell exploded in the British camp (during teatime, no less), a German soldier climbed out of his trench and crossed no-man's-land to apologize: "We hope no one was hurt. It is not our fault, it is that damned Prussian artillery."

Closer to home, it's not even clear why people obey traffic signals. Individually, there's not much motivation for stopping at red lights—short of the very off chance of being caught. Yet, most of the time, people do it anyway. They leave tips for waiters they may never see again, pick up after themselves when no one is looking, show kindness to total strangers.

To try to resolve the paradox, in 1980 Axelrod invited experts in game theory to a tournament of repeated games of prisoner's dilemma. Each entrant would submit a strategy, and the various strategies played against each other by means of computers. Points were assigned to outcomes and tabulated.

To almost everyone's surprise, the most successful strategy turned out to be an ingeniously simple program created by Anatol Rapoport at the University of Toronto. Called Tit for Tat, the program's first move is always to cooperate. After that, it simply echoes whatever its opposition does. If the opposition cooperates, Tit for Tat cooperates. If the opposition defects, Tit for Tat retaliates in kind.

In this sense, Tit for Tat embodies both biblical injunctions: an eye for an eye, and the Golden Rule. Or as William Poundstone sums it up in a book about classic game theory problems, the program's message is: "Do unto others as you would have them do unto you—or else!"

By not ever being the first to defect, Tit for Tat was what Axelrod called a "nice" program. As it turns out, most of the winners in computer simulations that Axelrod has run have been nice: most of the losers were not. Tit for Tat could also be forgiving—that is, even after the opposition defected, Tit for Tat would occasionally give cooperation another try. The lesson, says Axelrod, is "be nice and forgiving."

It is also important to be clear. Very complex computer programs fare no better than random ones in such simulated games because no one can figure out what their strategy is and respond in kind.

Axelrod then held a follow-up tournament. This time he got entries not only from game theorists, but also from researchers in biology, physics, and sociology. And this time, everyone knew about the success of Tit for Tat and other "nice" strategies. Nevertheless, Rapoport's simple program won again. The other experts, Axelrod concluded, all "made systematic errors of being too competitive for their own good, not being forgiving enough."

In a final round, Axelrod wanted to see what would happen if he pitted all the programs against each other in a kind of Darwinian evolution, where survival of the fittest meant success for those who produced the most viable offspring in the next generation—the number of offspring being determined by the number of points.

This time, Tit for Tat did well, but so, at first, did some very cut-throat, exploitative strategies. Then a funny thing happened: The exploitative strategies ran out of prey. There was no one left to gobble up. As Axelrod puts it, "in the long run [a strategy that is not nice] can destroy the very environment it needs for its own success."

The tournament also had lessons for the envious. If one strategy envied another's success and tried to do better, it would usually wind up cutting off its nose to spite its face. That is, the only way to get the better of an opponent would be to attack, and that would set off another round of nastiness that would make everyone worse off.

"There is no point in being envious of the success of the other player," says Axelrod, "since [in this kind of game] the other's success is virtually a prerequisite of your doing well yourself."

A final requirement for success was a stable, long-term relationship, where the same opponents would play each other again and again. In such a situation, it paid to be cooperative. This explains the relationship of the World War I soldiers, who faced each other month after month, or people in tight communities, or national leaders who need each other in an ongoing series of negotiations.

More recently, New York University's Steven Brams made great strides in making game theory more realistic.* While he was at it, he got interested in whether it might be possible to use mathematics to model human emotions—and therefore come up with strategies for getting out of frustrating situations.

In his "frustration" games, one player is stuck in a bad position, while another player is satisfied and has no incentive to change his tune. The first player can't get out of the situation without also hurting himself.

An example might be a family with an unruly teenager who refuses to follow any of the parents' rules. The parents don't want to become too Draconian, because that might hurt them, too. (Say the teenager uses the family car to take his little sister to school, and the parents would lose that service if they take away his keys. Or say they impose a no TV rule, but that means they must give up their favorite shows as well.)

If the parents get frustrated enough, however, they might be willing to hurt themselves (at least temporarily) simply to break out of the deadlock.

Another recent and socially relevant twist on game theory illuminates the effects of obvious labels on players—like skin color or nationality or gender. As described by

---

* Details can be found in his book, *Theory of Moves.*

Poundstone, this variation on Tit for Tat changes the rules slightly. Players would always cooperate with other players of the same group, but not with players bearing different labels. Thus, males, or blues, would always cooperate with other males, or blues, but not cooperate in encounter with females, or reds.

Not surprisingly, in this game of Discriminatory Tit for Tat, the majority group always did well, but minorities did very badly. The reason is not difficult to figure out: Where majorities had most of their daily encounters with others of their own kind, and thus were treated "nicely," minorities were forever bumping into their opposites, who would always "defect," or fail to cooperate.

It's possible, Poundstone concludes, that such behavioral dynamics could account for the compelling allure of minority communities—be they religious, racial, or even financial. Even a "ghetto," in this sense, can be "a safe haven where most interactions are likely to be positive."

Curiously, evidence from the world of the living—that is, biology and genetics—seems to confirm some of the "abstract" arguments to come out of game theory. If these notions are right, then the evolution of species has depended a great deal less on "dog eat dog" and a lot more on "dog learns to live cooperatively with other dogs" (not to mention humans) than anyone imagined.

Just because the "fittest" tend to survive, in other words, doesn't necessarily mean the "fittest" are the strongest, or meanest, or even the most reproductively profligate; the fittest may be those who learn best how to use cooperation for their own ends.

Controversial microbiologist Lynn Margulis has vastly extended the idea that symbiosis (living together without the benefit of clergy, one might call it) has been a major force in shaping organisms. From trees to fish to fungus, all kinds of living things take nourishment from each other, build communal housing, use each other, and generally form all sorts of lifelong partnerships and odd arrangements for the mutual benefit of all concerned.

Margulis has suggested that the cell itself arose from such cooperative arrangements among subcellular beings. Cells are packed full of specialized components that metabolize food, produce and store energy, propel the cell, shape its internal structure, and so forth. A good deal of evidence already supports Margulis's idea that cells are more like colonies of cooperating individuals than survivors of some fierce competitive race to "success."

Other biologists have argued—on a variety of different bases—that there is probably a gene for altruism and that humans (not to mention ants and bees and other intensely communal creatures) carry it within them as part of their genetic baggage. Altruism, wrote the late Lewis Thomas, "is essential for continuation of the species, and it exists as an everyday aspect of living."

After all, it's well known that creatures as various as vampire bats and stickleback fish put their own lives at risk to feed their fellows—even when the fellows happen to be unrelated.

In his usual lyric way, Thomas fashioned these facts into a lesson of near-biblical proportion:

I maintain that we are born and grow up with a fondness for each other, and that we have genes for that. We can be talked out of that fondness, for the genetic message is like a distant music, and some of us are hard-of-hearing. Societies are noisy affairs, drowning out the sound of ourselves and our connection. Hard-of-hearing, we go to war. Stone deaf, we make thermonuclear missiles. Nonetheless, the music is there, waiting for more listeners.

He may well be right, but the living genes aren't the only ones hearing the music. Carl Zimmer wrote in *Discover* magazine about a computer whiz named Maja Mataric of Brandeis University. She managed to get fourteen robots to cooperate in such simple tasks as retrieving a puck. Remarkably, cooperation wasn't a talent that she programmed into them. They learned it themselves. Instead of all ganging up on the same prize at the same time, she programmed them to pay attention to what the others were doing. Within fifteen minutes of practice, they acquired a taste for altruism.

What all this says about robots or vampire bats or even mathematicians, I'll leave to further study. Even if cooperation didn't steer human evolution, it probably wasn't completely absent from the picture, either. Perhaps the mathematicians' study of human interaction will someday help point the way out of what seems to be humanity's increasingly common lament—or as Rodney King puts it: "Why can't we all just get along?"

The Hero

Robert Creely

Robert Creeley was born in Arlington, Massachusetts, and he at-
tended Harvard University from 1943 to 1946, taking time out from
1944 to 1945 to work for the American Field Service in Burma and
India. He started publishing poetry in the Harvard magazine Wake.
He was friends with such famous poets as William Carlos Williams
and Ezra Pound. In his youth, he was interested in be-bop and
wrote poetry influenced by its rhythms. He was also an influential
professor at the experimental Black Mountain College, where he
edited the Black Mountain Review. *Between 1989–1991, he was*
the poet laureate of New York State. His numerous books of poetry
include: If I Were Writing This *(New Directions, 2003),* Just in Time:
Poems 1984–1994 *(2001),* Life & Death *(1998),* Echoes *(1994),* Selected Poems 1945–1990 *(1991),* Memory Gardens *(1986),* Mirrors
(1983), The Collected Poems of Robert Creeley, 1945–1975 *(1982),*
Later *(1979),* The Finger *(1968), and* For Love: Poems 1950–1960
(1962). He has also written a novel, short stories, and more than
a dozen books of prose, essays, and interviews. He was honored
with the Lannan Lifetime Achievement Award, the Frost Medal, the
Shelley Memorial Award, a National Endowment for the Arts grant,
a Rockefeller Foundation grant, and fellowships from the Guggen-
heim Foundation. He served as New York State Poet from 1989 to
1991 and since 1989 and he was elected a Chancellor of the Acad-
emy of American Poets in 1999.

Each voice which was asked
spoke its words, and heard
more than that, the fair question,
the onerous burden of the asking.

And so the hero, the
hero! stepped that gracefully
into his redemption, losing
or gaining life thereby.

Now we, now I
ask also, and burdened,
tied down, return
and seek the forest also.

Go forth, go forth,
saith the grandmother, the fire
of that old form, and turns
away from the form.

And the forest is dark,
mist hides it, trees
are dim, but I turn
to my father in the dark.

A spark, that spark of hope
which was burned out long ago,
the tedious echo
of the father image

— which only women bear,
also wear, old men, old cares,
and turn, and again find
the disorder in the mind.

Night is dark like the mind,
my mind is dark like the night.
O light the light! Old
foibles of the right.

Into that pit, now pit of
anywhere, the tears upon your hands,
how can you stand it,
I also turn.

I wear the face, I face
the right, the night, the way,
I go along the path
into the last and only dark,

hearing *hero! hero!*
a voice faint enough, a spark,
a glimmer grown dimmer through years
of old, old fears.

Videotape

Don DeLillo

Don DeLillo is one of the most valued American writers today. Son of Italian immigrants, he grew up in the Fordham section of the Bronx, an almost completely Italian American neighborhood at the time. DeLillo grew up Catholic, but as a boy, he lived a street life, playing games and shooting pool. He attended Fordham University, but he learned more on his own by reading books and visiting museums. DeLillo has written many novels dealing with American life and culture. His novel White Noise *won the National Book Award.* Libra, *an imaginative account of the Kennedy assassination, was honored with the* Irish Times-*Aer Lingus International Fiction Prize. His most recent books include* Underworld, The Body Artist, *and* Cosmopolis. *DeLillo is at best when he looks deeply into the influence of technology and consumerism on the attitudes and aspirations of ordinary Americans.*

It shows a man driving a car. It is the simplest sort of family video. You see a man at the wheel of a medium Dodge.

It is just a kid aiming her camera through the rear window of the family car at the wind-shield of the car behind her.

You know about families and their video cameras. You know how kids get involved, how the camera shows them that every subject is potentially charged, a million things they never see with the unaided eye. They investigate the meaning of inert objects and dumb pets and they poke at family privacy. They learn to see things twice.

It is the kid's own privacy that is being protected here. She is twelve years old and her name is being withheld even though she is neither the victim nor the perpetrator of the crime but only the means of recording it.

It shows a man in a sport shirt at the wheel of his car. There is nothing else to see. The car approaches briefly, then falls back.

You know how children with cameras learn to work the exposed moments that define the family cluster. They break every trust, spy out the undefended space, catching Mom coming out of the bathroom in her cumbrous robe and turbaned towel, looking bloodless and plucked. It is not a joke. They will shoot you sitting on the pot if they can manage a suitable vantage.

The tape has the jostled sort of noneventness that marks the family product. Of course the man in this case is not a member of the family but a stranger in a car, a random figure, someone who has happened along in the slow lane.

It shows a man in his forties wearing a pale shirt open at the throat, the image washed by reflections and sunglint, with many jostled moments.

It is not just another video homicide. It is a homicide recorded by a child who thought she was doing something simple and maybe halfway clever, shooting some tape of a man in a car.

He sees the girl and waves briefly, wagging a hand without taking it off the wheel—an underplayed reaction that makes you like him.

It is unrelenting footage that rolls on and on. It has an aimless determination, a persistence that lives outside the subject matter. You are looking into the mind of home video. It is innocent, it is aimless, it is determined, it is real.

He is bald up the middle of his head, a nice guy in his forties whose whole life seems open to the handheld camera.

But there is also an element of suspense. You keep on looking not because you know something is going to happen—of course you do know something is going to happen and you do look for that reason but you might also keep on looking if you came across this footage for the first time without knowing the outcome. There is a crude power operating here. You keep on looking because things combine to hold you fast—a sense of the random, the amateurish, the accidental, the impending. You don't think of the tape as boring or interesting. It is crude, it is blunt, it is relentless. It is the jostled part of your mind, the film that runs through your hotel brain under all the thoughts you know you're thinking.

The world is lurking in the camera, already framed, waiting for the boy or girl who will come along and take up the device, learn the instrument, shooting old Granddad at breakfast, all stroked out so his nostrils gape, the cereal spoon baby-gripped in his pale fist.

It shows a man alone in a medium Dodge. It seems to go on forever.

There's something about the nature of the tape, the grain of the image, the sputtering black-and-white tones, the starkness—you think this is more real, truer to life than anything around you. The things around you have a rehearsed and layered and cosmetic look. The tape is superreal, or maybe underreal is the way you want to put it. It is what lies at the scraped bottom of all the layers you have added. And this is another reason why you keep on looking. The tape has a searing realness.

It shows him giving an abbreviated wave, stiff-palmed, like a signal flag at a siding.

You know how families make up games. This is just another game in which the child invents the rules as she goes along. She likes the idea of videotaping a man in his car. She has probably never done it before and she sees no reason to vary the format or terminate early or pan to another car. This is her game and she is learning it and playing it at the same time. She feels halfway clever and inventive and maybe slightly intrusive as well, a little bit of brazenness that spices any game.

And you keep on looking. You look because this is the nature of the footage, to make a channeled path through time, to give things a shape and a destiny.

Of course if she had panned to another car, the right car at the precise time, she would have caught the gunman as he fired.

The chance quality of the encounter. The victim, the killer, and the child with a camera. Random energies that approach a common point. There's something here that speaks to you directly, saying terrible things about forces beyond you control, lines of intersection that cut through history and logic and every reasonable layer of human expectation.

She wandered into it. The girl got lost and wandered clear-eyed into horror. This is a children's story about straying too far from home. But it isn't the family car that serves as the instrument of the child's curiosity, her inclination to explore. It is the camera that puts her in the tale.

You know about holidays and family celebrations and how somebody shows up with a camcorder and the relatives stand around and barely react because they're numbingly accustomed to the process of being taped and decked and shown on the VCR with the coffee and cake.

He is hit soon after. If you've seen the tape many times you know from the handwave exactly when he will be hit. It is something, naturally, that you wait for. You say to your wife, if you're at home and she is there, Now here is where he gets it. You say, Janet, hurry up, this is where it happens.

Now here is where he gets it. You see him jolted, sort of wireshocked—then he seizes up and falls toward the door or maybe leans or slides into the door is the proper way to put it. It is awful and unremarkable at the same time. The car stays in the slow lane. It approaches briefly, then falls back.

You don't usually call your wife over to the TV set. She has her programs, you have yours. But there's a certain urgency here. You want her to see how it looks. The tape has been running forever and now the thing is finally going to happen and you want her to be here when he's shot.

Here it comes, all right. He is shot, head-shot, and the camera reacts, the child reacts—there is a jolting movement but she keeps on taping, there is a sympathetic response, a nerve response, her heart is beating faster but she keeps the camera trained on the subject as he slides into the door and even as you see him die you're thinking of the girl. At some level the girl has to be present here, watching what you're watching, unprepared—the girl is seeing this cold and you have to marvel at the fact that she keeps the tape rolling.

It shows something awful and unaccompanied. You want your wife to see it because it is real this time, not fancy movie violence—the realness beneath the layers of cosmetic perception. Hurry up, Janet, here it comes. He dies so fast. There is no accompaniment of any kind. It is very stripped. You want to tell her it is realer than real but then she will ask what that means.

The way the camera reacts to the gunshot—a startle reaction that brings pity and terror into the frame, the girl's own shock, the girl's identification with the victim.

You don't see the blood, which is probably trickling behind his ear and down the back of his neck. The way his head is twisted away from the door, the twist of the head gives you only a partial profile and it's the wrong side, it's not the side where he was hit.

And maybe you're being a little aggressive here, practically forcing your wife to watch. Why? What are you telling her? Are you making a little statement? Like I'm going to ruin your day out of ordinary spite. Or a big statement? Like this is the risk of existing. Either way you're rubbing her face in this tape and you don't know why.

It shows the car drifting toward the guardrail and then there's a jostling sense of two other lanes and part of another car, a split-second blur, and the tape ends here, either because the girl stopped shooting or because some central authority, the police or the district attorney or the TV station, decided there was nothing else you had to see.

This is either the tenth or eleventh homicide committed by the Texas Highway Killer. The number is uncertain because the police believe that one of the shootings may have been a copycat crime.

And there is something about videotape, isn't there, and this particular kind of serial crime? This is a crime designed for random taping and immediate playing. You sit there and wonder if this kind of crime became more possible when the means of taping and playing an event—playing it immediately after the taping—became part of the culture. The principal doesn't necessarily commit the sequence of crimes in order to see them taped and played. He commits the crimes as if they were a form of taped-and-played event. The crimes are inseparable from the idea of taping and playing. You sit there thinking that this is a crime that has found its medium, or vice versa—cheap mass production, the sequence of repeated images and victims, stark and glary and more or less unremarkable.

It shows very little in the end. It is a famous murder because it is on tape and because the murderer has done it many times and because the crime was recorded by a child. So the child is involved, the Video Kid as she is sometimes called because they have to call her something. The tape is famous and so is she. She is famous in the modern manner of people whose names are strategically withheld. They are famous without names or faces, spirits living apart from their bodies, the victims and witnesses, the underage criminals, out there somewhere at the edges of perception.

Seeing someone at the moment he dies, dying unexpectedly. This is reason alone to stay fixed to the screen. It is instructional, watching a man shot dead as he drives along on a sunny day. It demonstrates an elemental truth, that every breath you take has two possible endings. And that's another thing. There's a joke locked away here, a note of cruel slapstick that you are completely willing to appreciate. Maybe the victim's a chump, a dope, classically unlucky. He had it coming, in a way, like an innocent fool in a silent movie.

You don't want Janet to give you any crap about it's on all the time, they show it a thousand times a day. They show it because it exists, because they have to show it, because this is why they're out there. The horror freezes your soul but this doesn't mean that you want them to stop.

From *The Black Notebooks*

Toi Derricotte

Toi Derricotte was born in Detroit, Michigan, in 1941. Her books of poetry include Tender (1997), Captivity (1989), Natural Birth (1983), *and* The Empress of the Death House (1978). The Black Notebooks, *a literary memoir, from which the following excerpt was taken, was published in 1997. She has been honored with many awards, among which: Folger Shakespeare Library Poetry Book Award, the Lucille Medwick Memorial Award from the Poetry Society of America, a Pushcart Prize, and the Distinguished Pioneering of the Arts Award from the United Black Artists. She had fellowships from the National Endowment for the Arts, the New Jersey State Council on the Arts, and the Maryland State Arts Council.*

INTRODUCTION

The following selection of autobiographical prose is taken from *The Black Notebooks*, which I began writing in 1974 when we became one of the first black families to move into Upper Montclair, New Jersey. I began keeping journals in order to understand my inner responses to living in this environment which some part of me had been taught to think of as ideal: my feelings of depression, shame, anxiety, self-hatred, fear, isolation, as well as my desire for love and intimacy. Part of the complexity of my situation had to do with the fact that I appear to be white. I hoped that writing my feelings down, especially the ones which were the most disturbing, would exorcise their power over me.

Reprinted from *Kenyon Review,* 1991, by permission of the author.

Though the writing began strictly as a personal document, after several years, I came to think that the work probably had value for others too. Perhaps hidden fears and longings are under the surface of much behavior between blacks and whites, and many people are either unconscious or too ashamed to bring these parts of the self to light. Further, I came to believe that racism, and all its manifestations, is a reflection of deep psychic structures that have to be uncovered, addressed, and restructured before changes in the external world will be lasting.

Teachers Workshop

Today I did a teachers' workshop in a small town in New Jersey. Just about 99 44/100% "pure." I explained how I have the children write poems using oxymorons: "Think of something you can see very clearly, or feel very strongly. Now think of its opposite; like—Sun. Cold Sun. Or—rainbow. Black rainbow." One teacher said, "That's negative thinking. I don't like negative thinking. I want my rainbows to be colored good colors. Pretty colors. Not black. I don't like all this negative thinking." Immediately another teacher chimed in. "Yes. And what has happened to meter and rhyme?"

My stomach knotted up. They've found out what I am, what I bring to this lily-white happy town. Not that they know I'm black. But something subtle and unseen, something that comes out of my blackness. I bring the dreaded disease. In encourage their children to open their hearts to the "dark" side. To know the fear in them. To know the rage. To know the repression that has lopped off their brains—just as it has lopped off the brains of the children in the ghetto. But theirs is a painless death, the victims so anesthetized they don't kick.

The Woman from Audubon

Yesterday I did an in-service in Audubon. Afterward one of the teachers who spoke most intelligently during the meeting came over to speak to me. I was enjoying her remarks and, as we were talking, became aware of the tiny gold Star of David around her neck. This town is white. When I say white I mean white. The closest thing they have to something colored is an oriental restaurant. I have the feeling that Jews are rare. Why would she wear that, I thought.

For several years, I wore my identity like a banner. "Hello, I'm Toi Derricotte, I'm black." My black friends laughed at me and told me to grow up. But I was tired of the pleasant conversations at the bus stop with the white person who finally said: "Isn't it terrible? These colored people are taking over everything." I didn't want to get close and then be hurt. Better to put the truth out front.

When Bruce and I were looking for a house, I answered an ad for a rental property that I assumed was in an all-white neighborhood. I met the man who owned the property (I never take Bruce because I know from experience that if he comes, since he's obviously black, we never see what's available—only what they want us to see), and we drove to the house together. The lady who lived there, plump and matronly, became friendlier and friendlier as she took me through the rooms. Finally we sat down on the sofa and relaxed. "You're going to love it in this neighborhood," she assured me.

"Will I?"

"Oh yes," she answered. "You'll fit in perfectly."

Before I could imagine what she was talking about, she went on. "You're Catholic, aren't you?" I was floored. Nobody had ever guessed my religion before. I felt strangely flattered. Did I have a halo coming out of my head like the Blessed Virgin?

"I *am* Catholic," I said. "How did you know?"

"Oh, I'm just good at that sort of thing. What are you, anyway? Italian?"

Click, click, my brain went. So that's where she's heading. I had never had it done like this before—a real pro. OK, you bitch, I thought. I can play this game too.

"No," I replied politely.

A pause. She was waiting for me to volunteer.

"Are you Spanish?"

"No."

Another pause.

"Are you French?"

"No."

Another pause.

How many nationalities could she come up with?

"Are you Portuguese?"

"Syrian?"

"Greek?"

"Lebanese?"

"Armenian?"

"Turkish?"

"Are you Druze?"

She began naming sects I had never heard of.

"I'm black." Her face turned red as a hot towel.

"I didn't know blacks were Catholic!" she stammered.

I burst out laughing. She couldn't have said anything more able to defuse me if she had thought about it for months.

I wonder how many such situations have assaulted the woman from Audubon. Suddenly I feel a pang of desire that I should have a cross, a star, some sign of gold to wear, so that, before they wonder or ask, I can present them with evidence of my choice, a dignified response to the world's accusations. What would such a sign be for a black person? There are buttons:"I'm black and I'm proud." But I want something subtle, like the gold ornament, but able to be discerned, even if subconsciously.

Now I remember that the famous artist and naturalist Audubon, the man the town must have been named after, was rumored to have been black. The irony! How many of us are out here, with or without signs, moving back and forth over the line of sight?

Clarissa

Last night my friend Mady said how disturbed she is about racial problems in the small town she's teaching in. The community is largely white and upper middle class. However, there is a poor black section. Many of the mothers in this section are maids of other children in the school.

In each class there is one black child, and this child is also outstanding in terms of behavior. In one class the girl is super bright, super personality, in another the girl is the slowest. When asked to write something about her hand, she wrote: "My hand is clean." The teacher said: "That girl comes to school every day smelling and dirty." In the other classrooms, the black children are either the clowns or the "bad" kids. Almost all of them are far behind the whites in reading, writing, and speaking. When Mady talked to teachers, they looked at her like she was crazy. "There's no racism here!"

I remember Clarissa, that black girl who came to school each day starched and pressed all over—her kinky curls, her pinafore. I think of her oiled gold skin, her knobby knees and thin calves like a filly. She always talked at the wrong time, stood up at the wrong time, had to go to the bathroom. "Clarissa, didn't you go when the other children went?" And no matter how clean her mother sent her, no matter how many times she brought home bad reports, each day Clarissa screamed in class as if possessed.

I think of the teacher lifting her, screaming, away from the dollhouse where the other girl said: "She's taking my doll," holding her kicking feet away, carrying her as if she has the plague. Clarissa screams for her body lifted against her will, screams because her mother will beat her, screams because she will sit all morning in the window of the principal's office where everyone will look at her.

How did this happen, so that by the first grade it is already too late; and, in spite of her mother, who spent her maid's paycheck on a white pinafore so that Clarissa would fit in, she *doesn't* fit in. And her mother isn't strong enough to beat that devil out of her.

What makes Clarissa jump out of her skin?

Kinship

A black boy in the fourth grade said to me: "I'd like to be your son."

A white boy sitting near him responded: "You could never be her son."

"Why not," I asked.

"Because he's black."

"But I'm black too." He looked at me, his eyes swimming with pain and confusion.

It occurred to me that white children might have a more difficult time forming a concept of kinship to people of different colors than black children. Black children grow up in families where there is every conceivable color, texture of hair, thickness of feature. In white families there is much less variation.

I decided to test this. I asked the children: "How many in here have people in their family that are all different colors, some people as light as I am, some people as dark as Sheldon?" All the black kids raised their hands. "How many in here have people in their family that are all just about the same color as you are?" All the white children raised their hands.

Schools with predominantly white children want to teach the concept of the human family by including pictures of black people in textbooks. But valuing the other, learning we are all the same blood, is not a lesson one learns with the mind, but with the body—the way we first learn love through physical closeness.

I remember sleeping over at my best friend Amanda's when we were ten or eleven. We kicked her older sister out of bed, and talked far into the night. Summer nights I remember most. We would swing open the large door of the screened window; sometimes the moon would be out there with its shattering white grin. We would lie at the foot of her bed in a puddle of brightness. Her almond skin shone— as if a kind of luminous breath shined out of her.

She would soon go to sleep, but I would stay awake for hours, exuberant. Already I had sensed the darkness beyond the window, beyond the moonlight, and I was comforted. I was not alone.

September, 1973

Ariel Dorfman

Ariel Dorfman was born in Argentina, the son of Jewish parents who grew up speaking Yiddish and Russian as well as Spanish. In 1943, his father left Argentina and began working for the United Nations in New York. Soon after, Dorfman learned to speak English and refused to speak any other language with his parents. In 1954, his parents moved to Chile, where he continued to speak English but he was again attracted to Spanish. In 1968, Dorfman, who had married a Chilean and had a son, came back to the US to teach at Berkeley. After a year and a half of cultural experimentation, he returned to Chile and became involved with the effort of bringing Salvador Allende to power. In 1973 he narrowly missed being killed during the military coup against Allende. After the coup, Dorfman left Chile and now lives in exile in the US. His works include Death and the Maiden *and* Konfidenz, *both dealing with terrorism and its consequences on the personal lives of people. The following story is part of a memoir and refers to the events surrounding the military coup that overthrew Allende's government.*

It is late in September.

I have taken refuge in the house of the Israeli Ambassador.

You have said goodbye to me, my love, and now you are going down the stairs. Soon the sound of the door to the Embassy will be heard closing, your small figure will pass to the other side of the gates, and then you will cross the street. That's where the two men come up to speak to you. The conversation hardly lasts as long as it takes for a cigarette to be lit by the smaller man, the one with the checked jacket. The other one looks you in the eyes and your eyes must feel distant and startled

Reprinted from *Granta: The Magazine of New Writing* 60, 1998, by permission of The Wylie Agency.

at that instant. Then they invite you to get into the car. One of them takes your arm, but he does so with discretion, almost courteously. The motor is running, humming like a well-fed cat, but the car does not move. Now you're getting in, you and the smaller man in the back, and the other one in front. His strong, decisive shoulders form a contrast to his apologetic lips, to the thin impoverished wisp of his moustache. It will not be possible to see you. Only, all of a sudden, your hand which accepts a cigarette and then cups the flickering flame of the lighter. Your other hand can only be seen on one occasion, for a moment fluttering on the top of the back seat, fingers that hesitate, the shine of a wedding ring. Then it withdraws. The man in the front, seated next to the empty driver's seat, is the one asking the questions. Now, with his left hand, he turns off the engine and pockets the keys. That means they do not plan to leave right away. He will remain half-hunched up against the door, one leg raised, the shoe pushing against the upholstery, fingers intertwined at the knee. Once in a while, he scratches under his sock, rubs the skin compressed by his sock. They will not be in a hurry. Children will pass by on bikes calling each other by the names their parents gave them many years ago; the mailman will cross this spring day that seems like summer bringing news and ads and maybe letters from lost loves; mothers will go for a morning stroll and teach their kids how to stand up on two feet, take a step or two instead of crawling. Now a bird perches itself on the warm roof of the car and, without even a trill, flies off like an arrow. Maybe, inside, you've detected that slight presence, that slighter absence, like a leaf that falls from a tree out of season, a bit too late; maybe you've understood that a pair of wings opened up and then was gone. The man extracts a small notebook from a pocket in his jacket, and then a pencil. He passes it to you. During the briefest wave of time, your hand can be seen receiving the pencil, the notebook. Then, as if you were not really there in the back seat of the car, that extension of your body disappears and nothing more can be seen. The man tosses his keys up into the air and catches them neatly. He smiles. He points a key at you and says something, it must be a question. Impossible to know what you answered. A beggar woman stumbles down the street, a flock of ragtag kids in her wake. She approaches the car to ask for something, and then she backs off, half-understanding or not wanting to understand. Now the car window opens and the swarthy face of the smaller man appears, the man who has been sitting next to you. He hasn't slept much, hasn't slept well: there are bags under his eyes and his features are puffy. He blinks under that implacable daylight. Then he looks towards the Embassy for a while, giving the windows the once-over to see if there is somebody watching, if there is somebody behind half-drawn curtains trying to register and remember each movement, each gesture. He stays like that for a good while, motionless, as if he could guess what is happening behind those walls. He takes out a handkerchief and wipes it across his forehead, cleans the sweat from the rest of his face. He needs to shave, he needs to get home for a good shave. Maybe all night while he waited he's been thinking of the bath full of hot water. The air dances with white spores; he blinks his heavy eyelids. The breeze has begun to fall asleep under the spell of the day's heat. He emerges from the car quickly. A stream of sunlight slides down his body. Now he gets back into the car, into the driver's seat. He holds his hand out so the other man can give him the keys. The sound of the back door that opened and closed, the front door that opened and closed, does not disturb the quiet. It's almost like a sound of harmony, sweet metal. The car moves off, passes the house, passes the curtained windows, for an eternal white instant your petite face can be seen, the way your shoulders breathe, that dress which presses to your body like the skin of a lover. You will pass without looking towards the house, your face will pass, your eyes sinking into the abrupt horizon of the street which connects with other streets. But they will not take you away. Now the car brakes a bit further on, sheltered under the generous shade of that tree you have come to know so well, that you have heard moaning and dancing its branches below the weight of the wind last night. All that can be seen is the back of the car, and in a hollow opened by the leaves gently swaying with the rays of this spring that has quickened into summer, a blur of colour that could be your hair or your neck trembling under your hair. If it were not for the leisurely and merciless progress of the minute hand on your wristwatch, where the slow blood inside your arm finds and flows with the mysterious blood inside your hand, if it were not for the imperceptible rotation of this planet, it might be thought that time had stagnated, that all movement is paralysed, that silence is definitive, and that you will stay here for ever, you, the men, the car, the street. No beggar will pass. The mailman will not come back again. The children will have to put away their bicycles and go and eat lunch. When the sun begins to invade the top of the car, when midday has finally concluded and the afternoon has finally begun, when the intolerable heat forces the driver to seek a new refuge, nothing in the world, neither the buzzing of bees nor the yellow cheerful burst of the flowers, will be able to stop that engine from being started up again, that car from inching away from the kerb, and this time it will not pause under the shade or in the sun, this time the car will go on and on and on, nothing can stop it from losing itself there, far away, down the street which connects with other streets, taking you to that place from where you will never return.

This story, seemingly fictitious, really happened. It happened to us, to Angélica and to me, exactly as written here, exactly as I wrote it many years later. Except for the ending. They did not take her away, not for a day, not for a month, not for all time. But the rest is true: by the end of September I had taken temporary refuge in the residence of one of my mother's friends, the wife of the Israeli Ambassador, waiting during the next week for a chance to slip into one of the heavily guarded Latin American Embassies that could guarantee me safe conduct out of the country. And when Angélica had come to visit me and spend the night, the next morning she had been detained by two of Pinochet's secret policemen who had been watching the house under the impression that Senator Carlos Altamirano, the fugitive head of the Socialist party, thin and bespectacled like me, had sought refuge there. An absurd notion, given his pro-Palestinian sympathies. But Angélica managed to outwit those detectives without discussing international affairs and escaped the fate the character in the story was unable to avoid.

When many years later I came to write the experience, I ended it differently, tragically, partly because that is the way most episodes like this one do end, but mainly, I think, because that was the only way of transmitting to myself and others the horror of what went on in my mind during that hour when the woman I loved was in the hands of men who could do anything they wanted to her, anything they wanted and I could do nothing to stop them. That ending did not happen in reality but it did repeat itself over and over in my imagination as I watched from a window, praying I would not have to watch it over and over in the days and years to come in my memory, praying that I would not have to imagine a world without Angélica.

Discovering, after so many days obsessed with my ever-increasing distance from the country, that I would rather lose Chile than lose Angélica, that I could live without Chile but that I could not live without Angélica, beginning to understand that the private home I had built with her was more important and would outlast the public home I had sought to build with Chile and its people.

It was then, I think, that for the first time in my life I clearly separated my wife from the country where she had been born.

Ever since I had met her, Angélica had been confused, in my mind, with Chile. All the readings and all the trips and all the protests and all the snow on all the mountains did less to attach me to that country than this one frail human being.

There I was in early 1961, a stranger in a land that I had inhabited for seven years without finding a real gateway, whose songs and customs and people I hardly knew, no matter how much I had come to admire them, regard them as a potential avenue for liberation. And then, one day, Angélica. To be quite frank, what enchanted me about her to begin with were her dazzling looks and fiery spirit and extreme joy of life, the hot sexual thought of a lithe *moreno* body under her dress, that enchanting smile of hers that the gods of advertising couldn't have coached out of a woman if they had been given a thousand years and a ton of Max Factor make-up. How much of this I identified with the exotic Chile or Latin America that I had been secretly and transgressively hungering for all these years is anybody's guess. I experienced love with the metaphors available to males in Latin America—and elsewhere—at that time, no matter how suspect and gendered I may consider them now, more than thirty years later: the woman as the earth and earth-goddess to be excavated, a territory to be explored by a pioneer, a land in which to root your manhood like a tree, those were the images that surged inside me as we made love. I could never entirely rid myself of the feeling that I was somehow making mine something more than an individual woman, that I was making love to a community that was inside her, that through her body and her life I was binding myself to a permanent place on this planet.

Now that I write this, I have come to understand that it was ultimately not Chile that I desired in her. What attracted me most deeply in the woman who would become my wife were qualities that transcended national origins or boundaries, things I would have treasured in her life if she had been Lithuanian or from Mars. Her fierce loyalty, her amazing ability to see through people, her stubborn (and often exasperating) tendency to speak without minding the consequences, her almost animal loyalty, her fearlessness, her unpredictability—none of these were necessarily typical of Chile and some of them, such as her undiplomatic directness or her rejection of compromises, could even be construed as extremely un-Chilean.

And yet, if it was not Chile that finally ended up joining us, without Chile, nevertheless, the Chile I imagined inside her, it is probable that our love would not have lasted. Angélica is wonderful, but she was not then and certainly is not now, in spite of her name, an angel. Not that I was that easy either. We were attracted to each other precisely because we were opposites and if life was never boring and never will be while she is around, it was a constant clash. Given these circumstances and our immaturity, it is quite possible that we wouldn't have made it to marriage and beyond merely sustained by the dim intuition that each of us had found the long-lost half of their soul. An additional something was necessary for our love to survive those rough and desperate break-ups that all young lovers flounder through, and that something, for me, frequently seemed the vast Chile that I felt Angélica contained within herself. I could feel the country bringing me back for more, my need for this identity she gave me fastening me to her, Chile secretly gluing us together. It is the perverse logic of love that the reverse was true for Angélica: what kept her by my side when things didn't seem to work out was, she has told me, the very fact that I came from some other place, her intuition that I would not treat her the way Chilean males treat women, that I could be entirely trusted, that I was transparent, that I was naïve: in other words, that I was a gringo. A gringo who happened to be frantically searching for a country that would answer his loneliness and transience.

Angélica possessed that country merely by virtue of having been born here, simply because her forefathers and foremothers had made love under these mountains and mingled their many races and interbred their Iberian and Mediterranean and Indian and African stock at a time when mine had never even dreamed of emigrating; she possessed it in the nursery rhymes in Spanish she had sung when I had been reciting Old Mother Hubbard; she possessed it in the peasant proverbs she had absorbed in the dusty plaza of the small countryside town in the Aconcagua Valley where she had been brought up; she possessed it in every Chilean spice, every Chilean fruit, every Chilean meal that had nurtured her. That was Chile, all of that and more. She had been accumulating every drop of experience inside herself like a reservoir. At some point early in our fumbling and fearful and expectant movement towards one another, I sensed that reservoir, sensed that I could drink from its waters, drink Chile in her waters.

How vast were those waters and how insatiable my thirst was brought home to me the first night we became *'pololos'*—a word with which Chileans designate boys and girls who are going steady, a word that comes from a butterfly-like insect that goes from flower to flower making itself dizzy with sweetness. We had slunk into a sort of discotheque and started timidly to explore one another the way you do when you are under twenty and the universe has everything to teach you and an orchestra is remotely playing a bolero, *Bésame, bésame mucho, come si fuera esta noche la última vez,* kiss me, keep on kissing me, as if tonight were the last night, and then Angélica took her mouth from mine and began to sing (a bit off-key, but who cared) the words to that song of Latin American love that I had bypassed so often on the radio as I rushed to hum along with Frankie Avalon. A tango followed, which she also knew

by heart, and inside that brain of hers, behind those freckles, was the whole repertoire of popular Latin America that I had despised and that I now wanted to learn by
heart to prove my new-found identity. It may have been that very night when I asked
her if she danced *cueca,* the Chilean national dance, and she smiled mischievously and
grabbed a napkin from the table and waved it a bit in the air and hid her face behind
it and suggested that she could teach me some steps, that it was a matter of imagining a rooster out courting. That I had to try and corral her, corner her, that this was
the game. She was the treasure and I was the hunter. She would hide and I would seek.

It may have been the next day, when we went down to the centre of Santiago
together, that I realized that Angélica had within herself a treasure she barely knew
about, a treasure that I was seeking and that she was not even trying to hide. Her
presence by my side as we strolled through the centre of the city I had lived in for
seven years suddenly transformed me into a tourist arriving at this foreign destination
for the first time. I had often passed this café, for instance, and it meant absolutely nothing to me, but for Angélica it was the place where in the Forties her journalist father,
after he had put the paper to bed, would meet her mother and a group of Popular
Front friends and drink and talk till dawn. As Angélica casually told me the story of
the night her father had waited for the news of the Allied landing in Normandy, we
were interrupted by a pretty young woman. She came up to us, pecked Angélica's
cheek and was introduced to me as the daughter of her 'Mami Lolo', the woman who
had brought up Angélica when she was a little girl in the countryside. The two of them
chatted for a while about people I did not know and places I had never been. When
the young woman said goodbye and we continued on our way, Angélica sketched
out the story of her nanny, who had been brought very young into the family house
as a helper and later on had cared for the grandchildren, and who, it would turn out,
was in fact the illegitimate daughter of Angélica's grandfather. 'You have to come to
Santa Maria,' Angélica said, 'where I was raised, and meet my Mami Lolo.' Half a block
later, Angélica was greeted by someone else and so it went and so it would go. So many
people and so many conversations and so many stories, stories, stories. Perhaps it
was then that I began to understand that Angélica was a network of stories, a lineage
of stories, a wellspring of stories that had made her, that she was full to the brim with
people, with *Chileans,* who had made her. It may have been then or it may have been
later, but at some point rather early in our relationship, I realized that Angélica's connection to Chile was the opposite of mine, that it was not and never could be vol-
untary, that she could not discard it as I was in the process of discarding the United
States, that it was as much part of her as her lungs or her skin. In the months and years
to come, as she guided me into her life and her body, she also guided me into the mysteries of a continent that should have been mine by birthright but from which I had
cut myself off, a country I had seen for years as nothing more than a stop on the road
to somewhere else.

And when I had been faced with the loss of that country after the coup, when
I had finally agreed that yes, I would seek refuge in an embassy, what had ultimately
made that decision tolerable like a secret silhouette inside me was the promise of

Angélica, the certainty that I could wander the earth for ever if the woman who had taught Chile to me was by my side.

Now she was in that car with those two men and I had come face to face with the possibility that she would not accompany me in my wanderings, that she would not be there at all. I told myself that maybe this was the cruel and hidden reason behind my miraculous survival: death had spared me, because all along it was going to take Angélica instead. Death was going to punish me for having refused its gift and stayed in this country all this September. I was going to be punished for not having left immediately and sent my family away; this was what I deserved for pretending that I was untouchable and immortal.

But again I was given a reprieve.

When those two men released her and she came back into the residence and we trembled against each other, when I was able to hold my love, my best friend, my companion for life, in these arms that had already despaired of ever touching her again, my hand going through her hair over and over, closing my eyes and then opening them again to make sure that it was still true, that she was still here, I was finally ready to learn the lesson that death had sent me one more time, perhaps one last time. It was then that the coup finally caught up with me, that it descended on me as it had descended on La Moneda and exploded silently inside me like the bombs had exploded all over the city and made me understand, for the first time since Allende's overthrow, the full and irreversible reality of the evil that was visiting us and that would not go away. When I had anticipated my own death, I thought I had discovered what the Inferno is: the place where you suffer for ever without being able to escape. Now I knew I had been wrong: the Inferno is the one place in the world where the person you most love will suffer for all eternity while you are forced to watch, unable to intervene, responsible for having put her there.

And that Inferno was here, the country I had associated with Paradise.

It was time to leave Chile.

Indians on the Shelf

Michael Dorris

Michael Dorris, who sometimes wrote under the pseudonym Milou North, is known as an activist for the rights of American Indians as well as a talented writer. Born in Louisville, Kentucky, he is of Modoc Indian as well as English and French descent. He founded the Native American Studies Program at Dartmouth, and in 1971 became one of the first American bachelors to adopt a child, a boy with fetal alcohol syndrome. The trials and tribulations of raising his adopted son are described in his most famous book, The Broken Cord *(1989).*

In 1981, Dorris married Louise Erdrich and together they adopted two more American Indian children and had three of their own. In 1997, when the couple were about to divorce, Michael Dorris committed suicide in a motel in New Hampshire. It is unclear whether the cause of the suicide may have been the divorce or his chronic depression. When he died, Dorris was working on a book about fetal alcohol effect, a less debilitating condition that affected his other adopted children. He also wrote children's books and novels.

While on my way to do fieldwork in New Zealand several years ago, I stopped in Avarua, capital of the Cook Islands. To my tourist's eye it was a tropical paradise right out of Michener: palm trees, breadfruit and pineapples, crashing surf, and a profusion of flowers. Most people spoke Maori, and traditional Polynesian music and dance were much in evidence; there was no television, one movie theatre, one radio station, and a few private telephones.

There were, of course, gift shops, aimed primarily at people like myself who wanted to take with them some mememto of days spent sitting in the sun, eating arrowroot pudding and smelling frangipani in every breeze. And so I browsed, past the

Reprinted from *The American Indian and the Problem of History*, edited by Calvin Martin, (1987), Georges Borchardt, Inc.

Fijian tapa cloth, past the puka shell necklaces, past the coconut oil perfume, and came face to face with an all-too-familiar sight: perched in a prominent position on a shelf behind the cash register was an army of stuffed monkeys, each wearing a turkey-feather imitation of a Sioux war bonnet and clasping in right paw a plywood toma-hawk. "The Indians" had beaten *this* Indian to Rarotonga.

The salesperson replied to my startled question that, yes, indeed, these simian braves were a hot item, popular with tourist and native alike. She herself, she added with a broad smile, had played cowboys and Indians as a child.

More recently, I entertained in my home a young man from Zaire who was spending the summer at Dartmouth College in order to teach Swahili to students who would travel the next winter in Kenya on a foreign study program. My guest spoke very little English, a good deal more French, and three East African languages.

He was homesick for his tiny village on the west shore of Lake Tanganyika, and the Santa Clara pueblo chili I served reminded him of the spicy stews he ate as a child. We compared tribes, his and mine, and he listened with rare appreciation to recordings of southwestern Indian music. He had never met "real" Indians before, he reported, and was interested and curious about every detail. But it was not until I brought out an old eagle-feather headdress, a family treasure, that his eyes lit up with true recognition. Sweeping it out of my hand, and with an innocent and ingenuous laugh, he plopped it on his head, assumed a fierce expression and, patting his hand over his mouth, said "woo woo woo." He, too, in his radioless, roadless, remote village, had played cowboys and Indians; it was part of his culture, and he knew how to behave.

Generations of Germans have learned to read with Karl May's romanticized Indian novels; Hungarian intellectuals dressed in cultural drag cavort in imitation buckskin each summer, playing Indians for a week on a Danube island; and an un-pleasant, right-wing student newspaper at the college where I teach tries to make some symbolic "conservative" point by peddling "Indian-head" doormats for fifteen dol-lars each. Far from vanishing, as some once forecast, the First American seems if any-thing to be gaining ground as a cultural icon.

As folklore, Indians seem infinitely flexible; they can be tough and savage, as in the Washington Redskins football team, or, starring in environmental commercials, turn maudlin and weepy at the sight of litter. In advertising they are inextricably linked with those products (corn oil, tobacco) the general public acknowledges as indigenous to the Americas. Ersatz Indians have inspired hippies, Ralph Lauren designs, and boy scouts. But flesh and blood Native Americans have rarely participated in or benefit-ed from the creation of these imaginary Indians, whose recognition factor, as they say on Madison Avenue, outranks, on a world scale, that of Santa Claus, Mickey Mouse, and Coca Cola combined.

For most people, the myth has become real and a preferred substitute for ethno-graphic reality. The Indian mystique was designed for mass consumption by a European audience, the fulfillment of old and deep-seated expectations for "the Other." It is lit-tle wonder, then, that many non-Indians literally would not know a real Native Amer-ican if they fell over one, for they have prepared for a well-defined, carefully honed legend. Ordinary human beings, with widely variable phenotypes and personalities, fall short of the mold. Unless they talk "Indian" (a kind of metaphoric mumbo jumbo pidgin of English), ooze nostalgia for bygone days, and come bedecked with metallic or beaded jewelry, many native people who hold positions of respect and authority within their own communities are disappointments to non-Indians whose standards of ethnic validity are based on Pocahontas, Squanto, or Tonto.

In a certain sense, for five hundred years Indian people have been measured and have competed against a fantasy over which they have had no control. They are compared with beings who never really *were,* yet the stereotype is taken for truth. Last week my local mail carrier knocked at my door and announced that he was taking a group of little boys in the woods where they intended to live "like real Iroquois" for two days; did I have any advice, he wondered? In reply I suggested simply that they bring along their mommies, pointing out that in a matrilineal society children of that age would be entirely bound by the dictates of their associated clan mothers. This was not what he wanted to hear; it ran counter to his assumption of a macho, male-bonded Indian culture where men were dominant and women were "squaws," retiring and ineffectual unless there was a travois to pull. He and his group did not want to live like "real" Iroquois, and he was chagrined that the Six Nations did not conform to his version of proper savage behavior.

Such attitudes are difficult to rebut successfully, grounded as they are in long traditions of unilateral definitions. In the centuries since Columbus got lost in 1492, a plethora of European social philosophers have attempted to "place" Indians within the context of a Western intellectual tradition that never expected a Western Hemisphere, much less an inhabited one, to exist. It has been the vogue for hundreds of years for Europeans to describe Native Americans not in terms of themselves, but only in terms of who they are (or are not) vis-à-vis non-Indians. Hardly a possible explanation, from Lost Tribes of Israel to outer space or Atlantis refugees, has been eschewed in the quest for a properly rationalized explanation. Puritans viewed Indians as temptations from the devil; Frederick Jackson Turner, when he noticed them at all, saw them as obstacles to be overcome on the frontier; and expansionists, from President Andrew Jackson to Interior Secretary James Watt, have regarded them as simply and annoyingly in the way.

Popular American history, as taught in the schools, omits mention of the large precontact Indian population and its rapid decline due to the spread of European diseases. Instead, students are given the erroneous impression that the few indigenous people who did live in the Americas were dispatched to the Happy Hunting Ground due to conflict with stalwart pioneers and cavalrymen. Such a view of history, clearly at odds with well-documented facts, only serves to reinforce the myth of Indian aggressiveness and bellicosity and further suggests that they got what they deserved. In addition, by picturing Indians as a warlike and dangerous foe, Euro-American ancestors reap honor by having been victorious.

The pattern of Indian-European negotiation for land title in the seventeenth, eighteenth, and nineteenth centuries is also misrepresented; though students learn about the fifty states, they remain unaware of the existence of close to two hundred "domestic, dependent nations" within the country, and regard reservations, if they are conscious of them at all, as transitory poverty pockets "given" to the Indians by philanthropic bureaucrats. In many respects living Native Americans remain as mysterious, exotic, and unfathomable to their contemporaries in the 1980s as Powhatan appeared to John Smith over three hundred fifty years ago. Native rights, motives, customs, languages, and aspirations are misunderstood out of an ignorance that is both self-serving and self-righteous.

Part of the problem may well stem from the long-standing tendency of European or Euro-American thinkers to regard Indians as so "Other," so fundamentally and profoundly different, that they fail to extend to native peoples certain traits commonly regarded as human. A survey of literature dealing with Indians over the past two or three hundred years would seem to imply that Indians are motivated more often by mysticism than by ambition, are charged more by unfathomable visions than by intelligence or introspection, and in effect derive their understandings of the world more from an appeal to the irrational than to empiricism. Since the whys and wherefores of Native American society are not easily accessible to those culture-bound by Western traditional values, there is a tendency to assume that Indians are creatures either of instinct or whimsy.

This idea is certainly not new; Rousseau's noble savages wandered, pure of heart, through a preconcupiscent world, never having had so much as a bite of the fruit from the "tree of the knowledge of good and evil" (Genesis 2:17). Romantics, most of whom had never seen a living specimen, patronized Indians by eulogizing them, and thus denied them a common bond of humanity with other men and women. Since native people were assumed a priori to be incomprehensible, they were seldom comprehended; their societies were simply beheld, often through cloudy glasses, and rarely penetrated by the tools of logic and deductive analysis automatically reserved for cultures prejudged to be "civilized."

And on those occasions when Europeans did attempt to relate themselves to native societies, it was not, ordinarily, on a human being to human being basis, but rather through an ancestor-descendant model. Indians, though obviously contemporary with their observers, were somehow regarded as ancient, as examples of what Stone Age Europeans were like. In the paradigm of European confusion, Indians have been objects of mystery and speculation, not people.

It makes a great story, a real international crowd-pleaser that spans historical ages and generations, but there is a difficulty: Indians were, and are, *Homo sapiens sapiens.* Unless the presence of a shovel-shaped incisor, an epicanthic fold or an extra molar cusp (or the absence of Type B blood) affords one an extra toe in the metaphysical door, native people have had to cope, for the last 40,000 or so years, just like everyone else. Their cultures have had to make internal sense, their medicines have had to work consistently and practically, their philosophical explanations have had to be reasonably satisfying and dependable, or else the ancestors of those we call Indians really would have vanished long ago.

In other words, Native American societies rested upon intelligence. They developed and maintained usable, pragmatic views of the world. Those of their systems that had survived long enough to have been observed by fifteenth-century Europeans were certainly dynamic but clearly had worked for millennia.

The difficulty in accepting this almost tautological fact comes from the Euro-centric conviction that the West holds a virtual monopoly on "science," logic, and clear-thinking. To admit that other, culturally divergent viewpoints are equally plau-sible is to cast doubt on the monolithic center of Judeo-Christian belief: that there is but *one* of everything—God, right way, truth—and Europeans alone knew what that was. If Indian cultures were admitted to be possibly viable, then European societies were not the exclusive club they had always maintained they were.

It is little wonder, therefore, that Indian peoples were perceived not as they were but as they *had* to be, from a European point of view. They were whisked out of the realm of the real and into the land of make-believe. Indians became variably super and subhuman, never ordinary. They dealt in magic, not judgment. They were imagined to be stuck in their past, not guided by its precedents.

Such a situation argues strongly for the development and dissemination of a more accurate, more objective historical account of native people, but this is easier said than done. Inasmuch as the Indian peoples of North America were, before and during much of their contact period with Europe, non-literate, the requirements for recounting an emic native history are particularly demanding and, by the standards of most traditional methodology, unorthodox. There do not exist the familiar and reassuring kinds of written documentation that one finds in European societies of equivalent chronological periods, and the forms of tribal record preservation that are available—oral history, tales, mnemonic devices, and religious rituals—strike the average, university-trained academic as inexact, unreliable, and suspect. Culture-bound by their own approach to knowledge, they are apt to throw up their hands in despair and exclaim that *nothing* can be known of Indian history. By this logic, an absolute void is more acceptable than a reasonable, educated guess, and "evidence" is defined in only the most narrow sense.

Furthermore, it is naive to assume that most historians can view their subject without certain impediments to objectivity. Every professor in the last three hundred years, whether he or she was enculturated in Rarotonga or Zaire, in Hanover, New Hampshire or Vienna, was exposed at an early age to one or another form of folklore about Indians. For some it may well be that the very ideas about Native American cul-tures that initially attracted them to the field of American history are the items most firm-ly rooted in myth. They may have come to first "like" Indians because they believed them to be more honest, stoic, and brave than other people, and forever after have to strive against this bias in presenting their subjects as real, complicated people. Or they may discover to their disillusionment that all Indians are not pure of heart and have to suppress, consciously or unconsciously, their abiding resentment and disenchantment.

For most people, serious learning about Native American culture and history is different from acquiring knowledge in other fields, for it requires an initial, abrupt, and wrenching demythologizing. One does not start from point zero, but from minus ten, and is often required to abandon cherished childhood fantasies of super-heroes and larger-than-life villains.

There would seem to be a certain starting advantage here for historians or an-thropologists who also happen to be ethnically Native American, especially if they grew up in the context of tribal society. For them, at least, Indians have always been and are real, and they may have less difficulty in establishing links of continuity between contemporary and historical populations. They may have access to traditionally-kept records and escape some of the prejudice against non-Western methods. They may be more comfortable with taking analytical risks in hypothesizing explanations for traditional practices, basing their assumptions upon subtle but persuasive clues surviving in their own cultural experience.

Native scholars, of course, have their own special problems. For one thing, few of them have avoided exposure to the media blitz on folkloric or fantasy Indians. Indian children are as often tempted to "play Indian" as are their non-native contemporaries. They may be expected to live up to their mythic counterparts and feel like failures when they cry at pain or make noise in the woods. American Indians who deal as scholars with Indian materials are assumed by some non-natives to be hopelessly subjective and biased, and as such their work is dismissed as self-serving. Certainly it is true that most Native American scholarship could be termed "revisionist," but that in itself does not prove illegitimacy. Europeans and Euro-Americans have not felt shy in writing about their respective ancestors and are not automatically accused of aggrandizing them; why should native scholars be less capable of relatively impartial retrospection?

Whoever attempts to write Native American history must admit in advance to fallibility. There is not and never will be any proof, no possibility of "hard evidence" to support a conjecture based on deduction. David Bradley, in *The Chaneysville Incident,* writes wistfully of a firmly fixed chamber in Historian's Heaven in which all things are clear. "And we believe," he says, "if we have been good little historians, just before they do whatever it is they finally do with us, they'll take us in there and show us what was *really* going on. It's not that we want so much to know we were right. We *know* we're not right (although it would be nice to see exactly how close we came). It's just that we want to, really, truly, utterly, absolutely, completely, finally *know"* (1982:277).

Indian history hardly even offers purgatory. It depends on the imperfect evidence of archeology; the barely-disguised, self-focused testimony of traders, missionaries, and soldiers, all of whom had their own axes to grind and viewed native peoples through a narrow scope; and, last and most suspect of all, common sense. The making of cross-cultural, cross-temporal assumptions is enough to send every well-trained Western academic into catatonia, but there is no avoiding it. If we stipulate only a few givens—that Indian societies were composed of people of the normal range of intelligence; that human beings *qua* human beings, where and whenever they may live, share some traits; that Indians were and are human beings—then we have at least a start. We can dare, having amassed and digested all the hard data we can lay our hands on, to leap into the void and attempt to see the world through the eyes of our historical subjects. We can try to make sense out of practices and beliefs and reactions that do not conform to a Western model but must, within the configurations of their own cultures, have an explanation. We can stop treating Indians like sacred, one-dimensional European myths and begin the hard, terribly difficult and unpredictable quest of regarding them as human beings.

What Makes Superman So Darned American?

Gary Engle

Gary Engle is a professor of English at Cleveland State University. He specializes in popular culture and has written numerous magazine and journal articles. He has also published a book The Grotesque Essence: Plays from American Minstrel Style *(1978). The following essay was published in a collection entitled* Superman at Fifty! *co-authored with Dennis Dooley.*

When I was young I spent a lot of time arguing with myself about who would win in a fight between John Wayne and Superman. On days when I wore my cowboy hat and cap guns, I knew the Duke would win because of his pronounced superiority in the all-important matter of swagger. There were days, though, when a frayed army blanket tied cape-fashion around my neck signalled a young man's need to believe there could be no end to the potency of his being. Then the Man of Steel was the odds-on favorite to knock the Duke for a cosmic loop. My greatest childhood problem was that the question could never be resolved because no such battle could ever take place. I mean, how would a fight start between the only two Americans who never started anything, who always fought only to defend their rights and the American way?

Now that I'm older and able to look with reason on the mysteries of childhood, I've finally resolved the dilemma. John Wayne was the best older brother any kid could ever hope to have, but he was no Superman.

Superman is *the* great American hero. We are a nation rich with legendary figures. But among the Davy Crocketts and Paul Bunyans and Mike Finks and Pecos Bills and all the rest who speak for various regional identities in the pantheon of American folklore, only Superman achieves truly mythic stature, interweaving a pattern of beliefs, literary conventions, and cultural traditions of the American people more

Reprinted from *Superman at Fifty*, (1987), by permission of Octavia Press.

powerfully and more accessibly than any other cultural symbol of the twentieth century, perhaps of any period in our history.

The core of the American myth in *Superman* consists of a few basic facts that remain unchanged throughout the infinitely varied ways in which the myth is told—facts with which everyone is familiar, however marginal their knowledge of the story. Superman is an orphan rocketed to Earth when his native planet Krypton explodes; he lands near Smallville and is adopted by Jonathan and Martha Kent, who inculcate in him their American middle-class ethic; as an adult he migrates to Metropolis where he defends America—no, the world! no, the Universe!—from all evil and harm while playing a romantic game in which, as Clark Kent, he hopelessly pursues Lois Lane, who hopelessly pursues Superman, who remains aloof until such time as Lois proves worthy of him by falling in love with his feigned identity as a weakling. That's it. Every narrative thread in the mythology, each one of the thousands of plots in the fifty-year stream of comics and films and TV shows, all the tales involving the demigods of the Superman pantheon—Superboy, Supergirl, even Krypto the Superdog—every single one reinforces by never contradicting this basic set of facts. That's the myth, and that's where one looks to understand America.

It is impossible to imagine Superman being as popular as he is and speaking as deeply to the American character were he not an immigrant or an orphan. Immigration, of course, is the overwhelming fact in American history. Except for the Indians, all Americans have an immediate sense of their origins elsewhere. No nation on Earth has so deeply embedded in its social consciousness the imagery of passage from one social identity to another: the Mayflower of the New England separatists, the slave ships from Africa and the subsequent underground railroads toward freedom in the North, the sailing ships and steamers running shuttles across two oceans in the nineteenth century, the freedom airlifts in the twentieth. Somehow the picture just isn't complete without Superman's rocketship.

Like the peoples of the nation whose values he defends, Superman is an alien, but not just any alien. He's the consummate and totally uncompromised alien, an immigrant whose visible difference from the norm is underscored by his decision to wear a costume of bold primary colors so tight as to be his very skin. Moreover, Superman the alien is real. He stands out among the hosts of comic book characters (Batman is a good example) for whom the superhero role is like a mask assumed when needed, a costume worn over their real identities as normal Americans. Superman's powers—strength, mobility, x-ray vision and the like—are the comic-book equivalents of ethnic characteristics, and they protect and preserve the vitality of the foster community in which he lives in the same way that immigrant ethnicity has sustained American culture linguistically, artistically, economically, politically, and spiritually. The myth of Superman asserts with total confidence and a childlike innocence the value of the immigrant in American culture.

From this nation's beginnings Americans have looked for ways of coming to terms with the immigrant experience. This is why, for example, so much of American literature and popular culture deals with the theme of dislocation, generally focused in characters devoted or doomed to constant physical movement. Daniel Boone became an

American legend in part as a result of apocryphal stories that he moved every time his neighbors got close enough for him to see the smoke of their cabin fires. James Fenimore Cooper's Natty Bumppo spent the five long novels of the Leatherstocking saga drifting ever westward, like the pioneers who were his spiritual offspring, from the Mohawk Valley of upstate New York to the Great Plains where he died. Huck Finn sailed through the moral heart of America on a raft. Melville's Ishmael, Wister's Virginian, Shane, Gatsby, the entire Lost Generation, Steinbeck's Okies, Little Orphan Annie, a thousand fiddlefooted cowboy heroes of dime novels and films and television—all in motion, searching for the American dream or stubbornly refusing to give up their innocence by growing old, all symptomatic of a national sense of rootlessness stemming from an identity founded on the experience of immigration.

Individual mobility is an integral part of America's dreamwork. Is it any wonder, then, that our greatest hero can take to the air at will? Superman's ability to fly does more than place him in a tradition of mythic figures going back to the Greek messenger god Hermes or Zetes the flying Argonaut. It makes him an exemplar in the American dream. Take away a young man's wheels and you take away his manhood. Jack Kerouac and Charles Kurault go on the road; William Least Heat Moon looks for himself in a van exploring the veins of America in its system of blue highways; legions of gray-haired retirees turn Air Stream trailers and Winnebagos into proof positive that you can, in the end, take it with you. On a human scale, the American need to keep moving suggests a neurotic aimlessness under the surface of adventure. But take the human restraints off, let Superman fly unencumbered when and wherever he will, and the meaning of mobility in the American consciousness begins to reveal itself. Superman's incredible speed allows him to be as close to everywhere at once as it is physically possible to be. Displacement is, therefore, impossible. His sense of self is not dispersed by his life's migration but rather enhanced by all the universe that he is able to occupy. What American, whether an immigrant in spirit or in fact, could resist the appeal of one with such an ironclad immunity to the anxiety of dislocation?

In America, physical dislocation serves as a symbol of social and psychological movement. When our immigrant ancestors arrived on America's shores they hit the ground running, some to homestead on the Great Plains, others to claw their way up the socioeconomic ladder in coastal ghettos. Upward mobility, westward migration, Sunbelt relocation—the wisdom in America is that people don't, can't, mustn't end up where they begin. This belief has the moral force of religious doctrine. Thus the American identity is ordered around the psychological experience of forsaking or losing the past for the opportunity of reinventing oneself in the future. This makes the orphan a potent symbol of the American character. Orphans aren't merely free to reinvent themselves. They are obliged to do so.

When Superman reinvents himself, he becomes the bumbling Clark Kent, a figure as immobile as Superman is mobile, as weak as his alter ego is strong. Over the years commentators have been fond of stressing how Clark Kent provides an illusory image of wimpiness onto which children can protect their insecurities about their own personal (and, hopefully, equally illusory) weaknesses. But I think the role of Clark Kent is far more complex than that.

During my childhood, Kent contributed nothing to my love for the Man of Steel. If left to contemplate him for too long, I found myself changing from cape back into cowboy hat and guns. John Wayne, at least, was no sissy that I could ever see. Of course, in all the Westerns that the Duke came to stand for in my mind, there were elements that left me as confused as the paradox between Kent and Superman. For example, I could never seem to figure out why cowboys so often fell in love when there were obviously better options: horses to ride, guns to shoot, outlaws to chase, and savages to kill. Even on the days when I became John Wayne, I could fall victim to a never-articulated anxiety about the potential for poor judgment in my cowboy heroes. Then, I generally drifted back into a worship of Superman. With him, at least, the mysterious communion of opposites was honest and on the surface of things.

What disturbed me as a child is what I now think makes the myth of Superman so appealing to an immigrant sensibility. The shape-shifting between Clark Kent and Superman is the means by which this mid-twentieth-century, urban story—like the pastoral, nineteenth-century Western before it—addresses in dramatic terms the theme of cultural assimilation.

At its most basic level, the Western was an imaginative record of the American experience of westward migration and settlement. By bringing the forces of civilization and savagery together on a mythical frontier, the Western addressed the problem of conflict between apparently mutually exclusive identities and explored options for negotiating between them. In terms that a boy could comprehend, the myth explored the dilemma of assimilation—marry the school marm and start wearing Eastern clothes or saddle up and drift further westward with the boys.

The Western was never a myth of stark moral authority. Pioneers fled civilization by migrating west, but their purpose in the wilderness was to rebuild civilization. So civilization was both good and bad, what Americans fled from and journeyed toward. A similar moral ambiguity rested at the heart of the wilderness. It was an Eden in which innocence could be achieved through spiritual rebirth, but it was also the anarchic force that most directly threatened the civilized values America wanted to impose on the frontier. So the dilemma arose: In negotiating between civilization and the wilderness, between the old order and the new, between the identity the pioneers carried with them from wherever they came and the identity they sought to invent, Americans faced an impossible choice. Either they pushed into the New World wilderness and forsook the ideals that motivated them or they clung to their origins and polluted Eden.

The myth of the Western responded to this dilemma by inventing the idea of the frontier in which civilized ideals embodied in the institutions of family, church, law, and education are revitalized by the virtues of savagery: independence, self-reliance, personal honor, sympathy with nature, and ethical uses of violence. In effect, the mythical frontier represented an attempt to embody the perfect degree of assimilation in which both the old and new identities came together, if not in a single self-image, then at least in idealized relationships, like the symbolic marriage of reformed cowboy and displaced school marm that ended Owen Wister's prototypical *The Virginian,* or the mystical masculine bonding between representatives of an ascendant and a vanishing America—Natty Bumppo and Chingachgook, the Lone Ranger and Tonto. On the Western frontier, both the old and new identities equally mattered.

As powerful a myth as the Western was, however, there were certain limits to its ability to speak directly to an increasingly common twentieth-century immigrant sensibility. First, it was pastoral. Its imagery of dusty frontier towns and breathtaking mountainous desolation spoke most affectingly to those who conceived of the American dream in terms of the nineteenth-century immigrant experience of rural settlement. As the twentieth century wore on, more immigrants were, like Superman, moving from rural or small-town backgrounds to metropolitan environments. Moreover, the Western was historical, often elegiacally so. Underlying the air of celebration in even the most epic and romantic of Westerns—the films of John Ford, say, in which John Wayne stood tall for all that any good American boy could ever want to be—was an awareness that the frontier was less a place than a state of mind represented in historic terms by a fleeting moment glimpsed imperfectly in the rapid wave of westward migration and settlement. Implicitly, then, whatever balance of past and future identities the frontier could offer was itself tenuous or illusory.

Twentieth-century immigrants, particularly the Eastern European Jews who came to America after 1880 and who settled in the industrial and mercantile centers of the Northeast—cities like Cleveland where Jerry Siegel and Joe Shuster grew up and created Superman—could be entertained by the Western, but they developed a separate literary tradition that addressed the theme of assimilation in terms closer to their personal experience. In this tradition issues were clear-cut. Clinging to an Old World identity meant isolation in ghettos, confrontation with a prejudiced mainstream culture, second-class social status, and impoverishment. On the other hand, forsaking the past in favor of total absorption into the mainstream, while it could result in socioeconomic progress, meant a loss of the religious, linguistic, even culinary traditions that provided a foundation for psychological well-being. Such loss was particularly tragic for the Jews because of the fundamental role played by history in Jewish culture.

Writers who worked in this tradition—Abraham Cahan, Daniel Fuchs, Henry Roth, and Delmore Schwarz, among others—generally found little reason to view the experience of assimilation with joy or optimism. Typical of the tradition was Cahan's early novel *Yekl*, on which Joan Micklin Silver's film *Hester Street* was based. A young married couple, Jake and Gitl, clash over his need to be absorbed as quickly as possible into the American mainstream and her obsessive preservation of their Russian-Jewish heritage. In symbolic terms, their confrontation is as simple as their choice of headgear—a derby for him, a babushka for her. That the story ends with their divorce, even in the context of their gradual movement toward mutual understanding of one another's point of view, suggests the divisive nature of the pressures at work in the immigrant communities.

Where the pressures were perhaps most keenly felt was in the schools. Educational theory of the period stressed the benefits of rapid assimilation. In the first decades of this century, for example, New York schools flatly rejected bilingual education—a common response to the plight of non-English-speaking immigrants even today—and there were conscientious efforts to indoctrinate the children of immigrants with American values, often at the expense of traditions within the ethnic community. What resulted was a generational rift in which children were openly embarrassed by and even contemptuous of their parents' values, setting a pattern in American life in which second-generation immigrants migrate psychologically if not physically from their parents, leaving it up to the third generation and beyond to rediscover their ethnic roots.

Under such circumstances, finding a believable and inspiring balance between the old identity and the new, like that implicit in the myth of the frontier, was next to impossible. The images and characters that did emerge from the immigrant communities were often comic. Seen over and over in the fiction and popular theater of the day was the figure of the *yiddische Yankee,* a jingoistic optimist who spoke heavily accented American slang, talked baseball like an addict without understanding the game, and dressed like a Broadway dandy on a budget—in short, one who didn't understand America well enough to distinguish between image and substance and who paid for the mistake by becoming the butt of a style of comedy bordering on pathos. So engrained was this stereotype in popular culture that it echoes today in TV situation comedy.

Throughout American popular culture between 1880 and the Second World War the story was the same. Oxlike Swedish farmers, German brewers, Jewish merchants, corrupt Irish ward healers, Italian gangsters—there was a parade of images that reflected in terms often comic, sometimes tragic, the humiliation, pain, and cultural insecurity of people in a state of transition. Even in the comics, a medium intimately connected with immigrant culture, there simply was no image that presented a blending of identities in the assimilation process in a way that stressed pride, self-confidence, integrity, and psychological well-being. None, that is, until Superman.

The brilliant stroke in the conception of Superman—the sine qua non that makes the whole myth work—is the fact that he has two identities. The myth simply wouldn't work without Clark Kent, mild-mannered newspaper reporter and later, as the myth evolved, bland TV newsman. Adopting the white-bread image of a wimp is first and foremost a moral act for the Man of Steel. He does it to protect his parents from nefarious sorts who might use them to gain an edge over the powerful alien. Moreover, Kent adds to Superman's powers the moral guidance of a Smallville upbringing. It is Jonathan Kent, fans remember, who instructs the alien that his powers must always be used for good. Thus does the myth add a mainstream white Anglo-Saxon Protestant ingredient to the American stew. Clark Kent is the clearest stereotype of a self-effacing, hesitant, doubting, middle-class weakling ever invented. He is the epitome of visible invisibility, someone whose extraordinary ordinariness makes him disappear in a crowd. In a phrase, he is the consummate figure of total cultural assimilation, and significantly, he is not real. Implicit in this is the notion that mainstream cultural norms, however useful, are illusions.

Though a disguise, Kent is necessary for the myth to work. This uniquely American hero has two identities, one based on where he comes from in life's journey, one on where is going. One is real, one an illusion, and both are necessary for the myth

105

of balance in the assimilation process to be complete. Superman's powers make the hero capable of saving humanity; Kent's total immersion in the American heartland makes him want to do it. The result is an improvement on the Western: an optimistic myth of assimilation but with an urban, technocratic setting.

One must never underestimate the importance to a myth of the most minute elements which do not change over time and by which we recognize the story. Take Superman's cape, for example. When Joe Shuster inked the first Superman stories, in the early thirties when he was still a student at Cleveland's Glenville High School, Superman was strictly beefcake in tights, looking more like a circus acrobat than the ultimate Man of Steel. By June of 1938 when *Action Comics* no. 1 was issued, the image had been altered to include a cape, ostensibly to make flight easier to render in the pictures. But it wasn't the cape of Victorian melodrama and adventure fiction, the kind worn with a clasp around the neck. In fact, one is hard-pressed to find any precedent in popular culture for the kind of cape Superman wears. His emerges in a seamless line from either side of the front yoke of his tunic. It is a veritable growth from behind his pectorals and hangs, when he stands at ease, in a line that doesn't so much drape his shoulders as stand apart from them and echo their curve, like an angel's wings.

In light of this graphic detail, it seems hardly coincidental that Superman's real, Kryptonic name is Kal-El, an apparent neologism by George Lowther, the author who novelized the comic strip in 1942. In Hebrew, *el* can be both root and affix. As a root, it is the masculine singular word for God. Angels in Hebrew mythology are called *benei Elohim* (literally, sons of the Gods), or *Elyonim* (higher beings). As an affix, *el* is most often translated as "of God," as in the plenitude of Old Testament given names: Ishma-el, Dani-el, Ezeki-el, Samu-el, etc. It is also a common form for named angels in most Semitic mythologies: Israf-el, Aza-el, Uri-el, Yo-el, Rapha-el, Gabri-el and—the one perhaps most like Superman—Micha-el, the warrior angel and Satan's principal adversary.

The morpheme *Kal* bears a linguistic relation to two Hebrew roots. The first, *kal*, means "with lightness" or "swiftness" (faster than a speeding bullet in Hebrew?). It also bears a connection to the root *hal*, where *h* is the guttural *ch* of *chutzpah*. *Hal* translates roughly as "everything" or "all." *Kal-el*, then, can be read as "all that is God," or perhaps more in the spirit of the myth of Superman, "all that God is." And while we're at it, *Kent* is a form of the Hebrew *kana*. In its *k-n-t* form, the word appears in the Bible, meaning "I have found a son."

I'm suggesting that Superman raises the American immigrant experience to the level of religious myth. And why not? He's not just some immigrant from across the waters like all our ancestors, but a real alien, an extraterrestrial, a visitor from heaven if you will, which fact lends an element of the supernatural to the myth. America has no national religious icons nor any pilgrimage shrines. The idea of a patron saint is ludicrous in a nation whose Founding Fathers wrote into the founding documents the fundamental if not eternal separation of church and state. America, though, is pretty much as religious as other industrialized countries. It's just that our tradition of religious diversity precludes the nation's religious character from being embodied in objects or persons recognizably religious, for such are immediately identified by their attachment to specific sectarian traditions and thus contradict the eclecticism of the American religious spirit.

In America, cultural icons that manage to tap the national religious spirit are of necessity secular on the surface and sufficiently generalized to incorporate the diversity of American religious traditions. Superman doesn't have to be seen as an angel to be appreciated, but in the absence of a tradition of national religious iconography, he can serve as a safe, nonsectarian focus for essentially religious sentiments, particularly among the young.

In the last analysis, Superman is like nothing so much as an American boy's fantasy of a messiah. He is the male, heroic match for the Statue of Liberty, come like an immigrant from heaven to deliver humankind by sacrificing himself in the service of others. He protects the weak and defends truth and justice and all the other moral virtues inherent in the Judeo-Christian tradition, remaining ever vigilant and ever chaste. What purer or stronger vision could there possibly be for a child? Now that I put my mind to it, I see that John Wayne never had a chance.

The Hunting Years

Tom Franklin

Tom Franklin was born in Southern Alabama. He worked as a heavy equipment operator in a grit factory, a construction inspector in a chemical plant, and a clerk in a hospital morgue. His first book, Poachers *(1999), from which the following story has been excerpted, has attracted considerable attention. The title story, a novella, won the 1999 Edgar Allan Poe Award and was included in* New Stories From the South, Best American Mystery Stories *and* Best Mystery Stories of the Century.

The stories in Poachers *are set in southwest Alabama—an area where snake-infested swamps, polluting factories, and junked-up trailer parks pose equal challenges to people. The characters work in grit factories, drink a lot, spoil their marriages, or daydream of taking off for Alaska. Violence boils in their blood. As the following autobiographical piece shows, the violence and the drunkenness are all integral to an ideal of masculinity perverted by postindustrial life.*

Standing on a trestle in south Alabama, I look down into the coffee-brown water of the Blowout, a fishing hole I loved as a boy. It's late December, cold. A stiff wind rakes the water, swirls dead leaves and nods the tall brown cattails along the bank. Farther back in the woods it's very still, cypress trees and knees, thick vines, an abandoned beaver's lodge. Buzzards float overhead, black smudges against the gray clouds. Once, on this trestle, armed with only fishing rods, my brother Jeff and I heard a panther scream. It's a sound I've never forgotten, like a madwoman's shriek. After that, we brought guns when we came to fish. But today I'm unarmed, and the only noise is the groan and hiss of bulldozers and trucks on a new-cut logging road a quarter-mile away.

Reprinted from *Poachers*, (1999), by permission of HarperPerennial, a division of Harper-Collins, Inc.

I left the south four years ago, when I was thirty, to go to graduate school in Fayetteville, Arkansas, where among transplanted Yankees and westerners I realized how lucky I was to have been raised here in these southern woods among poachers and storytellers. I know, of course, that most people consider Arkansas the south, but it's not *my* south. My south—the one I haven't been able to get out of my blood or my imagination, the south where these stories take place—is lower Alabama, lush and green and full of death, the wooded counties between the Alabama and Tombigbee Rivers.

Yesterday at five A.M. I left Fayetteville and drove seven hundred miles south to my parents' new house in Mobile, and this morning I woke early and drove two more hours, past the grit factory and the chemical plants where I worked in my twenties, to Dickinson, the community where we lived until I was eighteen. It's a tiny place, one store (now closed) and a post office in the same building, a kudzu-netted graveyard, railroad tracks. I've been finishing a novella that takes place in these woods— in the story, a man is killed right beneath where I'm standing—and I'm here looking for details of the landscape, for things I might've forgotten.

To get to the Blowout, I picked through a half-mile of pine trees that twelve years ago had been one of my family's cornfields. I hardly recognized the place. I walked another half-mile along the new logging road, then climbed onto the railroad track, deep woods on both sides, tall patchwork walls of briar and tree, brown thrashers hopping along unseen like something pacing me. My father and aunts and uncles used to own this land. It was ours. When my grandfather died, he divided almost six hundred acres among his five children. He expected them to keep it in the family, but one by one they sold it for logging or to hunting dubs. Today none of it is ours.

I'm about to leave when I notice that fifty yards down the track something big is disentangling itself from the trees. For a moment I reexperience the shock I used to feel whenever I saw a deer, but this is only a hunter. I see that he's spotted me, is climbing onto the tracks and coming this way. Because I lived in these parts for eighteen years, I expect to know him, and for a moment I feel foolish: What am I doing here at the Blowout, during hunting season, without a gun?

It's a familiar sensation, this snag of guilt, because when I was growing up, a boy who didn't hunt was branded as a pussy. For some reason, I never wanted to kill things, but I wasn't bold enough to say so. Instead, I did the expected: went to church on Sundays and on Wednesday nights, said "Yes ma'am" and "No sir" to my elders. And I hunted.

Though I hated (and still hate) to get up early, I rose at four A.M. Though I hated the cold, I made my way through the icy woods, climbing into one of our family's deer stands or sitting at the base of a thick live oak to still hunt, which simply means waiting for a buck to walk by so you can shoot him. And because I came to hunting for the wrong reasons, and because I worried that my father, brother and uncles might see through my ruse, I became the most zealous hunter of us all.

I was the one who woke first in the mornings and shook Jeff awake. The first in the truck. The first to the railroad track, where we climbed the rocky hill and crept toward the Blowout, our splitting-up point. On those mornings, the stars still out, it would be too dark to see our breath, the cross ties creaking beneath our boots, and

109

I would walk the quietest, holding my double-barrel sixteen-gauge shotgun against my chest, my bare thumb on the safety and my left trigger finger on the first of its two triggers. When we got to the Blowout, I'd go left, without a word, and Jeff right. I'd creep down the loose rocks, every sound amplified in the still morning, and I'd step quietly over the frozen puddles below and into the dark trees.

In the woods, the stars disappeared overhead as if swiped away, and I inched forward with my hand before my face to feel for briars, my eyes watering from the cold. When I got far enough, I found a tree to sit beneath, shivering and miserable, thinking of the stories I wanted to write and hoping for something to shoot. Because at sixteen, I'd never killed a deer, which meant I was technically still a pussy.

Of course there were a lot of real hunters in my family, including my father. Though he no longer hunted, Gerald Franklin commanded the respect of the most seasoned woodsman because as a young man he'd been a legendary killer of turkeys (and we all knew that turkey hunters consider themselves the only serious sportsmen, disdaining deer or any other game the way fly fishermen look down on bait fishermen). Dad never bragged about the toms he'd shot, but we heard everything from our uncles. According to them, my father had been the wildest of us all, getting up earlier and staying in the woods later than any man in the county.

There's a story he tells where he woke on a spring Sunday to go hunting—he never used a clock, relying instead on his "built-in" alarm. Excited because he knew which tree a gobbler had roosted in the evening before, he dressed in the dark so he wouldn't wake my mother, pregnant with me. When he got to the woods it was still pitch black, so he settled down to wait for daylight. An hour passed, and no sign of light. Instead of going back home, though, he laid his gun aside, lit a cigarette and continued to wait for a dawn that wouldn't arrive for three more hours. Later, laughing, he told my uncles he'd gotten to the woods around one A.M.

But at some point, before I started first grade, he quit hunting. I always figured it was because he'd found religion. I grew up going to the Baptist church every Sunday with a father who was a deacon, not a hunter. Ours was a godly household—to this day I've never heard Dad curse—and we said grace at every meal (even if we ate out) and prayed as a family each night, holding hands. After church on Sunday mornings, Dad sat in our living room and read his Bible, wearing his tie all day, then loaded us in the big white Chrysler to head back to church in the evening.

If we passed the three Wiggins brothers, dressed in old clothes and carrying hand-cut fishing poles, Dad shook his head and gave us all a minisermon on the perils of fishing on the Lord's day. Though neither he nor anyone else has ever confirmed it, I've always thought that by not hunting he was paying a kind of self-imposed penance for the Saturday nights in his youth he'd spent in pool halls, and for the Sundays he'd skipped church to chase turkeys.

Sometimes, in my own hunting years, huddled against a sweet gum, waiting for noon or dusk to give me permission to leave the woods, I'd imagine my father as a younger man, slipping through the trees, still wearing his blue mechanic's shirt with his name stitched across the chest, grease from his garage under his fingernails, carrying in his callused hands the same sixteen-gauge shotgun he would later give me. He was heading toward where he'd heard a gobbler that morning before work.

When he got to the spot, he knelt and, cradling the shotgun, removed from the pocket of his old army jacket the little box turkey caller he would give my brother years later. It was wooden and hollow like a tiny guitar box. You drew a peg over its green surface as gently as you could, the way you'd peel an apple without breaking the skin. If you knew what you were doing, it made a quiet, perfect hen's cluck, something a man could barely hear, but a sound that would snap a gobbler's head around half a mile away. After Dad had clucked a time or two, he waited, and when he heard the distant answer—that mysterious lovely cry, half a rooster's crow and half the whinny of a horse—he worked his jaw like a man shifting his chewing tobacco, and from under his tongue he moved his "yepper" to the roof of his mouth.

Year after year, in our stockings for Christmas, he'd been giving Jeff and me our own yeppers, tiny plastic turkey callers the size of a big man's thumbnail, and he would try to teach us to "yep" the way turkeys do. Jeff caught on quickly, but it made me gag.

It was this kind of gift that let me know my father wanted me to hunt, though he never pressed, and let me know he was bothered by the fact that, until I was fifteen years old, I played with dolls. Not girls' dolls, but "action figures." The original G.I. Joe with his fuzzy crew cut and a scar on his chin, Johnny West with his painted-on clothes, Big Jim with his patented karate chop: I had them all. I loved playing with them, and because Jeff was two years younger than I was, he did whatever I did. But while he would wrench off G.I. Joe's head and hands to examine how the doll was put together, I would imagine that my G.I. Joe was Tarzan of the Apes. One of my sister's Barbie dolls, stripped to a skimpy jungle bikini, became Jane. A foot-tall Chewbacca was Kerchak, an ape. In the lush green summer afternoons, Jeff and I built African villages out of sticks and vines. We dug a wide trench across our backyard and with the garden hose made a muddy brown river filled with rubber snakes and plastic crocodiles.

When the Wiggins brothers pedaled up on their rusty bicycles—they were stringy, sun-yellowed boys who smelled like sweat and fish and never wore shirts or shoes in summer, who lived a mile away down a dirt road in the woods—Jeff and I would toss our dolls into the bushes and pretend to be cleaning up a mess in the backyard.

"Wanna go fishin'?" Kent Wiggins would ask, stuffing his lower lip with Skoal. His father worked for the lumber mill, and Kent would get a job there when he turned eighteen. I envied them the ease with which they accepted and handled their lives, the way they spit between their teeth, flicked a rod, fired a rifle.

Jeff and I always went wherever they asked us to go—I was afraid of being laughed at and being called a mama's boy for saying no, and Jeff enjoyed the fishing. And sitting on the trestle over the Blowout, watching the Wiginses and my little brother pull in catfish after catfish, I'd long for my G.I. Joe, and hate the longing.

Once, when I was newly fifteen in Kmart with ten birthday dollars to spend, Dad came up beside me.

"You could buy a hunting knife," he whispered.

"Gerald . . ." my mother warned.

He let go of my shoulders, put his hands in his pockets.

"He wants to get a new outfit for his G.I. Joe," Mom said to Dad.

I'd never felt more like a pussy.

So the hell with it, I thought, and headed for the tall line of fishing rods I could see beyond the toy aisle. Dad fell into step beside me. He let me shave the bristly hairs off his wrist in search of the sharpest knife while Mom stood with her arms folded near the stink bait, glaring into space. At the checkout counter, I watched Dad add another five to my ten dollars for the Old Timer Sharpfinger I'd picked. When we left the store, he had his arm around me.

As Dad drove us home, I asked him if he wished I didn't play with G.I. Joes. Mom sat far across the long seat, looking out her window. At my question, her head jerked toward Dad, who stopped whistling. He glanced at her before catching my eye in the rearview mirror.

"No," he said. "I'm real proud of you, son. I'm glad you've got . . . imagination."

When Jeff killed his first buck, a spike, I was there.

Despite being younger, Jeff has always been a much better shot than I am. I'd gotten Dad's sixteen-gauge at Christmas, but Jeff had unwrapped a Marlin thirty-thirty lever-action rifle. The fact that I was eighteen and still using a shotgun didn't go unnoticed—the boy with the weakest aim always gets the scattergun because its spray of buckshot gives more chances for a hit than a single bullet. Never mind that my sixteen-gauge was an antique that had belonged to my grandfather, a rare Foxboro crafted of blued Sterlingworth steel, a side-by-side model that broke open behind the walnut stock. The shells slid in and the breech closed with a muffled snap, a sound more like cloth than metal. It's a gun I can take apart—barrel, forearm, stock—and reassemble in thirty seconds. A gun worth over two thousand dollars. Yet in the woods, I was ashamed of it.

The high school closed on opening day of deer season, and on that first morning in 1980, Jeff and I sat in opposite tree stands—small seats built overlooking a wide field where deer came to graze—and from mine I watched my brother sight me with the scope of his rifle. I sat rigid, silent, ready for a deer, while a hundred yards away, Jeff waved at me. Gave me the finger. He pissed from off his stand, *twice.* He yawned. Slept. But as one hour became two, I stayed stock-still—I didn't have Jeff's instinct for knowing when to be ready, for being relaxed until it was time to raise your gun and aim. My limbs began to tingle, the blood slowing in my veins like a creek icing up. I didn't blink for so long that the woods blurred, and I began to feel that I was part of them, the trees and the leaves taking on a buzzing resonance and losing their sharp edges, the buzzing increasing like a hornet loose inside my head, and for an instant I hung there, the center of something, seeing from my ears, hearing from my eyes, the world around me a tangible glow of brindle noise. Then I blinked.

And from across the field came Jeff's gunshot.

From then on, I insisted on sitting in Jeff's lucky stand. A year later, early in the 1981 season, the sixteen-gauge in my lap, I was there, waiting. Tense. It was dusk, and I was losing hope again. I'd been hunting like a fanatic—once or twice a day. I'd stopped taking books with me. I'd seen deer and even missed a doe, the fabled buck fever claiming me with violent seizures, my gun barrel shaking, teeth clacking.

Now, on the lucky stand, I didn't see the deer when it walked into the field. You seldom do: they just appear. And if it's a buck, like this one, you notice the antlers first, the sleekest, sharpest things in the world, not bone but blood vessels dried and hard as stone. On the stand, I lifted the jittering shotgun, slowly, thumbing the safety, the buck less than twenty yards from where I sat trembling.

I aimed, blood roaring in my ears, and fired, not feeling the kick.

The buck raised his head, still chewing. His antlers seemed to unwind as he looked around, wondering where that blast had come from. At some point, I remembered that I had another barrel, and I began pulling the trigger again, before finally realizing that I had to pull the *second* trigger. When I fired, the deer buckled and recovered, then vanished, replaced by the noise of something tearing through the dead leaves behind me, a painful sound hacking down the gully.

From across the field, Jeff's voice: "Kill anything?"

I descended the ladder, my hands shaking. At the bottom, I struggled to break open the gun, and shells from my pocket fell to the ground. I reloaded, and, nearly crying, slid to the bottom of the gully.

The deer—thank God—was there. Still alive, but down. His side caving in and out and a hind leg quivering. Approaching him, I counted his points—six, seven, eight—an eight-point! What I was supposed to do now, what Dad and my uncles had drilled into me, was to cautiously approach the buck, draw my knife and cut his throat, watch him bleed to death. But in my excitement, I forgot this. Instead, I moved to within three feet of the deer's flagging side and flipped the sixteen-gauge's safety off. I put a finger on each of the shotgun's triggers, and, holding the gun at my hip, pulled them at the same time.

That night, my entire family admired the deer lying in the back of Dad's pickup, its black eyes turning foggy. It's traditional to rub blood on a boy's face when he kills his first deer, but Dad had a lesson to teach. I'd gut-shot the buck so badly that a lot of meat had been ruined. The hole I'd blown in his side was big enough to put my head in, and Dad came up behind me and did exactly that. When he pulled me out by my neck, I was almost sick, but I managed to hold it, like a man. That was when everyone gathered around me, my uncles and Jeff clapping my back, Mom and my aunts hugging me, trying not to get blood on their blouses.

When I tell this story, I end by saying that nothing except Beth Ann accepting my marriage proposal on a warm wine-and-cheese afternoon in Paris has surpassed the feeling I had that night. As Dad guided me through cleaning the deer, peeling down its skin, trimming away the small white pockets of fat, my eight-year-old cousin approached us. When the boy saw the buck's bloody, empty body cavity, he tumbled away, gagging. Dad rolled his eyes at me. Then we began to quarter the red meat, my face and neck still bloody, my hair stiff with gore.

Near the close of the same season, I sat on a wooded hill in a plot of land on which my father, when he sold it, had been wise enough to retain the mineral and hunting rights. It was only two months after I'd killed my eight-point, but now things were different because Jeff had bragged about the buck at school. Whenever I told the story, I always made myself seem foolish by giving the deer both barrels at such close range. People seemed to like that. I was discovering the power of self-depreciation and didn't mind being laughed at as long as everyone knew I'd killed the deer. And they did: Coach Horn had led me to his office behind the gym and shown me the antlers on his walls. For the first time in my life, I wasn't a pussy. No. Sitting on the hillside that evening, I was a man who'd enjoyed his first taste of blood and who wanted more.

It was a mild January day, the leaves crisp, stirred by the wind to an almost constant rustle. Suddenly, an even bigger eight-point buck had materialized at the bottom of the ravine, stealing among the live oaks. First I saw his rack of antlers as he nosed along the ground, eating acorns. Then his shoulders. His flat tail. The color of dead leaves, he blended so well into the hillside that I only saw him when he moved. My heart began to rattle, and, as if he heard it, the buck raised his head and looked right at me. He lifted his nose and snorted, his nostrils gleaming. For a moment he seemed to vanish, to have never been there, but before I could panic I saw him again as he took a step away from me.

Somehow, I did everything right—aimed when he put his head down, squeezed instead of jerked the trigger—and *still* damn near missed. My buckshot pellets sprayed the deer across his neck, face and antlers, chipping them, bringing bloody beads across his cheeks, putting out one eye and—we saw this later—injuring his spine so that he only had use of his front legs, the back two paralyzed. I stood and watched him drag himself through the leaves, trying to get away, pawing and stumbling down the gullyside.

From the next hollow over, Jeff called, "Kill anything?"

I half fell to the bottom of the ravine. The deer lay still, just a slight rippling of his big leathery sides, blood glistening on his black nose. While I circled him, gun ready, he watched me, his head up, turning to keep me in sight. One eye was red and bleeding, but the other remained bright and clear. From over the hill, I heard Jeff crashing through the leaves. I knew he'd heard my shot—my single shot—and I didn't want him to hear another.

Why didn't I cut the deer's throat? There was no shame in that, and it was the safest way to avoid the buck's deadly antlers. But instead I did something that shocks me to this day. I dropped the sixteen-gauge and drew my Sharpfinger. I approached the deer, watching him follow me with his good eye. Carefully, the way you'd reach to pin a snake with your foot, I stuck out my leg and put my boot on the buck's neck,

114

forcing his head down. I knelt on top of him, straddled his back. Now I heard his ragged breathing, felt his heat on my thighs. I took one thick tine of his antlers in my right hand and turned his good eye away so he couldn't see. He didn't resist. I raised the knife and began to stab him in the shoulder where I knew his heart was. The buck barely moved beneath me, and the blade cut cleanly, as if I were sticking soft dirt. I stabbed him twelve times, in what I thought a buckshot pattern would be. Then I laid my hand on the deer's hot shoulder, over the wounds I'd made, and felt that his heart had stopped.

By the time Jeff came running down the hill, I'd begun my first solo act of field dressing. It was—and still is—the biggest buck anyone in my family had killed, weighing over 220, seventy pounds more than I weighed at the time.

Later, as we hoisted the deer up beneath our skinning tree, Dad noticed the holes in the buck's side. He nodded to Jeff and me. "Now boys," he said, "*that* was a good shot." With my knife, I made a series of cuts along the deer's hind legs, and Jeff and Dad helped me peel down the buck's fur—a noise like Velcro makes—to reveal the nearly purple carcass beneath.

Night had fallen, and with a flashlight Dad looked at the deer's side. He bent, examining it more closely, working his finger into one of the knife slits. Then he stared me down.

"Son," he said, "is that what I think it is?"

I didn't answer.

He reached for the deer's head and lifted it by the giant, chipped, eight-point rack, a set of antlers so big I could step into it like pants. He grabbed me by the small of my back and jammed me into my dead deer. He brought the antlers against my stomach and pushed the points in so hard they hurt.

"Do you know what 'eviscerate' means?" he asked me.

Now, at the Blowout, the hunter approaches me on the trestle. I expect it's one of the Wiggins brothers, and here I am again, as gunless and guilty and foolish as if I'm holding a doll. But as the man draws closer, a scoped rifle in the crook of his arm, I see from his expensive camouflage, fluorescent orange hat and face paint that he's not from around here. The men who live in these parts hunt in work clothes, old boots and faded camo jackets passed down from their fathers or grandfathers. They would never wear face paint or an orange hat. When I hunted I used to carry such a cap in my pocket in case I ran into a game warden, but most of the hunters I grew up admiring simply never ran into game wardens. These men raise their own coon and squirrel dogs. Their rifles have taped stocks. Although they often kill out of season or at night, they usually eat what they kill. I admire them, and so I feel a flicker of distaste for this outsider.

"Hello," I say to the fellow, probably a lawyer from Mobile. "Kill anything?"

"Get out of here," he says.

I cock my head. "I'm sorry?"

"You heard me. This is private property. You're trespassing on our hunting club."
He swings his gun barrel toward the woods on the right, as if pointing to his buddies

lurking in the shadows, their faces green and black, twigs in their hair, expensive rifles aimed at my head.

I spit through my teeth. I don't tell him that this used to be my family's land, that I've dragged deer over this very track, spent hours on this goddamn trestle. Instead I say, "The railroad's not private property."

"The hell it's not," he says. And raises the rifle, aims at me.

We stand facing one another. It will be dark soon, and from the left side of the track comes the distant snarl of a logger's power saw. I try to see myself through the hunter's eyes: my ragged jeans, my leather jacket and hiking boots. To him I probably look like a hippie, like the last thing you'd expect to find out here.

Meanwhile, the hunter is edgy, glancing behind him in the woods. "I'm not gonna tell you again," he says.

The saw rattles to a stop, then revs up again.

"You hear that?" I ask. "That'll ruin your hunting more than I will."

I know I should leave, but instead I sit on the cold rail and look away from the hunter, at the woods. I recall a story my father told me. He was turkey hunting down here early on a Sunday morning. Creeping along, he heard a wavering voice, and it spooked him. He followed it through the trees until, in the distance, he saw an old black preacher standing on a stump, practicing his sermon. He had a giant white Bible in one hand and a red handkerchief for face-mopping in the other. Despite the forty-degree weather, his shirtsleeves were rolled up. Dad stopped and listened to the man's tremulous voice, knowing that every turkey for miles was gone, that his hunting was spoiled. He might as well have gone home. When I asked him if he was angry he said no, just spooked.

I turn and look at the hunter's camouflaged face. "You ever hunt turkeys?"

"Go to hell," he says, and walks away. He doesn't look back, just heads into the woods. When he's gone I stand up and close my coat. Take a last long look at the Blowout, then make my way carefully down the side of the tracks. I duck under the darkening magnolia branches on the other side and start back toward the logging road.

I know, as I walk, that I'm not the fancy-rifled lawyer in face paint and new camouflage, yet neither am I the dedicated native hunter I pretended to be all those years. Now when I return here, to Dickinson, it's as a kind of stranger—after all, I've left, gotten educated, lost some of my drawl. I even married a Yankee. And coming back like this to hunt for details for my stories feels a bit like poaching on land that used to be mine. But I've never lost the need to tell of my Alabama, to reveal it, lush and green and full of death. So I return, knowing what I've learned. I come back, where life is slow dying, and I poach for stories. I poach because I want to recover the paths while there's still time, before the last logging trucks rumble through and the old, dark ways are at last forever hewn.

Imperial Bedroom

Jonathan Franzen

Jonathan Franzen is a writer for New York Times. *He has also written two novels* The Twenty-Seventh City *(1988) and* Strong Motion *(1991) that have enjoyed success with readers and critics alike. Franzen was selected by* Granta *magazine as one of its 20 Best Young American Novelists.*

Our privacy panic isn't merely exaggerated. It's founded on a fallacy. Ellen Alderman and Caroline Kennedy, in "The Right to Privacy," sum up the conventional wisdom of privacy advocates like this: "There is less privacy than there used to be." The claim has been made or implied so often, in so many books and editorials and talk-show dens, that Americans, no matter how passive they are in their behavior, now dutifully tell pollsters that they're very much worried about privacy. From almost any historical perspective, however, the claim seems bizarre.

In 1890, an American typically lived in a small town under conditions of near-panoptical surveillance. Not only did his every purchase "register" but it registered in the eyes and in the memory of shopkeepers who knew him, his parents, his wife, and his children. He couldn't so much as walk to the post office without having his movements tracked and analyzed by neighbors. Probably he grew up sleeping in a bed with his siblings and possibly with his parents, too. Unless he was well-off, his transportation—a train, a horse, his own two feet—either was communal or exposed him to the public eye.

In the suburbs and exurbs where the typical American lives today, tiny nuclear families inhabit enormous houses, in which each person has his or her own bedroom and, sometimes, bathroom. Compared even with suburbs in the sixties and seventies, when I was growing up, the contemporary condominium development or gated community offers a striking degree of anonymity. It's no longer the rule that you know your neighbors. Communities increasingly tend to be virtual, the participants either faceless or firmly in control of the faces they present. Transportation is largely private: the latest S.U.V.s are the size of living rooms and come with onboard telephones, CD players, and TV screens; behind the tinted windows of one of these high-riding, I-see-you-but-you-can't-see-me mobile PrivacyGuard® units, a person can be wearing pajamas or a licorice bikini, for all anybody knows or cares. Maybe the government intrudes on the family a little more than it did a hundred years ago (social workers look in on the old and the poor, health officials require inoculations, the police inquire about spousal battery), but from a privacy perspective these intrusions don't begin to make up for the small-town snooping they've replaced.

"The right to be left alone"? Far from disappearing, it's exploding. It's the essence of modern American architecture, landscape, transportation, communications, and mainstream political philosophy. The real reason that Americans are passive about privacy is so big as to be almost invisible: we're flat-out *drowning* in privacy.

What's threatened isn't the private sphere. It's the public sphere. Much has been made of the discouraging effect that the Starr investigation may have on future aspirants to public office (only zealots and zeros need apply), but that's just half of it. The public world of Washington, because it's public, belongs to everyone. We're all invited to participate with our votes, our patriotism, our campaigning, and our opinions. The collective weight of a population makes possible our faith in the public world as something larger and more enduring and more dignified than any messy individual can be in private. But, just as one sniper in a church tower can keep the streets of an entire town empty, one real gross-out scandal can undermine that faith.

If privacy depends upon an expectation of invisibility, the expectation of *visibility* is what defines a public space. My "sense of privacy" functions to keep the public out of the private *and* to keep the private out of the public. A kind of mental Border collie yelps in distress when I feel that the line between the two has been breached. This is why the violation of a public space is so similar, as an experience, to the violation of privacy. I walk past a man taking a leak on a sidewalk in broad daylight (delivery-truck drivers can be especially self-righteous in their "Ya gotta go, ya gotta go" philosophy of bladder management), and although the man with the yawning fly is ostensibly the one whose privacy is compromised by the leak, I'm the one who feels the impingement. Flashers and sexual harassers and fellators on the pier and self-explainers on the cross-town bus all similarly assault our sense of the public by exposing themselves.

Since really serious exposure in public today is assumed to be synonymous with being seen on television, it would seem to follow that televised space is the premier public space. Many things that people say to me on television, however, would never be tolerated in a genuine public space—in a jury box, for example, or even on a city sidewalk. TV is an enormous, ramified extension of the billion living rooms and bedrooms in which it's consumed. You rarely hear a person on the subway talking loudly about, say, incontinence, but on television it's been happening for years. TV is devoid of shame, and without shame there can be no distinction between public and private. Last winter, an anchorwoman looked me in the eye and, in the tone of a close female relative, referred to a litter of babies in Iowa as "America's seven little darlin's." It was strange enough, twenty-five years ago, to get Dan Rather's reports on Watergate between spots for Geritol and Bayer aspirin, as if Nixon's impending resignation were somehow situated in my medicine chest. Now, shelved between ads for Promise margarine and Celebrity Cruises, the news itself is a soiled cocktail dress—TV the wardrobe and nothing but.

Reticence, meanwhile, has become an almost obsolete virtue. People now readily name their diseases, rents, and antidepressants. Sexual histories get spilled on first dates, Birkenstocks and cutoffs infiltrate the office on casual Fridays, telecommuting puts the boardroom in the bedroom, the "softer" modern office design puts the bedroom in the boardroom, salespeople unilaterally address customers by their first names, waiters won't bring me food until I've established a personal relationship with them, voice-mail machinery stresses the "I" in "I'm sorry, but I don't understand what you dialled," and cyberenthusiasts, in a particularly grotesque misnomer, designate as "public forums" pieces of etched silicon with which a forum's unshaved "participant" may communicate while sitting cross-legged in tangled sheets and wearing gym shorts. The networked world as a threat to privacy? It's the ugly spectacle of a privacy triumphant.

A genuine public space is a place where every citizen is welcome to be present, and where the purely private is excluded or restricted. One reason that attendance at art museums has soared in recent years is that museums still feel public in this way. After those tangled sheets, how delicious the enforced decorum and the hush, the absence of in-your-face consumerism. How sweet the promenading, the seeing and being seen. Everybody needs a promenade sometimes—a place to go when you want to announce to the world (not the little world of friends and family but the big world, the real world) that you have a new suit, or are in love, or suddenly realize that you stand a full inch taller when you don't hunch your shoulders.

Unfortunately, the fully public place is a nearly extinct category. We still have courtrooms and the jury pool, commuter trains and bus stations, here and there a small-town Main Street that really is a main street rather than a strip mall, certain coffee bars, and certain city sidewalks. Otherwise, for American adults the only halfway public space is the world of work. Here, especially in the upper echelons of business, codes of dress and behavior are routinely enforced, personal disclosures are penalized, and formality is still the rule. But these rituals extend only to the employees of the firm, and even they, when they become old, disabled, obsolete, or outsourceable, are liable to be expelled and thereby relegated to the tangled sheets.

The last big, steep-walled bastion of public life in America is Washington, D.C. Hence the particular violation I felt when the Starr report crashed in. Hence the feeling of being intruded on. It was privacy invasion, all right: private life brutally invading the most public of public spaces. I don't want to see sex on the news from Washington. There's sex everywhere else I look—on sitcoms, on the Web, on dust jackets, on the billboards in Times Square. Can't there be one thing in the national landscape that isn't about the bedroom? We all know there's sex in the cloakrooms of power, sex behind the pomp and circumstance, sex beneath the robes of justice; but can't we act like grownups and pretend otherwise? Pretend not that "no one is looking" but that *everyone* is looking?

For two decades now, business leaders and politicians across much of the spectrum, both Gingrich Republicans and Clinton Democrats, have extolled the virtues of privatizing public institutions. But what better word can there be for Lewinskygate and the ensuing irruption of disclosures (the infidelities of Helen Chenoweth, of Dan Burton, of Henry Hyde) than "privatization"? Anyone who wondered what a privatized Presidency might look like may now, courtesy of Mr. Starr, behold one.

In Denis Johnson's short story "Beverly Home," the young narrator spends his days working at a nursing home for the hopelessly disabled, where there is a particularly unfortunate patient whom no one visits:

> He was only thirty-three, I believe he said, but it was hard to guess what he told about himself because he really couldn't talk anymore, beyond clamping his lips repeatedly around his protruding tongue while groaning.
>
> No more pretending for him! He was completely and openly a mess. Meanwhile the rest of us go on trying to fool each other.

In a coast-to-coast, shag-carpeted imperial bedroom, we could all just be messes and save ourselves the trouble of pretending. But who wants to live in a pajama-party world? Privacy loses its value unless there's something it can be defined against. "Meanwhile the rest of us go on trying to fool each other"—and a good thing, too. The need to put on a public face is as basic as the need for the privacy in which to take it off. We need both a home that's not like a public space and a public space that's not like home.

Walking up Third Avenue on a Saturday night, I feel bereft. All around me, attractive young people are hunched over their StarTacs and Nokias with preoccupied expressions, as if probing a sore tooth, or adjusting a hearing aid, or squeezing a pulled muscle: personal technology has begun to look like a personal handicap. What I really want from a sidewalk is that people see me and let themselves be seen, but even this modest ideal is thwarted by cell-phone users and their unwelcome privacy. They say things like "Should we have couscous with that?" and "I'm on my way to Blockbuster." They aren't breaking any law by broadcasting these dining-nook conversations. There's no Publicity-Guard® that I can buy, no expensive preserve of public life to which I can flee. Seclusion, whether in a suite at The Plaza or in a cabin in the Catskills, is comparatively effortless to achieve. Privacy is protected as both commodity and right; public forums are protected as neither. Like old-growth forests, they're few and irreplaceable and should be held in trust by everyone. The work of maintaining them only gets harder as the private sector grows ever more demanding, distracting, and disheartening. Who has the time and energy to stand up for the public sphere? What rhetoric can possibly compete with the American love of "privacy"?

When I return to my apartment after dark, I don't immediately turn my lights on. Over the years, it's become a reflexive precaution on my part not to risk spooking exposed neighbors by flooding my living room with light, although the only activity I ever seem to catch them at is watching TV.

My skin-conscious neighbor is home with her husband tonight, and they seem to be dressing for a party. The woman, a vertical strip of whom is visible between the Levolors and the window frame, is wearing a bathrobe and a barrette and sitting in front of a mirror. The man, slick-haired, wearing suit pants and a white T-shirt, stands by a sofa in the other room and watches television in a posture that I recognize as uncommitted. Finally, the woman disappears into the bedroom. The man puts on a white shirt and a necktie and perches sidesaddle on an arm of the sofa, still watching television, more involved with it now. The woman returns wearing a strapless yellow dress and looking like a whole different species of being. Happy the transformation! Happy the distance between private and public! I see a rapid back-and-forth involving jewelry, jackets, and a clutch purse, and then the couple, dressed to the nines, ventures out into the world.

9.11.01
The Skyscraper and the Airplane

Adam Goodheart

Adam Goodheart is a free lance writer in Washington, D.C. and a member of the American Scholar's editorial board. He was a founding editor of Civilization *magazine, and his essays have appeared in the* Atlantic Monthly, *the* New York Times, The Washington Post, Outside, *and other publications.*

> *And as the smart ship grew*
> *In stature, grace, and hue,*
> *In shadowy silent distance grew the Iceberg too.*
>
> —Thomas Hardy,
> "The Convergence of the Twain" (1912)

Before the fire, before the ash, before the bodies tumbling solitary through space, one thin skin of metal and glass met another. Miles apart only moments before, then feet, and then, in an almost inconceivable instant, only a fraction of an inch. Try to imagine them there, suspended: two man-made behemoths joined in a fatal kiss.

Fatal, fated: perhaps even long foreseen. The skyscraper and the airplane were born side by side, and ever since then have occupied adjacent rooms in our collective unconscious. To call September 11th a nightmare is to be clinically precise about it, for like all true nightmares, it was grafted together out of preexisting elements, fragments of our waking lives and our imaginations.

Nearly a century ago, just five years after the first scrawny aircraft left the ground at Kitty Hawk, a widely circulated illustration by a Manhattan publisher named Moses King—"King's Dream of New York," he titled it—showed a fantasy cityscape in which biplanes buzzed among the down-town office towers and a vast dirigible brushed the uppermost cupola. In that same year, 1908, E. M. Forster wrote a short story envisioning a world of the future where humans lived in huge structures composed of tiny, airless chambers, each one "like the cell of a bee," leaving them to travel in airships that crisscrossed the globe (though the earth had become so drably uniform, he observed, that "what was the good of going to Pekin when it was just like Shrewsbury?"). In the last paragraph of the story, "The Machine Stops," Forster imagined this world coming to an end: "The whole city was broken like a honeycomb. An air-ship . . . crashed downwards, exploding as it went, rending gallery after gallery with its wings of steel."

Skyscraper and airplane: fragile containers for even-more-fragile flesh and blood. Each an artificial shell of our own manufacture—or not quite of our own manufacture, since, strictly speaking, very few of us, as individuals, have any direct involvement in their creation. Each a capsule of recycled air, with windows sealed shut against the blue. Each an innovation that, in Forsterian terms, has made Pekin more and more like Shrewsbury. Each a honeycomb that traps us side by side with strangers. Each a rig that suspends us far above the ground, half-willing aerialists, and then whispers: *Trust me*. Each a machine that teaches us, in similar ways, how to be modern.

What keeps it up? What, that is to say, keeps *us* up? Perhaps one person in a thousand really knows, understanding coolly why it is that the contraption doesn't plummet back to earth under our weight. For the rest of us, the precise functioning of wing and girder, the mathematical intricacies of gravitational thrust and counterthrust, remain lifelong mysteries. Our animal selves, quite sensibly, would rather stick close to solid ground. But this is where we must steel ourselves to be something more than animals. We must summon up the will to trust—not so much in the metal armature beneath us as in the faceless experts who designed and built it, in the corporations that own and maintain it, in the armature of civilization and science. No wonder we sometimes get dizzy.

The cultural critic Marshall Berman, in selecting a title for his 1982 treatise on the experience of modernity, borrowed a newly resonant phrase from Karl Marx: *All That Is Solid Melts Into Air*. "To be modern," he wrote, "is to find ourselves in an environment that promises us adventure, power, joy, growth, transformation of ourselves and the world—and, at the same time, that threatens to destroy everything we have, everything we know, everything we are." It is to ride atop a skyscraper, to soar in an airplane. And both threatened us with such destruction, not just on that machine-bright morning in September, but long before.

Both sprang from the late nineteenth century, and from the American Middle West (Louis Sullivan's Chicago, the Wright Brothers' Ohio)—a place where earth and sky were blank canvases waiting to be filled with movement and form. Yet both had deeper roots as well. In England in the 1780s, the decade in which the Montgolfiers took to the air in their balloons, and the young Wordsworth and Coleridge sharpened their pens at grammar school, the Duke of Bedford owned an exceptionally large racehorse that one of his grooms named Skyscraper—the first recorded appearance of the word. (The mare finished first at the Epsom Derby in 1789.) In the years that followed, *skyscraper* was used to describe the uppermost sail on a ship's rigging (1794), a high hat or bonnet (1800), or simply a very tall person (1857). After crossing the Atlantic, it was used by American sportswriters as early as the 1860s to describe a towering fly ball. Like so many of the next century's most important words (*computer, rocket, network*), *skyscraper* jostled around indecisively for a while, hesitating between one meaning and another before settling into its ultimate niche. However they used the word, people were clearly grasping toward the sky, toward something up there that they could almost brush with their fingertips—and that they were determined to reach by one contrivance or another.

When the earliest buildings to be called skyscrapers appeared, in the 1870s and 1880s, they sprang into shape so suddenly as to seem born in a single piece. The pioneering architects of Chicago, one recent historian has written, "learned almost everything of importance that would be known a century later about how to build skyscrapers." Yet the skyscraper was not, as it seems to us now, a single unified invention, but rather many inventions knit into one.

First and foremost, of course, was the ability to produce cheap, high-quality structural steel—the first truly revolutionary architectural innovation since the Romans invented the arch and the dome two millennia before. One nineteenth-century engineer couched this development in almost Darwinian terms: For the first time, he explained, tall buildings were designed as vertebrates instead of crustaceans. For the first time, their loads and stresses could be carried not by massive carapaces of masonry but by a web of slender struts and braces whose strength lay in its interconnectedness: a prototypical modern form, destined to be replicated in everything from computer chips to international airline routes. Louis Sullivan might have boasted of his buildings' pure functionalism, but in fact the skyscraper's exterior was merely its skin, its only function (besides shelter from the elements) to provide a kind of movie screen onto which the architect could project any embellishment he chose: rich Gothic traceries, Art Deco's silvery sheen, or, eventually, the stern theatrics of high modernism.

Still, if architects had had only steel to work with, the interiors of their skyscrapers would have just been little more than dark and dreary warrens. Office towers of ten and twenty stories required, for their basic functioning, a whole list of innovations that are now taken for granted, but that were still brand new in the second half of the nineteenth century: electric lights and central heating, passenger elevators and fire escapes, telephones and flush toilets. As fate had it, all of these appeared on the American scene at approximately the same time. And all of them, moreover, required a wholly new type of city to support them: one with reliable, centrally managed electric and gas companies, sewer systems, water mains, fire departments, elevator inspectors, telephone operators, trash collectors. Did the modern city give birth to the skyscraper, or vice versa? The answer, probably, is a bit of both.

Of all these varied accoutrements, none was more critical to the skyscraper's development than the passenger elevator. At New York's Crystal Palace exposition in 1854, a Yonkers mechanic named Elisha Graves Otis would periodically ascend high above the crowds on an open platform of wrought iron. As the machine creaked up to its zenith, the inventor gestured to an assistant, who cut through the hoisting rope with a hatchet. The spectators gasped in horror—but instead of plummeting to the ground, the elevator merely settled back into its ratcheted safety lock. "All safe, gentlemen, all safe," Otis announced.

Otis's words would become the constant refrain of the dawning era. In the nineteenth century, for the first time in human history, millions of ordinary people would be required to entrust their lives, on a daily basis, to technologies whose inner workings remained a mystery. They were a generation of pioneers, the men and women of New York and Chicago, no less than the settlers of the Great Plains. The odd thing, in retrospect, is how easily they seem to have taken the changes in stride. When the architect Bradford Gilbert, in 1888, topped off his Tower Building at eleven stories, many New York pedestrians avoided that block of Broadway, certain that the structure would topple in the first stiff breeze. But Gilbert, in an Otis-like show of confidence, moved his own office onto the uppermost floor; the building withstood a hurricane soon after, and before long was taken for granted. Barely two decades later, when the Metropolitan Life Building reached a record fifty stories, the only question was who would try for sixty. (It would be the retailing magnate Frank Woolworth, who began planning his skyscraper a few weeks after the Metropolitan tower opened.)

Even more remarkable, the mythology of the skyscraper was born full-fledged with the building itself. Here is the earliest recorded appearance of the word in its contemporary sense, from an 1883 issue of *American Architect and Building News:* "This form of sky-scraper gives that peculiar refined, independent, self-contained, daring, bold, heaven-reaching, erratic, piratic, Quixotic, American thought." (Those were the days when even trade journals waxed Whitmanesque.)

A century earlier, Thomas Jefferson, proclaiming American exceptionalism in his *Notes on Virginia*, cited the extraordinary size of native bears and elk, caverns and waterfalls. (He even vigorously defended American Indians against a French naturalist's insinuation that their "organs of generation" were smaller than average.) But the skyscraper rendered all of Jefferson's examples irrelevant. Here was the final proof of America's towering stature, in a tower raised not by God but by its citizens.

Before long, the race to scrape the sky lifted off the ground. And like the skyscraper's, the airplane's infancy was shortlived, its full maturity quick to arrive: Orville Wright would live to see the era of inflight movies. Strut and brace, spar and rib formed the bones of the plane as they did of the skyscraper, stiffening an outer shell designed to cut through hostile wind. And the airplane, too, would become a sort of capsule of human amenities, but to an even greater degree: a mobile life-support system, no less than a spaceship would be.

And yet, after nearly a century aloft, we have never learned to occupy planes as comfortably as we do skyscrapers. Antoine de Saint-Exupéry, in the 1930s, predicted that within a generation or two, the airplane would come to seem a perfectly commonplace thing, "an object as natural as a pebble polished by the waves." Instead, it still seems the very epitome of what is artificial and mechanical. Stepping aboard one, even the most habitual of flyers must exercise a small act of conscious will. The passenger never forgets that he is wagering his life on the journey, even if he knows that the odds in this type of roulette are relatively good.

Air travel is a unique experience in modern life, the sociologist Mark Gottdiener recently wrote, "because, deep down inside us, it is a 'near death' experience. It is the most common way individuals surrender control and voluntarily place themselves in harm's way in contemporary society. If they drive, they are also at risk, but they remain in control behind the wheel." Strapped into our seats, waiting on the runway, staring out the window at the stained frailty of the wing, we toy with fantasies of annihilation. We look at our fellow travelers and wonder what it would be like to face death alongside these strangers. A terribly intimate, terribly modern way to go: so close to one another in these well-lit rows, so far from family and home.

In a seminar for phobic flyers offered by American Airlines, participants spend ten consecutive hours being lectured by pilots, flight attendants, mechanics, and psychologists, who repeat this phrase like a mantra: "Airplanes do not drop, dive, plummet, or fall." In doing so, they merely voice the silent chant of every airborne congregation. For flying requires an act of almost religious faith, the surrender of oneself, in absolute trust, to the wisdom and benevolent expertise of corporations, pilots, governments, engineers—the whole apparatus of modernity. In this setting, the smallest acts take on ritual significance: the pantomimed instructions of flight attendants, the dimming of lights, the serving of food. Airline meals, tiny and perfectly formed, are like the Japanese tea ceremony, in which gesture is more important than nourishment. In giving us food, the airline offers us a promise of sustenance; in eating, we accept. All of us know one or two stiff-necked dissenters who refuse to fly at all, and they irritate us more than their mild neurosis would warrant, as if they had renounced their citizenship in the commonwealth of flight.

If the skyscraper, with its crudely phallic thrust, is male, the airplane is female. Entering, we pass into a place that promises—if rarely quite delivering—all the amenities of the womb: shelter, nourishment, warmth, dimness, sleep. The earliest flight attendants, in the 1920s, were men, but airlines quickly discovered that passengers preferred to be cared for by women, and before long they were openly competing with one another to provide the most beautiful and provocatively clad stewardesses. Erotic currents move among the passengers as well. Skyscrapers place us alongside strangers and demand that we work; airplanes seat us side by side and whisper idle fantasies of sex. This is the double face of modern alienation: the limitless pain of loneliness, the limitless promise of random encounters. Proximity, anonymity: the world of skyscrapers and airplanes is one in which terrorists stalk freely among their prey.

The architect of the World Trade Center, Minoru Yamasaki, was afraid of heights. He once wrote that in a world of perfect freedom, he'd have created nothing but one-story buildings overlooking fields of flowers. He designed the Trade Center with narrow windows framed by vertical columns like prison bars, close enough together that he could steady himself against them when looking out. Instead of one-story buildings overlooking fields of flowers, he built gargantuan monoliths overlooking a windswept plaza. Their scale was brutal, unsoftened by the slightest hint of stylishness. Only at a great distance did they impress, jutting like a double bowsprit from the prow of Manhattan, from the prow of America itself. Or, if you preferred, like a pair of middle fingers, raised against the hostile vastness of the Atlantic Ocean.

But to take in this view you had to stand far away: in Hoboken, or Hamburg, or Kabul. (Or to observe the towers through a lens. Like so many twentieth-century creations, they seemed designed to be seen not in person but on film, as though the cinematic eye were the only one that mattered.) Standing at the base of the towers and looking up, the human observer had the sense mostly not of their height, but of their immense weight. They were two mountains of trapped kinetic energy, perpetually poised at the brink of release. The irony of architecture, all architecture, is that we create structures to shelter ourselves, yet in building them, we set ourselves at risk. The surest way to stay safe from fires, earthquakes, and bombs is never to go indoors. The surest way not to fall is to stay on the ground.

In *Anna Karenina*, Levin is terrified by the birth of his first child, for he realizes that he has brought into the world a new means for him to be hurt beyond all previous imagining. Tolstoy recognized that every act of creation has its shadow double, a coequal act of destruction. When Yamasaki created buildings on an unprecedented scale, he also created the potential for disaster on an unprecedented scale, a nightmare knit into every cubic inch of glass and steel. (The man who would eventually engineer their destruction understood this: he came from a family of builders.) They fascinated us, as airplanes do, because part of us always imagined them falling. It is the same part of us that loves our children because we can imagine them dying.

And when the towers did fall, we watched with the horror of witnesses to a death half foreseen, in dreams and shadowy portents. They buckled, released their long-held burden, and wearily sank to earth.

The authors of the catastrophe—who can doubt it?—created something terrible and permanent: an image that will stand for as long as any tower. In a thousand years, anyone who knows anything at all about us, the ancient Modern Americans, will probably know about the skyscraper and the airplane, and about the bright September morning that welded them together.

Eight days after the collapse, I stood on lower Broadway near where the skyscrapers had been. The destruction was all strangely contained behind chain-link fences and squads of stolid cops: all the familiar markers of a Situation Under Control. The mounded ruins poured out a thick column of white smoke, its innards glowing sickly yellow under the slanting rays of late-afternoon sun. It looked exactly as if the crater of a volcano had somehow opened up among the downtown office buildings, and now was being probed and monitored by businesslike teams of geologists and seismologists, lest it erupt again without warning. I was reminded of being atop Mount Etna, and peering alongside other tourists into the gassy abyss of the caldera, looking fruitlessly for some deep-buried source of smoke and heat. Above everything, above the place where the towers had stood, a helicopter whirred, miraculously suspended, riding on a column of newly liberated air.

Revolution in the Library

Gertrude Himmelfarb

Before she retired, Gertrude Himmelfarb was distinguished professor of history and chairman of the doctoral program in history at the Graduate School of the City University of New York. She has written extensively on Victorian England and on contemporary society and culture. Her most recent book is The De-Moralization of Society: From Victorian Virtues to Modern Values *(1995). She has edited several other books and has contributed essays to many volumes and journals. A member of the Board of Trustees of the Woodrow Wilson International Center, she also sits on the Council of Scholars of the Library of Congress, the Council of Academic Advisers of the American Enterprise Institute, and the Board of Advisers of the Library of America.*

———————————————

Historians are notoriously wary of the word *revolution*. Unlike journalists, who find revolutions in every twist and turn of political events, intellectual movements, technological innovations, sartorial fashions, historians like to think that their revolutions last more than a month or two, or a year or two, or even a decade or two. Indeed, some historians, older historians like myself, are so sparing in their use of the word that they reserve it for changes that dramatically alter the course of entire centuries. Thus the Cromwellian revolution in England, complete with the decapitation of the king, is said to be not a serious revolution; at best it was only a civil war. Nor was the so-called Glorious Revolution that altered the succession to the throne; that was entirely too peaceful, too "glorious," to qualify as a revolution.

But there are, even the most cautious historian will agree, genuine revolutions. The French Revolution surely was one such, and probably the American Revolution (although this is still disputed; a colonial revolt, the English prefer to call it). And

———————————————

Reprinted from *The American Scholar*, (spring 1997), by permission of Gertrude Himmelfarb.

finally, after decades of indecision, the industrial revolution has been admitted into the pantheon of revolutions. When I was in graduate school, the term *industrial revolution* always appeared in quotation marks to suggest that it was not really a revolution. Today, even the most skeptical of historians agree that it was a real revolution. And having conceded that, some of us are prepared to say that we are now witnessing another revolution, a post-industrial revolution, the electronic revolution. Like all revolutions, this has ramifications far beyond its immediate context. For it may prove to be a revolution not only in the library itself—the way books are catalogued, stored, and circulated—but in the nature of learning and education.

The library is, and always has been, the heart of a college. I recall witnessing a demonstration at a university in the late 1960s, when the students demanded to be "empowered," as they said, and the professors protested, "But *we* are the university." In fact, librarians have as much right to make that claim. For professors—professors of the humanities, at any rate—as much as students, are the creatures of the library. Just as the laboratory is the domain of the sciences, so the library is of the humanities. For it is the library that is the repository of the learning and wisdom that are transmitted from the professors to the students.

If the library is now in the throes of a revolution—if desks and carrels in the library are being transformed into "workstations," and students and scholars find themselves consulting the Internet more often than books—something momentous is happening, something far more consequential than a mere technological innovation. The last time we experienced such an innovation was the invention of the printing press almost half a millennium ago. And that, as we now know, had momentous consequences. Among other things, it was responsible for the creation of libraries. There had been libraries, to be sure, before Gutenberg's invention. The most famous was the library in Alexandria founded by Ptolemy I in the fourth century B.C.—famous partly because of its infamous destruction by the Roman emperors in the third and fourth centuries A.D. But other libraries, public and private, survived and flourished, in Jerusalem, Greece, and Rome. At about the time that Gutenberg was perfecting his printing press, the Vatican Library was formed; its first catalogue listed twenty-five hundred volumes. Today, thanks to Gutenberg, a good many scholars have that many books or more in their home or office.

The print revolution is the perfect exemplar of the principle of quantity transmuted into quality. The quantum leap in the number of books now available to each individual or library is almost the least of the consequences of that revolution. More significant is its democratizing effect—the liberation of the culture from the control of clerics and scribes. The relative ease and cheapness of printing transferred the production of books to artisans and merchants, who were responsible neither to ecclesiastical nor to secular authorities but only to the dictates of the consumer and the market. Thus ephemeral popular books could be produced as cheaply as classical ones, and heretical tracts as readily as canonical ones.

Not only could numerous copies of each book be produced, but they could be produced in identical form. Thus every literate person could have access to the same text of the Bible, and could interpret and judge it without benefit of the mediating authorities of church or state. It is no accident, some historians suggest, that the print revolution preceded the Protestant Reformation; were it not for Gutenberg, they say, the Reformation might have petered out or been suppressed as so many medieval heresies were.

Now, with the electronic revolution, we are taking that democratizing process a giant step forward. It is not only the library catalogue that is computerized; the computer can call up a variety of other catalogues, indices, data bases, CD-Roms, the Internet, as well as books, journals, newspapers, archives, even manuscript collections from other libraries. Potentially, at least, the electronic revolution makes even smaller libraries the equivalent of libraries in major research universities and scholarly institutions. And it can do more than that. It can make those books, journals, data bases, and so on, "talk to each other," as cyberspace aficionados say. All you have to do is type in your request for information and the computer will collate the sources, synthesize them, and present the results for you on your screen.

And it can do still more. It can make you not only the recipient of all this information but the creator of it, an active partner in this "interactive process" (another cyberspace term). Your thoughts on any subject, your reflections, impressions, opinions, even your latest term paper, can find their way into the Internet by means of your "home page." Recently I heard a child on TV—an eight or nine year old—exult in the potentialities of this marvelous device. "It's wonderful," he said, "to be able to ask a question on your home page and have lots of people answer it for you." All of the adults on that program shared his enthusiasm. I wonder how many listeners recalled that only a few years ago he would have had to go to a textbook or encyclopedia for the answer to his question—an implicit recognition on his part that these sources were more reliable, more authoritative, than "lots of people."

By this time you will have suspected that I am of two minds about the new electronic revolution. Like a great many revolutions, it is salutary—up to a point. But, like most revolutions, it tends to go beyond that point. The democratization of knowledge is all to the good, if that means the democratization of *access* to knowledge. Anyone who spends a fair amount of time in the library is grateful for a computerized catalogue that gives information not only about the books and journals in that particular library but in all the libraries in the area or even in the country. And anyone who does not have access to a major research library, or who seeks information about a public figure or event in the recent past, or who wants to read or reread a particular book review or article, will be grateful to the Internet for retrieving that information quickly and efficiently.

But democratization of the access to knowledge should not be confused with the democratization of knowledge itself. And this is where the Internet, or any system of electronic networking, may be misleading and even pernicious. In cyberspace, every source seems as authoritative as every other. As that child on TV put it, "lots of people" will profess to have the answer to his question. The search for a name or phrase on the Internet will produce a comic strip or advertising slogan as readily as a quotation from the Bible or Shakespeare. The Internet is an equal opportunity resource; it recognizes no rank or status or privilege. In that democratic universe, all sources, all ideas, all theories seem equally valid and pertinent.

It takes a discriminating mind, a mind that is already stocked with knowledge and trained in critical discernment, to distinguish between Peanuts and Shakespeare—between the trivial and the important, the ephemeral and the enduring, the true and the false. It is just this sense of discrimination that the humanities have traditionally cultivated and that they must now cultivate even more strenuously if the electronic revolution is to do more good than bad.

The humanities have had much to contend with in recent years. The real revolution started even before the electronic one, and it started not with a technological revolution but with an intellectual one. It began a few decades ago with the attack on the "canon"—the great books that have traditionally been thought to constitute the heart of the humanities and the core of a liberal education. In the beginning, the criticism was leveled at the particular books in the canon—or, rather, at the authors of the books. Plato and Aristotle, Augustine and Aquinas, Shakespeare and Milton, Marx and Mill, all were derided as "Dead White Males"—"DWMS" or "Dweems," as they were familiarly known. The canon, it was charged, was sexist, elitist, and regressive, prejudiced against women, against blacks, and against the living.

But that was only the opening skirmish of the war. The attack escalated with an assault against the very idea of a canon. Any canon, the argument went, was objectionable because it was fixed, prescribed, imposed from without—therefore oppressive and authoritarian. When it was pointed out that the canon was not in fact fixed, that it differed from college to college and changed from one year to the next, that some old books were retired while new ones emerged (some by women, blacks, and even, horrors, the living), a new strategy came into play.

I first encountered this new turn of the argument some years ago when I participated in a panel discussion on the subject of the canon at a distinguished liberal arts college. One of the panelists, the head of the Women's Studies program at the college, explained that the problem was not only that the "Big Guys"—her variation on "Dead White Males"—were Guys, but also that they were Big, thus "privileging," as she put it, big books, great books. This, she complained, was what was really offensive in the canon. The canon—any canon—assumes that there is such a thing as great books containing great and enduring ideas and truths worthy of being studied and valued. Moreover, it assumes that these ideas and truths transcend time and place, race and ethnicity, class and gender, country and nationality. These assumptions, she said, are not only elitist; they are profoundly sexist, for they reflect a distinctively masculine view of how people think and feel, a masculine conception of ideas and reason. She concluded by calling upon women, and feminists particularly, to repudiate this masculine sensibility and adopt a uniquely feminine one, which celebrates not great ideas and truths but "the little things in women's lives . . . , the small nurturing things that women do."

131

I was taken aback by this argument when I first heard it. I could only protest that a retreat to "the little things in women's lives" is not my idea of what feminism is all about; it sounds to me suspiciously like a retreat to the kitchen. Nor do I agree that great books and ideas are distinctively masculine; nor that they are at all elitist. On the contrary, I believe them to be distinctively human and eminently democratic. They have survived the ages precisely because they are accessible to people of different backgrounds and characters, all of whom can aspire to understand them and to be elevated by them. This has been the principle inspiring the humanities, and, indeed, the very idea of a liberal education.

Since that episode, this challenge, not only to the canon but to the humanities and liberal education, has become all too familiar, and not only on the part of feminists. It is now espoused in a more sophisticated form by literary critics, philosophers, historians, and others under the banner of postmodernism, a doctrine that has become extremely influential, in some cases dominant, on many campuses and in many disciplines.

The mainspring of postmodernism is a radical—an absolute, one might say—relativism, skepticism, and subjectivism that rejects not only the idea of the canon, and not only the idea of greatness, but the very idea of truth. For the postmodernist, there is no truth, no knowledge, no objectivity, no reason, and, ultimately, no reality. Nothing is fixed, nothing is permanent, nothing is transcendent. Everything is in a state of total relativity and perennial flux. There is no correspondence between language and reality; indeed, there is no "essential" reality. What appears to be real is illusory, deceptive, problematic, indeterminate. What appears to be true is nothing more than what the power structure, the "hegemonic" authority in society, deems to be true.

To those of you who have been happily spared this latest intellectual fashion, it may seem bizarre and improbable. I can only assure you that it is all too prevalent in all fields of the humanities. This is not to say that all or even most professors of literature, history, or philosophy are postmodernists. But some of the most prestigious professors are, including the recent presidents of several important professional associations. And many of the brightest and most ambitious younger professors and graduate students are attracted to a mode of thought that they believe to be at the "cutting edge," the "vanguard" of their disciplines. More important is the fact that even those who do not think of themselves as postmodernists often share the extreme relativism and subjectivism that now pervade the humanities as a whole. In the leading professional journals today, the words "truth," "objectivity," "reason," and "reality" generally appear with quotation marks around them, suggesting how specious these concepts are.

What we are now confronting, therefore, is not one but two revolutions—an intellectual and a technological revolution which bear an uncanny resemblance to each other and have a symbiotic relationship to each other. If I were given to conspiratorial theories, I might speculate that Bill Gates, the chairman of Microsoft, is a secret agent of Jacques Derrida, the high priest of postmodernism. For the new technology is the perfect medium for the new ideology. Surfing through cyberspace is a truly postmodernist experience, a liberation from what the postmodernist calls "linear thinking"—a logical, rational mode of reasoning.

Words and images appear on the screen in rapid succession and in no predetermined or logical order. The reader, or rather viewer, patches them together as he likes, making of them what he will, connecting and disconnecting them at his pleasure. There is no fixed text, no authoritative source, no restrictions of space or time to confine him. (Compare the infinite capacity of the moving screen with the physical, spatial limitations of the book; or the speed of scrolling on the screen with turning the pages of a book.)

Another of the buzzwords of postmodernism is *intertextuality*—intruding into the text of a poem, for example, any words, ideas, or events, however remote or contradictory, that may come to the mind of the reader. The screen enormously facilitates such intertexuality, as it calls up other texts or images that may not even have occurred to the reader and that may have little or no bearing on the poem. The poem becomes, in the language of postmodernism, indeterminate, problematic, ironic. And the reading of the poem becomes, in effect, an exercise in Virtual Reality, having as little relation to the real poem as an electronic game of Virtual Reality has to the real world.

We are experiencing, then, a revolution, not only in library services but in the very conception of the library. And, like most revolutions, this one has enormous potentialities for good and bad. Among its undeniable virtues are the computerized catalogue, so much more efficient and informative than the old card catalogue; the ready access to other library holdings and data bases; the ability to retrieve rapidly information and material that otherwise would have taken days or would have been irrecoverable; the convenience of networking with colleagues working on similar subjects, exchanging ideas, information, and, let us admit it, the kind of professional and even personal gossip that goes with the trade.

But—and this is a large *but*—all this will be to the good only if the virtues of the new library are made to complement, rather than supplant, those of the old. And I am confident this can be done, although it will take a conscious effort to do it—to resist the seductions of the new medium, to refrain from mindless, endless cybersurfing, to withstand the tempting distractions along the way, to retain a sense of what is important, pertinent, and authoritative. Above all, it will mean keeping faith with the old library—with books that are meant to be read, not merely surfed. E-mail enthusiasts refer to postal mail as "snail-mail." Some books, to be sure, are better surfed ("skimmed," as we used to say) than read. But others should only be read at a snail's pace; anything faster than that defeats the purpose and violates the text.

This brings me to the heart of the matter—to the particular relationship between the library and the humanities. In theory, there is no reason why Milton's *Paradise Lost* or Rousseau's *Social Contract* cannot be called up on the screen, assuming they are "on line." (What is more likely is that something like a *Cliffs Notes* version of them is on line.) But even if they are on line, there is every reason to read them in book form—"hard copy," as we now say—rather than on the screen. With the physical volume in our hand, we are necessarily aware of the substantiality, the reality of the work, the text as it is, as Milton or Rousseau wrote it and meant us to read it. Of course, we will interpret and understand it within our own framework of reference; and of course we will draw upon other sources—critical, historical, biographical—to help us interpret and understand it. But we should always be brought back to the text, to the book in hand. The book is the reality; there is no Virtual Reality here. Moreover, each page of the book—in the case of a difficult work, each line of the page—has a distinctness, a hard reality of its own. Holding the book in hand, open at that page, it is easy to concentrate the mind upon it, to linger over it, mull over it, take as long as necessary to try to understand and appreciate it.

Reading it on the screen, however, is a quite different experience. There we tend to become postmodernists in spite of ourselves. It takes a great effort of will to concentrate on the text unaccompanied by whatever else may happen to be called up on the screen along with it. And it takes a still greater effort to remain fixed on a single page without scrolling on to the next, let alone to concentrate on a single passage, line, or word. The medium itself is too fluid, too mobile and volatile, to encourage any sustained effort of thought. It makes us impatient, eager to get on to the next visual presentation. And the more accustomed we become to the new medium, the more difficult it is to retain the old habits of study and thought. We become habituated to a fast pace, an ever-changing scene, a rapid succession of sensations and impressions. We become incapacitated for the longer, slower, less feverish tempo of the book.

We also become incapacitated for thinking seriously about ideas rather than amassing facts. For the purpose of retrieving facts, the Internet is enormously helpful, although even here some caveats are in order. We need to concentrate our mind on exactly what it is we want to know, to resist being distracted by fascinating but irrelevant facts, and—most important—to retain the ability to distinguish between facts and opinions, between reputable sources and dubious ones. The humanities, however, is about more than the retrieval of facts. It is also about appreciating a poem, understanding an idea, finding significance in a historical event, following the logic of an argument, reasoning about human nature, inquiring into ethical dilemmas, making rational and moral judgments—all of which require an exercise of mind that calls upon all the human faculties, and which no technology, however sophisticated, can satisfy. If we want, for example, a concordance to the Bible, we can find no better medium than the Internet. But if we want to read the Bible, to study it, think about it, reflect upon it, we should have it in our hands, for that is the only way of getting it into our minds and our hearts.

The humanities are an essentially human enterprise—an enterprise to which human beings have devoted themselves for all of civilized history. The record of that enterprise reposes in the library in the form of books—a vast multitude of books, including, to be sure, many worthless or meretricious ones, but also all the great ones. These are the books that sustain our mind and inspire our imagination. It is there that we look for truth, for knowledge, for wisdom. And it is these ideals that we hope will survive our latest revolution.

Novel Without a Name

Duong Thu Huong

*Duong Thu Huong was born in the area of Thai Binh in Vietnam.
As a singer, Duong Thu Huong was one of 30 people recruited for
an artistic troupe that performed for soldiers ("sing louder than the
bombs") near the central border, where much of the heaviest bombing took place. From this troupe, she was one of the three who survived the war. She was also the first female combatant/war
correspondent at the front when China attacked Vietnam in 1979.
Her career as a novelist has been very successful. Her novel* Beyond
Illusions *(1987) was actually the first of Huong's three novels—including also:* Paradise of the Blind *(1988), and* Fragments of Lost
Life *(1989)—written immediately after Vietnam's Communist Party
invited writers to participate in an era of openness and critical
analysis of the new nation. However,* Paradise of the Blind *was
banned by Communist Party authorities in its own country, because it depicted the disastrous 1953–56 land reforms. It was the
first novel from Vietnam ever published in the United States. Her
books have been banned in Vietnam ever since.* Novel without a
Name *(1995) is her chronicle of the Vietnam War. Her perspective
shows us what the war felt like for the Vietnamese.*

I listened all night to the wind howl through the Gorge of Lost Souls. Endless moans
punctuated by sobs. From time to time it whinnied like a mare in heat, whistling
through the broken shafts of the bamboo roof above me, sweeping through the countryside in a macabre symphony of sound.

The flame of our oil lamp flickered weakly. I poked my head from under the covers and blew it out, wishing I too could sink, body and soul, into the night. Against

Reprinted from *Novel Without a Name*, translated by Phan Huy Duong & Nina McPherson,
(1995), Penguin Putnam Inc.

the wall, a dead branch rapped a dull cadence. It was impossible to sleep, so I murmured a prayer. *Dear sisters, you who have lived and died here as human beings: Do not haunt us any longer. Protect us. Fortify our bodies, light the way for our spirits, so that in every battle we may conquer. When victory comes, when peace comes to our country, we will carry you back to the land of your ancestors.*

I buried my face in the blankets, trying to block out the wind. But it seemed to deepen and gather strength, howling through the Gorge of Lost Souls.

Two weeks earlier we had buried six girls. At dawn I had gone with Lanh's platoon to gather bamboo shoots. Shortly after midday we reached the Gorge of Lost Souls. A swarm of vultures circled in the air above us, diving earthward and rising again toward the sky, their cries shattering the silence. Lanh stopped suddenly, sniffing. "There must be a dead animal around here. It stinks!"

It did stink. The farther we advanced, the more the odor reeked. Someone proposed turning back, but Lanh urged us on. "It could be a man. Who knows? Maybe one of ours."

"Let's go see," I said.

We moved toward the corner of the forest from which the horrible odor seemed to emanate. We found six naked corpses. Women. Their breasts and genitals had been cut off and strewn on the grass around them. They were northern girls: We could tell by their scarves made out of parachute cloth and the lotus-shaped collars of their blouses. They must have belonged to a group of volunteers or a mobile unit that lost its way. Perhaps, like us, they had come here to search for bamboo shoots or vegetables.

The soldiers had raped them before killing them. The corpses were bruised violet. So this was how graceful, girlish bodies rotted, decomposing into swollen old corpses, puffy as dead toads. Maggots swarmed in their wounds, their eyes and mouths. Fat white larvae. They crawled over the corpses in waves, plunging in and out of them in a drunken orgy.

One of the soldiers covered his nose. "Goddamn worms. They're everywhere."

"Let's bury the girls," I said.

Vultures circled and shrieked overhead. The heat was suffocating. Sweat beaded and glistened on our faces. The odor of rotting flesh hung in the air. We gathered the corpses, fighting with the vultures and the maggots for each shred of flesh. We buried them. The girls' pockets were empty; not a single slip of paper, just a few pieces of red and blue yarn, a few betel nuts. The yarn to tie their hair, the betel nuts to clean their teeth. They must have believed they would see their men again . . .

The earth was shallow here, so we had to bury the corpses in a small circular pit. By the time we finished, the maggots had formed a dense mass. Lanh threw an armful of dead leaves over them in a pile and set fire to it. You could hear the maggots crackle. We stood around the blaze, exhausted, bathed in sweat.

We threw the bamboo shoots on the ground and returned to camp. Not a single vegetable. Just a clump of rice mixed with yams, a bit of salt, red chilies, and dried lemongrass. This was our life, our soldier's life. One day there would be nothing left of it.

"Quan, hey, Quan."

Luy's voice was a whine. I didn't move. He continued, "Hey, Quan. Quan, are you asleep already?"

I didn't answer, pretending to be asleep. But then I ended up drifting off. An odd slumber, like a train jerking along its tracks, ready to derail at any moment. A train without passengers, filled with youthful dreams, long letters written in violet ink. Red scarves litter the empty cars. Broken sticks of chalk. A pencil stub. The train rolls on, deaf, mute. Deserted fields spread out along both sides of the tracks as far as the eye can see. I want to scream for the conductor, to pull the emergency cord, to cry out. But I am invisible, paralyzed, formless, featureless. My face dissolves, my voice is smothered by the wind . . .

"Quan, hey, Quan."

A blow against my body. And as if from under water, I rise from the depths of the dream. Glistening waves lap at my body, gently molding me a face. I feel as if I could die of happiness. I have a face again . . .

"Quan, brother, wake up."

My arm felt paralyzed; it had fallen asleep. I struggled to pull up my covers. "What is it?"

"Quick, get up. I just saw an orangutan."

I wrapped myself more tightly under my covers. I was no longer some diluted substance in the depths of the water; I was lucid, but I didn't dare move. I wanted to wallow in this happiness, the warmth of these blankets; I was still alive, still myself, safe and sound, with my body, all thirty-two teeth, my sweat-damp feet in moldy socks, a belt around my waist.

"Get up, elder brother. We've got all the time in the world to sleep. The orangutan is huge. At least fifty pounds. Get up, quickly!"

I didn't move. Luy pleaded with me. "Please get up. We haven't had fresh meat in so long. Our knees go weak on patrol."

I didn't budge. Luy shook me. "Get up, elder brother. The men will finally be able to eat."

I peeled back the covers. "Why don't you just go by yourself?"

Luy winced. "I don't want to. It's a bit spooky. Come with me. I'll do the shooting. I never miss."

I sat upright. "You asshole. Why are you up so early?"

"I'm hungry. My stomach is screaming at me. Please, put your shoes on, elder brother. It'd be a shame if he got away."

I sighed, exasperated: Luy always called me "elder brother" when he wanted a favor. But I threw on my shoes and jacket and followed him. The forest was covered with a thick fog, and the cold, damp leaves brushed our faces as we walked. I was freezing. We advanced through eerie stands of trees. The shrieks of gibbons echoed in the distance.

"How can you see a monkey in this darkness?" I asked.

Luy laughed. "Chief, you forget that I've got the sharpest eyes in this company. Remember the time I shot those two bucks on the mountain? And the time on Mount Carambola, hunting wild goat? That was my rifle, after all."

I grumbled in acknowledgment.

"Boy, you sure have a short memory!" Luy continued. "It was on Mount Carambola that you first tasted orangutan."

I shuddered. I hadn't forgotten, I just didn't want to remember. But Luy wouldn't let me off so easily. He grinned, squinting at me mischievously: "I do have a good memory, don't I?"

I said nothing and bent down to pull a leech off the rim of my left boot. It was still dark, but I could see blood on the tip of my finger. The blood smell spread through the chill fog, nauseating and sweet like the narcotics used by the Montagnards. Luy had gone on ahead. "The trail is too narrow here. Let me trailblaze. We're going to have a great soup for lunch."

And he was off. The memory of the boiling-hot soup we had eaten at the foot of Mount Carambola came back to me. The soldiers had squatted down in a circle, banging their spoons against their mess tins, their eyes riveted on the steaming pot. Every now and then the cook stirred the clear broth, with its floating grains of puffy cooked rice . . . and tiny orangutan paws . . . like the hands of babies.

"Perfect. It looks perfect."

"Ten minutes more and it'll be ready. It's even more delicious than the famous swallow's-nest soup."

Everyone had congratulated one another. I just stared at the tiny hands spinning in circles on the surface of the soup. We had descended from the apes. The horror of it.

A long time ago, in the markets up north, I had seen some ghastly soups. There was always an immense cauldron perched on three blackened rocks over a searing bed of coals. A muddy gray scum gathered on the soup, pieces of buffalo, pieces of beef, entire livers, spleens, and horse hooves bobbed and floated to the surface.

The soup vendor wore a sooty black smock dripping with grease. His narrow eyes angled toward his temples like blades, his bald head glistened. He fished out huge chunks of the meat with a bamboo spear and placed them on a wooden board, where he hacked them up with a cleaver, the kind that could sever the thickest neck in ancient Annamite executions.

I used to stare furtively at those soups with a mixture of terror and awe. I had been raised in a different culture, in the famished, poverty-stricken Red River Delta. We only ate meat during ceremonies for the dead, or during Tet, the Lunar New Year. In the shadow of these dead souls, we took a little pleasure in existence. The lie extended even to the way the meat was served. We admired those who knew how to make the meat go farther by slicing it into fine strips; we congratulated those who could make rich-looking dishes out of our poor ingredients. To me, this mountain stew was a dish for giants from the depths of the forest, a barbarous dish that reminded me of the ancient legends about the famous inns where highway bandits came to dream to the strains of a Chinese lute.

The horror loomed large in my memory. Just like the horror of the orangutan soup. Orangutans are large apes, and they bear an uncanny resemblance to human beings. Their eyes can laugh maliciously or flare with hate, pain, or bitterness. Most of all, their hands are smooth and white, like the hands of a two-year-old child.

There were some real sharpshooters in my company. We often went hunting, and we always brought back lots of game—bucks, bears, polecats, and grouse. But sometimes we would cross uninhabited regions, places where the bombs had scared off all the animals. For months on end we forgot what meat even tasted like. At the foot of Mount Carambola, we killed two wild goats. Then there had been nothing for a long time. For eight weeks all we ate was rice with a bit of salt, red chilies, and root soup. And so the men had begun to hunt monkey.

On the first day out they killed an orangutan. That time, only the five hunters and the cook had dared to taste the soup. But the next time, the number doubled, and the time after that half the company joined the feast. By and by, everyone took part. The whole troop would go off hunting orangutan. Except me.

Soon they weren't just satisfied with the soup. They concocted other delicacies: a kind of monkey salad, minced-monkey dishes. They showered me with invitations to taste their cooking.

"Chief, if you only knew! After you've tasted it, everything else, the venison, all the wild fowl, seem as bland as snail soup. Orangutans are almost human. There's no tastier flesh."

"Aww, forget your inhibitions, Chief. Just try it once. A bowl of orangutan soup must be more nourishing than four ounces of monkey gelatin!"

We lived in a community. Anyone who stood apart stuck out like a nail that everyone—the cowards and the heroes, the vindictive and the tolerant alike—yearned to pry out. They wanted me to submit to the will of the group, if only to demonstrate its power . . .

That night Luy killed an orangutan that weighed almost forty-five pounds. The cooks minced the lean meat and made it into a salad with chilies, lemongrass, and aromatic herbs they had picked in the forest. They used the bones to make soup. I remember coming up to watch. It was cold outside, and the steam rose off the soup in fragrant, milky clouds.

The soldiers had gathered around the cauldron, their eyes gleaming hungrily. Teu, a private from Tien Hai, tugged at my shirttail: "Will you have a bowl of soup with us, Chief?"

I shook my head.

Teu insisted. "It's delicious, much better than venison."

"I don't feel like eating."

"Oh come on, it's not for lack of appetite, you don't have the guts, right?"

Teu had been stirring the soup with a ladle, and he scooped up a hand: "Like a child's, isn't it? It's scary. But I'm telling you, once you taste it, you'll be addicted."

The other soldiers joined in, jeering at me: "Go on, Chief, be a man. Try it, come on, try it."

"Okay, boys, this time we won't let him off. He has to try our orangutan soup."

My cheeks burned. I took the hand from the ladle and bit into it. I spat out a mouthful of tiny joints and bones.

"Bravo! Bravo, Chief!"

Exultant, they started to bang on their bowls and mess tins. I felt my neck, my back, burning. I glared at them and left the cave. The night was pitch-black. I groped my way to a nearby stream. I washed out my mouth several times, stuffing my fingers down my throat, trying to vomit up the hand. But nothing came up. It was done. I had eaten it; nothing could change that. I shuddered with horror at the thought of it: the taste of human flesh in my mouth. I quickly lit a cigarette. For an instant its flame lit up the darkness. My chest warmed. Curls of smoke lingered, caressing my face. My mind slowly settled.

I was five years old.

Of my childhood, I keep the memory of a distant hill, lush and green. Jack-fruit and longan trees hang over the worm-eaten roof of a pagoda; a broken roof panel sticks up through the leaves. It is evening. At the foot of the hill, a warm light flickers through the cassava vines.

Mother holds my hand as we climb the hill toward the pagoda. She is pregnant, her enormous belly sways under an ao dai dyed the chestnut color of mangrove bark. She clutches her belly, wincing as she walks. Her face is ashen, drenched in sweat.

"Hold the bottom of the sack tightly or the clothes and the blankets will fall out."

"Yes, Mother," I yell back. I yell to mask my fear. I have never seen my mother's face like this. To me she had always been young and beautiful. She used to rock me in a hammock, toss me in the air. Her laughter was like music. Even now she is inseparable from the memory of the cool water we poured from a coconut. She loved me; I adored her. When I wrapped my arms around her neck, nothing could frighten me; not even the shadows, the cries, or the gunshots. But now her face is as white as a drowned person's . . .

Her belly is strange and hideous to me, puffed out like a toad's. As she walks, her back curves oddly. I run behind her, out of breath, sweating.

"Quan, quickly, quickly." She suddenly screams. I am paralyzed. She puts her hand on her thigh and lifts her sweat-drenched face to the heavens. "My god, oh my god."

I see the sweat dripping down her neck.

Mother had come to this strange region after my father went off to join the anti-French resistance movement. She had taken refuge in this pagoda, where a Buddhist nun lived, supported by some distant relatives. My paternal grandparents were dead. My maternal grandparents lived somewhere beyond the horizon, where amber rice paddies were smothered in the smoke of war, where the sky was shattered by gunfire between troops sent by the French colonial puppet government and the Viet Minh. All this I had learned from my mother after she stopped working at the market to wait for the birth of her second child.

Back then, Mother took me in her arms murmuring and caressing me. I watched as her belly filled out. Curious, I used to put my hand over her stomach and draw it back whenever I felt something move. Mother would laugh: "That's your baby brother! You feel him moving? There, he just gave a kick. He's even more restless than you were. When you were here you didn't fidget so much."

I didn't understand. But somehow I knew that this warm, round belly held someone precious to me.

"Careful, Quan. Don't drop the satchel."

"Okay, okay."

Suddenly she collapses on the path, burying her face in the sand. I clutch her splayed thighs, whimpering. The back of her ao dai is drenched in sweat. Her hair sticks to her neck, and she rakes the dirt with her fingers, ripping loose clumps of grass from the path. I am trembling, lost.

"Mother, Mother."

She lets out another howl. "Oh, this is killing me."

I cling to her sweaty back. Suddenly, I don't even know why, I whisper to her in a low voice, "Please, Mother, don't go, don't leave me alone."

Mother raises herself, a haggard light flitted through her eyes. Her lips twist weakly, as if to smile. "My child."

Her voice is just a whisper. A smile flits across her contorted face. She lowers her head and crawls again toward the summit. I follow her, hugging the sack of clothes.

I don't remember how we got past the three doors that led inside the pagoda. I only remember the steps. Those high stones. So slippery.

The nun leads us to an abandoned shack at the back of the garden. The stone steps are covered with weeds and brush. Dust has gathered on the floor of the house, the window ledges, even the wooden altar to the ancestors. It hangs in huge spiderwebs, like in legends filled with monsters.

Mother lies down on an old mat covered with banana leaves and rags. Blood gushes from between her thighs, scarlet as the blood of the buffalo we sacrificed on festival days. I hear a child's cry. I see little hands, and then, kicking at the air, little reddened feet.

The nun's voice booms in my ears: "Your mother has given you a little brother. Go congratulate her instead of trembling like a little quail."

Another voice rings out. "Praise Buddha, isn't he cute! Don't scare him. Come here, child, come see your little brother."

141

She shoves a tiny red being under my nose. Its face, sticky and puckered, as wrinkled as an old man's, terrifies me. A few hairs stick to its forehead. Its feet kick the air, my face. Mother turns toward me. "Don't be afraid, my son, he's your little brother."

A final ray of sun lights her face; her eyes shine with tenderness. Her face is clear again. I grab the tiny red feet and rub them against my cheeks. "Little brother. Little brother."

The nun and the midwife start to laugh. My mother laughs too. Her teeth sparkle like jade. I always loved my mother's laugh.

I cry out with happiness. "I have a little brother."

My brother also begins to bawl, and I let go of his feet. The midwife places him in a clay basin, and he howls and wiggles, splashing water all around him.

My cigarette was half gone. Just beyond its glowing tip stood a dense stand of trees. A chameleon wriggled out of nowhere, a phosphorescent flash. Once more I felt the nausea, the desire to vomit up the orangutan hand. I took another drag on my cigarette and tried to reason with myself: *It has nothing to do with that . . . nothing to do with . . .*

But again I saw my brother's tiny feet kicking at the air. I watched a curl of smoke vanish, took a last drag on my cigarette, and flicked it into the stream. My mouth had a bitter taste. Something had wandered off beyond the horizon.

"What are you thinking about, elder brother?" I noticed Luy had again started to use that familiar term with me. He jabbed me in the ribs with his elbow.

"Nothing," I said, exasperated.

"So let's talk. We've been wandering like two lost bears. This is scary."

"Why don't you always call me 'elder brother'? Sometimes you call me 'Chief,' other times 'Commander.' "

Luy laughed insolently. "When I need to flatter, my tongue naturally reaches for the words 'Chief' and 'Commander.' "

"So that's it. 'Chief,' 'Commander'—you think those words are enough to get me out of bed, to drag me off hunting somewhere, to make me into your little deputy sharpshooter? You bastard."

"Don't be angry. Anyway, I only trick you when it comes down to little things, don't I? Careful—I'll bet you they've planted mines there in those bushes."

Dawn was breaking. Luy had gotten farther and farther ahead of me. His huge shoulders curved inward like bat's wings; he must have been almost six feet tall. His big body demanded fresh meat. For a long time we had lived on nothing but dried shrimp boiled with a few wild vegetables and lichen we scraped off rocks. Luy's skin was greenish. He would gather up all the grains of rice we had dropped from our bowls while eating. He would wolf down the burned, cindery rice crust on the bottom of the cooking pots.

"Ah, if I could just once eat my fill. A huge pot of sticky rice and a big braised ham hock. Or a big plate of rice noodles with lemon-and-shrimp sauce. Hey, Quan, let's see that box of sugar."

It was always the same story with him. Irritated, I snapped back: "Aren't you ashamed, a man your size? You licked it clean a long time ago."

"Not quite, not all of it . . . The other day I just scraped the surface."

"Well, go get it yourself, then. It's in the pack."

He got out the box of sugar and started to scrape it with a spoon. Then he licked it. Finally, he filled it with stream water, shook it, and drank it in one gulp. It was always like that with Luy. Later he wouldn't know what to do to tame his hunger. And at night he would dream of food he wanted to eat and wake up in a cold sweat, desperate.

An only son, Luy had been very spoiled. His mother had a few rice fields and ran her own small business, so she had a bit of money. Luy could easily down eight or nine bowls of rice at each meal.

"Careful, brother Quan, we're starting downhill."

We clutched tree roots and lowered ourselves down the precipice, which was wider and shallower than the Gorge of Lost Souls. Creeper vines with purple, trumpet-shaped flowers, flecked with velvety black patches, coiled around ancient trees. Inside each flower were stamens like octopus tentacles, swollen with pollen. They were translucent, dotted with gluey yellow beads of moisture that gave off a heavy, cloying perfume, a mixture of marsh weed and blood.

"We're here. Wait for me."

"Listen, just sit awhile and enjoy the view. I'll take care of the rest. That orangutan won't get out of here alive. I've been watching him. He's wandering among the trees at the bottom of that ravine. He must be hungry."

I sat down, hunching my shoulders for warmth. Dawn pierced through the fog, making it shimmer with icy silver shards of light. I followed the course of the stream with my eyes. I could see a cave covered with stunted trees, their dark branches stripped of leaves. Their trunks were thick with gnarled bulges, like deformed bodies. Why would orangutans come here to hunt for food?

The anxiety tree bears small, mushy yellow fruits shaped like canaries. It never bears much fruit, but in autumn it is covered with ash-colored flowers that bloom right through the winter, carpeting the earth with their cindery blossoms and giving off their nauseating, morbid scent. No one has ever succeeded in finding three fruits on an anxiety tree in a single season. The best climbers sometimes gather two. Everyone wants to taste the fruit at least once in their life; not just for its smooth, sugary flavor, but out of curiosity. It tastes good at first, but then a strange, drunken sensation comes over you, the heart suddenly beating faster and then slower in strange, irregular rhythms. People feel faint, sink into bizarre dreams. And all at once you feel the fragility of life, the uncertainty of it all, as you give yourself over to a strange expectancy:

a yearning for death. Could it be that apes, too, came here in search of this rare intoxication, this anxious desire for death?

Luy suddenly appeared on a large rock. He stood up and waved to me. I looked in the direction he had indicated. I saw a shadow in the branches of the anxiety tree. It looked like a bear waddling around, searching for honey. Luy signaled to me not to move. Hunched over, he sprinted forward and melted into a milky pocket of fog. I waited, arms crossed. The shadow lumbered about, moving back and forth among the branches of the tree. It climbed from branch to branch and, at the peak, stood up.

A shot rang out. A scream echoed off the rock face. Shivers shot up my spine, and I jumped as if under the flick of a whip. This was no animal cry; the howl had reverberated across the rock walls, amplified by the mountain's ravines and crevices, piercing through space like a sliver of bamboo through live flesh.

Luy ran toward me, his face white. "Quan, Quan . . ."

I couldn't meet his eyes. I too was trembling. "What's the matter?"

"I don't know. The orangutan, it screamed like a man. I'm so scared . . . Come with me." Luy fell back, lowering the barrel of his rifle. We moved down into the ravine toward the forest. My feet slipped on the clammy rocks. I staggered; I felt the sweat soaking my back.

The fog, still thick in the brush over our heads, was as cool and opaque as marble. I tripped over a root. A moan suddenly pierced the thicket.

"Chief, chief . . ." Luy grabbed me by the arm, and we rushed into the fog. Two emaciated legs stuck out of the underbrush, a pair of ripped old army boots on the feet. One had a sock on, the other was bare. My heart raced and I ran forward, pulling Luy behind me. The wounded man clutched his stomach. Under his arm was a bloodied parachute, the kind we used to drop flares. His abdomen and the front of his pants were soaked in blood. I recognized him: It was Phien, the shiest of all my soldiers. When he saw us, he raised his head. "Brother Luy, you shot me by mistake."

He smiled. His buck teeth glinted at the edge of his trembling lip. He looked up at me, his voice rasping. "Chief, don't punish me . . . I wanted to gather . . . A few parachutes . . . to . . ."

He choked and his neck fell limply to one side. I put my hand on his heart. It had stopped beating. I yanked out one of his hairs and held it under his nostrils. It didn't move. Luy let out a wail and began to weep, his head glued to Phien's chest, his huge body racked with sobs. "Oh no, oh no."

Phien's eyes remained open, indifferent, emptied of their last rays of joy or pain. Barely a minute before, he had looked up at me patiently, imploring me not to punish him. He must have gotten up early to get this far. For whom had he been looking for parachutes? Why had I known nothing about this? I looked down the list of the combatants in my unit. He was at the very end:

Nguyen Van Phien
Age: 19
Native village: Neo, Gia Vien commune, Ninh Binh province
Height: 5 feet

Traits: pockmarked face, prominent teeth
Character: patient, gentle

You could always find Phien in the worst places, doing the dirtiest work. Whether we were in the middle of the jungle or camped outside a village, he was the one who gathered the wood, who hunted for vegetables. Phien collected cinders, unblocked sewers, even cleaned the camp. The fast-talking young recruits liked to compete with one another over the pretty village girls. And when something went wrong, they sent Phien to make peace. He was a born martyr. No one who had set eyes on him would ever think of doing him any harm.

After our unit had set up camp, Phien would wander around with a two-stringed guitar. Whenever he had a free moment, he would settle under a tree and pluck a few tunes:

Oh, I'm climbing on Mount Quan Doc,
I'm sitting at the foot of the banyan tree . . .

Luy was still sobbing, doubled over. I shouted at him to get up. He looked at me, distraught, his face smeared with blood and tears. Suddenly I was overcome by fury: "What use is crying? They're going to court-martial you and put a bullet through your head."

Luy sat motionless. A blood-red tear fell onto his shirt collar.

"Wipe your face. Even if you do end up in court, I won't have to go looking like this."

Luy fumbled in his pants pocket and pulled out a crumpled swatch of dirty parachute cloth. He smoothed it out and wiped his face mechanically.

"So, what are you going to do?"

He stayed mute.

"No matter what, you'll end up in front of a firing squad. Maybe I should just put a bullet through your head right here."

He nodded and got up. He walked over until he stood face to face with me. "Shoot me. Go ahead, shoot me, elder brother. It's going to end like that anyway."

Luy closed his eyes. I looked over at Phien's corpse and then back at Luy. What a bitch, this life: The survivor had closed his eyes, waiting for a bullet, while the dead man stared wide-eyed into space.

"Go ahead, shoot. It'll be easier that way."

Luy's eyes were still firmly shut. It was now light out and I could see his face clearly. Wrinkles creased the skin on his cheeks and around his eyelids. It was the face of an old man. How could this bastard have aged so quickly? Perhaps I too had aged. After all, you never see your own face. I didn't allow myself to brood on these thoughts. I didn't have time. My arms and body went limp.

"Open your eyes," I said.

He opened them and stared at me.

"Do you really believe that I could turn my gun on you?"

145

He didn't respond. A green reflection of trees flitted across the surface of his eyes.

"Do you really believe that, you bastard?"

His eyes brimmed with tears; they rolled down his cheeks.

"Only the two of us know about this. Nobody meant this to happen. No one could have seen it coming. Now it's happened and we can't do anything about it. What good would it do to shoot you or throw you in prison for life? And then there's your mother."

Luy heaved a sob. His mother was a widow who lived and breathed for him. If he were to die in combat, she would waste away. If he were convicted, she would hang herself or jump in a river.

I had met her once, on the day of our mobilization. Back then Luy had the rosy cheeks of a young girl. He had walked awkwardly behind a huge woman whose body swam in an ao dai the yellowy color of chicken fat. This was his mother, his guardian angel, his slave, his best friend. An ugly, lonely, elephantine woman. Luy was her only pride, her sole reason for living. I turned back to him now, impatient: "Well?"

Luy was still sobbing. I exploded. "Shut up! I can just see it now: You die and your mother goes and commits suicide. No, I don't want to hear a word about this incident. We're going back to camp. Act as if nothing happened. At noon, before lunch, I'll ask Khiem to call roll. Then we'll make investigations. They'll find Phien just like we found those girls in the Gorge of Lost Souls. Understand?"

"I understand," Luy said, whimpering, "but you'd better just shoot me. How can I go on living after this?"

I grabbed him by the shoulders and shook him hard: "Get a grip on yourself. If this gets out, we'll both be in trouble. What good would that do? We're not traitors. We didn't intend to kill him. You're not the only one I'm making up this little fable for. Do you think I care if they pump you with lead? That's the easy way out. But there's your mother to think of. You understand? I'm doing this for her, not for you. Shut up and stop sniveling. And wipe your face. You look like a ghost."

At noon I asked Khiem to call roll. Everyone was whispering:

"Where has Phien gone to?"

"He's deserted, of course. I'd bet on that."

"That chicken? Impossible."

"Why not? It's always people like that who create scandals."

In Phien's pack they found a large parachute cloth and eight smaller ones from artillery flares. That evening, while Khiem sent out patrols to search for Phien, I was urgently summoned to division headquarters. Luy accompanied me part of the way. The liaison officer had gone off into the bushes to urinate. I asked Luy: "Why did Phien collect all those parachutes? It's crazy."

"Everyone collects parachutes. To make scarves, or just as souvenirs. He thought he could trade them later for real fabric. In his village, a scarf made out of parachute cloth is fashionable."

"How do you know?"

146

"He told me. He often talked about it, how after the war we wouldn't know how to make a living. So he thought we could trade the parachutes for fabric and make ourselves some clothes. You didn't know, but he was very poor. His parents died and left him with a two-year-old sister to raise. They made a living tending ducks, stealing a bit of paddy rice here and there, fishing in the rice paddies. He adored his sister."

Luy hiccuped.

"The liaison officer is coming back—shut up. If anyone hears about this, they'll shoot me first, you understand?"

Luy fell silent, then left. I followed the liaison officer to division headquarters.

The Geek Ascension

Jon Katz

Jon Katz started his career writing for The New York Times, The Wall Street Journal, Rolling Stone, *and* Wired. *He was a two-time finalist for the National Magazine Award and has written twelve books—six novels and six works of nonfiction. He is a contributing editor to public radio's* Marketplace *and to* Bark *magazine. One of Katz's most consuming preoccupations has been "geekness," by which he means the isolation and marginalization of young and talented people with interests in computers and science. His book* Geeks: How Two Lost Boys Rode the Internet Out of Idaho, *whose introduction is reproduced below, gathers together testimonies from many such young people, who have to deal with bullying from classmates. Presently, Katz is writing about technology and its impact on society.*

Where does it begin, this sense of being the Other? It can come early on, when you find yourself alone in your childhood bedroom, raising tropical fish, composing a poem, writing code, meeting friends mostly online, playing by yourself. Or in middle school, when the jocks turn on you and you pray you will get through gym class alive.

Or maybe it comes in high school, where you find yourself on the outside looking in, getting jostled in the halls, watching TV on weekends while everyone else goes to parties.

After some time, there's an accumulation of slights, hurts, realizations: You don't have a lot of friends; other kids avoid you; you're not good at sports or interested in shopping; the teachers seem to like their other students a lot more. There are few school activities you want to be part of, even if you could. The things you like aren't the same things most other people like.

The alienation is sometimes mild, sometimes savage. Sometimes it lasts a few years, sometimes a lifetime. It depends on where you live, who your parents are, whether there's single teacher who appreciates you, whether you can cling to one or two friends, how well you can hide your brains.

Increasingly, your lifeline is technology. Computers and the amazing power they give you—to install a new operating system, to confide in like-minded allies three time zones away, to slay tormentors on the screen even if you can't do much about the ones at school—are your passion. They give you skills and competence, or distraction and escape, or direction and stature, or all of the above.

Eventually, many of the people who call themselves geeks report a coming out, not unlike coming to terms with being gay or lesbian: a moment when you realize and acknowledge who you are and who you're never going to be.

"One day in my sophomore year," a kid named Jason e-mailed me, "I was sitting in the school cafeteria watching the kids at the other tables laugh and have fun, plotting how I was going to get home early and start playing Quake. And I suddenly got it. I was a geek. I was never going to be like them. They were never going to let me in. So I came out as a geek. . . . I can't say life has been a breeze, but after that, it was okay."

Some say they get comfortable with themselves afterward; many never do. But however long it lasts, at some point somewhere, you brush against this outsiderness—among geeks, it's the one common rite of passage. A few carry the scars around with them for good. Sometimes they hurt themselves. Sometimes—rarely—they hurt other people. But if you're lucky, you move past it, perhaps to a college where Others go. You find a community, a place where you're welcome.

For the first time, you're important, vital, on the inside; a citizen of an amazing new nation. You can instantly connect with the others like you. Being smart isn't a liability; it's usually the only thing that matters.

Whether you're a programmer or Web designer or developer, an artist, help-desk geek, or tech supporter, a filmmaker or writer, you're a part of the Geek Ascension. People need you. They hire you. They can't afford to be contemptuous. Life isn't a breeze, but it sure is different. You have an open invitation to what is, at the moment, the greatest party in the world: the Internet and the World Wide Web.

THE RISE OF THE GEEKS

I came face to face with the Geek Ascension at an ugly suburban Chicago cable-TV studio on a bitter winter morning in 1996, toward the end of a contentious tour for my first nonfiction book.

Virtuous Reality was a collection of essays about kids, culture, violence, and morality, a loosely focused defense of screen culture—the Net, the Web, TV, movies—against the politicians, journalists, and academics banging the drums, then and now, about the looming collapse of civilization. It was a position, therefore, that had prompted weeks of media sparring with members of the so-called intelligentsia and representatives of groups that had *decency* in their titles. I was the degenerate, the anti-Christ, a champion of porn and perversion.

The tour was winding down, thankfully, when I arrived for this predawn break-fast show. There was hardly anyone in the building but the anchorman, a handful of cameramen, the control-room techs, a producer, my book-tour escort, and me. Outside, the wind was howling; my fingers, though I was gripping a cup of coffee, were numb.

Watching the monitor in the green room, I saw Brain, the anchor, launch into the by-now-familiar tease of the segment as the inevitably frenetic producer guided me through makeup, prepped me for about ninety seconds, hustled me into the studio.

"Here's an interesting point of view," I heard the anchor say cheerfully just before I walked onto the set. "A former TV producer—and a father—who says the Internet *isn't* a dangerous place for your kids!"

I was wearing out, worn down by weeks of arguing. I was sick of myself, of the blah-blah coming out of my interviewers' mouths and my own. I was even more sick of people like this Parents for Decency flak, on the phone from Washington, D.C., where spokesmen for decency all seem to be.

"Just last week, a nine-year-old girl was lured into a park by some pervert online and raped," she announced in professional alarm. "Is that the kind of thing Mr. Katz wants us to ignore?"

Brian appeared stunned. "That sounds awful," he said, suddenly less friendly. "What about that?"

"Brian," I snapped, "it seems so dumb for us to be sitting here in a TV studio—with all the junk that you people put on the air all day, from soap operas to freeway shootings—and have to actually argue that the Internet isn't a dangerous place. Kids are more likely to have planes fall on their heads than to get hurt on the Net."

Brian and I were both startled to hear the sound of applause coming from some-where in the cavernous studio. Brian flushed, hesitated, then plowed on. Shocked, I looked around. Two cameramen were standing right on the studio floor clapping. So were a handful of techs inside the darkened control room, nodding at me, smiling and waving, giving me the thumbs-up, and yelping, "Yeah!" and "Awright!"

In a past life, I'd been executive producer of *The CBS Morning News*. I knew how CBS management—or I, for that matter—would have reacted to such an out-burst. Blood would have been spilled.

In fact, Brian was livid when we went to a commercial. "The bastards, I can't be-lieve they did that."

"Jeez," I said, still startled but pleased. "How do they get away with that? I would think they'd get fired."

"Are you kidding?" Brian muttered through gritted teeth. "We just built a new dig-italized control room and automated camera system. We're still working out the bugs. How could we fire those guys? Nobody else could possibly run the damn place!"

On the way out, I stopped by the control room. Three kids were sitting at the blinking, beeping, spaceship-like console, beaming at me and high-fiving each other.

They had scraggly longish hair and were wearing T-shirts—one *Star Trek*, one that said HACKERS DO WANT SEX! and one that really caught my attention: GEEK AND PROUD.

I made the rounds, shaking hands, collecting good wishes and slaps on the back like a candidate working the crowd. Nothing remotely like this had happened on any of my previous book tours. I liked it. "Hey thanks," I said, "I appreciate that. I hope you don't get in trouble."

The three of them snorted. "Hey, no sweat," one answered. "We're safe in here, man. There are a hundred pretty-boy anchors they could hire. And they change general managers every other month. But we've been here for two years. We set this control room up. The cameras, graphics, and commercial scripts are fully computerized, all digitalized. We worked up the programs that run the studio. We are the only irreplaceable people in the building. Welcome to the geek kingdom."

During the tour, I'd been filing daily *Virtuous Reality* book tour reports to Hotwired, the website I wrote for. Readers followed my travels, critiqued my press interviews, showed up at book signings, called in to chat on talk shows. So I reported my encounter with the control-room crew in a column headlined "The Rise of the Geeks." The next day, I had hundreds of e-mail messages from people all over the country, proudly claiming the name for themselves.

It was eye-opening. The definition of "geek" no longer had anything to do with biting the heads off chickens. These self-proclaimed geeks invited me to visit their offices, studios, and homes. "We run the systems that run the world," one e-mailed me from New York. "Until recently, most CEOs wouldn't have let us in the door. Now we sit next to the CEOs. We are the only people who know how the place operates, how to retrieve files, how to keep the neural systems running. We are the indispensables."

I'd been inducted, suddenly, into a previously secret society. Wherever I went—Wisconsin Public Radio, CNN, radio stations in L.A. and San Francisco—these mostly young men in T-shirts, more secure and cheerful than almost everybody around them, came up and introduced themselves, patted me on the back, offered to take me out for pizza, warned me about nasty anchors and interviewers. They were all walking billboards for *Star Wars*, various ISPs, *Beavis and Butt-Head*, diverse websites and computer games.

As I learned more, I wrote several additional Hotwired columns about geekhood, and e-mail responses poured in by the metric ton. They flowed in for months. I'm still getting them.

Theirs is an accidental empire. Almost no one foresaw the explosion of the Internet or its mushrooming importance. "The Internet's pace of adoption eclipses all other technologies that preceded it," a U.S. Commerce Department report declared in 1998. "Radio was in existence thirty-eight years before fifty million people tuned in; TV took thirteen years to reach that benchmark. Sixteen years after the first PC [personal computer] kit came out, fifty million people were using one. Once it was opened to the general public, the Internet crossed that line in four years." Although most Americans had never even heard the term a generation ago, the United States will have

151

more than 133 million Net users this year, according to the *Computer Industry Almanac.*

Historians can point to other periods of astonishing technological upheaval—the Renaissance, the Industrial Revolution—but they're hard pressed to find a similar convergence of a particular subculture and an explosive economic boom. Tech industries are growing so quickly that almost anything you publish about them is instantly dated. A finding like the American Electronics Association's 1997 estimate that the U.S. high-tech industry employed 4.3 million workers is inaccurate as this is being written and will be more inaccurate when it's read.

But the sense of limitless prospects for geeks is confirmed by the job market itself. At the beginning of 1998, the Commerce Department reported that about 190,000 U.S. information technology jobs were going begging at any given time, and that close to 100,000 new ones would be created annually for the next decade. The three fastest-growing occupations over the next several years, the Bureau of Labor Statistics added, will be computer scientists (who can work as theorists, researchers, or inventors), computer engineers (who work with the hardware or software of systems design and development, including programming or networking), and systems analysts (who solve specific computer problems, and adapt systems to individual and or corporate needs).

Geeks, then, are literally building the new global economy, constructing and expanding the Internet and the World Wide Web as well as maintaining it. They're paid well for their skills: Starting salaries for college grads with computer degrees average $35,000 to $40,000, says the National Association of Colleges and Employers, but the demand is so intense that many geeks forego or abandon college. Elite geek-incubators like Caltech, Stanford, and MIT complain that some of their best students abandon graduate school for lucrative positions in technology industries. Top-tier recruits not only command high salaries, but the prospect of stock-option wealth before they're thirty.

A society that desperately needs geeks, however, does not have to like them. In fact geeks and their handiwork generate considerable wariness and mistrust. Historians of technology like Langdon Winner have written that throughout history, widespread unease about science and technology has amounted almost to a religious upheaval.

Notice the moral outrage present in so much contemporary media coverage and political criticism of technology. Critics lambaste overdoses of TV-watching, violent video games, and porn on the Net; they warn of online thieves, perverts, vandals, and hatemongers; they call for V-chips, blocking and filtering software, elaborate ratings systems. They even want the Ten Commandments posted, like reassuring sprigs of wolfbane, in public schools.

If we are outraged and frightened by the spread of new technology, how are we supposed to feel about the new techno-elite busily making it all possible? "Why do I get this feeling that they—all of them, politicians, teachers, bosses—hate us more than ever?" e-mailed Rocket Roger in the week after the Columbine High School tragedy.

Not surprisingly, geeks can harbor a xenophobic streak of their own. Geeks often see the workplace, and the world, as split into two camps—those who get it and those who don't. The latter are usually derided as clueless "suits," irritating obstacles to efficiency and technological progress. "We make the systems that the suits screw up," is how one geek described this conflict.

The suits, in turn, view geeks as antisocial, unpredictable, and difficult, though they need them too badly to do much about it. They resent the way geeks' strong bargaining power exempts them from having to mainstream, to "grow up," the way previous generations did when they entered the workforce.

Why shouldn't they have autonomy and power? geeks respond; they can be unnervingly arrogant. Geeks know a lot of things most people don't know and can do things most people are only beginning to understand.

Until now, nerds and geeks (and their more conventional predecessors, the engineers), marginalized as unglamorous, have never had great status or influence. But the Internet is the hottest and hippest place in American culture, and the whole notion of outsiderness has been up-ended in a world where geeks are uniquely—and often solely—qualified to operate the most complex and vital systems, and where the demand for their work will greatly exceed their ability to fulfill it for years to come.

For the first time ever, it's a great time to be a geek.

DEFINING GEEKHOOD

What, exactly, is a geek?

After years of trying to grapple with the question, I still find it largely unanswerable. Continually meeting and corresponding with geeks has made my idea broader than the stereotype of the asocial, techno-obsessed loner.

For one thing, you can hardly be a geek all by yourself. The online world is one giant community comprised of hundreds of thousands of smaller ones, all involving connections to other people. The geekiest hangouts on the Net and Web—the open source and free software movement sites—are vast, hivelike communities of worker geeks patching together cheap and efficient new software that they distribute freely and generously to one another. That's not something loners could or would do.

In fact, the word "geek" is growing so inclusive as to be practically undefinable. I've met skinny and fat geeks, awkward and charming ones, cheerful and grumpy ones—but never a dumb one.

Still, in the narrowest sense, a contemporary geek is a computer-centered obsessive, one of the legions building the infrastructure of the Net and its related programs and systems. Geeks are at its white-hot epicenter.

Beyond them are the brainy, single-minded outsiders drawn to a wide range of creative pursuits—from raves to Japanese animation—who live beyond the contented or constrained mainstream and find passion and joy in what they do. Sometimes they feel like and call themselves geeks.

The truth is, geeks aren't like other people. They've grown up in the freest media environment ever. They talk openly about sex and politics, debate the future of technology, dump on revered leaders, challenge the existence of God, and are viscerally libertarian. They defy government, business, or any other institution to shut down their freewheeling culture.

And how could anyone? Ideas *are* free, literally and figuratively. Geeks download software, movies, and music without charge; they never pay for news or information; they swap and barter. Increasingly, they live in a digital world, one much more compelling than the one that has rejected or marginalized them. Being online has liberated them in stunning ways. Looks don't matter online. Neither does race, the number of degrees one has or doesn't have, or the cadence of speech. Ideas and personalities, presented in their purest sense, have a different dimension.

Geeks know—perhaps better than anyone—that computers aren't a substitute for human contact, for family and friends, for neighborhoods and restaurants and theaters. But cyberspace is a world, albeit a virtual one. Contact and community mean somewhat different things there, but they are real nonetheless.

The roots of the term are important. At the turn of the century, "geek" had a very particular meaning—geeks were the destitute nomads who bit the heads off chickens and rats at circuses and carnivals in exchange for food or a place to sleep.

For nearly seventy years, the term was unambiguously derisive, expanding to label freaks, oddballs, anyone distinctly nonconformist or strange.

But in the 1980s, a number of sometimes outcast or persecuted social groups in America—blacks, gays, women, nerds—began practicing language inversion as a self-defense measure. They adopted the most hateful words used against them as a badge of pride.

Rappers began singing about "niggas" and gay activists started calling themselves "queers." A motorcycle group called Dykes on Bikes roared proudly at the head of gay pride parades. Young women invoked "grrrl" power. The noxious terms became the coolest—a cultural trick that, for their targets, seemed to remove the words' painful sting.

Similarly, as hacker and writer Eric Raymond suggests, in the nineties the word "geek" evoked newer, more positive qualities.

As the Internet began to expand beyond its early cadre of hackers, some like-minded tenants in Santa Cruz, Austin, San Francisco, and Ann Arbor began dubbing their communal homes "geek houses." Formed at a time when the wide-bandwidth phone lines necessary to explore the Net were expensive and rare, these enclaves became techno-communities, sharing sometimes pirated T-1 lines and other requirements. The bright students they attracted used technology not to isolate themselves, as media stereotypes would have it, but to make connections.

The geek houses didn't last long. Faster and cheaper modems, ISDN and T-1 lines and other useful developments for data transmission became ubiquitous, spread to offices and university campuses, and made techno-communities almost instantly obsolete.

But the term kept spreading, picked up by the smart, obsessive, intensely focused people working to build the Internet and the World Wide Web—programmers, gamers, developers, and designers—and by their consumers and allies beyond. Geek chic—blackrimmed glasses, for instance—became a fashion trend. Bill Gates was a corporate geek, a category inconceivable a decade earlier, and no one was laughing. As the Web became culturally trendy, the image of its pale and asocial founders faded. Now it's amusing to see the term "geek" springing up almost everywhere—on TV shows (you know you've arrived when a network launches a primetime series called *Freaks and Geeks*), in advertising, on T-shirts and baseball caps. And appropriated by people who wouldn't have given a real geek the time of day just a few years ago.

People e-mail me all the time asking if they are geeks.

In this culture, I figure people have the right to name themselves; if you feel like a geek, you are one. But there are some clues: You are online a good part of the time. You feel a personal connection with technology, less its mechanics than its applications and consequences. You're a fan of *The Simpsons* and *The Matrix*. You saw *Phantom Menace* opening weekend despite the hype and despite Jar Jar. You are obsessive about pop culture, which is what you talk about with your friends or coworkers every Monday.

You don't like being told what to do, authority being a force you see as not generally on your side. Life began for you when you got out of high school, which, more likely than not, was a profoundly painful experience. You didn't go to the prom, or if you did, you certainly didn't feel comfortable there. Maybe your parents helped you get through, maybe a teacher or a soulmate.

Now, you zone out on your work. You solve problems and puzzles. You love to create things just for the kick of it. Even though you're indispensable to the company that's hired you, it's almost impossible to imagine yourself running it. You may have power of your own now—a family, money—yet you see yourself as one who never quite fits in. In many ways, geekdom is a state of mind, a sense of yourself in relation to the world that's not easily rewritten.

Domestic Gulags

Laura Kipnis

Laura Kipnis is a videomaker and cultural critic. She holds a BFA from San Francisco Art Institute and a MFA from Nova Scotia College of Art. She has received grants and fellowships from the Guggenheim Foundation, the Rockefeller Foundation, and the National Endowment for the Arts for both production and media criticism. Her videotapes have been screened and broadcast in the US, Europe, Japan, and Australia. In addition to her two books Bound and Gagged: Pornography and the Politics of Fantasy in America *(Grove, 1996 paperback, Duke, 1999) and* Ecstasy Unlimited: On Sex, Capital, Gender & Aesthetics *(Minnesota, 1993), her essays and reviews have appeared in* Critical Inquiry, Social Text, Wide Angle, The Village Voice, *and* Harper's. *The following excerpt is from her recent book* Against Love. A Polemic *(2003) published by Pantheon Books.*

Adultery is one way of protesting the confines of coupled life; of course there's always murder. (Neither is necessarily proposed as a *solution*.) Given the regularity with which episodes of spousal mayhem hit the newsstands, evidently opting for homicide over the indignities of divorce court or the travails of marriage counseling not infrequently strikes overwrought wives, husbands, lovers, and exes as the only available solution to the frustrating impasses of togetherness and the emotional thickets of relationships. From those early heady heartthrob days (the little gifts, the silly phone calls) to the guns and ammo catalogue, from lover's lane to the state pen, from the optimism of two souls merging to the impossibility of basic communication: "intimate violence" is such a regular occurrence that it merits its own statistical category in the Bureau of Justice annual compilation of crime figures, which helpfully sub-categorizes such forms of intimacy into "lethal" and "non-lethal" varieties.

No doubt we'd all prefer to think that such grisly fates always befall someone else. But logically speaking, *someone* must eventually play the unlucky role of "someone else." Will it be you? Will it be me? Is it just possible that at this very moment something we've said or done, inadvertently—or maybe not (if there's one thing every partner knows it's just how to push the other person's buttons)—is driving our secretly unhinged mates to contemplate putting our bodies through a wood chipper, or stabbing us and the kids and blaming it on hippie marauders, or haplessly trying to outsource the job to FBI agents impersonating killers-for-hire? All true stories of Love Gone Wrong and Good Spouses Gone Bad—terribly bad. (Remember, they always appear normal right up until they snap, just ask the neighbors. "*He was always out in front washing the car. I never thought anything about it, but you know, now it seems kind of suspicious.*")

Indeed, what would fill true crime's allotted bookstore shelves if not for all the inventively murderous mates in our midst? Would true crime even exist as a genre if not for the evident cultural fascination with every last lurid detail of lethal love? Celebrity murders or those among the society set never fail to captivate and are, needless to say, headline staples—all the better if they contain some kinky elements, or at least improbable alibis. Recent example: the washed-up television actor charged with hiring his bodyguard to shoot his wife in the parking lot of a Studio City restaurant where they had just dined, the actor having momentarily dashed back into the restaurant to retrieve the handgun he said he'd left there. (Handgun? Couldn't it have been . . . a wallet?) Non-celeb and local stories provide their own appeals, like the opportunity for artful headlines. "Man's Stabbed; Wife's Nabbed"—a nice bit of headline poetry from the *New York Daily News*. Of the numerous non-celeb spousal killings, it's interesting to note which stories get picked up by the wire services, elevated from the local crime beat to national attention; these tend to be the ones with an ironic twist or quirky cast of characters, sometimes so resembling stand-up punch lines—"Kill my wife, please"—or shaggy dog stories, so full of guilty amusement that you have to remind yourself that someone actually died. (Spouse murder often seems to have an unaccountably jokey aspect to it, assuming it's not someone you know.) In Irving, Texas, a 530-pound woman deliberately killed her husband by sitting on him during an argument. In Washington, D.C., a best-selling romance writer was murdered by her lawyer-husband. (Who could read this without wondering if he was tall, dark, and handsome?) In New York, a rabbi was convicted of hiring a member of his own congregation to kill his wife; it was the killer rather than the spiritual leader who was overcome by conscience and confessed.

"Non-lethal intimate violence" also provides macabre fascinations. You have your mutilations—a usually submissive Virginia wife takes butcher knife in hand to sever hubby from a favorite body part. Your disfigurements—a bereft Queens boyfriend pays three men to throw lye in his girlfriend's face when she tries to break it off with him. (She, left scarred and partially blinded by the attack, agreed for reasons known best to herself to marry him after he emerged from prison fourteen years later; then stood by him when he was accused, some thirty-five years later at age seventy, of threatening to kill his forty-two-year-old mistress, who had recently ended their five-year affair.) Your attempted poisonings—this a method typically favored by wives, featuring antifreeze, weed killer, and oleander tea (beware if served: highly lethal). Even your poignant moments—this one courtesy of the *Ottawa Citizen:* "Man Says Hatchet Attack No Reason For Divorce." ("I still love her, I don't care. If she gets crazy and cuts my head off, I still love her. I'd take her back.") Your eviscerations—a certain former New York mayor announces his plans to divorce his wife, to the press corps prior to actually informing the wife herself. Unfortunately, the Justice Department does not compile statistics on emotional violence or subcriminal forms of non-lethal intimate behavior: verbal abuse, or public undermining, or emotional blackmail, or everyday manipulations (often involving children), or all the other varieties of less-than-stellar couple conduct in our midst.

Should love come packaged with health advisories: Caution, May Be Addictive As Well As Harmful to Your Ongoing Survival? (Or to your dignity or self-worth?) Should coupling be categorized as a high-risk activity if it regularly leads habitués to such extremes of antisocial behavior and creative acts of mayhem? Or if it increases the likelihood of you becoming their object? Sometimes there's no getting out clean either: uncoupling too can prove dangerous. Recall the famous Scarsdale diet doctor shot to death by his diet-pill-addled headmistress-girlfriend after he took up with his nurse; the San Diego society matron who murdered her ex and his new young bride in their sleep; a certain notorious ex-football hero turned movie star, turned acquitted murderer.

Cultural explanations for the pervasiveness of mate-brutalizing and aggression tend to have an inherently non-explanatory quality to them. The bad apple theory gets the most play, but the problem is that we're clearly talking about bushels, not a few stray worms. Those in quest of better reasons may turn to psychological explanations about the proximity of love and hate, or eros and aggression; some find feminist analyses about sanctioned male violence to women useful (except that even if women are typically the victims of intimate violence, men are not entirely immune: in 1998 some 160,000 men were reported victims of violent assault by an intimate partner). But consider another explanation: perhaps these social pathologies and aberrations of love are the necessary fallout from the social conventions of love that we all adhere to and live out on a daily basis. The more cynical version of this position would be that something about love is inherently impossible; the more optimistic one would be that just the conventions are inherently impossible. Nevertheless, recall that Freud did derive the general workings of the psyche from studying hysterics and neurotics; perhaps we too will come to understand more about the normal conditions of love through our inquiries into love gone wrong.

Let's begin with the fact that falling in love, in the current intimacy regime, doesn't just mean committing to another person, it means committing to certain emotional bargains and trade-offs also, some of which prove more workable than others. It's generally understood that falling in love means committing to *commitment*. This might seem obvious, but actually it isn't. Different social norms could entail something entirely different: yearly renewable contracts, for example. And if we weren't so emotionally yoked to the social forms we've inherited that trying to envision different ways of having a love life seems intellectually impossible and even absurd, who knows what other options might present themselves?

Despite our paeans to commitment, clearly it proves not an entirely salutary experience across the board. Take the pervasiveness of intimate violence. The problem here is hardly lack of commitment; this is commitment in overdrive: being less committed might mean being able to walk away. But these emotional bargains of ours do prove obdurate, and few of us manage to uncommit, when this proves necessary, without leaving big bloody clumps of self behind. Because in the current emotional regime, as we know, falling in love also commits us to *merging*. Meaning that unmerging, when this proves necessary, is ego-shattering and generally traumatic. The fear and pain of losing love is so crushing that most of us will do anything to prevent it, especially when it's not our choice. And since forestalling trauma is what egos are designed to do, with anxiety as an advance warning system (unfortunately a largely ineffective one), this will mean that falling in love also commits us to anxiety—typically externalized in charming behaviors like jealousy, insecurity, control issues (the list goes on)—or, in some cases, to externalized violence—the response of a system in emotional overload. The ego experiencing intimations of impending loss—real or imagined—is not a pretty sight.

Perhaps the problem begins, as Freud and followers have variously implied, with the gloomy fact that adult love doesn't ever completely quell that constitutional human sense of lack and separation trauma that sets its quest in motion. Anxiety is not just endemic to the enterprise, it's also incurable: however assiduously we devote ourselves to love's pursuit and conquest, the fretful specter of loss permeates the scene. Nevertheless, there we are, chasing tantalizing glimpses of some lost imaginary wholeness in a lover's adoring gaze, or in the "types" that we favor, or in the romantic scenarios we reenact or repeat. There we are, hoping that the flimsy social safety nets we've committed ourselves to—monogamy, domesticity, maturity—resolve our anxieties; that "security" or "commitment" (or children, or real estate) are functional salves, even if the fetid quantities of apprehension pooled just beneath the floorboards bode a different story.

From George Cukor's *The Marrying Kind:*
Divorce court judge: Just what did you want out of marriage?
Florence: What I didn't get.

A society's lexicon of romantic pathologies invariably expresses its particular anxieties. High on our own list would be diagnoses like "immaturity," or "inability to settle down," leveled at those who stray from our domestic-couple norms, either by refusing entry in the first place, or pursuing various escape routes once installed: excess independence, ambivalence, "straying," divorce. For us modern lovers, *maturity* is not a depressing badge of early senescence and impending decrepitude; for us maturity is a sterling achievement, a sign of your worth as a person and your qualifications to love and be loved. (Though isn't this "maturity" business a bit of an anti-aphrodisiac in itself?—won't those geriatric years hobble along soon enough? Note that the American Association of Retired Persons calls its monthly publication *Modern Maturity*—just one more incentive to aspire to this enviable state. Never too early to make a down payment on those matching cemetery plots!) Clearly the injunction to achieve "maturity"—loose translation: 30-year mortgages, spreading waistlines, and shrunken libidos—finds its raison d'être in modern love's supreme anxiety, that structuring contradiction about the size of the San Andreas fault, upon which, unfortunately, the entirety of our emotional well-being rests, namely the expectation that romance and sexual attraction will persist throughout a lifetime of coupled togetherness, despite much hard evidence to the contrary.

Ever optimistic, heady with love's utopianism, most of us eventually pledge ourselves to unions that will, if successful, far outlast the desire that impelled them into being. The prevailing cultural wisdom is that even if sexual desire tends to be a short-lived phenomenon, nevertheless, that wonderful elixir "mature love" will kick in just in time to save the day, once desire flags. The question remaining unaddressed is whether cutting off other possibilities of romance and sexual attraction while there's still some dim chance of attaining them in favor of the more muted pleasures of "mature love" isn't similar to voluntarily amputating a healthy limb: a lot of anesthesia is required and the phantom pain never entirely abates. But if it behooves a society to convince its citizenry that wanting change means personal failure, starting over is shameful, or wanting more satisfaction than you have is illegitimate, clearly grisly acts of self-mutilation will be required.

Note that there hasn't always been quite such optimism about love's longevity, nor was the supposed fate of social stability tied to making it last beyond its given duration. For the Greeks, love was a disordering and thus preferably brief experience; the goal of marriage an orderly and well-managed household, not a path toward salvation or self-realization.

In the reign of courtly love, love was illicit and usually fatal. Passion meant suffering; the happy ending didn't yet exist in the cultural imagination. As for togetherness as an eternal ideal, the twelfth-century advice manual *De Amore et Amoris Remedio* (Treatise on Love and its Remedies) warned that too many opportunities to see or chat with the beloved would certainly decrease love. The innovation of happy love didn't even enter the vocabulary of romance until the seventeenth century; before the eighteenth century—when the family was primarily an economic unit instead of a hothouse of unmet needs—marriages were business alliances arranged between families and participants had little to say in the matter. (Passion was what you had *outside* marriage.) Wives were a form of property; wifely adultery was a breach of male property rights, and worse, it mucked up the orderly transmission of property via inheritance. It was only with the rise of the bourgeoisie—whose social power was no longer based on landholdings and inherited wealth—that marriages based on love rather than family alliances became the accepted practice. In other words, love matches became socially accepted once they no longer posed an economic threat to the class in power.

There are different ways to tell the story, and the historians all disagree, but it's evident from all accounts that our amatory predecessors didn't share our particular aspirations about their romantic lives—at least they didn't devote themselves to trying to sustain a fleeting experience past its shelf life or transform it into the basis of a long-term relationship. There may have been romantic torment, and the occasional intrepid romantic forerunner often paid the price—Heloise's lover, Peter Abelard: "They cut off those parts of my body with which I had committed the offense they deplored"—but the emphasis on love as a uniquely individual experience presupposes the existence of the modern individual. This is the one that comes equipped with specifically modern qualities like self-reflexiveness and psychological interiority: each one of us an embattled and unique personality, searching moors and countryside for that one beloved counterpart who will meet our unique psychological needs—conceptions of the self that, according to most historians, had little currency much before the late seventeenth century. In fact, a number of historians consider our version of romantic love a learned behavior that became fashionable only in the late eighteenth century, along with the new fashion for novel reading—the novel itself being a then-recent cultural form, invented precisely to explore all the hidden crevices of this newly burgeoning individuality. Other new cultural genres—autobiography, in particular—would figure here too. (Even archconservative Allan Bloom blames it all on Rousseau, who saw bourgeois love as a salve for the empty emotional center of restrained, law-bound societies and so elevated romance into a soul-saving experience.)

Fond as we are of projecting our own emotional quandaries backward through history, construing vivid costume dramas featuring medieval peasants or biblical courtesans tormented by our own longings and convoluted desires, sharing their feelings and dissecting their motives with the post-Freudian savvy of lifelong analysands, at least consider the fundamental social differences that provided the texture of premodern personal life: for instance, the near total absence of privacy prior to the eighteenth century (historian Phillipe Ariès: "Until the end of the seventeenth century, nobody was ever left alone"), or the complete legal subordination of women to men. Then there's sex. As literary scholar Ruth Perry points out, another eighteenth century innovation was sexual disgust: when Charlotte Lucas marries the repellent Mr. Collins in *Pride and Prejudice* in a "pragmatic match" and talks it over afterward with her girlfriends, there's no hint that sharing the bed of an odious man might cause a girl feelings of disgust. The point is that sex didn't have the same psychological resonance as it does for the contemporary psyche: physical revulsion at sex with the wrong person was a learned and socially instituted response. More than that, it was an effective social management tool, since once internalized it institutes the psychology of monogamy as a self-enforced system. As Perry puts it: "If women were to stay put as the sexual property of one man and one man only, they had to be trained to feel repugnance for physical relations with anyone else"—which also suggests that the psychology of sex is more of a historical contingency than we're often inclined to consider.

But it may be that other things have changed less than we like to imagine. However much the decline of arranged marriages is held up in this part of the globe as a sign of progress and enlightenment (including, lately, as propaganda for modernity when seeking to score political points against Islam), however much it flatters our illusions of independence to imagine that we get to love whomever and however we please, this story starts to unravel if you look too closely. Economic rationality was hardly eliminated when individuals began choosing their own mates instead of leaving the job to parents; it plays as much of a role as ever. Despite all the putative freedom, the majority of us select partners remarkably similar to ourselves—economically, and in social standing, education, and race. That is, we choose "appropriate" mates, and we precisely calculate their assets, with each party gauging just how well they can do on the open market, knowing exactly their own exchange value and that of prospective partners. (Exchange value includes your looks, of course. Look closely at newspaper engagement announcement photos—as social psychologists have in fact done and reported upon—and you will note that virtually every couple is quite precisely matched for degree of physical attractiveness.) Scratch the romantic veneer, and we're hard-nosed realists armed with pocket calculators, calipers, and magnifying glasses. The real transformation of modern love, as sociologist Eva Illouz points out, comes with the fact that ranking mates for material and social assets is now incorporated into the psychology of love and unconscious structures of desire, with individuals having now internalized the economic rationality once exerted by parents, thus "freely" falling in love with mates who are also—coincidentally—good investments. (Marrying down really isn't the norm, though certain assets are fungible categories—as we know, rich ugly men not infrequently nab beautiful women and vice versa.) Nevertheless, economic rationality in mate selection is now largely tacit in mainstream speech codes rather than the open matter it once was, and to ensure that it stays tacit we've devised a useful vocabulary of paralogical terms like "chemistry" and "clicking," as more descriptive terms like "economic self-interest" aren't considered polite. We do retain slightly dusty terms like "gold digger" or "fortune hunter" for those who jump rank or aren't subtle enough about their economic motives for current sensitivities. Terms like "good provider" or "security" may occasionally be invoked favorably in middle class culture, though their usage is strictly governed; discussing economic rationality in too much detail tends to be regarded as either déclassé or cold: it violates implicit personhood norms. (Speech codes may vary in different class strata or ethnic groups, but every social group has its codes and you breach them at the risk of exclusion.)

In other words, despite all the supposed freedom, the social rules governing mate selection are as finicky and precise as they were in Jane Austen's day. The difference is that it's now taboo to acknowledge them, which may amount to less freedom rather than more. What's now constrained isn't mate choice alone, it's any Austenesque acuity about the process. Falling in love itself is subject to the same bans on cognition: social protocols dictate that it be regarded as an elusive and slightly irrational procedure. Too much rationality or thinking risks killing the romance— and of course risks defying prevailing conceptions of the normal human: reptilian analogies like "cold-blooded" tend to be deployed against anyone displaying too much cognition where mooniness should prevail. But since falling in love *is* such a pleasure, and who wouldn't want to, clearly the only thing to do is to think as little as possible and hope for the best.

What Does It Mean to Be Well-Educated?

Alfie Kohn

Educated at Brown University and the University of Chicago, Alfie Kohn has written many articles and books on education and particularly about the effect of tests and exams on the minds and attitudes of students. His books include Punished by Rewards *(1993)*, No Contest: The Case against Competition *(1986)*, The Schools Our Children Deserve: Moving Beyond Traditional Classrooms and "Tougher Standards" *(1999), and* The Case against Standardized Testing *(2000)*. *His most recent books, published in the spring of 2004, are* What Does It Mean to Be Well Educated? *and* More Essays on Standards, Grading, and Other Follies. *In addition to writing books and articles, Kohn has appeared on TV and has lectured at many universities. His criticism of competition and rewards has helped shape the thinking of educators—as well as parents and managers—in this country and abroad.*

No one should offer pronouncements about what it means to be well-educated without meeting my wife. When I met Alisa, she was at Harvard, putting the finishing touches on her doctoral dissertation in anthropology. A year later, having spent her entire life in school, she decided to do the only logical thing . . . and apply to medical school. Today she is a practicing physician—and an excellent one at that, judging by feedback from her patients and colleagues.

She will, however, freeze up if you ask her what eight times seven is because she never learned the multiplication table. And forget about grammar ("Me and him went

Reprinted from *Principal Leadership*, (March 2003), by permission of the author. Copyright © 2003 by Alfie Kohn.

over her house today" is fairly typical) or literature ("Who's Faulkner?"). After a dozen years, I continue to be impressed on a regular basis by the agility of her mind as well as by how much she doesn't know. (I'm also bowled over by what a wonderful person she is, but that's beside the point.)

So what do you make of this paradox with whom I live? Is she a walking indictment of the system that let her get so far—29 years of schooling, not counting medical residency—without acquiring the basics of English and math? Or does she offer an invitation to rethink what it means to be well-educated because what she lacks hasn't prevented her from being a deep-thinking, high-functioning, multiply credentialed, professionally successful individual?

Of course, if those features describe what it means to be well-educated, then there is no dilemma to be resolved. She fits the bill. The problem arises only if your definition includes a list of facts and skills that one must have but that she lacks. In that case, however, my wife is not alone. Thanks to the Internet, which allows writers and researchers to circulate rough drafts of their manuscripts, I've come to realize just how many truly brilliant people cannot spell or punctuate. Their insights and discoveries may be changing the shape of their respective fields, but they can't use an apostrophe correctly to save their lives.

Or what about me (he suddenly inquired, relinquishing his comfortable perch from which issue all those judgments of other people)? I could embarrass myself pretty quickly by listing the number of classic works of literature I've never read. And I can multiply reasonably well, but everything mathematical I was taught after first-year algebra (and even some of that) is completely gone. How well-educated am I?

The issue is sufficiently complex that questions are easier to formulate than answers. So let's at least be sure we're asking the right questions and framing them well.

1. The Point of Schooling

Rather than attempting to define what it means to be well-educated, should we instead be asking about the *purposes of education?* The latter formulation invites us to look beyond academic goals. For example, Nel Noddings, professor emerita at Stanford University, urges us to reject "the deadly notion that the schools' first priority should be intellectual development" and contends that "the main aim of education should be to produce competent, caring, loving, and lovable people" (Noddings, 1992, pp. 17, 174).

Alternatively, we might wade into the dispute between those who see education as a means to creating or sustaining a democratic society and those who believe its primary role is economic, amounting to an investment in future workers and, ultimately, corporate profits. In short, perhaps the question "How do we know if education has been successful?" shouldn't be posed until we have asked what it's supposed to be successful *at*.

2. Evaluating People Versus Their Education

Does the phrase *well-educated* refer to a quality of the schooling you received or to something about you? Does it denote what you were taught or what you learned (and remember)? If the term applies to what you now know and can do, you could be poorly educated despite having received a top-notch education. However, if the term refers to the quality of your schooling, then we'd have to conclude that a lot of "well-educated" people sat through lessons that barely registered or at least are hazy to the point of irrelevance a few years later.

3. An Absence of Consensus

Is it even possible to agree on *a single definition* of what every high school student should know or be able to do to be considered well-educated? Is such a definition expected to remain constant across cultures (with a single standard for the United States and Somalia, for example) or even across subcultures (South-Central Los Angeles and Scarsdale [NY]; a Louisiana fishing community, the Upper East Side of Manhattan, and Pennsylvania Dutch country)? How about across historical eras: Would anyone seriously argue that our criteria for being well-educated today are exactly the same as those used a century ago—or that they should be?

To cast a skeptical eye on such claims is not necessarily to suggest that the term is purely relativistic: You like vanilla; I like chocolate. You favor knowledge about poetry; I prefer familiarity with the Gettysburg Address. Some criteria are more defensible than others. Nevertheless, we have to acknowledge a striking absence of consensus about what the term ought to mean. Further, any consensus that does develop is ineluctably rooted in time and place. It is misleading and even dangerous to justify our own pedagogical values by pretending they are grounded in some objective, transcendent Truth, as though the quality of being well-educated is a Platonic form waiting to be discovered.

4. Some Poor Definitions

Should we instead try to stipulate which answers *don't* make sense? I'd argue that certain attributes are either insufficient (possessing them isn't enough to make one well-educated) or unnecessary (one can be well-educated without possessing them)—or both. Let us therefore consider ruling out:

Seat time. Merely sitting in classrooms for x hours doesn't make one well-educated.

Job skills. It would be a mistake to reduce schooling to vocational preparation, if only because we can easily imagine graduates who are well-prepared for the workplace (at least for some workplaces) but whom we would not regard as well-educated. In any case, pressure to redesign secondary education to suit the demands of employers reflects little more than the financial interests—and the political power—of these corporations.

Test scores. To a disconcerting extent, high scores on standardized tests signify a facility with taking standardized tests. Most teachers can instantly name students who are talented thinkers but who just don't do well on these exams—as well as students whose scores seem to *over*estimate their intellectual gifts. Researchers have found a statistically significant correlation between high scores on a range of standardized tests and a shallow approach to learning (Anderman, 1992; Hall, Bolen, &

166

Gupton, 1995; Meece, Blumenfeld, & Hoyle, 1988). No single test is so valid, reliable, or meaningful that it can be treated as a marker for academic success.

Memorization of a bunch o' facts. Familiarity with a list of words, names, books, and ideas is a uniquely poor way to judge who is well-educated. As the philosopher Alfred North Whitehead (1967) observed long ago, "A merely well-informed man is the most useless bore on God's earth. . . . Scraps of information" are only worth something if they are put to use or, at least, "thrown into fresh combinations" (p. 1).

Look more carefully at the superficially plausible claim that you must be familiar with, say, *King Lear* to be considered well-educated. To be sure, it's a classic meditation on mortality, greed, belated understanding, and other important themes. But *how* familiar with it must you be? Is it enough that you can name its author or that you know it's a play? Do you have to be able to recite the basic plot? What if you read it once but barely remember it now?

If you don't like that example, pick another one. How much do you have to know about neutrinos or the Boxer Rebellion or the side-angle-side theorem? If deep understanding is required, then (a) very few people could be considered well-educated (which raises serious doubts about the reasonableness of such a definition) and (b) the number of items about which anyone could have that level of knowledge is sharply limited because time is finite. On the other hand, how can we justify a cocktail-party level of familiarity with all these items—reminiscent of Woody Allen's summary of *War and Peace* after taking a speed-reading course: "It's about Russia." What sense does it make to say that one person is well-educated for having a single sentence's worth of knowledge about the Progressive Era or photosynthesis, whereas someone who has to look them up is not?

Knowing a lot of stuff may seem harmless, albeit insufficient, but the problem is that efforts to shape schooling around this goal, dressed up with such pretentious labels as *cultural literacy*, have the effect of taking time away from more meaningful objectives, such as knowing how to think. If the Bunch o' Facts model proves a poor foundation on which to decide who is properly educated, it makes no sense to peel off items from such a list and assign clusters of them to students at each grade level. It is as poor a basis for designing curriculum as it is for judging the success of schooling.

The number of people who do confuse the possession of a storehouse of knowledge with being "smart"—the latter being a disconcertingly common designation for those who fare well on quiz shows—is testament to the naïve appeal that such a model holds. But there are also political implications to be considered here. To emphasize the importance of absorbing a pile of information is to support a larger worldview that sees the primary purpose of education as reproducing our current culture. It is probably not a coincidence that a Core Knowledge model wins rave reviews from Phyllis Schlafly's Eagle Forum and other conservative Christian groups as well as from the likes of *Investor's Business Daily*. To be sure, not every individual who favors this approach is a right-winger, but defining the notion of educational mastery in terms of the number of facts one can recall is well-suited to the task of preserving the status quo. By contrast, consider Dewey's suggestion that an educated person is

167

one who has "gained the power of reflective attention, the power to hold problems, questions, before the mind." Without this capability, he added, "the mind remains at the mercy of custom and external suggestions."

5. Attempting to Mandate a Single Definition

Who gets to decide what it means to be well-educated? Even assuming that you and I agree to include one criterion and exclude another, that doesn't mean our definition should be imposed with the force of law—for example, taking the form of requirements for a high school diploma. There are other considerations, such as the real suffering imposed on individuals who aren't permitted to graduate from high school, the egregious disparities in resources and opportunities available in different neighborhoods, and so on.

More to the point, the fact that so many of us *don't* agree suggests that a national or, better yet, international conversation should continue; that one definition may never fit all; and, therefore, that we should leave it up to local communities to decide who gets to graduate. But that is not what has happened. In about half the states, people sitting atop Mount Olympus have decreed that anyone who doesn't pass a certain standardized test will be denied a diploma and, by implication, classified as inadequately educated. This example of accountability gone haywire violates not only common sense but also the consensus of educational measurement specialists. And the consequences are entirely predictable: no high school graduation for a disproportionate number of students of color, from low-income neighborhoods, with learning disabilities, who attend vocational schools, or who are not yet fluent in English.

Less obviously, the idea of making diplomas contingent on passing an exam answers by default the question of what it means to be well- (or sufficiently) educated: Rather than grappling with the messy issues involved, we simply declare that standardized tests will tell us the answer. This is disturbing not only because of the inherent limits of the tests but also because teaching becomes distorted when passing those tests becomes the paramount goal. Students arguably receive an inferior education when pressure is applied to raise their test scores, which means that high school exit exams may actually *lower* standards.

Beyond proclaiming "Pass this standardized test or you don't graduate," most states now issue long lists of curriculum standards, containing hundreds of facts, skills, and subskills that all students are expected to master at a given grade level for a given subject. These standards are not guidelines but mandates (to which teachers are supposed to "align" their instruction). In effect, a Core Knowledge model, with its implication of students as interchangeable receptacles into which knowledge is poured, has become the law of the land in many places. Surely even defenders of this approach can appreciate the difference between *arguing* on its behalf and requiring that every school adopt it.

6. The Good School

Finally, instead of asking what it means to be well-educated, perhaps we should inquire into the *qualities of a school* likely to offer a good education. As I see it, the best sort of schooling is organized around problems, projects, and questions—as opposed to facts, skills, and disciplines. Knowledge is acquired, of course, but in a context and for a purpose. The emphasis is not only on depth rather than breadth but also on discovering ideas rather than on covering a prescribed curriculum. Teachers are generalists first and specialists (in a given subject matter) second; they commonly collaborate to offer interdisciplinary courses that students play an active role in designing. All of this happens in small, democratic schools that are experienced as caring communities.

Notwithstanding the claims of traditionalists eager to offer—and then dismiss—a touchy-feely caricature of progressive education, a substantial body of evidence exists to support the effectiveness of each of these components as well as the benefits of using them in combination. By contrast, it isn't easy to find *any* data to justify the traditional and still dominant model of secondary education: large schools, short classes, huge student loads for each teacher, a fact-transmission kind of instruction that is the very antithesis of student-centered, the virtual absence of any attempt to integrate diverse areas of study, the rating and ranking of students, and so on. Such a system acts as a powerful *obstacle* to good teaching, and it thwarts the best efforts of many talented educators on a daily basis.

Low-quality instruction can be assessed with low-quality tests, including home-grown quizzes and standardized exams designed to measure with faux objectivity the number of facts and skills students have crammed into their short-term memory. The effects of high-quality instruction are trickier, but not impossible, to assess. The most promising model turns on the notion of "exhibitions" of learning, in which students reveal their understanding by means of in-depth projects, portfolios of assignments, and other demonstrations—a model pioneered by Ted Sizer, Deborah Meier, and others affiliated with the Coalition of Essential Schools. By now we're fortunate to have access not only to essays about how this might be done (such as Sizer's invaluable *Horace* series) but also to books about schools that are actually doing it: *The Power of Their Ideas* by Meier, about Central Park East Secondary School in New York City; *Rethinking High School* by Harvey Daniels and his colleagues, about Best Practice High School in Chicago; and *One Kid at a Time* by Eliot Levine, about the Met in Providence, RI.

The assessments in such schools are based on meaningful standards of excellence, standards that may collectively offer the best answer to our original question simply because to meet those criteria is as good a way as any to show that one is well-educated. The Met School focuses on social reasoning, empirical reasoning, quantitative reasoning, communication, and personal qualities (such as responsibility, capacity for leadership, and self-awareness). Meier has emphasized the importance of developing five habits of mind: the value of raising questions about *evidence* (How do we know what we know?), *point of view* (Whose perspective does this represent?), *connections* (How is this related to that?), *supposition* (How might things have been otherwise?), and *relevance* (Why is this important?).

It's not only the ability to raise and answer those questions that matters, however, but also the disposition to do so. For that matter, any set of intellectual objectives, any description of what it means to think deeply and critically, should be accompanied by a reference to one's interest or intrinsic motivation to do such thinking. Dewey reminded us that the goal of education is more education. To be well-educated, then, is to have the desire as well as the means to ensure that learning never ends.

REFERENCES

Anderman, E. M. (1992). *Motivation and cognitive strategy use in reading and writing*. Paper presented at the National Reading Conference, San Antonio, Tex.

Hall, C. W., Bolen, L. M., & Gupton, R. H., Jr. (1995). Predictive validity of the study process questionnaire for undergraduate students. *College Student Journal 29* 234–239.

Meece, J. L., Blumenfeld, P. C., & Hoyle, R. H., (1988). Students' goal orientations and cognitive engagement in classroom activities. *Journal of Educational Psychology 80*, 514–523.

Noddings, N. (1992). *The challenge to care in schools: An alternative approach to education*. New York: Teachers College Press.

Whitehead, A. N. (1967). *The aims of education and other essays*. New York: Free Press.

A Story in Textbooks

Richard Lewontin

Richard Lewontin has a Ph.D. from Columbia University and is a professor of comparative zoology at Harvard University. He has written extensively about genetics, evolution, and the philosophical and social aspects of human behavior. His books include Biology as Ideology, *from which the chapter "A Story in Textbooks" has been excerpted here,* Not in Our Genes, *and* The Triple Helix: Gene, Organism, and Environment. *His opinions challenge the current views on genetics and expose misconceptions about the new advances in biology. Because of his convictions, soon after he was elected to the National Academy of Sciences, he removed himself in protest.*

The claim that all of human existence is controlled by our DNA is a popular one. It has the effect of legitimizing the structures of society in which we live, because it does not stop with the assertion that the differences in temperament, ability, and physical and mental health between us are coded in our genes. It also claims that the political structures of society—the competitive, entrepreneurial, hierarchical society in which we live and which differentially rewards different temperaments, different cognitive abilities, and different mental attitudes—is also determined by our DNA, and that it is, therefore, unchangeable. For after all, even if we were biologically different from one another, that in itself would not guarantee that society would have given different power and status to people who are different. That is, to make the ideology of biological determinism complete, we have to have a theory of unchangeable human nature, a human nature that is coded in our genes.

Every political philosophy has to begin with a theory of human nature. Surely, if we cannot say what it is to be truly human, we cannot argue for one or another form of social organization. Social revolutionaries, especially, must have a notion of what

Reprinted from *Biology as Ideology: The Doctrine of the DNA*, (1991), HarperCollins Publishers, Inc.

it is to be truly human because the call for revolution is the call for the spilling of blood and a wholesale reorganization of the world. One cannot call for a violent overthrow of what is, without claiming that what will be is more in accord with the true nature of human existence. So, even Karl Marx, whose view of society was an historical one, nevertheless believed that there was a true human nature and that human beings realize themselves in their essence by a planned social manipulation of nature for human welfare.

The problem for political philosophers has always been to try to justify their particular view of human nature. Before the seventeenth century, the appeal was made to divine wisdom. God had made people in a certain way. Indeed, they were made in God's image, although a rather blurred one, and moreover, human beings were basically sinful from the time of Adam and Eve's Fall. But modern secular technological society cannot draw its political claims from divine justification. From the seventeenth century onward, political philosophers have tried to create a picture of human nature based on some sort of appeal to a naturalistic view of the world. Thomas Hobbes in his *Leviathan*, which argued for the necessity of the king, built a picture of human nature from the simplest axioms about the nature of human beings as organisms. To Hobbes, human beings, like other animals, were self-enlarging, self-aggrandizing objects that simply had to grow and occupy the world. But the world was a place of finite resources, and so it necessarily would happen that human beings would come into conflict over those resources as they expanded and the result would be what he called "the war of all against all." The conclusion for Hobbes was that one needed a king to prevent this war from destroying everything.

The claims that organisms, especially human beings, grow without bound and that the world in which they grow is finite and limited are the two basic claims that have given rise to the modern biological theory of human nature. They resurfaced in the Reverend Malthus's treatise on population, in his famous law that organisms grow geometrically in numbers while the resources for their subsistence grow only arithmetically, and so again a struggle for existence must occur. As we all know, Darwin took over this notion of nature to build his theory of natural selection. Since all organisms are engaged in a struggle for existence, those that are better suited by their shape and form, by their physiology, and by their behavior to leave more offspring in that struggle will do so, and the consequence will be that their kind will take over the earth. The Darwinian view is that whatever human nature may be, it, like everything else about humans, who are after all living organisms, has evolved by natural selection. Therefore, what we truly are is the result of two billions years of evolution from the earliest rudimentary organisms to us.

As evolutionary theory has developed over the last one hundred years and become technologically and scientifically sophisticated, as vague notions of inheritance have become converted into a very precise theory of the structure and function of DNA, so the evolutionary view of human nature has developed a modern, scientific-sounding apparatus that makes it seem every bit as unchallengeable as the theories of divine providence seemed in an earlier age. What has happened in effect is that

Thomas Hobbes's war of all against all has been converted into a struggle between DNA molecules for supremacy and dominance over the structures of human life.

The most modern form of naturalistic human nature ideology is called sociobiology. It emerged onto the public scene about 15 years ago and has since become the ruling justifying theory for the permanence of society as we know it. It is an evolutionary and a genetic theory that uses the entire theoretical apparatus of modern evolutionary biology, including a great deal of abstruse mathematics, which is then translated for the inexpert reader in coffee-table books with beguiling pictures and in magazine articles and newspaper accounts. Sociobiology is the latest and most mystified attempt to convince people that human life is pretty much what is has to be and perhaps even ought to be.

The sociobiological theory of human nature is built in three steps. The first is a description of what human nature is like. One looks around at human beings and tries to build a fairly complete description of the features that are said to be common to all human beings in all societies in all places in all times.

The second step is to claim that those characteristics that appear to be universal in humans are, in fact, coded in our genes, that is, in our DNA. There are genes for religiosity, genes for entrepreneurship, genes for whatever characteristics are said to be built into the human psyche and human social organization.

These two claims—that there is a universal human nature and that it is coded in the genes and is unchangeable—would be sufficient as a biological theory of human nature in a purely descriptive sense. That is what we are; take it or leave it. But sociobiological theory, being built on evolutionary theory, goes one step further, as it must to fulfill its program. It must explain, and in some sense justify, how we come to have these particular genes rather than some other genes that might have given us quite a different human nature.

The theory thus goes on to the third step, the claim that natural selection, through the differential survival and reproduction of different kinds of organisms, has led inevitably to the particular genetic characteristics of individual human beings, characteristics that are responsible for the form of society. This claim strengthens the argument of legitimacy because it goes beyond mere description to assert that the human nature described is inevitable, given the universal law of the struggle for existence and the survival of the fittest. In this sense, the sociobiological theory of human nature puts on a mantle of universality and of utter fixity. After all, if 3 billion years of evolution have made us what we are, do we really think that a hundred days of revolution will change us?

Sociobiologists take the first step, the claimed correct description of what is universal in all human beings, more or less as every human nature theorist has done it, by looking around to see what people in their society are like and to some extent by telling their own life stories. Having looked inward at themselves and outward at modern capitalist society for a description of human nature, they then extend it a bit further by looking into the anthropological record in order to assure us that those very same elements that they find in twentieth-century North America and Britain are also, in one form or another, displayed by the Stone Age people of New Guinea. For some reason, they do not look much at the historical record of European society, of which they seem to be quite ignorant, but perhaps they feel that if New Guinea highlanders and Scottish highlanders show the same characteristics today, then there cannot have been much change in 1,500 years of recorded history.

And what are these human universals that sociobiologists find? One can hardly do better than look at the most influential, and in some sense, founding document of sociobiological theory, E.O. Wilson's *Sociobiology: The New Synthesis*.[1] Professor Wilson tells us, for example, that human beings are indoctrinable. He says, "Human beings are absurdly easy to indoctrinate. They seek it."[2] They are characterized by blind faith: "Man would rather believe than know."[3] That statement is, we must note, found in what is called a scientific work, used as a textbook in courses all over the world, filled with the mathematics of modern population biology, crammed with observations and facts about the behavior of all kinds of animals, based on what *Time* magazine has called the "iron laws of nature." But surely, "man would rather believe than know" is more in the line of barroom wisdom, the sort of remark one makes to one's friend at the local after work following a particularly frustrating attempt to persuade the person in the next office that he ought to do things in a different way. Among other aspects of human nature are said to be a universal spite and family chauvinism. We are told that "human beings are keenly aware of their own blood lines and the intelligence to plot intrigue."[4] Xenophobia, the fear of strangers, is part of our universal equipment. "Part of man's problem is that his intergroup responses are still crude and primitive and inadequate for the extending territorial relationship that civilization has thrust upon him."[5] One of the results of this, we are told, is that "the most distinctive human qualities have emerged during the phase of social evolution that occurred through intertribal warfare and through genocide."[6] And then there is the relationship between the sexes. Male dominance and superiority is part of human nature. Wilson writes that "among general social traits in human beings are aggressive dominance systems with males dominant over females."[7] The list is not complete. Nor is this simply the idiosyncratic view of one influential sociobiologist. The claims that human warfare, sexual dominance, love of private property, and hate of strangers are human universals are found over and over in the writings of sociobiologists, whether they be biologists, economists, psychologists, or political scientists.

But to make such claims, one must be quite blind even to the history of European society. Take, for example, the claim of a universal xenophobia. In fact, the attitudes of people toward foreign cultures and other countries have varied tremendously from social class to social class and time to time. Could the aristocracy of Russia in the nineteenth century, which thought all things Slavic to be inferior, which spoke French by preference, which looked to Germany for its military and technological resources, be described as xenophobic? Educated and upper classes in particular have often looked to other cultures for the highest and the best. English-speaking scientists on occasion are interviewed by Italian radio and television, and the answers given to the producer's questions are translated into Italian, which the listeners hear in a voice-over after a few moments of the scientist's English. When the producers are asked why they do not get an Italian scientist to do the program, they say that Italians simply do not believe any claims about science that are made in Italian and that they have to hear it in English if they are to believe it is true.

Nothing better reveals the narrow ahistorical claims of sociobiological description than the standard discussion of the economy of scarcity and unequal distribution. So, Professor Wilson writes that "the members of human societies sometimes cooperate closely in insectan fashion, but more frequently they compete for the limited resources allocated to their role sector. The best and the most entrepreneurial of the role actors usually gain a disproportionate share of the rewards while the least successful are displaced to other less desirable positions."[8] But this description completely ignores the immense amount of sharing of resources that occurs among a whole variety of modern hunting and gathering societies like Eskimos, and it completely distorts the history even of Europe. The concept of entrepreneurship does not work for, say, the thirteenth century in the Île-de-France, an agrarian feudal society in which land could not be bought and sold, in which labor could not be hired and fired, and in which the so-called market mechanism was a rudimentary form of exchange of a few goods. Of course, sociobiologists recognize that there are exceptions to these generalizations, but their claim is that those exceptions are temporary and unnatural, and that they will not persist in the absence of constant force and threat. So, societies may indeed, like blue-clad regimented Chinese, cooperate in so-called insectan fashion. But this can be managed only by constant supervision and force. The moment one relaxes one's vigil, people will revert to their natural ways. It is rather as if we could make a law saying that everyone would have to walk on their knees, which would be physically possible but terribly painful. The moment we relaxed our vigil, everyone would stand upright again.

At the surface of this theory of human nature is the obvious ideological commitment to modern entrepreneurial competitive hierarchical society. Yet underneath is a deeper ideology, and that is the priority of the individual over the collective. Despite the name *socio*biology, we are dealing with a theory not of social causation but of individual causation. The characteristics of society are seen as caused by the individual properties that its members have, and those properties, as we shall see, are said to derive from the members' genes. If human societies engage in war, that is because each individual in the society is aggressive. If men as a group dominate women or whites Blacks, it is because each man as an individual is desirous of dominating each woman and each white person has feelings of personal hostility set off by the sight of Black skin. The structures of society simply reflect these individual predispositions. Society is nothing but the collection of individuals in it, just as culture is seen as nothing but the collection of disarticulated bits and pieces, individual preferences and habits.

Such a view completely confuses, partly by linguistic confusion, very different phenomena. It is obviously not the case that Britain and Germany made war on each other in 1914 because individual Britons and individual Germans felt aggressive. If that were the case, we would not need conscription. Englishmen, Canadians, and Americans killed Germans and vice versa because the state put them in a position that made it inevitable they did so. A refusal to be conscripted meant a jail term and the refusal to obey orders in the field meant death. Great machines of propaganda, martial music, and stories of atrocities are manufactured by the state to convince its citizens that their lives and the chastity of their daughters are at risk in the face of the threat of barbarians. The confusion between individual aggression and national aggression is a confusion between the rush of hormones that may be felt if someone is slapped in the face and a national political agenda to control natural resources, lines of commerce, prices of agricultural goods, and the availability of labor forces that are the origins of warfare. It is important to realize that one does not have to have a particular view of the content of human nature to make this error of individuals causing society. Prince Kropotkin, a famous anarchist, also claimed that there was a universal human nature but one that would create cooperativeness and would be anti-hierarchical if only it were allowed free play.[9] But his theory was no less a theory of the dominance of the individual as the source of the social.

Having described a universal set of human social institutions that are said to be the consequence of individual natures, sociobiological theory then goes on to claim that those individual properties are coded in our genes. There are said to be genes for entrepreneurship, for male dominance, for aggressivity, so conflict between the sexes and parents and offspring is said to be genetically programmed. What is the evidence that these claimed human universals are in fact in the genes? Often, it is simply asserted that because they are universal they must be genetic. A classic example is the discussion of sexual dominance. Professor Wilson has written in *The New York Times*,"In hunter-gatherer societies, men hunt and women stay at home. This strong bias persists in most agricultural and industrial societies [apparently, he has not yet caught up with women in the workforce], and on that ground alone appears to have a genetic origin."[10] This argument confuses the observation with its explanation. If the circularity is not obvious, we might consider the claim that since 99 percent of Finns are Lutherans, they must have a gene for it.

ENDNOTES

[1] E.O. Wilson, *Sociobiology: The New Synthesis* (Cambridge, MA: Harvard University Press, 1975).

[2] Ibid., 562.

[3] Ibid., 561.

[4] Ibid., 119.

[5] Ibid., 556.

[6] Ibid., 575.

[7] Ibid., 552.

[8] Ibid., 554.

[9] P.A. Kropotkin, *Mutual Aid* (1901), Chapter 1.

[10] E. O. Wilson, "Human Decency Is Animal," *New York Times Magazine*, 12 October 1975, 38–50.

The First Snow

Daniel Lyons

Daniel Lyons has an MFA from the University of Michigan. His stories have appeared in Redbook *and* Playboy, *as well as literary magazines. He won first place in 1992 for the Playboy College Fiction contest. His first collection of stories,* The First Snow, *was published by the University of Massachusetts Press and won the 1992 Associated Writing Programs (AWP) Award in short fiction. His story "First Snow" was inspired by an article he read that reported on married men who were arrested for having sex in the woods in southern Michigan. The arrest caused quite a stir in the town. Gay rights advocates protested harassment and some of the men lost their jobs. Lyons imagined the plight of the families involved and immediately sat down to write his story after reading the article.*

The newspaper prints their names, and I admit that makes it worse. There are sixteen of them, and my father, whose name begins with A, is at the top of the list: Henry Abbott.

There was a rest area in Derry, apparently, and a path into the woods, and a giant hollow sycamore in the meeting place where they were arrested. The story in the *Gazette* says New Hampshire state troopers have been watching for weeks, camouflaged. They have videotapes.

The phone calls begin: more words for *fag* than I knew existed. Mom takes a call, listens, and slams down the phone. Her hair is matted to her head, her blouse is wrinkled, her eyes are bloodshot from not sleeping: she looks the way she did the time Jenny's appendix burst and we sat up all night in the hospital waiting room. She unplugs the phone.

Reprinted from *Story*, (winter 1993), by permission of the author.

"Visiting his mother," she says, disgusted. That was the excuse Dad used when he went out yesterday. I'm trying to remember how long he's been visiting Nana on Sundays.

She lights a cigarette and then stubs it out, so hard that it snaps. "Bob, I'm sorry," she tells me, "but I won't live with this."

Dad spent the night in jail. Mom said she couldn't handle the police station, all the smirks and snickers. He was arraigned this morning, and now, six hours later, he's still at his lawyer's office. I imagine this is a first for Mr. Pangione. He's a contract man: wills, taxes, divorces—the last, I think, may be of use when the criminal case is finished. I picture the two of them in their big leather chairs: Mr. Pangione embarrassed and looking down at his desk, my father fidgeting, afraid to go home.

Dad does more than jump into strange cars in rest areas. The big surprise is that he has a steady. All I can gather from the conversation taking place behind the bedroom door upstairs is that the steady is married, and that he too is shocked about Dad's adventures in the woods.

"What, and do you love him? Do you love him? I can't believe I'm asking this! My husband! I'm going to be sick."

Dad starts to cry. I can hear his wet words, but I can't make them out. Oddly, the news of the steady doesn't seem so bad.

Jenny and Nelson are in the family room playing Chutes and Ladders, oblivious. Jenny is seven and Nelson is five—both, I hope, too young to remember this. I, however, am seventeen.

I spread the *Gazette* out on the kitchen table and read the list of names again, wondering which one was the one with my father. What an image: all those men, moving silently in the woods, my father among them.

I fold the paper and put it up on top of the refrigerator, where Jenny and Nelson won't find it. I think about stupid things: Should I still do my homework? Will we have Thanksgiving? What are we doing for dinner tonight?

Mom solves the last one: Kentucky Fried Chicken. We sit, the five of us, at what I suppose will be our own Last Supper. Jenny and Nelson make castles with their mashed potatoes and Mom doesn't scold them; Dad grips the drumstick Mom gave him—at least she's got her sense of humor—and makes fake small talk about school, where he did not teach today; Mom gives him polite fake responses between gulps from her tumbler of gin; I watch for a while, then stare straight into my plate, not wanting to meet any of their eyes.

Later, Mom packs suitcases and duffel bags and moves with Jenny and Nelson to the Driscolls' house. I tell her I'm going to stay at home.

Mom puts the kids in the car, then comes in to ask me once more to come with her. For a moment I am literally standing between them: Mom at the open door, angry; Dad by the fireplace, drumming his fingers on the mantel, looking away. He is a schoolteacher, a man accustomed to dignity, which he is now working hard to maintain.

"Well?" she says.

The fact is, I feel bad for my father. I'm not going to leave him here alone.

"You go on without me," I say.

Just like any other night, Dad sits slack-gutted in his recliner in the family room, watching television. I go in and sit on the couch. The show is NFL highlights.

"Look at that hit," he says. "Jesus Christ."

There is a slow-motion replay: the arms stretching for the pass, the safety spearing in from behind, the tiny moment when there is no motion, then the legs lifting up, the head snapping back like a car crash dummy's, the ball tumbling free.

"Jesus Christ," he says again. He grabs a handful of peanuts from the can, shakes them in his hand like dice, and looks at me. "You going to stay for the game?" he says.

The air in the room feels over pressurized, like in a submarine that has surfaced too quickly.

"I don't know," I say.

"Well," he says, smiling, "I'm glad you decided to stay."

Suddenly I want to reach over and smack him for being so happy; I'd like to wipe that smile off his face.

"I'm glad you're in such a good mood," I say.

He sits up and says, "Bob, look—"

But I turn my back. I mumble something about homework and run upstairs to my room.

I'm on the phone with Drew—yes, everyone knows; some jerk has already started a joke—when another call comes in. It's Mr. Ryan, Dad's principal. I click back to Drew, tell him I've got to go, then call down to Dad.

"Well, I don't need to go to school tomorrow," he says when he arrives upstairs a few minutes later.

He tries to smile, then stands slope-shouldered in my doorway, looking old and paunchy in his cardigan sweater—more like an old fart at the Elks Club than some fairy running around in the woods. "I'm suspended," he says.

In homeroom there are eyes on me. I keep my head down. I write my name, over and over, in a spiral notebook. When Miss Moynihan calls my name there are snickers from the back of the room, but she stares them down. So she knows too, I think. We watch a video about nuclear weapons.

In the hall people make faces and whisper to each other, but they stay away, which is the best I can expect. It's not like I've got an army of friends who would rush to defend me. Drew comes up and fake punches me in the stomach—I guess to let me know that we're still manly men and to let everyone else know that he, at least, is on my side. He is five-foot-three and plays snare drum in the marching band. "So, Meester Elwood," he says. "You learn the Jetson's Theme?"

"The what?"

179

He pushes his glasses up the bridge of his nose. "Fuck you. The cartoon medley."

I make a face.

"For today? Rehearsal? The Turkey Day game?" He waves his hand back and forth in front of my face. "Hello? Hello?"

I explain that I am dropping band. Playing clarinet is just one of several things I will not do in public for a long, long time. Others: wear pink shirts, sharpen pencils, eat bananas. Beer in long-neck bottles. Anything to do with flowers.

On the door of my locker, in indelible black magic marker, is a drawing of a man, naked, kneeling down, with another man kneeling behind him, a giant third leg standing up from his abdomen. "Gee, Dad," the cartoon voice balloon says, "why can't we just go camping, like other families?"

The *Gazette* runs a front-page story about the arraignment. There is a priest, a banker, a man who runs a Sunoco station. Then there's my father, the menace of the J. G. Whittier Middle School.

A group of parents is calling for an investigation. "We want to know, has he ever chaperoned dances? Has he supervised gym?" a man named Ralph Leighton says.

A New Hampshire state trooper describes "the activities observed at the location." He uses words like "sodomy" and "fondling." During the arrest, he says, officers wore thick rubber gloves to keep from getting AIDS. Suddenly I think of our plates, our glasses, our toilet seat: but no, I think, that's ridiculous.

A Derry selectman says he doesn't care what these guys do as long as they do it in someone else's town. "I don't hate queers," he says.

After dinner, no kidding—Dad is cleaning his shotgun. He laughs when he sees the look on my face.

"For Christ's sake, Bob." He's wearing his most Dad outfit: corduroys from L. L. Bean, a polo shirt, and a golf sweater. "I thought we'd go down to Plum Island on Saturday. Ducks are open."

We really do hunt, he and I. Deer, ducks. But Jesus, I'm thinking—what's next? A pickup truck? Drinking contests? Washing whites with colors?

Dad is sunk so deep into his recliner that he and the chair look like all one piece, as if it grew out of his back. The remarkable thing is how much like a Dad he is. He is a little too fat in the belly and ass, and his brown hair is thin on top and shot with gray on the sides. He even wears brown tortoise-shell half-glasses when he reads the newspaper.

I study his face, looking for clues. For three days I've wondered how he managed to fool us all for so long. Wasn't there anything different about him? Yes, I realize now, there is a certain softness in his cheeks, a slackness at the edges of his mouth, which I hadn't noticed before.

"What?" he says, looking up from oiling the barrel.

"Nothing. Is that the Remington?"

He scowls. I turn back to the television and pretend to watch the commercial.

The phone rings. I jump up. "I'll unplug it."

"No," he says. He groans getting out of his chair. "Hello?" he says. Then, in a voice I've never heard: "Hi! Yes, I was hoping! I called this afternoon. Right. Oh, wait a minute." He hands me the phone. "Hang this up when I get upstairs?" Before I hang up I hear him say, "So, Mark."

In the night the phone rings. I reach, wondering how long it's been ringing.

A voice says, "You know how fags—"

I hang up. My breath rises in short, quick bursts. I think about school tomorrow. The phone rings again, and I unplug the cord, forgetting the other phones: the ringing continues in the kitchen, in the family room, in my father's room. My father says hello.

Then, groggy, he says, "Pardon me?"

I turn my face into my pillow. In the morning he pours me coffee and apologizes for the calls. "We'll get an answering machine," he says.

Mom says the Driscolls have room for me. I tell her I'm fine. "We're going hunting," I tell her. She rolls her eyes.

It's Wednesday. We're having dinner at Beshara's, a Lebanese place on South Union Street.

"Anyway, you can't all stay with the Driscolls," I say. "I mean, forever."

She says she is fully aware of what she can and can't do. She reminds me that she is my mother, I tell her I'm fully aware of that. I tell her that Dad is still Dad; that in most ways, nothing has changed. She uses words like "denial" and "trauma." She talks about lawyers and restraining orders. She pushes a cube of lamb back and forth on her plate.

"Are you going to eat that?" I say.

"Here." She slides her plate toward me.

I tell her my theory, which is that Dad has a brain tumor. Yesterday Drew told me about an uncle of his who one day at breakfast told his wife he was leaving her and the children to become a painter. And then did.

"That was Gauguin," she says.

"What?"

"Never mind."

"Anyway, something like a year later the guy had a seizure, and when they took him to the hospital they found out he had a tumor on his brain, the size of a grapefruit."

She lights a cigarette, "Why is it that tumors are always the size of a grapefruit? They're never the size of an orange. Or a cantaloupe."

This has been harder on her than I'd realized. I push on, though, explaining to her how Drew's uncle woke after surgery and didn't even know he'd left his family—the whole thing had been a mistake.

"And they all lived happily ever after," she says.

"Not really."

She raises an eyebrow. I shake my head.

"It doesn't matter. What *does* matter is that we get Dad in for a brain scan—fast." Finally, I make her laugh.

Our house leaks cold air through every joint, and the frame shudders and groans in the November wind. This house has been in the Abbott family since Ralph Waldo Emerson lived in our town. Emerson, in fact, ate dinner here, with my great-great-great uncle, Walter Henry Abbott.

I can't sleep. I lie still as a stone beneath two blankets and wonder whether my father fantasizes about me.

He must think about men. Young men: he must like the way we look. Does he think about me? Does he look at me? Has he ever? I cast back, but I can't remember any incidents. He sees me in the morning, though, scampering cold in a towel from the bathroom to my bedroom. I think about him eyeing me, wanting to take me in his mouth.

For a moment I wish him dead: I wonder what it would be like if he were gone. It is as if I have discovered that the man in the other room is not who he says he is; that he has been in a witness protection program and his real name is not Henry Abbott, but something else altogether, something sinister and Italian; that he is not my father at all.

I wonder if I will inherit this. I had a dream, once. But just once. And there was Art Brancato, a senior when I was a freshman: hairy-chested in the locker room, lounging naked, unafraid, a full-grown man at seventeen; I studied the way he squinted when he laughed, and for a while I tried to walk the way he did, rolling my shoulders. But no. That's not the same.

In the morning there is frost on the lawn and someone has spray-painted "Honk If You Love Men" on both sides of the Cutlass. The front of the house is spattered with eggs—it looks as if something big has sneezed on us.

Thanksgiving is a week away. Drew says I can come to his family's house, but I have to turn him down. Dad says he's going to cook dinner. He's counting on me. Secretly I'm hoping that someone will invite us—Aunt Marian, maybe—but I realize that's unlikely. We are pariahs, the unclean. So we will end up, the two of us, leaning over our little turkey and thanking God—for what? For not being run over by a train? For not being hit by lightning? "Well," I imagine Dad saying in his phony classroom voice, "we've still got two good arms and two good legs. That's more than some can say."

He calls the Driscolls to see if Mom and the kids will come home for the holiday. He has not spoken to her since she left. His hand shakes so much that he misses the number and has to hang up and dial again.

"Bill? Henry. Thanks," he says when Mr. Driscoll answers. "That means a lot right now. Right. I know. It's tough on all of us. I'm calling for Kate, actually. Oh. Well, I mean, you could tell her, all I want to do is talk. I mean, what harm—OK. All right. Maybe later, then."

But later she won't take his call, either.

He goes upstairs. I hear him on the phone with Mark. I imagine he's inviting him for Thanksgiving. Before our Norman Rockwell holiday scene can take form in my mind, I hear a sound like coughing from behind his door.

"For Christ's sake," he says. "For Christ's sake. All right then. I won't. I said I won't. Bye."

I dread gym but I don't ask to be excused. Afterward, in the locker room, I can't help it: I glance at their bodies. Not between their legs, but at the legs themselves. The long muscles of the thighs. The arms, the shoulders, the chests. The curved, wing-shaped backs.

I want to know if this excites me. I have always insisted that it doesn't, but I've never actually checked.

I look at their shapes, pink in the steam of the shower room. There is something, maybe. My looks are too furtive to tell. If I stared I might feel more. Or I might feel less.

It's Thursday afternoon. Walking home I hear the band practicing in the field behind the auditorium, and I hate my father for bringing me to this.

At home, Aunt Marian, Dad's sister, is sitting on the couch. She has brought a coffee cake; she makes them for funerals. She fidgets with the cellophane wrapping. Dad's family is pure Yankee, as tight with their feelings as they are with their money. They're not equipped for this.

"Well," she says.

He plants himself into his recliner. "So, yes," he says. "Nice of you."

Kindness lasts as long as a cup of tea. She avoids all references to Thanksgiving and instead chatters on about family gossip: which cousin got which piece of furniture from Grandmother Wilkinson's house in Gloucester, why Cousin Richard needed electroshock therapy. Then, her support shown, her duty endured, she rises to leave.

At the door she says, "Has Mom called?"

"Maybe I should call her."

"Poor dear Henry." She kisses his cheek. She turns to me and I get the same kiss. "Take care, Robert."

Twice that afternoon he starts to call, then hangs up. He putters. He fixes the leak in the roof in the back porch. He cleans leaves from the rain gutters.

Mom is taking Jenny and Nelson to spend Thanksgiving in Ohio with her sister. They might not come back, she says.

She and Dad are in the kitchen, Friday afternoon. I'm in the family room, wondering what we'll call this room now. Den, maybe.

Dad says she's using her children as bargaining chips.

"There's no bargaining going on here," she says. She tells him he should get a lawyer.

He sits at the kitchen table. He looks like a guy in a Vietnam movie, mumbling about all his dead friends, too shell-shocked to think straight.

She takes out a piece of paper and begins running down a list of what they own and what their debts are. Suddenly he interrupts her, slams his hand on the table, and says, "Look, you can't goddamn *do* this. You can't."

More and more he is angry. I take this as a good sign. At least he's acting like a man. In the scenario I dread, he slides the other way: he gets a fancy haircut, shrieks at jokes, flips his hands as he speaks.

Mom doesn't flinch. She folds the paper, puts it in her purse, and snaps it shut. "Good-bye, then," she says.

I walk her to the car. We sit in the driveway. She lights a new cigarette from the old one. Her hands tremble. She says, "I really don't think you should be staying here."

"Look," I say, "I'm not going to sleep on some couch in some basement."

"Does the other guy—" She drags, then exhales. "Does he come over?"

"I think they broke up."

"Broke up." She shakes her head. "Jesus Christ." She laughs. She seems fragile, as if she's grown old too fast, like the plants in those sped-up film clips. I can't look at her. "Bob," she says, "I want you to come with us to Ohio."

Don't do this, I'm thinking. Don't make me choose. In seven months I will finish school and then I will leave them all; but for now I want things to stay the same.

"I can get a court order," she says. "You're a minor."

Across the street, Mr. Gauthier is on his lawn, raking leaves and watching us. I wave at him. He looks away.

"Bob, please," she says.

"Reveille," Dad says. It's Saturday morning, still dark out. "Rise and shine."

We stop at Big Bear for coffee and cinnamon rolls. On the way to Plum Island I fall back to sleep, and when I wake up we are backing down the boat ramp. We have rented a Nissan Sentra while the Cutlass is being painted.

I winch out the boat, a twelve-foot Sears aluminum rowboat with a three-horse Evinrude motor, then drag it ashore with the bow line while Dad parks.

We sputter down the channel into the thick of the salt marsh, then sit and wait. The dawn sky is sick gray. I worry that it might rain. Dad loads five shells into the chamber of his gas-action Remington and hands me two for my over-and-under, the gun he used as a boy. We sit facing each other, barrels across our laps. We wait. We wait some more.

"Open those sardines," he says.

This is our hunting breakfast, a habit he got from his father. It's a tradition I don't plan to carry on.

The tin cover sticks at first. I take off my gloves to get a better grip, and when I pull harder the lid suddenly tears off in my hand and runs a long, curved slice across the meat of my thumb. "Fuck," I say, because we swear when we hunt. "Motherfucker," I say, as a line of blood fills the cut.

Dad reaches across and takes my hand. "Let's have a look," he says, but his touch is like a spark, and I pull away.

He stops. His eyes are wide open. He starts to say something, then doesn't. I look out over the marsh. There is nothing but water and sky, all gray. I imagine us from above, in black and white, so small on the water. I place the tin of sardines on the bench seat between us. I squeeze my thumb in the palm of my other hand. A drop of blood hits the bottom of the boat with a splat. Another falls; then another.

He reaches back to the first-aid box and takes out a Band-Aid. "Here," he says. I hold out my thumb, and he wraps the cut.

We sit. He doesn't say anything. He stares at me. I put my gloves back on. The wake from a boat crossing the marsh rocks us clumsily. He's still staring.

"I'm sorry," I say finally. "I just can't understand."

He fidgets with his wool cap. "I know."

"Maybe someday. I don't know."

"But you still love your old man, don't you?"

I kick my boots together. "Don't ask me things like that."

I look up. His eyes are reaching. I'm thinking that whatever happens, I don't want to see him cry.

"I need to know that," he says. "It's important."

He tries to take my hand again, but again I pull away.

"Stop it," I say. I sit back away from him. "Just don't."

He droops. I consider starting the engine and heading out of the marsh. But as awful as this moment is, I am unable to let it go. I feel on the edge of a discovery, as if some truth is about to reveal itself.

It doesn't. We sit and wait without talking. The water is calm, and now that the sun has come up, it's almost warm. We eat the sardines on crackers.

Suddenly shots are booming out over the water all around us—I realize now we're not alone here—and looking up I see the first line of ducks arcing down into the marsh. I point over his shoulder and he wheels and drops to one knee but already we're too late, they're past us and banking off, but he fires and fires anyway, long after the others have stopped. With each shot the recoil kicks his right shoulder back, as if it might spin him around. The spent shells leap from his chamber and hit the bottom of the boat still smoking, and he fires, fires, and fires into the empty sky.

He collapses into the curve of the bow. He turns his face away. I crawl over and kneel by him. "Dad," I say, "they're gone." He takes my hand, and this time I let him keep it.

Our new Code-A-Phone is chirping, and the message light blinks in time with it. Dad drops his hunting gear in the corner and, still in his plaid wool coat and right in front of me, he rushes to the machine like a schoolgirl. There is a man's voice, and I'm thinking, I really don't want to hear this.

But it's a man named Duncan Gardner, a lawyer. He represents Mom. "From now on, if you want to talk, I'd like you to talk to me," he says.

There are no other messages. Dad stands there, realizing, I guess, how foolish he looks. He takes a bottle to bed.

Later, past midnight, I lie awake in bed. Outside, the first snow of the season is falling against the night sky, tumbling through the tree branches and ticking against my window, and it's as if all the trouble in the world is coming down on us. Our old house creaks. I watch the snow toss and mingle in the air.

Dad is stirring in his room. Then his door opens and he pads down the stairs, through the hall and across the kitchen. I hold myself still, expecting—and I admit, half-hoping—to hear the crack of a muffled report from the garage. At least then we all could get over this. Instead there is the hum of the refrigerator, the clink of a bottle, a kitchen chair scraping on the linoleum floor. I cannot imagine why, but my poor father has decided to trudge on, and I know there are worse times ahead.

I think of him down there alone in the dark. I think of my mother, sleeping on a couch in someone's house. I think of Drew's uncle with the brain tumor, whose wife was so glad to have him back from the hospital that she decorated the house with balloons and streamers and threw a party for him. What they couldn't know, as they passed around the pieces of cake and danced to Ray Charles records, was that in three months his liver and lungs would be rotten with cancer, and that a month after that he'd be dead, leaving his friends to feel small and stupid—scared of the future, and stunned by the secrets life buries in us.

Magic Circle

Maria Mazziotti Gillan

Maria Mazziotti Gillan's work has appeared in Prairie Schooner,
The New York Times, Poetry Ireland, Connecticut Review, LIPS,
and Rattle, *as well as in numerous other journals and anthologies. She has published eight books of poetry, including* Where I
Come From, Things My Mother Told Me, *and* Italian Women in
Black Dresses, *from which the following poem has been selected.
With her daughter Jennifer, she has co-edited three anthologies:*
Unsettling America, Identity Lessons, *and* Growing up Ethnic in
America. *She is the editor of the* Paterson Literary Review. *Her
honors include the May Sarton Award, the Fearing Houghton
Award, New Jersey State Council on the Arts Fellowships in Poetry, and the American Literary Translator's Award through a
grant from the National Endowment for the Arts.*

My mother drew her magic circle around us, led us inside
where we were always safe. She told us stories,
spinning the thread back between herself and her mother
and her mother's mother and connecting that thread to us
her daughters and teaching us how to connect

the same thread to our daughters and granddaughters,
all those women baking bread and bearing children,
teaching us to love ourselves, love them. The stories,
save our lives, passing the meaning on from one
generation to the next, a silver thread, a silver

thread that strengthens us, all those women,
caught in our hearts, teaching us how to laugh,
how to make our arms into cradles
to hold each other and sing.

Lightning and the Lightning Bug:
The Craft of the Essay

Ved Mehta

Ved Mehta was born in India in 1934, and at the age of four, he lost his sight. He first came to the United States as a student at a school for the blind in Arkansas, and continued his education at Pomona College, Yale University, and finally, Oxford. He became a US citizen in 1975. Ved Mehta was a staff writer for The New Yorker *from 1961 to 1994 and has taught literature and history at half a dozen colleges and universities, including Williams, Vassar, and Yale. He is the author of an autobiographical series of books with the omnibus title* Continents of Exile, *of which the eighth book,* Remembering Mr. Shawn's *New Yorker*: The Invisible Art of Editing, *has just been published. Among his other books are* Portrait of India, Mahatma Gandhi and His Apostles, *and* Rajiv Gandhi and Rama's Kingdom, *all from Yale University Press.*

In 1956, when I was twenty-two, I graduated from Pomona College, in California, and went up to Oxford. There I started working for a second bachelor's degree, for in those days the best way to take full advantage of what Oxford offered and to enter into the stream of English life was to work for an undergraduate degree at the university. I was reading history and was required to submit one or two essays a week to the scrutiny of my tutors, most of whom were world-class scholars. While I was reading aloud to my medieval tutor one of my first essays, on the Anglo-Saxons, he stopped me after the word *motivation* and asked why I tended to reach for jargon when a good English word was to hand.

Reprinted from *The American Scholar* 67, no. 2 (spring 1998), by permission of Georges Borchardt, Inc.

"But everyone uses *motivation,*" I protested.

"Jargon is imprecise and encourages weak thought," said my tutor. "A careful writer would use a word like *impulse.*"

Until then, I had thought I was a tolerably good writer and had believed that after working over a draft several times I was able to say what I wanted to say. Indeed, before going up to Oxford, I had completed an entire book, an autobiography, much of which had been set down two years earlier, in the course of a summer. But I was so deeply in awe of Oxford and its tutorial system, and so impressionable, that my tutor's questioning of one infelicitous word effectively unraveled my confidence in my writing even as it began to sensitize me to the nuances of words. For some time thereafter, whenever I wrote a sentence, I would read it as my tutor might, and conclude that almost everything was wrong with it. I was reminded of an accomplished pianist friend who was then undergoing intense psychoanalysis and had become in the course of her treatment so self-conscious that she could scarcely play a five-finger exercise. But I felt sure that, just as her treatment contained the promise of her becoming a better pianist, so my Oxford education contained the promise of my becoming a better writer. The road, however, turned out to be a long and arduous one—and to stretch far beyond Oxford.

I recall how daunting were my first steps along that road. They led me to a chaos of randomly assembled materials that had to be subjected first to the elusive formulation of ideas and then to the untamable nature of language itself. I was constantly tempted to put off writing. There was always more to read, more to reflect on. I found I had first to decide what, exactly, I wanted to say, even if in the course of writing I should find myself saying something totally different. (All ideas grow and develop as one writes, I learned, since one's memory expands through the process of association.) Nevertheless, that initial idea, though it might be only the germ of one, enabled me to overcome the terror of the blank page. So as not to feel constrained or constricted, I would write what I came to call a "vomit draft," in which I would pour out everything I could think of without worrying about sense or grammar. Then I would start the process of revision. Cutting and shaping my thoughts helped me learn what, if anything, I knew about the subject. As I pressed on with my essay, I would try to come up with the most telling arguments or examples to buttress whatever point I was making. To locate them required me to interrupt the writing and go searching through many books. In time, I learned to find my way around indexes, tables of contents, and library catalogues. Sometimes I would put aside the essay and return later to cast a cold eye on it. The process as I describe it here may sound simple, but, as every student knows, it is turbulent and involves a lot of angst.

I remember that I was struck by the elegance and luster of many of the essays written by my English contemporaries. Compared to theirs, my best efforts came across as dull and lame. (In England, writing well in one's chosen subject is the foundation of a good education.) Before long, I discovered that many of the undergraduates I admired had developed their writing styles as schoolboys by imitating the styles of great authors or, if they were studying to be classicists, by translating Latin or Greek prose and verse into the styles of contemporary English authors, and vice versa. Sometimes these students wrote with a certain archness and artificiality, but I envied the facility and grace of expression that the best of them had developed. To cultivate ear and eye, some of them played a game that consisted of picking out characteristic passages from ancient and modern authors and seeing who could identify them. I tried to play the game, too, but because my knowledge of classical texts was either shaky or nonexistent, I was hopeless at it.

I confided my doubts about my schooling to my medieval tutor, and he said that he thought I needed to read more widely. I told him that since the age of fifteen, when I first started speaking English (I had grown up speaking Punjabi), I had done little besides read—and that, like many foreigners whose mother tongue was not English, I was an autodidact.

"Ah," he said. "But have you studied what makes one author's work different from another's?" My tutor explained that no piece of writing could prove effective and memorable unless its author found the right voice and the right style. For the study of these matters, he directed me to *The Oxford Book of English Prose,* a collection of choice morsels, mostly by British authors, culled and introduced by Sir Arthur Quiller-Couch and published in 1925. It was a feast: Chaucer, Shakespeare, Milton, Swift, Samuel Johnson, Lamb, Coleridge, Jane Austen, De Quincey, the Brontë sisters, Melville, Dickens, Arnold, Shaw, and many others. Over the next months and years, I returned to the book again and again. Genius being, by definition, inimitable and transcendent, the selections certainly didn't encourage me to attempt similar feats, but rather made anything I did attempt seem insipid by comparison.

Some young writers might find a study of the works of genius harmful, because it would discourage them from writing. They would do well to go their merry way and, like Walt Whitman, discover their inner resources on their own. How often have I met a mother who told me that her daughter wrote beautiful letters and would write a book if she could only find the time! Perhaps so. But, in my experience, for every natural writer there are ten or more writers who have to labor over their craft. Mark Twain once said, "The difference between the right word and the almost right word is the difference between lightning and the lightning bug." Even so, it is hard to imagine Mark Twain, who made a virtue of seeming artless, studying the great writers of the past.

I myself found my study of the masters very helpful. Because I could savor only a few pages of *The Oxford Book of English Prose* at a sitting, I dipped into the volume whenever I had a little time, reading and rereading a selection to ponder its tone and cadence, its diction and imagery, its movement and structure. It gradually became clear to me that well-wrought sentences from different authors had a distinctive logic and beauty that could no more be tampered with than could the authors' signatures. Unquestionably, no two writers were alike, yet it took me a long time to discern just what stylistic characteristics made every writer different from every other and then to be able to put those differences into words.

The precision and finish of prose became a passion with me. It led me on to grammar books, most notably Fowler's *Modern English Usage,* and to essays, not only by authors in Quiller-Couch's anthology, which included nothing published after 1914, but also by twentieth-century authors: Virginia Woolf, of whose ardent prose it may be said, among other things, that it launched a whole new way of thinking and writing; Edmund Wilson, who encapsulated in sinewy prose the life, work, and critical value of great authors as if no one else had ever written about them; V. S. Pritchett, who never wrote a book review that didn't contain an unexpected image; and E. B. White, whose homey yet elegant turns of phrase made you think that no one could convey, for instance, the feel of the day better than he could. . . .

Hagar

Toni Morrison

Toni Morrison was born in Lorain, Ohio. After she earned a Master's degree in English, she started teaching at Howard University in 1957. Later, while she worked as an editor at Random House, she started writing fiction. Her first novel, The Bluest Eye, *an expansion of an earlier short story, was published in 1970, and she attracted immediate attention as a promising writer. Her other novels include* Sula *(1973),* Song of Solomon *(1977), and* Tar Baby *(1981).* Beloved *(1987)—which won the 1988 Pulitzer Prize—is regarded by many as Morrison's most successful novel. The book explores many complex themes, including black Americans' relationship to slavery. The novel* Jazz *(1992) and the nonfiction book* Playing in the Dark: Whiteness and the Literary Imagination *(1992 were also well received. In 1993, Morrison won the Nobel Prize in literature. Her latest book is* Paradise *(1998). The following is a chapter from* Song of Solomon.

———————————

It was a long time after he left, that warm September morning, that she was able to relax enough to drop the knife. When it clattered to the linoleum, she brought her arms down, oh, so slowly, and cradled her breasts as though they were two mangoes thumbed over in the marketplace and pushed aside. She stood that way in the little rented room with the sunshine pouring in until Guitar came home. He could not get her to speak or move, so he picked her up in his arms and carried her downstairs. He sat her on the bottom step while he went to borrow a car to drive her home.

Terrible as he thought the whole business was, and repelled as he was by mindlessness in love, he could not keep the deep wave of sorrow from engulfing him as

———————————

Reprinted from *Song of Solomon*, (1987), by permission of Alfred A. Knopf, a division of Random House, Inc.

he looked at this really rather pretty woman sitting straight as a pole, holding her breasts, and staring in front of her out of hollow eyes.

The engine of the old car he'd borrowed roared, but Guitar spoke softly to her. "You think because he doesn't love you that you are worthless. You think because he doesn't want you anymore that he is right—that his judgment and opinion of you are correct. If he throws you out, then you are garbage. You think he belongs to you because you want to belong to him. Hagar, don't. It's a bad word, 'belong.' Especially when you put it with somebody you love. Love shouldn't be like that. Did you ever see the way the clouds love a mountain? They circle all around it; sometimes you can't even see the mountain for the clouds. But you know what? You go up top and what do you see? His head. The clouds never cover the head. His head pokes through, because the clouds let him; they don't wrap him up. They let him keep his head up high, free, with nothing to hide him or bind him. Hear me, Hagar?" He spoke to her as he would to a very young child. "You can't own a human being. You can't lose what you don't own. Suppose you did own him. Could you really love somebody who was absolutely nobody without you? You really want somebody like that? Somebody who falls apart when you walk out the door? You don't, do you? And neither does he. You're turning over your whole life to him. Your whole life, girl. And if it means so little to you that you can just give it away, hand it to him, then why should it mean any more to him? He can't value you more than you value yourself." He stopped. She did not move or give any sign that she had heard him.

Pretty woman, he thought. Pretty little black-skinned woman. Who wanted to kill for love, die for love. The pride, the conceit of these doormat women amazed him. They were always women who had been spoiled children. Whose whims had been taken seriously by adults and who grew up to be the stingiest, greediest people on earth and out of their stinginess grew their stingy little love that ate everything in sight. They could not believe or accept the fact that they were unloved; they believed that the world itself was off balance when it appeared as though they were not loved. Why did they think they were so lovable? Why did they think their brand of love was better than, or even as good as, anybody else's? But they did. And they loved their love so much they would kill anybody who got in its way.

He looked at her again. Pretty. Pretty little black girl. Pretty little black-skinned girl. What had Pilate done to her? Hadn't anybody told her the things she ought to know? He thought of his two sisters, grown women now who could deal, and the litany of their growing up. Where's your daddy? Your mama know you out here in the street? Put something on your head. You gonna catch your death a cold. Ain't you hot? Ain't you cold? Ain't you scared you gonna get wet? Uncross your legs. Pull up your socks. I thought you was goin to the Junior Choir. Your slip is showin. Your hem is out. Come back in here and iron that collar. Hush your mouth. Comb your head. Get up from there and make that bed. Put on the meat. Take out the trash. Vaseline get rid of that ash.

Neither Pilate nor Reba knew that Hagar was not like them. Not strong enough, like Pilate, nor simple enough, like Reba, to make up her life as they had. She needed what most colored girls needed: a chorus of mamas, grandmamas, aunts, cousins, sisters, neighbors, Sunday school teachers, best girl friends, and what all to give her the strength life demanded of her—and the humor with which to live it.

Still, he thought, to have the object of your love, worthy or not, despise you, or leave you . . .

"You know what, Hagar? Everything I ever loved in my life left me. My father died when I was four. That was the first leaving I knew and the hardest. Then my mother. There were four of us and she just couldn't cut it when my father died. She ran away. Just ran away. My aunt took care of us until my grandmother could get there. Then my grandmother took care of us. Then Uncle Billy came. They're both close to dead now. So it was hard for me to latch on to a woman. Because I thought if I loved anything it would die. But I did latch on. Once. But I guess once is all you can manage." Guitar thought about it and said, "But I never wanted to kill her. *Him,* yeah. But not her." He smiled, but Hagar wasn't looking, wasn't even listening, and when he led her out of the car into Reba's arms her eyes were still empty.

All they knew to do was love her and since she would not speak, they brought things to please her. For the first time in life Reba *tried* to win things. And, also for the first time, couldn't. Except for a portable television set, which they couldn't connect because they had no electricity, Reba won nothing. No raffle ticket, no Bingo, no policy slip, no clearing-house number, no magazine sweepstakes, no, nor any unpierced carnival balloon succumbed to her magic. It wore her down. Puzzled and luckless, she dragged herself home clutching stalks of anything that blossomed along the edges of lots and other people's gardens. These she presented to her daughter, who sat in a chair by the window or lay in bed fingering, fingering her hair.

They cooked special things for her; searched for gifts that they hoped would break the spell. Nothing helped. Pilate's lips were still and Reba's eyes full of panic. They brought her lipstick and chocolate milk, a pink nylon sweater and a fuchsia bed jacket. Reba even investigated the mysteries of making jello, both red and green. Hagar didn't even look at it.

One day Pilate sat down on Hagar's bed and held a compact before her granddaughter's face. It was trimmed in a goldlike metal and had a pink plastic lid.

"Look, baby. See here?" Pilate turned it all around to show it off and pressed in the catch. The lid sprang open and Hagar saw a tiny part of her face reflected in the mirror. She took the compact then and stared into the mirror for a long while.

"No wonder," she said at last. "Look at that. No wonder. No wonder."

Pilate was thrilled at the sound of Hagar's voice. "It's yours, baby," she said. "Ain't it pretty?"

"No wonder," said Hagar. "No wonder."

"No wonder what?" asked Pilate.

"Look at how I look. I look awful. No wonder he didn't want me. I look terrible." Her voice was calm and reasonable, as though the last few days hadn't been lived through at all. "I need to get up from here and fix myself up. No *wonder!*" Hagar threw back the bedcover and stood up. "Ohhh. I smell too. Mama, heat me some water. I need a bath. A long one. We got any bath salts left? Oh, Lord, my head. Look at that." She peered into the compact mirror again. "I look like a ground hog. Where's the comb?"

Pilate called Reba and together they flew through the house to find the comb, but when they found it Hagar couldn't get the teeth through her roped and matted hair.

"Wash it," said Reba. "Wash it and we'll comb it while it's wet."

"I need shampoo, then. Real shampoo. I can't use Mama's soap."

"I'll go get some." Reba was trembling a little. "What kind?"

"Oh, any kind. And get some hair oil, Reba. Posner's, and some . . . Oh, never mind. Just that. Mama? Have you seen my . . . Oh, my God. No wonder. No wonder."

Pilate pulled a piece of string from Hagar's bedspread and put it in her mouth. "I'll heat up the water," she said.

When Reba got back she washed Hagar's hair, brushed it, and combed it gently.

"Just make me two braids, Reba. I'm going to have to go to the beauty shop. Today. Oh, and I need something to wear." Hagar stood at the door of the little cardboard closet, running her hands over the shoulders of dresses. "Everything's a mess in here. A mess. All wrinkled . . ."

"Water's hot. Where you want the tub?"

"Bring it in here."

"You think you should be taking a bath so soon?" Reba asked. "You just got up."

"Hush, Reba," said Pilate. "Let the child take care of herself."

"But she's been in the bed three days."

"All the more reason."

"I can't put these things on. Everything's a mess." Hagar was almost in tears.

Reba looked at Pilate. "I hope you right. I don't approve of getting up too fast and jumping right in some water."

"Help me with this tub and stop grumbling."

"All wrinkled. What am I going to wear?"

"That ain't enough water to cover her feet."

"It'll grow when she sits down."

"Where's my yellow dress? The one that buttons all the way down?"

"Somewhere in there, I reckon."

"Find it for me and press it, would you? I know it's a mess. Everything's a mess."

Reba found and pressed the yellow dress. Pilate helped Hagar bathe. Finally a clean and clothed Hagar stood before the two women and said, "I have to buy some clothes. New clothes. Everything I have is a mess."

They looked at each other. "What you need?" asked Pilate.

"I need everything," she said, and everything is what she got. She shopped for everything a woman could wear from the skin out, with the money from Reba's diamond. They had seventy-five cents between them when Hagar declared her needs, and six dollars owed to them from customers. So the two-thousand-dollar two-carat diamond went to a pawnshop, where Reba traded it for thirty dollars at first and then, accompanied by a storming Pilate, she went back and got one hundred and seventy more for it. Hagar stuffed two hundred dollars and seventy-five cents into her purse and headed downtown, still whispering to herself every now and then, "No wonder."

She bought a Playtex garter belt, I. Miller No Color hose, Fruit of the Loom panties, and two nylon slips—one white, one pink—one pair of Joyce Fancy Free and one of Con Brio ("Thank heaven for little Joyce heels"). She carried an armful of skirts and an Evan-Picone two-piece number into the fitting room. Her little yellow dress that buttoned all the way down lay on the floor as she slipped a skirt over her head and shoulders, down to her waist. But the placket would not close. She sucked in her stomach and pulled the fabric as far as possible, but the teeth of the zipper would not join. A light sheen broke out on her forehead as she huffed and puffed. She was convinced that her whole life depended on whether or not those aluminum teeth would meet. The nail of her forefinger split and the balls of her thumbs ached as she struggled with the placket. Dampness became sweat and her breath came in gasps. She was about to weep when the saleswoman poked her head through the curtain and said brightly, "How are you doing?" But when she saw Hagar's gnarled and frightened face, the smile froze.

"Oh, my," she said, and reached for the tag hanging from the skirt's waist. "This is a five. Don't force it. You need, oh, a nine or eleven, I should think. Please. Don't force it. Let me see if I have that size."

She waited until Hagar let the plaid skirt fall down to her ankles before disappearing. Hagar easily drew on the skirt the woman brought back, and without further search, said she would take it and the little two-piece Evan-Picone.

She bought a white blouse next and a nightgown—fawn trimmed in sea foam. Now all she needed was make-up.

The cosmetics department enfolded her in perfume, and she read hungrily the labels and the promise. Myurgia for primeval woman who creates for him a world of tender privacy where the only occupant is you, mixed with Nina Ricci's L'Air du Temps. Yardley's Flair with Tuvaché's Nectaroma and D'Orsay's Intoxication. Robert Piguet's Fracas, and Calypso and Visa and Bandit. Houbigant's Chantilly. Caron's Fleurs de Rocaille and Bellodgia. Hagar breathed deeply the sweet air that hung over the glass counters. Like a smiling sleepwalker she circled. Round and round the diamond-clear counters covered with bottles, wafer-thin disks, round boxes, tubes, and phials. Lipsticks in soft white hands darted out of their sheaths like the shiny red penises of puppies. Peachy powders and milky lotions were grouped in front of poster after cardboard poster of gorgeous grinning faces. Faces in ecstasy. Faces somber with achieved seduction. Hagar believed she could spend her life there among the cut glass, shimmering in peaches and cream, in satin. In opulence. In luxe. In love.

It was five-thirty when Hagar left the store with two shopping bags full of smaller bags gripped in her hands. And she didn't put them down until she reached Lilly's Beauty Parlor.

"No more heads, honey." Lilly looked up from the sink as Hagar came in.

Hagar stared. "I have to get my hair done. I have to hurry," she said.

Lilly looked over at Marcelline. It was Marcelline who kept the shop prosperous. She was younger, more recently trained, and could do a light press that lasted. Lilly was still using red-hot irons and an ounce of oil on every head. Her customers were loyal but dissatisfied. Now she spoke to Marcelline. "Can you take her? I can't, I know."

Marcelline peered deeply into her customer's scalp. "Hadn't planned on any late work. I got two more coming. This is my eighth today."

No one spoke. Hagar stared.

"Well," said Marcelline. "Since it's you, come on back at eight-thirty. Is it washed already?"

Hagar nodded.

"Okay," said Marcelline. "Eight-thirty. But don't expect nothing fancy."

"I'm surprised at you," Lilly chuckled when Hagar left. "You just sent two people away."

"Yeah, well, I don't feel like it, but I don't want no trouble with that girl Hagar. No telling what she might do. She jump that cousin of hers, no telling what she might do to me."

"That the one going with Macon Dead's boy?" Lilly's customer lifted her head away from the sink.

"That's her. Ought to be shamed, the two of them. *Cousins.*"

"Must not be working out if she's trying to kill him."

"I thought he left town."

"Wouldn't you?"

"Well, I know I don't want to truck with her. Not me."

"She don't bother nobody but him."

"Well, Pilate, then. Pilate know I turned her down, she wouldn't like it. They spoil that child something awful."

"Didn't you order fish from next door?"

"All that hair. I hope she don't expect nothing fancy."

"Call him up again. I'm getting hungry."

"Be just like her. No appointment. No nothing. Come in here all late and wrong and want something fancy."

She probably meant to wait somewhere. Or go home and return to Lilly's at eight-thirty. Yet the momentum of the thing held her—it was all of a piece. From the moment she looked into the mirror in the little pink compact she could not stop. It was as though she held her breath and could not let it go until the energy and busyness culminated in a beauty that would dazzle him. That was why, when she left Lilly's, she looked neither right nor left but walked on and on, oblivious of other people, street lights, automobiles, and a thunderous sky. She was thoroughly soaked before she realized it was raining and then only because one of the shopping bags split. When she looked down, her Evan-Picone white-with-a-band-of-color skirt was lying in a neat half fold on the shoulder of the road, and she was far far from home. She put down both bags, picked the skirt up and brushed away the crumbs of gravel that stuck to it. Quickly she refolded it, but when she tried to tuck it back into the shopping bag, the bag collapsed altogether. Rain soaked her hair and poured down her neck as she stooped to repair the damage. She pulled out the box of Con Brios, a smaller package of Van Raalte gloves, and another containing her fawn-trimmed-in-seafoam shortie nightgown. These she stuffed into the other bag. Retracing her steps, she found herself unable to carry the heavier bag in one hand, so she hoisted it up to her stomach and hugged it with both arms. She had gone hardly ten yards when the bottom fell out of it. Hagar tripped on Jungle Red (Sculptura) and Youth Blend, and to her great dismay, saw her box of Sunny Glow toppling into a puddle. She collected Jungle Red and Youth Blend safely, but Sunny Glow, which had tipped completely over and lost its protective disk, exploded in light peach puffs under the weight of the raindrops. Hagar scraped up as much of it as she could and pressed the wilted cellophane disk back into the box.

Twice before she got to Darling Street she had to stop to retrieve her purchases from the ground. Finally she stood in Pilate's doorway, limp, wet, and confused, clutching her bundles in whatever way she could. Reba was so relieved to see her that she grabbed her, knocking Chantilly and Bandit to the floor. Hagar stiffened and pulled away from her mother.

"I have to hurry," she whispered. "I have to hurry."

Loafers sluicing, hair dripping, holding her purchases in her arms, she made it into the bedroom and shut the door. Pilate and Reba made no move to follow her.

Hagar stripped herself naked there, and without taking time to dry her face or hair or feet, she dressed herself up in the white-with-a-band-of-color skirt and matching bolero, the Maidenform brassiere, the Fruit of the Loom panties, the no color hose, the Playtex garter belt and the Joyce con brios. Then she sat down to attend to her face. She drew charcoal gray for the young round eye through her brows, after which she rubbed mango tango on her cheeks. Then she patted sunny glow all over her face. Mango tango disappeared under it and she had to put it on again. She pushed out her lips and spread jungle red over them. She put baby clear sky light to outwit the day light on her eyelids and touched bandit to her throat, earlobes, and wrists. Finally she poured a little youth blend into her palm and smoothed it over her face.

At last she opened the door and presented herself to Pilate and Reba. And it was in their eyes that she saw what she had not seen before in the mirror: the wet ripped hose, the soiled white dress, the sticky, lumpy face powder, the streaked rouge, and the wild wet shoals of hair. All this she saw in their eyes, and the sight filled her own with water warmer and much older than the rain. Water that lasted for hours, until the fever came, and then it stopped. The fever dried her eyes up as well as her mouth.

She lay in her little Goldilocks'-choice bed, her eyes sand dry and as quiet as glass. Pilate and Reba, seated beside the bed, bent over her like two divi-divi trees beaten forward by a wind always blowing from the same direction. Like the trees, they offered her all they had: love murmurs and a protective shade.

"Mama." Hagar floated up into an even higher fever.

"Hmmm?"

"Why don't he like my hair?"

"Who, baby? Who don't like your hair?"

"Milkman."

"Milkman does too like your hair," said Reba.

"No. He don't. But I can't figure out why. Why he never liked my hair."

"Of course he likes it. How can he not like it?" asked Pilate.

"He likes silky hair." Hagar was murmuring so low they had to bend down to hear her.

"Silky hair? Milkman?"

"He doesn't like hair like mine."

"Hush, Hagar."

"Silky hair the color of a penny."

"Don't talk, baby."

"Curly, wavy, silky hair. He don't like mine."

Pilate put her hand on Hagar's head and trailed her fingers through her granddaughter's soft damp wool. "How can he not love your hair? It's the same hair that grows out of his own armpits. The same hair that crawls up out his crotch on up his stomach. All over his chest. The very same. It grows out of his nose, over his lips, and if he ever lost his razor it would grow all over his face. It's all over his head, Hagar. It's his hair too. He got to love it."

"He don't love it at all. He hates it."

"No he don't. He don't know what he loves, but he'll come around, honey, one of these days. How can he love himself and hate your hair?"

"He loves silky hair."

"Hush, Hagar."

"Penny-colored hair."

"Please, honey."

"And lemon-colored skin."

"Shhh."

"And gray-blue eyes."

"Hush now, hush."

"And thin nose."

"Hush, girl, hush."

"He's never going to like my hair."

"Hush. Hush. Hush, girl, hush."

The neighbors took up a collection because Pilate and Reba had spent everything getting Hagar the things needed to fix herself up. It didn't amount to much, though, and it was touch and go whether she'd have a decent funeral until Ruth walked down to Sonny's Shop and stared at Macon without blinking. He reached into his cash drawer and pulled out two twenty-dollar bills and put them down on the desk. Ruth didn't stretch out her hand to pick them up, or even shift her feet. Macon hesitated, then wheeled around in his chair and began fiddling with the combination to his safe. Ruth waited. Macon dipped into the safe three separate times before Ruth unclasped her hands and reached for the money. "Thank you," she said, and marched off to Linden Chapel Funeral Home to make the fastest arrangements possible.

Two days later, halfway through the service, it seemed as though Ruth was going to be the lone member of the bereaved family there. A female quartet from Linden Baptist Church had already sung "Abide with Me"; the wife of the mortician had read the condolence cards and the minister had launched into his "Naked came ye into this life and naked shall ye depart" sermon, which he had always believed suitable for the death of a young woman; and the winos in the vestibule who came to pay their respects to "Pilate's girl," but who dared not enter, had begun to sob, when the door swung open and Pilate burst in, shouting, "Mercy!" as though it were a command. A young man stood up and moved toward her. She flung out her right arm and almost knocked him down. "I want mercy!" she shouted, and began walking toward the coffin, shaking her head from side to side as though somebody had asked her a question and her answer was no.

Halfway up the aisle she stopped, lifted a finger, and pointed. Then slowly, although her breathing was fast and shallow, she lowered her hand to her side. It was strange, the languorous, limp hand coming to rest at her side while her breathing was coming so quick and fast. "Mercy," she said again, but she whispered it now. The mortician scurried toward her and touched her elbow. She moved away from him and went right up to the bier. She tilted her head and looked down. Her earring grazed her shoulder. Out of the total blackness of her clothes it blazed like a star. The mortician tried to approach her again, and moved closer, but when he saw her inky, berry-black lips, her cloudy, rainy eyes, the wonderful brass box hanging from her ear, he stepped back and looked at the floor.

"Mercy?" Now she was asking a question. "Mercy?"

It was not enough. The word needed a bottom, a frame. She straightened up, held her head high, and transformed the plea into a note. In a clear bluebell voice she sang it out—the one word held so long it became a sentence—and before the last syllable had died in the corners of the room, she was answered in a sweet soprano: "I hear you."

The people turned around. Reba had entered and was singing too. Pilate neither acknowledged her entrance nor missed a beat. She simply repeated the word "Mercy," and Reba replied. The daughter standing at the back of the chapel, the mother up front, they sang.

> *In the nighttime.*
> *Mercy.*
> *In the darkness.*
> *Mercy.*
> *In the morning.*
> *Mercy.*
> *At my bedside.*
> *Mercy.*
> *On my knees now.*
> *Mercy. Mercy. Mercy. Mercy.*

They stopped at the same time in a high silence. Pilate reached out her hand and placed three fingers on the edge of the coffin. Now she addressed her words to the woman bordered in gray satin who lay before her. Softly, privately, she sang to Hagar the very same reassurance she had promised her when she was a little girl.

Who's been botherin my sweet sugar lumpkin?
Who's been botherin my baby?
Who's been botherin my sweet sugar lumpkin?
Who's been botherin my baby girl?

Somebody's been botherin my sweet sugar lumpkin.
Somebody's been botherin my baby.
Somebody's been botherin my sweet sugar lumpkin.
Somebody's been botherin my baby girl.

I'll find who's botherin my sweet sugar lumpkin.
I'll find who's botherin my baby.
I'll find who's botherin my sweet sugar lumpkin.
I'll find who's botherin my baby girl.

"My baby girl." The three words were still pumping in her throat as she turned away from the coffin. Looking about at the faces of the people seated in the pews, she fastened on the first pair of eyes that were directed toward her. She nodded at the face and said, "My baby girl." She looked for another pair of eyes and told him also, "My baby girl," Moving back down the aisle, she told each face turned toward her the same piece of news. "My baby girl. That's my baby girl. My baby girl. My baby girl. My baby girl."

Conversationally she spoke, identifying Hagar, selecting her away from everybody else in the world who had died. First she spoke to the ones who had the courage to look at her, shake their heads, and say, "Amen." Then she spoke to those whose nerve failed them, whose glances would climb no higher than the long black fingers at her side. Toward them especially she leaned a little, telling in three words the full story of the stumped life in the coffin behind her. "My baby girl." Words tossed like stones into a silent canyon.

Suddenly, like an elephant who has just found his anger and lifts his trunk over the heads of the little men who want his teeth or his hide or his flesh or his amazing strength, Pilate trumpeted for the sky itself to hear, "And she was *loved!*"

It startled one of the sympathetic winos in the vestibule and he dropped his bottle, spurting emerald glass and jungle-red wine everywhere.

Pet Fly

Walter Mosley

Walter Mosley was born in Los Angeles in 1952, but after high school he moved to Vermont, where he worked several jobs and attended several colleges before settling down to computer programming. From Vermont he moved to Boston and then, in 1982, to New York. He also moved from programming to establishing a consultancy in computer work with a partner.

Later he entered a writing workshop that led to his enrolling at City College to study with Frederic Tuten, the head of the college's writing program. While he was taking courses there, he wrote his first detective story, which eventually became Devil in a Blue Dress. *Walter Mosley is the author of the best selling* Easy Rawlins *series of mysteries, the novel* R.L.'s Dream, *and the story collection* Always Outnumbered, Always Outgunned, *for which he received the Anisfield-Wolf Book Award.*

Walter Mosley's novels are now published in eighteen countries. He is the president of the Mystery Writers of America, a member of the executive board of the PEN American Center and founder of its Open Book Committee, and is on the board of directors of the National Book Awards.

I had been seeing Mona Donelli around the building since my first day working in interoffice mail. Mona laughing, Mona complaining about her stiff new shoes or the air conditioning or her boyfriend refusing to take her where she wanted to go. She's very pretty. Mona wears short skirts and giggles a lot. She's not serious at all. When

Reprinted from *The New Yorker*, December 13, 1999, by permission of Watkins/Loomis Agency, Inc.

silly Mona comes in she says hello and asks how you are, but before you get a chance to answer she's busy talking about what she saw on TV last night or something funny that happened on the ferry from Staten Island that morning.

I would see Mona almost every day on my delivery route—at the coffee-break room on the fifth floor or in a hallway, never at a desk. So when I made a rare delivery to the third-floor mortgage department and saw her sitting there, wearing a conservative sweater buttoned all the way up to her throat, I was surprised. She was so subdued, not sad but peaceful, looking at the wall in front of her and holding a yellow pencil with the eraser against her chin.

"Air conditioning too high again?" I asked, just so she'd know that I paid attention to the nonsense she babbled about.

She looked at me and I got a chill, because it didn't feel like the same person I saw flitting around the office. She gave me a silent and friendly smile, even though her eyes seemed to be wondering what my question meant.

I put down the big brown envelope addressed to her department and left without saying anything else.

Back in the basement, I asked my boss, Ernie, what was wrong with Mona.

"Nothing," he said. "I think she busted up with some guy or something. No, no, I'm a liar. She went out with her boyfriend's best friend without telling him. Now she doesn't get why the boyfriend's mad. That's what she said. Bitch. What she think?"

Ernie didn't suffer fools, as my mother would say. He was an older black man who had moved to New York from Georgia thirty-three years ago. He had come to work at Carter's Home Insurance three days after he arrived. "I would have been here on day one," he told me, "but my bus got in on Friday afternoon."

I'd been there for only three weeks. After I graduated from Hunter College, I didn't know what to do. I had a B.A. in poli sci, but I didn't really have any skills. Couldn't type or work a computer. I wrote all my papers in longhand and used a typing service. I didn't know what I wanted to do, but I had to pay the rent. When I applied for a professional-trainee position that Carter's Home had advertised at Hunter, the personnel officer told me that there was nothing available, but maybe if I took the mailroom position something might open up.

"They hired two white P.T.s the day after you came," Ernie told me at the end of the first week. I decided to ignore that. Maybe those people had applied before me, or maybe they had skills with computers or something.

I didn't mind my job. Big Linda Washington and Little Linda Brown worked with me. The Lindas had earphones and listened to music while they wheeled around their canvas mail carts. Big Linda liked rap and Little Linda liked R & B. Neither one talked to me much.

My only friend at work was Ernie. He was the interoffice mail director. He and I would sit in the basement and talk for hours sometimes. Ernie was proud of his years at Carter's Home. He liked the job and the company, but he had no patience for most of the bosses.

"Workin' for white people is always the same thing," Ernie would say.

"But Mr. Drew's black," I said the first time I heard his perennial complaint. Drew was the supervisor for all postal and interoffice communication. He was a small man with hard eyes and breath that smelled of vitamins.

"Used to be," Ernie said. "Used to be. But ever since he got promoted he forgot all about that. Used to be he'd come down here and we'd talk like you 'n' me doin'. But now he just stands at the door and grins and nods. Now he's so scared I'm gonna pull him down that he won't even sit for a minute."

"I don't get it," I once said to Ernie. "How can you like the job and the company if you don't like the people you work for?"

"It's a talent," he replied.

"Why 'on't you tuck in your shirt?" Big Linda Washington said, sneering at me on the afternoon after I had seen Mona Donelli at her third-floor desk. "You look like some kinda fool, hangin' out all over the place."

Big Linda was taller than I, broader, too, and I'm pretty big. Her hair was straightened and frosted in gold. She wore dresses in primary colors, as a rule. Her skin was berry black. Her face, unless it was contorted from appraising me, was pretty.

We were in the service elevator, going up to the fifth floor. I tucked the white shirttails into my black jeans.

"At least you could make it even so the buttons go straight down," she remarked. "Just 'cause you light-skinned you can't go 'round lookin' like a mess."

I would have had to open up my pants to do it right, and I didn't want Big Linda to get any more upset than she already was.

She grunted and sucked a tooth.

The elevator opened, and she rolled out her cart. We had parallel routes, but I went in the opposite direction, deciding to take mail from the bottom of the stack rather than let her humiliate me.

The first person I ran into was Mona. Now she was wearing a one-piece deep red dress held up by spaghetti straps. Her breasts were free under the thin fabric, and her legs were bare. Mona was short, with thick black hair and green eyes. Her skin had a hint of olive but not so deep as what you think of as a Sicilian complexion.

"I can see why you were wearing that sweater at your desk," I said.

"What?" she replied, in a very unfriendly tone.

"That white sweater you were wearing," I said.

"What's wrong with you? I don't even own a white sweater."

She turned abruptly and clicked away on her red high heels. I wondered what had happened. I kept thinking that it was because of my twisted-up shirt. Maybe that's what made people treat me badly, maybe it was my appearance.

I continued along my route, pulling files from the bottom and placing them in the right "in" boxes.

"If the boxes ain't side by side, just drop it anywhere and pick up whatever you want to," Ernie had told me on my first day. "That's what I do. Mr. Averill put down the rules thirteen years ago, just before they kicked him upstairs."

Bernard Averill was the vice president in charge of all non-professional employees. He administered the cafeteria workers, the maintenance staff, secretarial services, and both the inter-office and postal mail departments. He was Ernie's hero because he was the only V.P. who had worked his way up from an entry level position.

When I'd finished the route, I went through the exit door at the far end of the hall to get a drink of water. I planned to wait there long enough for Big Linda to have gone back down. While I was at the water fountain, a fly buzzed by my head. It caught my attention because not many flies made it into the air-conditioned buildings around Wall Street, even in summer.

The fly landed on my hand, then flew to the cold aluminum bowl of the water fountain. He didn't have enough time to drink before zooming up to the ceiling. From there he lit on the doorknob, then landed on the baby finger of my left hand. After that he buzzed down to the floor. He took no more than a second to enjoy each perch.

"You sure jumpy, Mr. Fly," I said, as I might have when I was a child. "But you might be a Miss Fly, huh?"

The idea that the neurotic fly could be a female brought Mona to mind. I hustled my cart toward the elevator, passing Big Linda on the way. She was standing in the hall, talking to another young black woman.

"I got to wait for a special delivery from, um, investigations," Big Linda explained.

"I got to go see a friend on three," I replied.

"Oh." Big Linda seemed relieved.

I realized that she was afraid I'd tell Ernie that she was idling with her friends. Somehow that stung more than her sneers.

She was still wearing the beaded sweater, but instead of the eraser she had a tiny Wite-Out brush in her hand, half an inch from a sheet of paper on her violet blotter.

"I bet that blotter used to be blue, huh?"

"What?" She frowned at me.

"That blotter—it looks violet, purple, but that's because it used to be blue but the sun shined on it, from the window."

She turned her upper torso to look out the window. I could see the soft contours of her small breasts against the white fabric.

"Oh," she said, turning back to me. "I guess."

"Yeah," I said. "I notice things like that. My mother says that's why I never finish anything. She says I get distracted all the time and don't keep my eye on the job."

"Do you have more mail for me?"

"No, uh-uh, I was just thinking."

She looked at the drying Wite-Out brush and then jammed it back into the small bottle that was in her other hand.

"I was thinking about when I saw you this morning," I continued. "About when I saw you and asked about the air conditioning and your sweater and you looked at me like I was crazy."

"Yes," she said, "why did you ask that?"

"Because I thought you were Mona Donelli," I said triumphantly.

"Oh." She sounded disappointed. "Most people figure out that I'm not Mona because my nameplate says Lana Donelli."

"Oh," I said, suddenly crushed. I could notice a blotter turning violet, but I couldn't read a nameplate.

Lana was amused.

"Don't look so sad," she said. "I mean, even when they see the name some people still call me Mona."

"They do?"

"Yeah. It's a problem having an identical twin. They see the name and think that Mona's a nickname or something. Isn't that dumb?"

"I didn't know you had a sister, but I saw Mona on the fifth floor in a red dress, and then I saw a fly that couldn't sit still, and then I knew that you had to be somebody else," I said.

"You're funny," Lana said, crinkling up her nose, as if she were trying to identify a scent. "What's your name?"

"Rufus Coombs."

"Hi, Rufus," she said.

"Hey," I said.

My apartment is on 168th Street, in Washington Heights. It's pretty much a Spanish-speaking neighborhood. I don't know many people there, but the rent is all I can afford. My apartment—living room with a kitchen alcove, a small bedroom, and a toilet with a shower—is on the eighth floor and looks out over the Hudson. The $458 a month includes heat and gas, but I pay my own electric. I took it because of the view. There was a cheaper unit on the second floor, but it had windows that look out on a brick wall and I was afraid I'd be burglarized.

"Do you own a TV or a stereo?" my mother asked when I was trying to decide which apartment to take.

"You know I don't."

"Then you ain't got nuthin' to burgle," she said. I had called her in California, where she lives with my uncle.

"But they don't know that," I said. "I might have a color TV with VCR and a bad sound system."

"Lord," my mother prayed.

I didn't own much; she was right about that. Single mattress on the floor, an old oak chair that I found on the street, and kitchen shelving that I bought from a liquidator, four bookshelves, propped up in the corner. I also have a rice pot, a frying pan, and a kettle, with cutlery and enough plates for two.

I have Rachel, an ex-girlfriend living in the East Village, who will call me back at work if I don't call her too often. My two other friends are Eric Chen and Willy Jones. They both live in Brooklyn and still go to school.

That evening, I climbed the seven flights up to my apartment. The elevator had stopped working a month ago. I sat in my chair and looked at the water. It was peaceful and relaxing. A fly was buzzing against the glass, trying to get out.

I got up to kill him. But up close I hesitated. His coloring was unusual, a metallic green. The dull red eyes seemed too large for the body, as though he were an intelligent mutant fly from some far-flung future on late-night television.

He buzzed against the pane, trying to get away from me. When I returned to my chair, he settled. The red sun was hovering above the cliffs of New Jersey. The green fly watched. I thought of the fly I'd seen at work. That bug had been black and fairly small by fly standards. Then I thought about Mona and then Lana. The smallest nudge of an erection stirred. I thought of calling Rachel, but I didn't have the heart to walk the three blocks to a phone booth. So I watched the sunset gleaming around the fly, who was now just a black spot on the window. I fell asleep in the chair.

At three A.M. I woke up and made macaroni and cheese from a mix. The fly came into the cooking alcove, where I stood eating my meal. He lit on the big spoon I'd used to stir the dinner and joined me for supper.

Ernie told me that mortgaging didn't get much interoffice mail.

"Most of their correspondence comes by regular mail," he explained.

"Aren't they on the newsletter list?"

"She a white girl?"

"So?"

"Nuthin'. But I want you to tell me what it's like if you get it."

I didn't answer him.

I began delivering invitations to office parties, sales force newsletters, and productivity tips penned by Mr. Averill to Lana Donelli. We made small talk for thirty seconds or so, then she'd pick up the phone to make a call. I always looked back as I rounded the corner to make sure she really had a call to make. She always did.

The following Monday, I bought a glass paperweight with the image of a smiling Buddha's face etched in the bottom. When I got to Lana's desk, she wasn't there. I waited around for a while but she didn't appear, so I wrote her a note that said "From Rufus to Lana" and put the leaded-glass weight on it.

I went away excited and half scared. What if she didn't see my note? What if she did and thought it was stupid? I was so nervous that I didn't go back to her desk that day.

"I really shouldn't have left it," I said that night to the green fly. He was perched peacefully on the rim of a small saucer. I had filled the inner depression with a honey-and-water solution. I was eating a triple cheeseburger with bacon and fries from Wendy's. My pet fly seemed happy with his honey water and buzzed my sandwich only a few times before settling down to drink.

"Maybe she doesn't like me," I said. "Maybe it's just that she was nice to me because she feels sorry for me. But how will I know if I don't try and see if she likes me?"

"Hi," I said to Lana the next morning. She was wearing a jean jacket over a white T-shirt. She smiled and nodded. I handed her Mr. Averill's productivity tips newsletter.

"Did you see the paperweight?"

"Oh, yeah," she said without looking me in the eye. "Thanks." Then she picked up the phone and began pressing buttons. "Hi, Tristan? Lana. I wanted to know if . . ." She put her hand over the receiver and looked at me. "Can I do something else for you?"

"Oh," I said. "No. No," and I wheeled away in a kind of euphoria.

It's only now, when I look back on that moment, that I can see the averted eyes, the quick call, and the rude dismissal for what they were. All I heard then was "Thanks." I even remember a smile. Maybe she did smile for a brief moment, maybe not.

On Tuesday and Wednesday, I left three presents for her. I left them when she was away from her desk. I got her a small box of four Godiva chocolates, a silk rose, and a jar of fancy rose-petal jelly. I didn't leave any more notes. I was sure that she'd know who it was.

On Thursday evening, I went to a nursery on the East Side, just south of Harlem proper. There I bought a bonsai, a crab apple tree, for $347.52. I figured I'd leave it during Lana's Friday lunch break, and then she'd be so happy that on Monday she'd have to have lunch with me, no matter what.

I suspected that something was wrong when my pet fly went missing. He didn't even show up when I started eating a Beef Burrito Supreme from Taco Bell. I checked the big spiderweb near the bathroom window, but there were no little bundles that I could see.

That evening I was on edge, thinking I saw flies flitting into every corner.

"What's that?" Ernie asked me the next morning when I came in with the tiny crab apple tree.

"It's a tree."

"Tree for what?"

"My friend Willy wanted me to pick it up for him. He wants it for his new apartment, and the only place he could get it is up near me. I'm gonna meet him at lunch and give it to him."

"Uh-huh," Ernie said.

"You got my cart loaded?" I asked him.

Just then the Lindas came out of the service elevator. Big Linda looked at me and shook her head, managing to express contempt and pity at the same time.

"There's your carts," Ernie said to them.

They attached their earphones and rolled back to the service elevator. Little Linda was looking me in the eye as the slatted doors closed. She was still looking at me as the lift rose.

"What about me?"

"That's all I got right now. Why don't you sit here with me?"

"Okay." I sat down, expecting Ernie to bring up one of his regular topics, either something about Georgia, white bosses, or the horse races, which he followed but never wagered on. But instead of saying anything he just started reading the *Post*.

After a few minutes I was going to say something, but the big swinging door opened. Our boss, Mr. Drew, leaned in. He smiled and nodded at Ernie and then pointed at me.

"Rufus Coombs?"

"Yeah?"

"Come with me."

I followed the dapper little man through the messy service hall to the passenger elevator, which the couriers rarely took. It was a two-man elevator, so Drew and I had to stand very close to each other. He wore too much cologne, but otherwise he was perfect for his supervisory job, wearing a light gray suit with a shirt that hinted at yellow. I knew that he must have been in his forties, but he could have passed for a graduate student. He was light-skinned, like me, with what my mother called good hair. There were freckles around his eyes. I could see all of that because Mr. Drew avoided my gaze. He wouldn't engage me in any way.

We got out on the second floor and went to his office, which was at the far end of the mail-sorting room.

I looked around the room as Drew was entering his office. I saw Mona looking at me from the crevice of a doorway. I knew it was Mona because she was wearing a skimpy dress that could have been worn on a hot date. I got only a glimpse of her before she ducked away.

"Come on in, Coombs," Drew said.

The office was tiny. Drew actually had to stand on the tips of his toes and hug the wall to get behind his desk. There was a stool in front of the desk, not a chair.

By the time he said, "Sit down," I had lost my nervousness. I gauged the power of Mr. Leonard Drew by the size of his office.

"You're in trouble, Rufus," he said, looking as somber as he could.

"I am?"

He lifted a pink sheet of paper and shook it at me.

"Do you recognize this?" he asked.

"No."

"This is a sexual-harassment complaint form."

"Yeah?"

"It names you on the complaint."

"I don't get it."

"Lana Donelli . . ." He went on to explain everything that I had been doing and feeling for the last week as if they were crimes. Going to Lana's desk, talking to her, leaving gifts. Even remarking on her clothes had been construed as if there was a sexual innuendo attached. By the time he was finished, I was worried that the police might be called in.

"Lana says that she's afraid to come in to work," Drew said, his freckles disappearing into angry lines around his eyes.

I wanted to say that I didn't mean to scare her, but I could see that my intentions didn't matter, that a small woman like Lana would be afraid of a big, sloppy mail clerk hovering over her and leaving notes and presents.

"I'm sorry," I said.

"Sorry doesn't mean much when it's got to this point," he said. "If it was up to me, I'd send you home right now. But Mr. Averill says he wants to talk to you."

"Aren't you supposed to give me a warning?" I asked.

Drew twisted up his lips, as if he had tasted something so foul that he just had to spit it out. "You haven't been here a month. You're on probation."

"Oh," I said.

"Well?" he asked after a few moments.

"What?"

"Go back to the mailroom and stay down there. Tell Ernie that I don't want you in the halls. You're supposed to meet Mr. Averill at one-forty-five, in his office. I've given him my recommendation to let you go. After something like this, there's really no place for you here. But he can still refer the matter to the police. Lana might want a restraining order."

I wanted to tell him that a restraining order was ridiculous. I wanted to go to Lana and tell her the same thing. I wanted to tell her that I bought her a rose because she wore rose toilet water, that I bought her the tree because the sun on her blotter could support a plant. I really liked her. But even while I was imagining what I could say, I knew that it didn't matter.

"Well?" Drew said. "Go."

Ernie made busywork for us that morning. He told me that he was upset about what had happened, that he'd told Drew to go easy.

"You know if you was white this wouldn't never have happened," Ernie said. "That girl just scared you some Mandingo gonna rape her. You know that's a shame."

I went up to the third floor a little before twelve. Lana was sitting at her desk, writing on a yellow legal pad. I walked right up to her and started talking so she couldn't ignore what I had to say.

"I just wanted to tell you that I'm sorry if you think I was harassing you. I didn't mean it, but I can see how you might have thought I was. . . ."

Lana's face got hard.

". . . but I'm gonna get fired right after lunch and I just wanted to ask you one thing."

She didn't say anything, so I said, "Is it because I'm black that you're so scared'a me?"

"You're black?" she said. "I thought you were Puerto Rican or Spanish or something. I didn't know you were black. My boyfriend is black. You just give me the creeps. That's why I complained. I didn't think they were going to fire you."

She didn't care if I lived or died. She wasn't even scared, just disgusted. I thought I was in love, and I was about to be fired, and she'd never even looked close enough to see me.

I was so embarrassed that I went away without saying another word. I went down to the mailroom and sorted rubber bands until one-thirty-five.

Vice President Bernard Averill's office was on the forty-eighth floor of the Carter's Home Building. His secretary's office was larger by far than Mr. Drew's cubbyhole. The smiling blonde led me into Averill's airy room. Behind him was a giant window looking out over Battery Park, Ellis Island, and the Statue of Liberty. I would have been impressed if I wasn't empty inside.

211

Averill was on the phone.

"Sorry, Nick," he said into the receiver. "My one-forty-five is here."

He stood up, tall and thin. His gray suit looked expensive. His white shirt was crisp and bright under a rainbow tie. His gray hair was combed back, and his mustache was sharp enough to cut bread, as my mother is known to say.

"Sit down, Mr. Coombs."

He sat also. In front of him were two sheets of paper. At his left hand was the pink harassment form, at his right was a white form. Outside, the Budweiser blimp hovered next to Lady Liberty.

Averill brought his fingertips to just under his nose and gazed at a spot above my head.

"How's Ernie?" he asked.

"He's good," I said. "He's a great boss."

"He's a good man. He likes you."

I didn't know what to say to that.

Averill looked down at his desk. "This does not compute."

"What?"

He patted the white page. "This says that you're a college graduate, magna cum laude in political science, that you came here to be a professional trainee." He patted the pink sheet. "This says that you're an interoffice-mail courier who harasses secretaries in the mortgage department."

Averill reached into his vest pocket and came out with an open package of cigarettes. At orientation they'd told us that there was absolutely no smoking anywhere in the building, but he took one out anyway. He lit up and took a deep drag, holding the smoke in his lungs for a long time before exhaling.

"Is there something wrong with you?" he asked.

"I don't think so," I said, swallowing hard.

Averill examined me through the tobacco haze. He seemed disgusted.

Staring directly into my eyes, he said, "Do you see this desk?"

The question petrified me, but I couldn't say why. Maybe it was the intensity of his gaze.

"I could call five or six women into this office right now and have them right here on this desk. Right here." He jabbed the desk with his middle finger.

My heart was racing. I had to open my mouth to get enough air.

"They're not going to fill out any pink slips," he said. "Do you know why?"

I shook my head.

"Because I'm a man. I don't go running around leaving chocolates on empty desks like bait. I don't fake reasons to come skulking around with newsletters."

Averill seemed angry as well as offended. I wondered if he knew Lana, or maybe her family. Maybe he wanted to fight me. I wanted to quit right then, to stand up and walk out before anything else happened. I was already thinking of where I could apply for another job when Averill sat back and smiled.

"Why are you in the interoffice-mail room?" he asked, suddenly much friendlier.

"No P.T. positions were open when I applied," I said.

"Nonsense. We don't have a limit on P.T s."

"But Ms. Worth said —"

"Oh." Averill held up his hand. "Reena. You know, Ernie helped me out when I got here, twenty-three years ago. I was just a little older than you. They didn't have the P.T. program back then, just a few guys like Ernie. He never even finished high school, but he showed me the ropes."

Averill drummed the fingers of his free hand between the two forms that represented me.

"I know this Lana's sister," he said. "Always wearing those cocktail dresses in to work. Her boss is afraid to say anything, otherwise he might get a pink slip, too." He paused to ponder some more. "How would you like to be a P.T. floater?"

"What's that?" I asked.

"Bumps you up to a grade seven and lets you move around in the different departments until you find a fit."

I was a grade B1.

"I thought you were going to fire me."

"That's what Drew suggested, but Ernie says that it's just a mixup. What if I talked to Lana? What if I asked her to hold this back, to give you a second chance?"

"I'd like that," I said. "Thanks."

"Probably be better if I let Drew fire you, you know," he said, standing up. I stood, too. "I mean if you fuck up once you'll probably just do it again, right?"

He held out his hand.

Watching the forbidden smoke curl around his head, I imagined that Averill was some kind of devil. When I thanked him and shook his hand, something inside me wanted to scream.

I found six unused crack vials a block from the subway stop near my apartment. I knew they were unused because they still had the little plastic stoppers in them.

When I got upstairs, I spent hours searching my place. I looked under the mattress and behind the toilet, under the radiator, and even down under the burners on the stove. Finally, after midnight, I decided to open the windows.

The fly had crawled down into the crack between the window frame and the sill in my bedroom. His green body had dried out, which made his eyes even bigger. He'd gone down there to die, or maybe, I thought, he was trying to get away from me. Maybe I had killed him. Later, I found out that flies have a very short life span. He probably died of old age.

I took his small, dried-out corpse and put it in one of the crack vials. I stoppered him in the tiny glass coffin and buried him among the roots of the bonsai crab apple.

"So you finally bought something nice for your house," my mother said after I told her about the changes in my life. "Maybe next you'll get a real bed."

How to Tell a True War Story

Tim O'Brien

Tim O'Brien is best known for his writings about the Vietnam War. Born in Minnesota, he grew up in Worthington and was a college student when the war started. Although he participated in anti-war protests, he found himself drafted, became an infantry sergeant in Vietnam, and came home with a Purple Heart. Upon returning, he wrote his recollections of the war and published them under the title If I Die in a Combat Zone, Box Me Up and Ship Me Home *(1973). Among his other works are* Northern Lights *(1975)* Going after Cacciato *(1978),* Speaking of Courage *(1980), and* The Things They Carried *(1990), from which the following story has been selected. More recent works include,* In the Lake of the Woods *(1994),* Tomcat in Love *(1998), and* July, July *(2002).*

This is True.

I had a buddy in Vietnam. His name was Bob Kiley, but everybody called him Rat.

A friend of his gets killed, so about a week later Rat sits down and writes a letter to the guy's sister. Rat tells her what a great brother she had, how together the guy was, a number one pal and comrade. A real soldier's soldier, Rat says. Then he tells a few stories to make the point, how her brother would always volunteer for stuff nobody else would volunteer for in a million years, dangerous stuff, like doing recon or going out on these really badass night patrols. Stainless steel balls, Rat tells her. The guy was a little crazy, for sure, but crazy in a good way, a real daredevil, because he liked the challenge of it, he liked testing himself, just man against gook. A great, great guy, Rat says.

Anyway, it's a terrific letter, very personal and touching. Rat almost bawls writing it. He gets all teary telling about the good times they had together, how her brother

made the war seem almost fun, always raising hell and lighting up villes and bringing smoke to bear every which way. A great sense of humor, too. Like the time at this
river when he went fishing with a whole damn crate of hand grenades. Probably the
funniest thing in world history, Rat says, all that gore, about twenty zillion dead gook
fish. Her brother, he had the right attitude. He knew how to have a good time. On
Halloween, this real hot spooky night, the dude paints up his body all different colors and puts on this weird mask and hikes over to a ville and goes trick-or-treating
almost stark naked, just boots and balls and an M-16. A tremendous human being,
Rat says. Pretty nutso sometimes, but you could trust him with your life.

And then the letter gets very sad and serious. Rat pours his heart out. He says
he loved the guy. He says the guy was his best friend in the world. They were like soul
mates, he says, like twins or something, they had a whole lot in common. He tells the
guy's sister he'll look her up when the war's over.

So what happens?

Rat mails the letter. He waits two months. The dumb cooze never writes back.

A true war story is never moral. It does not instruct, nor encourage virtue, nor suggest models of proper human behavior, nor restrain men from doing the things men
have always done. If a story seems moral, do not believe it. If at the end of a war
story you feel uplifted, or if you feel that some small bit of rectitude has been sal-
vaged from the larger waste, then you have been made the victim of a very old and
terrible lie. There is no rectitude whatsoever. There is no virtue. As a first rule of
thumb, therefore, you can tell a true war story by its absolute and uncompromising
allegiance to obscenity and evil. Listen to Rat Kiley. Cooze, he says. He does not say
bitch. He certainly does not say woman, or girl. He says cooze. Then he spits and
stares. He's nineteen years old—it's too much for him—so he looks at you with those
big sad gentle killer eyes and says *cooze*, because his friend is dead, and because it's
so incredibly sad and true: she never wrote back.

You can tell a true war story if it embarrasses you. If you don't care for obscenity, you don't care for the truth; if you don't care for the truth, watch how you
vote. Send guys to war, they come home talking dirty.

Listen to Rat: "Jesus Christ, man, I write this beautiful fuckin' letter, I slave over
it, and what happens? The dumb cooze never writes back."

The dead guy's name was Curt Lemon. What happened was, we crossed a muddy
river and marched west into the mountains, and on the third day we took a break along
a trail junction in deep jungle. Right away, Lemon and Rat Kiley started goofing. They
didn't understand about the spookiness. They were kids; they just didn't know. A nature hike, they thought, not even a war, so they went off into the shade of some giant
trees—quadruple canopy, no sunlight at all—and they were giggling and calling each
other yellow mother and playing a silly game they'd invented. The game involved
smoke grenades, which were harmless unless you did stupid things, and what they
did was pull out the pin and stand a few feet apart and play catch under the shade of

those huge trees. Whoever chickened out was a yellow mother. And if nobody chickened out, the grenade would make a light popping sound and they'd be covered with smoke and they'd laugh and dance around and then do it again.

It's all exactly true.

It happened, to *me*, nearly twenty years ago, and I still remember that trail junction and those giant trees and a soft dripping sound somewhere beyond the trees. I remember the smell of moss. Up in the canopy there were tiny white blossoms, but no sunlight at all, and I remember the shadows spreading out under the trees where Curt Lemon and Rat Kiley were playing catch with smoke grenades. Mitchell Sanders sat flipping his yo-yo. Norman Bowker and Kiowa and Dave Jensen were dozing, or half dozing, and all around us were those ragged green mountains.

Except for the laughter things were quiet.

At one point, I remember, Mitchell Sanders turned and looked at me, not quite nodding, as if to warn me about something, as if he already *knew*, then after a while he rolled up his yo-yo and moved away.

It's hard to tell you what happened next.

They were just goofing. There was a noise, I suppose, which must've been the detonator, so I glanced behind me and watched Lemon step from the shade into bright sunlight. His face was suddenly brown and shining. A handsome kid, really. Sharp gray eyes, lean and narrow-waisted, and when he died it was almost beautiful, the way the sunlight came around him and lifted him up and sucked him high into a tree full of moss and vines and white blossoms.

In any war story, but especially a true one, it's difficult to separate what happened from what seemed to happen. What seems to happen becomes its own happening and has to be told that way. The angles of vision are skewed. When a booby trap explodes, you close your eyes and duck and float outside yourself. When a guy dies, like Curt Lemon, you look away and then look back for a moment and then look away again. The pictures get jumbled; you tend to miss a lot. And then afterward, when you go to tell about it, there is always that surreal seemingness, which makes the story seem untrue, but which in fact represents the hard and exact truth as it *seemed*.

In many cases a true war story cannot be believed. If you believe it, be skeptical. It's a question of credibility. Often the crazy stuff is true and the normal stuff isn't, because the normal stuff is necessary to make you believe the truly incredible craziness.

In other cases you can't even tell a true war story. Sometimes it's just beyond telling.

I heard this one, for example, from Mitchell Sanders. It was near dusk and we were sitting at my foxhole along a wide muddy river north of Quang Ngai. I remember how peaceful the twilight was. A deep pinkish red spilled out on the river, which moved without sound, and in the morning we would cross the river and march west into the mountains. The occasion was right for a good story.

"God's truth," Mitchell Sanders said. "A six-man patrol goes up into the mountains on a basic listening-post operation. The idea's to spend a week up there, just lie low and listen for enemy movement. They've got a radio along, so if they hear anything suspicious—anything—they're supposed to call in artillery or gunships, whatever it takes. Otherwise they keep strict field discipline. Absolute silence. They just listen."

Sanders glanced at me to make sure I had the scenario. He was playing with his yo-yo, dancing it with short, tight little strokes of the wrist.

His face was blank in the dusk.

"We're talking regulation, by-the-book LP. These six guys, they don't say boo for a solid week. They don't got tongues. *All* ears."

"Right," I said.

"Understand me?"

"Invisible."

Sanders nodded.

"Affirm," he said. "Invisible. So what happens is, these guys get themselves deep in the bush, all camouflaged up, and they lie down and wait and that's all they do, nothing else, they lie there for seven straight days and just listen. And man, I'll tell you—it's spooky. This is mountains. You don't *know* spooky till you been there. Jungle, sort of, except it's way up in the clouds and there's always this fog—like rain, except it's not raining—everything's all wet and swirly and tangled up and you can't see jack, you can't find your own pecker to piss with. Like you don't even have a body. Serious spooky. You just go with the vapors—the fog sort of takes you in . . . And the sounds, man. The sounds carry forever. You hear stuff nobody should *ever* hear."

Sanders was quiet for a second, just working the yo-yo, then he smiled at me.

"So after a couple days the guys start hearing this real soft, kind of wacked-out music. Weird echoes and stuff. Like a radio or something, but it's not a radio, it's this strange gook music that comes right out of the rocks. Faraway, sort of, but right up close, too. They try to ignore it. But it's a listening post, right? So they listen. And every night they keep hearing that crazyass gook concert. All kinds of chimes and xylophones. I mean, this is wilderness—no way, it can't be real—but there it *is*, like the mountains are tuned in to Radio fucking Hanoi. Naturally they get nervous. One guy sticks Juicy Fruit in his ears. Another guy almost flips. Thing is, though, they can't report music. They can't get on the horn and call back to base and say, 'Hey, listen, we need some firepower, we got to blow away this weirdo gook rock band.' They can't do that. It wouldn't go down. So they lie there in the fog and keep their mouths shut. And what makes it extra bad, see, is the poor dudes can't horse around like normal. Can't joke it away. Can't even talk to each other except maybe in whispers, all hush-hush, and that just revs up the willies. All they do is listen."

Again there was some silence as Mitchell Sanders looked out on the river. The dark was coming on hard now, and off to the west I could see the mountains rising in silhouette, all the mysteries and unknowns.

"This next part," Sanders said quietly, "you won't believe."

"Probably not," I said.

"You won't. And you know why?" He gave me a long, tried smile. "Because it happened. Because every word is absolutely dead-on true."

Sanders made a sound in his throat, like a sigh, as if to say he didn't care if I believed him or not. But he did care. He wanted me to feel the truth, to believe by the raw force of feeling. He seemed sad, in a way.

"These six guys," he said, "they're pretty fried out by now, and one night they start hearing voices. Like at a cocktail party. That's what it sounds like, this big swank gook cocktail party somewhere out there in the fog. Music and chitchat and stuff. It's crazy, I know, but they hear the champagne corks. They hear the actual martini glasses. Real hoity-toity, all very civilized, except this isn't civilization. This is Nam.

"Anyway, the guys try to be cool. They just lie there and groove, but after a while they start hearing—you won't believe this—they hear chamber music. They hear violins and cellos. They hear this terrific mama-san soprano. Then after a while they hear gook opera and a glee club and the Haiphong Boys Choir and a barbershop quartet and all kinds of weird chanting and Buddha-Buddha stuff. And the whole time, in the background, there's still that cocktail party going on. All these different voices. Not human voices, though. Because it's the mountains. Follow me? The rock—it's *talking*. And the fog, too, and the grass and the goddamn mongooses. Everything talks. The trees talk politics, the monkeys talk religion. The whole country. Vietnam. The place talks. It talks. Understand? Nam—it truly *talks*.

"The guys can't cope. They lose it. They get on the radio and report enemy movement—a whole army, they say—and they order up the firepower. They get arty and gunships. They call in air strikes. And I'll tell you, they fuckin' crash that cocktail party. All night long, they just smoke those mountains. They make jungle juice. They blow away trees and glee clubs and whatever else there is to blow away. Scorch time. They walk napalm up and down the ridges. They bring in the Cobras and F-4s, they use Willie Peter and HE and incendiaries. It's all fire. They make those mountains burn.

"Around dawn things finally get quiet. Like you never even *heard* quiet before. One of those real thick, real misty days—just clouds and fog, they're off in this special zone—and the mountains are absolutely dead-flat silent. Like Brigadoon—pure vapor, you know? Everything's all sucked up inside the fog. Not a single sound, except they still *hear* it.

"So they pack up and start humping. They head down the mountain, back to base camp, and when they get there they don't say diddly. They don't talk. Not a word, like they're deaf and dumb. Later on this fat bird colonel comes up and asks what the hell happened out there. What'd they hear? Why all the ordnance? The man's ragged out, he gets down tight on their case. I mean, they spent six trillion dollars on firepower, and this fatass colonel wants answers, he wants to know what the fuckin' story is.

"But the guys don't say zip. They just look at him for a while, sort of funny like, sort of amazed, and the whole war is right there in that stare. It says everything you can't ever say. It says, man, you got *wax* in your ears. It says, poor bastard, you'll never know—wrong frequency—you don't *even* want to hear this. Then they salute the fucker and walk away, because certain stories you don't ever tell."

You can tell a true war story by the way it never seems to end. Not then, not ever. Not when Mitchell Sanders stood up and moved off into the dark.

It all happened.

Even now, at this instant, I remember that yo-yo. In a way, I suppose, you had to be there, you had to hear it, but I could tell how desperately Sanders wanted me to believe him, his frustration at not quite getting the details right, not quite pinning down the final and definitive truth.

And I remember sitting at my foxhole that night, watching the shadows of Quang Ngai, thinking about the coming day and how we would cross the river and march west into the mountains, all the ways I might die, all the things I did not understand.

Late in the night Mitchell Sanders touched my shoulder.

"Just came to me," he whispered. "The moral, I mean. Nobody listens. Nobody hears nothin'. Like that fatass colonel. The politicians, all the civilian types. Your girlfriend. My girlfriend. Everybody's sweet little virgin girlfriend. What they need is to go out on LP. The vapors, man. Trees and rocks—you got to *listen* to your enemy."

And then again, in the morning, Sanders came up to me. The platoon was preparing to move out, checking weapons, going through all the little rituals that preceded a day's march. Already the lead squad had crossed the river and was filing off toward the west.

"I got a confession to make," Sanders said. "Last night, man, I had to make up a few things."

"I know that."

"The glee club. There wasn't any glee club."

"Right."

"No opera."

"Forget it, I understand."

"Yeah, but listen, it's still true. Those six guys, they heard wicked sound out there. They heard sound you just plain won't believe."

Sanders pulled on his rucksack, closed his eyes for a moment, then almost smiled at me. I knew what was coming.

"All right," I said, "What's the moral?"

"Forget it."

"No, go ahead."

For a long while he was quiet, looking away, and the silence kept stretching out until it was almost embarrassing. Then he shrugged and gave me a stare that lasted all day.

"Hear that quiet, man?" he said. "That quiet—just listen. There's your moral."

In a true war story, if there's a moral at all, it's like the thread that makes the cloth. You can't tease it out. You can't extract the meaning without unraveling the deeper meaning. And in the end, really, there's nothing much to say about a true war story, except maybe "Oh."

True war stories do not generalize. They do not indulge in abstraction or analysis.

For example: War is hell. As a moral declaration the old truism seems perfectly true, and yet because it abstracts, because it generalizes, I can't believe it with my stomach. Nothing turns inside.

It comes down to gut instinct. A true war story, if truly told, makes the stomach believe.

This one does it for me. I've told it before—many times, many versions—but here's what actually happened.

We crossed that river and marched west into the mountains. On the third day, Curt Lemon stepped on a booby-trapped 105 round. He was playing catch with Rat Kiley, laughing, and then he was dead. The trees were thick; it took nearly an hour to cut an LZ for the dustoff.

Later, higher in the mountains, we came across a baby VC water buffalo. What it was doing there I don't know—no farms or paddies—but we chased it down and got a rope around it and led it along to a deserted village where we set up for the night. After supper Rat Kiley went over and stroked its nose.

He opened up a can of C rations, pork and beans, but the baby buffalo wasn't interested.

Rat shrugged.

He stepped back and shot it through the right front knee. The animal did not make a sound. It went down hard, then got up again, and Rat took careful aim and shot off an ear. He shot it in the hindquarters and in the little hump at its back. He shot it twice in the flanks. It wasn't to kill; it was to hurt. He put the rifle muzzle up against the mouth and shot the mouth away. Nobody said much. The whole platoon stood there watching, feeling all kinds of things, but there wasn't a great deal of pity for the baby water buffalo. Curt Lemon was dead. Rat Kiley had lost his best friend in the world. Later in the week he would write a long personal letter to the guy's sister, who would not write back, but for now it was a question of pain. He shot off the tail. He shot away chunks of meat below the ribs. All around us there was the smell of smoke and filth and deep greenery, and the evening was humid and very hot. Rat went to automatic. He shot randomly, almost casually, quick little spurts in the belly and butt. Then he reloaded, squatted down, and shot it in the left front knee. Again the animal fell hard and tried to get up, but this time it couldn't quite make it. It wobbled and went down sideways. Rat shot it in the nose. He bent forward and whispered something, as if talking to a pet, then he shot it in the throat. All the while the baby buffalo was silent, or almost silent, just a light bubbling sound where the nose had been. It lay very still. Nothing moved except the eyes, which were enormous, the pupils shiny black and dumb.

Rat Kiley was crying. He tried to say something, but then cradled his rifle and went off by himself.

The rest of us stood in a ragged circle around the baby buffalo. For a time no one spoke. We had witnessed something essential, something brand-new and profound, a piece of the world so startling there was not yet a name for it.

Somebody kicked the baby buffalo.

It was still alive, though just barely, just in the eyes.

"Amazing," Dave Jensen said. "My whole life, I never seen anything like it."

"Never?"

"Not hardly. Not once."

Kiowa and Mitchell Sanders picked up the baby buffalo. They hauled it across the open square, hoisted it up, and dumped it in the village well.

Afterward, we sat waiting for Rat to get himself together.

"Amazing," Dave Jensen kept saying. "A new wrinkle. I never seen it before."

Mitchell Sanders took out his yo-yo. "Well, that's Nam," he said. "Garden of Evil. Over here, man, every sin's real fresh and original."

How do you generalize?

War is hell, but that's not the half of it, because war is also mystery and terror and adventure and courage and discovery and holiness and pity and despair and long-ing and love. War is nasty; war is fun. War is thrilling; war is drudgery. War makes you a man; war makes you dead.

The truths are contradictory. It can be argued, for instance, that war is grotesque. But in truth war is also beauty. For all its horror, you can't help but gape at the awful majesty of combat. You stare out at tracer rounds unwinding through the dark like brilliant red ribbons. You crouch in ambush as a cool, impassive moon rises over the nighttime paddies. You admire the fluid symmetries of troops on the move, the har-monies of sound and shape and proportion, the great sheets of metal-fire streaming down from a gunship, the illumination rounds, the white phosphorus, the purply or-ange glow of napalm, the rocket's red glare. It's not pretty, exactly. It's astonishing. It fills the eye. It commands you. You hate it, yes, but your eyes do not. Like a killer for-est fire, like cancer under a microscope, any battle or bombing raid or artillery bar-rage has the aesthetic purity of absolute moral indifference—a powerful, implacable beauty—and a true war story will tell the truth about this, though the truth is ugly.

To generalize about war is like generalizing about peace. Almost everything is true. Almost nothing is true. At its core, perhaps, war is just another name for death, and yet any soldier will tell you, if he tells the truth, that proximity to death brings with it a corresponding proximity to life. After a firefight, there is always the im-mense pleasure of aliveness. The trees are alive. The grass, the soil—everything. All around you things are purely living, and you among them, and the aliveness makes you tremble. You feel an intense, out-of-the-skin awareness of your living self—your truest self, the human being you want to be and then become by the force of wanting it. In the midst of evil you want to be a good man. You want decency. You want justice and courtesy and human concord, things you never knew you wanted. There is a kind of largeness to it, a kind of godliness. Though it's odd, you're never more alive than when you're almost dead. You recognize what's valuable. Freshly, as if for the first time, you love what's best in yourself and in the world, all that might be lost. At the hour of dusk you sit at your foxhole and look out on a wide river turning pinkish red, and at the mountains beyond, and although in the morning you must cross the river and

221

go into the mountains and do terrible things and maybe die, even so, you find your-self studying the fine colors on the river, you feel wonder and awe at the setting of the sun, and you are filled with a hard, aching love for how the world could be and always should be, but now is not.

Mitchell Sanders was right. For the common solider, at least, war has the feel—the spiritual texture—of a great ghostly fog, thick and permanent. There is no clar-ity. Everything swirls. The old rules are no longer binding, the old truths no longer true. Right spills over into wrong. Order blends into chaos, love into hate, ugliness into beauty, law into anarchy, civility into savagery. The vapors suck you in. You can't tell where you are, or why you're there, and the only certainty is overwhelming ambiguity.

In war you lose your sense of the definite, hence your sense of truth itself, and therefore it's safe to say that in a true war story nothing is ever absolutely true.

Often in a true war story there is not even a point, or else the point doesn't hit you until twenty years later, in your sleep, and you wake up and shake your wife and start telling the story to her, except when you get to the end you've forgotten the point again. And then for a long time you lie there watching the story happen in your head. You listen to your wife's breathing. The war's over. You close your eyes. You smile and think, Christ, what's the *point?*

This one wakes me up.

In the mountains that day, I watched Lemon turn sideways. He laughed and said something to Rat Kiley. Then he took a peculiar half step, moving from shade into bright sunlight, and the booby-trapped 105 round blew him into a tree. The parts were just hanging there, so Dave Jensen and I were ordered to shinny up and peel him off. I remember the white bone of an arm. I remember pieces of skin and something wet and yellow that must've been the intestines. The gore was horrible, and stays with me. But what wakes me up twenty years later is Dave Jensen singing "Lemon Tree" as we threw down the parts.

You can tell a true war story by the questions you ask. Somebody tells a story, let's say, and afterward you ask, "Is it true?" and if the answer matters, you've got your answer.

For example, we've all heard this one. Four guys go down a trail. A grenade sails out. One guy jumps on it and takes the blast and saves his three buddies.

Is it true?

The answer matters.

You'd feel cheated if it never happened. Without the grounding reality, it's just a trite bit of puffery, pure Hollywood, untrue in the way all such stories are untrue. Yet even if it did happen—and maybe it did, anything's possible—even then you know it can't be true, because a true war story does not depend upon that kind of truth. Absolute occurrence is irrelevant. A thing may happen and be a total lie; another thing may not happen and be truer than the truth. For example: Four guys go down a trail. A grenade sails out. One guy jumps on it and takes the blast, but it's a killer grenade and everybody dies anyway. Before they die, though, one of the dead guys says, "The fuck you do *that* for?" and the jumper says, "Story of my life, man," and the other guy starts to smile but he's dead.

That's a true story that never happened.

Twenty years later, I can still see the sunlight on Lemon's face. I can see him turning, looking back at Rat Kiley, then he laughed and took that curious half step from shade into sunlight, his face suddenly brown and shining, and when his foot touched down, in that instant, he must've thought it was the sunlight that was killing him. It was not the sunlight. It was a rigged 105 round. But if I could ever get the story right, how the sun seemed to gather around him and pick him up and lift him high into a tree, if I could somehow recreate the fatal whiteness of that light, the quick glare, the obvious cause and effect, then you would believe the last thing Curt Lemon believed, which for him must've been the final truth.

Now and then, when I tell this story, someone will come up to me afterward and say she liked it. It's always a woman. Usually it's an older woman of kindly temperament and humane politics. She'll explain that as a rule she hates war stories; she can't understand why people want to wallow in all the blood and gore. But this one she liked. The poor baby buffalo, it made her sad. Sometimes, even, there are little tears. What I should do, she'll say, is put it all behind me. Find new stories to tell.

I won't say it but I'll think it.

I'll picture Rat Kiley's face, his grief, and I'll think, *You dumb cooze.*

Because she wasn't listening.

It *wasn't* a war story. It was a *love* story.

But you can't say that. All you can do is tell it one more time, patiently, adding and subtracting, making up a few things to get at the real truth. No Mitchell Sanders, you tell her. No Lemon, no Rat Kiley. No trail junction. No baby buffalo. No vines or moss or white blossoms. Beginning to end, you tell her, it's all made up. Every goddamn detail—the mountains and the river and especially that poor dumb baby buffalo. None of it happened. *None* of it. And even if it did happen, it didn't happen in the mountains, it happened in this little village on the Batangan Peninsula, and it was raining like crazy, and one night a guy named Stink Harris woke up screaming with a leech on his tongue. You can tell a true war story if you just keep on telling it.

And in the end, of course, a true war story is never about war. It's about sunlight. It's about the special way that dawn spreads out on a river when you know you must cross the river and march into the mountains and do things you are afraid to do. It's about love and memory. It's about sorrow. It's about sisters who never write back and people who never listen.

The Genetic Archaeology of Race

Steve Olson

Born in San Diego, CA, Steve Olson is a science journalist who has worked for the National Academy of Sciences, the White House Office of Science and Technology, and the Institute for Genomic Research. He is the author of several books, including Shaping the Future *and* Biotechnology, *and has written for the* Atlantic Monthly, Science, *and other magazines. Steve Olson's work,* Mapping Human History *was nominated for the 2002 National Book Award. The article "The Genetic Archeology of Race," a large portion of which is printed here, follows the efforts of the scientists engaged in the Human Diversity Genome project, which was dedicated to collecting DNA from various groups in order to study their differences.*

Over the past decade or so genetics researchers have been undermining the wide-spread belief that groups of people differ genetically in character, temperament, or intelligence. They have shown that all human beings are incredibly similar genetically—much more so than other species of large mammals. They have revealed the folly of attributing group behavioral differences to biology rather than culture.

But that's not how many of the news stories have read. On the contrary, here are the kinds of headlines you might have seen: "RESEARCHERS FIND GENETIC MARKER UNIQUE TO AFRICANS." "ASIANS BIOLOGICALLY LESS SUSCEPTIBLE TO ALCOHOLISM." "ALL NATIVE AMERICANS DESCENDED FROM A SMALL NUMBER OF FOUNDERS." In other words, given how journalists, pundits, and bigots have interpreted genetics research, people are probably more convinced than ever that group differences are significant.

We will continue to be inundated with DNA-sequence information—and with interpretations of that information—for many years to come. These genetic data have immense medical potential (though that potential will probably take much longer to realize than most people suspect). By studying the genetic differences among individuals, researchers will eventually find many DNA variants that contribute to health or disease.

But genetics research is also producing results of an entirely different kind. Differences in DNA sequences from person to person reflect the cumulative effects of human history. The patterns of genetic variation in the world today therefore carry a record of that history. They document the evolution of an African ape that began walking on two legs about four million years ago. They record the existence, sometime between 100,000 and 200,000 years ago, of a small group of people who are the ancestors of every person alive today. They chronicle the origins of "races" and "ethnic groups" and describe how those groups have both blended and separated over time.

Most genetics researchers are well aware of the historical dimensions of their work. But because these considerations raise uncomfortable issues, particularly issues of race, they tend to be downplayed. The White House news conference held on June 26 of last year to celebrate the sequencing of the human genome was filled with stirring but vague homages to human unity. "The human genome is our shared inheritance," said Francis Collins, the head of the publicly funded Human Genome Project, at the National Institutes of Health. "Race has no genetic or scientific basis," said Craig Venter, whose company, Celera Genomics, has been sequencing and analyzing human DNA.

The reality is considerably more complex. Genetics research is demonstrating that the differences in appearance among groups are profoundly incidental, but these differences *do* have a genetic basis. And although it's true that all people have inherited the same genetic legacy, the genetic differences among groups have important implications for our understanding of history and for biomedical research. These complications in an otherwise reassuring story have thoroughly spooked the leaders of the public and private genome efforts. The NIH has been collecting information about genetic variants from different ethnic groups in the United States, but it has refused to link specific variants with ethnicity. Celera has been sequencing DNA from an Asian, a Hispanic, a Caucasian, and an African-American, but it, too, declines to say which DNA is which.

This strategy of avoiding the issue is almost sure to backfire. It seems to imply that geneticists have something to hide. But the message emerging from laboratories around the world should be hailed, not muzzled. It is one of great hope and promise for our species.

One reason for the caution displayed by the genome sequencers is a largely overlooked drama that has been playing out on the fringes of the Human Genome Project for the past ten years. Unlike most scientific dramas, this one has a clear protagonist: Luigi Luca Cavalli-Sforza, a genial but sharp-tongued professor of genetics at Stanford University. Now seventy-nine, with thick silver hair and a perpetually inquisitive expression, Cavalli-Sforza combines the demeanor of a man accustomed to respect with a natural openness that has won him many friends. Born and educated in Italy, he went to Stanford University in 1971. There he quickly became a leader in the fledgling field of anthropological genetics, which draws inferences about the past based on the patterns observed in human DNA. His former students are now scattered around the world, carrying on the work he began. Yet he still rides his bike to campus each morning to write, read, and analyze the latest results from the lab. "He'll work until he drops," an associate says. "He's curious about the science."

In 1991 Cavalli-Sforza and a group of colleagues proposed a comprehensive study of human genetic differences, which they called the Human Genome Diversity Project. The study would involve gathering cells from several thousand people around the world, "immortalizing" the cells by converting them into laboratory cell lines, and using the cells' DNA to reconstruct human evolution and history. For Cavalli-Sforza, the Human Genome Diversity Project was to be the culmination of a lifetime of work.

The proposal loosed a flood of controversy. Aboriginal groups in the United States, New Guinea, and other countries accused the HGDP of stealing their genes, destroying their culture, and even contributing to genocide. Academic critics claimed that the project could encourage racist thinking, by oversimplifying issues of great complexity. "The idea of studying human genetic diversity is a good one," says one outspoken critic, Jonathan Marks, an anthropologist at the University of North Carolina at Charlotte. "But the way that Cavalli-Sforza has conceptualized it has problems at all levels."

Cavalli-Sforza has been baffled by the reaction to his proposal. He has always believed that the HGDP will help to end racism, not inflame it. In the 1970s he participated in public debates with the Stanford physicist William Shockley to dispute Shockley's racist ideas. He has worked closely with various African groups and cares deeply about their well-being. He protests that his intentions have always been purely scientific.

For almost a decade Cavalli-Sforza has been trapped in the paradox at the heart of human genetics: The only way to understand how similar we are is to learn how we differ. Yet any study of human differences seems to play into the hands of those who would accentuate those differences. Researchers might claim that the genetic differences they identify among groups have no biological significance. Yet simply by dividing human beings into categories—whether sub-Saharan Africans, Jews, Germans, or Australian aborigines—they reinforce the distinctions they would seek to minimize. How to resolve this dilemma is quickly becoming one of the most difficult problems facing the study of human genetics.

A THEORY OF MUTATION

More than 10,000 years ago, on the frigid, windswept plains of northeastern Siberia, a genetic accident occurred in a testicle of a particular man. As one of the man's sperm cells divided, the Y chromosome in the cell underwent a copying error. One of the chemical units making up his DNA changed from a molecule called cytosine to one called thymine. An elaborate biochemical proofreading apparatus is supposed to correct such copying errors, which geneticists call mutations. But there are so many individual chemical units, or nucleotides, in human DNA—about 60 million in the Y chromosome, and about three billion in the other chromosomes in a human sperm or egg cell—that a few mutations inevitably creep in every time a cell divides.

Within the next couple of months the man impregnated a woman. The sperm cell that combined with her egg was the one with the mutated Y. The woman gave birth to a son, each of whose cells had the mutated Y he got from his father. The son was no different from the other men in his tribe (the mutation in his Y had no effect on his body), yet he was a pivotal figure in human genetic history.

At some point, according to one interpretation of events, the son of the man whose Y had mutated crossed what was then a broad plain leading from Asia to North America—presumably with a small band of others. Before him stretched a continent that was largely, or perhaps completely, devoid of human beings. This man had sons himself, and his sons had sons. Over subsequent centuries his descendants spread down the length of North America, across the Isthmus of Panama, and into South America. All of them carried their forebear's distinctive Y chromosome, to which they added their own mutations. Today more than half of Native American males have this mutated Y chromosome.

Genetic reconstructions of historical events can always be interpreted in somewhat different ways, observes Peter Underhill, the geneticist in Cavalli-Sforza's lab who first detected this and many other variations in Y chromosomes. The mutation could have occurred in Siberia some generations before the migration along the Bering land bridge, or it could have occurred in North America. Nevertheless, we know that this man existed and that his Y chromosome differed from any previous Y chromosome in this way. His particular mutation could not have originated in more than one of the ancestors of today's Native Americans, and the mutation occurred in no other group in the world. Yet DNA is such a long and complex molecule that every act of human procreation produces at least some unique mutations. These mutations spill across the generations like an unusually shaped jaw or distinctively colored eyes. The result is an elaborate human genealogy, an intricately branching tree of genetic alterations.

When Cavalli-Sforza first became interested in genetics, the detailed mechanisms of human heredity were completely unknown. In 1938, at the age of sixteen, he had enrolled in medical school at the University of Pavia, in Italy, largely because of a fascination with microscopes. "It turned out to be a very lucky choice," he says. "Had I not gone to medical school, I would have been conscripted at the beginning of the war."

But when he graduated, in 1944, he found that he disliked the practice of medicine. So he took a part-time faculty position at the University of Parma and did research on bacterial genetics. He is still well known among geneticists for his contributions to the discovery that microbes have sex—or at least can engage in the kind of genetic exchanges involved in human couplings.

In 1951 a chance remark by one of his students redirected his research toward human beings. "Throughout my life I've been very lucky in finding good students," he recalled recently, when I met with him in his office at the Stanford medical school. "This particular student was also a priest. He mentioned to me that there were some data he thought would be of interest for human genetics." For more than three centuries the Catholic Church had collected information on births, marriages, and deaths in many Italian parishes. It was the ideal data set, Cavalli-Sforza realized, for the study of a particularly contentious issue in twentieth-century genetics—the role of genetic drift in evolution.

Most descriptions of evolution emphasize natural selection, in which a beneficial mutation becomes more common over time because bearers of this mutation are more likely to survive and procreate. But if an organism just happens to have lots of descendants, its genetic variants will become more common whether they are selected for or not. That's what happened with the Siberian forefather of many Native Americans. His Y chromosome did not have an advantage over any others—it simply prospered through the vagaries of genetic chance.

In the 1950s many geneticists believed that natural selection would almost always squelch genetic drift. The parish records gave Cavalli-Sforza a way to test the idea. They showed that most people in the mountain valleys high above Parma married within their own small villages. Genetic drift is more obvious in small, relatively insular populations, because an individual who happens to have lots of children can flood a population with his or her distinctive genetic variants. In contrast, on the plains around the university, for example, the genetic effects of any one person are reduced, because the population is larger and more mixed. There genetic drift should be less obvious.

One way to measure genetic drift is to look at the relative proportions of blood types within certain communities. So Cavalli-Sforza and a few assistants took needles and test tubes and fanned out over the countryside. With the help of parish priests they gathered blood samples, often in sacristies after Sunday mass. They found that the distribution of blood types varied much more from village to village in the mountains than in the valley, just as predicted by the theory of genetic drift.

His success led Cavalli-Sforza to consider the matter more broadly. If he could link genetics with mating and migrations among the people around Parma, why couldn't he do the same thing on a larger scale? In fact, he ought to be able to determine the genetic relationship between any two groups of people. A group should carry many of its predecessors' variants, just as children bear the genetic legacies of their parents. By detailing the genetic similarities and differences among groups, Cavalli-Sforza could trace humanity's spread across the planet.

More and more kinds of blood were being discovered in the 1950s. In 1961 Cavalli-Sforza decided that he had enough data to try his idea. He and a colleague analyzed published data on blood types in fifteen populations—three each from Europe, Africa, Asia, and the Americas, and one each from Australia, New Guinea, and New Zealand—and produced a tree showing how the various groups were related.

The results looked reasonable. The Native Americans from Venezuela and Arizona were related to Eskimos and Koreans in the sample, squaring with a migration across what is now the Bering Strait. The Africans and Europeans were genetically close, reflecting their continents' relative proximity. But to find out more, Cavalli-Sforza needed new kinds of data.

DECODING HUMAN HISTORY

The best way to determine the genetic relationships among people is to compare the sequences of the nucleotides in their DNA. But in the early 1960s those sequences were inaccessible. Manipulating DNA in the laboratory at that time was like playing the piano with a baseball bat—existing tools were far too awkward to examine individual nucleotides. Cavalli-Sforza therefore turned to the next best thing: the many thousands of proteins in the human body. The sequence of nucleotides in DNA dictates the sequence of the amino acids that constitute proteins, though the translation between the two is a convoluted process that partially obscures the underlying DNA sequence. Still, by studying proteins Cavalli-Sforza could learn at least a little about the DNA differences among people.

The result was a decades-long string of remarkable, though in some cases still hotly contested, discoveries. In the early 1970s, for example, Cavalli-Sforza and the archaeologist Albert Ammerman proposed a radical new hypothesis for the peopling of Europe. At that time most anthropologists believed that modern Europeans were descended largely from the continent's Stone Age inhabitants, who replaced the Neanderthal people starting about 40,000 years ago. By analyzing the genetic variation of modern Europeans, Cavalli-Sforza and Ammerman came to a different conclusion. They decided that Europeans are descended largely from populations of farmers who started migrating out of the Middle East 9,000 years ago. As the sons and daughters of farming families left their parents' farms and moved into new territory, they interbred with the existing hunter-gatherer populations, which produced gradients of genetic change radiating from the Middle East. Only in mountainous areas unattractive to farmers—the Pyrenees homelands of the Basques, for example—were the genes of the indigenous peoples comparatively intact.

Other historical events, too, appeared to have influenced the European gene pool. For example, a genetic trail leads from the area north of the Black and Caspian Seas into the rest of Europe. Cavalli-Sforza linked this trail to the spread of the descendants of nomadic warriors and herders who first domesticated the horse, about 4,000 B.C.

Similar traces of historical events showed up on every other continent. The genetic history of China is dominated by a split between northern and southern people, despite the official position that all ethnic Chinese are descended from common ancestors. Native American proteins point to three major waves of migration, suggesting connections among groups that had never considered themselves related. And wherever Cavalli-Sforza looked, the fragmentary protein evidence hinted at much-greater detail to come.

Cavalli-Sforza didn't know it when he moved to Stanford in 1971, but a series of experiments then going on at the university and elsewhere were about to transform anthropological genetics—and much of the rest of biology. The Stanford biochemist Stanley Cohen and the University of California at San Francisco biochemist Herbert Boyer were figuring out how to cut DNA in precise locations, combine DNA from different organisms, and grow the resulting hybrid DNA in bacteria. For the first time, human beings could control DNA nucleotide by nucleotide. The age of genetic engineering had begun.

New tools followed rapidly, with names like fluorescent DNA sequencing and polymerase chain reaction. By the mid-1980s biologists had realized that they had the means to pursue a goal that would have been unthinkable just a decade earlier: with sufficient effort they could read the entire multibillion-nucleotide sequence of human DNA. In 1990 an international consortium of governments launched the Human Genome Project to determine the sequence. Spurred by competition from the private sector, the project is today more or less finished (some cleanup work is still needed to complete the sequence).

As far as Cavalli-Sforza was concerned, the Human Genome Project was a good idea but didn't go far enough. The DNA that was sequenced is a pastiche of chromosomal fragments from various unidentified donors, and the project has produced just a single generic sequence to represent all of humanity. To trace human history Cavalli-Sforza needed to know how DNA sequences vary among people from different parts of the world. He began to think about the best way to gather such data, and he traded ideas with friends and colleagues. The result was the Human Genome Diversity Project, which was proposed in 1991 and fleshed out over the next two years. According to the planning document for the project, the goal would be to collect DNA from several hundred distinct groups, including many indigenous groups. Immortalized in cell lines, this DNA would be used primarily to study human history, but it would also have more-practical applications. Medical researchers could use it to investigate the connections between genetics and disease. And according to the planning document, by demonstrating the nature of the genetic differences among people, research on genetic variation would "help to combat the widespread popular fear and ignorance of human genetics and will make a significant contribution to the elimination of racism." Who could be opposed to that?

Cavalli-Sforza has always believed that if people understood genetics, they couldn't possibly be racists. For that he must certainly be judged naive. Then again, geneticists think in terms of generations, and over that time scale even the staunchest opinions can change. In the 1950s only four percent of white Americans approved of marriages between members of different races. Today the number is close to 50 percent, and it is undoubtedly much higher among young people.

Changing attitudes and new social forces are already having an influence on the collective genome of our species. Barriers that in the past have limited intermarriage among groups are breaking down. Cavalli-Sforza believes that many societies are moving toward what he calls the American model. "Two hundred years from now," he says, "people all over the world will be mixing in the same way that people in the United States are today."

A greater rate of intermarriage will generate great cultural upheavals. Genetically it will matter not a whit. Human beings are so similar that it makes no difference biologically for a white to marry a black, or for an Asian to marry an Australian. More intermarriage will make it harder to figure out an individual's ancestry. But it can only hasten the approach of a color-blind society.

Today most people still bear some traces of group biological history in their faces and skin. Perhaps someday our species will lose those distinguishing characteristics, through either intermarriage or genetic engineering. Until then the study of our genetic differences, if interpreted with care and understanding, could be one of the best ways to appreciate our biological unity.

Orientation

Daniel Orozco

Daniel Orozco was raised in San Francisco and studied at the University of Washington, Seattle. He has published stories in The Santa Clara Review, Story *magazine and others. His story "The Bridge" was included in* Pushcart Prize XXI *(1997), and "Orientation," which appeared in* The Seattle Review, *was selected for inclusion in* The Best American Short Stories *1995. Presently, he teaches writing at San Francisco State University and is a Stegner Fellow in fiction at Stanford University.*

Those are the offices and these are the cubicles. That's my cubicle there, and this is your cubicle. This is your phone. Never answer your phone. Let the Voicemail System answer it. This is your Voicemail System Manual. There are no personal phone calls allowed. We do, however, allow for emergencies. If you must make an emergency phone call, ask your supervisor first. If you can't find your supervisor, ask Phillip Spiers, who sits over there. He'll check with Clarissa Nicks, who sits over there. If you make an emergency phone call without asking, you may be let go.

These are your IN and OUT boxes. All the forms in your IN box must be logged in by the date shown in the upper left-hand corner, initialed by you in the upper right-hand corner, and distributed to the Processing Analyst whose name is numerically coded in the lower left-hand corner. The lower right-hand corner is left blank. Here's your Processing Analyst Numerical Code Index. And here's your Forms Processing Procedures Manual.

You must pace your work. What do I mean? I'm glad you asked that. We pace our work according to the eight-hour workday. If you have twelve hours of work in your IN box, for example, you must compress that work into the eight-hour day. If you have one hour of work in your IN box, you must expand that work to fill the eight-hour day. That was a good question. Feel free to ask questions. Ask too many questions, however, and you may be let go.

That is our receptionist. She is a temp. We go through receptionists here. They quit with alarming frequency. Be polite and civil to the temps. Learn their names, and invite them to lunch occasionally. But don't get close to them, as it only makes it more difficult when they leave. And they always leave. You can be sure of that.

The men's room is over there. The women's room is over there. John LaFountaine, who sits over there, uses the women's room occasionally. He says it is accidental. We know better, but we let it pass. John LaFountaine is harmless, his forays into the forbidden territory of the women's room simply a benign thrill, a faint blip on the dull flat line of his life.

Russell Nash, who sits in the cubicle to your left, is in love with Amanda Pierce, who sits in the cubicle to your right. They ride the same bus together after work. For Amanda Pierce, it is just a tedious bus ride made less tedious by the idle nattering of Russell Nash. But for Russell Nash, it is the highlight of his day. It is the highlight of his life. Russell Nash has put on forty pounds, and grows fatter with each passing month, nibbling on chips and cookies while peeking glumly over the partitions at Amanda Pierce, and gorging himself at home on cold pizza and ice cream while watching adult videos on TV.

Amanda Pierce, in the cubicle to your right, has a six-year-old son named Jamie, who is autistic. Her cubicle is plastered from top to bottom with the boy's crayon artwork—sheet after sheet of precisely drawn concentric circles and ellipses, in black and yellow. She rotates them every other Friday. Be sure to comment on them. Amanda Pierce also has a husband, who is a lawyer. He subjects her to an escalating array of painful and humiliating sex games, to which Amanda Pierce reluctantly submits. She comes to work exhausted and freshly wounded each morning, wincing from the abrasions on her breasts, or the bruises on her abdomen, or the second-degree burns on the backs of her thighs.

But we're not supposed to know any of this. Do not let on. If you let on, you may be let go.

Amanda Pierce, who tolerates Russell Nash, is in love with Albert Bosch, whose office is over there. Albert Bosch, who only dimly registers Amanda Pierce's existence, has eyes only for Ellie Tapper, who sits over there. Ellie Tapper, who hates Albert Bosch, would walk through fire for Curtis Lance. But Curtis Lance hates Ellie Tapper. Isn't the world a funny place? Not in the ha-ha sense, of course.

Anika Bloom sits in that cubicle. Last year, while reviewing quarterly reports in a meeting with Barry Hacker, Anika Bloom's left palm began to bleed. She fell into a trance, stared into her hand, and told Barry Hacker when and how his wife would die. We laughed it off. She was, after all, a new employee. But Barry Hacker's wife is dead. So unless you want to know exactly when and how you'll die, never talk to Anika Bloom.

Colin Heavey sits in that cubicle over there. He was new once, just like you. We warned him about Anika Bloom. But at last year's Christmas Potluck, he felt sorry for her when he saw that no one was talking to her. Colin Heavey brought her a drink.

He hasn't been himself since. Colin Heavey is doomed. There's nothing he can do about it, and we are powerless to help him. Stay away from Colin Heavey. Never give any of your work to him. If he asks to do something, tell him you have to check with me. If he asks again, tell him I haven't gotten back to you.

This is the Fire Exit. There are several on this floor, and they are marked accordingly. We have a Floor Evacuation Review every three months, and an Escape Route Quiz once a month. We have our Biannual Fire Drill twice a year, and our Annual Earthquake Drill once a year. These are precautions only. These things never happen.

For your information, we have a comprehensive health plan. Any catastrophic illness, any unforeseen tragedy is completely covered. All dependents are completely covered. Larry Bagdikian, who sits over there, has six daughters. If anything were to happen to any of his girls, or to all of them, if all six were to simultaneously fall victim to illness or injury—stricken with a hideous degenerative muscle disease or some rare toxic blood disorder, sprayed with semiautomatic gunfire while on a class field trip, or attacked in their bunk beds by some prowling nocturnal lunatic—if any of this were to pass, Larry's girls would all be taken care of. Larry Bagdikian would not have to pay one dime. He would have nothing to worry about.

We also have a generous vacation and sick leave policy. We have an excellent disability insurance plan. We have a stable and profitable pension fund. We get group discounts for the symphony, and block seating at the ballpark. We get commuter ticket books for the bridge. We have Direct Deposit. We are all members of Costco.

This is our kitchenette. And this, this is our Mr. Coffee. We have a coffee pool, into which we each pay two dollars a week for coffee, filters, sugar, and CoffeeMate. If you prefer Cremora or half-and-half to CoffeeMate, there is a special pool for three dollars a week. If you prefer Sweet'n Low to sugar, there is a special pool for two-fifty a week. We do not do decaf. You are allowed to join the coffee pool of your choice, but you are not allowed to touch the Mr. Coffee.

This is the microwave oven. You are allowed to *heat* food in the microwave oven. You are not, however, allowed to *cook* food in the microwave oven.

We get one hour for lunch. We also get one fifteen-minute break in the morning, and one fifteen-minute break in the afternoon. Always take your breaks. If you skip a break, it is gone forever. For your information, your break is a privilege, not a right. If you abuse the break policy, we are authorized to rescind your breaks. Lunch, however, is a right, not a privilege. If you abuse the lunch policy, our hands will be tied, and we will be forced to look the other way. We will not enjoy that.

This is the refrigerator. You may put your lunch in it. Barry Hacker, who sits over there, steals food from this refrigerator. His petty theft is an outlet for his grief. Last New Year's Eve, while kissing his wife, a blood vessel burst in her brain. Barry Hacker's wife was two months pregnant at the time, and lingered in a coma for half a year before dying. It was a tragic loss for Barry Hacker. He hasn't been himself since. Barry Hacker's wife was a beautiful woman. She was also completely covered. Barry Hacker did not have to pay one dime. But his dead wife haunts him. She haunts all of us. We have seen her, reflected in the monitors of our computers, moving past our cubicles. We have seen the dim shadow of her face in our photocopies. She pencils herself in in the receptionist's appointment book, with the notation: To see Barry Hacker. She has left messages in the receptionist's Voicemail box, messages garbled by the electronic chirrups and buzzes in the phone line, her voice echoing from an immense distance within the ambient hum. But the voice is hers. And beneath her voice, beneath the tidal *whoosh* of static and hiss, the gurgling and crying of a baby can be heard.

In any case, if you bring a lunch, put a little something extra in the bag for Barry Hacker. We have four Barrys in this office. Isn't that a coincidence?

This is Matthew Payne's office. He is our Unit Manager, and his door is always closed. We have never seen him, and you will never see him. But he is here. You can be sure of that. He is all around us.

This is the Custodian's Closet. You have no business in the Custodian's Closet.

And this, this is our Supplies Cabinet. If you need supplies, see Curtis Lance. He will log you in on the Supplies Cabinet Authorization Log, then give you a Supplies Authorization Slip. Present your pink copy of the Supplies Authorization Slip to Ellie Tapper. She will log you in on the Supplies Cabinet Key Log, then give you the key. Because the Supplies Cabinet is located outside the Unit Manager's office, you must be very quiet. Gather your supplies quietly. The Supplies Cabinet is divided into four sections. Section One contains letterhead stationery, blank paper and envelopes, memo and note pads, and so on. Section Two contains pens and pencils and typewriter and printer ribbons, and the like. In Section Three we have erasers, correction fluids, transparent tapes, glue sticks, et cetera. And in Section Four we have paper clips and push pins and scissors and razor blades. And here are the spare blades for the shredder. Do not touch the shredder, which is located over there. The shredder is of no concern to you.

Gwendolyn Stich sits in that office there. She is crazy about penguins, and collects penguin knickknacks: penguin posters and coffee mugs and stationery, penguin stuffed animals, penguin jewelry, penguin sweaters and T-shirts and socks. She has a pair of penguin fuzzy slippers she wears when working late at the office. She has a tape cassette of penguin sounds which she listens to for relaxation. Her favorite colors are black and white. She has personalized license plates that read PEN GWEN. Every morning, she passes through all the cubicles to wish each of us a *good* morning. She brings Danish on Wednesdays for Hump Day morning break, and doughnuts on Fridays for TGIF afternoon break. She organizes the Annual Christmas Potluck, and is in charge of the Birthday List. Gwendolyn Stich's door is always open to all of us. She will always lend an ear, and put in a good word for you; she will always give you a hand, or the shirt off her back, or a shoulder to cry on. Because her door is always open, she hides and cries in a stall in the women's room. And John LaFountaine—who, enthralled when a woman enters, sits quietly in his stall with his knees to his chest— John LaFountaine has heard her vomiting in there. We have come upon Gwendolyn Stich huddled in the stairwell, shivering in the updraft, sipping a Diet Mr. Pibb and hugging her knees. She does not let any of this interfere with her work. If it interfered with her work, she might have to be let go.

Kevin Howard sits in that cubicle over there. He is a serial killer, the one they call the Carpet Cutter, responsible for the mutilations across town. We're not supposed to know that, so do not let on. Don't worry. His compulsion inflicts itself on strangers only, and the routine established is elaborate and unwavering. The victim must be a white male, a young adult no older than thirty, heavyset, with dark hair and eyes, and the like. The victim must be chosen at random, before sunset, from a public place; the victim is followed home, and must put up a struggle; et cetera. The carnage inflicted is precise: the angle and direction of the incisions; the layering of skin and muscle tissue; the rearrangement of the visceral organs; and so on. Kevin Howard does not let any of this interfere with his work. He is, in fact, our fastest typist. He types as if he were on fire. He has a secret crush on Gwendolyn Stich, and leaves a red-foil-wrapped Hershey's Kiss on her desk every afternoon. But he hates Anika Bloom, and keeps well away from her. In his presence, she has uncontrollable fits of shaking and trembling. Her left palm does not stop bleeding.

In any case, when Kevin Howard gets caught, act surprised. Say that he seemed like a nice person, a bit of a loner, perhaps, but always quiet and polite.

This is the photocopier room. And this, this is our view. It faces southwest. West is down there, toward the water. North is back there. Because we are on the seventeenth floor, we are afforded a magnificent view. Isn't it beautiful? It overlooks the park, where the tops of those trees are. You can see a segment of the bay between those two buildings there. You can see the sun set in the gap between those two buildings over there. You can see this building reflected in the glass panels of that building across the way. There. See? That's you, waving. And look there. There's Anika Bloom in the kitchenette, waving back.

Enjoy this view while photocopying. If you have problems with the photocopier, see Russell Nash. If you have any questions, ask your supervisor. If you can't find your supervisor, ask Phillip Spiers. He sits over there. He'll check with Clarissa Nicks. She sits over there. If you can't find them, feel free to ask me. That's my cubicle. I sit in there.

Brownies

ZZ Packer

*ZZ Packer is an emerging talented writer. She was born in Chicago
but raised in Atlanta and Louisville, Kentucky. Currently a Stegner
fellow at Stanford, she holds degrees from Johns Hopkins and from
the University of Iowa. "Brownies" was inspired by her childhood
in the suburbs of Atlanta, where newly middle class African Americans tried to give their children a "proper" education sending them
to ballet and gymnastics lessons. At that early age, Packer and her
friends realized that they were made to imitate white models and
began to resent whites, particularly white girls. "In 'Brownies,'" she
says, "I wanted to capture how such bitterness was inherited and
incubated."*

By the end of our first day at Camp Crescendo, the girls in my Brownie troop had decided to kick the asses of each and every girl in Brownie Troop 909. Troop 909 was
doomed from the first day of camp; they were white girls, their complexions like a
blend of ice cream: strawberry, vanilla. They turtled out from their bus in pairs, their
rolled-up sleeping bags chromatized with Disney characters—Sleeping Beauty, Snow
White, Mickey Mouse—or the generic ones cheap parents bought—washed-out rainbows, unicorns, curly-eyelashed frogs. Some clutched Igloo coolers and still others
held on to stuffed toys like pacifiers, looking all around them like tourists determined
to be dazzled.

Our troop wended its way past their bus, past the ranger station, past the col-
orful trail guide drawn like a treasure map, locked behind glass.

"Man, did you smell them?" Arnetta said, giving the girls a slow once-over. "They
smell like Chihuahuas. *Wet* Chihuahuas." Although we had passed their troop by yards,
Arnetta raised her nose in the air and grimaced.

Arnetta said this from the very rear of the line, far away from Mrs. Margolin, who strung our troop behind her like a brood of obedient ducklings. Mrs. Margolin even looked like a mother duck—she had hair cropped close to a small ball of a head, almost no neck, and huge, miraculous breasts. She wore enormous belts that looked like the kind weight lifters wear, except hers were cheap metallic gold or rabbit fur or covered with gigantic fake sunflowers. Often these belts would become nature lessons in and of themselves. "See," Mrs. Margolin once said to us, pointing to her belt. "This one's made entirely from the feathers of baby pigeons."

The belt layered with feathers was uncanny enough, but I was more disturbed by the realization that I had never actually seen a baby pigeon. I searched for weeks for one, in vain—scampering after pigeons whenever I was downtown with my father.

But nature lessons were not Mrs. Margolin's top priority. She saw the position of troop leader as an evangelical post. Back at the A.M.E. church where our Brownie meetings were held, she was especially fond of imparting religious aphorisms by means of acrostics—Satan was the "Serpent Always Tempting And Noisome"; she'd refer to the Bible as "Basic Instructions Before Leaving Earth." Whenever she occasionally quizzed us on these at the beginning of the Brownie meeting, expecting to hear the acrostics parroted back to her, only Arnetta's correct replies soared over our vague mumblings. "Jesus?" Mrs. Margolin might ask expectantly, and Arnetta alone would dutifully answer, "Jehovah's Example, Saving Us Sinners."

Arnetta made a point of listening to Mrs. Margolin's religious talk and giving her what she wanted to hear. Because of this, Arnetta could have blared through a megaphone that the white girls of Troop 909 were "wet Chihuahuas" without arousing so much as a blink from Mrs. Margolin. Once Arnetta killed the troop goldfish by feeding it a French fry covered in ketchup, and when Mrs. Margolin demanded an explanation, Arnetta claimed that the goldfish had been eyeing her meal for hours, until—giving in to temptation—it had leapt up and snatched the whole golden fry from her fingertips.

"*Serious* Chihuahua," Octavia added—though neither Arnetta nor Octavia could *spell* "Chihuahua" or had ever *seen* a Chihuahua. Trisyllabic words had gained a sort of exoticism within our fourth-grade set at Woodrow Wilson Elementary. Arnetta and Octavia, compelled to outdo each other, would flip through the dictionary, determined to work the vulgar-sounding ones like "Djibouti" and "asinine" into conversation.

"*Caucasian* Chihuahuas," Arnetta said.

That did it. Drema and Elise doubled up on each other like inextricably entwined kites; Octavia slapped the skin of her belly; Janice jumped straight up in the air, then did it again, just as hard, as if to slam-dunk her own head. No one had laughed so hard since a boy named Martez had stuck his pencil in the electric socket and spent the whole day with a strange grin on his face.

"Girls, girls," said our parent helper, Mrs. Hedy. Mrs. Hedy was Octavia's mother. She wagged her index finger perfunctorily, like a windshield wiper. "Stop it now. Be good." She said this loudly enough to be heard, but lazily, nasally, bereft of any feeling or indication that she meant to be obeyed, as though she would say these words again at the exact same pitch if a button somewhere on her were pressed.

But the girls didn't stop laughing; they only laughed louder. It was the word "Caucasian" that had got them all going. One day at school, about a month before the Brownie camping trip, Arnetta had turned to a boy wearing impossibly high-ankled floodwater jeans, and said "What are *you? Caucasian?*" The word took off from there, and soon everything was Caucasian. If you ate too fast, you ate like a Caucasian; if you ate too slow, you ate like a Caucasian. The biggest feat anyone at Woodrow Wilson could do was to jump off the swing in midair, at the highest point in its arc, and if you fell (like I had, more than once) instead of landing on your feet, knees bent Olympic-gymnast-style, Arnetta and Octavia were prepared to comment. They'd look at each other with the silence of passengers who'd narrowly escaped an accident, then nod their heads, and whisper with solemn horror and haughtiness, *"Caucasian."*

Even the only white kid in our school, Dennis, got in on the Caucasian act. That time when Martez stuck the pencil in the socket, Dennis had pointed, and yelled, "That was *so* Caucasian!"

Living in the south suburbs of Atlanta, it was easy to forget about whites. Whites were like those baby pigeons: real and existing, but rarely thought about. Everyone had been to Rich's to go clothes shopping, everyone had seen white girls and their mothers coocooing over dresses; everyone had gone to the downtown library and seen white businessmen swish by importantly, wrists flexed in front of them to check the time on their watches as though they would change from Clark Kent into Superman any second. But those images were as fleeting as cards shuffled in a deck, whereas the ten white girls behind us—*invaders,* Arnetta would later call them—were instantly real and memorable, with their long shampoo-commercial hair, as straight as spaghetti from the box. This alone was reason for envy and hatred. The only black girl most of us had ever seen with hair that long was Octavia, whose hair hung past her butt like a Hawaiian hula dancer's. The sight of Octavia's mane prompted other girls to listen to her reverentially, as though whatever she had to say would somehow activate their own follicles. For example, when, on the first day of camp, Octavia made as if to speak, a silence began. "Nobody," Octavia said, "calls us niggers."

At the end of that first day, when half of our troop made its way back to the cabin after tag-team restroom visits, Arnetta said she'd heard one of the girls in Troop 909 call Daphne a nigger. The other half of the girls and I were helping Mrs. Margolin clean up the pots and pans from the ravioli dinner. When we made our way to the restrooms to wash up and brush our teeth, we met up with Arnetta midway.

"Man, I completely heard the girl," Arnetta reported. "Right, Daphne?"

Daphne hardly ever spoke, but when she did her voice was petite and tinkly, the voice one might expect from a shiny new earring. She'd written a poem once, for Langston Hughes Day, a poem brimming with all the teacher-winning ingredients—trees and oceans, sunsets and moons—but what cinched the poem for the grown-ups, snatching the win from Octavia's musical ode to Grandmaster Flash and the Furious Five, were Daphne's last lines:

You are my father, the veteran
When you cry in the dark
It rains and rains and rains in my heart

She'd worn clean, though faded, jumpers and dresses when Chic jeans were the fashion, but when she went up to the dais to receive her prize journal, pages trimmed in gold, she wore a new dress with a velveteen bodice and a taffeta skirt as wide as an umbrella. All the kids clapped, though none of them understood the poem. I'd read encyclopedias the way others read comics, and I didn't get it. But those last lines pricked me, they were so eerie, and as my father and I ate cereal, I'd whisper over my Froot Loops, like a mantra, *"You are my father, the veteran. You are my father, the veteran, the veteran, the veteran,"* until my father, who acted in plays as Caliban and Othello and was not a veteran, marched me up to my teacher one morning, and said, "Can you tell me what the hell's wrong with this kid?"

I had thought Daphne and I might become friends, but she seemed to grow spooked by me whispering those lines to her, begging her to tell me what they meant, and I had soon understood that two quiet people like us were better off quiet alone.

"Daphne? Didn't you hear them call you a nigger?" Arnetta asked, giving Daphne a nudge.

The sun was setting through the trees, and their leafy tops formed a canopy of black lace for the flame of the sun to pass through. Daphne shrugged her shoulders at first, then slowly nodded her head when Arnetta gave her a hard look.

Twenty minutes later, when my restroom group returned to the cabin, Arnetta was still talking about Troop 909. My restroom group had passed by some of the 909 girls. For the most part, they had deferred to us, waving us into the restrooms, letting us go even though they'd gotten there first.

We'd seen them, but from afar, never within their orbit enough to see whether their faces were the way all white girls appeared on TV—ponytailed and full of energy, bubbling over with love and money. All I could see was that some rapidly fanned their faces with their hands, though the heat of the day had long passed. A few seemed to be lolling their heads in slow circles, half-purposefully, as if exercising the muscles of their necks, half-ecstatically, rolling their heads about like Stevie Wonder.

"We can't let them get away with that," Arnetta said, dropping her voice to a laryngitic whisper. "We can't let them get away with calling us niggers. I say we teach them a lesson." She sat down cross-legged on a sleeping bag, an embittered Buddha, eyes glimmering acrylic black. "We can't go telling Mrs. Margolin, either. Mrs. Margolin'll say something about doing unto others and the path of righteousness and all. Forget that shit." She let her eyes flutter irreverently till they half closed, as though ignoring an insult not worth returning. We could all hear Mrs. Margolin outside, gathering the last of the metal campware.

Nobody said anything for a while. Arnetta's tone had an upholstered confidence that was somehow both regal and vulgar at once. It demanded a few moments of silence in its wake, like the ringing of a church bell or the playing of taps. Sometimes Octavia would ditto or dissent whatever Arnetta had said, and this was the signal that others could speak. But this time Octavia just swirled a long cord of hair into pretzel shapes.

"*Well?*" Arnetta said. She looked as if she had discerned the hidden severity of the situation and was waiting for the rest of us to catch up. Everyone looked from Arnetta to Daphne. It was, after all, Daphne who had supposedly been called the name, but Daphne sat on the bare cabin floor, flipping through the pages of the Girl Scout handbook, eyebrows arched in mock wonder, as if the handbook were a catalogue full of bright and startling foreign costumes. Janice broke the silence. She clapped her hands to broach her idea of a plan.

"They gone be sleeping," she whispered conspiratorially, "then we gone sneak into they cabin, then we gone put daddy longlegs in they sleeping bags. Then they'll wake up. Then we gone beat 'em up till they flat as frying pans!" She jammed her fist into the palm of her hand, then made a sizzling sound.

Janice's country accent was laughable, her looks homely, her jumpy acrobatics embarrassing to behold. Arnetta and Octavia volleyed amused, arrogant smiles whenever Janice opened her mouth, but Janice never caught the hint, spoke whenever she wanted, fluttered around Arnetta and Octavia futilely offering her opinions to their departing backs. Whenever Arnetta and Octavia shooed her away, Janice loitered until the two would finally sigh, "What is it, Miss Caucasoid? What do you want?"

"Oh shut up, Janice," Octavia said, letting a fingered loop of hair fall to her waist as though just the sound of Janice's voice had ruined the fun of her hair twisting.

"All right," Arnetta said, standing up. "We're going to have a secret meeting and talk about what we're going to do."

The word "secret" had a built-in importance. Everyone gravely nodded her head. The modifier form of the word had more clout than the noun. A secret meant nothing; it was like gossip: just a bit of unpleasant knowledge about someone who happened to be someone other than yourself. A secret *meeting* or a secret *club*, was entirely different.

That was when Arnetta turned to me, as though she knew doing so was both a compliment and a charity.

"Snot, you're not going to be a bitch and tell Mrs. Margolin, are you?"

I had been called "Snot" ever since first grade, when I'd sneezed in class and two long ropes of mucus had splattered a nearby girl.

"Hey," I said. "Maybe you didn't hear them right—I mean—"

"Are you gonna tell on us or not?" was all Arnetta wanted to know, and by the time the question was asked, the rest of our Brownie troop looked at me as though they'd already decided their course of action, me being the only impediment. As though it were all a simple matter of patriotism.

Camp Crescendo used to double as a high school band and field hockey camp until an arching field hockey ball landed on the clasp of a girl's metal barrette, knifing a skull nerve, paralyzing the right side of her body. The camp closed down for a few years, and the girl's teammates built a memorial, filling the spot on which the girl fell with hockey balls, upon which they had painted—all in nail polish—get-well tidings, flowers, and hearts. The balls were still stacked there, like a shrine of ostrich eggs embedded in the ground.

On the second day of camp, Troop 909 was dancing around the mound of nail polish-decorated hockey balls, their limbs jangling awkwardly, their cries like the constant summer squeal of an amusement park. There was a stream that bordered the field hockey lawn, and the girls from my troop settled next to it, scarfing down the last of lunch: sandwiches made from salami and slices of tomato that had gotten waterlogged from the melting ice in the cooler. From the stream bank, Arnetta eyed the Troop 909 girls, scrutinizing their movements to glean inspiration for battle.

"Man," Arnetta said, "we could bum-rush them right now if that damn lady would *leave.*"

The 909 troop leader was a white woman with the severe pageboy hairdo of an ancient Egyptian. She lay sprawled on a picnic blanket, Sphinxlike, eating a banana, sometimes holding it out in front of her like a microphone. Beside her sat a girl slowly flapping one hand like a bird with a broken wing. Occasionally, the leader would call out the names of girls who'd attempted leapfrogs and flips, or of girls who yelled too loudly or strayed far from the circle.

"I'm just glad Big Fat Mama's not following us here," Octavia said. "At least we don't have to worry about her." Mrs. Margolin, Octavia assured us, was having her Afternoon Devotional, shrouded in mosquito netting, in a clearing she'd found. Mrs. Hedy was cleaning mud from her espadrilles in the cabin.

"I handled them." Arnetta sucked on her teeth and proudly grinned. "I told her we was going to gather leaves."

"Gather leaves," Octavia said, nodding respectfully. "That's a good one. They're so mad-crazy about this camping thing." She looked from ground to sky, sky to ground. Her hair hung down her back in two braids like a squaw's. "I mean, I really don't know why it's even called *camping*—all we ever do with Nature is find some twigs and say something like, 'Wow, this fell from a tree.'" She then studied her sandwich. With two disdainful fingers, she picked out a slice of dripping tomato, the sections congealed with red slime. She pitched it into the stream embrowned with dead leaves and the murky effigies of other dead things, but in the opaque water a group of small silver-brown fish appeared. They surrounded the tomato and nibbled.

"Look!" Janice cried. "Fishes! Fishes!" As she scrambled to the edge of the stream to watch, a covey of insects threw up tantrums from the wheatgrass and nettle, a throng of tiny electric machines, all going at once. Octavia snuck up behind Janice as if to push her in. Daphne and I exchanged terrified looks. It seemed as though only we knew that Octavia was close enough—and bold enough—to actually push Janice into the stream. Janice turned around quickly, but Octavia was already staring serenely into the still water as though she were gathering some sort of courage from it. "What's so funny?" Janice said, eyeing them all suspiciously.

Elise began humming the tune to "Karma Chameleon," all the girls joining in, their hums light and facile. Janice began to hum, against everyone else, the high-octane opening chords of "Beat It."

"I love me some Michael Jackson," Janice said when she'd finished humming, smacking her lips as though Michael Jackson were a favorite meal. "I will marry Michael Jackson."

Before anyone had a chance to impress upon Janice the impossibility of this, Arnetta suddenly rose, made a sun visor of her hand, and watched Troop 909 leave the field hockey lawn.

"Dammit!" she said. "We've got to get them *alone.*"

"They won't ever be alone," I said. All the rest of the girls looked at me. If I spoke even a word, I could count on someone calling me Snot, but everyone seemed to think that we could beat up these girls; no one entertained the thought that they might fight *back.* "The only time they'll be unsupervised is in the bathroom."

"Oh shut up, Snot," Octavia said.

But Arnetta slowly nodded her head. "The bathroom," she said. "The bathroom," she said, again and again. "The bathroom! The bathroom!" She cheered so blissfully that I thought for a moment she was joking.

According to Octavia's watch, it took us five minutes to hike to the restrooms, which were midway between our cabin and Troop 909's. Inside, the mirrors above the sinks returned only the vaguest of reflections, as though someone had taken a scouring pad to their surfaces to obscure the shine. Pine needles, leaves, and dirty flattened wads of chewing gum covered the floor like a mosaic. Webs of hair matted the drain in the middle of the floor. Above the sinks and below the mirrors, stacks of folded white paper towels lay on a long metal counter. Shaggy white balls of paper towels sat on the sink tops in a line like corsages on display. A thread of floss snaked from a wad of tissues dotted with the faint red-pink of blood. One of those white girls, I thought, had just lost a tooth.

The restroom looked almost the same as it had the night before, but it somehow seemed stranger now. We had never noticed the wooden rafters before, coming together in great V's. We were, it seemed, inside a whale, viewing the ribs of the roof of its mouth.

"Wow. It's a mess," Elise said.

"You can say that again."

Arnetta leaned against the doorjamb of a restroom stall. "This is where they'll be again," she said. Just seeing the place, just having a plan, seemed to satisfy her. "We'll go in and talk to them. You know, 'How you doing? How long will you be here?' that sort of thing. Then Octavia and I are gonna tell them what happens when they call any one of us a nigger."

"I'm going to say something, too," Janice said.

Arnetta considered this. "Sure," she said. "Of course. Whatever you want."

Janice pointed her finger like a gun at Octavia and rehearsed the line she'd thought up, "'We're gonna teach you a *lesson.*' That's what I'm going to say." She narrowed her eyes like a TV mobster. "'We're gonna teach you little girls a lesson!'"

With the back of her hand, Octavia brushed Janice's finger away. "You couldn't teach me to shit in a toilet."

"But," I said, "what if they say, 'We didn't say that. We didn't call anyone a N-I-G-G-E-R'?"

"Snot," Arnetta sighed. "Don't think. Just fight. If you even know how."

Everyone laughed while Daphne stood there. Arnetta gently laid her hand on Daphne's shoulder. "Daphne. You don't have to fight. We're doing this for you."

Daphne walked to the counter, took a clean paper towel, and carefully unfolded it like a map. With this, she began to pick up the trash all around. Everyone watched.

"C'mon," Arnetta said to everyone. "Let's beat it." We all ambled toward the restroom doorway, where the sunshine made one large white rectangle of light. We were immediately blinded and shielded our eyes with our hands, our forearms.

"Daphne?" Arnetta asked. "Are you coming?"

We all looked back at the girl, who was bending, the thin of her back hunched like a maid caught in stage limelight. Stray strands of her hair were lit nearly transparent, thin fiber-optic threads. She did not nod yes to the question, nor did she shake her head no. She abided, bent. Then she began again, picking up leaves, wads of paper, the cotton fluff innards from a torn stuffed toy. She did it so methodically, so exquisitely, so humbly, she must have been trained. I thought of those dresses she wore, faded and old, yet so pressed and clean; I then saw the poverty in them, I then could imagine her mother, cleaning the houses of others, returning home, weary.

"I guess she's not coming."

We left her, heading back to our cabin, over pine needles and leaves, taking the path full of shade.

"What about our secret meeting?" Elise asked.

Arnetta enunciated in a way that defied contradiction: "We just had it."

Just as we caught sight of our cabin, Arnetta violently swerved away from Octavia. "You farted," she said.

Octavia began to sashay, as if on a catwalk, then proclaimed, in a Hollywood-starlet voice, "My farts smell like perfume."

It was nearing our bedtime, but in the lengthening days of spring, the sun had not yet set.

"Hey, your mama's coming," Arnetta said to Octavia when she saw Mrs. Hedy walk toward the cabin, sniffling. When Octavia's mother wasn't giving bored, parochial orders, she sniffled continuously, mourning an imminent divorce from her husband. She might begin a sentence, "I don't know what Robert will do when Octavia and I are gone. Who'll buy him cigarettes?" and Octavia would hotly whisper *"Mama"* in a way that meant: Please don't talk about our problems in front of everyone. Please shut up.

But when Mrs. Hedy began talking about her husband, thinking about her husband, seeing clouds shaped like the head of her husband, she couldn't be quiet, and no one could ever dislodge her from the comfort of her own woe. Only one thing could perk her up—Brownie songs. If the rest of the girls were quiet, and Mrs. Hedy was in her dopey sorrowful mood, she would say, "Y'all know I like those songs, girls.

Why don't you sing one?" Everyone would groan except me and Daphne. I, for one, liked some of the songs.

"C'mon, everybody," Octavia said drearily. "She likes 'The Brownie Song' best." We sang, loud enough to reach Mrs. Hedy:

I've something in my pocket;
It belongs across my face.
And I keep it very close at hand in a most convenient place.
I'm sure you couldn't guess it
If you guessed a long, long while.
So I'll take it out and put it on—
It's a great big Brownie Smile!

"The Brownie Song" was supposed to be sung as though we were elves in a workshop, singing as we merrily cobbled shoes, but everyone except me hated the song and sang it like a maudlin record, played at the most sluggish of rpms.

"That was good," Mrs. Hedy said, closing the cabin door behind her. "Wasn't that nice, Linda?"

"Praise God," Mrs. Margolin answered without raising her head from the chore of counting out Popsicle sticks for the next day's session of crafts.

"Sing another one," Mrs. Hedy said, with a sort of joyful aggression, like a drunk I'd once seen who'd refused to leave a Korean grocery.

"God, Mama, get over it," Octavia whispered in a voice meant only for Arnetta, but Mrs. Hedy heard it and started to leave the cabin.

"Don't go," Arnetta said. She ran after Mrs. Hedy and held her by the arm. "We haven't finished singing." She nudged us with a single look. "Let's sing 'The Friends Song.' For Mrs. Hedy."

Although I liked some of the songs, I hated this one:

Make new friends
But keep the o-old,
One is silver
And the other gold.

If most of the girls in my troop could be any type of metal, they'd be bunched-up wads of tinfoil maybe, or rusty iron nails you had to get tetanus shots for.

"No, no, no," Mrs. Margolin said before anyone could start in on "The Friends Song." "An uplifting song. Something to lift her up and take her mind off all these earthly burdens."

Arnetta and Octavia rolled their eyes. Everyone knew what song Mrs. Margolin was talking about, and no one, no one, wanted to sing it.

"Please, no," a voice called out. "Not 'The Doughnut Song.'"

"Please not 'The Doughnut Song,'" Octavia pleaded.

"I'll brush my teeth twice if I don't have to sing 'The Doughnut—'"

"Sing!" Mrs. Margolin demanded.

We sang:

Life without Jesus is like a do-ough-nut!
Like a do-ooough-nut!
Like a do-ooough-nut!
Life without Jesus is like a do-ough-nut!
There's a hole in the middle of my soul!

There were other verses, involving other pastries, but we stopped after the first one and cast glances toward Mrs. Margolin to see if we could gain a reprieve. Mrs. Margolin's eyes fluttered blissfully, half-asleep.

"Awww," Mrs. Hedy said, as though giant Mrs. Margolin were a cute baby. "Mrs. Margolin's had a long day."

"Yes indeed," Mrs. Margolin answered. "If you don't mind, I might just go to the lodge where the beds are. I haven't been the same since the operation."

I had not heard of this operation, or when it had occurred, since Mrs. Margolin had never missed the once-a-week Brownie meetings, but I could see from Daphne's face that she was concerned, and I could see that the other girls had decided that Mrs. Margolin's operation must have happened long ago in some remote time unconnected to our own. Nevertheless, they put on sad faces. We had all been taught that adulthood was full of sorrow and pain, taxes and bills, dreaded work and dealings with whites, sickness, and death.

"Go right ahead, Linda," Mrs. Hedy said. "I'll watch the girls." Mrs. Hedy seemed to forget about divorce for a moment; she looked at us with dewy eyes, as if we were mysterious, furry creatures. Meanwhile, Mrs. Margolin walked through the maze of sleeping bags until she found her own. She gathered a neat stack of clothes and pajamas slowly, as though doing so were almost painful. She took her toothbrush, her toothpaste, her pillow. "All right!" Mrs. Margolin said, addressing us all from the threshold of the cabin. "Be in bed by nine." She said it with a twinkle in her voice, as though she were letting us know she was allowing us to be naughty and stay up till nine-fifteen.

"C'mon, everybody," Arnetta said after Mrs. Margolin left. "Time for us to wash up."

Everyone watched Mrs. Hedy closely, wondering whether she would insist on coming with us since it was night, making a fight with Troop 909 nearly impossible. Troop 909 would soon be in the bathroom, washing their faces, brushing their teeth—completely unsuspecting of our ambush.

"We won't be long," Arnetta said. "We're old enough to go to the restroom by ourselves."

Mrs. Hedy pursed her lips at this dilemma. "Well, I guess you Brownies are almost Girl Scouts, right?"

"Right"

"Just one more badge," Drema said.

"And about," Octavia droned, "a million more cookies to sell." Octavia looked at all of us. *Now's our chance,* her face seemed to say, but our chance to do *what* I didn't exactly know.

Finally, Mrs. Hedy walked to the doorway where Octavia stood, dutifully waiting to say good-bye and looking bored doing it. Mrs. Hedy held Octavia's chin. "You'll be good?"

"Yes, Mama."

"And remember to pray for me and your father? If I'm asleep when you get back?"

"Yes, Mama."

When the other girls had finished getting their toothbrushes and washcloths and flashlights for the group restroom trip, I was drawing pictures of tiny birds with too many feathers. Daphne was sitting on her sleeping bag, reading.

"You're not going to come?" Octavia asked.

Daphne shook her head.

"I'm also gonna stay, too," I said. "I'll go to the restroom when Daphne and Mrs. Hedy go."

Arnetta leaned down toward me and whispered so that Mrs. Hedy, who had taken over Mrs. Margolin's task of counting Popsicle sticks, couldn't hear. "No, Snot. If we get in trouble, you're going to get in trouble with the rest of us."

We made our way through the darkness by flashlight. The tree branches that had shaded us just hours earlier, along the same path, now looked like arms sprouting menacing hands. The stars sprinkled the sky like spilled salt. They seemed fastened to the darkness, high up and holy, their places fixed and definite as we stirred beneath them.

Some, like me, were quiet because we were afraid of the dark; others were talking like crazy for the same reason.

"Wow," Drema said, looking up. "Why are all the stars out here? I never see stars back on Oneida Street."

"It's a camping trip, that's why," Octavia said. "You're supposed to see stars on camping trips."

Janice said, "This place smells like the air freshener my mother uses."

"These woods are *pine,*" Elise said. "Your mother probably uses pine air freshener."

Janice mouthed an exaggerated "Oh," nodding her head as though she just then understood one of the world's great secrets.

No one talked about fighting. Everyone was afraid enough just walking through the infinite deep of the woods. Even without seeing anyone's face, I could tell this wasn't about Daphne being called a nigger. The word that had started it all seemed melted now into some deeper, unnameable feeling. Even though I didn't want to fight, was afraid of fighting, I felt as though I were part of the rest of the troop, as though I were defending something. We trudged against the slight incline of the path, Arnetta leading the way. I wondered, looking at her back, what she could be thinking.

"You know," I said, "their leader will be there. Or they won't even be there. It's dark already. Last night the sun was still in the sky. I'm sure they're already finished."

"Whose flashlight is this?" Arnetta said, shaking the weakening beam of the light she was holding. "It's out of batteries."

Octavia handed Arnetta her flashlight. And that's when I saw it. The bathroom was just ahead.

But the girls were there. We could hear them before we could see them.

"Octavia and I will go in first so they'll think there's just two of us. Then wait till I say, 'We're gonna teach you a lesson,'" Arnetta said. "Then bust in. That'll surprise them."

"That's what I was supposed to say," Janice said.

Arnetta went inside, Octavia next to her. Janice followed, and the rest of us waited outside.

They were in there for what seemed like whole minutes, but something was wrong. Arnetta hadn't given the signal yet. I was with the girls outside when I heard one of the Troop 909 girls say, "NO. That did NOT happen!"

That was to be expected, that they'd deny the whole thing. What I hadn't expected was *the voice* in which the denial was said. The girl sounded as though her tongue were caught in her mouth. "That's a BAD word!" the girl continued. "We don't say BAD words!"

"Let's go in," Elise said.

"No," Drema said. "I don't want to. What if we get beat up?"

"Snot?" Elise turned to me, her flashlight blinding. It was the first time anyone had asked my opinion, though I knew they were just asking because they were afraid.

"I say we go inside, just to see what's going on."

"But Arnetta didn't give us the signal," Drema said. "She's supposed to say, 'We're going to teach you a lesson,' and I didn't hear her say it."

"C'mon," I said. "Let's just go in."

We went inside. There we found the white girls, but about five girls were huddled up next to one big girl. I instantly knew she was the owner of the voice we'd heard. Arnetta and Octavia inched toward us as soon as we entered.

"Where's Janice?" Elise asked, then we heard a flush. "Oh."

"I think," Octavia said, whispering to Elise, "they're retarded."

"We ARE NOT retarded!" the big girl said, though it was obvious that she was. That they all were. The girls around her began to whimper.

"They're just pretending," Arnetta said, trying to convince herself. "I know they are."

Octavia turned to Arnetta. "Arnetta. Let's just leave."

Janice came out of a stall, happy and relieved, then she suddenly remembered her line, pointed to the big girl, and said, "We're gonna teach you a lesson."

"Shut up, Janice," Octavia said, but her heart was not in it. Arnetta's face was set in a lost, deep scowl. Octavia turned to the big girl, and said loudly, slowly, as if they were all deaf, "We're going to leave. It was nice meeting you, okay? You don't have to tell anyone that we were here. Okay?"

"Why not?" said the big girl, like a taunt. When she spoke, her lips did not meet, her mouth did not close. Her tongue grazed the roof of her mouth, like a little pink fish. "You'll get in trouble. I know. I know."

Arnetta got back her old cunning. "If you said anything, then you'd be a tattletale."

The girl looked sad for a moment, then perked up quickly. A flash of genius crossed her face: "I *like* tattletale."

"It's all right, girls. It's gonna be all right!" the 909 troop leader said. It was as though someone had instructed all of Troop 909 to cry at once. The troop leader had girls under her arm, and all the rest of the girls crowded about her. It reminded me of a hog I'd seen on a field trip, where all the little hogs would gather about the mother at feeding time, latching on to her teats. The 909 troop leader had come into the bathroom shortly after the big girl threatened to tell. Then the ranger came, then, once the ranger had radioed the station, Mrs. Margolin arrived with Daphne in tow.

The ranger had left the restroom area, but everyone else was huddled just outside, swatting mosquitoes.

"Oh. They *will* apologize," Mrs. Margolin said to the 909 troop leader, but Mrs. Margolin said this so angrily, I knew she was speaking more to us than to the other troop leader. "When their parents find out, every one a them will be on punishment."

"It's all right. It's all right," the 909 troop leader reassured Mrs. Margolin. Her voice lilted in the same way it had when addressing the girls. She smiled the whole time she talked. She was like one of those TV cooking show women who talk and dice onions and smile all at the same time.

"See. It could have happened. I'm not calling your girls fibbers or anything." She shook her head ferociously from side to side, her Egyptian-style pageboy flapping against her cheeks like heavy drapes. "It *could* have happened, see. Our girls are *not* retarded. They are *delayed* learners." She said this in a syrupy instructional voice, as though our troop might be delayed learners as well. "We're from the Decatur Children's Academy. Many of them just have special needs."

"Now we won't be able to walk to the bathroom by ourselves!" the big girl said.

"Yes you will," the troop leader said, "but maybe we'll wait till we get back to Decatur—"

"I don't want to wait!" the girl said. "I want my Independence patch!"

The girls in my troop were entirely speechless. Arnetta looked as though she were soon to be tortured but was determined not to appear weak. Mrs. Margolin pursed her lips solemnly and said, "Bless them, Lord. Bless them."

In contrast, the Troop 909 leader was full of words and energy. "Some of our girls are echolalic—" She smiled and happily presented one of the girls hanging on to her, but the girl widened her eyes in horror and violently withdrew herself from the center of attention, as though she sensed she were being sacrificed for the village sins. "Echolalic," the troop leader continued. "That means they will say whatever they hear, like an echo—that's where the word comes from. It comes from 'echo.'" She ducked her head apologetically. "I mean, not all of them have the most progressive of parents, so if they heard a bad word they might have repeated it. But I guarantee it would not have been *intentional.*"

Arnetta spoke. "I saw her say the word. I heard her." She pointed to a small girl, smaller than any of us, wearing an oversized T-shirt that read: EAT BERTHA'S MUSSELS.

The troop leader shook her head and smiled. "That's impossible. She doesn't speak. She can, but she doesn't."

Arnetta furrowed her brow. "No. It wasn't her. That's right. It was *her.*"

The girl Arnetta pointed to grinned as though she'd been paid a compliment. She was the only one from either troop actually wearing a full uniform: the mocha-colored A-line shift, the orange ascot, the sash covered with patches, though all the same one—the Try-It patch. She took a few steps toward Arnetta and made a grand sweeping gesture toward the sash. "See," she said, full of self-importance, "I'm a Brownie." I had a hard time imagining this girl calling anyone a "nigger"; the girl looked perpetually delighted, as though she would have cuddled up with a grizzly if someone had let her.

On the fourth morning, we boarded the bus to go home.

The previous day had been spent building miniature churches from Popsicle sticks. We hardly left the cabin. Mrs. Margolin and Mrs. Hedy guarded us so closely, almost no one talked for the entire day.

Even on the day of departure from Camp Crescendo, all was serious and silent. The bus ride began quietly enough. Arnetta had to sit beside Mrs. Margolin, Octavia had to sit beside her mother. I sat beside Daphne, who gave me her prize journal without a word of explanation.

"You don't want it?"

She shook her head no. It was empty.

Then Mrs. Hedy began to weep. "Octavia," Mrs. Hedy said to her daughter without looking at her, "I'm going to sit with Mrs. Margolin. All right?"

Arnetta exchanged seats with Mrs. Hedy. With the two women up front, Elise felt it safe to speak. "Hey," she said, then she set her face into a placid vacant stare, trying to imitate that of a Troop 909 girl. Emboldened, Arnetta made a gesture of mock pride toward an imaginary sash, the way the girl in full uniform had done. Then they all made a game of it, trying to do the most exaggerated imitations of the Troop 909 girls, all without speaking, all without laughing loud enough to catch the women's attention.

Daphne looked at her shoes, white with sneaker polish. I opened the journal she'd given me. I looked out the window, trying to decide what to write, searching for lines, but nothing could compare with the lines Daphne had written, *"My father, the veteran,"* my favorite line of all time. The line replayed itself in my head, and I gave up trying to write.

By then, it seemed as though the rest of the troop had given up making fun of the 909 girls. They were now quietly gossiping about who had passed notes to whom in school. For a moment the gossiping fell off, and all I heard was the hum of the bus as we sped down the road and the muffled sounds of Mrs. Hedy and Mrs. Margolin talking about serious things.

"You know," Octavia whispered, 'why did *we* have to be stuck at a camp with retarded girls? You know?"

"*You* know why," Arnetta answered. She narrowed her eyes like a cat. "My mama and I were in the mall in Buckhead, and this white lady just kept looking at us. I mean, like we were foreign or something. Like we were from China."

"What did the woman say?" Elise asked.

"Nothing," Arnetta said. "She didn't say nothing."

A few girls quietly nodded their heads.

"There was this time," I said, "when my father and I were in the mall and—"

"Oh, shut up, Snot," Octavia said.

I stared at Octavia, then rolled my eyes from her to the window. As I watched the trees blur, I wanted nothing more than to be through with it all: the bus ride, the troop, school—all of it. But we were going home. I'd see the same girls in school the next day. We were on a bus, and there was nowhere else to go.

"Go on, Laurel," Daphne said to me. It was the first time she'd spoken the whole trip, and she'd said my name. I turned to her and smiled weakly so as not to cry, hoping she'd remember when I'd tried to be her friend, thinking maybe that her gift of the journal was an invitation of friendship. But she didn't smile back. All she said was, "What happened?"

I studied the girls, waiting for Octavia to tell me to "shut up" again before I even had a chance to utter another word, but everyone was amazed that Daphne had spoken. I gathered my voice. "Well," I said. "My father and I were in this mall, but *I* was the one doing the staring." I stopped and glanced from face to face. I continued. "There were these white people dressed like Puritans or something, but they weren't Puritans. They were Mennonites. They're these people who, if you ask them to do a favor, like paint your porch or something, they have to do it. It's in their rules."

"That sucks," someone said.

"C'mon," Arnetta said. "You're lying."

"I am not."

"How do you know that's not just some story someone made up?" Elise asked, her head cocked, full of daring. "I mean, who's gonna do whatever you ask?"

"It's not made up. I know because when I was looking at them, my father said, "See those people. If you ask them to do something, they'll do it. Anything you want.'"

No one would call anyone's father a liar. Then they'd have to fight the person, but Drema parsed her words carefully. "How does your *father* know that's not just some story? Huh?"

"Because," I said, "he went up to the man and asked him would he paint our porch, and the man said, 'Yes.' It's their religion."

"Man, I'm glad I'm a Baptist," Elise said, shaking her head in sympathy for the Mennonites.

"So did the guy do it?" Drema asked, scooting closer to hear if the story got juicy.

"Yeah," I said. "His whole family was with him. My dad drove them to our house. They all painted our porch. The woman and girl were in bonnets and long, long skirts with buttons up to their necks. The guy wore this weird hat and these huge suspenders."

"Why," Arnetta asked archly, as though she didn't believe a word, "would someone pick a *porch*? If they'll do anything, why not make them paint the whole *house*? Why not ask for a hundred bucks?"

I thought about it, and I remembered the words my father had said about them painting our porch, though I had never seemed to think about his words after he'd said them.

"He said," I began, only then understanding the words as they uncoiled from my mouth, "it was the only time he'd have a white man on his knees doing something for a black man for free."

I remembered the Mennonites bending like Daphne had bent, cleaning the restroom. I remembered the dark blue of their bonnets, the black of their shoes. They painted the porch as though scrubbing a floor. I was already trembling before Daphne asked quietly, "Did he thank them?"

I looked out the window. I could not tell which were the thoughts and which were the trees. "No," I said, and suddenly knew there was something mean in the world that I could not stop.

Arnetta laughed. "If I asked them to take off their long skirts and bonnets and put on some jeans, they would do it?"

And Daphne's voice—quiet, steady: "Maybe they would. Just to be nice."

Sequence, Sometimes Metaphysical

Theodore Roethke

As a child, Theodore Roethke spent much time in the greenhouse owned by his father and uncle. The subjects and imagery of his verse were profoundly influenced by his impressions of the natural world. Roethke attended the University of Michigan and took a few classes at Harvard. His first book, Open House *(1941), was well received by critics. He was awarded the Pulitzer Prize in 1954 for the volume* The Waking. *Roethke taught at various colleges and universities, including Lafayette, Pennsylvania State, and Bennington, and worked last at the University of Washington, where he was mentor to a generation of Northwest poets that included David Wagoner, Carolyn Kizer, and Richard Hugo.*

IN A DARK TIME

In a dark time, the eye begins to see,
I meet my shadow in the deepening shade;
I hear my echo in the echoing wood—
A lord of nature weeping to a tree.
I live between the heron and the wren,
Beasts of the hill and serpents of the den.

What's madness but nobility of soul
At odds with circumstance? The day's on fire!
I know the purity of pure despair,
My shadow pinned against a sweating wall.
That place among the rocks—is it a cave,
Or winding path? The edge is what I have.

A steady storm of correspondences!
A night flowing with birds, a ragged moon,
And in broad day the midnight come again!
A man goes far to find out what he is—
Death of the self in a long, tearless night,
All natural shapes blazing unnatural light.

Dark, dark my light, and darker my desire.
My soul, like some heat-maddened summer fly,
Keeps buzzing at the sill. Which I is *I*?
A fallen man, I climb out of my fear.
The mind enters itself, and God the mind,
And one is One, free in the tearing wind.

MY PAPA'S WALTZ

The whiskey on your breath
Could make a small boy dizzy;
But I hung on like death:
Such waltzing was not easy.

We romped until the pans
Slid from the kitchen shelf;
My mother's countenance
Could not unfrown itself.

The hand that held my wrist
Was battered on one knuckle;
At every step you missed
My right ear scraped a buckle.

You beat time on my head
With a palm caked hard by dirt,
Then waltzed me off to bed
Still clinging to your shirt.

Prologue

Philip Roth

Philip Roth was born (in 1933) and raised in Newark, New Jersey. He began writing for literary magazines while studying for a Ph.D. in English at the University of Chicago. His first published work was a collection of short stories entitled Goodbye Columbus *(1959). Since then, Roth has written and published numerous novels among which* Portnoy's Complaint *(1969),* The Great American Novel *(1973), the trilogy* Zuckerman Bound *(1985), and* I Married a Communist *(1998). The following is the Prologue to his autobiographical book* Patrimony *(1994).*

One day in late October 1944, I was astonished to find my father, whose workday ordinarily began at seven and many nights didn't end until ten, sitting alone at the kitchen table in the middle of the afternoon. He was going into the hospital unexpectedly to have his appendix removed. Though he had already packed a bag to take with him, he had waited for my brother, Sandy, and me to get home from school to tell us not to be alarmed. "Nothing to it," he assured us, though we all knew that two of his brothers had died back in the 1920s from complications following difficult appendectomies. My mother, the president that year of our school's parent-teacher association, happened, quite unusually, to be away overnight in Atlantic City at a statewide PTA convention. My father had phoned her hotel, however, to tell her the news, and she had immediately begun preparations to return home. That would do it, I was sure: my mother's domestic ingenuity was on a par with Robinson Crusoe's, and as for nursing us all through our illnesses, we couldn't have received much better care from Florence Nightingale. As was usual in our household, everything was now under control.

Reprinted from *The Facts: A Novelist's Autobiography*, (1988), by permission of Farrar, Straus & Giroux.

By the time her train pulled into Newark that evening, the surgeon had opened him up, seen the mess, and despaired for my father's chances. At the age of forty-three, he was put on the critical list and given less than a fifty-fifty chance to survive.

Only the adults knew how bad things were. Sandy and I were allowed to go on believing that a father was indestructible—and ours turned out to be just that. Despite a raw emotional nature that makes him prey to intractable worry, his life has been distinguished by the power of resurgence. I've never intimately known anyone else—aside from my brother and me—to swing as swiftly through so wide a range of moods, anyone else to take things so hard, to be so openly racked by a serious setback, and yet, after the blow has reverberated down to the quick, to clamber back so aggressively, to recover lost ground and get going again.

He was saved by the new sulfa powder, developed during the early years of the war to treat battlefront wounds. Surviving was an awful ordeal nonetheless, his weakness from the near-fatal peritonitis exacerbated by a ten-day siege of hiccups during which he was unable to sleep or to keep down food. After he'd lost nearly thirty pounds, his shrunken face disclosed itself to us as a replica of my elderly grandmother's, the face of the mother whom he and all his brothers adored (toward the father—laconic, authoritarian, remote, an immigrant who'd trained in Galicia to be a rabbi but worked in America in a hat factory—their feelings were more confused). Bertha Zahnstecker Roth was a simple old-country woman, good-hearted, given to neither melancholy nor complaint, yet her everyday facial expression made it plain that she nursed no illusions about life's being easy. My father's resemblance to his mother would not appear so eerily again until he himself reached his eighties, and then only when he was in the grip of a struggle that stripped an otherwise physically youthful old man of his seeming impregnability, leaving him bewildered not so much because of the eye problem or the difficulty with his gait that had made serious inroads on his self-sufficiency but because he felt all at once abandoned by that masterful accomplice and overturner of obstacles, his determination.

When he was driven home from Newark's Beth Israel Hospital after six weeks in bed there, he barely had the strength, even with our assistance, to make it up the short back staircase to our second-story apartment. It was December 1944 by then, a cold winter day, but through the windows the sunlight illuminated my parents' bedroom. Sandy and I came in to talk to him, both of us shy and grateful and, of course, stunned by how helpless he appeared seated weakly in a lone chair in the corner of the room. Seeing his sons together like that, my father could no longer control himself and began to sob. He was alive, the sun was shining, his wife was not widowed nor his boys fatherless—family life would now resume. It was not so complicated that an eleven-year-old couldn't understand his father's tears. I just didn't see, as he so clearly could, why or how it should have turned out differently.

I knew only two boys in our neighborhood whose families were fatherless, and thought of them as no less blighted than the blind girl who attended our school for a while and had to be read to and shepherded everywhere. The fatherless boys seemed almost equally marked and set apart; in the aftermath of their fathers' deaths, they too struck me as scary and a little taboo. Though one was a model of obedience and the other a troublemaker, everything either of them did or said seemed determined by his being a boy with a dead father and, however innocently I arrived at this notion, I was probably right.

I knew no child whose family was divided by divorce. Outside of the movie magazines and the tabloid headlines, it didn't exist, certainly not among Jews like us. Jews didn't get divorced—not because divorce was forbidden by Jewish law but because that was the way they were. If Jewish fathers didn't come home drunk and beat their wives—and in our neighborhood, which was Jewry to me, I'd never heard of any who did—that too was because of the way they were. In our lore, the Jewish family was an inviolate haven against every form of menace, from personal isolation to gentile hostility. Regardless of internal friction and strife, it was assumed to be an indissoluble consolidation. *Hear, O Israel, the family is God, the family is One.*

Family indivisibility, the first commandment.

In the late 1940s, when my father's younger brother, Bernie, proclaimed his intention of divorcing the wife of nearly twenty years who was the mother of his two daughters, my mother and father were as stunned as if they'd heard that he'd killed somebody. Had Bernie committed murder and gone to jail for life, they would probably have rallied behind him despite the abominable, inexplicable deed. But when he made up his mind not merely to divorce but to do so to marry a younger woman, their support went instantly to the "victims," the sister-in-law and the nieces. For his transgression, a breach of faith with his wife, his children, his entire clan—a dereliction of his duty as a Jew *and* as a Roth—Bernie encountered virtually universal condemnation.

That family rupture only began to mend when time revealed that no one had been destroyed by the divorce; in fact, anguished as they were by the breakup of their household, Bernie's ex-wife and his two girls were never remotely as indignant as the rest of the relatives. The healing owed a lot to Bernie himself, a more diplomatic man than most of his judges, but also to the fact that for my father the demands of family solidarity and the bond of family history exceeded even *his* admonishing instincts. It was to be another forty-odd years, however, before the two brothers threw their arms around each other and hungrily embraced in an unmistakable act of unqualified reconciliation. This occurred a few weeks before Bernie's death, in his late seventies, when his heart was failing rapidly and nobody, beginning with himself, expected him to last much longer.

I had driven my father over to see Bernie and his wife, Ruth, in their condominium in a retirement village in northwestern Connecticut, twenty miles from my own home. It was Bernie's turn now to wear the little face of his unillusioned, stoical old mother; when he came to the door to let us in, there in his features was that stark resemblance that seemed to emerge in all the Roth brothers when they were up against it.

Ordinarily the two men would have met with a handshake, but when my father stepped into the hallway, so much was clear both about the time that was left to Bernie and about all those decades, seemingly stretching back to the beginning of time, during which they had been alive as their parents' offspring, that the handshake was swallowed up in a forceful hug that lasted minutes and left them in tears. They seemed to be saying goodbye to everyone already gone as well as to each other, the last two surviving children of the dour hatblocker Sender and the imperturbable *balabusta* Bertha. Safely in his brother's arms, Bernie seemed also to be saying goodbye to himself. There was nothing to guard against or defend against or resent anymore, nothing even to remember. In these brothers, men so deeply swayed, despite their dissimilarity, by identical strains of family emotion, everything remembered had been distilled into pure, barely bearable feeling.

In the car afterward my father said, "We haven't held each other like that since we were small boys. My brother's dying, Philip. I used to push him around in his carriage. There were nine of us, with my mother and father. I'll be the last one left."

While we drove back to my house (where he was staying in the upstairs back bedroom, a room in which he says he never fails to sleep like a baby) he recounted the struggles of each of his five brothers—with bankruptcies, illnesses, and in-laws, with marital dissension and bad loans, and with children, with their Gonerils, their Regans, and their Cordelias. He recalled for me the martyrdom of his only sister, what she and all the family had gone through when her husband the bookkeeper who liked the horses had served a little time for embezzlement.

It wasn't exactly the first time I was hearing these stories. Narrative is the form that his knowledge takes, and his repertoire has never been large: family, family, family, Newark, Newark, Newark, Jew, Jew, Jew. Somewhat like mine.

I naïvely believed as a child that I would always have a father present, and the truth seems to be that I always will. However awkward the union may sometimes have been, vulnerable to differences of opinion, to false expectations, to radically divergent experiences of America, strained by the colliding of two impatient, equally willful temperaments and marred by masculine clumsiness, the link to him has been omnipresent. What's more, now, when he no longer commands my attention by his bulging biceps and his moral strictures, now, when he is no longer the biggest man I have to contend with—and when I am not all that far from being an old man myself—I am able to laugh at his jokes and hold his hand and concern myself with his well-being, I'm able to love him the way I wanted to when I was sixteen, seventeen, and eighteen but when, what with dealing with him and feeling at odds with him, it was simply an impossibility. *The* impossibility, for all that I always respected him for his particular burden and his struggle within a system that he didn't choose. The mythological role of a Jewish boy growing up in a family like mine—to become the hero one's father failed to be—I may even have achieved by now, but not at all in the way that was preordained. After nearly forty years of living far from home, I'm equipped at last to be the most loving of sons—just, however, when he has another agenda. He is trying to die. He doesn't say that, nor, probably, does he think of it in those words, but that's his job now and, fight as he will to survive, he understands, as he always has, what the real work is.

Trying to die isn't like trying to commit suicide—it may actually be harder, because what you are trying to do is what you least want to have happen; you dread it but there it is and it must be done, and by no one but you. Twice in the last few years he has taken a shot at it, on two different occasions suddenly became so ill that I, who was then living abroad half the year, flew back to America to find him with barely enough strength to walk from the sofa to the TV set without clutching at every chair in between. And though each time the doctor, after a painstaking examination, was unable to find anything wrong with him, he nonetheless went to bed every night expecting not to awaken in the morning and, when he did awaken in the morning, he was fifteen minutes just getting himself into a sitting position on the edge of the bed and another hour shaving and dressing. Then, for God knows how long, he slouched unmoving over a bowl of cereal for which he had absolutely no appetite.

I was as certain as he was that this was it, yet neither time could he pull it off and, over a period of weeks, he recovered his strength and became himself again, loathing Reagan, defending Israel, phoning relatives, attending funerals, writing to newspapers, castigating William Buckley, watching MacNeil-Lehrer, exhorting his grown grandchildren, remembering in detail our own dead, and relentlessly, exactingly—and without having been asked—monitoring the caloric intake of the nice woman he lives with. It would seem that to prevail here, to try dying and to *do* it, he will have to work even harder than he did in the insurance business where he achieved a remarkable success for a man with his social and educational handicaps. Of course, here too he'll eventually succeed—though clearly, despite his record of assiduous application to every job he has ever been assigned, things won't be easy. But then they never have been.

Needless to say, the link to my father was never so voluptuously tangible as the colossal bond to my mother's flesh, whose metamorphosed incarnation was a sleek black sealskin coat into which I, the younger, the privileged, the pampered papoose, blissfully wormed myself whenever my father chauffeured us home to New Jersey on a winter Sunday from our semiannual excursion to Radio City Music Hall and Manhattan's Chinatown: the unnameable animal-me bearing her dead father's name, the protoplasm-me, boy-baby, and body-burrower-in-training, joined by every nerve ending to her smile and her sealskin coat, while his resolute dutifulness, his relentless industriousness, his unreasoning obstinacy and harsh resentments, his illusions, his innocence, his allegiances, his fears were to constitute the original mold for the American, Jew, citizen, man, even for the writer, I would become. To be at all is to be her Philip, but in the embroilment with the buffeting world, my history still takes its spin from beginning as his Roth.

Under the Influence

Paying the Price of My Father's Booze

Scott Russell Sanders

Scott Russell Sanders teaches at Indiana University and he is a valued writer of nonfiction. He has written numerous books, among which the most recent are: Writing from the Center *(1995)* Hunting for Hope *(1999),* The Force of Spirit *(2001), and* Crowded Creek *(2002). He has also written numerous children's books. Scott Russell Sanders contributes frequently to journals such as* Audubon, Harper's, Orion, North American Review, Georgia Review, Gettysburg Review, Kenyon Review, Parabola *and* Utne Reader. *He has served as literary editor of* The Cambridge Review, *as fiction editor of* The Minnesota Review, *and as columnist on new fiction for the* Chicago Sun-Times. *He is a contributing editor for* Audubon *and an editorial adviser for* Orion. *In addition to writing, Scott Russell Sanders has done hundreds of public readings and lectures.*

My father drank. He drank as a gut-punched boxer gasps for breath, as a starving dog gobbles food—compulsively, secretly, in pain and trembling. I use the past tense not because he ever quit drinking but because he quit living. That is how the story ends for my father, age sixty-four, heart bursting, body cooling, slumped and forsaken on the linoleum of my brother's trailer. The story continues for my brother, my sister, my mother, and me, and will continue as long as memory holds.

In the perennial present of memory, I slip into the garage or barn to see my father tipping back the flat green bottles of wine, the brown cylinders of whiskey, the cans of beer disguised in paper bags. His Adam's apple bobs, the liquid gurgles, he wipes the sandy-haired back of a hand over his lips, and then, his bloodshot gaze bumping into me, he stashes the bottle or can inside his jacket, under the workbench, between two bales of hay, and we both pretend the moment has not occurred.

"What's up, buddy?" he says, thick-tongued and edgy.

"Sky's up," I answer, playing along.

"And don't forget prices," he grumbles. "Prices are always up. And taxes."

In memory, his white 1951 Pontiac with the stripes down the hood and the Indian head on the snout lurches to a stop in the driveway; or it is the 1956 Ford station wagon, or the 1963 Rambler shaped like a toad, or the sleek 1969 Bonneville that will do 120 miles per hour on straightaways; or it is the robin's-egg-blue pickup, new in 1980, battered in 1981, the year of his death. He climbs out, grinning dangerously, unsteady on his legs, and we children interrupt our game of catch, our building of snow forts, our picking of plums, to watch in silence as he weaves past us into the house, where he drops into his overstuffed chair and falls asleep. Shaking her head, our mother stubs out a cigarette he has left smoldering in the ashtray. All evening, until our bedtimes, we tiptoe past him, as past a snoring dragon. Then we curl fearfully in our sheets, listening. Eventually he wakes with a grunt, Mother slings accusations at him, he snarls back, she yells, he growls, their voices clashing. Before long, she retreats to their bedroom, sobbing—not from the blows of fists, for he never strikes her, but from the force of his words.

Left alone, our father prowls the house, thumping into furniture, rummaging in the kitchen, slamming doors, turning the pages of the newspaper with a savage crackle, muttering back at the late-night drivel from television. The roof might fly off, the walls might buckle from the pressure of his rage. Whatever my brother and sister and mother may be thinking on their own rumpled pillows, I lie there hating him, loving him, fearing him, knowing I have failed him. I tell myself he drinks to ease the ache that gnaws at his belly, an ache I must have caused by disappointing him somehow, a murderous ache I should be able to relieve by doing all my chores, earning A's in school, winning baseball games, fixing the broken washer and the burst pipes, bringing in the money to fill his empty wallet. He would not hide the green bottles in his toolbox, would not sneak off to the barn with a lump under his coat, would not fall asleep in the daylight, would not roar and fume, would not drink himself to death, if only I were perfect.

I am forty-four, and I know full well now that my father was an alcoholic, a man consumed by disease rather than by disappointment. What had seemed to me a private grief is in fact, of course, a public scourge. In the United States alone, some ten or fifteen million people share his ailment, and behind the doors they slam in fury or disgrace, countless other children tremble. I comfort myself with such knowledge, holding it against the throb of memory like an ice pack against a bruise. Other people have keener sources of grief: poverty, racism, rape, war. I do not wish to compete to determine who has suffered most. I am only trying to understand the corrosive mixture of helplessness, responsibility, and shame that I learned to feel as the son of an alcoholic. I realize now that I did not cause my father's illness, nor could I have cured it. Yet for all this grownup knowledge, I am still ten years old, my own son's age, and as that boy I struggle in guilt and confusion to save my father from pain.

261

Consider a few of our synonyms for *drunk*: tipsy, tight, pickled, soused, and plowed; stoned and stewed, lubricated and inebriated, juiced and sluiced; three sheets to the wind, in your cups, out of your mind, under the table; lit up, tanked up, wiped out; besotted, blotto, bombed, and buzzed; plastered, polluted, putrefied; loaded or looped, boozy, woozy, fuddled, or smashed; crocked and shit-faced, corked and pissed, snockered and sloshed.

It is a mostly humorous lexicon, as the lore that deals with drunks—in jokes and cartoons, in plays, films, and television skits—is largely comic. Aunt Matilda nips elderberry wine from the sideboard and burps politely during supper. Uncle Fred slouches to the table glassy-eyed, wearing a lampshade for a hat and murmuring, "Candy is dandy, but liquor is quicker." Inspired by cocktails, Mrs. Somebody recounts the events of her day in a fuzzy dialect, while Mr. Somebody nibbles her ear and croons a bawdy song. On the sofa with Boyfriend, Daughter Somebody giggles, licking gin from her lips, and loosens the bows in her hair. Junior knocks back some brews with his chums at the Leopard Lounge and stumbles home to the wrong house, wonders foggily why he cannot locate his pajamas, and crawls naked into bed with the ugliest girl in school. The family dog slurps from a neglected martini and wobbles to the nursery, where he vomits in Baby's shoe.

It is all great fun. But if in the audience you notice a few laughing faces turn grim when the drunk lurches onstage, don't be surprised, for these are the children of alcoholics. Over the grinning mask of Dionysus, the leering face of Bacchus, these children cannot help seeing the bloated features of their own parents. Instead of laughing, they wince, they mourn. Instead of celebrating the drunk as one freed from constraints, they pity him as one enslaved. They refuse to believe *in vino veritas*, having seen their befuddled parents skid away from truth toward folly and oblivion. And so these children bite their lips until the lush staggers into the wings.

My father, when drunk, was neither funny nor honest; he was pathetic, frightening; deceitful. There seemed to be a leak in him somewhere, and he poured in booze to keep from draining dry. Like a torture victim who refuses to squeal, he would never admit that he had touched a drop, not even in his last year, when he seemed to be dissolving in alcohol before our very eyes. I never knew him to lie about anything, ever, except about this one ruinous fact. Drowsy, clumsy, unable to fix a bicycle tire, balance a grocery sack, or walk across a room, he was stripped of his true self by drink. In a matter of minutes, the contents of a bottle could transform a brave man into a coward, a buddy into a bully, a gifted athlete and skilled carpenter and shrewd businessman into a bumbler. No dictionary of synonyms for *drunk* would soften the anguish of watching our prince turn into a frog.

Father's drinking became the family secret. While growing up, we children never breathed a word of it beyond the four walls of our house. To this day, my brother and sister rarely mention it, and then only when I press them. I did not confess the ugly, bewildering fact to my wife until his wavering and slurred speech forced me to. Recently, on the seventh anniversary of my father's death, I asked my mother if she ever spoke of his drinking to friends. "No, no, never," she replied hastily. "I couldn't bear for anyone to know."

The secret bores under the skin, gets in the blood, into the bone, and stays there. Long after you have supposedly been cured of malaria, the fever can flare up, the tremors can shake you. So it is with the fevers of shame. You swallow the bitter quinine of knowledge, and you learn to feel pity and compassion toward the drinker. Yet the shame lingers and, because of it, anger.

For a long stretch of my childhood we lived on a military reservation in Ohio, an arsenal where bombs were stored underground in bunkers and vintage airplanes burst into flames and unstable artillery shells boomed nightly at the dump. We had the feeling, as children, that we played within a minefield, where a heedless footfall could trigger an explosion. When Father was drinking, the house, too, became a minefield. The least bump could set off either parent.

The more he drank, the more obsessed Mother became with stopping him. She hunted for bottles, counted the cash in his wallet, sniffed at his breath. Without meaning to snoop, we children blundered left and right into damning evidence. On afternoons when he came home from work sober, we flung ourselves at him for hugs and felt against our ribs the tell-tale lump in his coat. In the barn we tumbled on the hay and heard beneath our sneakers the crunch of broken glass. We tugged open a drawer in his workbench, looking for screwdrivers or crescent wrenches, and spied a gleaming six-pack among the tools. Playing tag, we darted around the house just in time to see him sway on the rear stoop and heave a finished bottle into the woods. In his goodnight kiss we smelled the cloying sweetness of Clorets, the mints he chewed to camouflage his dragon's breath.

I can summon up that kiss right now by recalling Theodore Roethke's lines about his own father:

> The whiskey on your breath
> Could make a small boy dizzy;
> But I hung on like death:
> Such waltzing was not easy.

Such waltzing was hard, terribly hard, for with a boy's scrawny arms I was trying to hold my tipsy father upright.

For years, the chief source of those incriminating bottles and cans was a grimy store a mile from us, a cinder-block place called Sly's, with two gas pumps outside and a mangy dog asleep in the window. Inside, on rusty metal shelves or in wheezing coolers, you could find pop and Popsicles, cigarettes, potato chips, canned soup, raunchy postcards, fishing gear, Twinkies, wine, and beer. When Father drove anywhere on errands, Mother would send us along as guards, warning us not to let him out of our sight. And so with one or more of us on board, Father would cruise up to Sly's, pump a dollar's worth of gas or plump the tires with air, and then, telling us to wait in the car, he would head for the doorway.

Dutiful and panicky, we cried, "Let us go with you!"

"No," he answered. "I'll be back in two shakes."

"Please!"

"No!" he roared. "Don't you budge or I'll jerk a knot in your tails!"

So we stayed put, kicking the seats, while he ducked inside. Often, when he had parked the car at a careless angle, we gazed in through the window and saw Mr. Sly fetching down from the shelf behind the cash register two green pints of Gallo wine. Father swigged one of them right there at the counter, stuffed the other in his pocket, and then out he came, a bulge in his coat, a flustered look on his reddened face.

Because the mom and pop who ran the dump were neighbors of ours, living just down the tar-blistered road, I hated them all the more for poisoning my father. I wanted to sneak in their store and smash the bottles and set fire to the place. I also hated the Gallo brothers, Ernest and Julio, whose jovial faces beamed from the labels of their wine, labels I would find, torn and curled, when I burned the trash. I noted the Gallo brothers' address in California and studied the road atlas to see how far that was from Ohio, because I meant to go out there and tell Ernest and Julio what they were doing to my father, and then, if they showed no mercy, I would kill them.

While growing up on the back roads and in the country schools and cramped Methodist churches of Ohio and Tennessee, I never heard the word *alcoholic*, never happened across it in books or magazines. In the nearby towns, there were no addiction-treatment programs, no community mental-health centers, no Alcoholics Anonymous chapters, no therapists. Left alone with our grievous secret, we had no way of understanding Father's drinking except as an act of will, a deliberate folly or cruelty, a moral weakness, a sin. He drank because he chose to, pure and simple. Why our father, so playful and competent and kind when sober, would choose to ruin himself and punish his family we could not fathom.

Our neighborhood was high on the Bible, and the Bible was hard on drunkards. "Woe to those who are heroes at drinking wine and valiant men in mixing strong drink," wrote Isaiah. "The priest and the prophet reel with strong drink, they are confused with wine, they err in vision, they stumble in giving judgment. For all tables are full of vomit, no place is without filthiness." We children had seen those fouled tables at the local truck stop where the notorious boozers hung out, our father occasionally among them. "Wine and new wine take away the understanding," declared the prophet Hosea. We had also seen evidence of that in our father, who could multiply seven-digit numbers in his head when sober but when drunk could not help us with fourth-grade math. Proverbs warned: "Do not look at wine when it is red, when it sparkles in the cup and goes down smoothly. At the last it bites like a serpent and stings like an adder. Your eyes will see strange things, and your mind utter perverse things." Woe, woe.

Dismayingly often, these biblical drunkards stirred up trouble for their own kids. Noah made fresh wine after the flood, drank too much of it, fell asleep without any clothes on, and was glimpsed in the buff by his son Ham, whom Noah promptly cursed. In one passage—it was so shocking we had to read it under our blankets with flashlights—the patriarch Lot fell down drunk and slept with his daughters. The sins of the fathers set their children's teeth on edge.

Our ministers were fond of quoting St. Paul's pronouncement that drunkards would not inherit the kingdom of God. These grave preachers assured us that the wine referred to in the Last Supper was in fact grape juice. Bible and sermons and hymns combined to give us the impression that Moses should have brought down from the mountain another stone tablet, bearing the Eleventh Commandment: Thou shalt not drink.

The scariest and most illuminating Bible story apropos of drunkards was the one about the lunatic and the swine. We knew it by heart: When Jesus climbed out of his boat one day, this lunatic came charging up from the graveyard, stark naked and filthy, frothing at the mouth, so violent that he broke the strongest chains. Nobody would go near him. Night and day for years, this madman had been wailing among the tombs and bruising himself with stones. Jesus took one look at him and said, "Come out of the man, you unclean spirits!" for he could see that the lunatic was possessed by demons. Meanwhile, some hogs were conveniently rooting nearby. "If we have to come out," begged the demons, "at least let us go into those swine." Jesus agreed, the unclean spirits entered the hogs, and the hogs raced straight off a cliff and plunged into a lake. Hearing the story in Sunday school, my friends thought mainly of the pigs. (How big a splash did they make? Who paid for the lost pork?) But I thought of the redeemed lunatic, who bathed himself and put on clothes and calmly sat at the feet of Jesus, restored—so the Bible said—to "his right mind."

When drunk, our father was clearly in his wrong mind. He became a stranger, as fearful to us as any graveyard lunatic, not quite frothing at the mouth but fierce enough, quick-tempered, explosive; or else he grew maudlin and weepy, which frightened us nearly as much. In my boyhood despair, I reasoned that maybe he wasn't to blame for turning into an ogre: Maybe, like the lunatic, he was possessed by demons.

If my father was indeed possessed, who would exorcise him? If he was a sinner, who would save him? If he was ill, who would cure him? If he suffered, who would ease his pain? Not ministers or doctors, for we could not bring ourselves to confide in them; not the neighbors, for we pretended they had never seen him drunk; not Mother, who fussed and pleaded but could not budge him; not my brother and sister, who were only kids. That left me. It did not matter that I, too, was only a child, and a bewildered one at that. I could not excuse myself.

On first reading a description of delirium tremens—in a book on alcoholism I smuggled from a university library—I thought immediately of the frothing lunatic and the frenzied swine. When I read stories or watched films about grisly metamorphoses—Dr. Jekyll becoming Mr. Hyde, the mild husband changing into a werewolf, the kindly neighbor inhabited by a brutal alien—I could not help but see my own father's mutation from sober to drunk. Even today, knowing better, I am attracted by the demonic theory of drink, for when I recall my father's transformation, the emergence of his ugly second self, I find it easy to believe in being possessed by unclean spirits.

We never knew which version of Father would come home from work, the true or the tainted, nor could we guess how far down the slope toward cruelty he would slide.

How far a man *could* slide we gauged by observing our back-road neighbors—the out-of-work miners who had dragged their families to our corner of Ohio from the desolate hollows of Appalachia, the tightfisted farmers, the surly mechanics, the balked and broken men. There was, for example, whiskey-soaked Mr. Jenkins, who beat his wife and kids so hard we could hear their screams from the road. There was Mr. Lavo the wino, who fell asleep smoking time and again, until one night his disgusted wife bundled up the children and went outside and left him in his easy chair to burn; he awoke on his own, staggered out coughing into the yard, and pounded her flat while the children looked on and the shack turned to ash. There was the truck driver, Mr. Sampson, who tripped over his son's tricycle one night while drunk and got mad, jumped into his semi, and drove away, shifting through the dozen gears, and never came back. We saw the bruised children of these fathers clump onto our school bus, we saw the abandoned children huddle in the pews at church, we saw the stunned and battered mothers begging for help at our doors.

Our own father never beat us, and I don't think he beat Mother, but he threatened often. The Old Testament Yahweh was not more terrible in His rage. Eyes blazing, voice booming, Father would pull out his belt and swear to give us a whipping, but he never followed through, never needed to, because we could imagine it so vividly. He shoved us, pawed us with the back of his hand, not to injure, just to clear a space. I can see him grabbing Mother by the hair as she cowers on a chair during a nightly quarrel. He twists her neck back until she gapes up at him, and then he lifts over her skull a glass quart bottle of milk, the milk spilling down his forearm, and he yells at her, "Say just one more word, one goddamn word, and I'll shut you up!" I fear she will prick him with her sharp tongue, but she is terrified into silence, and so am I, and the leaking bottle quivers in the air, and milk seeps through the red hair of my father's uplifted arm, and the entire scene is there to this moment, the head jerked back, the club raised.

When the drink made him weepy, Father would pack, kiss each of us children on the head, and announce from the front door that he was moving out. "Where to?" we demanded, fearful each time that he would leave for good, as Mr. Simpson had roared away for good in his diesel truck. "Someplace where I won't get hounded every minute," Father would answer, his jaw quivering. He stabbed a look at Mother, who might say, "Don't run into the ditch before you get there," or "Good riddance," and then he would slink away. Mother watched him go with arms crossed over her chest, her face closed like the lid on a box of snakes. We children bawled. Where could he go? To the truck stop, that den of iniquity? To one of those dark, ratty flophouses in town? Would he wind up sleeping under a railroad bridge or on a park bench or in a cardboard box, mummied in rags like the bums we had seen on our trips to Cleveland and Chicago? We bawled and bawled, wondering if he would ever come back.

He always did come back, a day or a week later, but each time there was a sliver less of him.

266

In Kafka's *Metamorphosis*, which opens famously with Gregor Samsa waking up from uneasy dreams to find himself transformed into an insect, Gregor's family keep reassuring themselves that things will be just fine again "when he comes back to us." Each time alcohol transformed our father we held out the same hope, that he would really and truly come back to us, our authentic father, the tender and playful and competent man, and then all things would be fine. We had grounds for such hope. After his tearful departures and chapfallen returns, he would sometimes go weeks, even months, without drinking. Those were glad times. Every day without the furtive glint of bottles, every meal without a fight, every bedtime without sobs encouraged us to believe that such bliss might go on forever.

Mother was fooled by such a hope all during the forty-odd years she knew Greeley Ray Sanders. Soon after she met him in a Chicago delicatessen on the eve of World War II and fell for his butter-melting Mississippi drawl and his wavy red hair, she learned that he drank heavily. But then so did a lot of men. She would soon coax or scold him into breaking the nasty habit. She would point out to him how ugly and foolish it was, this bleary drinking, and then he would quit. He refused to quit during their engagement, however, still refused during the first years of marriage, refused until my older sister came along. The shock of fatherhood sobered him, and he remained sober through my birth at the end of the war and right on through until we moved in 1951 to the Ohio arsenal. The arsenal had more than its share of alcoholics, drug addicts, and other varieties of escape artists. There I turned six and started school and woke into a child's flickering awareness, just in time to see my father begin sneaking swigs in the garage.

He sobered up again for most of a year at the height of the Korean War, to celebrate the birth of my brother. But aside from that dry spell, his only breaks from drinking before I graduated from high school were just long enough to raise and then dash our hopes. Then during the fall of my senior year—the time of the Cuban Missile Crisis, when it seemed that the nightly explosions at the munitions dump and the nightly rages in our household might spread to engulf the globe—Father collapsed. His liver, kidneys, and heart all conked out. The doctors saved him, but only by a hair. He stayed in the hospital for weeks, going through a withdrawal so terrible that Mother would not let us visit him. If he wanted to kill himself, the doctors solemnly warned him, all he had to do was hit the bottle again. One binge would finish him.

Father must have believed them, for he stayed dry the next fifteen years. It was an answer to prayer, Mother said, it was a miracle. I believe it was a reflex of fear, which he sustained over the years through courage and pride. He knew a man could die from drink, for his brother Roscoe had. We children never laid eyes on doomed Uncle Roscoe, but in the stories Mother told us he became a fairy-tale figure, like a boy who took the wrong turn in the woods and was gobbled up by the wolf.

The fifteen-year dry spell came to an end with Father's retirement in the spring of 1978. Like many men, he gave up his identity along with his job. One day he was a boss at the factory, with a brass plate on his door and a reputation to uphold; the next day he was a nobody at home. He and Mother were leaving Ontario, the last of the many places to which his job had carried them, and they were moving to a new house in Mississippi, his childhood stomping ground. As a boy in Mississippi, Father sold Coca-Cola during dances while the moonshiners peddled their brew in the parking lot; as a young blade, he fought in bars and in the ring, winning a state Golden Gloves championship; he gambled at poker, hunted pheasant, raced motorcycles and cars, played semiprofessional baseball, and, along with all his buddies—in the Black Cat Saloon, behind the cotton gin, in the woods—he drank hard. It was a perilous youth to dream of recovering.

After his final day of work, Mother drove on ahead with a car full of begonias and violets, while Father stayed behind to oversee the packing. When the van was loaded, the sweaty movers broke open a six-pack and offered him a beer.

"Let's drink to retirement!" they crowed. "Let's drink to freedom! to fishing! hunting! loafing! Let's drink to a guy who's going home!"

At least I imagine some such words, for that is all I can do, imagine, and I see Father's hand trembling in midair as he thinks about the fifteen sober years and about the doctors' warning, and he tells himself, *Goddamnit, I am a free man,* and *Why can't a free man drink one beer after a lifetime of hard work?* and I see his arm reaching, his fingers closing, the can tilting to his lips. I even supply a label for the beer, a swaggering brand that promises on television to deliver the essence of life. I watch the amber liquid pour down his throat, the alcohol steal into his blood, the key turn in his brain.

Soon after my parents moved back to Father's treacherous stomping ground, my wife and I visited them in Mississippi with our four-year-old daughter. Mother had been too distraught to warn me about the return of the demons. So when I climbed out of the car that bright July morning and saw my father napping in the hammock, I felt uneasy, and when he lurched upright and blinked his bloodshot eyes and greeted us in a syrupy voice, I was hurled back into childhood.

"What's the matter with Papaw?" our daughter asked.

"Nothing," I said. "Nothing!"

Like a child again, I pretended not to see him in his stupor, and behind my phony smile I grieved. On that visit and on the few that remained before his death, once again I found bottles in the workbench, bottles in the woods. Again his hands shook too much for him to run a saw, to make his precious miniature furniture, to drive straight down back roads. Again he wound up in the ditch, in the hospital, in jail, in the treatment center. Again he shouted and wept. Again he lied. "I never touched a drop," he swore. "Your mother's making it up."

I no longer fancied I could reason with the men whose names I found on the bottles—Jim Beam, Jack Daniel's—but I was able now to recall the cold statistics about alcoholism: ten million victims, fifteen million, twenty. And yet, in spite of my age, I reacted in the same blind way as I had in childhood, by vainly seeking to erase through my efforts whatever drove him to drink. I worked on their place twelve and sixteen hours a day, in the swelter of Mississippi summers, digging ditches, running electrical wires, planting trees, mowing grass, building sheds, as though what nagged at him was some list of chores, as though by taking his worries upon my shoulders I could redeem him. I was flung back into boyhood, acting as though my father would not drink himself to death if only I were perfect.

I failed of perfection; he succeeded in dying. To the end, he considered himself not sick but sinful. "Do you want to kill yourself?" I asked him. "Why not?" he answered. "Why the hell not? What's there to save?" To the end, he would not speak about his feelings, would not or could not give a name to the beast that was devouring him.

In silence, he went rushing off the cliff. Unlike the biblical swine, however, he left behind a few of the demons to haunt his children. Life with him and the loss of him twisted us into shapes that will be familiar to other sons and daughters of alcoholics. My brother became a rebel, my sister retreated into shyness, I played the stalwart and dutiful son who would hold the family together. If my father was unstable, I would be a rock. If he squandered money on drink, I would pinch every penny. If he wept when drunk—and only when drunk—I would not let myself weep at all. If he roared at the Little League umpire for calling my pitches balls, I would throw nothing but strikes. Watching him flounder and rage, I came to dread the loss of control. I would go through life without making anyone mad. I vowed never to put in my mouth or veins any chemical that would banish my everyday self. I would never make a scene, never lash out at the ones I loved, never hurt a soul. Through hard work, relentless work, I would achieve something dazzling—in the classroom, on the basketball court, in the science lab, in the pages of books—and my achievement would distract the world's eyes from his humiliation. I would become a worthy sacrifice, and the smoke of my burning would please God.

It is far easier to recognize these twists in my character than to undo them. Work has become an addiction for me, as drink was an addiction for my father. Knowing this, my daughter gave me a placard for the wall: WORKAHOLIC. The labor is endless and futile, for I can no more redeem myself through work than I could redeem my father. I still panic in the face of other people's anger, because his drunken temper was so terrible. I shrink from causing sadness or disappointment even to strangers, as though I were still concealing the family shame. I still notice every twitch of emotion in those faces around me, having learned as a child to read the weather in faces, and I blame myself for their least pang of unhappiness or anger. In certain moods I blame myself for everything. Guilt burns like acid in my veins.

I am moved to write these pages now because my own son, at the age of ten, is taking on himself the griefs of the world, and in particular the griefs of his father. He tells me that when I am gripped by sadness, he feels responsible; he feels there must be something he can do to spring me from depression, to fix my life. And that crushing sense of responsibility is exactly what I felt at the age of ten in the face of my father's drinking. My son wonders if I, too, am possessed. I write, therefore, to drag into the light what eats at me—the fear, the guilt, the shame—so that my own children may be spared.

I still shy away from nightclubs, from bars, from parties where the solvent is alcohol. My friends puzzle over this, but it is no more peculiar than for a man to shy away from the lions' den after seeing his father torn apart. I took my own first drink at the age of twenty-one, half a glass of burgundy. I knew the odds of my becoming an alcoholic were four times higher than for the children of nonalcoholic fathers. So I sipped warily.

I still do—once a week, perhaps, a glass of wine, a can of beer, nothing stronger, nothing more. I listen for the turning of a key in my brain.

On Reading a Videotext

Robert Scholes

Robert Scholes is Andrew W. Melon Professor of Humanities at Brown University, based in the Department of Modern Cultures and Media. He teaches courses in modernism, modern literature, art, opera, and thought. Scholes has a Ph.D. from Cornell University and has written numerous academic books and articles on literature, theory, and the media. His most recent books are Protocols of Reading *(1989),* Hemingway's Genders *(1994) and* The Rise and Fall of English *(1998). Recently, Scholes has started experimenting with publishing on line, taking advantage of the possibility of including color pictures within his essays about painters. For the past several years, he has been working with the College Board, the ETS, the NCTE and a group of energetic and creative teachers to develop a new version of a final course in English for all high school students. This course is now being taught in programs all over the country. It is called Pacesetter English. "On Reading a Videotext" is an excerpt from* Protocols of Reading.

We must consider the rhetoric of video, because it is so powerful, so ubiquitous in our culture, and because it brings into play the temporal or narrative dimension of evaluative discourse in a very vivid manner. Appealing, as it does, to a wide audience, it will also provide an appropriate occasion to consider the relation of specific texts to the cultural codes against which they must be read.

The moments of surrender proposed to us by video texts come in many forms, but all involve a complex dynamic of power and pleasure. We are, for instance, offered a kind of power through the enhancement of our vision. Close-ups position us where we could never stand. Slow motion allows us an extraordinary penetration into the

Reprinted from *Protocols of Reading*, (1989), by permission of Yale University Press.

mechanics of movement, and, combined with music, lends a balletic grace to ordinary forms of locomotion. Filters and other devices cause us to see the world through jaundiced or rose-colored optics, coloring events with emotion more effectively than verbal pathetic fallacy and less obtrusively. These derangements of normal visual processing can be seen as either constraints or extensions of visual power—that is, as power over the viewer or as extensions of the viewer's own optical power, or both. Either way they offer us what is perhaps the greatest single virtue of art: change from the normal, a defense against the ever-present threat of boredom. Video texts, like all except the most utilitarian forms of textuality, are constructed upon a base of boredom, from which they promise us relief.

Visual fascination—and I have mentioned only a few of its obvious forms—is just one of the matrices of power and pleasure that are organized by video texts. Others include narrativity and what I should like to call, at least tentatively, cultural reinforcement. By narrativity, of course, I mean the pleasures and powers associated with the reception of stories presented in video texts. By cultural reinforcement, I mean the process through which video texts confirm viewers in their ideological positions and reassure them as to their membership in a collective cultural body. This function, which operates in the ethical-political realm, is an extremely important element of video textuality and, indeed, an extremely important dimension of all the mass media. This is a function performed throughout much of human history by literature and the other arts, but now, as the arts have become more estranged from their own culture and even opposed to it, the mass media have come to perform this role. What the epic poem did for ancient cultures, the romance for feudalism, and the novel for bourgeois society, the media—and especially television—now do for the commodified, bureaucratized world that is our present environment.

It is time, now, to look at these processes as they operate in some specific texts. Let us begin with a well-known Budweiser commercial, which tells—most frequently in a format of twenty-eight seconds, though a longer version also exists—the life story of a black man pursuing a career as a baseball umpire. In this brief period of time, we are given enough information to construct an entire life story—provided we have the cultural knowledge upon which this construction depends. The story we construct is that of a young man from the provinces, who gets his "big break," his chance to make it in the big city, to rise to the top of his profession. We see him working hard in the small-time, small-town atmosphere of the minor leagues, where the pace of events is slower and more relaxed that it is "at the top." He gets his chance for success—the voice-over narrator says, "In the minors you got to make all the calls, and then one day you *get* the call"—after which we see him face his first real test. He must call an important and "close" play correctly and then withstand the pressure of dispute, neither giving ground by changing his mind (which would be fatal) nor reacting too vigorously to the challenge of his call by an offended manager. His passing of this test and being accepted is presented through a later scene in a bar, in which the manager who had staged the protest "toasts" the umpire with a bottle of Budweiser beer, with a chorus in the background singing, "You keep America working. This Bud's for you." From this scene we conclude that the ump has now "made it" and will live happily ever after. From a few scenes, then, aided by the voice-over narration and a music track, we construct an entire life. How do we do this? We draw upon a storehouse of cultural information that extends from fairy tales and other basic narrative structures to knowledge about the game and business of baseball.

In processing a narrative text we actually construct the story, bringing a vast repertory of cultural knowledge to bear upon the text that we are contemplating. Our pleasure in the narrative is to some extent a constructive pleasure, based upon the sense of accomplishment we achieve by successfully completing this task. By "getting" the story, we prove our competence and demonstrate our membership in a cultural community. And what is the story that we "get"? It is the myth of America itself, of the racial melting pot, of upward mobility, of justice done without fear or favor. The corporate structure of baseball, with minor leagues offering a path for the talented to the celebrity and financial rewards of the majors, embodies values that we all possess, we Americans, as one of the deepest parts of our cultural heritage or ideology. It is, of course, on the playing field that talent triumphs most easily over racial or social barriers. Every year in baseball new faces arrive. Young men, having proved themselves in the minors, get their chance to perform at the highest level. Yale graduates and high-school dropouts who speak little or no English are judged equally by how well they hit, run, throw, and react to game situations. If baseball is still the national pastime, it is because in it our cherished myths materialize—or appear to materialize.

The commercial we are considering is especially interesting because it shows us a black man competing not with his body but with his mind, his judgment and his emotions, in a cruelly testing public arena. Americans who attend to sports are aware that black athletes are just beginning to find acceptance at certain "leadership" positions, such as quarterback in professional football, and that there is still an active scandal over the slender representation of blacks at baseball's managerial and corporate levels. The case of the black umpire reminds viewers of these problems, even as it suggests that here, too, talent will finally prevail. The system works, America works. We can take pride in this. The narrative reduces its story to the absolutely bare essentials, making a career turn, or seem to turn, on a single decision. The ump must make a close call, which will be fiercely contested by a manager who is deliberately testing him. This is a story of initiation, in that respect, an ordeal that the ump must meet successfully. The text ensures that we know this is a test, by showing us the manager plotting in his dugout, and it gives us a manager with one of those baseball faces (Irish? German?) that have the history of the game written on them. This is not just partisan versus impartial judge, it is old man against youth, and white against black. We root for the umpire because we want the system to work—not just baseball but the whole thing: America. For the story to work, of course, the ump must make the right call, and we must know it to be right. Here, the close-up and slow motion come into play—just as they would in a real instant replay—to let us see both how close the call is and that the umpire has indeed made the right call. The runner is out. The manager's charge from dugout is classic baseball protest, and the ump's self-control and slow walk away from the angry manager are gestures in a ritual we all know. That's right, we think, that's the way it's done. We know these moves the way the contem-

273

poraries of Aeschylus and Sophocles knew the myths upon which the Greek tragedies were based. Baseball is already a ritual, and a ritual we partake of mostly through the medium of television. The commercial has only to organize these images in a certain way to create a powerful narrative.

At the bar after the game, we are off stage, outside that ritual of baseball, but we are still in the world of myth. The manager salutes the ump with his tilted bottle of beer; the old man acknowledges that youth has passed its test. The sword on the shoulder of knighthood, the laying on of hands, the tilted Bud—all these are ritual gestures in the same narrative structure of initiation. To the extent that we have wanted this to happen we are gratified by this closing scene of the narrative text, and many things, as I have suggested, conspire to make us want this ending. We are dealing with an archetypal narrative that has been adjusted for maximum effect within a particular political and social context, and all this has been deployed with a technical skill in casting, directing, acting, photographing, and editing that is of a high order. It is very hard to resist the pleasure of this text, and we cannot accept the pleasure without, for the bewildering minute at least, also accepting the ideology that is so richly and closely entangled with the story that we construct from the video text. To accept the pleasure of this text is to believe that America works; and this is a comforting belief, itself a pleasure of an even higher order—for as long as we can maintain it. Does the text also sell Budweiser? This is something only market research (if you believe it) can tell. But it surely sells the American way first and then seeks to sell its brand of beer by establishing a metonymic connection between the product and the nation: a national beer for the national pastime.

An audience that can understand this commercial, successfully constructing the ump's story from the scenes represented in the text and the comments of the narrative voice, is an audience that understands narrative structure and has a significant amount of cultural knowledge as well, including both data (how baseball leagues are organized, for instance, and how the game is played) and myth (what constitutes success, for example, and what initiation is). At a time when critics such as William Bennett and E. D. Hirsch are bewailing our ignorance of culture, it is important to realize that many Americans are not without culture; they simply have a different culture from that of Bennett and Hirsch. What they really lack, for the most part, is any way of analyzing and criticizing the power of a text like the Budweiser commercial—not its power to sell beer, which is easily resisted, especially once you have tasted better beer—but its power to sell America. For the sort of analysis that I am suggesting, it is necessary to recover (as Eliot says) from the surrender to this text, and it is also necessary to have the tools of ideological criticism. Recovery, in fact, may depend upon critical analysis, which is why the analysis of video texts needs to be taught in all our schools.

Before moving on to the consideration of a more complex textual economy; we would do well to pause and consider the necessity of ideological criticism. One dimension of the conservative agenda for this country has been conspicuously anti-critical. The proposals of William Bennett and E. D. Hirsch, for instance, different as they are in certain respects, are both recipes for the indoctrination of young people in certain cultural myths. The great books of past ages, in the eyes of Bennett, Hirsch, and Allan Bloom, are to be mythologized, turned into frozen monuments of Greatness in which our "cultural heritage" is embodied. This is precisely what Bloom does to Plato, for instance, turning the dialectical search for truth into a fixed recipe for "greatness of soul." The irony of this is that Plato can only die in this process. Plato's work can better be kept alive in our time by such irreverent critiques as that of Jacques Derrida, who takes Plato seriously as an opponent, which is to say, takes him dialectically. In this age of massive manipulation and disinformation, criticism is the only way we have of taking something seriously. The greatest patriots in our time will be those who explore our ideology critically, with particular attention to the gaps between mythology and practice. Above all, we must start with our most beloved icons, not the ones we profess allegiance to, but those that really have the power to move and shake us.

Surrounded by Sleep

Akhil Sharma

Akhil Sharma was born in Delhi, India, in 1971. He grew up in Edison, New Jersey. Sharma Akhil has published short stories in The New Yorker, *and many of them have been selected for the collection of Best American Short Stories in 1996, 1998, and 2002. His novel,* The Obedient Father, *published in 2000, won the PEN/ Hemingway Award and the Sue Kaufman Prize from the Academy of Arts and Letters. He lives in New York and works as an investment banker.*

One August afternoon, when Ajay was ten years old, his elder brother, Aman, dove into a pool and struck his head on the cement bottom. For three minutes, he lay there unconscious. Two boys continued to swim, kicking and splashing, until finally Aman was spotted below them. Water had entered through his nose and mouth. It had filled his stomach. His lungs collapsed. By the time he was pulled out, he could no longer think, talk, chew, or roll over in his sleep.

Ajay's family had moved from India to Queens, New York, two years earlier. The accident occurred during the boys' summer vacation, on a visit with their aunt and uncle in Arlington, Virginia. After the accident, Ajay's mother came to Arlington, where she waited to see if Aman would recover. At the hospital, she told the doctors and nurses that her son had been accepted into the Bronx High School of Science, in the hope that by highlighting his intelligence she would move them to make a greater effort on his behalf. Within a few weeks of the accident, the insurance company said that Aman should be transferred to a less expensive care facility, a long-term one. But only a few of these were any good, and those were full, and Ajay's mother refused to move Aman until a space opened in one of them. So she remained in Arlington, and Ajay stayed too, and his father visited from Queens on the weekends when he wasn't working. Ajay was enrolled at the local public school and in September he started fifth grade.

Before the accident, Ajay had never prayed much. In India, he and his brother used to go with their mother to the temple every Tuesday night, but that was mostly because there was a good *dosa* restaurant nearby. In America, his family went to a temple only on important holy days and birthdays. But shortly after Ajay's mother came to Arlington, she moved into the room that he and his brother had shared during the summer and made an altar in a corner. She threw an old flowered sheet over a cardboard box that had once held a television. On top she put a clay lamp, an incense-stick holder, and postcards depicting various gods. There was also a postcard of Mahatma Gandhi. She explained to Ajay that God could take any form; the picture of Mahatma Gandhi was there because he had appeared to her in a dream after the accident and told her that Aman would recover and become a surgeon. Now she and Ajay prayed for at least half an hour before the altar every morning and night.

At first she prayed with absolute humility. "Whatever you do will be good because you are doing it," she murmured to the postcards of Ram and Shivaji, daubing their lips with water and rice. Mahatma Gandhi got only water, because he did not like to eat. As weeks passed and Aman did not recover in time to return to the Bronx High School of Science for the first day of classes, his mother began doing things that called attention to her piety. She sometimes held the prayer lamp until it blistered her palms. Instead of kneeling before the altar, she lay face down. She fasted twice a week. Her attempts to sway God were not so different from Ajay's performing somersaults to amuse his aunt, and they made God seem human to Ajay.

One morning as Ajay knelt before the altar, he traced an Om, a crucifix, and a Star of David into the pile of the carpet. Beneath these he traced an *S*, for Superman, inside an upside-down triangle. His mother came up beside him.

"What are you praying for?" she asked. She had her hat on, a thick gray knitted one that a man might wear. The tracings went against the weave of the carpet and were darker than the surrounding nap. Pretending to examine them, Ajay leaned forward and put his hand over the *S*. His mother did not mind the Christian and Jewish symbols—they were for commonly recognized gods, after all—but she could not tolerate his praying to Superman. She'd caught him doing so once several weeks earlier and had become very angry, as if Ajay's faith in Superman made her faith in Ram ridiculous. "Right in front of God," she had said several times.

Ajay, in his nervousness, spoke the truth. "I'm asking God to give me a hundred percent on the math test."

His mother was silent for a moment. "What if God says you can have the math grade but then Aman will have to be sick a little while longer?" she asked.

Ajay kept quiet. He could hear cars on the road outside. He knew that his mother wanted to bewail her misfortune before God so that God would feel guilty. He looked at the postcard of Mahatma Gandhi. It was a black-and-white photo of him walking down a city street with an enormous crowd trailing behind him. Ajay thought of how, before the accident, Aman had been so modest that he would not leave the bathroom until he was fully dressed. Now he had rashes on his penis from the catheter that drew his urine into a translucent bag hanging from the guardrail of his bed.

His mother asked again, "Would you say, 'Let him be sick a little while longer'?"

"Are you going to tell me the story about Uncle Naveen again?" he asked.

"Why shouldn't I? When I was sick, as a girl, your uncle walked seven times around the temple and asked God to let him fail his exams just as long as I got better."

"If I failed the math test and told you that story, you'd slap me and ask what one has to do with the other."

His mother turned to the altar. "What sort of sons did you give me, God?" she asked. "One you drown, the other is this selfish fool."

"I will fast today so that God puts some sense in me," Ajay said, glancing away from the altar and up at his mother. He liked the drama of fasting.

"No, you are a growing boy." His mother knelt down beside him and said to the altar, "He is stupid, but he has a good heart."

Prayer, Ajay thought, should appeal with humility and an open heart to some greater force. But the praying that he and his mother did felt sly and confused. By treating God as someone to bargain with, it seemed to him, they prayed as if they were casting a spell.

This meant that it was possible to do away with the presence of God entirely. For example, Ajay's mother had recently asked a relative in India to drive a nail into a holy tree and tie a saffron thread to the nail on Aman's behalf. Ajay invented his own ritual. On his way to school each morning, he passed a thick tree rooted half on the sidewalk and half on the road. One day Ajay got the idea that if he circled the tree seven times, touching the north side every other time, he would have a lucky day. From then on he did it every morning, although he felt embarrassed and always looked around beforehand to make sure no one was watching.

One night Ajay asked God whether he minded being prayed to only in need.

"You think of your toe only when you stub it," God replied. God looked like Clark Kent. He wore a gray cardigan, slacks, and thick glasses, and had a forelock that curled just as Ajay's did.

God and Ajay had begun talking occasionally after Aman drowned. Now they talked most nights while Ajay lay in bed and waited for sleep. God sat at the foot of Ajay's mattress. His mother's mattress lay parallel to his, a few feet away. Originally God had appeared to Ajay as Krishna, but Ajay had felt foolish discussing brain damage with a blue god who held a flute and wore a dhoti.

"You're not angry with me for touching the tree and all that?"

"No. I'm flexible."

"I respect you. The tree is just a way of praying to you," Ajay assured God.

God laughed. "I am not too caught up in formalities."

Ajay was quiet. He was convinced that he had been marked as special by Aman's accident. The beginnings of all heroes are distinguished by misfortune. Superman and Batman were both orphans. Krishna was separated from his parents at birth. The

278

god Ram had to spend fourteen years in a forest. Ajay waited to speak until it would not appear improper to begin talking about himself.

"How famous will I be?" he asked finally.

"I can't tell you the future," God answered.

Ajay asked, "Why not?"

"Even if I told you something, later I might change my mind."

"But it might be harder to change your mind after you have said something will happen."

God laughed again. "You'll be so famous that fame will be a problem."

Ajay sighed. His mother snorted and rolled over.

"I want Aman's drowning to lead to something," he said to God.

"He won't be forgotten."

"I can't just be famous, though. I need to be rich too, to take care of Mummy and Daddy and pay Aman's hospital bills."

"You are always practical." God had a soulful and pitying voice, and God's sympathy made Ajay imagine himself as a truly tragic figure, like Amitabh Bachchan in the movie *Trishul*.

"I have responsibilities," Ajay said. He was so excited at the thought of his possible greatness that he knew he would have difficulty sleeping. Perhaps he would have to go read in the bathroom.

"You can hardly imagine the life ahead," God said.

Even though God's tone promised greatness, the idea of the future frightened Ajay. He opened his eyes. There was light coming from the street. The room was cold and had a smell of must and incense. His aunt and uncle's house was a narrow two-story home next to a four-lane road. The apartment building with the pool where Aman had drowned was a few blocks up the road, one in a cluster of tall brick buildings with stucco fronts. Ajay pulled the blanket tighter around him. In India, he could not have imagined the reality of his life in America: the thick smell of meat in the school cafeteria, the many television channels. And, of course, he could not have imagined Aman's accident, or the hospital where he spent so much time.

The hospital was boring. Vinod, Ajay's cousin, picked him up after school and dropped him off there almost every day. Vinod was twenty-two. In addition to attending county college and studying computer programming, he worked at a 7-Eleven near Ajay's school. He often brought Ajay hot chocolate and a comic from the store, which had to be returned, so Ajay was not allowed to open it until he had wiped his hands.

Vinod usually asked him a riddle on the way to the hospital. "Why are manhole covers round?" It took Ajay half the ride to admit that he did not know. He was having difficulty talking. He didn't know why. The only time he could talk easily was when he was with God. The explanation he gave himself for this was that just as he couldn't chew when there was too much in his mouth, he couldn't talk when there were too many thoughts in his head.

When Ajay got to Aman's room, he greeted him as if he were all right. "Hello, lazy. How much longer are you going to sleep?" His mother was always there. She got up and hugged Ajay. She asked how school had been, and he didn't know what to say. In music class, the teacher sang a song about a sailor who had bared his breast before jumping into the sea. This had caused the other students to giggle. But Ajay could not say the word *breast* to his mother without blushing. He had also cried. He'd been thinking of how Aman's accident had made his own life mysterious and confused. What would happen next? Would Aman die or would he go on as he was? Where would they live? Usually when Ajay cried in school, he was told to go outside. But it had been raining, and the teacher had sent him into the hallway. He sat on the floor and wept. Any mention of this would upset his mother. And so he said nothing had happened that day.

Sometimes when Ajay arrived his mother was on the phone, telling his father that she missed him and was expecting to see him on Friday. His father took a Greyhound bus most Fridays from Queens to Arlington, returning on Sunday night in time to work the next day. He was a bookkeeper for a department store. Before the accident, Ajay had thought of his parents as the same person: MummyDaddy. Now, when he saw his father praying stiffly or when his father failed to say hello to Aman in his hospital bed, Ajay sensed that his mother and father were quite different people. After his mother got off the phone, she always went to the cafeteria to get coffee for herself and Jell-O or cookies for him. He knew that if she took her coat with her, it meant that she was especially sad. Instead of going directly to the cafeteria, she was going to go outside and walk around the hospital parking lot.

That day, while she was gone, Ajay stood beside the hospital bed and balanced a comic book on Aman's chest. He read to him very slowly. Before turning each page, he said, "Okay, Aman?"

Aman was fourteen. He was thin and had curly hair. Immediately after the accident, there had been so many machines around his bed that only one person could stand beside him at a time. Now there was just a single waxy yellow tube. One end of this went into his abdomen; the other, blocked by a green bullet-shaped plug, was what his Isocal milk was poured through. When not being used, the tube was rolled up and bound by a rubber band and tucked beneath Aman's hospital gown. But even with the tube hidden, it was obvious that there was something wrong with Aman. It was in his stillness and his open eyes. Once, in their house in Queens, Ajay had left a plastic bowl on a radiator overnight and the sides had dropped and sagged so that the bowl looked a little like an eye. Aman reminded Ajay of that bowl.

Ajay had not gone with his brother to the swimming pool on the day of the accident, because he had been reading a book and wanted to finish it. But he heard the ambulance siren from his aunt and uncle's house. The pool was only a few minutes away, and when he got there a crowd had gathered around the ambulance. Ajay saw his uncle first, in shorts and an undershirt, talking to a man inside the ambulance. His aunt was standing beside him. Then Ajay saw Aman on a stretcher, in blue shorts with a plastic mask over his nose and mouth. His aunt hurried over to take Ajay home. He cried as they walked, although he had been certain that Aman would be fine in a few days: in a Spider-Man comic he had just read, Aunt May had fallen into a coma and she had woken up perfectly fine. Ajay had cried simply because he felt crying was called for by the seriousness of the occasion. Perhaps this moment would mark the beginning of his future greatness. From that day on, Ajay found it hard to cry in front of his family. Whenever tears started coming, he felt like a liar. If he loved his brother, he knew, he would not have thought about himself as the ambulance had pulled away, nor would he talk with God at night about becoming famous.

When Ajay's mother returned to Aman's room with coffee and cookies, she sometimes talked to Ajay about Aman. She told him that when Aman was six he had seen a children's television show that had a character named Chunu, which was Aman's nickname, and he had thought the show was based on his own life. But most days Ajay went into the lounge to read. There was a TV in the corner and a lamp near a window that looked out over a parking lot. It was the perfect place to read. Ajay liked fantasy novels where the hero, who was preferably under the age of twenty-five, had an undiscovered talent that made him famous when it was revealed. He could read for hours without interruption, and sometimes when Vinod came to drive Ajay and his mother home from the hospital it was hard for him to remember the details of the real day that had passed.

One evening when he was in the lounge, he saw a rock star being interviewed on *Entertainment Tonight*. The musician, dressed in a sleeveless undershirt that revealed a swarm of tattoos on his arms and shoulders, had begun to shout at the audience, over his interviewer, "Don't watch me! Live your life! I'm not you!" Filled with a sudden desire to do something, Ajay hurried out of the television lounge and stood on the sidewalk in front of the hospital entrance. But he did not know what to do. It was cold and dark and there was an enormous moon. Cars leaving the parking lot stopped one by one at the edge of the road. Ajay watched as they waited for an opening in the traffic, their brake lights glowing.

"Are things getting worse?" Ajay asked God. The weekend before had been Thanksgiving. Christmas soon would come, and a new year would start, a year during which Aman would not have talked or walked. Suddenly Ajay understood hopelessness. Hopelessness felt very much like fear. It involved a clutching in the stomach and a numbness in the arms and legs.

"What do you think?" God answered.

"They seem to be."

"At least Aman's hospital hasn't forced him out."

"At least Aman isn't dead. At least Daddy's Greyhound bus has never skidded off a bridge." Lately Ajay had begun talking much more quickly to God than he used to. Before, when he had talked to God, Ajay would think of what God would say in response before he said anything. Now Ajay spoke without knowing how God might respond.

"You shouldn't be angry at me." God sighed. God was wearing his usual cardigan. "You can't understand why I do what I do."

"You should explain better, then."

"Christ was my son. I loved Job. How long did Ram have to live in a forest?"

"What does that have to do with me?" This was usually the cue for discussing Ajay's prospects. But hopelessness made the future feel even more frightening than the present.

"I can't tell you what the connection is, but you'll be proud of yourself."

They were silent for a while.

"Do you love me truly?" Ajay asked.

"Yes."

"Will you make Aman normal?" As soon as Ajay asked the question, God ceased to be real. Ajay knew then that he was alone, lying under his blankets, his face exposed to the cold dark.

"I can't tell you the future," God said softly. These were words that Ajay already knew.

"Just get rid of the minutes when Aman lay on the bottom of the pool. What are three minutes to you?"

"Presidents die in less time than that. Planes crash in less time than that."

Ajay opened his eyes. His mother was on her side and she had a blanket pulled up to her neck. She looked like an ordinary woman. It surprised him that you couldn't tell, looking at her, that she had a son who was brain-dead.

In fact, things were getting worse. Putting away his mother's mattress and his own in a closet in the morning, getting up very early so he could use the bathroom before his aunt or uncle did, spending so many hours in the hospital—all this had given Ajay the reassuring sense that real life was in abeyance, and that what was happening was unreal. He and his mother and brother were just waiting to make a long-delayed bus trip. The bus would come eventually to carry them to Queens, where he would return to school at P.S. 20 and to Sunday afternoons spent at the Hindi movie theater under the trestle for the 7 train. But now Ajay was starting to understand that the world was always real, whether you were reading a book or sleeping, and that it eroded you every day.

He saw the evidence of this erosion in his mother, who had grown severe and unforgiving. Usually when Vinod brought her and Ajay home from the hospital, she had dinner with the rest of the family. After his mother helped his aunt wash the dishes, the two women watched theological action movies. One night, in spite of a headache that had made her sit with her eyes closed all afternoon, she ate dinner, washed dishes, sat down in front of the TV. As soon as the movie was over, she went upstairs, vomited, and lay on her mattress with a wet towel over her forehead. She asked Ajay to massage her neck and shoulders. As he did so, Ajay noticed that she was crying. The tears frightened Ajay and made him angry. "You shouldn't have watched TV," he said accusingly.

"I have to," she said. "People will cry with you once, and they will cry with you a second time. But if you cry a third time, people will say you are boring and always crying."

Ajay did not want to believe what she had said, but her cynicism made him think that she must have had conversations with his aunt and uncle that he did not know about. "That's not true," he told her, massaging her scalp. "Uncle is kind. Auntie Aruna is always kind."

"What do you know?" She shook her head, freeing herself from Ajay's fingers. She stared at him. Upside down, her face looked unfamiliar and terrifying. "If God lets Aman live long enough, you will become a stranger too. You will say, 'I have been unhappy for so long because of Aman, now I don't want to talk about him or look at him.' Don't think I don't know you," she said.

Suddenly Ajay hated himself. To hate himself was to see himself as the opposite of everything he wanted to be: short instead of tall, fat instead of thin. When he brushed his teeth that night, he looked at his face: his chin was round and fat as a heel. His nose was so broad that he had once been able to fit a small rock in one nostril.

His father was also being eroded. Before the accident, Ajay's father loved jokes— he could do perfect imitations—and Ajay had felt lucky to have him as a father. (Once, Ajay's father had convinced his own mother that he was possessed by the ghost of a British man.) And even after the accident, his father had impressed Ajay with the patient loyalty of his weekly bus journeys. But now his father was different.

One Saturday afternoon, as Ajay and his father were returning from the hospital, his father slowed the car without warning and turned into the dirt parking lot of a bar that looked as though it had originally been a small house. It had a pitched roof with a black tarp. At the edge of the lot stood a tall neon sign of an orange hand lifting a mug of sudsy golden beer. Ajay had never seen anybody drink except in the movies. He wondered whether his father was going to ask for directions to somewhere, and if so, to where.

His father said, "One minute," and they climbed out of the car.

They went up wooden steps into the bar. Inside, it was dark and smelled of cigarette smoke and something stale and sweet. The floor was linoleum like the kitchen at his aunt and uncle's. There was a bar with stools around it, and a basketball game played on a television bolted against the ceiling, like the one in Aman's hospital room.

His father stood by the bar waiting for the bartender to notice him. His father had a round face and was wearing a white shirt and dark dress pants, as he often did on the weekend, since it was more economical to have the same clothes for the office and home.

The bartender came over. "How much for a Budweiser?" his father asked.

It was a dollar fifty. "Can I buy a single cigarette?" He did not have to buy; the bartender would just give him one. His father helped Ajay up onto a stood and sat down himself. Ajay looked around and wondered what would happen if somebody started a knife fight. When his father had drunk half his beer, he carefully lit the cigarette. The bartender was standing at the end of the bar. There were only two other men in the place. Ajay was disappointed that there were no women wearing dresses slit all the way up their thighs. Perhaps they came in the evenings.

His father asked him if he had ever watched a basketball game all the way through.

"I've seen the Harlem Globetrotters."

His father smiled and took a sip. "I've heard they don't play other teams, be-cause they can defeat everyone else so easily."

"They only play against each other, unless there is an emergency—like in the car-toon, when they play against the aliens to save the Earth," Ajay said.

"Aliens?"

Ajay blushed as he realized his father was teasing him.

When they left, the light outside felt too bright. As his father opened the car door for Ajay, he said, "I'm sorry." That's when Ajay first felt that his father might have done something wrong. The thought made him worry. Once they were on the road, his fa-ther said gently, "Don't tell your mother."

Fear made Ajay feel cruel. He asked his father, "What do you think about when you think of Aman?"

Instead of becoming sad, Ajay's father smiled. "I am surprised by how strong he is. It's not easy for him to keep living. But even before, he was strong. When he was interviewing for high school scholarships, one interviewer asked him, 'Are you a thinker or a doer?' He laughed and said, 'That's like asking, "Are you an idiot or a moron?"'"

From then on they often stopped at the bar on the way back from the hospital. Ajay's father always asked the bartender for a cigarette before he sat down, and dur-ing the ride home he always reminded Ajay not to tell his mother.

Ajay found that he himself was changing. His superstitions were becoming ex-treme. Now when he walked around the good-luck tree he punched it, every other time, hard, so that his knuckles hurt. Afterward, he would hold his breath for a mo-ment longer than he thought he could bear, and ask God to give the unused breaths to Aman.

In December, a place opened in one of the good long-term care facilities. It was in New Jersey. This meant that Ajay and his mother could move back to New York and live with his father again. This was the news Ajay's father brought when he arrived for a two-week holiday at Christmas.

Ajay felt the clarity of panic. Life would be the same as before the accident but also unimaginably different. He would return to P.S. 20, while Aman continued to be fed through a tube in his abdomen. Life would be Aman's getting older and growing taller than their parents but having less consciousness than even a dog, which can be-come excited or afraid.

Ajay decided to use his devotion to shame God into fixing Aman. The fact that two religions regarded the coming December days as holy ones suggested to Ajay that prayers during this time would be especially potent. So he prayed whenever he thought of it—at his locker, even in the middle of a quiz. His mother wouldn't let him fast, but he started throwing away the lunch he took to school. And when his mother prayed in the morning, Ajay watched to make sure that she bowed at least once to-ward each of the postcards of deities. If she did not, he bowed three times to the possibly offended god on the postcard. He had noticed that his father finished his prayers in less time than it took to brush his teeth. And so now, when his father began praying in the morning, Ajay immediately crouched down beside him, because he knew his father would be embarrassed to get up first. But Ajay found it harder and harder to drift into the rhythm of sung prayers or into his nightly conversations with God. How could chanting and burning incense undo three minutes of a sunny August afternoon? It was like trying to move a sheet of blank paper from one end of a table to the other by blinking so fast that you started a breeze.

On Christmas Eve his mother asked the hospital chaplain to come to Aman's room and pray with them. The family knelt together beside Aman's bed. Afterward the chaplain asked her whether she would be attending Christmas services. "Of course, Father," she said.

"I'm also coming," Ajay said.

The chaplain turned toward Ajay's father, who was sitting in a wheelchair because there was nowhere else to sit.

"I'll wait for God at home," he said.

That night, Ajay watched *It's a Wonderful Life* on television. To him, the movie meant that happiness arrived late, if ever. Later, when he got in bed and closed his eyes, God appeared. There was little to say.

"Will Aman be better in the morning?"

"No."

"Why not?"

"When you prayed for the math exam, you could have asked for Aman to get better, and instead of your getting an A, Aman would have woken."

This was so ridiculous that Ajay opened his eyes. His father was sleeping nearby on folded-up blankets. Ajay felt disappointed at not feeling guilt. Guilt might have contained some hope that God existed.

When Ajay arrived at the hospital with his father and mother the next morning, Aman was asleep, breathing through his mouth while a nurse poured a can of Isocal into his stomach through the yellow tube. Ajay had not expected that Aman would have recovered; nevertheless, seeing him that way put a weight in Ajay's chest.

The Christmas prayers were held in a large, mostly empty room: people in chairs sat next to people in wheelchairs. His father walked out in the middle of the service.

Later, Ajay sat in a corner of Aman's room and watched his parents. His mother was reading a Hindi women's magazine to Aman while she shelled peanuts into her lap. His father was reading a thick red book in preparation for a civil service exam. The day wore on. The sky outside grew dark. At some point Ajay began to cry. He tried to be quiet. He did not want his parents to notice his tears and think that he was crying for Aman, because in reality he was crying for how difficult his own life was.

His father noticed first. "What's the matter, hero?"

His mother shouted, "What happened?" and she sounded so alarmed it was as if Ajay were bleeding.

"I didn't get any Christmas presents. I need a Christmas present," Ajay shouted. "You didn't buy me a Christmas present." And then, because he had revealed his own selfishness, Ajay let himself sob. "You have to give me something. I should get some-thing for all this." Ajay clenched his hands and wiped his face with his fists. "Each time I come here I should get something."

His mother pulled him up and pressed him into her stomach. His father came and stood beside them. "What do you want?" his father asked.

Ajay had no prepared answer for this.

"What do you want?" his mother repeated.

The only thing he could think was "I want to eat pizza and I want candy."

His mother stroked his hair and called him her little baby. She kept wiping his face with a fold of her sari. When at last he stopped crying, they decided that Ajay's father should take him back to his aunt and uncle's. On the way, they stopped at a mini-mall. It was a little after five, and the streetlights were on. Ajay and his father did not take off their winter coats as they ate, in a pizzeria staffed by Chinese people. While he chewed, Ajay closed his eyes and tried to imagine God looking like Clark Kent, wearing a cardigan and eyeglasses, but he could not. Afterward, Ajay and his father went next door to a magazine shop and Ajay got a bag of Three Musketeers bars and a bag of Reese's peanut butter cups, and then he was tired and ready for home.

He held the candy in his lap while his father drove in silence. Even through the plastic, he could smell the sugar and chocolate. Some of the houses outside were dark, and others were outlined in Christmas lights.

After a while Ajay rolled down the window slightly. The car filled with wind. They passed the building where Aman's accident had occurred. Ajay had not walked past it since the accident. When they drove by, he usually looked away. Now he tried to spot the fenced swimming pool at the building's side. He wondered whether the pool that had pressed itself into Aman's mouth and lungs and stomach had been drained, so that nobody would be touched by its unlucky waters. Probably it had not been emptied until fall. All summer long, people must have swum in the pool and sat on its sides, splashing their feet in the water, and not known that his brother had lain for three minutes on its concrete bottom one August afternoon.

Blood

Naomi Shihab Nye

Naomi Shihab Nye is a prolific poet. Her poems and short stories have appeared in various journals and reviews throughout North America, Europe, and the Middle and Far East. She has published numerous books of poems, including 19 Varieties of Gazelle: Poems of the Middle East *(Greenwillow Books, 2002),* Fuel *(1998),* Red Suitcase *(1994), and* Hugging the Jukebox *(1982). She was born in St. Louis, Missouri, to a Palestinian father and an American mother and was educated at Trinity University in San Antonio, Texas. Her work explores her dual heritage and the hybrid quality of American culture. She has twice traveled to the Middle East and Asia for the United States Information Agency promoting international goodwill through the arts. Nye has received awards from the Texas Institute of Letters, the Carity Randall prize, and the International Poetry Forum.*

"A true Arab knows how to catch a fly in his hands,"
my father would say. And he'd prove it,
cupping the buzzer instantly
while the host with the swatter stared.

In the spring our palms peeled like snakes.
True Arabs believed watermelon could heal fifty ways.
I changed these to fit the occasion.

Reprinted from *Yellow Glove*, (1986), by permission of the author.

Years before, a girl knocked,
wanted to see the Arab.
I said we didn't have one.
After that, my father told me who he was,
"Shihab"—"shooting star"—
a good name, borrowed from the sky.
Once I said, "when we die, we give it back?"
He said that's what a true Arab would say.

Today the headlines clot in my blood.
A little Palestinian dangles a truck on the front page.
Homeless fig, this tragedy with a terrible root
is too big for us. What flag can we wave?
I wave the flag of stone and seed,
table mat stitched in blue.

I call my father, we talk around the news.
It is too much for him,
neither of his two languages can reach it.
I drive into the country to find sheep, cows,
to plead with the air:
Who calls anyone *civilized?*
Where can the crying heart graze?
What does a true Arab do now?

Regeneration Through Violence: The Language of the Myth

Richard Slotkin

Richard Slotkin, a Ph. D. from Brown University, teaches interdisciplinary courses on American culture, literature, film, and history. He recently completed the last volume of a trilogy on the American myth of the frontier: Gunfighter Nation: The Myth of the Frontier in Twentieth Century America *(1992). Both the first volume,* Regeneration through Violence: The Mythology of the American Frontier *(1973), and the second,* The Fatal Environment: The Myth of the Frontier in the Age of Industrialization *(1985) received academic prizes. He also wrote and published two historical novels:* The Crater *(1980), a novel of the civil war; and* The Return of Henry Starr *(1988), about the end of the Old West and the beginning of the Western. The essay below is an excerpt from* Gunfighter Nation.

The Myth of the Frontier is our oldest and most characteristic myth, expressed in a body of literature, folklore, ritual, historiography, and polemics produced over a period of three centuries. According to this myth-historiography, the conquest of the wilderness and the subjugation or displacement of the Native Americans who originally inhabited it have been the means to our achievement of a national identity, a democratic polity, an ever-expanding economy, and a phenomenally dynamic and "progressive" civilization. The original ideological task of the Myth was to explain and justify the establishment of the American colonies; but as the colonies expanded and developed, the Myth was called on to account for our rapid economic growth,

Reprinted from *Gunfighter Nation: The Myth of the Frontier in Twentieth Century America*, (1992) University of Oklahoma Press. Copyright © 1992 by Richard Slotkin.

our emergence as a powerful nation-state, and our distinctively American approach to the socially and culturally disruptive processes of modernization.

The peculiarities of the American version of this myth/ideology derived from our original condition as a settler-state, a colonial outpost of the European "metropolis." In America, all the political, social, and economic transformations attendant on modernization began with outward movement, physical separation from the originating "metropolis." The achievement of "progress" was therefore inevitably associated with territorial expansion and colored by the experience, the politics, and the peculiar psychology of emigration.

Euro-American history begins with the self-selection and abstraction of particular European communities from their metropolitan culture, and their transplantation to a wilderness on the other side of the ocean where conditions were generally more primitive than those at home. These colonies in turn would expand by reproducing themselves in subcolonial settlements, projected at some distance from the colonial metropolis into a further and more primitive wilderness. Thus the processes of American development in the colonies were linked from the beginning to a historical narrative in which repeated cycles of *separation* and *regression* were necessary preludes to an improvement in life and fortune.

Conflict was also a central and peculiar feature of the process. To establish a colony or settlement, the Europeans had to struggle against an unfamiliar natural environment and against the non-European, non-White natives for whom the wilderness was home. Violence is central to both the historical development of the Frontier and its mythic representation. The Anglo-American colonies grew by displacing Amerindian societies and enslaving Africans to advance the fortunes of White colonists. As a result, the "savage war" became a characteristic episode of each phase of westward expansion.

Conflict with the Indians defined one boundary of American identity: though we were a people of "the wilderness" we were *not* savages. The other boundary was defined by the emergence of conflicts between the colonies and the "mother country," and (later) between the regional concerns of the "borderers" and those of American metropolitan regimes. The compleat "American" of the Myth was one who had defeated and freed himself from both the "savage" of the western wilderness and the metropolitan regime of authoritarian politics and class privilege.

In each stage of its development, the Myth of the Frontier relates the achievement of "progress" to a particular form or scenario of violent action. "Progress" itself was defined in different ways: the Puritan colonists emphasized the achievement of spiritual regeneration through frontier adventure; Jeffersonians (and later, the disciples of Turner's "Frontier Thesis") saw the frontier settlement as a re-enactment and democratic renewal of the original "social contract"; while Jacksonian Americans saw the conquest of the Frontier as a means to the regeneration of personal fortunes and/or of patriotic vigor and virtue. But in each case, the Myth represented the redemption of American spirit or fortune as something to be achieved by playing through a scenario of separation, temporary regression to a more primitive or "natural" state, and *regeneration through violence.*

At the core of that scenario is the symbol of "savage war," which was both a mythic trope and an operative category of military doctrine. The premise of "savage war" is that ineluctable political and social differences—rooted in some combination of "blood" and culture—make coexistence between primitive natives and civilized Europeans impossible on any basis other than that of subjugation. Native resistance to European settlement therefore takes the form of a fight for survival; and because of the "savage" and bloodthirsty propensity of the natives, such struggles inevitably become "wars of extermination" in which one side or the other attempts to destroy its enemy root and branch. The seventeenth-century Puritans envisioned this struggle in biblical terms—"Two Nations [are in] the Womb and will be striving"—and urged their soldiers to exterminate the Wampanoags as God commanded Israel to wipe out the Amalekites. But similar ideas informed the military thinking of soldiers in the Age of Reason, like Colonel Henry Bouquet, who described an "American war" as "a rigid contest where all is at stake and mutual destruction the object . . . [where] everything is terrible; the face of the country, the climate, the enemy . . . [where] victories are not decisive but defeats are ruinous; and simple death is the least misfortune that can happen." Military folklore from King Philip's War to Braddock's Defeat to Custer's Last Stand held that in battle against a savage enemy you always saved the last bullet for yourself; for in savage war one side or the other must perish, whether by limitless murder or by the degrading experience of subjugation and torture.

In its most typical formulations, the myth of "savage war" blames Native Americans as instigators of a war of extermination. Indians were certainly aggressors in particular cases, and they often asserted the right to exclude settlers from particular regions. But with the possible exception of Tecumseh's abortive attempt at a confederacy of western tribes, after 1700 no tribe or group of tribes pursued (or was capable of pursuing) a general "policy" of exterminating or removing White settlements on a large-scale basis. The accusation is better understood as an act of psychological projection that made the Indians scapegoats for the morally troubling side of American expansion: the myth of "savage war" became a basic ideological convention of a culture that was itself increasingly devoted to the extermination or expropriation of the Indians and the kidnaping and enslavement of black Africans.

In American mythology, the Indian war also provides a symbolic surrogate for a range of domestic social and political conflicts. By projecting the "fury" of class resentment outward against the Indian, the American expands his nation's resources and thereby renders class struggle unnecessary. All the antipathies that make for Revolutionary Terror and/or dictatorial oppression in Europe are projected onto the American savage, who becomes the only obstacle to the creation of a perfect republic. But this historical myth and its hopeful political scenario can only be realized so long as a frontier exists: a reservoir of natural resources sufficient to requite the ambitions of all classes without prejudice to the interests of any.

In analyzing the structure and meaning of this mythology of violence, it is vital that we not confuse mythic representation with political reality. The mythic tales and polemics we will be examining are rife with visions of border wars that turn overnight into preludes to Armageddon and with proposals for genocide and wars of extermination. And there has been enough actual violence along these lines—the Indian wars, the slave trade, "lynch law" and race riots, the labor/management violence of 1880—1920, and our currently high levels of domestic and criminal violence—to support the belief that America has been a peculiarly violent nation. However, most of these apparently distinctive forms of political and social violence have also figured with comparable prominence in the histories of other settler-states, and of Europe. Neither the slave trade nor the subjugation/extermination of natives by colonists was an exclusively Anglo-American enterprise. The mass genocides of modern times belong not to the history of the Americas, but to Europe, Asia, and Africa. What is distinctively "American" is not necessarily the amount or kind of violence that characterizes our history but the mythic significance we have assigned to the kinds of violence we have actually experienced, the forms of symbolic violence we imagine or invent, and the political uses to which we put that symbolism.

When history is translated into myth, the complexities of social and historical experiences are simplified and compressed into the action of representative individuals or "heroes." The narrative of the hero's action exemplifies and tests the political and/or moral validity of a particular approach to the use of human powers in the material world. The hero's inner life—his or her code of values, moral or psychic ambivalence, mixtures of motive—reduces to personal motive the complex and contradictory mixture of ideological imperatives that shape a society's response to a crucial event. But complexity and contradiction are focused rather than merely elided in the symbolizing process. The heroes of myth embody something like the full range of ideological contradictions around which the life of the culture revolves, and their adventures suggest the range of possible resolutions that the culture's lore provides.

The moral landscape of the Frontier Myth is divided by significant borders, of which the wilderness/civilization, Indian/White border is the most basic. The American must cross the border into "Indian country" and experience a "regression" to a more primitive and natural condition of life so that the false values of the "metropolis" can be purged and a new, purified social contract enacted. Although the Indian and the Wilderness are the settler's enemy, they also provide him with the new consciousness through which he will transform the world. The heroes of this myth-historical quest must therefore be "men (or women) who know Indians"—characters whose experiences, sympathies, and even allegiances fall on both sides of the Frontier. Because the border between savagery and civilization runs through their moral center, the Indian wars are, for these heroes, a spiritual or psychological struggle which they win by learning to discipline or suppress the savage or "dark" side of their own human nature. Thus they are mediators of a double kind who can teach civilized men how to defeat savagery on its native grounds—the natural wilderness, and the wilderness of the human soul.

Picture This: Can Photographs Change the Way We Think?

Susan Sontag

Susan Sontag was born in New York City, but she grew up in Tucson, Arizona, and attended high school in Los Angeles. She received her B.A. from the College of the University of Chicago and did graduate work in philosophy, literature, and theology at Harvard University and Saint Anne's College, Oxford. Her books include novels (The Benefactor, Death Kit, The Volcano Lover, *and* In America), *and nonfiction* (Against Interpretation, On Photography, Illness as Metaphor). *Her stories and essays have appeared in* The New Yorker, The New York Review of Books, The Times Literary Supplement, Art in America, Antaeus, Parnassus, The Threepenny Review, The Nation, Granta, *and many other magazines here and abroad. Her books have been translated into thirty-two languages. The following essay is an excerpt from her new book* Regarding the Pain of Others.

Often something looks, or is felt to look, "better" in a photograph. Indeed, it is one of the functions of photography to improve the normal appearance of things. (Hence, one is always disappointed by a photograph that is not flattering.) Beautifying is one classic operation of the camera, and tends to bleach out a moral response to what is shown. Uglifying, showing something at its worst, is a more modern function, it is didactic and invites an active response. For photographs to accuse, and possibly to alter conduct, they must shock.

Reprinted from *The Guardian*, July 26, 2003.

An example: a few years ago, the public health authorities in Canada, where it had been estimated that smoking kills 45,000 people a year, decided to supplement the warning printed on every pack of cigarettes with a shock photograph—of cancerous lungs, a stroke-clotted brain, a damaged heart or a bloody mouth in acute periodontal distress. A pack with such a picture accompanying the warning about the deleterious effects of smoking would be 60 times more likely to inspire smokers to quit, a research study had somehow calculated, than a pack with only the verbal warning.

Let's assume this is true. Still one might wonder, for how long? Does shock have time limits? Right now the smokers of Canada are recoiling in disgust, if they do look at these pictures. Will those smoking five years from now still be upset? Shock can become familiar. Shock can wear off. Even if it doesn't, one need not look. People have means of defending themselves against what is upsetting—in this instance, unpleasant information for those wishing to continue to smoke. This seems normal, that is, adaptive. As one can become habituated to horror in real life, one can also become habituated to the horror of certain images.

Yet there are cases where repeated exposure to what shocks, saddens, appals does not use up a full-hearted response. Habituation is not automatic, for images (portable, insertable) obey different rules than does real life. Representations of the Crucifixion do not become banal to believers, if they really are believers. This is even more true of staged representations. Performances of Chushingura, probably the best-known narrative in all of Japanese culture, can be counted on to make a Japanese audience sob when Lord Asano admires the beauty of the cherry blossoms on his way to where he must commit seppuku, no matter how often they have followed the story (as a Kabuki or Bunraku play, as a film); the drama of the betrayal and murder of Imam Hussayn in the Taziyah does not cease to bring an Iranian audience to tears no matter how many times they have seen the martyrdom enacted. On the contrary. They weep, in part, because they have seen it many times. People want to weep. Pathos, in the form of a narrative, does not wear out.

But do people want to be horrified? Probably not. Still, there are pictures whose power does not abate, in part because one cannot look at them often. Pictures of ruined faces that will testify always to a great iniquity that was survived at a cost: the faces of horribly disfigured first world war veterans who survived the inferno of the trenches; the faces melted and thickened with scar tissue of survivors of the American atomic bombs dropped on Hiroshima and Nagasaki; the faces cleft by machete blows of Tutsi survivors of the genocidal rampage launched by the Hutus in Rwanda—is it correct to say that people get used to these?

Indeed, the very notion of atrocity, of war crime, is associated with the expectation of photographic evidence. Such evidence is, usually, of something posthumous. The remains, as it were—the mounds of skulls in Pol Pot's Cambodia, the mass graves in Guatemala and El Salvador, Bosnia and Kosovo. And this posthumous reality is often the keenest of summations. As Hannah Arendt pointed out soon after the end of the second world war, all the photographs and newsreels of the concentration camps are misleading because they show the camps at the moment the Allied troops marched in. What makes the images unbearable—the piles of corpses and the skeletal survivors—was not at all typical for the camps, which, when they were functioning, exterminated their inmates systematically (by gas, not starvation and illness), then cremated them immediately. And photographs echo photographs: it was inevitable that the photographs of emaciated Bosnian prisoners at Omarska, the Serb death camp created in northern Bosnia in 1992, would recall memories of the photographs taken in the Nazi death camps in 1945.

Photographs of atrocity illustrate as well as corroborate. Bypassing disputes about exactly how many were killed (numbers are often inflated at first), the photograph gives the indelible sample. The illustrative function of photographs leaves opinions, prejudices, fantasies, misinformation untouched. The information that many fewer Palestinians died in the assault on Jenin than had been claimed by Palestinian officials (as the Israelis had said all along) made much less impact than the pictures of the razed centre of the refugee camp. And, of course, atrocities that are not secured in our minds by well-known photographic images, or of which we simply have had very few images—the total extermination of the Herero people in Namibia decreed by the German colonial administration in 1904; the Japanese onslaught in China, notably the massacre of nearly 400,000 and the rape of 80,000 Chinese in December 1937, the so-called Rape of Nanking; the rape of some 130,000 women and girls (10,000 of whom committed suicide) by victorious Soviet soldiers unleashed by their commanding officers in Berlin in 1945—seem more remote. These are memories that few have cared to claim.

The familiarity of certain photographs builds our sense of the present and immediate past. Photographs lay down routes of reference, and serve as totems of causes: sentiment is more likely to crystallise around a photograph than around a verbal slogan. And photographs help construct, and revise, our sense of a more distant past, with the posthumous shocks engineered by the circulation of hitherto unknown photographs. Photographs that everyone recognises are now a constituent part of what a society chooses to think about, or declares that it has chosen to think about. It calls these ideas "memories" and, in the long run, that is a fiction. Strictly speaking, there is no such thing as collective memory—it is part of the same family of spurious notions as collective guilt. But there is collective instruction.

All memory is individual, unreproducible, it dies with each person. What is called collective memory is not a remembering but a stipulating—that this is important, this is the story of how it happened—with the pictures that lock the story in our minds. Ideologies create substantiating archives of images, representative images, which encapsulate common ideas of significance and trigger predictable thoughts, feelings. Poster-ready photographs—the mushroom cloud of an A-bomb test, Martin Luther King speaking at the Lincoln memorial in Washington DC, the astronaut on the moon—are the visual equivalent of sound bites. They commemorate, in a no less blunt fashion than postage stamps, important historical moments; indeed, the triumphalist ones (the picture of the A-bomb excepted) become postage stamps. Fortunately, there is no one signature picture of the Nazi death camps.

As art has been redefined during a century of modernism as an activity whose destiny it is to end in some kind of museum, so it is now the destiny of many photographic troves to be exhibited and preserved in museum-like institutions. Among such archives of horror, the photographs of genocide have undergone the greatest institutional development. The point of creating public repositories for these and other relics is to ensure that the crimes they depict will continue to figure in people's consciousness. This is called remembering, but in fact it is a good deal more than that.

The memory museum in its current proliferation is a product of a way of thinking about, and mourning, the destruction of European Jewry in the 1930s and 1940s, which came to institutional fruition in Yad Vashem in Jerusalem, the Holocaust Memorial Museum in Washington DC, and the Jewish Museum in Berlin. Photographs and other memorabilia of the Shoah have been committed to a perpetual recirculation, to ensure that what they show will be remembered. Photographs of the suffering and martyrdom of a people are more than reminders of death, of failure, of victimisation, they invoke the miracle of survival. To aim at the perpetuation of memories means, inevitably, that one has undertaken the task of continually renewing, of creating memories—aided, above all, by the impress of iconic photographs. People want to be able to visit—and refresh—their memories.

Now many victims of oppression want a memory museum, a temple that houses a comprehensive, organised, illustrated narrative of their sufferings. Armenians, for example, have long been clamouring for a museum in Washington DC to institutionalise the memory of the genocide of Armenian people by the Ottoman Turks. But why is there no museum of the history of slavery in the nation's capital, a city whose population is overwhelmingly African-American? Indeed, there is no museum of the history of slavery—the whole story, starting with the slave trade in Africa itself, not just selected parts, such as the Underground Railroad—anywhere in the United States. This, it seems, is a memory judged too dangerous to social stability to activate and to create. The Holocaust Memorial Museum and the future Armenian Genocide Museum and Memorial are about events that didn't happen in America, so the memory-work runs no risk of rousing an embittered domestic population against authority.

To have a museum chronicling the great crime that was African slavery in the United States of America would be to acknowledge that the evil was here. Americans prefer to picture the evil that was there, and from which the United States—a unique nation, one without any certifiably wicked leaders throughout its entire history—is exempt. That the US, like every other country, has its tragic past does not sit well with the founding, still all-powerful, belief in American exceptionalism. The national consensus on American history as a history of progress is a new setting for distressing photographs—one that focuses our attention on wrongs, both here and elsewhere, for which America sees itself as the solution or cure.

In Novel Conditions:
The Cross-Dressing Psychiatrist

Allucquère Rosanne Stone

Allucquère Rosanne (Sandy) Stone is Associate Professor and Director of the Advanced Communication technologies Laboratory (ACTLab) in the department of Radio-TV-Film at the University of Texas at Austin, where she studies issues related to interface, interaction, and desire. She was program chair and organizer for the 1991 Second International Conference on Cyberspace, member of the program committee for the Third International Conference on Cyberspace in 1993, and director of the subsequent Conferences on Cyberspace up to and including the present ones. Her academic publications include numerous articles on psychoanalysis and cyberspace. Her book The War of Desire and Technology at the Close of the Mechanical Age *was published by MIT Press in September 1995 (hardcover) and September 1996 (paperback), and it is currently available in English, Italian, Japanese, Swedish, and Chinese. The following essay is a chapter from this book.*

One of our Western industrialized cultural assumptions is that subjectivity is invariably constituted in relation to a physical substance—that social beings, people, exist by virtue of possessing biological bodies through which their existence is warranted in the body politic. Another is that we know unproblematically what "body" is. Let me tell you a boundary story, a tale of the nets, as a means of anchoring one corner of the system of discourse within which this discussion operates. It is also a fable of loss of innocence—which, I have begun to notice, is the tenor of more than one story

Reprinted from *The War of Desire and Technology at the Close of the Mechanical Age*, (1996), by permission of MIT Press.

here. In the course of this essay a number of chapters partake of the loss-of-innocence motif . . . in retrospect, a surprising number. People who still believe that I have some sort of rosy vision of the future of virtual systems are advised to reread a few of the origin myths I present in these pages. Herewith, another.

This one begins in 1982, on the CompuServe conference system. CompuServe is owned by Reader's Digest and Ziff-Davis. CompuServe began in 1980 as a generalized information service, offering such things as plane reservations, weather reports, and the "Electronic Shopping Mall," which is simply lists of retail items that can be purchased through CompuServe and ordered on-line. It was one of perhaps three major formation services that started up within a year or so of each other. The others were The Source, Prodigy, and America Online. All of these were early attempts by business to capture some of the potential market formed by consumers with computers and modems, an attempt to generate business of a kind that had not previously existed. None of the on-line services knew what this market was or where it lay, but their thinking, as evidenced by reports in the *Wall Street Journal,* was along the lines of television. That is, computers would be media in which goods could be sold visually, like a shopping service. Prodigy implemented this theory by having banners advertising products running along the bottom of the screen, while permitting conferencing to go on in the main screen area. The companies who financed The Source seem to have believed that unrestricted conversation was against the American Way, because it was never permitted to occur within the system. Both Prodigy and The Source saw their primary mission as selling goods. They attracted audiences in the same way that broadcasters did, as a product to be delivered to manufacturers in the form of demographic groups meant to watch commercials. The Source went quietly bankrupt in 1986. Prodigy, by virtue of having permitted on-line conferencing, weathered the storms of the shakeout days in which it became clear that whatever on-line services were good for, it was *not* to deliver audiences to manufacturers. CompuServe, however, found out quite early that the thing users found most interesting was on-line conferencing and chat—that is, connectivity. Or, as an industry observer put it, "People are willing to pay money just to connect. Just for the opportunity to communicate." America Online never saw itself as a medium for selling goods and concentrated on connectivity in various forms from the beginning.

Most on-line conferences now offer what are called chat lines, which are virtual places where many people can interact simultaneously in real time. In the Internet world there are many such places with quite elaborately worked out geographies; these are known as multiple-user thisses-and-thats. The first of these were direct descendants of real-life things called role-playing games, or RPGs.

Role-playing games were developed within a rather small community whose members shared certain social traits. First, most were members of the Society for Creative Anachronism, or SCA, one of the driving forces behind the Renaissance Faires. The SCA sponsors medieval tournaments with full regalia as well as medieval banquets in medieval style, which is to say, 16-course meals of staggering richness. Once one has attended such a banquet, the shorter life span of people in the Middle Ages becomes much more understandable.

Participants are extremely dedicated to the principles of the SCA, one of which is that tournaments go on as scheduled, rain or shine. In California, where many SCA members live, this can be risky. There is something not exactly bracing about watching two grown men in full armor trying to whack each other with wooden swords while thrashing and wallowing through ankle-deep mud and pouring rain. During this phase of my research I got a glimpse of what it must be like to be trained as a traditional anthropologist, and finally to be sent to some godforsaken island where one thrashes out one's fieldwork in a soggy sleeping bag while being wracked by disabling parasites and continuous dysentery.

Second, many of the people who belong to the SCA also consider themselves part of what is sometimes called the neopagan movement. And third, particularly in California, many of the people who participate in SCA events and who belong to the neopagan movement are also computer programmers.

Originally RPGs seemed to be a way for SCA members to continue their fantasy roles between tournaments. Role-playing games are also a good deal less expensive and more energy efficient than tournaments. They have tremendous grab for their participants, are open-ended, and improve with the players' imaginations. Some RPG participants have kept a good game going for years, meeting monthly for several days at a time to play the game, eating, sleeping, and defecating in role. For some, the game has considerably more appeal than reality. They express an unalloyed nostalgia for a time when roles were clearly defined, folks lived closer to nature, life was simpler, magic was afoot, and adventure was still possible. They are aware, to a certain extent, that their Arthurian vision of the Middle Ages is thoroughly bogus, but they have no intention of allowing reality to temper their enthusiasm.

The first RPG was published as a set of rules and character descriptions in 1972 and was called, appropriately enough, Dungeons and Dragons. It was an extension, really, of SCA into a textual world. D&D, as it quickly became known, used a set of rules invented by the Austin game designer Steve Jackson called the Generic Universal Role Playing System, or GURPS, for constructing characters, and voluminous books containing lists of character attributes, weapons, and powers. A designated Dungeon Master acted as arbiter of disputes and prognosticator of events and had considerable effect on the progress of the game; creative Dungeon Masters, like good tops, were hard to find and, once discovered, were highly prized.

The first 120- and 300-baud modems became available in the mid-1970s, and virtually the instant that they became available, the programmers among the D&D community began to develop versions of the game that could be played on-line. The first on-line systems ran on small personal computers (the very first were developed for Apple II's). Because of the problems of writing multitasking operating systems, which allow several people to log in on-line at once, the first systems were time-aliased; that is, only one person could be on-line at a time, so simultaneous real-time interaction was impossible. The first of these to achieve a kind of success was an on-line game called *Mines of Moria.* The program contained most of the elements that are still ubiquitous in on-line RPG systems: Quests, Fearsome Monsters, Treasure,

Wizards, Twisty Mazes, Vast Castles, and, because the systems were written by young heterosexual males, the occasional Damsel in Distress.

As the Internet came into being from its earlier and more cloistered incarnation as ARPANET, more people had access to multitasking systems. The ARPANET had been built around multitasking systems such as Bell Laboratories' UNIX and had packet-switching protocols built in; these enabled multiple users to log in from widely separated locations. The first on-line multiple-user social environments were written in the early 1980s and were named, after their origins, Multiple-User Dungeons or MUDs. When the staid academics and military career persons who actually oversaw the operation of the large systems began to notice the MUDs in the mid-1980s, they took offense at such cavalier misuse of their equipment. The writers of the MUDs then tried the bald public-relations move of renaming their systems Multiple-User *Domains* in an effort to distance themselves from the offensive odor of play that accompanied the word *dungeon*. The system administrators were unimpressed by this move. Later multiple-user social environments came to be called MUSEs (for Multiple-User Social Environment), MUSHes (for Multiple-User Social Host), MUCKs, and MOOs (MUD Object-Oriented). Of these, all are somewhat similar except for the MOO, which uses a different and much more flexible method of creating objects within the simulation. Unlike MUDs, objects and attributes in a MOO are persistent; when the MOO crashes, everything is still in place when it comes back up. This property has importance for large systems such as Fujitsu's *Habitat* and smaller ones that contain many complex objects, such as the MIT Media Lab's MediaMOO and the U. Texas ACTLab's PointMOOt.

The multiple-user social environments written for the large, corporate-owned, for-pay systems betray none of their origins in low culture. They do not contain objects, nor can objects be constructed within them. They are thoroughly sanitized, consisting merely of bare spaces within which interactions can take place. They are the Motel 6 of virtual systems. Such an environment is the CB chat line on the CompuServe. It was on CompuServe, some time early in 1982, that a New York psychiatrist named Sanford Lewin opened an account.

In the conversation channels, particularly the real-time chat conferences such as CB, it is customary to choose an on-line name, or "handle," that may have no relationship to one's "real" name, which CompuServe does not reveal. Frequently, however, participants in virtual conversations choose handles that express some part of their personalities, real or imagined. Lewin, with his profession in mind, chose the handle "Doctor."

It does not appear to have dawned on him that the term was gender-neutral until a day not long after he first signed on. He had been involved in a general chat in public virtual space, had started an interesting conversation with a woman, and they had decided to drop into private mode for a few minutes. In private mode two people who have chosen to converse can only "hear" each other, and the rest of the people in the vicinity cannot "hear" them. The private conversation was actually under way for a few minutes before Lewin realized it was profoundly different from any conversation he'd been in before. Somehow the woman to whom he was talking had mistaken him for a *woman* psychiatrist. He had always felt that even in his most personal conversations with women there was always something missing, some essential connection. Suddenly he understood why, because the conversation he was now having was deeper and more open than anything he'd experienced. "I was stunned," he said later, "at the conversational mode. I hadn't known that women talked among themselves that way. There was so much more vulnerability, so much more depth and complexity. And then I thought to myself, Here's a terrific opportunity to help people, by catching them when their normal defenses are down and they're more able to hear what they need to hear."

Lewin reasoned, or claimed to have reasoned, that if women were willing to let down their conversational barriers with other women in the chat system, then as a psychiatrist he could use the chat system to do good. The obvious strategy of continuing to use the gender-neutral "Doctor" handle didn't seem like the right approach. It appears that he became deeply intrigued with the idea of interacting with women *as a woman,* rather than using a female persona as a masquerade. He wanted to become a female persona to such an extent that he could feel what it was like to be a woman in some deep and essential way. And at this point his idea of helping women by becoming an on-line woman psychiatrist took a different turn.

He opened a second account with CompuServe under the name Julie Graham. He spent considerable time working out Julie's persona. He needed someone who would be fully functioning on-line, but largely unavailable off-line in order to keep her real identity secret. For the most part, he developed an elaborate and complex history for Julie, but creating imaginary personae was not something with which he had extensive experience. So there were a few minor inconsistencies in Julie's history from time to time; and it was these that provided the initial clues that eventually tipped off a few people on the net that something was wrong. As it turned out, though, Julie's major problems didn't arise from the inconsistencies in her history, but rather from the consistencies—from the picture-book life Lewin had developed for her.

Julie first signed on in 1982. She described herself as a New York neuropsychologist who, within the last few years, had been involved in a serious automobile accident caused by a drunken driver. Her boyfriend had been killed, and she had suffered severe neurological damage to her head and spine, in particular to Broca's area, which controls speech. She was now mute and paraplegic. In addition, her face had been severely disfigured, to the extent that plastic surgery was unable to restore her appearance. Consequently she never saw anyone in person. She had become a recluse, embittered, slowly withdrawing from life, and seriously planning suicide, when a friend gave her a small computer and modem and she discovered CompuServe.

After being tentatively on-line for a while, her personality began to flourish. She began to talk about how her life was changing, and how interacting with other women in the net was helping her reconsider her situation. She stopped thinking of suicide and began planning her life. Although she lived alone and currently held no job, she had a small income from an inheritance; her family had made a fortune in a mercantile business, so at least she was assured of a certain level of physical comfort. She was an atheist, who enjoyed attacking organized religion; smoked dope, and was occasionally quite stoned on-line late at night; and was bisexual, from time to time coming on to the men and women with whom she talked. In fact, as time went on, she became flamboyantly sexual. Eventually she was encouraging many of her friends to engage in net sex with her.

Some time during this period Julie changed her handle, or sign-on pseudonym, as a celebration of her return to an active social life, at least on the net. She still maintained her personal privacy, insisting that she was too ashamed of her disfigurements and her inability to vocalize, preferring to be known only by her on-line persona. People on the chat system held occasional parties at which those who lived in reasonable geographic proximity would gather to exchange a few socialities in biological mode, and Julie assiduously avoided these. Instead she ramped up her social profile on the net even further. Her standard greeting was a huge, expansive "HI!!!!!!!!!!!!"

Julie started a women's discussion group on CompuServe. She also had long talks with women outside the group, and her advice was extremely helpful to many of them. Over the course of time several women confided to her that they were depressed and thinking about suicide, and she shared her own thoughts about her brush with suicide and helped them to move on to more life-affirming attitudes. She also helped several women with drug and chemical dependencies. An older woman confided her desire to return to college and her fear of being rejected; Julie encouraged her to go through with the application process. Once the woman was accepted, Julie advised her on the writing of several papers (including one on MPD) and in general acted as wise counsel and supportive sister.

She also took it upon herself to ferret out pretenders in the chat system, in particular men who masqueraded as women. As Van Gelder pointed out in her study of the incident, Julie was not shy about warning women about the dangers of letting one's guard down on the net. "Remember to be careful," Van Gelder quotes her as saying, "Things may not be as they seem."

There is a subtext here, which has to do with what I have been calling the on-line persona. Of course we all change personae all the time, to suit the social occasion, although with on-line personae the act is more purposeful. Nevertheless, the societal imperative with which we have been raised is that there is one primary persona, or "true identity," and that in the off-line world—the "real world"—this persona is firmly attached to a single physical body, by which our existence as a social being is authorized and in which it is grounded. The origin of this "correct" relationship between body and persona seems to have been contemporaneous with the Enlightenment, the same cultural moment that gave birth to what we like to call the sovereign subject. True, there is no shortage of examples extending far back in time of a sense of something in the body other than just meat. Usually this has to do with an impalpable soul or a similar manifestation—some agency that carries with it the seat of consciousness, and that normally may be decoupled from the body only after death. For many people, though, the soul or some impalpable avatar routinely journeys free of the body, and a certain amount of energy is routinely expended in managing the results of its travels. Partly the Western idea that the body and the subject are inseparable is a worthy exercise in wish fulfillment—an attempt to explain why ego-centered subjectivity terminates with the substrate *and* to enforce the termination. Recently we find in science fiction quite a number of attempts to refigure this relationship, notably in the work of authors like John Varley, who has made serious tries at constructing phenomenologies of the self (e.g., Varley 1986).

Julie worked off her fury at drunk drivers by volunteering to ride along in police patrol cars. Because of her experience at neuropsychology, she was able to spot erratic driving very quickly, and by her paralysis she could offer herself as a horrible example of the consequences. During one of these forays she met a young cop named John. Her disability and disfigured face bothered him not a whit, and they had a whirlwind romance. Shortly he proposed to her. After Julie won his mother over (she had told him "he was throwing his life away by marrying a cripple"), they were married in a joyous ceremony. Rather than having a live reception, they held the reception online, toasting and being toasted by friends from remote sites around the country. They announced that they intended to honeymoon in the Greek Islands, and soon real postcards from Greece began showing up in their friends' mailboxes.

Julie's professional life began to bloom. She began attending conferences and giving papers around the States, and shortly in Europe as well. Of course there were problems, but John was the quintessential caring husband, watching out for her, nurturing her. Her new popularity on the conference circuit allowed them to take frequent trips to exotic places. While they were on safari, if there was a place her wheelchair couldn't reach, he simply carried her. When they were home he was frequently out on stakeouts in the evenings, which gave her lots of time to engage with her on-line friends. Occasionally he would talk to her friends on the chat system.

Julie began talking about becoming a college teacher. She felt that she could overcome her handicap by using a computer in the classroom. This would be hooked to a large screen to "talk" with her students. Throughout the planning of her new career, John was thoroughly supportive and caring.

It was some time during this period that Julie's friends first began to become suspicious. She was always off at conferences, where presumably she met face to face with colleagues. And she and John spent a lot of time on exotic vacations, where she must also be seeing people face to face. It seemed that the only people who never got to see her were her on-line friends. With them she maintained a firm and unyielding invisibility. There were beginning to be too many contradictions. But it was the other disabled women on-line who pegged her first. They knew the real difficulties—personal and interpersonal—of being disabled. Not "differently abled," that wonderful term, but rather the brutal reality of the way most people—including some friends—related to them. In particular they knew the exquisite problems of negotiating friendships, not to mention love relationships, in close quarters with the "normally" abled. In that context, Julie's relationship with the unfailingly caring John was simply impossible. John was a Stepford husband.

Still, nobody had yet pegged Julie as other than a disabled woman. The other disabled women on-line thought that she was probably a disabled woman, but also felt that she was probably lying about her romantic life and about her frequent trips. But against that line of argument they had to deal with the reality that they had hard evidence of some of those trips—real postcards from Greece—and in fact Julie and John had gone back to Greece next year, accompanied by another flurry of postcards.

Julie, John, Joan—they are all wonderful examples of the war of desire and technology. Their complex virtual identities are real and productive interventions into our cultural belief that the unmarked social unit, besides being white and male, is a single self in a single body. Multiple personality "disorder" is another such intervention. As I tried to make clear in "Identity in Oshkosh," MPD is generally considered to be pathological, the result of trauma. But we can look to the construction and management of pathology for the circumstances that constitute and authorize the unmarked, so that we may take the pathologization of MPD and in general the management and control of any manifestations of body-self, other than the one body—one self norm, to be useful tools to take apart discourses of the political subject so we can see what makes them work. There are other interventions to be made, and here we interrogate a few Harawayan elsewheres—in this case, virtual space, the phantasmic "structure" within which real social interactions take place—for information. Of course, the virtual environment of the chat lines is just beginning, a look at a single event when such events were still singular.

Julie's friends weren't the only ones who were nervous over the turns her life was taking and the tremendous personal growth she was experiencing. In fact, Lewin was getting nervous too. Apparently he'd never expected the impersonation to succeed so dramatically. He thought he'd make a few contacts on-line, and maybe offer helpful advice to some women. What had happened instead was that he'd found himself deeply engaged in developing a whole new part of himself that he'd never known existed. His responses had long since ceased to be a masquerade; with the help of the on-line mode and a certain amount of textual prosthetics, he was in the process of *becoming* Julie. She no longer simply carried out his wishes at the keyboard; she had her own emergent personality, her own ideas, her own directions. Not that he was losing his own identity, but he was certainly developing a parallel one, one of considerable puissance. Jekyll and Julie. As her friendships deepened and simultaneously the imposture began to unravel, Lewin began to realize the enormity of his deception.

And the simplicity of the solution.

Julie had to die.

And so events ground inexorably onward. One day Julie became seriously ill. With John's help, she was rushed to the hospital. John signed on to her account to tell her on-line friends and to explain what was happening: Julie had been struck by an exotic bug to which she had little resistance, and in her weakened state it was killing her. For a few days she hovered between life and death, while Lewin hovered, setting up her demise in a plausible fashion.

The result was horrific. Lewin, as John, was deluged with expressions of shock, sorrow, and caring. People offered medical advice, offered financial assistance, sent cards, sent flowers. Some people went into out-and-out panic. The chat lines became jammed. So many people got seriously upset, in fact, that Lewin backed down. He couldn't stand to go through with it. He couldn't stand to engineer her death. Julie recovered and came home.

The relief on the net was enormous. Joyous messages were exchanged. Julie and John were overwhelmed with caring from their friends. In fact, sometime during the great outpouring of sympathy and concern, while Julie was at death's door, one of her friends managed to find out the name of the hospital where she was supposed to be staying. He called, to see if he could help out, and was told there was no one registered by that name. Another thread unraveled.

Lewin was still stuck with the problem that he hadn't had the guts to solve. He decided to try another tack, one that might work even better from his point of view. Shortly, Julie began to introduce people to her new friend, Sanford Lewin, a New York psychiatrist. She was enormously gracious about it, if not downright pushy. To hear her tell it, Lewin was absolutely wonderful, charming, graceful, intelligent, and eminently worthy of their most affectionate attention. Thus introduced, Lewin then began trying to make friends with Julie's friends himself.

He couldn't do it.

Sanford simply didn't have the personality to make friends easily on-line. Where Julie was freewheeling and jazzy, Sanford was subdued and shy. Julie was a confirmed atheist, an articulate firebrand of rationality, while Sanford was a devout conservative Jew. Julie smoked dope and occasionally got a bit drunk on-line; Sanford was, how shall we say, drug-free—in fact, he was frightened of drugs—and he restricted his drinking to a little Manischewitz on high holy days. And to complete the insult, Julie had fantastic luck with sex on-line, while when it came to erotics Sanford was a hopeless klutz who didn't know a vagina from a virginal. In short, Sanford's Sanford persona was being defeated by his Julie persona.

What do you do when your imaginary playmate makes friends better than you do?

With Herculean efforts Lewin had succeeded in striking up at least a beginning friendship with a few of Julie's friends when the Julie persona began to come seriously unraveled. First the disabled women began to wonder aloud, then Lewin took the risk of revealing himself to a few more women with whom he felt he had built a friendship. Once he started the process, word of what was happening spread rapidly through the net. But just as building Julie's original persona had taken some time, the actual dismantling of it took several months, as more clearly voiced suspicion gradually turned to factual information and the information was passed around the conferences, repeated, discussed, and picked over. Shortly the process reached a critical level where it became self-supporting. In spite of the inescapable reality of the deception, though, or rather in spite of the inescapable unreality of Julie Graham, there was a kind of temporal and emotional mass in motion that, Newton-like, tended to remain in motion. Even as it slowly disintegrated like one of the walking dead, the myth of Julie still tended to roll ponderously ahead on its own, shedding shocked clots of ex-Julie fans as it ran down. The effect, though spread out over time, was like a series of bombing raids interspersed throughout a ground war.

Perhaps to everyone's surprise, the emotion that many of those in the chat system felt most deeply was mourning. Because of the circumstances in which it occurred, Julie's unmasking as a construct, a cross-dressing man, had been worse than a death. There was no focused instant of pain and loss. There was no funeral, no socially supported way to lay the Julie persona to rest, to release one's emotions and to move on. The help Julie had given people in that very regard seemed inappropriate in the circumstance. Whatever else Julie was or wasn't, she had been a good friend and a staunch supporter to many people in need, giving unstintingly of her time and virtual energy wherever it was required. Her fine sense of humor and ability to see the bright side of difficulties had helped many people, mostly women, over very difficult places in their lives. At least some of her charm and charisma should have rubbed off on Lewin. But it didn't. And, quite understandably, some of the women did not bounce back with forgiveness. At least one said that she felt a deep emotional violation which, in her opinion, was tantamount to sexual assault. "I felt raped," she said, "I felt as if my deepest secrets were violated. The good things Julie did . . . were all done by deception." Some of the women formed a support group to talk about their sense of betrayal and violation, which they referred to wryly as "Julie-anon."

The Julie incident produced a large amount of Monday morning quarterbacking among the habitués of CompuServe's chat system. In retrospect, several women felt that Julie's helpfulness had exceeded the bounds of good sense—that what she had actually fostered was dependency. Others focused on her maneuvers for net sex, which sometimes amounted to heavy come-ons even with old friends. Perhaps most telling was the rethinking, among Julie's closest friends, of their attitudes toward Julie's disability. One said, "In retrospect, we went out of our way to believe her. We wanted to give her all the support we could, because of what she was trying to do. So everybody was bending over backward to extend praise and support and caring to this disabled person. We were all so supportive when she got married and when she was making all the speaking engagements . . . in fact there was a lot of patronizing going on that we didn't recognize at the time."

Sanford Lewin retained his CompuServe account. He has a fairly low profile on the net, not least because the Sanford person is inherently low-key. Many of Julie's friends made at least a token attempt to become friends with him. Not too many succeeded, because, according to them, there simply wasn't that much in common between them. Several of the women who were friends of Julie have become acquaintances of Lewin, and a few have become friends. One said, "I've been trying to forget about the Julie thing. We didn't think it through properly in the first place, and many of the women took risks that they shouldn't have. But whether he's Julie or Sanford, man or woman, there's an inner person that must have been there all along. That's the person I really like."

The hackers in my study population, the people who wrote the programs by means of which the nets exist, just smiled tiredly. A few sympathized with the women whom Julie had taken in, and understood that it takes time to realize, through experience, that social rules do not necessarily map across the interface between the physical and virtual worlds. But all of them had understood from the beginning that the nets presaged radical changes in social conventions, some of which would go unnoticed. That is, until an event like a disabled woman who is revealed to be "only" a persona—not a true name at all—along with the violated confidences that resulted from the different senses in which various actors understood the term *person,* all acted together to push these changes to the foreground. Some of these engineers, in fact, wrote software for the utopian possibilities it offered. Young enough in the first days of the net to react and adjust quickly, they had long ago taken for granted that many of the pre-net assumptions about the nature of identity had quietly vanished. Even though they easily understood and assimilated conflictual situations such as virtual persona as mask for an underlying identity, few had yet thought very deeply about what underlay the underlying identity. There is an old joke about a woman at a lecture on cosmology who said that she understood quite clearly what kept the earth hanging in space; it actually rested on the back of a giant turtle. When asked what the turtle was standing on, she replied that the turtle was standing on the back of yet another turtle, and added tartly, "You can't confuse me, young man; it's turtles all the way down."

Is it personae all the way down?

Say amen, somebody.

Rules of the Game

Amy Tan

Daughter of Chinese immigrants, Amy Tan was born in 1952 in Oakland, California. She grew up in the San Francisco Bay Area, graduated from high school in Montreux, Switzerland, and received her master's degree in Linguistics from San Jose State University. She won an essay contest at the age of eight, and from that day on, she dreamed of becoming a fiction writer. After becoming a free-lance business writer, a job she found unfulfilling, she began to write fiction as a hobby. For her first book, The Joy Luck Club, *from which the following story has been selected, Amy Tan was a finalist for The National Book Award and the winner of the L.A. Times Book Award in 1989. Other books by Tan include the novels* The Kitchen God's Wife *(1991),* The Hundred Secret Senses *(1995),* The Bonesetter's Daughter *(2001), and a collection of essays,* The Opposite of Fate: A Book of Musings *(2003). Her work has been translated into twenty languages.*

I was six when my mother taught me the art of invisible strength. It was a strategy for winning arguments, respect from others, and eventually, though neither of us knew it at the time, chess games.

"Bite back your tongue," scolded my mother when I cried loudly, yanking her hand toward the store that sold bags of salted plums. At home, she said, "Wise guy, he not go against wind. In Chinese we say, Come from South, blow with wind—poom!—North will follow. Strongest wind cannot be seen."

The next week I bit back my tongue as we entered the store with the forbidden candies. When my mother finished her shopping, she quietly plucked a small bag of plums from the rack and put it on the counter with the rest of the items.

My mother imparted her daily truths so she could help my older brothers and me rise above our circumstances. We lived in San Francisco's Chinatown. Like most of the other Chinese children who played in the back alleys of restaurants and curio shops, I didn't think we were poor. My bowl was always full, three five-course meals every day, beginning with a soup full of mysterious things I didn't want to know the names of.

We lived on Waverly Place, in a warm, clean, two-bedroom flat that sat above a small Chinese bakery specializing in steamed pastries and dim sum. In the early morning, when the alley was still quiet, I could smell fragrant red beans as they were cooked down to a pasty sweetness. By daybreak, our flat was heavy with the odor of fried sesame balls and sweet curried chicken crescents. From my bed, I would listen as my father got ready for work, then locked the door behind him, one-two-three clicks.

At the end of our two-block alley was a small sandlot playground with swings and slides well-shined down the middle with use. The play area was bordered by wood-slat benches where old-country people sat cracking roasted watermelon seeds with their golden teeth and scattering the husks to an impatient gathering of gurgling pigeons. The best playground, however, was the dark alley itself. It was crammed with daily mysteries and adventures. My brothers and I would peer into the medicinal herb shop, watching old Li dole out onto a stiff sheet of white paper the right amount of insect shells, saffron-colored seeds, and pungent leaves for his ailing customers. It was said that he once cured a woman dying of an ancestral curse that had eluded the best of American doctors. Next to the pharmacy was a printer who specialized in gold-embossed wedding invitations and festive red banners.

Farther down the street was Ping Yuen Fish Market. The front window displayed a tank crowded with doomed fish and turtles struggling to gain footing on the slimy green-tiled sides. A hand-written sign informed tourists, "Within this store, is all for food, not for pet." Inside, the butchers with their bloodstained white smocks deftly gutted the fish while customers cried out their orders and shouted, "Give me your freshest," to which the butchers always protested, "All are freshest." On less crowded market days, we would inspect the crates of live frogs and crabs which we were warned not to poke, boxes of dried cuttlefish, and row upon row of iced prawns, squid, and slippery fish. The sanddabs made me shiver each time; their eyes lay on one flattened side and reminded me of my mother's story of a careless girl who ran into a crowded street and was crushed by a cab. "Was smash flat," reported my mother.

At the corner of the alley was Hong Sing's, a four-table café with a recessed stairwell in front that led to a door marked "Tradesmen." My brothers and I believed the bad people emerged from this door at night. Tourists never went to Hong Sing's, since the menu was printed only in Chinese. A Caucasian man with a big camera once posed me and my playmates in front of the restaurant. He had us move to the side of the picture window so the photo would capture the roasted duck with its head dangling from a juice-covered rope. After he took the picture, I told him he should go into Hong Sing's and eat dinner. When he smiled and asked me what they served,

309

I shouted, "Guts and duck's feet and octopus gizzards!" Then I ran off with my friends, shrieking with laughter as we scampered across the alley and hid in the entryway grotto of the China Gem Company, my heart pounding with hope that he would chase us.

My mother named me after the street that we lived on: Waverly Place Jong, my official name for important American documents. But my family called me Meimei, "Little Sister." I was the youngest, the only daughter. Each morning before school, my mother would twist and yank on my thick black hair until she had formed two tightly wound pigtails. One day, as she struggled to weave a hard-toothed comb through my disobedient hair, I had a sly thought.

I asked her, "Ma, what is Chinese torture?" My mother shook her head. A bobby pin was wedged between her lips. She wetted her palm and smoothed the hair above my ear, then pushed the pin in so that it nicked sharply against my scalp.

"Who say this word?" she asked without a trace of knowing how wicked I was being. I shrugged my shoulders and said, "Some boy in my class said Chinese people do Chinese torture."

"Chinese people do many things," she said simply. "Chinese people do business, do medicine, do painting. Not lazy like American people. We do torture. Best torture."

My older brother Vincent was the one who actually got the chess set. We had gone to the annual Christmas party held at the First Chinese Baptist Church at the end of the alley. The missionary ladies had put together a Santa bag of gifts donated by members of another church. None of the gifts had names on them. There were separate sacks for boys and girls of different ages.

One of the Chinese parishioners had donned a Santa Claus costume and a stiff paper beard with cotton balls glued to it. I think the only children who thought he was the real thing were too young to know that Santa Claus was not Chinese. When my turn came up, the Santa man asked me how old I was. I thought it was a trick question; I was seven according to the American formula and eight by the Chinese calendar. I said I was born on March 17, 1951. That seemed to satisfy him. He then solemnly asked if I had been a very, very good girl this year and did I believe in Jesus Christ and obey my parents. I knew the only answer to that. I nodded back with equal solemnity.

Having watched the other children opening their gifts, I already knew that the big gifts were not necessarily the nicest ones. One girl my age got a large coloring book of biblical characters, while a less greedy girl who selected a smaller box received a glass vial of lavender toilet water. The sound of the box was also important. A ten-year-old boy had chosen a box that jangled when he shook it. It was a tin globe of the world with a slit for inserting money. He must have thought it was full of dimes and nickels, because when he saw that it had just ten pennies, his face fell with such undisguised disappointment that his mother slapped the side of his head and led him out of the church hall, apologizing to the crowd for her son who had such bad manners he couldn't appreciate such a fine gift.

As I peered into the sack, I quickly fingered the remaining presents, testing their weight, imagining what they contained. I chose a heavy, compact one that was wrapped in shiny silver foil and a red satin ribbon. It was a twelve-pack of Life Savers and I spent the rest of the party arranging and rearranging the candy tubes in the order of my favorites. My brother Winston chose wisely as well. His present turned out to be a box of intricate plastic parts; the instructions on the box proclaimed that when they were properly assembled he would have an authentic miniature replica of a World War II submarine.

Vincent got the chess set, which would have been a very decent present to get at a church Christmas party, except it was obviously used and, as we discovered later, it was missing a black pawn and a white knight. My mother graciously thanked the unknown benefactor, saying, "Too good. Cost too much." At which point, an old lady with fine white, wispy hair nodded toward our family and said with a whistling whisper, "Merry, merry Christmas."

When we got home, my mother told Vincent to throw the chess set away. "She not want it. We not want it," she said, tossing her head stiffly to the side with a tight, proud smile. My brothers had deaf ears. They were already lining up the chess pieces and reading from the dog-eared instruction book.

I watched Vincent and Winston play during Christmas week. The chessboard seemed to hold elaborate secrets waiting to be untangled. The chessmen were more powerful than old Li's magic herbs that cured ancestral curses. And my brothers wore such serious faces that I was sure something was at stake that was greater than avoiding the tradesmen's door to Hong Sing's.

"Let me! Let me!" I begged between games when one brother or the other would sit back with a deep sign of relief and victory, the other annoyed, unable to let go of the outcome. Vincent at first refused to let me play, but when I offered my Life Savers as replacements for the buttons that filled in for the missing pieces, he relented. He chose the flavors: wild cherry for the black pawn and peppermint for the white knight. Winner could eat both.

As our mother sprinkled flour and rolled out small doughy circles for the steamed dumplings that would be our dinner that night, Vincent explained the rules, pointing to each piece. "You have sixteen pieces and so do I. One king and queen, two bishops, two knights, two castles, and eight pawns. The pawns can only move forward one step, except on the first move. Then they can move two. But they can only take men by moving crossways like this, except in the beginning, when you can move ahead and take another pawn."

"Why?" I asked as I moved my pawn. "Why can't they move more steps?"

"Because they're pawns," he said.

"But why do they go crossways to take other men? Why aren't there any women and children?"

"Why is the sky blue? Why must you always ask stupid questions?" asked Vincent. "This is a game. These are the rules. I didn't make them up. See. Here. In the book." He jabbed a page with a pawn in his hand. "Pawn. P-A-W-N. Pawn. Read it yourself."

311

My mother patted the flour off her hands. "Let me see book," she said quietly. She scanned the pages quickly, not reading the foreign English symbols, seeming to search deliberately for nothing in particular.

"This American rules," she concluded at last. "Every time people come out from foreign country, must know rules. You not know, judge say, Too bad, go back. They not telling you why so you can use their way go forward. They say, Don't know why, you find out yourself. But they knowing all the time. Better you take, it, find out why yourself." She tossed her head back with a satisfied smile.

I found out about all the whys later. I read the rules and looked up all the big words in a dictionary. I borrowed books from the Chinatown library. I studied each chess piece, trying to absorb the power each contained.

I learned about opening moves and why it's important to control the center early on; the shortest distance between two points is straight down the middle. I learned about the middle game and why tactics between two adversaries are like clashing ideas; the one who plays better has the clearest plans for both attacking and getting out of traps. I learned why it is essential in the endgame to have foresight, a mathematical understanding of all possible moves, and patience; all weaknesses and advantages become evident to a strong adversary and are obscured to a tiring opponent. I discovered that for the whole game one must gather invisible strengths and see the endgame before the game begins.

I also found out why I should never reveal "why" to others. A little knowledge withheld is a great advantage one should store for future use. That is the power of chess. It is a game of secrets in which one must show and never tell.

I loved the secrets I found within the sixty-four black and white squares. I carefully drew a handmade chessboard and pinned it to the wall next to my bed, where at night I would stare for hours at imaginary battles. Soon I no longer lost any games or Life Savers, but I lost my adversaries. Winston and Vincent decided they were more interested in roaming the streets after school in their Hopalong Cassidy cowboy hats.

On a cold spring afternoon, while walking home from school, I detoured through the playground at the end of our alley. I saw a group of old men, two seated across a folding table playing a game of chess, others smoking pipes, eating peanuts, and watching. I ran home and grabbed Vincent's chess set, which was bound in a cardboard box with rubber bands. I also carefully selected two prized rolls of Life Savers. I came back to the park and approached a man who was observing the game.

"Want to play?" I asked him. His face widened with surprise and he grinned as he looked at the box under my arm.

"Little sister, been a long time since I play with dolls," he said, smiling benevolently. I quickly put the box down next to him on the bench and displayed my retort.

Lau Po, as he allowed me to call him, turned out to be a much better player than my brothers. I lost many games and many Life Savers. But over the weeks, with each diminishing roll of candies, I added new secrets, Lau Po gave me the names. The Double Attack from the East and West Shores. Throwing Stones on the Drowning Man.

The Sudden Meeting of the Clan. The Surprise from the Sleeping Guard. The Humble Servant Who Kills the King. Sand in the Eyes of Advancing Forces. A Double Killing Without Blood.

There were also the fine points of chess etiquette. Keep captured men in neat rows, as well-tended prisoners. Never announce "Check" with vanity, lest someone with an unseen sword slit your throat. Never hurl pieces into the sand-box after you have lost a game, because then you must find them again, by yourself, after apologizing to all around you. By the end of the summer, Lau Po had taught me all he knew, and I had become a better chess player.

A small weekend crowd of Chinese people and tourists would gather as I played and defeated my opponents one by one. My mother would join the crowds during these outdoor exhibition games. She sat proudly on the bench, telling my admirers with proper Chinese humility, "Is luck."

A man who watched me play in the park suggested that my mother allow me to play in local chess tournaments. My mother smiled graciously, an answer that meant nothing. I desperately wanted to go, but I bit back my tongue. I knew she would not let me play among strangers. So as we walked home I said in a small voice that I didn't want to play in the local tournament. They would have American rules. If I lost, I would bring shame on my family.

"Is shame you fall down nobody push you," said my mother.

During my first tournament, my mother sat with me in the front row as I waited for my turn. I frequently bounced my legs to unstick them from the cold metal seat of the folding chair. When my name was called, I leapt up. My mother unwrapped something in her lap. It was her *chang*, a small tablet of red jade which held the sun's fire. "Is luck," she whispered, and tucked it into my dress pocket. I turned to my opponent, a fifteen-year-old boy from Oakland. He looked at me, wrinkling his nose.

As I began to play, the boy disappeared, the color ran out of the room, and I saw only my white pieces and his black ones waiting on the other side. A light wind began blowing past my ears. It whispered secrets only I could hear.

"Blow from the South," it murmured. "The wind leaves no trail." I saw a clear path, the traps to avoid. The crowd rustled. "Shhh! Shhh!" said the corners of the room. The wind blew stronger. "Throw sand from the East to distract him." The knight came forward ready for the sacrifice. The wind hissed, louder and louder. "Blow, blow, blow. He cannot see. He is blind now. Make him lean away from the wind so he is easier to knock down."

"Check," I said, as the wind roared with laughter. The wind died down to little puffs, my own breath.

My mother placed my first trophy next to a new plastic chess set that the neighborhood Tao society had given to me. As she wiped each piece with a soft cloth, she said, "Next time win more, lose less."

"Ma, it's not how many pieces you lose," I said. "Sometimes you need to lose pieces to get ahead."

"Better to lose less, see if you really need."

At the next tournament, I won again, but it was my mother who wore the triumphant grin.

"Lost eight piece this time. Last time was eleven. What I tell you? Better off lose less!" I was annoyed, but I couldn't say anything.

I attended more tournaments, each one farther away from home. I won all games, in all divisions. The Chinese bakery downstairs from our flat displayed my growing collection of trophies in its window, amidst the dust-covered cakes that were never picked up. The day after I won an important regional tournament, the window encased a fresh sheet cake with whipped-cream frosting and red script saying "Congratulations, Waverly Jong, Chinatown Chess Champion." Soon after that, a flower shop, headstone engraver, and funeral parlor offered to sponsor me in national tournaments. That's when my mother decided I no longer had to do the dishes. Winston and Vincent had to do my chores.

"Why does she get to play and we do all the work," complained Vincent.

"Is new American rules," said my mother. "Meimei play, squeeze all her brains out for win chess. You play, worth squeeze towel."

By my ninth birthday, I was a national chess champion. I was still some 429 points away from grand-master status, but I was touted as the Great American Hope, a child prodigy and a girl to boot. They ran a photo of me in *Life* magazine next to a quote in which Bobby Fischer said, "There will never be a woman grand master." "Your move, Bobby," said the caption.

The day they took the magazine picture I wore neatly plaited braids clipped with plastic barrettes trimmed with rhinestones. I was playing in a large high school auditorium that echoed with phlegmy coughs and the squeaky rubber knobs of chair legs sliding across freshly waxed wooden floors. Seated across from me was an American man, about the same age as Lau Po, maybe fifty. I remember that his sweaty brow seemed to weep at my every move. He wore a dark, malodorous suit. One of his pockets was stuffed with a great white kerchief on which he wiped his palm before sweeping his hand over the chosen chess piece with great flourish.

In my crisp pink-and-white dress with scratchy lace at the neck, one of two my mother had sewn for these special occasions, I would clasp my hands under my chin, the delicate points of my elbows poised lightly on the table in the manner my mother had shown me for posing for the press. I would swing my patent leather shoes back and forth like an impatient child riding on a school bus. Then I would pause, suck in my lips, twirl my chosen piece in midair as if undecided, and then firmly plant it in its new threatening place, with a triumphant smile thrown back at my opponent for good measure.

I no longer played in the alley of Waverly Place. I never visited the playground where the pigeons and old men gathered. I went to school, then directly home to learn new chess secrets, cleverly concealed advantages, more escape routes.

But I found it difficult to concentrate at home. My mother had a habit of standing over me while I plotted out my games. I think she thought of herself as my protective ally. Her lips would be sealed tight, and after each move I made, a soft "Hm-mmmph" would escape from her nose.

"Ma, I can't practice when you stand there like that," I said one day. She retreated to the kitchen and made loud noises with the pots and pans. When the crashing stopped, I could see out of the corner of my eye that she was standing in the door-way. "Hmmmph!" Only this one came out of her tight throat.

My parents made many concessions to allow me to practice. One time I complained that the bedroom I shared was so noisy that I couldn't think. Thereafter, my brothers slept in a bed in the living room facing the street. I said I couldn't finish my rice; my head didn't work right when my stomach was too full. I left the table with half-finished bowls and nobody complained. But there was one duty I couldn't avoid. I had to accompany my mother on Saturday market days when I had no tournament to play. My mother would proudly walk with me, visiting many shops, buying very little. "This my daughter Wave-ly Jong," she said to whoever looked her way.

One day after we left a shop I said under my breath, "I wish you wouldn't do that, telling everybody I'm your daughter." My mother stopped walking. Crowds of people with heavy bags pushed past us on the sidewalk, bumping into first one shoulder, then another.

"Aiii-ya. So shame be with mother?" She grasped my hand even tighter as she glared at me.

I looked down. "It's not that, it's just so obvious. It's just so embarrassing."

"Embarrass you be my daughter?" Her voice was cracking with anger.

"That's not what I meant. That's not what I said."

"What you say?"

I knew it was a mistake to say anything more, but I heard my voice speaking, "Why do you have to use me to show off? If you want to show off, then why don't you learn to play chess?"

My mother's eyes turned into dangerous black slits. She had no words for me, just sharp silence.

I felt the wind rushing around my hot ears. I jerked my hand out of my mother's tight grasp and spun around, knocking into an old woman. Her bag of groceries spilled to the ground.

"Aii-ya! Stupid girl!" my mother and the woman cried. Oranges and tin cans careened down the sidewalk. As my mother stooped to help the old woman pick up the escaping food, I took off.

I raced down the street, dashing between people, not looking back as my mother screamed shrilly, "Meimei! Meimei!" I fled down an alley, past dark, curtained shops and merchants washing the grime off their windows. I sped into the sunlight, into a large street crowded with tourists examining trinkets and souvenirs. I ducked into another dark alley, down another street, up another alley. I ran until it hurt and I realized I had nowhere to go, that I was not running from anything. The alleys contained no escape routes.

My breath came out like angry smoke. It was cold. I sat down on an upturned plastic pail next to a stack of empty boxes, cupping my chin with my hands, thinking hard. I imagined my mother, first walking briskly down one street or another looking for me, then giving up and returning home to await my arrival. After two hours, I stood up on creaking legs and slowly walked home.

The alley was quiet and I could see the yellow lights shining from our flat like two tiger's eyes in the night. I climbed the sixteen steps to the door, advancing quietly up each so as not to make any warning sounds. I turned the knob; the door was locked. I heard a chair moving, quick steps, the locks turning—click! click! click!—and then the door opened.

"About time you got home," said Vincent. "Boy, are you in trouble."

He slid back to the dinner table. On a platter were the remains of a large fish, its fleshy head still connected to bones swimming upstream in vain escape. Standing there waiting for my punishment, I heard my mother speak in a dry voice.

"We not concerning this girl. This girl not have concerning for us."

Nobody looked at me. Bone chopsticks clinked against the inside of bowls being emptied into hungry mouths.

I walked into my room, closed the door, and lay down on my bed. The room was dark, the ceiling filled with shadows from the dinnertime lights of neighboring flats.

In my head, I saw a chessboard with sixty-four black and white squares. Opposite me was my opponent, two angry black slits. She wore a triumphant smile. "Strongest wind cannot be seen," she said.

Her black men advanced across the plane, slowly marching to each successive level as a single unit. My white pieces screamed as they scurried and fell off the board one by one. As her men drew closer to my edge, I felt myself growing light. I rose up into the air and flew out the window. Higher and higher, above the alley, over the tops of tiled roofs, where I was gathered up by the wind and pushed up toward the night sky until everything below me disappeared and I was alone.

I closed my eyes and pondered my next move.

Superassassin

Lysley Tenorio

*Born in the Philippines, Lysley Tenorio grew up in San Diego, CA.
He earned a BA degree in English from the University of California
at Berkeley and an MFA degree from the University of Oregon. He
has published stories in* The Atlantic Monthly, Ploughshares, *the*
Chicago Tribune, *and* Best New American Voices *2001. He has received the Nelson Algren Award, a Stegner Fellowship, the George
Bennett Fellowship and the Jacob K. Javits Fellowship.*

September, 1958. Coast City, California. The noble alien Abin Sur, protector of sector 2814 of our galaxy, crash-lands on Earth. Buried beneath the
rubble of his spacecraft, he uses his last flicker of energy to summon test
pilot Hal Jordan and offers him the fabled Ring of Power, a weapon created
by the Guardians of Oa. With his dying breath Abin Sur asks, "Will you be
my successor, Hal Jordan? Will you swear to use this ring to uphold justice
throughout the universe?"

"I swear it," Jordan promises. He slips the ring onto his finger, and
takes the Guardians' Oath:

> In brightest day, in blackest night
> No evil shall escape my sight
> Let those who worship evil's might
> Beware my power—Green Lantern's Light!

For nearly four decades Hal Jordan will save the universe on countless occasions as the Green Lantern, establishing himself as one of Earth's greatest champions. But in the 1990s, just years from the new millennium, his
intentions and heroism become questionable. By 1994 he has turned on
the Guardians and become the most powerful villain in the galaxy. The
question remains: Did the Green Lantern die a villain or a hero? This ques-

tion has stumped historians in recent years. This essay will retrace the history of the Green Lantern, and conclude once and for

Black ink gashes my paper when Brandon DeStefano swipes it from beneath the point of my pen. "May I?" he asks. His eyes rush side to side over my words. "Listen to this crazy shit," he tells Tenzil Jones, his best friend. Brandon reads my paper to Tenzil in what is supposed to be my voice, adding an accent that isn't mine. Then he looks up at me, shaking his head in disapproval. "It's supposed to be about a real person in history, freak. What's wrong with you?"

"Hey," Tenzil whispers from behind me, "maybe I'll do mine on the Tooth Fairy."

I don't waste my time with talk. I put my hand out for the paper's return. Brandon makes sure that Mr. Cosgrove isn't looking and then crumples my paper, hurling it at me like a grenade. It hits my face and falls dead to the ground. "*Ka-pow!*" Brandon says, pointing his finger at me like a gun. "Why didn't you use your power ring to stop it?" Tenzil holds up his palm, and the two high-five each other, as if they've accomplished some great feat of teamwork.

"You are no Dynamic Duo," I tell them.

"What?" Brandon asks.

"You are"—I lean into him, aligning my eyes with his—"no Dynamic Duo." I say each word slowly, every syllable getting equal time. It's not my place to make terrible truths easier to hear; all I do is reveal them.

Suddenly Tenzil's finger flicks my ear, fast and hard. My neck jerks, my back stiffens. I feel the heat just below my right temple. "You're whacked, man," he says.

I know better than to tell Mr. Cosgrove. Not because I'm afraid; I just prefer another kind of justice.

I pick up my essay from the floor, pulling at opposite corners to undo the crumpled mass. It's wrinkled, like old skin, so I rub it between my hands, up and down until my palms burn from friction. When the page is smooth, I continue to write, even after the bell rings and the classroom has emptied. Only when Mr. Cosgrove starts locking up windows and shutting mini-blinds do I stop.

"Mr. Cosgrove?" He can't hear me above his whistling, so I say his name again.

"What? Oh, sorry." He turns to me. "Didn't realize you were still here."

"I know." I start erasing the chalkboard for him. "I just wanted to tell you that I'm excited about this assignment. I think I'll learn a lot from this."

He nods. "I'm sure you will."

"I used to hate your class, this subject."

"History changes," he says, smiling.

"And I used to hate you."

For four seconds Mr. Cosgrove is silent. Then he says, "I guess we change too, depending on how you look at things." He looks me in the eyes, smiling, and I think he means it.

"Right." I wipe chalk dust from my shirt and offer to help him with the windows, but he says they've been done, and explains that he needs to get home soon.

I grab my backpack from my chair, and before I leave, I tell him that his class is my favorite, the only one that's useful in the real world.

Long before the heckling from classmates and neighborhood children, the questioning stares from old churchwomen, and long, long before I knew the true story of my father, I was aware of the strange mutant abilities that my body possesses: though my skin is fair, I never burn in the sun, can barely manage a midsummer tan. When seasons change, so does the color of my hair, back and forth from brown to black. Despite my roundish face I have a unique bone structure that captures both shadow and light in just the right places, so that in the proper lighting my face can be startling. And my eyes—somewhere between slanted gashes and perfect ovals—are of two colors: the right is as brown as wet earth, and the left is jet black, a perfect obsidian orb. I keep them behind slightly tinted eyeglasses.

Fifteen years ago, at the moment of my spawning, no one could have guessed the potency of my hybridity.

"What are you goofing about now?" Luc asks me. He is quick to interrupt my meditations, dismissing them as daydreams. He shoots a rubber band at me from across the table. It bounces off my right lens. When I tell him to quit, to stop or I will kill him, I am shushed by the librarian, who frowns at me like an archenemy whose plans I have just foiled. "You're zoning out again," Luc says, sliding his grammar book over to me. "You said you would help me, so help." Though Luc is the most intelligent and perceptive student in the ninth grade (and the only other person I've ever known who is able to comprehend the theories of an anti-matter universe), his counselor insists that he take ESL classes. His English, standardized testing says, is not up to speed. In grade school they said the same thing about me. I knew the words—I had a tenth-grade vocabulary by the time I was eight. I just chose not to speak.

We muddle through the textbook examples of passive voice, and I even devise my own exercises, in comic-book format. *"Superman has been killed mercilessly by me," proclaimed Doomsday*. But today I am in no mood to be a champion of standard written English. "Later," I promise. Luc shrugs his shoulders, thinking that I have given up, that surrendering is a possibility. So I rescue the moment by suggesting "Dystopia?," and his frown morphs into a smile. In a flash we cram books into our backpacks, slip on our raincoats, and pull hoods over our heads. As we exit the library, the words "psychos," "faggots," and "losers" reach us from behind study carrels. Luc and I stop to face our accusers, giving them looks that we will substantiate when the time is right. Then we are out the library door, off the campus, and under the afternoon drizzle. We stand at the bus stop, two secret heroes on the fringes of winter, waiting for the sun, any source of rejuvenation, just one outbound bus away from here and into the city.

Dystopia Comics is the only all-used–comic-book store in Daly City. Most stores file their back issues away in neat alphabetized rows, each one sealed in a plastic bag with rigid backing. But Dystopia lives up to its name. Comics are stuffed into shoddy cardboard boxes, and Luc and I spend hours rummaging through bin after bin. We always win in the end: in the past half hour Luc has found issues of *Justice League* and *Sandman*, even a water-damaged issue of *The Watchmen*, and I've started a small stack of old issues of *Green Lantern*, precisely what I need for my research. I sometimes think that Luc and I possess an extra sense, an instinct for finding small treasures among the slightly torn and the discarded.

"Closing time," a husky voice mutters from behind and above me. I do a quick one-eighty, fists clenched and ready. I face the cashier, who stands just inches away from me. His globular, fleshy belly is even closer, oozing over the elastic waistband of his Bermuda shorts. "If you're going to read it, then buy it."

I give Luc the signal and then shift my eyes back to the cashier. "Pardon me, sir," I say, "but your volume is infringing upon my space."

He blinks. "My what?"

"The amount of space your cubic units are occupying."

He blinks again. "So?" Already I've confused him, thrown him off, and all he can do is point to the clock. "Just hurry it up, all right?"

My eye catches the exposed belly once more. With the proper serrated edge I could carve into the flesh, cut a tunnel right through it.

I smile at the mass before me. "Let's go, Luc."

We walk out the door and turn the corner into a narrow alley. We crouch down to the ground, shielded between Dumpsters, and Luc unzips his backpack. From between textbooks and folders he pulls out our stack of comics and gives me my half. "Distract him longer next time," he says. "He almost turned around too soon."

"No backtalk from the sidekick." I tuck my comics away in the secret pocket of my backpack.

The rain has stopped, but we don our hoods anyway. We proceed into the street, outside the crosswalk lines, defying the blinking red hand before us. "Nice work," I tell Luc. "See you tomorrow, oh seven hundred hours."

"Oh seven hundred hours," he confirms.

On sad nights my mother listens to her 45 rpm of "Johnny Angel" over and over again until she passes out. Tonight is going to be one of those nights. Before I can even lock the door behind me, she starts screaming, asking where I've been. "Nowhere," I tell her. "Just out."

"And what should I do if something happened to you out there?" she asks, one hand on her hip, the other tugging at the neckline of her Las Vegas sweatshirt. "What should I do then?" She takes heavy, staggered breaths and begins to empty out the kitchen cupboards, throwing food we need over the fire escape, weeping, uttering profanities about men and why they are the way they are.

I give her five quick shots of Johnny Walker and put her to bed. I take off her shoes, pull the sheets over her, and press REPLAY on her turntable. She puts her arms around my neck and pulls my face to hers, telling me what a good boy I've been. "Don't you change," she whispers. I can feel the tears on her lips wetting my ear.

"Go to sleep, Mom," I whisper. I pull down the shades, shutting out the last bits of daylight.

She got left again. I knew my mother was feeling hopeful this time around. This guy lasted almost four weeks.

When I warn her, she tells me I'm crazy, so this time I kept quiet. But I saw it coming. Her strategy was faulty: she had been making domestic offerings—a home-cooked meal of lumpia and pinakbet, Filipino delicacies she calls her love potions. But they lack any magical properties. Her men always see the food as alien and weird, a little too far from home. So they take what they want and then vanish. "Ride a rocket to the moon, that's fine," she once slurred to some guy on the phone, "but baby, baby, won't you please come back?" It was my twelfth birthday party, but I wasn't the one who wanted him there: I took the receiver from her hands. "Accidents happen, bastard," I warned, "so watch your back." She grabbed the phone, hit me with it, and then apologized for my rudeness. But he'd already hung up.

Mom's messed-up universe started with one bad star: a nine-month marriage to the man who was my father. He brought her to the States, a living knickknack from his military days. Their union, brief as it was, spawned me and all my biological peculiarities. "You're like Aquaman," Luc said when I told him the story—"cool." But Aquaman's mother was a mermaid, his father a human being. Nothing is human within the man who was my father. He disappeared from her life just hours before I was born. What I imagine, what I've even dreamed, is that he is a sinister breed of assassin, with white hair, white skin, and white eyes, invading alien streets, sent to find and fuck my mother and then finish her off. When she is drunk, she talks about my origin, sticking the sick story in my head, panel after panel after panel.

And then she'll break in half, Johnny Angel and Johnny Walker to the rescue. But I forgive her. Like all heroes, she needs her Fortress of Solitude, her Paradise Island, any place tucked away from the evil in the world. Not to worry: I keep a lookout.

From 1958 to 1965 the Green Lantern thwarts villains from every quadrant of the galaxy. At the end of the sixties he is ordered by the Guardians to return home, to uphold good on Earth. For the first time he encounters evils that the Guardians themselves cannot defeat: racism, poverty, over-population. "Ironic," he thinks in Green Lantern #187, carrying the dead body of a black man beaten by racist thugs, "with my power ring I can drain an entire ocean, shrink an entire galaxy to the size of a penny. Yet hatred and human cruelty are still impervious to it!"

This is a turning point in the Green Lantern's history. Though many claim it is the defining experience of his career, I will argue that it distracted him from his primary objective: the upholding and protection of justice at the galactic level. This paper will show that his return to Earth was a mistake, one we would pay for decades later.

Rain dots my paper, so I put it inside. I'm wet but warm, wrapped up in a black Army-issue blanket. I remain on the fire escape.

I can hear mothers' voices screaming for their kids to come in, old homeless men arguing for space beneath an awning. Ten minutes later and twenty yards beyond, a teenager holds a knife against an old woman's neck while his friend rummages through her purse. When they're done, they shove her to the ground, light their cigarettes, and walk away.

Nourished by the elements, bloated with stars, our universe is still a hungry one; even I can feel it. So why did the Guardians send him back? With our region of space abounding in alien threats, why did the Green Lantern return? I was resistant at first, but I'm beginning to see the point of the assignment: *This is the inquiry of history*, just like Mr. Cosgrove says. It changes when the perspective changes. It's too late to repair the as-is of planet Earth. In the end we're the residue that the Green Lantern's ring can't penetrate.

Drizzle turns to storm, but I'll sit here for another hour before I go in.

This morning I knock on my mother's door, three times, but she's out cold. She's already late for work, so I go into her bedroom and lay her pink waitress uniform on a chair. I whisper good-bye and then leave for school.

Luc meets me on the corner. "Ready?" I ask.

He opens his backpack. "It's all here."

"Good," I nod. "Let's go."

We have our enemies. Today Luc and I will deliver Brandon DeStefano to justice.

Last week we were reading comics at lunch on the football-field bleachers when Brandon and Tenzil walked by. "It's Luc the Gook!" Brandon screamed. I gave him the finger, and Luc told him to run along with the other nonsentients. "Non*what*?" Brandon said, climbing up toward us, bleacher by bleacher. "I don't understand Korean, gook." Then Tenzil reached from behind and snatched Luc's comic (an almost valuable issue of *Swamp Thing* #12) right out of his hands. He tossed it to Brandon, who stuffed it down the back of his pants, farted on it, and then dropped it in a puddle beneath the bleachers. "Freaks," he said. Then they walked toward the lunch courtyard, a trail of sinister *ha-ha-has* ricocheting behind them.

Luc went down to rescue the comic, but I kept Brandon in my eye when I noticed that something about him wasn't quite right: his head started twitching, shoulder and ear crashing against each other. His spine arched him forward and back, forward and back, each vertebra breaking through skin until the body was no more. Then, in a sudden flash of light, Brandon deStefano became The Gas, a force able to release methane-based emissions powerful enough to stun an enemy or wipe out an entire planet. Luc and I vowed revenge, and I intend to get it every time I can.

We get to school early, while the boys' locker room is still empty. We find The Gas's locker, and in seventy-four seconds Luc picks the lock. I pull the impostor Right Guard deodorant from my backpack and make the switch.

Later, when PE is over, Luc and I dress quickly, taking position by our lockers. We keep an eye out for The Gas, who has just emerged from the showers. He comes closer and closer but pays us no mind. In regular street clothes we are anonymous, merely mortal men.

The Gas dries himself off and reaches into his locker for his deodorant. He shakes the can once, twice, and removes the cap. He raises his arm above his head, positioning the Right Guard at his armpit. Before he can spray, Luc and I vanish.

The Gas has no idea of the power that's about to befall him; no one ever does. But this is how I like it. First my enemies underestimate me; then I smash them.

Do you think it'll heal?" On this team Luc is the conscience.

"No one has ever died from a scorched armpit," I tell him, stashing another swiped teacher's edition in my locker. He knows I speak the truth. I don't say things just to be reassuring.

The final bell rings. By tomorrow morning we'll hear snippets of talk here and there about the incident. Campus security will circulate in homerooms and PE classes, spouting the same refrain: If we work together, we can prevent this from happening again.

Feeble heroism from the crooked authorities. This is what they said last time and the time before that, and no one suspected our true identities then. "We ought to celebrate," I decide. "Meet me at Kingpin Donuts before school tomorrow."

Luc stares into my eyes as if he means to challenge me. "You said you would change the deodorant into spray paint, not a blowtorch," he whispers. "You said you wouldn't do this anymore."

"Shut up." I slam my locker shut. "We're done for today. Go home."

After school I check on my mother at the restaurant. I take my station on an adjacent rooftop, over what was once a tropical-fish store. I would stop in after school just to watch the fish, tracing their paths with my finger. I liked the bubble aquariums best— the fish looked airborne, flying around in their Plexiglas globes like lovely winged mutants. Four months ago the store was bombed (by a Filipino gang, the newspapers suspected), and the next day I walked by to find half the storefront missing, the floor blanketed with aquarium shards. I entered and walked among the ruins, the crunch of glass beneath my feet. Beams of morning light seeped through broken windows and cracks in the wall, teleporting me to a kaleidoscopic world: ruby- and sapphire- and emerald-colored fish lay on the ground, lifeless, but still reflecting the brilliant sun in each tiny scale. I took out my lunch, threw away the sandwich, and stashed as many fish as I could fit into the Ziploc bag. Had they been alive, I would have been carrying nearly $400 worth of fish; dead, they were worth nothing. I didn't care. I took them home and kept them tucked away for three months, behind the ice trays and TV dinners, and took them out late at night to look at them. Bathed in freezer light, they were like life-giving stones, alien and cold. When Mom found them, their color had finally faded, and she flushed them down the toilet.

The store remains vacant, but the roof is sturdy, and my vantage point is good. From up here I can see down into the restaurant, beyond the gaudy-lettered window, which reads BARRY ALLEN'S though the owners are a Vietnamese couple by the name of Ngoc-Tran. "They probably needed something catchier, for business purposes," Luc said, explaining why they used the name. "Koreans do it all the time."

So do superheroes.

The last of the afternoon regulars finally leaves, and my mother takes a cigarette break at a corner booth. She stares out at the street, taking greedy drags of a Marlboro. She exhales smoke against the window, and it dances before her face like some sort of phantom lover that I can see too. I often catch my mother in these moments, a sad woman in pink, looking into nothing, waiting. "That's how I met your father," she once confessed in a stupor. She was one of Manila Rosie's Beauties, the best dancing girls the Navy boys could find in the city. "And I was your daddy's favorite," she said. After a two-week courtship he proposed to my mother, promising her citizenship in the U.S.A. "United Stars of America" is what she called it. I have had longing dreams about this incarnation of my mother, seeing her asleep and afloat in outer space, the constellations reforming themselves around her. I try to locate this part of her in myself, to isolate it from all the other stuff.

Then suddenly, from nowhere, a man in a uniform invades the picture. He sits down at her booth, lights my mother another cigarette, lights his own. They begin to talk. I don't need to hear what they're saying; I can read the words, frame by frame. My mother laughs, her hand over her breast, as if she is gasping for air. She is weakening.

Oh, stop! You're too much, do you know that? she says, giggling.

He tosses his head back, his shoulders bouncing up and down, up and down, laughing at his own jokes with a villain's arrogance. Then he grabs my mother's hand and brings it close to his face. He is acquainting himself with my mother's biology, remembering the texture of her skin, her scent. *My little tropical gardenia*, he says to her. But his thoughts betray him. *So easy* bubbles from his head. *This bitch will be so easy*.

I'm too far and high up above. There's no way to warn her in time, no hope for a last-minute rescue.

Having discussed the Green Lantern's shift in crime-fighting focus, this paper will now examine its consequences. In 1976 the Green Lantern returns to the stars. This is a difficult time for him. Realizing that he is unable to wipe out the societal ills of the era, he falters in his ability to wield the power ring. He is summoned to Oa, where the Guardians put him on trial and consider finding a replacement. The following dialogue is an excerpt from that trial:

"Perhaps Abin Sur was mistaken in selecting you, Hal Jordan."

"Please, Guardians. Allow me to prove myself worthy of the ring. Allow me to be your champion once more."

The world jerks to a stop, and my pencil slips from my hands. I pick it up from the littered bus floor. "Brake more gently next time, please!" I shout to the bus driver. Baldie shoots me a look from his extended rearview mirror.

He does it again at the next stop. "Hey!" I rise from my seat. "I said brake more gently next time!" I walk toward the front. "Did you hear me?" Baldie ignores me and slams on the brakes at the light. I keep him in my eye as I fight gravity, but I lose my footing; I fall. Just as quickly I'm up again, and I almost manage to dig the point of my pencil into his arm, but two of his henchmen passengers force me off before I can make contact with his skin. I walk the rest of the way home against traffic so loud that it smothers and suffocates the battle cries in my head.

When I call, Luc's grandmother picks up the phone. I don't bother identifying myself; she always drops the receiver at the sound of my voice, and I have to wait two or three minutes until Luc finds out it's for him. To his grandmother, I'm The Filipino, the mutant friend who is too different for her to speak with, too weird to be allowed to come over.

Luc finally picks up, and I tell him what happened. "Just breathe for a sec," he says, competing with loud kitchen noises in the background. "It'll be fine."

"He had to be stopped," I explain. "He's putting other lives at risk. Better the driver die than a busload of innocents." If I have to be the one to do it, then I'll do it.

Luc understands the good of my intentions and says so. "But it's over now. You kept all those passengers safe."

"Let's hope."

Then Luc says he's sorry but he has to go, his mother needs to call his aunt about a Korean variety show on cable. "No problemo," I say, "and thanks again. Old chum." I wait for the click on his end and then I hang up.

With my mother at the restaurant, I have time to work in my lab. I can construct bombs and explosives, but these require the proper chemicals and materials, and I can use the bathroom for only so many hours in a day before my mother becomes suspicious. When she pounds on the door, asking what I am doing, I tell her nothing, to please give me five or ten minutes. She guesses that I am masturbating and tells me to stop. I tell her okay.

My favorite weapon is my slingshot. I stole it from a high-quality sporting-goods store six months back: lightweight, aerodynamic, potential of elasticity twenty times as great as the average sling. It angers me how a lesser comic like *Dennis the Menace* has reduced the slingshot to a mischief-making toy kept in a child's back pocket. People forget that David killed Goliath with a slingshot. With the proper ammunition I could kill from afar too.

But I am at work on what I hope will be the greatest addition to my arsenal. Centuries ago Filipino warriors created the yo-yo as a weapon, emitting from their hands stone-heavy objects at the ends of twenty-foot-long ropes. They learned to hunt with it, to kill. Eventually the yo-yo immigrated to America. The story goes that a traveling salesman named Duncan saw one and introduced it to the country as a new hobby, a toy to pass the time.

I intend to get it back.

I will fuse together my native ingenuity with modern technology to create a weapon of deadly hybridity. My yo-yo will be of marble, attached to string at least fifty feet long, so that even from rooftops I can stun my enemies far, far below. My father, too, had weapons. In the framed photo my mother keeps on her bureau, he holds a rifle in one hand, my mother in the other.

Suddenly I hear movement in the apartment. "Come out here!" my mother shouts, pounding on the bathroom door. "Come out and meet my new friend!"

"You're early! Hold on a sec!" I stash everything behind the toilet paper under the sink, hiding it next to the Windex and Lysol.

I open the door and find my mother standing before me, her head resting dreamily on his arm. "Honey," she says, smiling at me, "this is Alex. He's our mailman. We met today at the restaurant."

At least six feet tall, Lex towers over my mother and over me. He is well-postured, undoubtedly strong and agile. His uniform shows a badge of a bald eagle, and another badge tells me that he has proudly delivered U.S. mail for five years. "Hey, champ," he says. He fixes his eyes, as blue and sharp as lasers, on me. Five milky-white fingers reach out.

Armed with addresses and ZIP codes, Lex can track down anyone, anywhere. If my mother and I were to escape, he could follow the trail of our forwarding address to find us. It's the extra sense, the instinct, of a hunter.

Villain.

But I accept his challenge and take his hand. I tilt my head down just a bit, so that my glasses slide down the bridge of my nose. "Nice to meet you," I say with a smile. Lex does a double take at my nonmatching eyes. Already I have the upper hand.

My mother and Lex want privacy, so tonight I'm a bedroom shut-in. But I can still hear them laughing, dancing clumsily around the front room to old Motown love songs. Luckily, I have the ability to phase out any and all distractions, to teleport my thoughts, even my senses, elsewhere. I believe this is another of my mutant abilities, the active residue of my father's genetic imprint. It's the power he used on Mom and me.

I use that power tonight. I have homework to do.

I research, going through issue after old issue of *Green Lantern*. Already I feel like the Green Lantern's biographer. I recognize the earnestness of the early years, when he is made up of simple, clean strokes of a pen, when the green of his costume is bright and the black is bold, and the villains are easy to tell from the heroes. In the sixties he is more weathered, and in the seventies the battle scars are painfully obvious in the inking of his musculature: the mementos of victories are also the reminders of loved ones lost. I feel sad for him, for all the time he's been forced to see.

And now I'm at that difficult point in my project where his status as a hero comes into question. "It's where history stops becoming fact," Mr. Cosgrove would say, "and you have to choose what's true and what isn't."

Brought to Oa, he stands before a jury of Guardians, on trial for abusing his power, for attempting to alter history to save his city and the woman he loved. "*Hal Jordan, Green Lantern of sector 2814, for misuse of the power of Oa, you are hereby asked to surrender the ring to us,*" they say. Half of Hal Jordan's face fills the next panel, and his rage is clear even behind the mask. Next is a Guardian's bony, blue-skinned hand reaching out, palm open. "*You will surrender the ring, Hal Jordan,*" he says.

"*THE RING!*" five voices echo through the same voice bubble.

And then Hal Jordan's face, the mask, one eye, and nothing. Only a frightening flash of green.

I take the bottom corner of the page between my fingers. I turn the page slowly, knowing what comes next: an exploding sky, fallen emerald towers, the lifeless bodies of Guardians long thought to be immortal scattered among the debris. "*Traitor!*" one accuses with his dying breath. But Hal Jordan admits nothing, denies nothing. He takes their rings, all of them, and explodes into space, Earthbound, a furious green light trailing behind him.

History is to be interpreted; that's the rule. What makes me so angry is that the decision has already been made for us. The cover's depiction of Hal Jordan proves the bias: his eyebrows are sharp-pointed arches, his lips stretch in a sinister grin, and behind the mask his eyes are vacant, blank with madness and power. It's the face of a villain, the kind I've seen a million times.

But consider what Hal Jordan has seen. Consider the burden he bears: *he got there too late.* He got there in time only to see his city wiped out by an enemy he couldn't defeat. You don't recover from that; you fix it. If I could rewrite the comic, I'd do the same.

The following pages are panels of green: he wipes out a building in the background, *KRAZAAKK!*, one in the foreground, *BLAZAAAM!* He destroys another, and another. Then—*CRASH!*—something made of glass falls to the floor in the living room. I hear my mother and Lex whirling around to the music, bumping into bookshelves and walls, causing fragile things to fall. They laugh through loud kisses.

"Could you please be quiet out there?" They don't answer. "Would you be quiet, please?" Still nothing, only the soft sounds of my mother being taken yet again. "Be quiet."

At 2:43 A.M. I wake from weird dreams. Dehydrated and dizzy, I get a glass of milk. On the way back to my room I peek through my mother's half-closed door. She's curled up in Lex's arms; the sheets are wrapped around their bodies, binding them together. In her sleep her hands still clamp around his neck.

I walk toward them, silent in bare feet, invisible in the blue glow of the digital clock. I stand at the foot of the bed, watching their bodies just barely rise from breath. If I wanted to, I could crawl in between them, my head in the circle of my mother's arms, my knee rammed into Lex's balls.

My mother mumbles something in her sleep, taking quick breaths, and slowly she turns away from Lex. I go to her. I can feel her pupils shift side to side beneath the skin of her eyelids, and I press down on them just enough until the panic in her head subsides. I move a strand of black hair away from her face, looping it slowly around my finger.

I float to the other side of the bed, over to Lex. In the moonlight he is even paler, and the stubble on his chin is like metallic bristles against my knuckles. I kneel next to him and set my head down beside his. I can see my mother's lipstick smeared along his neck, trailing down to the center of his chest. It's the residue of what she thinks is love, and I can imagine my mother kissing him, just inches above the spot where the heart should be. I lay my palm flat on that spot, just barely touching skin. I can feel the life beating inside him. Maybe this is how my father felt. "What do you want from us?" I whisper to him. "Who sent you here?" But like my mother, he is drowned in sleep or just passed out.

So I test him. I tip my almost-empty glass, letting a tiny drop of milk fall onto his ear. The white liquid dot slides from the outer edge and vanishes into the black hole of his ear canal. His neck and shoulders jerk, lightning-quick. Then he is still again. "Assassin," I say. I return to the kitchen to wash my glass.

We have not seen The Gas for almost two weeks since the battle. At lunch Luc and I split up, eavesdropping on conversations, trying to piece together the fate of our nemesis.

After school we regroup on the library roof. "I heard Suzy Cheerleader talking to one of the vice-principals," Luc says. "Brandon's in the hospital."

"The Gas will be fine," I tell him, staring out onto the campus quad. We stay low, speaking in whispers.

"Did you hear me? He's in the hospital now. His arm needs some sort of operation. Skin grafts or something. What did you put in that thing anyway?"

Skin grafts. Then the body of my enemy is mutating as well. Fascinating. "Mercury fulminate, chloride of azode, some other chemicals. The usual."

I keep an eye out until I finally spot Tenzil, blanketing the school with his propaganda. I blame Tenzil, an ally of The Gas, for our corrupt student government. As vice-president, he's the person who rejected my proposal for a school trip to the San Francisco Comic Book Convention, and gave my money to varsity track instead.

I pull the yo-yo from my bag. "What the hell is that?" Luc asks.

"Quiet." This moment requires silence and the utmost precision.

Tenzil comes closer as I loop the string round and round my finger until I've cut off circulation. I raise my hand over the edge. But suddenly Luc grabs my wrist. "Don't," he says, trying to bring me back.

I take a quick foot to his stomach, freeing myself from his clutches. "If we don't get him, he'll get us."

"What are you talking about?" Luc asks, as if he doesn't already know. He rises from the ground and reaches for my wrist again, but he's too slow: I snap my hand forward, letting go the yo-yo for its spectacular debut.

Marble-heavy, the double disk drops straight to the ground. But Tenzil is gone, and the yo-yo dangles at the string's end, lifeless, refusing to wind its way back up to me. "Where is he?" I say. "Where the fuck did he go?" I crane my neck over the edge, scanning the quad, the locker bay, anywhere someone might hide from me. But Tenzil is nowhere to be found. "Traitor," I accuse Luc. "This is your fault." But when I turn, he, too, is gone. I take a quick inventory of the rooftop. No traces.

I run through the campus, taking down Tenzil's posters and flyers. I return to the roof, where I tear them into a pile of tiny pieces. Then I scoop them up and throw them to the sky, letting them fall like ashes on the spot where the chalk outline of Tenzil Jones's body should have been. I want to mourn today's loss.

I keep no school ID, have no driver's permit. I tossed my Social Security card once I had committed the number to memory. If I have no money, then there's nothing in my wallet. I have my anonymity to keep me safe.

Today my wallet is empty but I'm hungry, so I stop by Ollie's Market on the way home. Ollie stands behind the counter, a sixty-something grump in a dirty undershirt, venting his frustrations on his customers. At his side is Sasha the Amputee, Ollie's half retriever, half something else. Sasha's right hind leg was the only casualty of the last holdup, which Ollie swears, despite the ski masks, was done by Filipino gangsters. "Filipinos!" he curses to the air. "Stealing this and stealing that!"

He makes this so easy.

My mutant biology hides that part of me he would fear. It is, after all, layered with the skin of my father, fused with that of my mother, and it gives me chameleonic powers. Ollie continues complaining and accusing, unaware that a shapeshifter stands before him. I tell him I know exactly how he feels, that they really can't be trusted, that they're a dangerous and deadly breed, and I keep Ollie in my eye, drowning out his sound as my hand fingers its way to the mini-rack of candy bars at my side.

But Sasha sees. The mutt snarls, her snout pointed at me, accusing me. *Go ahead,* I dare her. *Hobble after me and you'll lose another, you damaged bitch.* Mission accomplished, I tell Ollie good-bye, and press my heel onto Sasha's front paw as I walk out the door. She lets out a pathetic yelp. "Sorry." I smile at Ollie, petting the dog's head.

I exit the store and make a sharp right into an alleyway. I walk through and cross a four-way intersection diagonally, dodging cars and buses. I make a left, a right, and another right. I round corner after corner until the geometry of the city swallows me whole and it's safe for me to eat.

The shades are drawn when I enter our apartment. I hear movement from the bedroom. "Mom?"

I open her door. "Mom." She's on the floor, lying on her side. Laid out beside her is my father's uniform, still wrapped in plastic on a wire hanger. She reaches out to it, moving her thumb back and forth over a shiny gold button.

I give her a shot of whisky. I pour her another and then another, and she goes on about how Lex doesn't love her, that the evil in men will always kill her, more and more slowly each time. "All the time. All the time this happens. Tell your father to stop it, please." She weeps into my chest, clinging to my shirt. Streaks of blood stain her hands. She's been cutting herself again.

An orphaned boy sees a bat flying through a window. The last son of Krypton dreams of the afterglow of his dead home world. All heroes have their omens; this blood will be mine.

"I will," I tell her. "I swear it." But she cannot hear my oath.

In conclusion, he is no longer the Green Lantern. With a final surge of power, Hal Jordan transforms himself into Parallax, a master of space and dimension, wielder of the greatest power ever known. His only agenda: to destroy time, to interrupt for good the linearity of history. With one hand he will knock past, present, and future out of order; he will be the judge of who may live, who will die, and who will never have existed at all. Time will move forward, time will move back, until it collides with itself, until what is left is the Zero Hour, and all that has gone wrong can finally be set right.

Villains and heroes don't ask for the power they're given: Destiny, Fate, and Luck drop it on us like a star, and we have no choice but to use it.

It's due tomorrow, but fuck the paper. Tonight I must enter the fray.

I paint black around my eyes, like a domino mask, erasing the traces of who I am.

Mother's future slips into Mother's past as I don my father's uniform jacket. It fits perfectly; I never knew our bodies were the same. Gold buttons sparkle on my chest, badges adorn my arms. To the collar I attach a cape, a long piece of cloth light enough that it does not impede my speed, dark enough that it keeps me wrapped in night shadows. All superassassins rely on the darkness.

I place my ammunition—segments of aluminum pipe filled with impact-sensitive explosives—in a tiny suede pouch attached to my belt. I secure the slingshot in my front belt loop; the yo-yo I keep in an oversized pocket on my pant leg.

Midnight strikes. I climb out the window, descend the fire escape, and run through the city, staying in back alleys and unlit streets. I keep an eye out for any and all enemies who dare to venture into the night. Though they are many and I am one, I will fight this battle alone. I have no need for Luc anymore. Sidekicks are extraneous; they give up the fight too easily. Robin was killed off for a reason after all.

I make my way to the abandoned projects. I enter through the back, and blast open the door to the stairwell. I fly up seven, eight, nine flights. I need to go higher.

Fourteen, fifteen, sixteen flights. I must go higher.

I reach the roof. I walk along its perimeter, to be sure I am alone. Night wind howls all around, blowing my cape behind me like a black ghost in tow.

I peer over the edge; the city itself has become a grid. Black streets and white sidewalks crisscross, framing city blocks like tiny pictures, a page of panels with too many scenes. But somewhere in all of this I know my enemy lurks, waiting for me to strike, daring me to cross the white borders and enter the battle. I will wait for him every night if I have to.

I take out the slingshot. I load the ammunition and pull back the sling. I aim, ready at any moment to let go.

A Trip to Warsaw

Tzvetan Todorov

Bulgarian-born Tzvetan Todorov is a major thinker in the French humanities. He started as a literary critic but he branched out into history and culture. The themes of his books include morality, ethics, displacement, memory, democracy and so on. His publication record is impressive and the success of many of his books phenomenal. His publications include: The Fantastic: A Structural Approach to a Literary Genre, The Poetics of Prose, Mikhail Bakhtin: The Dialogical Principle, The Conquest of America: The Question of the Other, Literature and its Theorists: A Personal View of Twentieth-Century Criticism, Facing the Extreme: Moral Life in the Concentration Camps, The Morals of History, A French Tragedy: Scenes of Civil War, Summer 1944, *etc. He has also written books on Jean-Jacques Rousseau, Benjamin Constant, and French humanism. The following essay is from his book* Facing the Extreme: Moral Life in the Concentration Camps *(1996).*

SUNDAY VISITS

It began very simply, in November of 1987. A friend had offered to show us some sights that were not on the official tour of Warsaw. We had accepted eagerly, glad for the opportunity to escape the program to which we had been bound by the conference, our reason for being in this city. So it was that we arrived on a Sunday around noon at the church where Father Popieluszko—the priest who had been killed by the secret police for his ties to the Solidarity movement—had officiated and where he now lay buried. It was a striking scene. Merely on entering the courtyard of the church, it seemed, we were in a different world, overflowing with banners and posters we had seen nowhere else in the city. Inside, in the semicircle of the choir, was an exhibit documenting the life of the martyred priest, each of the glass cases—like so many personal stations of the cross—illustrating a moment in his career. There were pictures of him in private meetings and pictures of him in crowds; there was a map that traced the route of his last journey, and then a photograph of the bridge from which he had been thrown into the river. A little further on, a crucifix with Popieluszko in place of Christ. Outside was the tombstone itself, around which a heavy chain, riveted to stones, formed the outline of a map of greater Poland (reaching into Lithuania and the Ukraine). All in all, there was an intensity here that stuck in your throat. And everywhere around us the crowd, endless: the service had just concluded, and we waited a long time for the flood of people leaving the building to subside so that we could enter, but when we finally did we found that the church, miraculously, was still full.

I could not help thinking then of the visit we had made that same morning to the Jewish cemetery in Warsaw. We were alone. A step or two off the central path and we were plunged into indescribable chaos: trees had grown up between the graves; weeds and wild grasses had crowded in, erasing all the boundaries between them, and the tombstones themselves had gone the way of the coffins and sunk into the earth. We suddenly understood that, by contrast, other cemeteries were full of life, because in them the past remained present, whereas here even the tombstones—those petrifications of memory—were dying. The extermination of the Jews during the war, marked by a few monuments at the entrance to the graveyard, had had this further effect: it had killed a second time those who had died the century before, for it had killed the memories in which they might have lived on. There was total silence around us, and yet our voices seemed not to carry. Hardly had we entered the cemetery when we lost one another. The trees that had pushed up between the graves blocked our view, and our shouts went unanswered. And then, just as suddenly, we found one another again and began to wander about silently, pausing here and there before the funerary monuments that sprang out at us from this fantastic forest.

There was an emotional connection between these two parts of the morning, but also a difference I could not define. Several days later, back in Paris, I continued to feel unsettled by my inability to understand. I thought that by reading some books on Polish history I could put an end to my confusion and overcome my feeling of uneasiness. During my stay in Warsaw I had been told, on separate occasions, of two books that might interest me. Perhaps, I thought, these books contained the key to this feeling that puzzled me. And so I bought them and began to read, immersing myself in them. As it happens, they dealt with two events in recent history—the Warsaw ghetto uprising of 1943 and the Warsaw Rising of 1944. I felt that they did indeed shed some light on the present; I wanted to know more and looked for other books on these events. This is what I found.

WARSAW, 1944

The first of the two books, *Varsovie 44,* contains interviews that Jean-François Steiner conducted with people who either had taken part in the Warsaw Rising or had witnessed it or were experts on Polish history. (The revolt took place in the summer of

1944 when the Red Army had reached the eastern suburbs of Warsaw; the Polish re-sisters hoped to bring down the German occupation force on their own, thereby confirming Poland's independence from Russia. They fought heroically for months but failed.) These interviews, interspersed with various documents from the period as well as excerpts from literary works, form a long montage of texts, all revolving around the question of how the decision to revolt was reached. In the detailed accounts de-scribing the rising fervor, I realized I was actually reading a reflection on heroism. Cer-tainly the rebels were heroes, but, more than that, the hold that heroic values had on their spirit seemed to have played a decisive role in the outbreak of the revolt and in its progress. This heroic spirit had acted as a kind of drug; it kept the fighters in a state of exaltation that helped them withstand even the most difficult ordeals.

But what exactly *is* heroism, I asked myself as I read. With respect to the great antinomy underlying human actions—necessity versus freedom, or impersonal law ver-sus individual will—heroism clearly falls on the side of freedom and free will. Where, to the eyes of ordinary people, the situation seems to offer no alternative, where it seems that one must bow to circumstances, the hero fights the odds and, through some extraordinary deed, manages to bend destiny to his own ends. The hero is the opposite of the fatalist; he is on the side of the revolutionary, never the conservative, for he has no particular respect for the status quo and believes people can attain any goal they choose, provided they have the will to do so.

The leaders of the Warsaw Rising, those who gave the orders for it to begin, plainly acted in this heroic spirit. Colonel Okulicki was the chief of operations for the Polish Home Army (the Armia Krajowa, the underground organization that spear-headed the revolt and that, unlike the smaller Armia Ludowa, the Communist People's Army, had links to London, not Moscow); his fate was especially tragic—he died not from Hitler's bullets, as he would have wished, but in Stalin's prisons, which he feared above all else. According to recollections of survivors, Okulicki embraced a heroic out-look from the start. "He wanted things to be the way he thought they ought to be," states a witness, "and he refused to accept their being otherwise" (Steiner 101). Okulicki's concern for what ought to be far outweighed his attention to what was. The same was true of Brigadier-General Tadeusz Pelczynski, the chief of staff. In his interview with Steiner thirty years later, he recalls, "We knew Poland was doomed, but we could not accept that verdict" (241). Similarly, General Tadeusz Bor-Komorowski, the commander in chief, remembers that on the eve of the uprising he simply "dis-counted the possibility that it might fail," believing that things would turn out just as they should (Ciechanowski 247). When, after the fighting had begun, someone told Colonel Antoni Monter, the Home Army region commander for Warsaw, that a certain neighborhood had fallen into German hands, he shot back, "I do not accept this in-formation" (Zawodny 22). That attitude is typical of the hero: he may know that his ideal is unrealizable (in this case, both Poland's position on the map and the Red Army's military potential made Soviet occupation a foregone conclusion), but be-cause he desires it above all else, he pursues it with all his might.

Pelczynski turns this heroic principle into something like a military code of honor. "For a soldier," he asserts, "there is no order that cannot be carried out if he has the will to do so" (Steiner 112). There is no distinguishing between reasonable and unreasonable orders, between those that do and those that do not take account of the situation as it really is. All that matters, according to this code, is whether or not there is a sufficient measure of will. This, it seems, was the Polish military tradition. Steiner cites a prewar general who explains to his subordinates that material shortages can always be compensated for by an effort of will, by the soldiers' capacity for self-sacrifice. "Let there be an inverse relation between your munitions and Polish blood," he admonishes them. "Anytime you lack some of the former, make up for it with some of the latter" (122). Okulicki's position was identical: in the hands of people with sufficient determination, sticks and bottles would be perfectly adequate against German tanks. Later, Pelczynski would say the same: "We saw their material superiority over us. But . . . the Polish people had the advantage of better morale." The Poles, moreover, were not alone in their choice. As another Polish official put it, "When the people of Paris were marching on the Bastille, they did not count their clubs" (Ciechanowski 261).

Heroes, then, prefer the ideal to the real—that much is certain. During the Warsaw Rising, the ideal went by several names. Clearly the rebels were fighting for the freedom of Warsaw (and, if possible, its survival); more often, however, they spoke in terms of a loftier ideal, that of "the nation." "We must fight," says Okulicki, "without regard for anything or anyone, and in our heart of hearts there can be only one thought—Poland" (Steiner 108). To claim that one's ideal is "the nation" is not enough, however, for the nation can be many things: a group of human beings—my family and friends or my compatriots, for instance—or a certain number of places and houses and roads. These interpretations Okulicki rejects: the uprising, he argues, must not be postponed "under the pretext of saving a few lives or a few houses" (108). It is a question of saving not the people of Warsaw but the idea of Warsaw, not individual Poles or Polish territory but an abstraction called Poland. "For us, Poland was the object of a genuine cult," another rebel commander declares. "We loved her not simply as a country; we loved her as a mother, a queen, a virgin" (10). Thus the country was deified (and feminized); in the process many of its real characteristics were simply ignored.

And so it was not the Polish people who had to be saved but, rather, certain qualities of theirs: their will to freedom, their desire for independence, their national pride. "If we do not fight," Pelczynski warns, "the Polish nation risks a terrible moral collapse" (121). And as it was becoming impossible to defend material values, he states on another occasion, the Polish people had to content themselves with moral values (Ciechanowski 277). Kazimierz Sosnkowski, the Polish supreme commander in chief in London, writes the following in a letter to Prime Minister Stanislaw Mikolajczyk: "Acts of despair are sometimes unavoidable in the lives of nations, in view of the common feelings of the population, the political symbolism of such acts, and their moral significance for posterity" (158). In other words, people must die so that moral and political values can survive. A further implication, of course, is that there must be someone to define what is moral and what is not and to determine—with an eye to history and to the future—what course of action to take in the present.

But even Poland the abstraction is not always enough; Poland must itself be offered up to an even more distant ideal—that of the West, which, in its turn, comes to stand for civilization, or even "humanity." The Russians are the forces of barbarism and Poland the last line of defense against them. Thus it becomes possible to sacrifice the lives of any number of people in the name of defending humanity. In a letter to Bor-Komorowski, Sosnkowski reveals his desire to make the Polish question "a problem for the conscience of the world, a test-case for the future of European nations" (185). Bor himself recalls, "We felt that the battle for Warsaw would have to call for a response from the world" (269). Okulicki justifies the revolt in a similar fashion: "An effort was needed which would stir the conscience of the world" (211). The insurrection becomes a sacrificial act in the name of a series of increasingly remote and always impersonal beneficiaries or audiences—Warsaw, Poland, the West, the world. Lives are sacrificed not for other human beings but for ideas. In the final analysis, nothing less than the absolute can satisfy these heroic spirits.

In the lives of the heroes, certain human qualities are more highly prized than others. Foremost among them is loyalty to an ideal—loyalty that is valued in and of itself, independent of the nature of the ideal. (That is why we can admire a heroic enemy.) The hero, in this sense, is the opposite of the traitor: whatever the circumstances, he never betrays (behavior that is no doubt a vestige of the chivalric code of honor). Thus when Okulicki was arrested and interrogated by the Soviet secret police, he remained silent; of course, such restraint also requires a great capacity to withstand physical suffering. The hero is a solitary figure, in fact, doubly so: not only does he fight for abstractions rather than for individuals, but family and friends, by their very existence, make him vulnerable. The hero's education is an apprenticeship in isolation; it is also, of course, the time when his courage hardens and grows strong. The courageous act is, in fact, the most direct manifestation of heroism. Once again, Okulicki serves as example: in the heat of battle, he volunteers to attack an enemy machinegun nest; his pockets stuffed with hand grenades, he races alone across the open field. Here, courage is simply the willingness to risk one's life to attain a goal. Life is not the supreme value; indeed, it can be sacrificed at any time. When a clear goal is absent, however, or when the goal is an insignificant one, what we have is no longer heroism and bravery but bravado: one risks one's life for no particular reason. Okulicki, for example, hated to hide. "Bombs and shells were falling all around us," a witness reports. "The few people we came upon were dashing from one shelter to the next, and there was Okulicki strolling calmly down the middle of the street as though unaware of the danger" (Steiner 98). Conversely, a lack of courage is what the hero most despises in others.

The hero, then, is prepared to sacrifice his own life as well as the lives of others, provided the sacrifice advances the chosen goal. But even this stipulation ceases to matter—and here we are not speaking of bravado—the instant the hero decides to act on behalf of a beneficiary as remote as history or humanity: there is little risk of abstractions like these ever disappointing heroic expectations. That is why the leaders of the Warsaw Rising decided that it should take place "whatever the cost" (215). When the battle is fought for the benefit of no real, concrete individual, or

335

particular group of individuals, it becomes an end in itself, irrefutable proof of the heroic spirit of those who wage it. We must fight, Stefan Grot-Rowecki, who preceded Bor-Komorowski as commander of the Home Army, used to say, "even if a hopeless struggle awaits us" (Ciechanowski 137). "We shall all be massacred," predicts one of the rebels as events begin to unfold, "but at least we will have fought" (Steiner 190). Similarly, though in hindsight, Pelczynski declares, "It was our duty to fight; as far as I was concerned, nothing else mattered" (241).

Okulicki's reasoning is more elaborate. If the insurrection begins and the Russians come to our aid, he argues, the wager is won, but if they don't intervene, if they let the Germans massacre us, all is still not lost: Warsaw will be destroyed, many Poles will die, but the Soviet perfidy will be obvious to everyone; the Western powers will fight the Russians in a Third World War, and out of the ashes a new Poland will arise. . . . His predictions, of course, proved only partially correct: the Soviet forces did not support the Warsaw Rising, which, it bears repeating, was not only directed against the Germans, but also had the Russians in mind. The Germans put down the insurrection, killing 200,000 people, deporting 700,000, and leveling Warsaw. But World War III did not take place, and Poland became a satellite of the Soviet Union much as if the insurrection had never taken place. The goal, then, was not attained, yet if it had been, would it have been justified at such a price? What kinds of acts are those that must be done "whatever the cost"?

The leaders of the Warsaw Rising often seemed to be following the slogan "Better dead than Red." They felt their choice was either to revolt and die or to surrender and live. They preferred the first solution. "For a Pole," Okulicki declares, "it is better to die than to be a coward," and it was said of Pelczynski that "when he suddenly understood that he had no choice but to surrender or die, he chose to die" (107, 238). Bor-Komorowski also preferred action, however futile, to inaction. And Monter's order to the commanders of the Mokotow sector of Warsaw on the fifty-sixth day of the fighting reflects a similar outlook: "You are forbidden to withdraw," he said (Zawodny 22). This kind of heroic stance commands respect. Still, one wonders if the choice set out above reflected the real possibilities. "Red" is the opposite not of "dead" but of "white" or "brown" or "black," and in the final analysis it is only the living who have a color. One of the fighters who opposed the uprising put it this way: "If all of us continue trying to die for Poland, one day soon there won't be any Poles left to live here" (Steiner 108). And when the heroes of the Warsaw Rising were dead, Warsaw went Red all the same.

To the hero, death has more value than life. Only through death—whether one's own or that of others—is it possible to attain the absolute: by dying for an ideal one proves that one holds it dearer than life itself. "Despair had driven them to aspire to the absolute," one witness says, "and at that level there was no solution but to die" (230). Measured against aspirations for the absolute, real life necessarily seems an unsatisfactory compromise. As another witness observes, "Heroes are not made to live" (11).

Perhaps life and death are opposites in another sense as well. In certain exceptional circumstances like the Warsaw Rising dying is easy, particularly if one believes in the resurrection of the soul. But even if one does not, death remains an unknown, and that is its fascination. To sacrifice one's life is to put all one's courage into a single definitive act, whereas staying alive can require a daily, moment-by-moment kind of courage. Life, too, is sometimes a sacrifice, but it is not a flamboyant one: to sacrifice my time and energy, if that is what is demanded of me, I have to stay alive. In this sense, it can be more difficult to live than to die.

Those who opposed the plans for the Warsaw Rising did not do so in the name of some slogan that would have merely stood the heroic principle on its head; they did not say, "Better Red than dead" or "It is better to surrender than to die." That was what their adversaries wanted people to believe. After Okulicki had heard the objections, he "started calling us cowards, telling us we were dragging our feet on the decision because we weren't brave enough to fight" (248). As a result, there was no way to protest. "We hardly dared criticize the slightest proposal for fear of making ourselves seem like cowards or traitors" (171). This last comment is revealing: one can act like a hero for fear of seeming a coward. The hero is not necessarily intrepid. It is simply that he feels a particular kind of fear, the fear of being afraid, and that feeling takes priority over all others and finally eclipses them.

Those who disagreed with Okulicki chose not the other alternative but rather a different set of options entirely. According to one dissenter whom Steiner interviewed, the real choice was between "a serious political and military action" and "a suicide perpetrated by irresponsible leaders who sought refuge in a glorious death because they didn't have the courage to face the difficulties of life" (221). For this man, the courage to live is rarer and more precious than the courage to die. Another of Okulicki's opponents uses the term *responsibility* (249). Politics and war must not be carried out in the name of what Weber calls the ethics of conviction, because these things are not matters of principle. The fact that I hold a belief does not guarantee that the community as a whole will benefit if I go ahead and act on it. One needs to anticipate the consequences of one's decisions while keeping in mind the actual course of events, not merely what one wishes would happen. Here, the word *responsibility* recovers its original meaning—a leader *is responsible for* the lives and well-being of those he commands; at the same time, he *responds to* appeals from many different sources.

The hero's world—and perhaps herein lies his weakness—is one-dimensional; it is composed of pairs of opposites: us and them, friend and foe, courage and cowardice, hero and traitor, black and white. That outlook best befits situations in which the orientation is death, not life. In Warsaw of 1944, it was not simply the forces of good and evil that confronted each other but the Russians and the Germans, the Home Army and the People's Army, the government in exile and the civilian population. In circumstances this complex, reaching the best solution—in this instance, unfortunately, merely the lesser evil—requires a careful consideration of all sides rather than unswerving loyalty to an ideal. The values of life are not absolute values: life is diverse, and every situation is heterogeneous. Choices are made not out of concession or cowardly compromise but from a recognition of this multiplicity.

There is, however, a drawback to the nonheroic attitude: it does not lend itself well to stories, at least not to those in the traditional mold. Narratives, however, are indispensable for any society; in fact, heroes are themselves invariably inspired by literary or legendary example, usually impressed upon them in childhood. Even in the heat of the moment, the hero already foresees the effect his deed will produce once translated into words: the future story, the story that will one day be told, shapes the present. Okulicki, for example, criticizes other plans for the revolt as "not being spectacular enough," while his own plan is one of which "the whole world will speak" (106, 107). The insurgents' bulletin of October 3, 1944, declares, "Nobody in Poland, or in Warsaw, or in the whole world can . . . say that we surrendered too soon" (Zawodny 194). Concern for what will later be said is present at the very moment of action. The rebels understood themselves to be writing, as the time-honored formula has it, "one of the most glorious pages in the history of Poland." Thus, when Pelczynski realizes that Steiner, his interviewer, has no compelling interest in glorifying heroes, he becomes indignant: "If this is how you plan to write your book," he complains, "we might as well end this conversation right now" (Steiner 260). Beautiful tales need unblemished heroes. Spirits of a more practical bent, who take the constraints of reality into account, do not make particularly good narrative subjects. Prime Minister Mikolajczyk seems to have been such a man. "He didn't see himself as Christ or Saint George or the Virgin Mary," a witness says (58). How, then, is someone like him to be made into the hero of a tale?

THE GHETTO, 1943

The relation between heroism and narrative is also one of the main themes in *Shielding the Flame*, the second book that had been recommended to me in Poland. Written in the 1970s, this book, too, is constructed around a series of interviews, but between just two people, Hanna Krall and Marek Edelman, a leader of the other uprising in Warsaw, the ghetto revolt of 1943. And whereas *Varsovie 44* presents a montage in which the author does not appear, Krall decided that she herself should figure in the text.

The Warsaw ghetto uprising is another of the most glorious pages of history, in this case, the history of Jewish heroism; this has been said a thousand times. But it so happens that Edelman could not produce a truly heroic account of the events, at least not until some time after they had occurred. Krall describes Edelman's very first attempt to do so, three days after escaping from the ghetto, as he delivers a report to the representatives of various underground political parties. He gives a neutral account, flat and colorless, a simple description of what had just taken place. We lacked weapons and experience, he says. The Germans fought well. Deeply disappointed by the mediocre quality of the narrative, Edelman's audience attributed it to the state of shock its author must have been in at the time. "He was not talking the way he was supposed to talk. 'How is one supposed to talk?' Edelman asked me. One is supposed to talk with hatred and grandiloquence—one is supposed to scream. There's no other way to express all this except by screaming. And so, from the very beginning, he was no good at talking about it because he was unable to scream. He was no good as a hero because he lacked grandiloquence" (Krall and Edelman 14–15).

Hatred of the enemy, high emotion (pathos), a feverish tone (shouting, scream-ing): these are the ingredients missing from Edelman's report. On the other hand, they are not entirely absent from his text of 1945, a sober account (included in the French edition of the book) that nonetheless seeks to bring out the rebels' heroism. Thirty years later, when Edelman looks back on these events in his interview with Krall, he sees himself as a young man who wanted to imitate the conventional hero. Back then, he says, his dream was to run around "with two guns strapped to [his] body; the guns completed the outfit, very *de rigueur*. You figured in those days if you had two guns, you had everything" (1–2). He realizes now to what extent this desire to see himself as a hero figured in his attraction to firearms, in the very act of pulling the trigger. "People have always thought that shooting is the highest form of heroism," Edelman says. "So we shot" (3).

But now he sees things very differently. What actually took place seems to him to belie the official, heroic version of events. "Can you even call that an uprising?" he asks. "All it was about, finally, was our not letting them slaughter us when our turn came. It was only a choice as to the manner of dying" (10). Mordechai Anielewicz, the principal leader of the uprising, whose "heroic posture" Edelman had celebrated thirty years before, now appears in a different light: he is no less sympathetic a char-acter, of course, but neither is he so completely an object of idolatry. If Anielewicz was elected to lead the uprising, Edelman says, it was "because he very much wanted to be a commander." And, he adds, "he was a little childish in this ambition" (22). Edel-man also tells how Anielewicz, as a young boy, would apply red dye to the gills of the fish his mother sold, so that the fish would look fresh. This anecdote, translated into several languages, "angered many people," for Edelman "had stripped everything of its magnitude" (4, 10). The public—like Pelczynski, in his interview with Steiner—wants its heroes heroic.

Edelman insists on telling his story exactly as he remembers it, however, and not according to the conventions of heroic narrative. The desire for absolute accuracy leads him to observations like "In the Ghetto, there should only have been martyrs and Joan of Arcs, right? But if you want to know, in the bunker on Mila Street, together with Anielewicz's group, there were some prostitutes and even a pimp. A big tattooed guy, with huge biceps . . ." (42). Edelman claims, moreover, that he survived not be-cause of some act of heroism but because the SS man who shot at him must have had an uncorrected astigmatism: all the bullets fell a little too far to the right (43).

This is not to say, of course, that the ghetto uprising did not give rise to acts of heroism like those of Okulicki. There was Michal Klepfisz, for instance, who threw himself onto a German machine gun so that his comrades could escape. While Edel-man clearly admires acts of this sort, they do not truly capture his imagination. What interests him are actions of a different sort, equally virtuous but distinct enough from those with which we have been dealing that we need a different term to describe them. Let us then use the term *heroic virtues* in speaking of Okulicki and the term *ordinary virtues* to describe the cases that Edelman reports.

Like heroic virtues, the ordinary virtues are acts of will, individual efforts of re-fusal to accept what seems an implacable necessity. But such willful determination does not lead to the conclusion that "there is no order that cannot be carried out." In truth, it doesn't *lead* anywhere at all, because it provides its own justification. Edelman describes how he decided one day to become a resistance fighter. Walking down Zelazna Street in the ghetto, he saw an old man who had been hoisted up onto a barrel by two German officers; they were cutting off his beard with a huge pair of tailor's scissors and were doubled over with laughter. "At that moment, I realized that the most important thing was never letting myself be pushed onto the top of that barrel. Never, by anybody" (38). What Edelman understood is, first, that there is no qualitative difference between great and small humiliations and, second, that one can always express one's will, choose one's actions—and refuse to follow orders. The uprising may have been nothing more than a way for us to choose our death, he says. But the difference between choosing death and submitting to it is enormous; it is this difference that separates human beings from animals. In choosing one's death, one performs an act of will and thereby affirms one's membership in the human race. The Jews of Warsaw took no pride in the fact that Jews in some of the other Polish cities had let themselves be slaughtered; they decided that they, for their part, would act. In so doing, they had already achieved their goal: they had affirmed their humanity.

"To choose between life and death is the last chance to hold onto one's dignity," Hanna Krall observes (46). *Dignity:* this, then, is the first ordinary virtue, and it simply means the capacity of the individual to remain a subject with a will; that fact, by itself, is enough to ensure membership in the human race. To choose death means something very different from what it means in the context of the heroic virtues. For the hero, death eventually becomes a value and a goal, because it embodies the absolute better than life does. From the standpoint of the ordinary virtues, however, death is a means, not an end: it is the ultimate recourse of the individual who seeks to affirm his dignity.

Thus, suicide is valued not in itself but rather as an expression of will. Yet even the suicide that has the assertion of dignity as its goal is not always, from the perspective of the ordinary virtues, a truly admirable act. Dignity is a necessary but not a sufficient condition, as Edelman's description of two very famous suicides suggests. The first is that of Adam Czerniakow, president of the Jewish Council set up by the Germans, who killed himself in his office on learning of the decision to deport the residents of the ghetto to Treblinka. "We reproached him for having made his death his own private business. We were convinced that it was necessary to die publicly, in the eyes of the world" (9–10). In *Notes from the Warsaw Ghetto*, Emmanuel Ringelblum, the great historian of the ghetto, echoes that opinion: "The suicide of Czerniakow—too late, a sign of weakness—should have called for resistance—a weak man" (327). In choosing to take his own life without revealing to the community the fate that awaited it, without exhorting the people to fight back, Czerniakow acted with dignity but without real concern for others. It's not that he was oblivious to his community; the journal in which he set down his thoughts and impressions makes that clear. And in his suicide note, he writes, "I am powerless, my heart trembles in sorrow and compassion. I can no longer bear all this. My act will show everyone the right thing to do" (Hilberg et al. 344). Czerniakow means to address his contemporaries, but he chooses to do so in such a way that they cannot hear him. Was suicide really his only option?

The second suicide (which in fact may not have been a suicide at all) is that of Mordechai Anielewicz, the young commander of the ghetto rebels. "He should never have done it," Edelman says. "Even though it was a very good symbol. You don't sacrifice your life for a symbol" (6). (Sosnkowski says the exact opposite, that the symbol is precisely the thing one should die for.) Two suicides, in many ways different—one too private, the other too symbolic—but with much in common nevertheless: each takes into consideration the remote beneficiary of the act, history, and each neglects those who are most directly affected, the other inhabitants of the ghetto. Thus, instead of serving as a means of helping others, the suicides were acts that began and ended with themselves.

This further requirement of virtuous acts, that they not only demonstrate the dignity of their authors but also contribute to the welfare of others, might be called *caring*. Caring, or concern, is the second ordinary virtue: acts of ordinary virtue are undertaken not in behalf of humanity or the nation but always for the sake of an individual human being. Concern for others carries with it certain rewards. There are things we can do for others that we are incapable of doing solely for ourselves, and so concern for others can keep us from giving up. "Everybody had to have somebody to act for, somebody to be the center of his life," Edelman recounts. "To be with someone was the only way to survive in the ghetto. . . . So if someone, somehow, by some miracle escaped and was still alive, he had to stick to some other human being" (42–43, 48).

On the subject of those who died because they cared for someone else, Edelman is no longer reticent at all; on the contrary, it is precisely these acts of ordinary virtue that make the strongest impression on him. And so we learn of a young girl named Pola Lifszyc and what she did as the transport convoys began to leave for Treblinka. "She went to her house and . . . saw that her mother wasn't there," Edelman says. "Her mother was already in a column marching toward the *Umschlagplatz*. Pola ran after the column alone, from Leszno Street to Stawki Street. Her fiancé gave her a lift in his *riksa* so that she could catch up—and she made it. At the last minute, she managed to merge into the crowd so as to be able to get on the train with her mother" (45). (The train, of course, was one of those whose passengers never returned to their point of departure.) Why was Pola in such a hurry? Did her fiancé have any idea what his bicycle was being used for?

Edelman tells us of a nurse named Mrs. Tenenbaum who had obtained a pass that permitted its bearer to avoid deportation—temporarily. Her daughter did not have one, and so Mrs. Tenenbaum handed the pass to her, asking her to hold it for a moment, then went upstairs and swallowed a fatal dose of Luminal, thereby avoiding any and all discussion. During the three months following what amounted to a temporary stay of execution, the time afforded her by the pass, Mrs. Tenenbaum's daughter fell in love and knew real happiness. Edelman tells another story, of a niece of Tosia Goliborska, one of his colleagues, who, immediately after her wedding ceremony, found the barrel of a soldier's rifle shoved up against her belly. Her new husband put out his hand to protect her, only to have it blown off. "But this was precisely what mattered," Edelman says, "that there be someone ready to cover your belly with his hand should it prove necessary" (48–49).

Most often, the beneficiary of such concern was a family member—a mother or daughter, brother or sister, husband or wife. But with so many loved ones gone, other "relatives" were found, people who acted as "surrogates." And even when the surrogate beneficiary was not one person but many—like the children whom Dr. Janusz Korczak accompanied from his orphanage to Treblinka so that they would not go alone or the fellow Jews whom Abraham Gepner, a rich industrialist, chose to remain with—the beneficiaries were never an abstraction but individuals of flesh and blood, personally known to the subject. To fall short of such concern was not necessarily cause for blame, but it did mean a tacit breach of the human contract, as an episode related by one of Steiner's eyewitnesses illustrates. After the uprising of 1943 and before the Warsaw Rising of 1944, this witness came upon the Christian husband of a Jewish woman in the ruins of the ghetto. Like Pola, this woman had made the decision to go with her relatives on the transport train; her husband chose to stay behind. Although she did not reproach him for his decision, something between them had been severed nonetheless. "What she wanted," said the husband, "was for me to have gone to die with her. Instead, I let her go and I let her die. And I've been atoning ever since" (Steiner 202).

Sometimes caring can lead people to take not their own lives but, paradoxically, the lives of others. A doctor poisons the children in the hospital where she works, before the SS has a chance to take them away. "She saved these children from the gas chamber," Edelman says. But in order to do so, she had to sacrifice her own poison. "[The nurses] were saving this poison for their closest relatives. And this doctor had given her *own* cyanide to kids who were complete strangers!" (9). It is precisely in this sense that to live can be more difficult than to die. Edelman also tells of the nurse who was attending a woman in childbirth on the second floor of a hospital as the Germans were clearing out the first. When the baby was born, "the doctor handed it to the nurse, and the nurse laid it on one pillow, then smothered it with another one. The baby whimpered a little, and then fell silent" (47). The nurse did what had to be done; no one reproached her for it. Nevertheless, forty-five years later this nurse, Adina Blady Szwajger, now a pediatrician, cannot forget that she began her medical career by taking a life.

Ordinary virtues, then, have distinct characteristics very much in evidence even after the end of the war. Edelman's circumstances are less dramatic now, and he is no longer called upon to risk his life; his earlier choices, however, have steered him toward a new profession: he has become a cardiologist. "As a doctor, I can now be responsible for human lives," he declares. "But why would I want this responsibility? Doubtless because everything else seems unimportant to me" (126). Responsibility is a particular form of caring, the form incumbent on people in privileged positions, like doctors or leaders. Indeed, it is for not having seen their responsibilities through that Anielewicz and Czerniakow fell short—although in different ways—of what caring demanded.

These two kinds of virtue—the ordinary and the heroic—differ with respect to the beneficiaries of the acts they inspire: acts of ordinary virtue benefit individuals, a Miss Tenenbaum, for example, whereas acts of heroism can be undertaken for the benefit of something as abstract as a certain concept of Poland. Both kinds of virtue, however, demand courage and the sacrifice of energy or life. And both can call for a split-second decision—whether Okulicki's attack on an enemy machine-gun nest or Pola's leap onto her fiancé's bicycle. Heroic virtues tend to be the province of men, while ordinary virtues are equally if not more characteristic of women (but it is true that the physical abilities required are different). Yet the real difference comes down to the question of whether it is for people or ideas that one has chosen to die (or live).

This opposition is not to be confused with the opposition between the particular and the general, that is, between loyalty to one's own group and a love of humanity as a whole. To be loyal to one's compatriots alone means not to care about foreigners; but foreigners are individuals like everyone else. And "humanity" need not be interpreted as a mere abstraction, the way the leaders of the 1944 Warsaw Rising understood it; it can also mean the community of all concrete human beings. Moral obligation—to care for a person—can be universal without being abstract. Therefore, those who prefer their own kind exclusively, who act out of blind loyalty, do not necessarily value people more than ideas; they value certain individuals more than others. Yet by the same token, those who see humanity as an abstraction can also commit crimes in its name—and all the more easily in that, depending on the moment and the people involved, ideas can mask very different realities. Indeed, those ideas that seem the purest and most generous and disinterested are often made to serve the most tragic ventures. After all, Hitler used to say that he was fighting the Russians in order to halt barbarism and rescue civilization. With human beings, however, there is no such danger: they represent only themselves.

Wouldn't You Rather Be at Home?

The Internet and the Myth of the Powerful Self

Ellen Ullman

Ellen Ullman is a software engineering consultant and writer based in San Francisco, who has been involved in the computer industry since 1978. She is the author of Close to the Machine: Technophilia and Its Discontents *(City Lights, 1997). Her writings have also appeared in* Harper's *magazine and in several anthologies among which* Resisting the Virtual Life, *and* Wired Women: Gender and New Realities in Cyberspace *(ed. Lynn Cherny and Elizabeth Reba Wise, Seal Press, 1996), as well as at* salon.com. *She is a commentator on National Public Radio's "All Things Considered."*

Years ago, before the Internet as we know it had come into existence—I think it was around Christmas, in 1990—I was at a friend's house, where her nine-year-old son and his friend were playing the video game that was the state of the art at the time, Sonic the Hedgehog. They jumped around in front of the TV and gave off the sort of rude noises boys tend to make when they're shooting at things in a video game, and after about half an hour they stopped and tried to talk about what they'd just been doing. The dialogue went something like this:

"I wiped out at that part with the ladders."

"Ladders? What ladders?"

"You know, after the rooms."

"Oh, you mean the stairs?"

"No, I think they were ladders. I remember, because I died there twice."

"I never killed you around any ladders. I killed you where you jump down off this wall."

"Wall? You mean by the gates of the city?"

"Are there gates around the city? I always called it the castle."

The boys muddled along for several more minutes, making themselves more confused as they went. Finally they gave up trying to talk about their time with Sonic the Hedgehog. They just looked at each other and shrugged.

I didn't think about the two boys and Sonic again until I watched my clients try out the World Wide Web. By then it was 1995, the Internet as we know it was beginning to exist, but the two women who worked for my client, whom I'd just helped get online, had never before connected to the Internet or surfed the Web. They took to it instantly, each disappearing into nearly an hour of obsessive clicking, after which they tried to talk about it:

"It was great! I clicked that thing and went to this place. I don't remember its name."

"Yeah. It was a link. I clicked here and went there."

"Oh, I'm not sure it was a link. The thing I clicked was a picture of the library."

"Was it the library? I thought it was a picture of City Hall."

"Oh, no. I'm sure it was the library."

"No, City Hall. I'm sure because of the dome."

"Dome? Was there a dome?"

Right then I remembered Sonic and the two boys; my clients, like the two boys, had experienced something pleasurable and engaging, and they very much wanted to talk about it—talking being one of the primary ways human beings augment their pleasure. But what had happened to them, each in her own electronic world, resisted description. Like the boys, the two women fell into verbal confusion. How could they speak coherently about a world full of little wordless pictograms, about trails that led off in all directions, of idle visits to virtual places chosen on a whim-click?

Following hyperlinks on the Web is like the synaptic drift of dreams, a loosening of intention, the mind associating freely, an experience that can be compelling or baffling or unsettling, or all of those things at once. And like dreams, the experience of the Web is intensely private, charged with immanent meaning for the person inside the experience, but often confusing or irrelevant to someone else.

At the time, I had my reservations about the Web, but not so much about the private, dreamlike state it offered. Web surfing seemed to me not so much antisocial as asocial, an adventure like a video game or pinball, entertaining, sometimes interesting, sometimes a trivial waste of time; but in a social sense it seemed harmless, since only the person engaged in the activity was affected.

Something changed, however, not in me but in the Internet and the Web and in the world, and the change was written out in person-high letters on a billboard on the corner of Howard and New Montgomery Streets in San Francisco. It was the fall of 1998. I was walking toward Market Street one afternoon when I saw it, a background of brilliant sky blue, with writing on it in airy white letters, which said: *now the world really does revolve around you.* The letters were lower-case, soft-edged, spaced irregularly, as if they'd been skywritten over a hot August beach and were already drifting off into the air. The message they left behind was a child's secret wish, the ultimate baby-world narcissism we are all supposed to abandon when we grow up: the world really does revolve around me.

What was this billboard advertising? Perfume? A resort? There was nothing else on it but the airy, white letters, and I had to walk right up to it to see a URL written at the bottom; it was the name of a company that makes semiconductor equipment, machinery used by companies like Intel and AMD to manufacture integrated circuits. Oh, chips, I thought. Computers. Of course. What other subject produces such hyperbole? Who else but someone in the computer industry could make such a shameless appeal to individualism?

The billboard loomed over the corner for the next couple of weeks. Every time I passed it, its message irritated me more. It bothered me the way the "My Computer" icon bothers me on the Windows desktop, baby names like "My Yahoo" and "My Snap"; my, my, my; two-year-old talk; infantilizing and condescending.

But there was something more disturbing about this billboard, and I tried to figure out why, since it simply was doing what every other piece of advertising does: whispering in your ear that there is no one like you in the entire world, and what we are offering is for you, special you, and you alone. What came to me was this: Toyota, for example, sells the idea of a special, individual buyer ("It's not for everyone, just for you"), but chip makers, through the medium of the Internet and the World Wide Web, are creating the actual infrastructure of an individualized marketplace.

What had happened between 1995, when I could still think of the Internet as a private dream, and the appearance of that billboard in 1998 was the near-complete commercialization of the Web. And that commercialization had proceeded in a very particular and single-minded way: by attempting to isolate the individual within a sea of economic activity. Through a process known as "disintermediation," producers have worked to remove the expert intermediaries, agents, brokers, middlemen, who until now have influenced our interactions with the commercial world. What bothered me about the billboard, then, was that its message was not merely hype but the reflection of a process that was already under way: an attempt to convince the individual that a change currently being visited upon him or her is a good thing, the purest form of self, the equivalent of freedom. The world really does revolve around you.

In Silicon Valley, in Redmond, Washington, the home of Microsoft, and in the smaller silicon alleys of San Francisco and New York, "disintermediation" is a word so common that people shrug when you try to talk to them about it. Oh, disintermediation, that old thing. Everyone already knows about that. It has become accepted wisdom, a process considered inevitable, irrefutable, good.

I've long believed that the ideas embedded in technology have a way of percolating up and outward into the nontechnical world at large, and that technology is made by people with intentions and, as such, is not neutral. In the case of disintermediation, an explicit and purposeful change is being visited upon the structure of the global marketplace. And in a world so dominated by markets, I don't think I go too far in saying that this will affect the very structure of reality, for the Net is no longer simply a zone of personal freedoms, a pleasant diversion from what we used to call "real life"; it has become an actual marketplace that is changing the nature of real life itself.

Removal of the intermediary. All those who stand in the middle of a transaction, whether financial or intellectual: out! Brokers and agents and middlemen of every description: good-bye! Travel agents, real-estate agents, insurance agents, stockbrokers, mortgage brokers, consolidators, and jobbers, all the scrappy percentniks who troll the bywaters of capitalist exchange—who needs you? All those hard-striving immigrants climbing their way into the lower middle class through the penny-ante deals of capitalism, the transfer points too small for the big guys to worry about—find yourself some other way to make a living. Small retailers and store clerks, salespeople of every kind—a hindrance, idiots, not to be trusted. Even the professional handlers of intellectual goods, anyone who sifts through information, books, paintings, knowledge, selecting and summing up: librarians, book reviewers, curators, disc jockeys, teachers, editors, analysts—why trust anyone but yourself to make judgments about what is more or less interesting, valuable, authentic, or worthy of your attention? No one, no professional interloper, is supposed to come between you and your desires, which, according to this idea, are nuanced, difficult to communicate, irreducible, unique.

The Web did not cause disintermediation, but it is what we call an "enabling technology": a technical breakthrough that takes a difficult task and makes it suddenly doable, easy; it opens the door to change, which then comes in an unconsidered, breathless rush.

We are living through an amazing experiment: an attempt to construct a capitalism without salespeople, to take a system founded upon the need to sell ever greater numbers of goods to ever growing numbers of people, and to do this without the aid of professional distribution channels—without buildings, sidewalks, shops, luncheonettes, street vendors, buses, trams, taxis, other women in the fitting room to tell you how you look in something and to help you make up your mind, without street people panhandling, Santas ringing bells at Christmas, shop women with their perfect makeup and elegant clothes, fashionable men and women strolling by to show you the latest look—in short, an attempt to do away with the city in all its messy stimulation, to abandon the agora for home and hearth, where it is safe and everything can be controlled.

The first task in this newly structured capitalism is to convince consumers that the services formerly performed by myriad intermediaries are useless or worse, that those commissioned brokers and agents are incompetent, out for themselves, dishonest. And the next task is to glorify the notion of self-service. Where companies once vied for your business by telling you about their courteous people and how well they would serve you—"Avis, We Try Harder"—their job now is to make you believe that only you can take care of yourself. The lure of personal service that was dangled before the middle classes, momentarily making us all feel almost as lucky as the rich, is being withdrawn. In the Internet age, under the pressure of globalized

347

capitalism and its slimmed-down profit margins, only the very wealthy will be served by actual human beings. The rest of us must make do with Web pages, and feel happy about it.

One evening while I was watching television, I looked up to see a commercial that seemed to me to be the most explicit statement of the ideas implicit in the disiater-mediated universe. I gaped at it, because usually such ideas are kept implicit, hidden behind symbols. But this commercial was like the sky-blue billboard: a shameless and naked expression of the Web world, a glorification of the self, at home, alone.

It begins with a drone, a footstep in a puddle, then a ragged band pulling a dead car through the mud—road warriors with bandanas around their foreheads carrying braziers. Now we see rafts of survivors floating before the ruins of a city, the sky dark, red-tinged, as if fires were burning all around us, just over the horizon. Next we are outside the dead city's library, where stone lions, now coated in gold and come to life, rear up in despair. Inside the library, red-coated Fascist guards encircle the readers at the table. A young girl turns a page, loudly, and the guards say, "Shush!" in time to their march-step. We see the title of the book the girl is reading: *Paradise Lost.* The bank, too, is a scene of ruin. A long line snakes outside it in a dreary rain. Inside, the teller is a man with a white, spectral face, who gazes upon the black spider that is slowly crawling up his window. A young woman's face ages right before us, and in response, in ridicule, the bank guard laughs. The camera now takes us up over the roofs of this post-apocalyptic city. Lightning crashes in the dark, red-tinged sky. On a telephone pole, where the insulators should be, are skulls.

Cut to a cartoon of emerald-green grass, hills, a Victorian house with a white picket fence and no neighbors. A butterfly flaps above it. What a relief this house is after the dreary, dangerous, ruined city. The door to this charming house opens, and we go in to see a chair before a computer screen. Yes, we want to go sit in that chair, in that room with candy-orange walls. On the computer screen, running by in teasing succession, are pleasant virtual reflections of the world outside: written text, a bank check, a telephone pole, which now signifies our connection to the world. The camera pans back to show a window, a curtain swinging in the breeze, and our sense of calm is complete. We hear the Intel-Inside jingle, which sounds almost like chimes. Cut to the legend: Packard Bell. Wouldn't you rather be at home?

In sixty seconds, this commercial communicates a worldview that reflects the ultimate suburbanization of existence: a retreat from the friction of the social space to the supposed idyll of private ease. It is a view that depends on the idea that desire is not social, not stimulated by what others want, but generated internally, and that the satisfaction of desires is not dependent upon other persons, organizations, structures, or governments. It is a profoundly libertarian vision, and it is the message that underlies all the mythologizing about the Web: the idea that the civic space is dead, useless, dangerous. The only place of pleasure and satisfaction is your home. You, home, family; and beyond that, the world. From the intensely private to the global, with little in between but an Intel processor and a search engine.

In this sense, the ideal of the Internet represents the very opposite of democracy, which is a method for resolving differences in a relatively orderly manner through the mediation of unavoidable civil associations. Yet there can be no notion of resolving differences in a world where each person is entitled to get exactly what he or she wants. Here all needs and desires are equally valid and equally powerful. I'll get mine and you'll get yours; there is no need for compromise and discussion. I don't have to tolerate you, and you don't have to tolerate me. No need for messy debate and the whole rigmarole of government with all its creaky, bothersome structures. There's no need for any of this, because now that we have the World Wide Web the problem of the pursuit of happiness has been solved! We'll each click for our individual joys, and our only dispute may come if something doesn't get delivered on time. Wouldn't you really rather be at home?

But who can afford to stay at home? Only the very wealthy or a certain class of knowledge worker can stay home and click. On the other side of this ideal of work-anywhere freedom (if indeed it is freedom never to be away from work) is the reality that somebody had to make the thing you ordered with a click. Somebody had to put it in a box, do the paperwork, carry it to you. The reality is a world divided not only between the haves and have-nots but between the ones who get to stay home and everyone else, the ones who deliver the goods to them.

The Net ideal represents a retreat not only from political life but also from culture—from that tumultuous conversation in which we try to talk to one another about our shared experiences. As members of a culture, we see the same movie, read the same book, hear the same string quartet. Although it is difficult for us to agree on what we might have seen, read, or heard, it is out of that difficult conversation that real culture arises. Whether or not we come to an agreement or understanding, even if some decide that understanding and meaning are impossible, we are still sitting around the same campfire.

But the Web as it has evolved is based on the idea that we do not even want a shared experience. The director of San Francisco's Museum of Modem Art once told an audience that we no longer need a building to house works of art; we don't need to get dressed, go downtown, walk from room to room among crowds of other people. Now that we have the Web, we can look at anything we want whenever we want, and we no longer need him or his curators. "You don't have to walk through *my* idea of what's interesting to look at," he said to a questioner in the audience named Bill. "On the Web," said the director, "you can create the museum of Bill."

And so, by implication, there can be the museums of George and Mary and Helene. What then will this group have to say to one another about art? Let's say the museum of Bill is featuring early Dutch masters, the museum of Mary is playing video art, and the museum of Helene is displaying French tapestries. In this privatized world, what sort of "cultural" conversation can there be? What can one of us possibly say to another about our experience except, "Today I visited the museum of me, and I liked it."

Why Literature?

Mario Vargas Llosa

Mario Vargas Llosa was born in Arequipa, Peru. After his parents separated he was brought up by his mother and maternal grandparents in Cochabamba, Bolivia, Piura, northern Peru, and then in Lima. He attended Leoncio Prado Military Academy, and Colegio Nacional San Miguel de Piura. He later moved to Europe and lived in Spain and France. He worked as a journalist, an editor, and broadcaster. From the late 1960s, Vargas Llosa worked as a visiting professor at many American and European universities. He has always been politically engaged, and in 1990 he was a conservative candidate (Fredemo, the Democratic Front) for the Peruvian presidency. He was not elected and continued his life as a writer and teacher of literature on the international scene. His books include: The Time of the Hero *(1962)*, Aunt Julia and the Scriptwriter *(1977)*, The Green House *(1966)*, The War of the End of the World *(1981)*, The Real life of Alejandro Mayta *(1984)*, The Storyteller *(1984)*, The Language of Passion *(2001)*, and many others.*

It has often happened to me, at book fairs or in bookstores, that a gentleman approaches me and asks me for a signature. "It is for my wife, my young daughter, or my mother," he explains. "She is a great reader and loves literature." Immediately I ask: "And what about you? Don't you like to read?" The answer is almost always the same: "Of course I like to read, but I am a very busy person." I have heard this explanation dozens of times: this man and many thousands of men like him have so many important things to do, so many obligations, so many responsibilities in life, that they cannot waste their precious time buried in a novel, a book of poetry, or a literary essay for hours and hours. According to this widespread conception, literature is a dispensable

Reprinted from *The New Republic*, May 14, 2001.

activity, no doubt lofty and useful for cultivating sensitivity and good manners, but essentially an entertainment, an adornment that only people with time for recreation can afford. It is something to fit in between sports, the movies, a game of bridge or chess; and it can be sacrificed without scruple when one "prioritizes" the tasks and the duties that are indispensable in the struggle of life.

It seems clear that literature has become more and more a female activity. In bookstores, at conferences or public readings by writers, and even in university departments dedicated to the humanities, the women clearly outnumber the men. The explanation traditionally given is that middle-class women read more because they work fewer hours than men, and so many of them feel that they can justify more easily than men the time that they devote to fantasy and illusion. I am somewhat allergic to explanations that divide men and women into frozen categories and attribute to each sex its characteristic virtues and shortcomings; but there is no doubt that there are fewer and fewer readers of literature, and that among the saving remnant of readers women predominate.

This is the case almost everywhere. In Spain, for example, a recent survey organized by the General Society of Spanish Writers revealed that half of that country's population has never read a book. The survey also revealed that in the minority that does read, the number of women who admitted to reading surpasses the number of men by 6.2 percent, a difference that appears to be increasing. I am happy for these women, but I feel sorry for these men, and for the millions of human beings who could read but have decided not to read.

They earn my pity not only because they are unaware of the pleasure that they are missing, but also because I am convinced that a society without literature, or a society in which literature has been relegated—like some hidden vice—to the margins of social and personal life, and transformed into something like a sectarian cult, is a society condemned to become spiritually barbaric, and even to jeopardize its freedom. I wish to offer a few arguments against the idea of literature as a luxury pastime, and in favor of viewing it as one of the most primary and necessary undertakings of the mind, an irreplaceable activity for the formation of citizens in a modern and democratic society, a society of free individuals.

We live in the era of the specialization of knowledge, thanks to the prodigious development of science and technology and to the consequent fragmentation of knowledge into innumerable parcels and compartments. This cultural trend is, if anything, likely to be accentuated in years to come. To be sure, specialization brings many benefits. It allows for deeper exploration and greater experimentation; it is the very engine of progress. Yet it also has negative consequences, for it eliminates those common intellectual and cultural traits that permit men and women to coexist, to communicate, to feel a sense of solidarity. Specialization leads to a lack of social understanding, to the division of human beings into ghettos of technicians and specialists. The specialization of knowledge requires specialized languages and increasingly arcane codes, as information becomes more and more specific and compartmentalized. This is the particularism and the division against which an old proverb warned us: do not

351

focus too much on the branch or the leaf, lest you forget that they are part of a tree, or too much on the tree, lest you forget that it is part of a forest. Awareness of the existence of the forest creates the feeling of generality, the feeling of belonging, that binds society together and prevents it from disintegrating into a myriad of solipsistic particularities. The solipsism of nations and individuals produces paranoia and delirium, distortions of reality that generate hatred, wars, and even genocide.

In our time, science and technology cannot play an integrating role, precisely because of the infinite richness of knowledge and the speed of its evolution, which have led to specialization and its obscurities. But literature has been, and will continue to be, as long as it exists, one of the common denominators of human experience through which human beings may recognize themselves and converse with each other, no matter how different their professions, their life plans, their geographical and cultural locations, their personal circumstances. It has enabled individuals, in all the particularities of their lives, to transcend history: as readers of Cervantes, Shakespeare, Dante, and Tolstoy, we understand each other across space and time, and we feel ourselves to be members of the same species because, in the works that these writers created, we learn what we share as human beings, what remains common in all of us under the broad range of differences that separate us. Nothing better protects a human being against the stupidity of prejudice, racism, religious or political sectarianism, and exclusivist nationalism than this truth that invariably appears in great literature: that men and women of all nations and places are essentially equal, and that only injustice sows among them discrimination, fear, and exploitation.

Nothing teaches us better than literature to see, in ethnic and cultural differences, the richness of the human patrimony, and to prize those differences as a manifestation of humanity's multifaceted creativity. Reading good literature is an experience of pleasure, of course; but it is also an experience of learning what and how we are, in our human integrity and our human imperfection, with our actions, our dreams, and our ghosts, alone and in relationships that link us to others, in our public image and in the secret recesses of our consciousness.

This complex sum of contradictory truths—as Isaiah Berlin called them—constitutes the very substance of the human condition. In today's world, this totalizing and living knowledge of a human being may be found only in literature. Not even the other branches of the humanities—not philosophy, history, or the arts, and certainly not the social sciences—have been able to preserve this integrating vision, this universalizing discourse. The humanities, too, have succumbed to the cancerous division and subdivision of knowledge, isolating themselves in increasingly segmented and technical sectors whose ideas and vocabularies lie beyond the reach of the common woman and man. Some critics and theorists would even like to change literature into a science. But this will never happen, because fiction does not exist to investigate only a single precinct of experience. It exists to enrich through the imagination the entirety of human life, which cannot be dismembered, disarticulated, or reduced to a series of schemas or formulas without disappearing. This is the meaning of Proust's observation that "real life, at last enlightened and revealed, the only life fully lived, is literature." He was not exaggerating, nor was he expressing only his love for his own vocation. He was advancing the particular proposition that as a result of literature life is better understood and better lived; and that living life more fully necessitates living it and sharing it with others.

The brotherly link that literature establishes among human beings, compelling them to enter into dialogue and making them conscious of a common origin and a common goal, transcends all temporal barriers. Literature transports us into the past and links us to those who in bygone eras plotted, enjoyed, and dreamed through those texts that have come down to us, texts that now allow us also to enjoy and to dream. This feeling of membership in the collective human experience across time and space is the highest achievement of culture, and nothing contributes more to its renewal in every generation than literature.

It always irritated Borges when he was asked, "What is the use of literature?" It seemed to him a stupid question, to which he would reply: "No one would ask what is the use of a canary's song or a beautiful sunset." If such beautiful things exist, and if, thanks to them, life is even for an instant less ugly and less sad, is it not petty to seek practical justifications? But the question is a good one. For novels and poems are not like the sound of birdsong or the spectacle of the sun sinking into the horizon, because they were not created by chance or by nature. They are human creations, and it is therefore legitimate to ask how and why they came into the world, and what is their purpose, and why they have lasted so long.

Literary works are born, as shapeless ghosts, in the intimacy of a writer's consciousness, projected into it by the combined strength of the unconscious, and the writer's sensitivity to the world around him, and the writer's emotions; and it is these things to which the poet or the narrator, in a struggle with words, gradually gives form, body, movement, rhythm, harmony, and life. An artificial life, to be sure, a life imagined, a life made of language—yet men and women seek out this artificial life, some frequently, others sporadically, because real life falls short for them, and is incapable of offering them what they want. Literature does not begin to exist through the work of a single individual. It exists only when it is adopted by others and becomes a part of social life—when it becomes, thanks to reading, a shared experience.

One of its first beneficial effects takes place at the level of language. A community without a written literature expresses itself with less precision with less richness of nuance, and with less clarity than a community whose principal instrument of communication, the word, has been cultivated and perfected by means of literary texts. A humanity without reading, untouched by literature, would resemble a community of deaf-mutes and aphasics, afflicted by tremendous problems of communication due to its crude and rudimentary language. This is true for individuals, too. A person who does not read, or reads little, or reads only trash, is a person with an impediment: he can speak much but he will say little, because his vocabulary is deficient in the means for self-expression.

This is not only a verbal limitation. It represents also a limitation in intellect and in imagination. It is a poverty of thought, for the simple reason that ideas, the concepts through which we grasp the secrets of our condition, do not exist apart from words. We learn how to speak correctly—and deeply, rigorously, and subtly—from good literature, and only from good literature. No other discipline or branch of the arts can substitute for literature in crafting the language that people need to communicate. To speak well, to have at one's disposal a rich and diverse language, to be able to find the appropriate expression for every idea and every emotion that we want to communicate, is to be better prepared to think, to teach, to learn, to converse, and also to fantasize, to dream, to feel. In a surreptitious way, words reverberate in all our actions, even in those actions that seem far removed from language. And as language evolved, thanks to literature, and reached high levels of refinement and manners, it increased the possibility of human enjoyment.

Literature has even served to confer upon love and desire and the sexual act itself the status of artistic creation. Without literature, eroticism would not exist. Love and pleasure would be poorer, they would lack delicacy and exquisiteness, they would fail to attain to the intensity that literary fantasy offers. It is hardly an exaggeration to say that a couple who have read Garcilaso, Petrarch, Góngora, or Baudelaire value pleasure and experience pleasure more than illiterate people who have been made into idiots by television's soap operas. In an illiterate world, love and desire would be no different from what satisfies animals, nor would they transcend the crude fulfillment of elementary instincts.

Nor are the audiovisual media equipped to replace literature in this task of teaching human beings to use with assurance and with skill the extraordinarily rich possibilities that language encompasses. On the contrary, the audiovisual media tend to relegate words to a secondary level with respect to images, which are the primordial language of these media, and to constrain language to its oral expression, to its indispensable minimum, far from its written dimension. To define a film or a television program as "literary" is an elegant way of saying that it is boring. For this reason, literary programs on the radio or on television rarely capture the public. So far as I know, the only exception to this rule was Bernard Pivot's program *Apostrophes*, in France. And this leads me to think that not only is literature indispensable for a full knowledge and a full mastery of language, but its fate is linked also and indissolubly with the fate of the book, that industrial product that many are now declaring obsolete.

This brings me to Bill Gates. He was in Madrid not long ago and visited the Royal Spanish Academy, which has embarked upon a joint venture with Microsoft. Among other things, Gates assured the members of the academy that he would personally guarantee that the letter "ñ" would never be removed from computer software—a promise that allowed four hundred million Spanish speakers on five continents to breathe a sigh of relief, since the banishment of such an essential letter from cyberspace would have created monumental problems. Immediately after making his amiable concession to the Spanish language, however, Gates, before even leaving the premises of the academy, avowed in a press conference that he expected to accomplish his highest goal before he died. That goal, he explained, is to put an end to paper and then to books.

In his judgment, books are anachronistic objects. Gates argued that computer screens are able to replace paper in all the functions that paper has heretofore assumed. He also insisted that, in addition to being less onerous, computers take up less space and are more easily transportable, and also that the transmission of news and literature by these electronic media, instead of by newspapers and books, will have the ecological advantage of stopping the destruction of forests, a cataclysm that is a consequence of the paper industry. People will continue to read, Gates assured his listeners, but they will read on computer screens, and consequently there will be more chlorophyll in the environment.

I was not present at Gates's little discourse; I learned these details from the press. Had I been there I would have booed Gates for proclaiming shamelessly his intention to send me and my colleagues, the writers of books, directly to the unemployment line. And I would have vigorously disputed his analysis. Can the screen really replace the book in all its aspects? I am not so certain. I am fully aware of the enormous revolution that new technologies such as the Internet have caused in the fields of communication and the sharing of information, and I confess that the Internet provides invaluable help to me every day in my work; but my gratitude for these extraordinary conveniences does not imply a belief that the electronic screen can replace paper, or that reading on a computer can stand in for literary reading. That is a chasm that I cannot cross. I cannot accept the idea that a nonfunctional or nonpragmatic act of reading, one that seeks neither information nor a useful and immediate communication, can integrate on a computer screen the dreams and the pleasures of words with the same sensation of intimacy, the same mental concentration and spiritual isolation, that may be achieved by the act of reading a book.

Perhaps this is a prejudice resulting from lack of practice, and from a long association of literature with books and paper. But even though I enjoy surfing the Web in search of world news, I would never go to the screen to read a poem by Góngora or a novel by Onetti or an essay by Paz, because I am certain that the effect of such a reading would not be the same. I am convinced, although I cannot prove it, that with the disappearance of the book, literature would suffer a serious blow, even a mortal one. The term "literature" would not disappear, of course. Yet it would almost certainly be used to denote a type of text as distant from what we understand as literature today as soap operas are from the tragedies of Sophocles and Shakespeare.

There is still another reason to grant literature an important place in the life of nations. Without it, the critical mind, which is the real engine of historical change and the best protector of liberty, would suffer an irreparable loss. This is because all good literature is radical, and poses radical questions about the world in which we live. In all great literary texts, often without their authors' intending it, a seditious inclination is present.

Literature says nothing to those human beings who are satisfied with their lot, who are content with life as they now live it. Literature is the food of the rebellious spirit, the promulgator of nonconformities, the refuge for those who have too much or too little in life. One seeks sanctuary in literature so as not to be unhappy and so as not to be incomplete. To ride alongside the scrawny Rocinante and the confused

355

Knight on the fields of La Mancha, to sail the seas on the back of a whale with Captain Ahab, to drink arsenic with Emma Bovary, to become an insect with Gregor Samsa: these are all ways that we have invented to divest ourselves of the wrongs and the impositions of this unjust life, a life that forces us always to be the same person when we wish to be many different people, so as to satisfy the many desires that possess us.

Literature pacifies this vital dissatisfaction only momentarily—but in this miraculous instant, in this provisional suspension of life, literary illusion lifts and transports us outside of history, and we become citizens of a timeless land, and in this way immortal. We become more intense, richer, more complicated, happier, and more lucid than we are in the constrained routine of ordinary life. When we close the book and abandon literary fiction, we return to actual existence and compare it to the splendid land that we have just left. What a disappointment awaits us! Yet a tremendous realization also awaits us, namely, that the fantasized life of the novel is better—more beautiful and more diverse, more comprehensible and more perfect—than the life that we live while awake, a life conditioned by the limits and the tedium of our condition. In this way, good literature, genuine literature, is always subversive, unsubmissive, rebellious: a challenge to what exists.

How could we not feel cheated after reading *War and Peace* or *Remembrance of Things Past* and returning to our world of insignificant details, of boundaries and prohibitions that lie in wait everywhere and, with each step, corrupt our illusions? Even more than the need to sustain the continuity of culture and to enrich language, the greatest contribution of literature to human progress is perhaps to remind us (without intending to, in the majority of cases) that the world is badly made; and that those who pretend to the contrary, the powerful and the lucky, are lying; and that the world can be improved, and made more like the worlds that our imagination and our language are able to create. A free and democratic society must have responsible and critical citizens conscious of the need continuously to examine the world that we inhabit and to try, even though it is more and more an impossible task, to make it more closely resemble the world that we would like to inhabit. And there is no better means of fomenting dissatisfaction with existence than the reading of good literature; no better means of forming critical and independent citizens who will not be manipulated by those who govern them, and who are endowed with a permanent spiritual mobility and a vibrant imagination.

Still, to call literature seditious because it sensitizes a reader's consciousness to the imperfections of the world does not mean—as churches and governments seem to think it means when they establish censorship—that literary texts will provoke immediate social upheavals or accelerate revolutions. The social and political effects of a poem, a play, or a novel cannot be foreseen, because they are not collectively made or collectively experienced. They are created by individuals and they are read by individuals, who vary enormously in the conclusions that they draw from their writing and their reading. For this reason, it is difficult, or even impossible, to establish precise patterns. Moreover, the social consequences of a work of literature may have little to do with its aesthetic quality. A mediocre novel by Harriet Beecher Stowe seems

356

to have played a decisive role in raising social and political consciousness of the horrors of slavery in the United States. The fact that these effects of literature are difficult to identify does not imply that they do not exist. The important point is that they are effects brought about by the actions of citizens whose personalities have been formed in part by books.

Good literature, while temporarily relieving human dissatisfaction, actually increases it, by developing a critical and nonconformist attitude toward life. It might even be said that literature makes human beings more likely to be unhappy. To live dissatisfied, and at war with existence, is to seek things that may not be there, to condemn oneself to fight futile battles, like the battles that Colonel Aureliano Buendía fought in *One Hundred Years of Solitude,* knowing full well that he would lose them all. All this may be true. Yet it is also true that without rebellion against the mediocrity and the squalor of life, we would still live in a primitive state, and history would have stopped. The autonomous individual would not have been created, science and technology would not have progressed, human rights would not have been recognized, freedom would not have existed. All these things are born of unhappiness, of acts of defiance against a life perceived as insufficient or intolerable. For this spirit that scorns life as it is—and searches with the madness of Don Quixote, whose insanity derived from the reading of chivalric novels—literature has served as a great spur.

Let us attempt a fantastic historical reconstruction. Let us imagine a world without literature, a humanity that has not read poems or novels. In this kind of atrophied civilization, with its puny lexicon in which groans and apelike gesticulations would prevail over words, certain adjectives would not exist.

When one imagines such a world, one is tempted to picture primitives in loincloths, the small magic-religious communities that live at the margins of modernity in Latin America, Oceania, and Africa. But I have a different failure in mind. The nightmare that I am warning about is the result not of underdevelopment but of overdevelopment. As a consequence of technology and our subservience to it, we may imagine a future society full of computer screens and speakers, and without books, or a society in which books—that is, works of literature—have become what alchemy became in the era of physics: an archaic curiosity, practiced in the catacombs of the media civilization by a neurotic minority. I am afraid that this cybernetic world, in spite of its prosperity and its power, its high standard of living and its scientific achievement would be profoundly uncivilized and utterly soulless—a resigned humanity of postliterary automatons who have abdicated freedom.

It is highly improbable, of course, that this macabre utopia will ever come about. The end of our story, the end of history, has not yet been written, and it is not predetermined. What we will become depends entirely on our vision and our will. But if we wish to avoid the impoverishment of our imagination, and the disappearance of the precious dissatisfaction that refines our sensibility and teaches us to speak with eloquence and rigor, and the weakening of our freedom, then we must act. More precisely, we must read.

357

Unraveled

Liza Ward

Liza Ward grew up in Brooklyn, New York. She graduated from Middlebury College in 1998 with a degree in English; her under-graduate thesis took the form of short stories. Ward got an intern-ship to The Atlantic Monthly *a year later, after stints in the editorial department of J. Crew and at the Bread Loaf Writers' Conference. "Unraveled" was her first story to be published. She also published other stories in* The Atlantic Monthly *and is now at work on a novel.*

I was an angel in the fourth-grade Christmas pageant, and my mother didn't come. I wasn't just any angel. I had a solo. I blew the trumpet when Jesus was born. Back-stage somebody else's mother pinned on my wings. Her hair was gray, and she had glasses. She sat on a chair, her fat spilling around her. She took the pins out of her mouth and turned me around. She said, 'There. Don't you look like a real little angel. Won't your mother be proud!"

I said, "She's not here." I looked the lady straight in her dog-brown eyes. I said, "My mother is in a coma."

The lady's eyes went watery, as if someone had pinched her. I said, "All I want for Christmas is my mother back." That made her cry. My mother would cry when she heard about these lies. She would hold her drink in front of her face, run her fingers through my hair, and shake her head. She would say, "What a messed-up little kid I made."

In seventh grade I got suspended, for writing out verb conjugations on my leg. I wrote them all the way to my underwear, and during the test I pulled my skirt up over my thigh. Danny Costar was watching me. I cinched it up higher so that he could see the

---

Reprinted from *The Atlantic Monthly* 286, no. 3, September 2000, by permission of the author.

conjugation of *vouloir*, and Madame Bauvais said, "*Mademoiselle Holmes! Qu'est-ce que tu fais?*" My mother was asked to come into school for this. She got called, but she never came. She was staring at herself in the bedroom mirror. She was tracing the small wrinkles that creased her face.

The bedroom door was ajar when I came home from school. Through the crack I could see her sitting on a chair in front of the vanity table, and smoke from an ashtray curling up through the light. I walked in. The room smelled stale, like cigarettes and lilies from the silk sachets in her drawers. This was the scent of my mother. I said, "I got suspended."

She didn't turn around. She just kept staring at her reflection in the mirror. She said, "I'm sorry I didn't go." She wasn't even mad. She said, "I thought I would cry. And who wants to see a crying mother when the mother should be yelling?" My mother lifted the cigarette to her lips and sucked. She viciously jabbed the stub against the face of the mirror. It left a dark smudge and rained ashes over her makeup case.

I said, "What did you do that for?"

"Who knows." This was her answer. My mother said, "Why does anybody do the things they do?" She turned her face away from the mirror. She pushed back her chair and stood up. So did Snowy, our Persian cat, who had been sleeping all white and plush on the rug. My mother was still wearing her thin robe, though it was already afternoon. It was the Ginger Rogers one, light and flowing, the one she wore when she wanted to feel wanted. She said a man had given it to her because it clung to her curves. "For example," my mother asked, "why is the sky blue?" She threw off her robe. She let it fall into a heap by the vanity table, and over the twitching tail of our cat. "Or better yet, why"—she turned away and faced the mirror—"did I get left alone?" She didn't wait for an answer, though I could have given her one.

My mother stumbled naked into her dressing room. I could hear her pulling open drawers and banging them shut too loudly. I could smell the lily clouds and powder, and over them the faint scent of gin. I could see her arms extend through tight blue sleeves, her legs push through clinging dark denim. Then she was standing, dressed, in the doorway. She began searching around the room, stepping through the thick pink rug on high-heeled boots. I sat on the bed with my legs hanging. My mother picked up a scarf from beside my feet and tied it over her mane of blonde hair. She didn't look at me. She bent to straighten the scarf in the mirror.

I had been swinging my legs, kicking the dust ruffle, watching her move quickly around the room. Now I stood up. I tried to stop her from leaving. I said, "Where are you going?"

"It doesn't matter," she answered. "Nowhere. You're old enough to not know everything I do."

I followed her out into the hall. I followed her down the soft carpeted stairs. She was digging through her purse by the door. I grabbed the hem of her coat. It wasn't long and muted, like other mothers' coats. It was red. I said, "Are you coming back ever?"

She didn't turn around. She was looking for her keys. "Yes, I'm coming back," she snapped. "When have I ever not?" She paused beside the open door in winter light. She pulled gloves on over her slim hands. She lit a cigarette in the frame of the door. The breeze filled the corner of her scarf behind her head and lifted her hair. Then she turned and smiled. Her blue eyes were glassy and bitten by frost. "Hey," she said to me. "Sammy, sweetie—" She sucked in against the wind. "I need to be free. Feel the ground move under my feet a little—the earth spin in Central Park. I'll be back."

I watched my mother disappear down the block, between faceless forms fighting toward Fifth Avenue. When she was out of sight, I turned off the lights. The house was narrow and dark. It was dead. I picked up Snowy and bounced her up and down like a baby. She hissed, so I let her go. I went up to my mother's room and turned on the lights. I watched pools of warmth pierce dusky pinks. I went through her closet. I opened her drawers. I tried on her clothes in front of the mirror. Her shirts were too big. The bras hung flat like deflated balloons. I put on her robe and tied it over my bony hips. The hem rippled into pools around my feet. It was silky and cool on my skin and I imagined it caressing soft curves. I lay down in it on her bed, on the rose comforter that caught dry skin in its delicate folds. I let the hem trail out over my pointed toes. I reached for the pack of cigarettes on her nightstand, and the lighter. I rested my neck against the lacy white pillows. I lit a cigarette and let the smoke roll around in my mouth. I forced it out in light gray clouds that drifted toward the ceiling. I let the ashes fall into the marble bowl beside the picture in its silver frame. It was a picture of my mother and father sitting in the sand on the beach at Quogue. It had always been there by the bed. It was beside his untouched pillow, like a trophy. He spent his nights in safety behind the closed door of another woman's room. I lay there as the room grew darker and shadows melted across the rug. I was listening for the sound of the downstairs door, and her faltering steps across the floor. But she didn't come back until late. I fell asleep like that, lying there in her clothes.

I didn't hear her come in until the bedroom door banged open. I sat up, shaken out of sleep. My mother stood there, leaning on the arm of a man. I rubbed my eyes. The man was someone I had seen at the Christmas party at Mrs. Brink's, in The Dakota. All the distinguished and lonely people gathered there around a tree. My mother took me every year. She would say, "Here's the place to find him, just you wait." The man had poured my mother champagne. He had looked down her dress. He had rested his hand on her forearm and fingered the shiny red sleeve. His hair was gray around the sides. He looked like someone's father, or a teacher who smoked cigars. I covered myself with the comforter, pulling it up over my chin. I was hiding the robe. My mother was swaying slightly, and the man was helping to hold her up. His arm was around her shoulders. She said, "What are you doing in here, Samantha?" Her hair was falling over her face. She said, "That's my daughter. She's playing Mother."

I said, "I'm not. I've been waiting up."

The man pushed my mother forward. He urged her gently into the room. My mother pulled him across the carpet. She dragged him over to the bed, where I was still sitting, hidden beneath the comforter. She snaked her arms up around his neck. She pressed her lips to his cheek. She dangled there. She swung her hair back through the air. I imagined his neck smelling of the musk that rich men wear. I supposed that she would never want to lift her head up from it. The man was laughing. I thought he might drop her. He said, "I think you should get in bed, Linda." He rubbed her shoulders. He said, "Lie down."

She turned around. She bent down. She leaned her arm on the side of the mattress. She pushed her hair out of her eyes. She stared at me. She said, "I can't, Frankie. Someone is sleeping in my bed."

I rolled over to the other side, where the sheets were cold. I kneaded the feather folds with my fingers. My mother threw herself down on the bed. She crawled toward me, across the comforter. She put her face up to mine and pointed her finger toward the door. Her hot breath was bathed in bourbon. "Get out," she said. "We want to be alone."

"*I* want to be alone." I said this. I spun out from under the covers and landed on the floor, spread-eagled, with the gauze robe around my thighs.

My mother peered down at me over the edge of the bed. She said, "Take that off—it's mine."

But I didn't. I ran out of her room and slammed the door.

Late in the morning I heard him leave. I heard my mother follow his heavy steps, softly down the stairs. I heard her laugh. I heard the gentle rise of her voice in the hall, heard the door close quickly on a gust of winter wind. I was sitting in the kitchen doing homework. I put my name at the top, with the date in French. I drew a straight line down the center of the sheet to separate words. I organized definitions and dotted my *i*s.

My mother said, "Sammy?" She was standing in a patch of sunlight on the tile floor. Everything was soft. Her hair fell around her face in luscious, long ripples. She didn't look like anyone's mother. She looked sugarcoated and candy-floss sweet. She was smiling. The cat was winding around her ankles. My mother said, "I forgot to feed Snowy. I guess she's hungry." She bent down and ran her finger over the head of our cat and down to the end of her sassy tail.

I said, "I did it," even though I hadn't. I was looking at the dictionary. I said, "I did it when you were asleep with him." I turned some pages.

"Him—" My mother pulled out a chair and sat down. "His name is Frank. Mr. Cooke." She rested her elbows on the surface of the table and leaned her face in the cup of her hands: She said, "Look at me." I looked up from the page, though I didn't want to. To look at her hurt. My mother was soft where I was angles. "I want you to like him, Sammy," she said. "I think he'll be good for us."

I said, "Okay." Just like that.

"He's going to be around a lot. He's not just someone I met in a bar." My mother stood up. She turned to go. She said, "So no guilt. I'm doing this for you." She said it over her shoulder. She didn't even mention my suspension.

In the following days my mother dressed before noon. She would kiss me on both cheeks. She would ask about school. She fluttered over floors in floppy white slippers, straightening slipcovers and beating cushions. She would say, "Consuela doesn't get it. I can't believe it. I never knew." She hired the Clean Team. They were dressed in white suits. They ran through the house in droves like ants. They polished windows and oiled hinges. They rearranged the rooms. My mother stood with one hand on her hip, nodding her head. She said things were coming together. She said she loved feeling that her life was under control.

My mother was cooking. She was trying out recipes. She would leave them warming in china terrines. She would bend over the stove. She would shove spoons in my mouth and tell me to try, taste, savor, smell. She said, "I want things to be perfect for him. I want to do everything I can, Sammy."

My mother was having Frank to dinner. She said, "Call him Mr. Cooke. I'm cooking for Mr. Cooke." She laughed. She spent the day stirring over the stove, and the early evening getting ready. I sat on the edge of the bed watching my mother pull heavy hangers from the closet. She was standing in front of her full-length mirror. She was turning around, looking over her shoulder at the curve of her back in a red silk dress. She said, "Frank likes me in red." She said, "Sammy, do you think I'm sagging?" She went over to the nightstand and took a sip from her drink. The ice cubes chimed happily. They hit the curved sides of the glass. She looked at me. She was holding the glass up close to her neck. She ran one finger around the smooth wet rim. She said, "Sincerely, how old do I look?"

I said, "I don't know. You're my mother." I stared at the wall.

My mother raised the drink to her lips. She said, "You know just what to say." She swallowed. Her lips left a deep full print on the edge of the glass. She crossed the room slowly, over the warm, lamplit rug. She sat down at the vanity table and moved her face close to the mirror. She was tracing her fingers over her skin, running them lightly along the creases of time. She kissed the edges of her eyes with her fingertips, and traced the faint lines that ran from her nose to the corners of her mouth. She lit a cigarette. She said, "I don't think Frank likes me to smoke."

I said, "Then why are you?"

"Because I have to," my mother answered. "Because I'm nervous. You wouldn't understand what that means. You don't understand much, you're so young." She turned around in her chair and looked at me. She sucked in hard on her cigarette. She said, "You know what the greatest thing about being young is?"

I said, "No."

"You have no idea what it's like to be old." The ice was melting in her drink. The lime was growing tired in the glass.

I got up off the bed. I said, "Is Frank going to sleep here again?"

"Yes!" My mother stood up. "That's what boyfriends do." She flipped her hair over her shoulders then, and smiled sweetly. She moved closer to where I stood. Her face went warm. She was going to try to make me understand it. "Do you have a boyfriend, Sammy?" she said.

I wasn't going to answer this. I made a face. I wrinkled up my nose.

"Come on," my mother teased. "I bet you do." She moved closer. She lunged forward. She grabbed my shoulder fiercely. She smelled like lilies and gin and ashes. She ran her hand quickly over the flat front of my shirt, over the aching points on my chest. She laughed. "You have little boobies, Sammy!" She crowed.

"I don't!" I said. I shook myself free from her grasp.

"Oh, but you do, you do." My mother's teeth gleamed white beneath heavy red lips.

I ran out of the room. I slammed the door.

When I came downstairs, my mother was stirring something on the stove. She was wearing an apron over her dress, and cursing to herself quietly. She said, "I should have known I couldn't handle this shit!" She turned around when she heard my steps. The combs were falling out of her frizzing hair. Sweat was forming on her brow, and her makeup was smeared. She said, "Don't you look pretty." She said, "Will you go talk to Frank, please? He's sitting in the living room." She turned her attention back to the stove. She said, "Ask him what he'd like to drink."

I was wearing a dress my mother had bought for me, red like hers. It had long sleeves and a scoop neck. It fell above my knees, and I could feel it cool and smooth on my skin. I could feel the hem rustle against my thighs, over the thin nylon that clung to my legs. I stepped across the cold tile, over the black and white squares in the hall. I listened to the sound of the heels of my shoes graze the surface of the glassy floor. I tucked my smooth hair behind my ears. I opened the living room doors. He was sitting on the couch my father used to like. It was the one by the fireplace with the heavy arms and the high back. He was turning pages in a photography book about Long Island Sound.

I said, "We go there sometimes. We have a house in the Hamptons."

He looked up. He smiled at me. He said, "Well, if it isn't the little bedroom wonder."

I could feel my cheeks grow hot like my dress. I brushed my hair over the sides of my face. I looked at the floor.

Frank cleared his throat. He said, "I go there in the summers too." He said, "That's where I first saw your mother. I fell in love with her from afar. She was wearing a flowered bathing suit at the beach." He smiled. He said, "I never saw you."

I said, "Oh, I didn't know you knew her before." I walked toward the fire. I said, "My mother's making coquilles Saint-Jacques."

Frank had on a turtleneck and a blazer, and the book was in his lap. He closed the heavy cover and put the book on the floor. The fire's shadows and light danced over his face. The flames reflected in his spectacles. He took them off. He folded them gently in his large hands. He put them in his breast pocket. He looked at me. I was watching the fire. He said, "What in the world is Cocky Saint Jack?" I thought he was funny. I laughed.

He said, "I'm not very good at French. Not like you."

I said, "I'm not either. I'm really not." I told Frank I had been kicked out of French class. I said, "I got in trouble for writing out verbs on my thigh, all the way up to here." I put my hand on my hip. I said, "I was wearing a skirt."

Frank laughed. He said, "You're a clever girl, then. That's how you make it in this world. You've got it all figured out."

I could hear my mother banging pots in the kitchen. I smiled. I brushed my hair back behind my ears. I let my little pearls twinkle in the light. I said, "I'm supposed to ask you what you want to drink."

He said, "Well Samantha." The way he said my name sounded old. He let it roll off his tongue. He softened the sound. He made it round. He said, "I would like to have a Mount Gay and tonic, with a twist of lime. Do you think you could make that?"

I went over to the bar behind the piano. I searched through the bottles. I lifted them up in the dim light and stared at the names. I set them down heavily, and they clinked together on the mirrored shelf. Clear amber liquid swayed in the bottoms of mysterious bottles. I said, "I found it, Frank." I smiled at myself in the mirrored shelf. I was wearing lipstick. It made my skin look pale and smooth.

Frank said, "Half and half. Half rum, half tonic, on ice."

I bent over low beneath the shelf to reach the tonic. I felt my dress rise over the backs of my thighs. I dropped the ice cubes slowly into the bottom of the heavy glass, hearing the sound of each one fall crisply against another. I poured in rum. It swelled slowly around the cubes. I poured in tonic. I watched the bubbles rise and break through the tinted drink. I said, "Now lime?"

"Yes," he said. "Just squeeze a little in."

I rubbed the green slice between my thumb and forefinger. I kneaded out the juice and the seeds onto the surface of the drink. I walked over to Frank. I held the cool glass back from him, against my chest. I said, "I hope it doesn't taste bad."

He said, "You taste it, and then tell me."

I lifted the drink to my lips. It smelled strong, biting. I curled my lips slowly around the smooth rim. I tilted the glass, felt the coldness drip between my lips. It stung. It brought tears to my eyes. I swallowed. "I think it's good," I said. I gave it to him.

He took it in one hand. It was a large hand with wrinkles. It was rough like a cowboy's, like the hand of a man who throws lassos, like Ralph Lauren. Frank sipped his drink. He said, "Perfect. Sit down." He patted the cushion beside him.

I sat. The softness melted beneath me. Frank smelled like after-shave, like musk, and I felt warm beside him there by the fire. He reached out. He ran his fingers through my hair. The roughness made my scalp tickle. He cleared his throat. He said, "You look so much like your mother, except for the hair, your lovely brown hair."

I leaned over. I snuggled up close to his ear. I shielded the side of my mouth with my hand. I whispered, "My mother's hair is only dyed blonde. It's not real."

I saw the smile spread across the side of his face, and his mouth opened slowly as he began to laugh.

I said, "And she smokes cigarettes all the time."

His eyes crinkled at the corners. He said, "I won't tell. The secret's between you and me." He put his hand on my shoulder. He squeezed it gently.

My mother was standing in the doorway with her hands on her hips. The light was behind her, and it made her hair glow softly. She had let it down to fall around her long neck and smooth shoulders. She said, "Dinner's ready." She smiled sweetly.

On the way in, she pinched my arm hard. She pushed me up against the side of the doorway. She put her mouth close to my ear. She smelled of gin. Her voice was thick. She said, "Go away, Sammy. We want to be alone."

I sat upstairs with Snowy. Our stomachs rumbled. I closed the door of the den. Neither of us could get out. The cat kept rubbing against it, as if the wood were a person she could charm. It wasn't. She wasn't charming me. I could still hear through the closed door. Their voices were that loud. The sound of my mother laughing furiously, trying too hard, traveled up the stairs. I imagined her drink clutched like a pillow, lipstick staining her teeth. The thought made my stomach hurt. They would be eating dessert if my mother remembered to serve it. I smoothed my hair in the soft face of the mirror. I pinched my cheeks to make them red. I opened the door. I went downstairs.

I crossed the light-stained marble. The dishes were strewn over the dining-room table. My mother's hair was tossed wildly. She was talking too loudly. Frank was quiet at the other end of the table. One hand was supporting his chin. My mother had her elbows on the table. She had told me never to do this. She would say, "Men don't like it when women act like them. It's not demure."

I stood in the doorway only for a moment, but my mother saw me. She started to stand. She said, "Sammy," as if she were pleased to see me. "Isn't she young and pretty, Frank?" My mother reached her arm out to welcome me in. Her heavy rings hit the wine bottle with a sudden chime. The bottle teetered and fell. The liquid spilled over the white tablecloth. It coursed toward her quickly. My mother moved to catch it with her napkin but it spilled over the end of the table, staining her dress a deeper red, as if someone had shot her. Frank stood up. He looked embarrassed. She said, "No, no. Don't move. Really, I'm such a klutz." My mother had already forgotten I was there. She moved toward the door. "I'll just go change."

"Are you sure you're all right, Linda?' He started to take her arm. My mother was unsteady. She brushed away his hand. "I'll be just a minute." She breezed by me. She tossed her hair. I saw her stumble when she reached the banister. She clutched the mahogany with one hand, the molding with the other. She led herself upstairs.

I said, "She gets nervous when she cooks."

Frank said, "I understand." He walked toward the hall closet and reached for his coat.

I said, "Do you want me to make you another drink?"

"No, thank you, Samantha." He turned around to face me, his coat over his arm. He said, "I think your mother's had enough for the both of us." He winked at me, as if we had a secret joke between us. "She should sleep it off." Frank pushed his arms into the sleeves of his coat. He really was leaving.

I tried to get between him and the door. I touched his arm. I fingered the wool. I looked up into his face. I said, "You didn't have dessert."

He stepped around me. He said, "That's all right. I'm sure it's good." He had the knob in his hand.

I said, "She'll be down."

He smiled. He chucked me under my chin. "Tell her thank you." He said it just like that. He opened the door. The pane of glass rattled when his shoe knocked wood. He closed it behind him. Frank was gone, and he didn't look back.

My mother was standing at the top of the stairs. She was wearing her robe. "Where is he?"

I didn't answer. I watched her descend. The thin white robe trailed behind her, illuminated sheer and gauzy by the lamp in the alcove. "What did you say to him?"

I said, "He left. I was trying to stop him."

My mother just stood there. She touched her face to make sure all the features were in place. She smoothed the front of her Ginger Rogers robe. All at once her cheeks were smudged with black mascara. Her face unraveled with tears. "Well, what did he say?"

"He said thank you," I answered. "He said he was sorry but he had to go. He said he had fun."

My mother stared at her reflection in the clear face of the door.

"He said he'd call you." I added this, but it didn't work.

My mother sobbed. She crumpled. The glass pane shook. She was beating her fists on it. The cat, perched on a step, was staring, mesmerized by my mother's motion. I wanted to kick it. Instead I opened the door. I stepped out into the night. For a few paces I followed a figure. The figure retreating might have been anyone's. I stopped where I was. I called, "Hey!" But I hated the sound of my voice, small and shaking. Snow was beginning to fall in soft flakes.

The city was silent, as if it had died. I knew my mother was standing behind me, there in the cold draft by the door, searching frozen patches of light. I imagined her breath held in her chest in the darkness. She was staring out at the street, at me standing there in my red dress just like hers. Car lights rounding corners played across wet cheeks. She was waiting, praying he'd turn around and come back. I was waiting too. I was wearing my mother's disappointment like a tired old face. I turned around in the sleeping street. I faced our house, tall and thin. It was spotted with one lone light, breathless, awake, and silent.

Aftermath

Mary Yukari Waters

A promising talent, Mary Yukari Waters won the Pushcart Prize and was chosen for Barnes and Noble's summer 2003 Discover Great New Writers program for her volume of short stories, The Laws of Evening. *Born in Tokyo, she is half Japanese and half Irish American. She has an MFA from the University of California at Irvine. She has published short stories in various magazines, which have often been selected for the yearly collection Best American Short Stories. She is the recipient of an NEA literature grant.*

In Imamiya Park the boys are playing dodge ball, a new American game. Behind them tall poplars rise up through the low-lying dusk, intercepting the last of the sun's rays, which dazzle the leaves with white and gold.

Makiko can hardly believe her son, Toshi, belongs with these older boys. Seven years old! Once, his growth had seemed commensurate with the passage of time. These last few years, however, with the war and surrender, the changes have come too fast, skimming her consciousness like pebbles skipped over water.

Makiko is grateful the war is over. But she cannot ignore a nagging sense that Japan's surrender has spawned a new threat—one more subtle, more diffuse. She can barely articulate it, even to herself; feels unmoored, buffeted among invisible forces surging all around her. As if caught up in these energies, her son's thin body is rapidly lengthening. Look! Within that circle in the dirt he is dodging, he is feinting; his body twists with an unfamiliar grace, foreshadowing that of a young man.

Toshi's growth is abetted by a new lunch program at school that is subsidized by the American government, which has switched, with dizzying speed, from enemy to ally. Each day her son comes home with alien food in his stomach: bread, cheese, bottled milk. Last week, in the pocket of his shorts Makiko found a cube of condensed

---

peanut butter—an American dessert, Toshi explained—which he had meant to save for later. It was coated with lint from his pocket, which he brushed off, ignoring her plea to "get rid of that dirty thing."

And each day Toshi comes home with questions she cannot answer: Who was Magellan? How do you say "My name is Toshi" in English? How do you play baseball?

Makiko shows him the ball games her own mother taught her. She bounces an imaginary ball, chanting a ditty passed down from the Edo period:

> Yellow topknots
> of the Portuguese wives
>
> spiraled like seashells
> and stuck atop their heads,
>
> hold one up to your ear,
> shake it up and down—
>
> a little shrunken brain
> is rattling inside.

In the old days, she tells him, they used to put something inside the rubber balls—maybe a scrap of iron, she wasn't sure—that made a rattling noise. Toshi, too old now for this sort of amusement, sighs with impatience.

Just four years ago, Toshi's head had been too big for his body—endearingly out of proportion, like the head of a stuffed animal. Even then he had a manly, square-jawed face, not unlike that of a certain city council candidate appearing on election posters at the time. Her husband, Yoshitsune, nicknamed his son "Mr. Magistrate." Before going off to war, Yoshitsune had developed a little routine with their son. "*Oi*, Toshi! Are you a man?" Yoshitsune would prompt in his droll tone, using the word *otoko,* with its connotations of male bravery, strength, and honor. He would ask this question several times a day, often before neighbors and friends.

"*Hai,* Father! I am a man!" little Toshi would cry, stiffening at soldierly attention as he had been coached, trembling with eagerness to please. His short legs, splayed out from the knees as if buckling under the weight of his head, were still dimpled with baby fat.

"*Maaa!* An excellent, manly answer!" the grownups praised, through peals of laughter.

Makiko had laughed too, a faint constriction in her throat, for Yoshitsune had remarked to her, "When I'm out fighting in the Pacific, that's how I'm going to remember him." After that, she began watching their child closely, trying to memorize what Yoshitsune was memorizing. Later, when her husband was gone, it comforted her to think that the same images swam in both their minds at night. Even today, Toshi's three-year-old figure is vivid in her mind. On the other hand, she has not fully absorbed the war years, still shrinks from those memories and all that has followed.

Foreigners, for instance, are now a familiar sight. American army jeeps with beefy red arms dangling out the windows roar down Kagane Boulevard, the main thoroughfare just east of Toshi's school. "Keep your young women indoors," the neighbors say. Occasionally Makiko has seen a soldier offering chocolates or peanuts to little children, squatting down to their level, holding out the treat—it seems to her they all have hairy arms—as if to a timid cat. Just yesterday Toshi came home, smiling broadly and carrying chocolates—not one square but three. Bile had surged up in Makiko's throat, and before she knew it, she had struck them right out of his hand and onto the kitchen floor. "How could you!" she choked as Toshi, stunned, burst into sobs. "How could you! Those men killed your *father*!"

This evening Makiko has come to the park with a small box of caramels, bought on the black market with some of the money she was hoarding to buy winter yarn. "In the future," she will tell him, "if you want something so badly, you come to me. *Ne?* Not to them."

On a bench in the toddlers' section, now deserted, she waits for her son to finish his game with the other boys. All the other mothers have gone home to cook dinner. The playground equipment has not been maintained since the beginning of the war. The swing set is peeling with rust; the freestanding animals—the ram, the pig, the rooster—have broken-down springs, and their carnival paint has washed away, exposing more rusted steel.

Ara maaa! Her Toshi has finally been hit! Makiko feels a mother's pang. He is crossing the line to the other side now, carrying the ball, Makiko notes the ease with which the fallen one seems to switch roles in this game, heaving the ball at his former teammates without the slightest trace of disloyalty.

This year Makiko is allowing Toshi to light the incense each evening before the family altar. He seems to enjoy prayer time much more now that he can use matches. She also regularly changes which photograph of her husband is displayed beside the miniature gong. This month's photograph shows Yoshitsune in a cotton *yukata*, smoking under the ginkgo tree in the garden. Sometimes, in place of a photograph, she displays an old letter or one of his silk scent bags, still fragrant after a bit of massaging. To keep Toshi interested, Makiko presents his father in the light of constant renewal.

"Just talk to him inside your mind," she tells her son. "He wants to know what you're learning in school, what games you're playing. Just like any other father, *ne*? Don't leave him behind, don't ignore him, just because he's dead." She wonders if Toshi secretly considers his father a burden, making demands from the altar, like a cripple from a wheelchair.

"Your father's very handsome in this picture, *ne?*" she says tonight. Within the lacquered frame, her son's father glances up from lighting a cigarette, a bemused half-smile on his face, as if he is waiting to make a wry comment.

Toshi nods absently. Frowning, he slashes at the matchbox with the expert flourish of a second-grade boy. The match rips into flames.

"Answer properly! You're not a little baby anymore."

"*Hai*, Mother." Toshi sighs with a weary, accommodating air, squaring his shoulders in a semblance of respectful attention. Makiko remembers with sorrow the big head, the splayed legs of her baby boy.

It amazes her that Toshi has no memory of the routine he once performed with his father. "What *do* you remember of him?" she prods every so often, hoping to dislodge some new memory. But all that Toshi remembers of his father is being carried on one arm before a sunny window.

"*Maaa*, what a wonderful memory!" Makiko encourages him each time. "It must have been a very happy moment!"

When would this have taken place: which year, which month? Would even Yoshitsune have remembered it, this throwaway moment that, inexplicably, has outlasted all the others in their son's mind? She tries conjuring it up, as if the memory is her own. For some reason she imagines autumn, the season Yoshitsune sailed away: October 1942. How the afternoon sun would seep in through the nursery window, golden, almost amber, advancing with the viscous quality of Hiezan honey or of nostalgia, overtaking sluggish dust motes and even sound. She wishes Toshi could remember the old view from that upstairs window: a sea of gray tiled roofs drowsing in the autumn haze, as yet unravaged by the fires of war.

"I'm done," Toshi says.

"What! Already? Are you sure?"

"*Hai*, Mother." Already heading for the dining room, where supper lies waiting on the low table, he slides back the *shoji* door in such a hurry that it grates on the grooves. Makiko considers calling him back—his prayers are getting shorter and shorter—but the incident with the chocolates is still too recent for another reprimand.

She follows him into the dining room. "A man who forgets his past," she quotes as she scoops rice into his bowl, "stays at the level of an animal." Toshi meets her eyes with a guilty, resentful glance. "Go on," she says blandly, "eat it while it's hot."

Toshi falls to. In order to supplement their meager rice ration, Makiko continues to mix in chopped *kabura* radishes—which at least resemble rice in color—as she did during the war. Sometimes she switches to chopped turnips. At first, before the rationing became strict, Toshi would hunch over his rice bowl with his chopsticks, fastidiously picking out one bit of vegetable after another and discarding it on another plate. Now he eats with gusto. It cuts her, the things he has grown used to. As a grown man he will reminisce over all the wrong things, things that should never have been a part of his childhood: this shameful pauper food; a block of peanut paste covered with lint; enemy soldiers amusing themselves by tossing chocolate and peanuts to children.

Later, Toshi ventures a question. Makiko has noticed that night-time—the black emptiness outside, the hovering silence—still cows him a little, stripping him of his daytime cockiness. After his goodnight bow, Toshi remains kneeling on the *tatami* floor. He says, "I was thinking, Mama, about how I'm seven—and how I only remember things that happened after I was three. So that means I've forgotten a whole half of my life—right?"

"That's right," Makiko says. He is looking up at her, his brows puckered in a look of doleful concentration, which reminds her of his younger days. "But it's perfectly normal, Toshi-*kun*. It's to be expected."

He is still thinking. "So when I get older," he says, "am I going to keep on forgetting? Am I going to forget you too?"

Makiko reaches out and strokes his prickly crewcut. "From this age on," she says, "you'll remember everything, Toshi-*kun*. Nothing more will ever be lost."

In the middle of the night, Makiko awakens from a dream in which Yoshitsune is hitting her with a fly swatter. She lies paralyzed under her *futon,* outrage buzzing in her chest. Details from the dream wash back into her mind: Yoshitsune's smile, distant and amused; the insolent way he wielded the swatter, as if she were hardly worth the effort.

A blue sheet of moonlight, slipping in through the space between two sliding panels, glows in the dark.

In the first year or two after his death, this sort of thing would happen often, and not always in the form of dreams. There were times—but hardly ever anymore; why tonight?—when, in the middle of washing the dishes or sweeping the alley, some small injustice from her past, long forgotten, would rise up in her mind, blocking out all else till her heart beat hard and fast. Like that time, scarcely a month after their wedding, when Yoshitsune had run into his old girlfriend at Nanjin Station and made such a fuss: his absurd, rapt gaze; the intimate timbre of his voice as he inquired after her welfare.

And there was the time—the only time in their entire marriage—when Yoshitsune had grabbed Makiko by the shoulders and shaken her hard. He'd let go immediately, but not before she had felt the anger in his powerful hands and her throat had choked up with fear. That too was early on in the marriage, before Makiko learned to tolerate his sending sizable sums of money to his mother each month.

What is to be done with such memories?

They get scattered, left behind. Over the past few years, more pleasant recollections have taken the lead, informing all the rest, like a flock of birds, heading as one body along an altered course of nostalgia.

She has tried so hard to remain true to the past. But the weight of her need must have been too great: her need to be comforted, her need to provide a legacy for a small, fatherless boy. Tonight she senses how far beneath the surface her own past has sunk, its outline distorted by deceptively clear waters.

Toshi has been counting the days till Tanabata Day. A small festival is being held at the riverbank—the first since the war. It will be a meager affair, of course, nothing like it used to be: no goldfish scooping, no *soba* noodles, no fancy fireworks. However, according to the housewives at the open-air market, there will be a limited number of sparklers—the nicest kind, Makiko tells her son—and traditional corn grilled with *shoyu*, which can be purchased out of each family's food allowance.

Because of an after-dark incident near Kubota Temple involving an American soldier and a young girl, Makiko's younger brother has come by this evening to accompany them to the festival. Noboru is a second-year student at the local university.

"*Ne*, Big Sister! Are you ready yet?" he keeps calling from the living room. Makiko is inspecting Toshi's nails and the back of his collar.

"Big Sister," Noboru says, looking up as Makiko finally appears in the doorway, "your house is too immaculate. I get nervous every time I come here!" He is sitting stiffly on a floor cushion, sipping homemade persimmon tea.

"Well," Makiko answers, "I hate dirt." She has switched, like most women, to Western dresses—they require less fabric—but it makes her irritable, having to expose her bare calves in public. She tugs down her knee-length dress.

"*Aaa*," says young Noboru from his floor cushion, "but I, for one, am fascinated by it. The idea of it, I mean. What's that old saying—'Nothing grows in a sterile pond'? Just think, Big Sister, of the things that come out of dirty water. A lotus, for example. Or a pearl. Just think: a pearl's nothing more than a grain of dirt covered up by an oyster! And life itself, Big Sister, billions of years ago—emerging from the primordial muck!"

"*Maa maa*, Nobo-*kun*." She sighs, double-checking her handbag for coin purse, ration tickets, and handkerchief. "You seem to be learning some very interesting concepts at the university."

Toshi is waiting by the front door in shorts and a collared shirt, impatiently pulling the door open and then shut, open and then shut.

Finally they are on their way, strolling down the narrow alley in the still, muggy evening. The setting sun angles down on the east side of the alley, casting a pink-and-orange glow on the charred wooden lattices, where shadows stretch like the long heads of snails from the slightest of protrusions. In the shadowed side of the alley, one of the bucktoothed Kimura daughters ladles water from a bucket onto the asphalt around her door, pausing, with a good-evening bow, to let them pass. The water, colliding with warm asphalt, has released a smell of many layers: asphalt, earth, scorched wood, tangy dragon's beard moss over a mellower base of tree foliage; prayer incense and *tatami* straw, coming from the Kimuras' half-open door; and mixed in with it all, some scent from far back in Makiko's own childhood that falls just short of definition.

"We Japanese," Noboru is saying, "must reinvent ourselves. We must change to fit the modern world. We mustn't remain an occupied nation." He talks of the new constitution, of the new trade agreements. Makiko has little knowledge of politics. She is amused—disquieted too—by this academic young man, who before the war was a mere boy loping past her window with a butterfly net over his shoulder.

"Fundamental shifts . . . ," Noboru is saying, " . . . outdated pyramidal structures." He has just begun wearing hair pomade with an acrid metallic scent. It seems to suggest fervor, fundamental shifts.

"Toshi-*kun!*" Makiko calls. "Don't go too far." The boy stops running. He walks, taking each new step in exaggerated slow motion.

"So much change!" she says to Noboru as she tugs at her cotton dress. "And so fast. Other countries had centuries to do it in."

"*Sō, sō,* Big Sister!" Noboru says. "*Sō, sō.* But we have no choice—that's a fact. You jettison from a sinking ship if you want to survive."

The pair approaches Mr. Watanabe, watering his potted morning glories in the twilight. Holding his watering can in one hand, the old man gives them a genteel bow over his cane. "Yoshitsune-*san,*" he murmurs politely, "Makiko-*san.*" He then turns back to his morning glories, bending over them with the tenderness of a mother with a newborn.

"Poor Watanabe-*san, ne?*" Noboru whispers. "He gets more and more confused every time we see him."

Yes, poor Mr. Watanabe, Makiko thinks. Bit by bit he is being pulled back in, like a slowing planet, toward some core, some necessary center of his past. Laden with memory, his mind will never catch up to Noboru's new constitution or those trade agreements, or even the implications of that billboard with English characters—instructions for arriving soldiers?—rising above the blackened rooftops and blocking his view of the Hiezan hills.

Oddly, Mr. Watanabe's greeting has triggered a memory: Makiko is strolling with Yoshitsune on a summer evening. For one heart-beat she experiences exactly how things used to be—their commonplace existence, before later events imposed their nostalgia—with a stab of physical recognition that is indefinable, impossible to call up again. Then it is gone, like the gleam of a fish, having stirred up all the waters around her.

They walk on in silence. "Toshi-*kun!*" she calls out again. "Slow down." Toshi pauses, waiting for them; he swings at the air with an imaginary bat. "*Striku! Striku!*" he hisses.

It occurs to Makiko how artificial this war has been, suspending people in the same, unsustainable state of solidarity. For a while everyone had clung together in the bomb shelter off Nijiya Street, thinking the same thoughts, breathing in the same damp earth and the same warm, uneasy currents made by bodies at close range. But that is over now.

Makiko thinks of her future. She is still full of life and momentum. There is no doubt that she will pass through this period and into whatever lies beyond it, but at a gradually slowing pace; a part of her, she knows, will lag behind in the honeyed light of prewar years.

"Toshi-*kun!*" she cries. "Wait!" Her son is racing ahead, his long shadow sweeping the sunlit fence as sparrows flutter up from charred palings.

Makiko stands out on the veranda, fanning herself with a paper *uchiwa.* Toshi is already asleep. The night garden is muggy; the mosquitoes are out in full force. She can hear their ominous whine from the hydrangea bush, in between the rasping of crickets, but they no longer target her as they did in her youth. She is thinner now, her skin harder from the sun, her blood watered down from all the rationing.

It was a wonderful festival. Shadowy adults bent over their children, helping them to hold sparklers over the glassy water. The sparklers sputtered softly in the dark, shedding white flakes of light. Makiko had watched from a distance; Toshi was old enough, he had insisted, to do it by himself. She had remarked to Noboru how there is something in everyone that responds to fireworks: so fleeting, so lovely in the dark.

It was a fine night for Toshi. "This corn is so *good, ne,* Mama?" he kept saying, looking up from his rationed four centimeters of corncob. "This sure tastes *good, ne?*" The joy on his face, caught in the glow of red paper lanterns, brought a lump to her throat.

Tonight there is a full moon. Earlier, at dusk, it was opaque and insubstantial. Now, through shifting moisture in the air, it glows bright and strong, awash with light.

Makiko, the festival owed its luster to all that lay beneath, to all those other evenings of her life and their lingering phosphorescence. Which long-ago evenings exactly? They are slowly losing shape, merging together in her consciousness.

Perhaps Toshi will remember this night. Perhaps it will rise up again once he is grown. Some smell, some glint of light will bring texture and emotion to a future summer evening. As will his memory of praying before his father's picture or being carried by his father before an open window.

The Distribution of Distress

Patricia Williams

*Patricia Williams is a professor of Law. She received a B.A. (1972)
from Wellesley College and a J.D. (1975) from Harvard University.
She has worked both as a lawyer and a professor of law. She is the
author of* The Alchemy of Race and Rights: A Diary of a Law Professor *(1991),* The Rooster's Egg: On the Persistence of Prejudice
(1995), and Seeing a Color-Blind Future: The Paradox of Race
*(1997). Influential not only in legal circles but in the public do-
main as well, she is a columnist for* The Nation. *Her essays and
columns have challenged what many take for granted in our society, particularly with regard to race and gender.*

Many years ago, I was standing in a so-called juice bar in Berkeley, California. A young
man came in whom I had often seen begging in the neighborhood. A more bruised-
looking human one could not imagine: he was missing several teeth, his clothes were
in rags, his blond hair was matted, his eyes red-rimmed, his nails long and black and
broken. On this particular morning he came into the juice bar and ordered some sort
of protein drink from the well-scrubbed, patchouli-scented young woman behind the
counter. It was obvious that his presence disturbed her, and when he took his drink
and mumbled, "Thanks, little lady," she exploded.

"Don't you dare call me 'little lady'!" she snarled with a ferocity that turned
heads. "I'm a *woman* and you'd better learn the difference!"

"Sorry," he whispered with his head bowed, like a dog that had been kicked, and
he quite literally limped out of the store.

"Good riddance," the woman called after him.

This took place some fifteen years ago, but I have always remembered the in-
terchange because it taught me a lot about the not so subliminal messages that can

Reprinted from *Seeing a Color-Blind Future*, (1998), Farrar, Straus & Giroux.

be wrapped in the expression of Virtue Aggrieved, in which antibias of one sort is used to further the agenda of bias of another kind.

In an abstract sense, I understood the resentment for girlish diminutives. Too often as a lawyer I have been in courtroom situations where coy terms of endearment were employed in such a way that "the little lady, God-bless-her" became a marginalizing condescension, a precise condensation of "She thinks she's a lawyer, poor thing." Yet in this instance, gender power was clearly not the issue, but rather the emotional venting of a revulsion at this man's dirty and bedraggled presence. It wasn't just that he had called her a little lady; she seemed angry that he had dared address her at all.

If, upon occasion, the ploughshare of feminism can be beaten into a sword of class prejudice, no less can there be other examples of what I call battling biases, in which the impulse to antidiscrimination is defeated by the intrusion or substitution of a different object of enmity. This revolving door of revulsions is one of the trickiest mechanisms contributing to the enduring nature of prejudice; it is at heart, I suppose, a kind of traumatic reiteration of injurious encounters, preserving even as it transforms the overall history of rage.

I was in England several years ago when a young Asian man was severely beaten in East London by a young white man. I was gratified to see the immediate renunciation of racism that ensued in the media. It was a somewhat more sophisticated and heartfelt collective self-examination than sometimes occurs in the United States in the wake of such incidents, where, I fear, we are much more jaded about all forms of violence. Nevertheless, what intrigued me most about the media coverage of this assault was the unfortunate way in which class bias became a tool for the denunciation of racism.

"Racial, Ethnic, or Religious Prejudice Is Repugnant," screamed the headlines.

Hooray, I thought.

And then the full text: "It is repugnant, *particularly*"—and I'm embellishing here—"when committed by a miserable low-class cockney whose bestial nature knows no plummeted depth, etc. etc."

Oh dear, I thought.

In other words, the media not only defined anti-Asian and anti-immigrant animus as ignorance, as surely it is, but went on to define that ignorance as the property of a class, of "the" lower classes, implying even that a good Oxbridge education inevitably lifts one above that sort of thing. As surely it does not.

And therein lies a problem, I think. If race or ethnicity is not a synonym for either ignorance or foreignness, then neither should class be an explanatory trashbin for racial prejudice, domestic incivility, and a host of other social ills. If the last fifty years have taught us nothing else, it is that our "isms" are no less insidious when beautifully polished and terribly refined.

None of us is beyond some such pitfalls, and in certain contexts typecasting can even be a necessary and helpful way of explaining the social world. The hard task is to untangle the instances where the categoric helps us predict and prepare for the world from those instances where it verges on scapegoating, projection, and prejudice.

To restate the problem, I think that the persistence of racism, ethnic and religious intolerance, as well as gender and class bias, is dependent upon recirculating images in which the general and the particular duel each other endlessly.

"En garde, you heathenish son of an inferior category!"

"Brute!" comes the response. "I am inalienably endowed with the unique luminosity of my rational individualism; it is you who are the guttural eruption of an unspeakable subclassification . . ."

Thrust and parry, on and on, the play of race versus ethnicity versus class versus blood feud. One sword may be sharper or quicker, but neither's wound is ever healed.

Too often these tensions are resolved simply by concluding that stereotyping is just our lot as humans so let the consequences fall where they may. But stereotyping operates as habit not immutable trait, a fluid project that rather too easily flows across the shifting ecology of human relations. And racism is a very old, very bad habit.

This malleability of prejudice is underscored by a little cultural comparison. If class bias has skewed discussions of racism in the British examples I have just described, it is rather more common in the United States for race to consume discussions of class altogether. While I don't want to overstate the cultural differences between the United States and the United Kingdom—there is enough similarity to conclude that race and class present a generally interlocking set of problems in both nations—the United States does deem itself classless with almost the same degree of self-congratulation that the United Kingdom prides itself on being largely free of a history of racial bias. Certainly these are good impulses and desirable civic sentiments, but I am always one to look closely at what is deemed beyond the pale. *It will never happen here* . . . The noblest denials are at least as interesting study as the highest ideals.

Consider: for a supposedly classless society, the United States nevertheless suffers the greatest gap of any industrialized nation between its richest and poorest citizens. And there can be no more dramatic and ironic class consciousness than the Dickensian characteristics ascribed to those in the so-called underclass, as opposed to the rest—what are we to call them, the *over*class? Those who are deemed to have class versus those who are so far beneath the usual indicia of even lower class that they are deemed to have no class at all.

If this is not viewed by most Americans as a problem of class stasis, it is perhaps because class denominations are so uniformly understood to be stand-ins for race. The very term *underclass* is a *euphemism* for blackness, class operating as euphemism in that we Americans are an upbeat kind of people and class is usually thought to be an easier problem than race.

Middle-classness, on the other hand, is so persistently a euphemism for whiteness, that middle-class black people are sometimes described as "honorary whites" or as those who have been deracinated in some vaguely political sense. More often than I like to remember, I have been told that my opinion about this or that couldn't possibly be relevant to "real," "authentic" black people. Why? Simply because I don't sound like a Hollywood stereotype of the way black people are "supposed" to talk. "Speaking white" or "Talking black." No in-between. Speaking as a black person while

377

sounding like a white person has, I have found, engendered some complicated sense of betrayal. "*You're* not black! You're not *white!*" No one seems particularly interested in the substantive ideas being expressed; but everyone is caught up with the question of whether anyone should have to listen to a white-voiced black person.

It is in this way that we often talk about class and race such that we sometimes end up talking about neither, because we insist on talking about race as though it were class and class as though it were race, and it's hard to see very clearly when the waters are so muddied with all that simile and metaphor.

By the same token, America is usually deemed a society in which the accent with which one speaks Does Not Matter. That is largely true, but it is not so where black accents are concerned. While there is much made of regional variations—New Yorkers, Minnesotans, and Southerners are the butts of a certain level of cheap satire—an accent deemed "black" is the one with some substantial risk of evoking outright discrimination. In fact, the speech of real black people ranges from true dialects to myriad patois, to regional accents, to specific syntactical twists or usages of vocabulary. Yet language identified as black is habitually flattened into some singularized entity that in turn becomes synonymous with ignorance, slang, big lips and sloppy tongues, incoherent ideas, and very bad—terribly unruly!—linguistic acts. Black speech becomes a cipher for all the other stereotypes associated with racial discrimination; the refusal to understand becomes rationalized by the assumption of incomprehensibility.

My colleague Professor Mari Matsuda has studied cases involving accent discrimination. She writes of lawsuits whose transcripts revealed an interesting paradox. One case featured a speaker whose accent had been declared incomprehensible by his employer. Nevertheless, his recorded testimony, copied down with no difficulty by the court reporter, revealed a parlance more grammatically accurate, substantively coherent, and syntactically graceful than any other speaker in the courtroom, including the judge. This paradox has always been the subject of some interest among linguists and sociolinguists, the degree to which language is understood in a way that is intimately linked to relations among speakers.

"Good day," I say to you. Do you see me as a genial neighbor, as part of your day? If so, you may be generously disposed to return the geniality with a hearty "Hale fellow, well met."

"Good day," I say. Do you see me as an impudent upstart the very sound of whose voice is an unwelcome intrusion upon your good day? If so, the greeting becomes an act of aggression; woe betide the cheerful, innocent upstart.

"Shall we consider race?" I say to you. If you are disposed to like me, you might hear this as an invitation to a kind of conversation we have not shared before, a leap of faith into knowing more about each other.

"Shall we consider race?" I say. *Not* "Shall I batter you with guilt before we riot in the streets?" But only: "Shall we *consider* race?" Yet if I am that same upstart, the blood will have boiled up in your ears by now, and very shortly you will start to have tremors from the unreasonable audacity of my meddlesome presumption. Nothing I actually say will matter, for what matters is that I am out of place . . .

This dynamic, this vital ingredient of the willingness to hear, is apparent in the contradiction of lower-status speech being simultaneously understood yet not understood. Why is the sound of black voices, the shape of black bodies so overwhelmingly agreeable, so colorfully comprehensible in some contexts, particularly in the sports and entertainment industries, yet deemed so utterly incapable of effective communication or acceptable presence when it comes to finding a job as a construction worker?

This is an odd conundrum, to find the sight and the sound of oneself a red flag. And it is a kind of banner, one's face and one's tongue, a banner of family and affiliation—that rhythm and stress, the buoyance of one's mother's tongue; that plane of jaw, that prominence of brow, the property of one's father's face. What to make of those social pressures that would push the region of the body underground in order to allow the purity of one's inner soul to be more fully seen? When Martin Luther King, Jr., urged that we be judged by the content of our character, surely he meant that what we looked like should not matter. Yet just as surely that enterprise did not involve having to deny the entirely complicated symbolic character of one's physical manifestation. This is a hard point, I confess, and one fraught with risk of misunderstanding. The color of one's skin is a part of ourselves. It does not matter. It is precious, and yet it should not matter; it is important and yet it must not matter. It is simultaneously our greatest vanity and anxiety, and I am of the opinion, like Martin Luther King, that none of this should matter.

Yet let me consider the question of self-erasure. I've written elsewhere about my concern that various forms of biotechnological engineering have been turned to such purposes—from skin lighteners to cosmetic surgery to the market for sperm with blond hair and eggs with high IQs. Consider the boy I read about who had started some sort of computer magazine for children. A young man of eleven, celebrated as a computer whiz, whose family had emigrated from Puerto Rico, now living in New York. The article recounted how much he loved computers because, he said, nobody judged him for what he looked like, and he could speak without an accent. What to make of this freedom as disembodiment, this technologically purified mental communion as escape from the society of others, as neutralized social space. What a delicate project, this looking at each other, seeing yet not staring. Would we look so hard, judge so hard, be so hard—what would we look like?—if we existed unself-consciously in our bodies—sagging, grayhaired, young, old, black, white, balding and content?

Let me offer a more layered illustration of the way in which these issues of race and class interact, the markers of class distinction and bias in the United Kingdom emerging also in the United States as overlapping substantially with the category of race. A few years ago, I purchased a house. Because the house was in a different state than where I was located at the time, I obtained my mortgage by telephone. I am a prudent little squirrel when it comes to things financial, always tucking away sufficient stores of nuts for the winter, and so I meet all the criteria of a quite good credit risk. My loan was approved almost immediately.

A short time after, the contract came in the mail. Among the papers the bank forwarded were forms documenting compliance with what is called the Fair Housing Act. It is against the law to discriminate against black people in the housing market, and one of the pieces of legislation to that effect is the Fair Housing Act, a law that monitors lending practices to prevent banks from doing what is called "red-lining." Redlining is a phenomenon whereby banks circle certain neighborhoods on the map and refuse to lend in those areas for reasons based on race. There are a number of variations on the theme. Black people cannot get loans to purchase homes in white areas; or black people cannot get start-up money for small businesses in black areas. The Fair Housing Act thus tracks the race of all banking customers to prevent such discrimination. Unfortunately, some banks also use the racial information disclosed on the Fair Housing forms to engage in precisely the discrimination the law seeks to prevent.

I should repeat that to this point my entire mortgage transaction had been conducted by telephone. I should also say that I speak what is considered in the States a very Received-Standard-English, regionally northeastern perhaps, but not marked as black. With my credit history, with my job as a law professor, and no doubt with my accent, I am not only middle-class but match the cultural stereotype of a good white person. It is thus perhaps that the loan officer of this bank, whom I had never met in person, had checked off a box on the Fair Housing form indicating that I *was* "white."

Race shouldn't matter, I suppose, but it seemed to in this case, and so I took a deep breath, crossed out "white," checked the box marked "black," and sent the contract back to the bank. That will teach them to presume too much, I thought. A done deal, I assumed.

Suddenly said deal came to a screeching halt. The bank wanted more money as a down payment, they wanted me to pay more points, they wanted to raise the rate of interest. Suddenly I found myself facing great resistance and much more debt.

What was most interesting about all this was that the reason the bank gave for its newfound recalcitrance was not race, heaven forbid—racism doesn't exist anymore, hadn't I heard? No, the reason they gave was that property values in that neighborhood were suddenly falling. They wanted more money to cover the increased risk.

Initially, I was surprised, confused. The house was in a neighborhood that was extremely stable; prices in the area had not gone down since World War II, only slowly, steadily up. I am an extremely careful shopper and I had uncovered absolutely no indication that prices were falling at all.

It took my real estate agent to make me see the fight. "Don't you get it," he sighed. "This is what they always do."

And even though I work with this sort of thing all the time, I really hadn't gotten it: for of course, *I* was the reason the prices were in peril.

The bank was proceeding according to demographic data that show any time black people move into a neighborhood in the States, whites are overwhelmingly likely to move out. In droves. In panic. In concert. Pulling every imaginable resource with them, from school funding to garbage collection to social workers who don't want to work in black neighborhoods to police whose too frequent relation to black communities is a corrupted one of containment rather than protection.

It's called a tipping point, this thing that happens when black people move into white neighborhoods. The imagery is awfully catchy you must admit: the neighborhood just tipping right on over like a terrible accident, whoops! Like a pitcher I suppose. All that nice fresh wholesome milk spilling out, running away . . . leaving the dark, echoing, upended urn of the inner city.

This immense fear of "the black" next door is one reason the United States is so densely segregated. Only two percent of white people have a black neighbor, even though black people constitute approximately thirteen percent of the population. White people fear black people in big ways, in small ways, in financial ways, in utterly incomprehensible ways.

As for my mortgage, I threatened to sue and eventually procured the loan on the original terms. But what was fascinating to me about this whole incident was the way in which it so exemplified the new problems of the new rhetoric of racism. For starters, the new rhetoric of racism never mentions race. It wasn't race but risk with which the bank was concerned. Second, since financial risk is all about economics, my exclusion got reclassified as just a consideration of class, and there's no law against class discrimination, after all, for that would present a restraint on one of our most precious liberties, the freedom to contract or not. If public schools, trains, buses, swimming pools, and neighborhoods remain segregated, it's no longer a racial problem if someone who just happens to be white keeps hiking the price for someone who just accidentally and purely by the way happens to be black. White people set higher prices for the "right," the "choice" of self-segregation. If black people don't move in, it's just that they can't *afford* to. Black people pay higher prices for the attempt to integrate, even as the integration of oneself is a threat to one's investment by lowering its value.

By this measure of mortgage worthiness, the ingredient of blackness is cast not just as a social toll but as an actual tax. A fee, an extra contribution at the door, an admission charge for the higher costs of handling my dangerous propensities, my inherently unsavory properties. I was not judged based on my independent attributes or individual financial worth as a client; nor even was I judged by statistical profiles of what my group actually do. (For, in fact, anxiety-stricken, middle-class black people make grovelingly good cake-baking neighbors when not made to feel defensive by the unfortunate, historical welcome strategies of bombs, burnings, or abandon.)

Rather, I was being evaluated based on what an abstraction of White Society writ large thinks we—or I—do, and that imagined "doing" was treated and thus established as a self-fulfilling prophecy.

However rationalized, this form of discrimination is a burden: one's very existence becomes a lonely vacuum when so many in society not only devalue *me,* but devalue *themselves* and their homes for having me as part of the landscaped view from the quiet of their breakfast nook.

I know, I know, I exist in the world on my own terms surely. I am an individual and all that. But if I carry the bank's logic out with my individuality rather than my collectively imagined effect on property values as the subject of this type of irrational economic computation, then I, the charming and delightful Patricia J. Williams, become a bit like a car wash in your backyard. Only much worse in real price terms. I am more than a mere violation of the nice residential comfort zone in question; my blackness can rezone altogether by the mere fortuity of my relocation.

"Dumping district," cringes the nice, clean actuarial family next door; "there goes the neighborhood . . ." as whole geographic tracts slide into the chasm of impecuniousness and disgust. I am the economic equivalent of a medical waste disposal site, a toxic heap-o'-home.

In my brand-new house, I hover behind my brand-new kitchen curtains, wondering whether the very appearance of my self will endanger my collateral yet further. When Benetton ran an advertisement that darkened Queen Elizabeth II's skin to a nice rich brown, the *Sun* newspaper ran an article observing that this "obviously cheapens the monarchy." Will the presentation of my self so disperse the value of my own, my ownership, my property?

This is madness, I am sure, as I draw the curtain like a veil across my nose. In what order of things is it *rational* to thus hide and skulk?

It is an intolerable logic. An investment in my property compels a selling of myself.

I grew up in a white neighborhood where my mother's family had been the only black people for about fifty years. In the 1960s, Boston began to feel the effects of the great migration of Southern blacks to the north that came about as a result of the Civil Rights Movement. Two more black families moved into the neighborhood. There was a sudden churning, a chemical response, a collective roiling with streams of froth and jets of steam. We children heard all about it on the playground. The neighborhood was under siege. The blacks were coming. My schoolmates' parents were moving out *en masse.*

It was remarkable. The neighborhood was entirely black within about a year.

I am a risk pool. I am a car wash.

I was affected, I suppose, growing up with those children who frightened themselves by imagining what it would be like to touch black bodies, to kiss those wide unkissable lips, to draw the pure breath of life through that crude and forbidden expanse of nose; is it really possible that a gentle God—their God, dear God—would let a *human* heart reside within the wet charred thickness of black skin?

I am, they told me, a jumble of discarded parts: low-browed monkey bones and infected, softly pungent flesh.

In fact, my price on the market is a variable affair. If I were crushed and sorted into common elements, my salt and juice and calcinated bits are worth approximately five English pounds. Fresh from the kill, in contrast, my body parts, my lungs and liver, heart and healthy arteries, would fetch some forty thousand. There is no demand for the fruit of my womb, however; eggs fresh from their warm dark sanctuary are worthless on the open market. "Irish Egg Donor Sought," reads an ad in the little weekly newspaper that serves New York City's parent population. And in the weird economy of bloodlines, and with the insidious variability of prejudice, "Irish eggs" command a price of upwards of five thousand pounds.

This silent market in black worth is pervasive. When a certain brand of hiking boots became popular among young people in Harlem, the manufacturer pulled the product from inner-city stores, fearing that such a trend would "ruin" the image of their boot among the larger market of whites.

It's funny . . . even shoes.

Last year I had a funny experience in a shoe store. The salesman would bring me only one shoe, not two.

"I can't try on a pair?" I asked in disbelief.

"When you pay for a pair," he retorted. "What if there were a hundred of you," he continued. "How would we keep track?"

I was the only customer in the store, but there were a hundred of me in his head.

In our Anglo-American jurisprudence there is a general constraint limiting the right to sue to cases and controversies affecting the individual. As an individual, I could go to the great and ridiculous effort of suing for the minuscule amount at stake in waiting for the other shoe to drop from his hand; but as for the real claim, the group claim, the larger defamation to all those other hundreds of me . . . well, that will be a considerably tougher row to hoe.

I am one, I am many.

I am amiable, orderly, extremely honest, and a very good neighbor indeed. I am suspect profile, market cluster, actuarial monster, statistical being.

My particulars battle the generals.

"Typecasting!" I protest.

"Predictive indicator," assert the keepers of the gate.

"Prejudice!" I say.

"Precaution," they reply.

Hundreds, even thousands, of me hover in the breach.

Virtual Worlds

Benjamin Woolley

British author Benjamin Woolley, a correspondent for The Late Show, *was the first to introduce the idea of virtual reality in Britain. He has contributed numerous articles to national newspapers and magazines on technology. He also writes 'Signs of Life,' an edition of* Horizon *on the use of computers in the study and simulation of life forms. In 1992, Benjamin Woolley won the BP Arts Journalism television award.* Virtual Worlds. A Journey in Hyperreality *examines the dramatic intellectual and cultural changes brought about by the development of technology.*

In our days everything seems pregnant with its contrary.

Karl Marx, 1856.

On 7 May, 1987, the US multinational Proctor & Gamble submitted Olestra, a new food substitute, to the American Food and Drug Administration (FDA) for approval. Olestra was, in the judgement of the world's media as well as Proctor & Gamble's publicity, potentially one of the most significant nutritional breakthroughs of its time. It promised what every dieter desired, the realization of an impossible dream: fat-free fat.

For a dietary aid, Olestra is made out of unpromising ingredients, sugar and fat. However, when they are chemically bonded together in the correct way, they form a new and very strange substance: sucrose polyester. It may sound better suited to manufacturing shirts than food, but sucrose polyester has interesting nutritional qualities. It retains the culinary and textural qualities of the fat, but in a form that the body is unable to digest. Result: a fat that passes straight through the body. In tests,

Reprinted from *Virtual Worlds: A Journey in Hype and Hyperreality*, (1992), Blackwell Publishing, Ltd.

obese subjects who ate a diet that used Olestra lost weight even if they were allowed to supplement the diet with conventional fatty snacks.

Fat-free fat. It is a concept pregnant with its own contrary. When Marx used the phrase in 1856, he was commenting on an era that was having to come to terms with the violent impact of industrialization on the order of nature. This book is about the impact of an even more disorientating era: artificialization, of making dreams come true, of 'imagineering' as the Disney Corporation calls it. What are the extent and limits of the artificial? Is there, can there be, any contact with reality when it is possible to make fat that is not fat, when the fake becomes indistinguishable from—even more authentic than—the original, when computers can create synthetic worlds that are more realistic than the real world, when technology scorns nature?

Evidence of artificialization seemed to be abundant at the time of writing this book. Wherever one looked, artificiality was triumphing over reality. In the closing months of 1991, as the Soviet Union broke apart, the fate of the embalmed body of Lenin, which had been lying in state since 1924, was in doubt. Some had questioned whether, indeed, it was his 'real' body at all, Lenin's unblemished facial complexion suggesting that it might be a waxwork. But who cares? Most British politicians would happily become a waxwork if it meant a position at Madame Tussaud's, the most popular tourist site in London. In an artificial world, there is no need for Lenin's material substance any more than there is a need for the great materialist state he founded. It is, perhaps, a fitting symbol of the triumph of the land of dreams over the empire of iron, the 'end of history', that Lenin should be left to decay while the cryogenically preserved Walt Disney waits in suspended animation (an appropriate state for a cartoonist) to return to the world that is now his.

As the worms awaited Lenin, a book entitled *Fly Fishing* by J. R. Hartley entered the British bestseller list. Unremarkable though it may have seemed, this was no ordinary book. British Telecom had run a series of television commercials featuring an elderly man locating a copy of the out-of-print *Fly Fishing* by J. R. Hartley using the Yellow Pages. The man turns out at the end of the commercial to be J. R. Hartley. So moved was the audience by this story that bookshops and even the British Library were reportedly overwhelmed with requests for it—even though, of course, no such book and no such author had ever existed. So the publisher Random Century decided to create one. It commissioned the writer Michael Russell to ghost write the book, and hired the actor Norman Lumsden, who had played Hartley in the original advertisement, to pose as the author. The result was a fiction turned into fact—artificial reality.

Few of us think about 'reality' much—those of us who intend to write books about it have to keep reminding ourselves that we are rare exceptions. It is, perhaps, the conceptual equivalent of unconscious motor functions such as breathing. It is vital to life—without it, we would be unable to distinguish the real from the imaginary, the true from the false, the natural from the artificial. But we do not have to think about it to use it—indeed, as soon as we do start thinking about it, it becomes extremely difficult to continue using it. For this reason, perhaps, some may regard it as a peculiar subject for any sort of analysis: it is a given, a fact of life, and best left hidden behind the curtain of unconsciousness.

To extend (but I hope not exhaust) the breathing metaphor, the problem is that just as a polluted environment can make us short of breath, so an increasingly complex, artificial environment can diminish our sense of reality. And, as that sense diminishes, so innumerable troubling side-effects start to creep in. Soon after Olestra's announcement, an American pressure group, the Center for Science in the Public Interest, quoted the results of tests using rats which showed that nearly a half of the rats fed on Olestra died during the period of the experiment, compared with under a third of the rats fed a normal diet. 'Aha!' said the critics, 'There you have it: you think you can have fat for free, but there is really a price, the price that nature usually exacts, cancer.'

The prejudice that favours the products of nature over our own is, perhaps, understandable. Nature's approvals process is slower even that the FDA's, working at the pace of evolutionary time to separate dangerous substances from those to whom they are a danger. We are part of a natural order poised in a state of delicate equilibrium, safe as long as we keep to our position within it. This 'natural order' is a very basic, important structure. It is independent of us, uncontaminated by us. The problem with synthetic substances like Olestra is that they are not a part of it—worse, that they seem to ignore it, even violate it. Fat-free fat, like alcohol-free alcoholic drinks, sugar-free sweets and caffeine-free coffee, flouts the reality principle, the principle that you cannot have something for nothing, that everything has its price, that nothing in life is free, that there is no such thing as a free lunch, that there can be no gain without pain. Science and technology have arrogantly ignored this principle, and the result is a world filled with disease and pollution.

But must it be thus? Surely there *could* be gain without pain or, more appropriately given that Olestra is a dietary aid, less without distress, crapulence without corpulence? As the *US News & World Report* put it in a rather breathless report about food substitutes entitled 'Have your cake and eat it, too', 'the foodstuffs of which dieters dream are fast becoming realities'. And why not? A few cancerous rats prove nothing: there is no law of science (though perhaps one of logic) that says a fat-free fat is impossible.

It is this sort of debate, and what for most of us is a genuine feeling of uncertainty as to exactly what we can believe that makes any secure, unexamined notion of reality increasingly troublesome. How is it possible to hold a clear view of the distinction between reality and fantasy when the unreal is continually being realized?

There has never been a totally secure view of reality, certainly not in the industrial era of history. People say that the world is not as real than it used to be. Well, to adapt what an editor of *Punch* said in response to a tiresome criticism of his magazine: the world was *never* as real as it used to be. Indeed, it is industry, the power to manufacture what previously had to be taken from nature, that has made the world progressively more artificial and less real, that provided the wealth and energy to change the natural landscape, even to replace it with one of our own making. But equally the industrial era has been about the discovery of reality. The ability to manipulate nature, to turn its operation to our own ends, shows how successful science has been in discovering how it works, and technology in exploiting that discovery. The industrial experience, in other words, seems to have both destroyed reality and reinforced it.

As we enter the so-called post-industrial era, the crisis continues. It is a favourite theme of nearly all commentaries about the times we live in. There is a 'legitimation crisis', a 'crisis of representation', and one great big 'crisis of modernity'. As Umberto Eco observed: 'Crisis sells well. During the last few decades we have witnessed the sale (on newsstands, in bookshops, by subscription, door-to-door) of the crisis of religion, of Marxism, of representation, the sign, philosophy, ethics, Freudianism, presence, the subject . . . Whence the well-known quip: "God is dead, Marxism is undergoing crisis, and I don't feel so hot myself." The question such crises pose is whether this means that attitudes to reality have been undermined by the experience of modernity, or whether reality itself, something firm and objective, something underpinning the uncertain world of appearance, has been shown to be an illusion. Is the lesson we should have learnt from the last century that *there is no reality?* When the newspapers and the food manufacturers tell us that dreams are fast becoming realities, does that really mean that reality is fast becoming a dream?

For centuries the issue of what does and does not count as real has been a matter of philosophy. There have been two main questions, what could be called the ontological and epistemological questions. The ontological question is about being: what is real? Is there a reality behind appearance? The epistemological question is about knowing: what is truth? Is knowledge the product of reason or of experience? For most people, and certainly for most scientists, neither question is particularly relevant, because there are working systems that are used to tell reality from appearance, truth from falsity. When a court assesses the truth of a witness's evidence, epistemology does not come into it. The judge does not ask the members of the jury whether or not they are rationalists or empiricists. Similarly, the result of an experiment does not rest on whether the scientist performing the experiment is an idealist or materialist.

At Britain's first virtual reality conference, held in the summer of 1991, the chairman, Tony Feldman, tried to emphasize that the agenda he had drawn up was concerned with hard-headed, pragmatic business issues, but conceded that 'the metaphysics are inescapable'. Technology, he and the subsequent speakers observed, could manipulate reality to the point of being able to create it. Artificialization is no longer just a matter of cultural observation or intellectual angst, it had become, well, real. It is for this reason that reality is no longer secure, no longer something we can simply assume to be there.

Most people probably now have some idea of what virtual reality is. It is the technology used to provide a more intimate 'interface' between humans and computer imagery. It is about simulating the full ensemble of sense data that make up 'real' experience. Ideally, the user wears a device that substitutes the sense data coming from the natural world with that produced by a computer. Computer screens are placed before the eyes, 'effectors' cover the body, providing the sights of this artificial world, and the feelings that result from touching it. Furthermore, tracking devices attached to the body monitor its movements, so, as the user moves, so what he or she sees and feels is altered accordingly. This book does not provide a technical description or assessment of this technology. I am more concerned with the two issues that underlie its emergence as one of the 'Big Ideas' of the 1990s, issues that remain neglected by the computer industry, but which I hope to show are essential to making sense of the developments that have lead to this rude instrusion of metaphysics into ordinary life.

The first issue is simulation. Computers are unique in that they are all, in a sense, simulations of some ideal computer, a 'universal machine'. Everything a computer does can be seen as a simulation, except that many of the things it simulates do not exist beyond the simulation. What, then, is simulation? Is it just another form of imitation or representation, fiction for the computer age? Can anything be simulated—even reality and human intelligence? These questions raise important mathematical and scientific questions, and in attempting to answer them I hope to show what is 'special' about the computer, why it is not just a glorified calculator, and why those who have developed it have attributed to it such extraordinary creative powers.

The second issue concerns artificial reality. It is a strange, provocative notion. It is hard to tell on first acquaintance whether it is meaningful or meaningless. It could be a new paradigm, it could be pretentious. It could be an oxymoron, a figure of speech that uses what sounds like a contradiction to suggest a much deeper truth. It could just be a contradiction. It has become a general-purpose metaphor for both the present and the future, one that is easy to pick up but impossible to put down. Its attractions are obvious. It is a term full of novelty and puzzle, provocatively coined to intensify a deep-seated insecurity as well as capture a sense of technological adventure.

The term's origin is generally attributed to Myron Krueger, an American 'computer artist and educator' (his own description), who used it as the title of a book written in the 1970s but not published until 1983. The book's subject was what he called 'responsive environments', art installations in which lighting and sound would change according to the movement of people walking around them. He did not, however, use the term 'artificial reality' as a technological label. He had a more ambitious use for it: 'The world described in Genesis, created by mysterious cosmic forces, was a volatile and dangerous place. It moulded human life through incomprehensible caprice. Natural beneficence tempered by natural disaster defined reality. For centuries, the goal of human effort was to tap Nature's terrible power. Our success has been so complete, that a new world has emerged. Created by human ingenuity, it is an artificial reality.'

The champions of virtual reality and computer simulation—who are not just pioneering visionaries but powerful commercial interests—are wanting to make artificial reality real. To them, it promises not just a world where you can eat fat without getting fat, not just a metaphor, but the actual creation of any world you could ever want or imagine—fantastical, fabulous, terrifying, infinite, enclosed, utopian, Stygian. I want to look at the validity of such promises, and to discover their influence over the whole notion of reality. Artificial reality has acquired the role of a sort of Barium meal ingested by the body of society and culture, its spreading glow revealing, under the X-ray of critical examination, the growths and malfunctions of the internal organs.

Just like a Barium meal, some people find any discussion about artificial or virtual reality hard to swallow. Upon introducing the idea to innocent members of the lay public, I discovered that, far from showing mild interest or no interest, they would look at me as though I had announced myself to be the risen Messiah. Life, they seemed to say, is complicated enough without making it more complicated with such outlandish ideas. Such an attitude has a proud and long tradition in Anglo-Saxon culture. You could say it was formulated as long ago as the fourteenth century, when it came to be known as 'Occam's razor', after the English philosopher William of Occam. Occam was a ferociously ascetic Franciscan, so ascetic he actually led a revolt in favour of poverty, when Pope John XXII threatened to end it as a monastical principle. He was an equally ferocious intellectual ascetic, demanding that in philosophical theory, 'entities are not to be multiplied beyond necessity', a principle more economically expressed in the phrase 'cut the crap'. Judged in such terms, most contemporary theory, especially that coming from the fields of information technology and cultural criticism, seems in need of a good shave.

Some contemporary theorists positively encourage the multiplication of entities. One of the most enthusiastic is the influential French sociologist Roland Barthes, who died in 1980. His most important work was *Mythologies,* a book that unblushingly used the most sophisticated analytical techniques to examine the most commonplace objects and activities: wrestling, margarine, photos of Greta Garbo, polystyrene. It was Barthes's explicit aim to break the illusion of 'naturalness' that is used by mass media to dress up reality. He wanted to show that our notion of the natural and the real is really a highly political construction, a product of history. 'In short, in the account given of our contemporary circumstances . . . I wanted to track down, in the decorative display of *what-goes-without-saying,* the ideological abuse which, in my view, is hidden there.' He set out to be reality's party pooper, to show that, in his language, it is the product of myth.

Neologisms are, Barthes claims, essential precisely because of this myth. What we take to be fixed and certain is, in fact, constantly changing, and so the language used to analyse it must change too. The words that appear in dictionaries, words that are presented as having meaning independent of history, are no use. We need new ones: 'neologism is therefore inevitable. China is one thing, the idea which a French petit-bourgeois could have of it not so long ago is another: for this peculiar mixture of bells, rickshaws and opium-dens, no other word is possibly but *Sininess.* Unlovely? One should at least get some consolation from the fact that conceptual neologisms are never arbitrary: they are built according to a highly sensible proportional rule'. Artificial reality. Unlovely, or built according to a highly sensible proportional rule? Just another example of intellectual stubble and a candidate for Occam's cut-throat, or a perfectly legitimate example of a new term for something that has not been previously recognized or expressed?

My belief is that artificial reality does reveal a great deal about the 'myth' of reality—about the way that the idea of reality is used and understood, at least within the Western culture that gave birth to it. If nothing else, it reveals that much of what we take to be reality *is* myth, just as Olestra reveals that the idea of fat is a myth. It reveals that the things we assume to be independent of us are actually constructed by us. It reveals that being 'real', like being 'natural', is not simply a value-free, un-problematic, apolitical, objective state—though part of its mythology is to make itself appear to be so. It reveals that, like 'new' and, indeed, 'natural', 'real' has been abducted by business as a marketing term.

Artificial reality, then, expresses the ambiguity of current attitudes to reality. But that ambiguity is not, as most commentators on the subject have taken it to be, evidence that there is no reality. Just because there is a reality myth does not mean that reality is a myth. The absurdity of such a position is revealed in attempts by some antirealists to argue that they cannot assert reality to be a myth because that would be to assert that what is real is that reality is a myth, which cannot be asserted as there is no reality (because it is a myth).

I want to show that such denials of reality are mistaken, that there is a reality, and that the virtual form of it, far from releasing us from it, can help us recover it. I also believe we need it. Take away reality, and all that is left is relativism, a belief that truth can be established simply by asserting it, that the self is all that exists—no, that *myself* is all that exists. The computing industry was built on the liberal belief in the individual as the only legitimate political entity, and virtual reality has, in some hands, been promoted as the ultimate embodiment of that principle. What better way of expressing your individualism than by creating your own, individual reality? Empowered by the personal computer, liberated by virtual reality, the individual becomes the God of his or her own universe. The sight of someone wearing a virtual reality headset is the ultimate image of solipsistic self-absorption, their movements and gestures meaningless to those left outside.

We have to look, then, at how virtual reality and artificial reality, the technology and culture, are changing public reality. Because the formidable might of commerce and in particular the computing industry have been deployed in defining reality, we need to look at what they mean to do with it.

For Anne Gregory

William Butler Yeats

Irish poet, dramatist, and prose writer, William Butler Yeats was one of the greatest English-language poets of the 20th century. Yeats received the Nobel Prize for Literature in 1923. Born in Dublin in 1865, he moved with his family to London in 1867. In 1881 they returned to Dublin, where Yeats studied at the Metropolitan School of Art. In 1885, Yeats published his first poems in The Dublin University Review. *His volumes of poetry include* The Wanderings of Oisin and Other Poems *(1889), He also wrote plays:* Cathleen Ni Houlihan *(1902) and* The Land of Heart's Desire *(1894), and a book of mystical philosophy called* A Vision *(1925). Yeats often mixes Irish mythology, mysticism, and Christian belief in his poems.*

'Never shall a young man,
Thrown into despair
By those great honey-coloured
Ramparts at your ear,
Love you for yourself alone
And not your yellow hair.'

'But I can get a hair-dye
And set such colour there,
Brown, or black, or carrot,
That young men in despair
May love me for myself alone
And not my yellow hair.'

'I heard an old religious man
But yesternight declare
That he had found a text to prove
That only God, my dear,
Could love you for yourself alone
And not your yellow hair.'

THE MOTHER OF GOD

The threefold terror of love; a fallen flare
Through the hollow of an ear;
Wings beating about the room;
The terror of all terrors that I bore
The Heavens in my womb.

Had I not found content among the shows
Every common woman knows,
Chimney corner, garden walk,
Or rocky cistern where we tread the clothes
And gather all the talk?

What is this flesh I purchased with my pains,
This fallen star my milk sustains,
This love that makes my heart's blood stop
Or strikes a sudden chill into my bones
And bids my hair stand up?

NEW CONCATENATIONS

The following writing assignments are based on successive connections between individual texts, which can lead to sets of interrelated essays. The assignments are called *links,* because they connect texts to each other. A set of assignments is called a *concatenation,* because the assignments are connected to each other like links in a chain, that is, loosely, not rigidly. The word "link" is also used to indicate the places in a hypertext from which one can connect to a different site. The navigation from text to text enabled by the links is a good metaphor for the activity of developing and connecting ideas. Both *link* and *concatenation* suggest freedom in selecting and relating concepts, but they also emphasize the connectedness necessary for a piece of writing to make sense.

Every concatenation has five links, and each link can include from one to four texts. Some links include movies, and some include research. A concatenation of links gives you the opportunity to consider the texts included in it from different angles and to discover new layers of meaning with each new essay you write. The number of possible links between texts in this book is virtually unlimited. You are invited both to test some of the links bellow and to create your own by generating other combinations.

Each link has a theme that can become the topic of your paper. The first paragraph of the link contains a quotation, whose interpretation can serve as a map for constructing an argument with examples from all the texts. The second paragraph in the link asks questions that you may use to start brainstorming and discovering ideas for your paper. You may also use them to free write in preparation for writing the essay. Finally, the last paragraph asks the central question of the assignment that has to be answered in an essay form.

This format gives you the freedom to take the premise of the assignment in whichever direction you find interesting and appealing to you. The use of a quotation as a starting point for your work on the paper emphasizes the importance of interpretation in generating new and original ideas. Although rooted in the texts, the assignments ask you to construct an original argument. But original ideas usually develop in a context, that is, they result from contact with other peoples' ideas. Even though you need to explore the texts and use them as sources of examples or concepts, the essays you write will show your own interpretation of the readings, and will make claims determined by your point of view. Your reactions to the texts as wholes, or to passages from the texts, together with the connections you can make between different texts, are steps toward generating new ideas.

The original argument grows from your interpretations of various passages from the texts, but it is very important that your voice should be heard in the paper above the voices of the authors included. Your voice can be heard if you have a thesis, or make a claim that you can later support. It is a good idea to give your paper a title that would reflect its main message in a word or a phrase. When you use the words or ideas of the authors studied, it is advisable that you comment on them critically, and make your references clear.

In high school, you may have learned to analyze a text and critique it, or to compare two texts, or to describe an object. In a college essay, however, you have to combine all these skills to build a more complex argument. Analysis, comparison, and description are discrete operations that contribute to the building of a case or to supporting a thesis. In addition to those, you must learn the skill of interpretation, which represents your relation to the text as well as the connections you can make between various texts.

You can establish relations between texts by looking closely at details. The closer you read, the more connections you will be able to make, and the more ideas you will generate. Before starting to write your essay, reread the texts with the assignment in mind and mark the passages relevant to the topic. Free write about them: translate them into your own terms, relate them to your experience, ask questions, and raise objections. At this stage, you will also start noticing the connections that can be made between details from various texts. Write mini comparisons, and explain the relations between such details. Later, you may use some of these passages as quotations in your paper. Play the believing and doubting game: look for examples and arguments in favor of what you read and then look for examples or arguments that contradict what you read.

When you are done taking notes, you can start thinking about your first draft. When you write, you practically go backward on your preparation process. In other words, once you have arrived at some conclusions, you can start with them as claims and explain your reader how you have arrived at them. By analyzing the quotations, you can support the claims that you will be making. By the time you get to the final draft, all those claims must converge into a unitary and coherent argument. Your essay will thus contain an original argument supported by your interpretations of passages from the texts, and it will reveal the relations you have established between them. It will, above all, show your contribution to the conversation of the world.

It is important to think of your writing as part of a larger conversation, and of yourself as an author among other authors. Since you are a student, it is normal to think that you write for your teacher. Yet when you finish college, you will not be writing for a teacher any more. To practice for the future writing tasks, you have to imagine that you write for an audience that is not part of the class. You can think of that audience as people interested in what you have to say, because they do not have access to your readings and your discussions with your classmates. Such an audience will obviously need details and explanations, but you must not think they need to be told everything. On the contrary, it will help them focus on your ideas, if you give only the relevant details from the readings.

Writing is hard work, but it can also give you great satisfaction, especially when you find out that your reader is interested and pleased.

CONCATENATION I

Link 1

Texts: Tim O'Brien, "How to Tell a True War Story"

Tim O'Brien speaks about the experiences of soldiers during the Vietnam War, and the difficulties in "telling a true war story" become apparent in the structure and style of his own short story. At the end, he imagines a woman evaluating his story and his attempt to clear her misunderstandings. He speculates she did not understand, "Because she wasn't listening. It *wasn't* a war story. It was a *love* story" (223).

What does O'Brien want us to listen to in his story? And in what sense is this a "love story"?

Study the text well and try to figure out what O'Brien means by applying the word "love" to war. Look for passages that could confirm his statement. Look also for passages that can contradict his statement. Mark those passages and write notes and comments on them.

Write an essay to explain the meaning of O'Brien's statement. The essay can be about the difficulty to communicate an extraordinary experience; or about the bonds that war fosters among soldiers; or about the relation between truth, experience, and telling story.

In order to develop your ideas and communicate effectively, you will have to write at least three pages for this assignment.

Link 2

Texts: Tim O'Brien, "How to Tell a True War Story"
          Duong Thu Huong, from *Novel without a Name*

Tim O'Brien explains that one cannot generalize about war:

> How do you generalize?
>   War is hell, but that's not the half of it, because war is also mystery and terror and adventure and courage and discovery and holiness and pity and despair and longing and love. War is nasty; war is fun. War is thrilling; war is drudgery. War makes you a man; war makes you dead. (221)

O'Brien and Huong tell stories of war from enemy camps. What conclusions can we draw about any war from these two stories? To what extent can we generalize about war based on their similarities?

Examine O'Brien's statements and see how apparently contradictory notions can be reconciled. Find passages in both stories that either confirm or contradict O'Brien's statements. Take notes and make comments on the passages you have marked. Establish relations between them and describe them in your notes.

After you have finished taking notes, write an essay in which you respond to O'Brien's statement by using the examples from both his story and the excerpt from Huong's novel. You may want to focus on the dehumanizing aspects of war, on violence, on the relationships among the soldiers, on the environment, etc. Whatever your focus will be, make it clear from the start and make sure you arrive at a conclusion about it! For a full development of this assignment you will need to write at least four pages.

Link 3

Texts: Tim O'Brien, "How to Tell a True War Story"
Duong Thu Huong, from *Novel without a Name*
Tzvetan Todorov, "A Trip to Warsaw"

In "A Trip to Warsaw," Tzvetan Todorov ponders on heroes and heroism:

> The hero's world—and perhaps therein lies its weakness—is one-dimensional; it is composed of pairs of opposites: us and them, friend and foe, courage and cowardice, hero or traitor, black and white. That outlook best befits situations in which the orientation is death, not life.
>
> The values of life are not absolute values: life is diverse and any situation is heterogeneous. Choices are made not out of concession or cowardly compromise but from a recognition of this multiplicity. (337)

What does heterogeneity mean in this context? What is the implied definition of the hero?

Todorov refers to a different war that O'Brien and Huong, yet his observations may apply to any war. Look over their stories and mark the passages where you find the aspects of war that Todorov speaks about. Find instances of heroism or its contrary, examples of heterogeneity, of moral choices, etc. Mark the passages and take notes on them. Compare the examples you find and establish relations between them.

After you have finished taking notes, write an essay in which you discuss Todorov's notion of "hero" and the way it is illustrated and/or contradicted by the examples in the stories written by O'Brien and Huong. You may focus on the notion of hero, or on moral choices that people have to make during a war, or on the pairs of opposites that guide a hero's choices, or on the complexity of real life war situations, or whatever else in Todorov's statement you find appropriate. In order to develop an argument and support it with evidence form the texts, you will need to write at least four pages.

Link 4

Texts: Tim O'Brien, "How to Tell a True War Story"
Tzvetan Todorov, "A Trip to Warsaw"
Breyten Breytenbach, "Write and Wrong"
Movie: *Full Metal Jacket* (Dir. Stanley Kubrick)

After visiting the former concentration camps, Breytenbach concludes: "It should have been burned to the ground and left to the wind. The town, too, should have been given over to the dark ink of time. No memorial, no ceremonies, just the salted earth forever. Because we have no right to remember" (36). Why does Breytenbach decide in favor of forgetting the past?

Carefully reconsider Breytenbach's objections against remembering and his statements about writing in relation to the recordings of wars done by O'Brien, Todorov, and the movie. Mark those passages where remembrance seems difficult or problematic. Look at scenes from the movie where the characters consider the ways in which they will remember the war. Write notes on the passages or scenes you have selected.

After you have finished taking notes, write an essay focusing on recording the events of the past, or interpreting experience, or active remembrance, or the uses of history. Whatever your focus, construct a thesis around it and support it with evidence from the texts and the movie. In order to construct an argument and support it with evidence, you will need to write at least four pages.

Link 5

Texts: Tim O'Brien, "How to Tell a True War Story"
Tzvetan Todorov, "A Trip to Warsaw"
Breyten Breytenbach, "Write or Wrong"
Susan Sontag, "Picture This: Can Photographs Change the Way we Think?"
Research on famous photographs from wars.

Susan Sontag attracts our attention that the camera can be used in two ways: "Beautifying is one classic operation of the camera, and tends to bleach out a moral response to what is shown. Uglifying, showing something at its worst, is a more modern function, it is didactic and invites an active response" (293). Do all representations, whether in writing or images, obey this rule?

Consider Sontag's statement in relation to the representations of the war in the texts you have read. Mark the passages where representations are made or discussed. Take notes and make comments on these passages. Establish connections between the statements of the writers. Examine the photographs you have selected and write an analysis of each image, relating it to Sontag's statement.

After you have finished taking notes, write an essay to show how Sontag's characterization of representations works in the texts above and in photographs that you may find in the archives on the Internet. You may focus your essay on techniques of representation, the notion of beauty and its opposite—ugliness, or on the importance of the angle or point of view in representing something, or anything related to representations and memory. In order to develop your ideas and use all the evidence, you will need to write at least five pages for this assignment.

CONCATENATION II

Link 1

Texts: Lysley Tenorio, "Superassassin"

The narrator of Tenorio's story defines himself as a "mutant":

> Long before the heckling of classmates and neighborhood children, the questioning stares from old churchwomen, and long before I knew the true story of my father, I was aware of the strange mutant abilities my body possesses: though my skin is fair, I never burn in the sun, can barely manage a midsummer mutant. (319)

Analyze the above description in your notes. Then, look for other passages in the story where the narrator/character reveals things about himself, whether in a direct or indirect manner. If you are not a reader of comic books, you may want to look up some of the superheroes he mentions in order to understand his references.

After you have done this groundwork, write a paper in which you use the above description to explore the narrator/character of Tenorio's story. Keep in mind that he might not always be telling the truth. If he is lying or fantasizing, try to figure out the reasons why he is not sticking to the facts. In order to complete this character study, and support it with evidence from the story, you will have to write at least three pages.

Link 2

Texts: Lysley Tenorio, "Superassassin"
Akhil Sharma, "Surrounded by Sleep"

Akhil Sharma's character, Ajay, is as attracted to super-heroes as the boy in Tenorio's story: "He was convinced he had been marked as special by Aman's accident. The beginnings of all heroes are distinguished by misfortune. Superman and Batman were both orphans. Krishna was separated from his parents at birth. The god Ram had to spend fourteen years in a forest." (278–79)

Ajay finds a similarity between himself and the super-heroes, just as Tenorio's narrator relates to the Green Lantern. Why do they need super-heroes in their lives? And on what basis do they identify with super-heroes?

Study the ways in which the two characters regard super-heroes, their need for such heroes, and the things they miss in their lives. Make sure you have all the passages where the two characters interact with or speak about the super-heroes marked and commented upon before you start writing.

After you have drawn some conclusions about the two characters, write an essay in which you discuss the role of the super-heroes in the imagination of all young people. In order to develop all the conclusions drawn from evidence, you will need to write at least four pages.

Link 3

Texts: Lysley Tenorio, "Superassassin"
Ved Mehta, "Lightning and the Lightning Bug"
Movie: *Bullets over Broadway* (Dir. Woody Allen)

Mehta talks about his experience at Oxford:

I was so deeply in awe of Oxford and its tutorial system, and so impressionable, that my tutor's questioning of one infelicitous word effectively unraveled my confidence in my writing even as it began to sensitize me to the nuances of words. For some time thereafter, whenever I wrote a sentence, I would read it as my tutor might, and conclude that everything was wrong with it. I was reminded of an accomplished pianist friend who was undergoing psychoanalysis and had become in the course of her treatment so self-conscious that he could hardly play a five-finger exercise. (190)

Like Mehta, Tenorio's narrator writes in response to a class assignment. David Shayne, in the movie, is a professional writer, who is confronted with the audience represented by Cheech. To what extent are their experiences similar? Analyze the quotation above and think of Mehta's experience with writing in relation to the writing experiences of Tenorio's narrator and David Shayne. Consider the different situations under which they write, the audiences they address, and their different motivations.

After you have finished these considerations in your notes, and arrived at a conclusion, write an essay about the importance of the audience and the consequences of writing for an audience for the resulting piece.

The topic of your essay lends itself to self-reflection: you too are writing and keeping an audience in mind. The audience is someone outside the class, who has not read the texts or heard about your assignment. In order to fully develop your ideas on this topic and examine the evidence from the texts and your own experience, you need to write at least four pages.

Link 4

Texts: Lysley Tenorio, "Superassassin"
Ved Mehta, "Lightning and the Lightning Bug"
J. M. Coetzee, "Emerging from Censorship"

Meditating on censorship, Coetzee has this to say about the inner life of the self:

> The self, as we understand the self today, is not the unity it was assumed to be by classical rationalism. On the contrary, it is multiple and multiply divided against itself. It is, to speak in figures, a zoo in which a multitude of beasts have residence, over which the anxious, overworked zookeeper of rationality exercises a rather limited control. (66)

First, read this quotation with the utmost attention and analyze it to figure out what Coetzee is saying and what he implies. You can do this in writing, if you prefer. Note that he speaks "in figures" and the figures of speech normally need interpretation. Then look back on the other texts we have read and see what issues related to identity emerge from them. Consider the way in which each character or narrator thinks about himself, the things or people he identifies with, the way he relates to other people, is seen by other people and so on. You might also want to think about your own self and how you define yourself.

After you have considered all the aspects of identity in all the texts, write an essay in which you test the validity of Coetzee's remark against the examples in the texts and your experience. Your interpretation of his words will determine your thesis. In order to develop this topic fully, and to support your argument with evidence, you will need to write at least four pages.

Link 5

Texts: Lysley Tenorio, "Superassassin"
Akhil Sharma, "Surrounded by Sleep"
Ved Mehta, "Lightning and the Lightning Bug"
Gary Engle, "What Makes Superman So Darned American?"
Research: ethnic and racial identity

Gary Engle relates immigrant identity to,

> … a separate literary tradition that addressed the theme of assimilation in terms closer to their personal experience. In this tradition issues were clear-cut. Clinging to an Old World identity meant isolation in the ghettos, confrontation with prejudiced mainstream culture, second-class social status, and impoverishment. On the other hand, forsaking the past in favor of total absorption into the mainstream, while it could result in socioeconomic progress, meant a loss of the religious, linguistic, even culinary traditions that provided a foundation for psychological well-being" (104).

Why can't immigrants adapt without losing some of their traditions? How do they solve their dilemma?

Look closer at Engle's description of the immigrants' dilemma and seek examples of immigrants in the stories by Tenorio, Sharma, Mehta, and your research that have the same or similar problems. Then, look at the ways in which immigrants try to cope with harsh conditions and at the role writing and fantasy play in the solutions they find.

After you have arrived at a conclusion, write a paper about immigration and its problems, or ways of adapting to a new country, or the role of writing and fantasy in the process of forming a new identity. In order to fully develop this topic and support your thesis with evidence from the texts, you will need to write at least five pages.

CONCATENATION III

Link 1

Text: Toi Dericotte, from *The Black Notebooks*

In her introduction, Toi Derricotte says, "I came to believe that racism, and all its manifestations, is a reflection of deep psychic structures that have to be uncovered, addressed, and restructured before changes in the external world will be lasting" (83). What does she mean by "psychic structures," and what structures of this kind does she reveal in her notes?

Examine closely the quotation above and look through all the subdivisions in Derricotte's narrative. Underline the passages that make you think of "psychic structures" and write freely about them to show the psychological processes involved in the attitudes of people toward the narrator.

Write an essay in which you discuss Derricotte's statement in the quotation above and show how her opinions about racial attitudes are confirmed or contradicted by the evidence in her writing. You may use additional examples from your own experience to make your case. In order to develop an argument and examine all the evidence in the text, you will need to write at least three pages.

Link 2

Texts: Toi Dericotte, from *The Black Notebooks*
Patricia Williams, "The Distribution of Distress"

In her essay, Patricia Williams raises the issue of individual racial characteristics:

When Martin Luther King, Jr. urged that we be judged by the content of our character, surely he meant what we looked like should not matter. Yet just as surely that enterprise did not involve having to deny the entirely complicated symbolic character of one's physical manifestation. This is a hard point, I confess, and one fraught with risk of misunderstanding. The color of one's skin is a part of ourselves. It does not matter. It is precious, and yet it should not matter; it is important and yet it must not matter. (379)

What does Williams mean by "the entirely complicated symbolic character of one's physical manifestation"? Why is there a risk of misunderstanding? And how can color be precious and not matter at the same time?

Examine Williams' words in the quotation above and construct your own interpretation of what she says. Look back in both her text and in Toi Derricotte's *Notebooks* and find examples that help you understand the quotation better or prove the points that you make in your interpretation.

After you have marked the relevant passages and written notes on them, you may proceed to write an essay of your own based on the interpretation you have given to the quotation above. The topic of your essay can be the importance of physical appearance in the relationships between people, the psychological effect of racial difference, social and racial equality, or whatever else you have read in Williams' quotation above. In order to be able to develop a thorough interpretation of the quote and to support your points with evidence from the texts, you will need to write at least four pages.

Link 3

Texts: Toi Dericotte, from *The Black Notebooks*
Patricia Williams, "The Distribution of Distress"
Steve Olson, "The Genetic Archeology of Race"

Olson points out that, at the heart of human genetics, there is a paradox: "The only way to understand how similar we are is to learn how we differ" (226). How would you explain this paradox? And how does this paradox relate to the more complicated psychological and social aspects of racial difference?

Try to clarify Olson's statement in your own terms and then look for evidence in his essay as well as Patricia Williams's and in Derricotte's *Notebooks*. Make notes on the passages that you find relevant to your interpretation of Olson's statement. Look also for evidence of what he is not saying: other complexities of racial issues. Take notes on the underlined passages and make connections between them.

Then write an essay of your own in which you discuss the paradox pointed out by Olson in relation to the texts written by Derricotte and Williams. In order to be able to construct an argument and support it with evidence from the three texts, you will need to write at least four pages.

Link 4

Texts: Steve Olson, "The Genetic Archeology of Race"
          Richard Lewontin, "A Story in Textbooks"
Movie: *Hulk* (Dir. Ang Lee)

Lewontin's argument against the misunderstanding of scientific data concerning genetics is directed against socio-biological theories:

> Having described a universal set of human social institutions that are said to be the consequences of individual natures, socio-biological theory then goes on to claim that those individual properties are coded in our genes. There are said to be genes for entrepreneurship, for male dominance, for aggressivity, so the conflict between the sexes and parents and offspring is said to be genetically programmed. What is the evidence that these claimed human universals are in fact in the genes? (176)

At this point in his essay, Lewontin is summarizing his entire argument and draws some broad general conclusions himself. To what extent are his conclusions valid? In what way do they apply to the work of the scientists described in Olson's essay? How are the generalizations Lewontin condemns illustrated by the movie?

Examine Lewontin's entire argument starting from his conclusions and check to see how some of his assertions might apply to the facts that Olson reports in his article. Make notes on the passages where Olson seems to agree with Lewontin's ideas and passages where he gives facts that can support or contradict Lewontin. Watch the movie and note the visual clues of what is happening to David Banner at the molecular level. Note also the progress of the Hulk toward more and more aggressive attitudes.

After you have finished taking notes, write an essay of your own in which you explore the uses of genetic theory and research. In order to develop an argument and support it with evidence from the two essays and the movie, you need to write at least four pages.

Link 5

Texts: Steve Olson, "The Genetic Archeology of Race"
          Richard Lewontin, "A Story in Textbooks"
          Greg Bear, "Blood Music"
          Research on genetics

Greg Bear opens his story with a statement about the hierarchy of beings in nature: "Within the ranks of magnitude of all creatures, small as microbes or great as humans, there is an equality of "élan," just as the branches of a tall tree, gathered together, equal the bulk of the limbs below, and all the limbs equal the bulk of the trunk" (153). How does this description foreshadow what happens in the whole story? How does it relate to genetic theory?

Think about the opening of Greg Bear's story, about the way it maps out the course of its action, and then think about genetic theory, the archeology of the human race, and the uses to which the discovery of the genetic code can be put. Mark the passages in the texts we have read and the texts you have found in the library that can be related to each other and can help you support the ideas that you have generated.

Then write an essay in which you explore one particular aspect of genetic theory presented in the texts and related to Bear's story. Use both the articles and the story to explain the benefits and the dangers of applying genetic theories. In order to develop an argument and support it with evidence from the texts, you will need to write at least five pages.

CONCATENATION IV

Link 1

Text: Liza Ward, "Unraveled"

The narrator of the story is a young girl, who is not yet able to understand her mother's problems. Her mother is aware of her daughter's inability to figure out her behavior when she says: "You wouldn't understand what that means. You don't understand much, you're so young" (362). Yet she continues to behave erratically. Do you understand her behavior? Is her behavior typical for a whole category of women?

Because the narrating voice belongs to the daughter, the explanation for the mother's behavior comes from vague clues and naive perceptions. Re-read the story and mark the passages that give you clues as to the reasons for the mother's behavior. Try not to judge her, but to explain what might have happened to her to bring her to where she is in her life. Write about the passages you have underlined speculating about the mother's motives.

When you are done taking notes, try to pinpoint the main reason for the mother's behavior. This reason may be individual or it may be derived from a whole network of social relations and rules of behavior. Write an essay focusing on the mother's behavior and her main reason for acting the way she does. In order to develop a full explanation and to support it with evidence from the text, you will need to write at least three pages.

Link 2

Texts: Liza Ward, "Unraveled"
Toni Morrison, "Hagar"

On his way to Hagar's house, her friend, Guitar, generalizes about women like her:

> The pride, the conceit of these doormat women amazed him. They were always women who had been spoiled as children. Whose whims had been taken seriously by adults and who grew up to be the stingiest, greediest people on earth and out of their stinginess grew their stingy little love that ate everything in sight. They could not believe or accept that they were unloved; they believed that the world itself was off balance when it appeared as though they were not loved. Why did they think they were so lovable? Why did they think their brand of love was better than anybody else's? But they did. And they loved their love so much they would kill anybody who got in its way. (194)

Guitar makes this judgment from the outside. What leads him to be so harsh with women? How would the women themselves describe their plight?

Look close at what Guitar is saying here and try to figure out his assumptions and his point of view. Think back on the two stories and respond to Guitar with explanations of the women's behavior that show their own point of view and their own assumptions. Locate the passages in the stories that would support the new explanations. Write notes on them and compare the similar situations.

After you have finished taking notes, write an essay exploring the behavior of women and the social conditions that determine it. In order to develop an argument and to support it with evidence from the texts, you will need to write at least four pages.

Link 3

Texts: Liza Ward, "Unraveled"
Toni Morrison, "Hagar"
Ariel Dorfman, "September, 1973"
Movie: *Miss Congeniality* (Dir. Donald Petrie)

Dorfman confesses that his attraction to his wife followed a pattern common to all males:

> To be quite frank, what enchanted me about her to begin with were her dazzling looks and fiery spirit and extreme joy of life, the hot sex-

ual thought of a lithe *moreno* body under her dress, that enchanting smile of hers that the gods of advertising couldn't have coached out of a woman if they had given her a thousand years and a ton of Max Factor make-up. (90)

To what extent are all people attracted to the physical attributes of a person when they fall in love? What are the consequences of knowing that physical attraction counts, for women in particular?

Analyze Dorfman's quotation here and then look at the way his opinions change as he goes along in his account of his relationship to his wife. Look also for passages in the other two stories and scenes in the movie where the physical appearance of women is an issue. Make notes on the way the beliefs about beauty are expressed and the way women try to meet beauty standards. Write notes on the passages you have selected.

Write an essay in which you explore the notion of feminine beauty and its importance for individuals and society, or the attitudes of men toward women, or the way women tend to think of themselves, or whatever aspect of men/women relationships you find most interesting. Use evidence from all texts and the movie, as well as personal experience, to support your argument. In order to develop an argument and support it with evidence, you will need to write at least four pages.

Link 4

Texts: Liza Ward, "Unraveled"
Toni Morrison, "Hagar"
Ariel Dorfman, "September, 1973"
Laura Kipnis, "Domestic Gulags"

Laura Kipnis is looking for an understanding of wide-spread spousal abuse and comes up with an alternative to the prevailing explanations:

But consider another explanation: perhaps these social pathologies and aberrations of love are the necessary fallout from the social conventions of love that we adhere to and live out on a daily basis. The more cynical version of this position would be that something about love is inherently impossible; the more optimistic one would be that the conventions are inherently impossible. (158)

What is the difference between the cynical and the optimistic versions of her statement?

Read the quotation carefully and re-read Kipnis's essay to reconsider the context in which she makes this statement. Look back on the stories and mark the passages dealing with what Kipnis calls "aberrations of love." Mark also the passages that attempt to define love. Write notes to explain the implications contained in those passages.

After you have finished writing your notes, write an essay in which you explore the conventions of love in our society based on the texts you have read and personal experience. In order to develop an argument and support it with evidence from the texts, you will need to write at least four pages.

Link 5

Texts: Ariel Dorfman, "September, 1973"
Laura Kipnis, "Domestic Gulags"
Jonathan Franzen, "Imperial Bedroom"
Research about privacy

When he says that, "What is threatened is not the private sphere. It's the public sphere" (118), Franzen reveals a usually ignored relation between the notions of public and private. What is the relationship between the private and public domains?

Re-read Franzen's essay to understand his definitions of private and public spheres! Go back to the other texts and look for the passages where Dorfman or Kipnis talk about the same issues. Make notes on the passages and try to infer how they define the two concepts and what kind of relationship they see between private and public issues. Add notes from your research as well.

After you have finished writing notes, write an essay exploring the relationship between the public and private spheres. You may want to also explore such notions as love, home, nation, etc. In order to develop an argument and support it with evidence from the texts you will need to write at least five pages.

CONCATENATION V

Link 1

Text: Don DeLillo, "Videotape"

DeLillo describes a very common occurrence—watching a videotape—and points to the quality of the images:

> There is something about the nature of the tape, the grain of the image, the sputtering black-and-white tones, the starkness—you think this is more real, truer to life than anything around you. The things around you have a rehearsed and layered and cosmetic look.

The tape is superreal, or maybe underreal is the way you want to put it. It is what lies at the scraped bottom of all the layers you have added. And this is another reason why you keep looking. The tape has a searing realness. (78)

Look closer at the quotation above. Besides the watching of the tape, a new topic creeps in: reality. How can a tape, which is obviously created by technological means, be real?

Work on interpreting this quotation and look for other instances in the story where DeLillo makes references to reality or real things. Underline the relevant passages and write freely about them in your notebook.

After you have finished reexamining the story with special attention to the "reality" issue, write an essay in which you discuss either the definition of reality, or the way we perceive reality, or the reasons we consider something to be real. Use examples from the story to make your point, but feel free to bring in other examples from your experience which are relevant to the topic. In order to develop an argument and support it with evidence and reasoning, you will have to write at least three pages.

Link 2

Texts: Don DeLillo, "Videotape"
Brooks Brown and Robert Merritt, "The Videotapes"

In the conclusion of this chapter from his book, Brooks Brown voices his opinion about the videotapes: "I believe the tapes can help us understand what happened and should be released to the public" (45). Do videotapes or other recordings of events help us understand what happened?

Look over Brown and Merritt's chapter to find those passages where some understanding of the events at Columbine surfaces. Look back on DeLillo's "Videotape" and see whether the repeated watching of the tape brings about an understanding of the event. Take notes on the relevant passages and compare the similar situations in both texts.

After you have finished taking notes, write an essay exploring the value of video-recording. You may think about the extent to which we trust videotapes, the way in which they can be manipulated, or the extent to which they can mislead us. Whatever your focus, make sure you express it clearly and you support your argument with evidence from the text. Of course, you may think of other famous videotapes that you have seen on the news, such as the Kennedy assassination, the beating of Rodney King, the falling of the twin towers. In order to be able to set up an argument and support it with evidence, you will need to write at least four pages.

Link 3

Texts: Don DeLillo, "Videotape"
          Brooks Brown and Robert Merritt, "The Videotapes"
          Jon Katz, "The Geek Ascension"
Movie: *The Matrix* (Dir. Andy and Larry Wachowski)

Jon Katz discusses the "screen culture" that has been on the rise since the beginnings of cinema. One consequence of the existence of this culture is that traditional notions of community and relationships become different though they do not disappear: "But cyberspace is a world, albeit a virtual one. Contact and community mean somewhat different things there, but they are real nonetheless" (154).

What are the differences between an actual community and a community in cyberspace?

Re-read Katz's essay for clues about such differences! Reread DeLillo and Brown and Merritt to see how other notions have changed, such as the notions of reality and understanding that you have examined in the previous papers. Examine scenes from the movie where the notions of reality, perceptions, and cyberspace are discussed or illustrated. Take notes on all these and see if you can create connections between them and make comparisons.

After you have finished taking notes, write an essay in which you explore the changes brought about by recent technologies, or as Katz put it, "screen culture." You may use some of the insights from your previous papers and any examples from your experience that you find relevant, in addition to the examples from the texts and the movie. In order to develop an argument and support it with evidence, you need to write at least four pages.

Link 4

Texts: Don DeLillo, "Videotape"
          Brooks Brown and Robert Merritt, "The Videotapes"
          Jon Katz, "The Geek Ascension"
          Gertrude Himmelfarb, "Revolution in the Library"

When Gertrude Himmelfarb says that, "The Internet is an equal opportunity resource; it recognizes no rank or status or privilege. In that democratic universe, all sources, all ideas, all theories seem equally valid and pertinent" (131), she sounds very much like Katz, who proclaims that, "Looks don't matter on line. Neither does race, the number of degrees one has or doesn't have, or the cadence of speech. Ideas and personalities, presented in their purest sense, have a different dimension" (154). But look closer at what they are saying: do they agree?

Compare the assumptions behind the quotations above and think about the effects of technology on intellectual activities. Look through all the texts for passages that show the authors' support or disapproval of technology, and try to figure out what determines their positions regarding social changes determined by technology. Take notes and comment on the relevant passages. Try to create connections between them.

After you have finished taking notes, write an essay exploring the impact of technology on society, or the reasons why people oppose or welcome new technologies, or whatever aspect of the relationship between society and technology interests you most. Use the texts as sources of ideas and examples. In order to make an argument and support it with evidence from the texts, you will have to write at least four pages.

Link 5

Texts: Brooks Brown and Rob Merritt, "The Videotapes"
Jon Katz, "The Geek Ascension"
Gertrude Himmelfarb, "Revolution in the Library"
Mario Vargas Llosa, "Why Literature?"
Research: the evolution and culture of the book

In your previous papers you have explored the social impact of technology, but Vargas Llosa attracts our attention to a different consequence of technology's presence: "The solipsism of nations and individuals produces paranoia and delirium, distortions of reality that generate hatred, wars, and even genocide" (352).

If you have not looked up some of these words in the dictionary, do so now. Give some thought to this sentence and consider the author's position. Look back on the other texts and your research to find examples that can either endorse or contradict his opinion. Play a believing and doubting game. First, believe Llosa and look for examples in his favor. Then doubt what he is saying and look for counter examples. Take many notes on the passages you select and try to find ways to relate them to each other.

After you have finished taking notes, write an essay in which you consider the relation between technologies and imagination, technology and human relationships, or whatever aspect discussed by Vargas Llosa has interested you most. In order to create and support an argument, you need to write at least five pages.

411

CONCATENATION VI

Link 1

Texts: Z.Z. Packer, "Brownies"

A summer camp is not exactly school, but it is meant to be educational. In Packer's story, the narrator recognizes this purpose, when she talks about Mrs. Margolin: "She wore enormous belts that looked like the kind weight lifters wear, except hers were cheap metallic gold or rabbit fur or covered with gigantic fake sunflowers. Often, these belts would become nature lessons in and of themselves" (238). What do the brownies learn from their environment? What are the most important lessons they learn and where do those lessons come from?

Examine the story for instances where the girls are instructed by their camp supervisors and for the kind of activities supposed to teach them important lessons. Look also for other opportunities the girls have to learn. Think about the kind of lessons the girls actually need and find passages where such needs become evident. Take notes and write comments on these passages.

After you have finished taking notes, write an essay regarding the way we acquire knowledge as children, or the way we are taught, or the kind of knowledge we need to have. You may want to distinguish the learning process from what is generally called education. In order to develop an argument and support it with evidence from the story, you will need to write at least three pages.

Link 2

Texts: Z.Z. Packer, "Brownies"
Walter Mosley, "Pet Fly"

Mosley's narrator is surprised by the remarks of a co-worker. Speaking about Mr. Drew, Ernie refers to him as white. When the narrator objects by saying, "But Mr. Drew is black," Ernie answers: "Used to be, but ever since he got promoted he forgot all about that. Used to be he's come down here and we'd talk like you 'n' me doin'. But now he just stands in the door and grins and nods. Now he is so scared I'm gonna pull him down that he won't even sit for a minute" (205). What does Ernie mean? What does Mr. Drew's job have to do with his skin color?

Give some thought to Ernie's words and think about the social realities they reflect. Examine both stories for instances where you can see how power is associated with race. Take notes and comment on the passages that you find relevant to what Ernie says about Mr. Drew.

After you are done taking notes and establishing relations between the two stories, write an essay based on your interpretation of Ernie's words. You may focus on power and hierarchy in a segment of society, racial relations based on power, ways of imposing or exerting power, or other aspect of power and race. In order to develop an argument and support it with evidence from the stories, you need to write at least four pages.

Link 3

Texts: Z.Z. Packer, "Brownies"
Walter Mosley, "Pet Fly"
Patricia Williams, "The Distribution of Distress"
Movie: *The Crying Game* (Dir. Neil Jordan)

Patricia Williams's argument focuses on competing biases:

> If, upon occasion, the ploughshare of feminism can be beaten into the sword of class prejudice, no less can there be other examples of what I call battling biases, in which the impulse to antidiscrimination is defeated by the intrusion or substitution of a different object of enmity. This revolving door of revulsions is one of the trickiest mechanisms contributing to the enduring nature of prejudice; it is at the heart, I suppose, a kind of traumatic reiteration of injurious encounters, preserving even as it transforms the overall history of rage. (376)

How do biases relate to power? What is the purpose of prejudice? Examine the quotation above and use it to map Patricia Williams's entire argument. You may need to use a dictionary or encyclopedia. Then examine the two stories again and find the passages where Williams's words seem to resonate. Look at the scenes in the movie where prejudices seem to compete with each other. Take notes on such passages and scenes and create connections between them.

After you have finished taking notes, write an essay in which you consider Williams's argument and the way it is or is not illustrated by the two stories. In order to develop an argument and support it with evidence, you will have to write at least four pages.

Link 4

Texts: Walter Mosley,   "Pet Fly"
        Patricia Williams,   "The Distribution of Distress"
        Alluquere Rosanne Stone, "In Novell Conditions: The Cross-Dressing
                                  Psychiatrist"

Commenting on the adventure of Dr. Lewin in cyberspace, Stone states:

> The societal imperative with which we have been raised is that
> there is one primary persona, or "true identity," and that in the off-
> line world—the "real world"—this persona is firmly attached to a sin-
> gle physical body, by which our existence as social beings is
> authorized and in which it is grounded. The origin of this "correct"
> relationship between body and persona seems to have been con-
> temporaneous with the Enlightenment, the same cultural moment
> that gave birth to what we like to call the sovereign subject. . . .
> Partly the Western idea that the body and the subject are insepara-
> ble is a worthy exercise in wish fulfillment—an attempt to explain
> why ego-centered subjectivity terminates with the substrate *and* to
> enforce the termination. (302–303)

What is the relationship between identity, persona, ego, and subject in Stone's statement above?

Examine Stone's statement and find definitions for all the terms she
uses. You may need to consult a dictionary or encyclopedia for the purpose. After you have come up with your own interpretation of this quotation, look in the other texts for ways to illustrate, support, or contradict
Stone's statement. Write notes and comments on the passages you find
relevant and make connections between them.

After you have finished analyzing your materials and taking notes,
write an essay about an aspect of identity that you find most interesting.
You may focus on the idea of selfhood or identity, the divisions within the
self, the role of the body in identifying someone, or any other issue related
to identity. In order to develop an argument and support it with evidence, you will need to write at least four pages.

Link 5

Texts: Patricia Williams,   "The Distribution of Distress"
         Alluquere Rosanne Stone,   "In Novell Conditions: The Cross-Dressing
                                        Psychiatrist"
         Ellen Ullman,   "Wouldn't You Rather Be at Home?"
         Research on the impact of the Internet

In her analysis of recent changes due to the Internet, Ullman relates it to democracy:

> In this sense, the ideal of the Internet represents the very opposite of democracy, which is a method of resolving differences in a relatively orderly manner through the mediation of unavoidable civil associations. Yet there can be no notion of resolving differences in a world where each person is entitled to go exactly what he or she wants. Here all needs and desires are equally powerful. I'll get mine, and you'll get yours; there is no need for compromise and discussion. I don't have to tolerate you, and you don't have to tolerate me. No need for messy debate and the whole rigmarole of government with all its creaky, bothersome structures. There's no need for any of this, because now that we have the World Wide Web the problem of the pursuit of happiness has been solved! (349)

Examine Ullman's words here carefully and try to see what definition of democracy is at work in her reasoning. Look back both on her texts and the texts written by Williams and Stone. Do some research on the impact of the Internet on various social and economic domains! Make connections and comparisons between the various arguments to decide where you stand in relation to them. Write notes and comments on the passages that you find relevant to Ullman's statement.

After you have finished taking notes and making connections, write an essay on the impact of the Internet on society, economy, culture, or the individual. You may choose to focus on any one or several of these aspects. In order to develop an argument and support it with evidence, you will need to write at least five pages.